BUSINESS
LOGISTICS

Third Edition

BUSINESS LOGISTICS

Third Edition

Nicholas A. Glaskowsky, Jr.
University of Miami

Donald R. Hudson
University of Miami

Robert M. Ivie
Director of International Market Development
E & J Gallo Winery

The Dryden Press
A Harcourt Brace Jovanovich College Publisher

*Fort Worth   Philadelphia   San Diego   New York   Orlando   Austin   San Antonio
Toronto   Montreal   London   Sydney   Tokyo*

For Elizabeth, Ofelia, and Kristi.

Acquisitions Editor: John E. Anderson
Production Editor: Leslie Leland
Designer: Diana Jean Parks
Art Editor: Susan Holtz
Production Manager: Mary Kay Yearin

ISBN: 0-15-505652-2

Library of Congress Number: 91-71489

Printed in the United States of America

PREFACE

The purpose of this book is to provide a comprehensive and up-to-date survey of business logistics system design and management. It has been planned to help develop the ability to organize and analyze logistics information, to aid in making logistics decisions, and to provide insights that will assist in making recommendations or taking actions that will effectively resolve a logistics problem situation.

Our treatment of the field of business logistics deals with the management of physical supply and physical distribution activities. These activities constitute the total effort required to make particular kinds and specific quantities of goods available in acceptable condition at the place and time desired by the customer.

The field of business logistics has evolved from concepts developed by transportation economists, geographers, electrical and industrial engineers, electronic and computer engineers, and students of production and marketing management. Each of these areas continues to contribute significantly to the knowledge base that underlies the discipline of logistics system management.

Marshall McLuhan has pointed out that it is difficult to describe and discuss a system, any system, in the linear format of a book. Our approach in this third edition is to begin by considering the logistics system scope and the relationships of logistics to other functions of a business. From there we proceed to the operation of logistics systems. The third part of the book addresses the management issues of logistics system strategy, organization, and control. We conclude with a look to the future of logistics management and the challenges it will face in the remainder of this century and on into the next.

We have included a set of discussion questions at the end of each chapter that are intended as learning devices; their answers will confirm the reader's understanding of the material just presented. We have also included a short case at the end of twelve of the eighteen chapters in the book, the purpose of these being to stimulate the development of alternative solutions to the problem presented in each case.

The basic concepts involved in the management of business logistics certainly have not changed since the publication of the second edition. However, there have been many major changes in the logistics management environment, such as the deregulation of transportation and extraordinary developments in the area of computers and electronic data interchange, that have had profound effects on the operation of logistics systems.

Other developments are also having a significant impact on logistics management. Examples of these include the shift from an emphasis on production (output) measurement to productivity and performance quality measurement, a very great increase in the demand for better customer service, continued and growing emphasis on interorganizational coordination (much of this being made possible by transportation deregulation), the rapidly increasing globalization of business, and the impact of environmental considerations on logistics operations.

We are happy for this opportunity to thank those members of the editorial staff of Harcourt Brace Jovanovich, Inc. who put their fine professional abilities to work to bring this book to print. They did not try our patience and hopefully we did not try theirs. In particular we wish to thank John Anderson, Eleanor Garner, Susan Holtz, Leslie Leland, Diana Jean Parks, and Mary Kay Yearin.

We also wish to thank Joseph L. Cavinato of the Pennsylvania State University and John Ozmet of the University of Arkansas for reviewing the manuscript and for their many helpful suggestions for improving it. Their input of time and effort is much appreciated.

Those familiar with the earlier editions of this book will note the absence of Professor James L. Heskett from the group of coauthors of this third edition. This was Jim's decision, as he wished to devote his time and energy to other projects. However, we must acknowledge the major contributions he made to the first and second editions, and therefore to this edition also. Jim was one of the leading pioneers in the development of the theory and practice of business logistics, and he continues to make very significant contributions to the field.

All three editions of this book have benefitted from the contributions of hundreds of students, academic researchers, business executives, and individuals in trade associations and government agencies. To them, and for their help, we are grateful. However, as we said in the prefaces to earlier editions, for any errors, misconceptions, or fuzzy thinking that appears between these covers, the buck stops with us.

Nicholas A. Glaskowsky, Jr.
Donald R. Hudson
Robert M. Ivie

Coral Gables, Florida
Modesto, California
July, 1991

CONTENTS

3

PRODUCT PRICING POLICIES   *75*

6

INVENTORY MANAGEMENT   167

PART TWO

INTEGRATED LOGISTICS SYSTEM OPERATIONS

7

TRANSPORT FACILITIES

8

TRANSPORTATION RATES AND SERVICES   *231*

9

TRAFFIC MANAGEMENT   259

10

PACKAGING AND MATERIAL HANDLING   295

11

WAREHOUSING MANAGEMENT   *333*

12

INFORMATION PROCESSING AND COMMUNICATION SERVICES   *393*

13

MULTINATIONAL LOGISTICS STRATEGY AND OPERATIONS   **423**

PART THREE

INTEGRATED LOGISTICS SYSTEM STRATEGY, ORGANIZATION, AND CONTROL   479

14

LOCATION THEORY AND PRACTICE   481

15

INTEGRATED LOGISTICS SYSTEM STRATEGY AND DESIGN 533

16

ORGANIZATION FOR LOGISTICS MANAGEMENT   *573*

17

SYSTEM PERFORMANCE MEASUREMENT AND CONTROL

601

18

A LOOK TO THE FUTURE   639

PART ONE

INTEGRATED LOGISTICS SYSTEM SCOPE AND RELATIONSHIPS

CHAPTER ONE

1

Logistics in the Economy and the Enterprise

LEARNING OBJECTIVES

The objectives of this chapter are to:

➢ Trace the history and development of business logistics.

➢ Show the role and importance of logistics activities in the economy.

➢ Explain the differences between mercantile and logistics activities, and the significance of these differences.

➢ Define the scope of logistics activities in business firms.

➢ Review the development of the logistics management function.

➢ Analyze and explain the reasons for the steadily increasing concern with logistics.

➢ Discuss the relative importance of logistics costs and activities in the light of various corporate strategies.

On a summer day in June, at points widely scattered across a continent, various events occur. A teenager in Orlando, Florida, walking because of the failure of the brake cable on his tenspeed bike, goes to the local bike shop to buy a replacement cable made in Westfield, Massachusetts. A chemical plant manager in St. Paul, Minnesota, is counting on the arrival of a tank car of sulfuric acid from Wilmington, Delaware; without it, production will come to a halt before the week is out. The sales manager of a soft drink franchise in Denver checks with the production manager to make sure that extra large inventories of canned and bottled products will be available to accommodate the upcoming Fourth of July weekend demand for soft drinks in eastern Colorado. And, in her office at a department store in San Francisco, California, a buyer of sportswear is determining the size of the order she will send to a manufacturer in Seattle, and also what percentages of the order should be for which styles, colors, and sizes.

All of these events have something in common: each involves logistics activities designed to insure that goods produced are given value by distribution to points where and when they are needed. Without logistics the effort and resources put into producing more than could be used locally would be wasted. And, lacking economies of scale, the costs of producing goods in small quantities for purely local consumption would be much higher.

With this in mind, business logistics is, for the purposes of this book, defined as *the management of all activities that facilitate product movement and the coordination of supply and demand in the creation of time and place utility in goods*. It may be noted that activities of packaging or final assembly performed in warehouse facilities (whether for specific customers or otherwise) constitute the creation of *form utility* and are actually *manufacturing* activities. Even though they may be carried on in a warehouse, they are *not* logistics activities.

Currently, managers are showing an ever increasing deep concern with the costs and management of logistics. As Sharman points out, product life cycles are contracting, product lines are proliferating, the customer — not the manufacturer — is calling the shots in the marketplace, and low-cost, high-volume data processing and transmission is revolutionizing logistics control systems.[1] Further, there is now, as never before, a clear recognition by managers that logistics can (and should) play an important role in the formulation and implementation of corporate strategy. Shapiro asserts that ''for want of an appropriate logistics system, many a good corporate strategy has been lost,'' and notes that ''managers have once again begun to look to logistics systems as a potential source of competitive advantage.''[2]

LOGISTICS IN THE ECONOMY

History and Development

In the United States the technologies of mass manufacture that came into use following the Industrial Revolution provided the potential for expanding production capacities far beyond the ability of nearby customers to use the consequent output. The late-nineteenth century forces that made wider distribution of goods possible included a rapidly growing labor force, the construction of a national railroad system, and new and rapidly growing markets inland as well as along the eastern seaboard.

The industrial development that propelled the United States into a position of world industrial leadership continued apace until the 1930s, when the Great Depression made it clear that we could not concentrate forever on productive capacity without comparable attention being paid to the desires of the market and the ability and inclination of individuals to consume the output of the industrial machine.

It was at this point that observers of the scene began to point to the inefficiencies of the distribution system. A pioneering voice of concern was that of Ralph Borsodi, who in 1929 concluded that:

> . . . in 50 years between 1870 and 1930 the cost of distributing necessities and luxuries has nearly trebled, while production costs have gone down by one-fifth . . . what we are saving in production we are losing in distribution. . . .[3]

Yet, at precisely this point in time, retailers and wholesalers were developing concepts of chain-store marketing and cooperative wholesaling organizations to make their operations more efficient through economies of scale, mechanization, and better organization and control of efforts.

As the pent-up demand for durables and other goods subsided in the aftermath of World War II, the nation was left with a greatly expanded production capability. Attention shifted to satisfying more varied customer wants (more models, colors, sizes, etc.) as a means of encouraging consumption that would take up the slack in unused production capacity. The "age of marketing," which had its genesis in the 1930s, bloomed from the early 1950s onward.

It was natural for logistics activities to come under review as a part of the growing emphasis on the marketing and distribution system. By the mid-1950s, it was obvious to informed executives that logistics offered a very fruitful area for improvement of industrial and commercial activity, in terms of both quality and cost of output, and this potential was not to be overlooked. However, the realization of the potential was to take many years.

The first textbook did not appear in the field until 1961.[4] In 1962 Peter Drucker, perhaps the world's foremost management consultant and writer, correctly termed logistics as being "The Economy's Dark Continent."[5] And in 1964, the first textbook using the word "logistics" in its title was published.[6] In the two decades since the 1960s, logistics management has steadily grown in terms of management concern, attention, and importance.

Logistics in Economic Activity

Once products or services in excess of need are created at any one location, they must be made available elsewhere or remain unused. Economists have long emphasized the need to capitalize on comparative cost advantages in the production of goods and services. The ability to utilize lower labor costs, favorable locations with regard to raw material sources, and low costs for construction and land depends on the degree to which barriers to exchange and the physical transfer of goods from one place to another can be lowered.

Magnitude of Logistics in the Economy A comprehensive study of physical distribution costs was made by A. T. Kearney, Inc. for the National Council of Physical Distribution Management (NCPDM).[7] The Kearney data was developed using a very extensive questionnaire completed by 418 firms (plus 27 field interviews), U.S. Census of Manufacturers data, and cross references to previous studies by others for comparison and validation purposes. Table 1–1 presents the several published estimates of aggregate logistics costs cited in the NCPDM study by A. T. Kearney. To quote the Kearney study, "Clearly, there is a wide range of estimates for the costs of logistics depending on the source and the methodology chosen. However, the conclusion to be drawn from these data is that the $650 billion estimate of total logistics cost by Kearney is reasonable and perhaps even on the conservative side."[8]

TABLE 1–1: Range of Estimates, U.S. Logistics Cost: 1982

Source/Methodology	$ Billions	
	Low Estimate	High Estimate
Herbert W. Davis & Co. (1980)	$624.1	$ 730.4
Herbert W. Davis & Co. (1982)		
Arithmetic Total %	580.8	679.8
Weighted Total %	548.4	641.8
LaLonde and Zinzer (NCPDM, 1976)		
"Commonly Recognized" Costs	623.5	729.7
"Total" Costs	941.6	1,102.0
Donald J. Bowersox (1978)	611.9	611.9+
1983 NCPDM Productivity Study Survey Respondents	623.5	729.7
Average	650.5	746.5

SOURCE: *Measuring and Improving Productivity in Physical Distribution*, NCPDM, 1984, p. 336.

Although focusing on productivity, the Kearney study is perhaps the best compilation and analysis of macroeconomic physical distribution costs achieved thus far. Kearney estimated 1982 logistics expenditures in the United States to have been $650 billion, including transportation ($300 billion), storage and warehousing ($180 billion), inventory carrying costs ($130 billion), and administration ($40 billion).[9] This translates to about 20% of the gross national product of $3.17 trillion in 1982. An update of the 1984 Kearney study has been commissioned by the Council of Logistics Management. The results of this new study will likely be available in late 1991 or shortly thereafter.

The Flow Concept One way of viewing the economic process is as a variety of flows involving material, money (transactions), information, people, and title to goods. Through the flow process, combinations of the basic "factors of production" (using a traditional term from economics) — land, labor, materials, and money — are merged into new combinations to yield rent, wages, product, and profit. Some have claimed that a fifth factor of production, *management*, is the means by which the necessary flows are achieved. This concept is diagrammed in Figure 1–1.

The Functional Concept So far, so good. But there is no mention of logistics in Figure 1–1. It is not until one turns to *functions* performed as a result of economic activity that logistics can be positioned in the scheme of business activity.

Economic activity can be viewed as being composed of the core activities of production, distribution and facilitation. Production involves the manufacture of goods, the extraction of minerals from the earth, agriculture and fishing, and the creation of skills and services (for example, through education). Distribution involves both the creation of demand (transactions) through promotional effort and the logistics of making goods and services available once they are "sold." Facilitation — provision of finance and information — makes production and distribution possible. Viewed in this light, all three core functions create value, and all are productive. Our interest centers on distribution.

FIGURE 1–1: The flow concept of economic activity

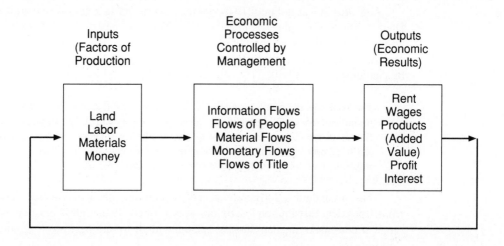

Distribution   Paul D. Converse articulated the distinctly different areas of activity in distribution this way:

> Marketing (distribution) has been defined as matter in motion. There are two kinds of motion in moving goods from the farm, the mine, and the factory into the hands of the ultimate consumers. Goods must be moved through the trade channel and gotten into the possession of customers — that is they must be bought and sold. . . . [Second,] goods must be moved physically.[10]

In doing so, Converse revived a long-dormant discussion begun by Arch Shaw, who wrote in 1916:

> The problem of distribution today is . . . complex. Broadly speaking, it divides into two sub-problems closely related and interdependent but each having to do with a different set of factors and reactions. The first takes shape in the question: given a particular article, how can a demand for it be created of sufficient volume to make its production and distribution profitable? The second is: through what channels can the article itself be conveyed from the factory warehouse where it is of least value, into the hands of those consumers who will pay the most profitable price for it, though this price may not be the highest at which a more limited volume could be sold?[11]

In answering his two questions, Shaw concluded that distribution was composed of two types of effort: demand creation and physical supply. For our purposes, activities of demand creation and physical supply will be referred to as marketing activities and logistics.

Marketing Activities   Marketing activities include all ways by which organizations and individuals create awareness of real or perceived attributes of a product or service on the part of a potential customer. They are concerned with buying and selling and the maintenance of customer loyalty and post-purchase satisfaction. The end objective of such efforts is to increase a firm's sales, hopefully at a profit.

Logistics   It was not until 1948 that the American Marketing Association (AMA) formulated a definition for physical distribution: ''The movement and handling of goods from the point of production to the point of consumption or use.''[12] The AMA's Definitions Committee also made a special effort to differentiate the terms ''physical distribution'' and ''distribution'' by cautioning:

> The word ''distribution'' is sometimes used to describe this activity. In view of the technical meaning of the word ''distribution'' in economic theory and of the fact that it is used by the Bureau of the Census and increasingly by marketing students and businessmen as synonymous with ''marketing,'' the Committee recommends that its use as a synonym of, or substitute for, ''physical distribution'' be discouraged.[13]

Thus, a standard and generally accepted definition that distinguished ''demand creation'' from ''physical distribution'' activities was formed. Although it did not represent the full range of non-marketing activities associated with distribution, it was a significant conceptual step forward.

Distinctions between Marketing and Logistics Activities   Although marketing and logistics activities appear to be related fields of study, there are several reasons why they should be treated separately.

Utility Creation   Marketing and logistics efforts are undertaken to create different types of utilities in goods. Through contact with the market, marketing efforts increase conscious or latent desire on the part of the customer to possess a good or benefit from a service. This effort leads to sales transactions or some type of exchange. Thus, marketing activities are concerned primarily with creating *possession utility*.

Logistics creates *place and time utility* in goods and services. Place utility is created primarily by transportation, and inventory management and the strategic location of goods and service operations primarily create time utility. Logistics activities are the means by which customer demands for time and place utility in goods and services are translated into a supply of these types of utility.

Channel Composition   The study of marketing has long included consideration of the institutions through which goods pass on their way from producers to ultimate customers. A linked series of such institutions is said to make up a channel of distribution. However, marketing and logistics channels for the same item frequently involve different institutions.

Marketing and logistics channels for wheat seed, wheat, and flour are illustrated in Figure 1–2. The marketing channel includes firms that buy and sell this family of products, often taking title in the process. The logistics channel includes those firms involved in the physical transfer of the products, those that actually take physical possession of the wheat seed, wheat, or flour.

Note that the sets of firms included in these two channels are not the same. Only in recent years has industry clearly recognized and truly differentiated between marketing and logistics activities within channels of distribution. Such differentiation has opened the door for the improved design of both marketing and logistics efforts, as will be shown later.

FIGURE 1–2: Logistics and marketing channels and costs for wheat seed, wheat, and flour, plus production or operations costs

Cost[a] Allocated by Function			Contribution to Overhead and Profit	Economic Institution		Product Form
Logistics	Production	Marketing		Logistics Channel	Marketing Channel	
.6 ¢	3.0 ¢	.2 ¢	1.0 ¢	Wheat seed producer		
.6			.2	Transport company		
.4		.2	.2	Merchant wholesaler		Wheat Seed
1.0			.4	Transport Company		
.2		.8	.4	Retailer		
2.0	10.0	.4	3.6	Wheat producer		
1.0			.2	Grain elevator		
9.0			3.3	Transport company		Wheat
		3.1	.6	Grain broker		
9.6	33.9	15.7	10.8	Flour miller		
17.4			1.9	Transport company		
4.2			.7	Public warehouse		
		4.5	.6	Food broker		
4.5		9.2	2.3	Merchant wholesaler		Flour
11.4			.9	Transport company		
3.8		10.5	2.9	Retailer		
13.0		10.0		Ultimate consumer		
78.5 ¢	46.9 ¢	54.6 ¢	30.0 ¢			

The total cost of a 10-pound bag of flour to the consumer = $2.10

[a]Costs are illustrative only

    In Figure 1–2, each transfer of goods from one business entity to the next requires the coordination of demand and supply among many different institutions in the channel, from the original grower of wheat seed to the ultimate consumer of flour. The length of time required from the original planting of wheat for seed to the ultimate consumption of flour may be as much as three years or more. Allowing for two growing seasons, storage time of nearly two years may be required, with attendant costs of storage and investment in inventory. Transportation and material handling activities are also repeated six or more times.

    Figure 1–2 is a vastly oversimplified representation of what goes on in a channel of distribution and in its component marketing and logistics channels. Management in the logistics channel has as its basic objectives (1) providing the customer the desired level of product availability in terms of quantity and delivery time; (2) having on hand the product assortments desired by the customer; and (3) offering the desired service levels at an attractive cost (often through the consolidation of products for physical movement) wherever it can be accomplished.

The importance of product assortments — for ''merchandising'' as well as for consolidation for storage and transportation — means that related products and product families are assembled and then dispersed from each of several institutions in logistics channels. This allows producing organizations to specialize in the goods they produce, and various types of wholesaling and retailing institutions, for example, to specialize in selling different assortments of products from a variety of sources.

Further, each institution in a logistics channel encompasses one or more facilities or terminals to and from which goods flow in a physical sense. The terminal for a trucker may be just that; for retailers, ''terminals'' are their warehouses and retail stores. Even though the assortment of goods may change at each level in the channel, the total volume of economic activity in an industry is typically large enough to allow for the efficient movement of a given product to and from channel ''terminals'' by means of its consolidation with changing assortments of other products.

Overall, a logistics channel may disperse goods from relatively few sources to many eventual users, as would be the case with flour. Or it might be the reverse, as is typical of a company offering solid waste disposal services, such as collection from many sources for transportation to a single disposal point. Or, as in the case of a department store chain, there will be many inbound shipments from various sources to the chain's warehouses and then a great many outbound shipments to individual stores in the chain.

LOGISTICS IN THE ENTERPRISE

The Systems Approach

In large measure, American industry owes its relative success in managing logistics activities to the systems approach formulated in the 1950s. However, because a prosperous seller's economy makes marketing easier and cost control gets less attention, the implementation of this approach often sputtered badly. Professor LaLonde of Ohio State University is aptly quoted as saying, ''American management's philosophy has typically been: 'If you're smart enough to make it, aggressive enough to sell it — then any dummy can get it there!' And now we're paying for [that philosophy].''[14]

Proponents of the systems approach view logistics as a set of interrelated activities. The performance of one activity influences, and is influenced by, the performance of other activities. Therefore, judging the parts of a system individually may lead to undesirable results because system performance depends on the ''balance'' that is achieved between system components. This balance can be measured in terms of capacity, timing, economics, or various other means. Often, performance reflects the effectiveness of the weakest or least efficient element in the system, regardless of the degree of technical sophistication or capability associated with other elements in such a system.

Because optimum system performance is a result of the integration of all the system's elements, it does not necessarily depend on (1) the optimum performance of each individual system component; (2) the ability to cut the single most important cost item in the system budget; or (3) the use of the most advanced technology for system components. Any of these may result in optimization of a particular activity but may denigrate the performance of the system as a whole.

According to the systems approach, the management of systems involves cost trade-offs, relying on the belief that all activities and results can be translated into costs and benefits. Finally, systems management often is not compatible with existing (historical) organizational arrangements (see those discussed in Chapter 16).

Approach of the Book

This book takes a system-oriented approach to the subject of logistics. In looking at logistics-system scope and relationships, integrated system design, operations, logistics strategy, and organization and control, the book moves from the somewhat descriptive (designed to provide necessary background) to the analytical; from the technical aspects of design to the real pay-off, strategic systems management; from the management of logistics systems in individual firms to those encompassing several firms doing business with one another. The essential scheme of the book is laid out in Figure 1–3.

FIGURE 1–3: Plan of the book

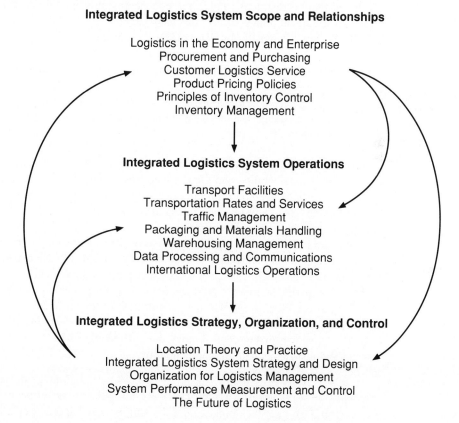

Integrated Logistics System Scope and Relationships

Logistics in the Economy and Enterprise
Procurement and Purchasing
Customer Logistics Service
Product Pricing Policies
Principles of Inventory Control
Inventory Management

Integrated Logistics System Operations

Transport Facilities
Transportation Rates and Services
Traffic Management
Packaging and Materials Handling
Warehousing Management
Data Processing and Communications
International Logistics Operations

Integrated Logistics Strategy, Organization, and Control

Location Theory and Practice
Integrated Logistics System Strategy and Design
Organization for Logistics Management
System Performance Measurement and Control
The Future of Logistics

A system-oriented approach to study means more than a fancy diagram. It means that when examining individual system elements and activities, the important interactions between related logistics elements will be highlighted wherever possible.

The military provides the origin of the term "logistics." Together with tactics and strategy, logistics is one of the three major functions of the military mission. Many of the military's logistics management concepts have been adopted and modified by business to meet a variety of commercial needs.

Military logistics has been defined as "the process by which human effort and facilitating resources are directed toward the objective of *creating and supporting* combat forces and weapons."[15] Logistics, as a function of the business enterprise, devotes primary attention to the movement and storage of products and supplies and is concerned only incidentally with the movement of people, for example, business travel.*

The military logistician often must set up priorities for filling demand, making possible a degree of "customer control" that is virtually impossible in business except under extraordinary circumstances. In most businesses all customer orders are considered "top priority" due to the pressures of competition. In recent years, the excess of supply (capacity) over demand in many industries has encouraged this philosophy.

Business Logistics vis-a-vis Logistics Engineering

Because of its distinctive and different concerns, it is appropriate to identify and discuss briefly an additional branch of logistics management: *logistics engineering*.

The Society of Logistics Engineers (SOLE), a professional organization, comprises about 10,000 practitioners of logistics engineering from government, the armed forces, and defense-related corporations. SOLE offers an engineering-oriented definition of logistics as:

> The art and science of management, engineering, and technical activities concerned with requirements, design, and supplying and maintaining resources to support objectives, plans and operations.[16]

Among the most important concepts of logistics engineering are those of reliability, availability, maintainability, and life-cycle costing.[17] These concepts deal with the trade-offs among the costs of keeping a product or system operational and the costs associated with system failure. The major question involved is how much of a safety factor to build into the logistics engineering support program.

Of major importance for logistics engineering decision making is the concept of life-cycle costing, a calculation that takes into account the total flow of cash expended for the acquisition, operation, and maintenance of a system or piece of equipment over its expected life as a basis for comparing alternative products or systems for possible procurement.

Thus, it is correct to say that the general field of logistics encompasses two major sub-fields. These two sub-fields are commonly referred to as *business logistics* and *logistics engineering*. As shown in Figure 1–4, they are sufficiently different in their orientation as to warrant and justify this definitional dichotomy.

---

*Intercity and international business travel by Americans, most often arranged by company travel departments or by travel agents, represents a substantial volume of traffic for the airline industry, probably more than $30 billion annually. However, business travel involves no inventory management, no warehousing, no customer service and is therefore not a corporate logistics management function.

FIGURE 1-4: Business logistics–logistics engineering continuum illustrating levels of post-purchase logistics support

```
◄——————— BUSINESS LOGISTICS >————— < LOGISTICS ENGINEERING ——————►

1     2     3     4     5     6     7     8     9    10    11    12    13    14    15    16
```

1 Canned Goods[a]   Light Aircraft[e] 9
   2 Textbooks[b]   Industrial Machinery[e] 10
      3 Clothing[c]   Diesel Locomotives[e] 11
        4 Shoes[c]   Helicopters[e] 12
          5 Simple Appliances[d]   Minicomputers[e] 13
            6 Complex Appliances[d]   Commercial Aircraft[e] 14
              7 Automobiles[d]   Combat Aircraft[e] 15
                8 Truck-Tractors[d]   Spacecraft[e] 16

[a]purchased and consumed

[b]purchased and used/retained

[c]post-purchase repair by local tailor shops/shoe repair shops

[d]post-purchase repair and maintenance by local firms using manufacturer-supplied repair parts and manuals

[e]post-purchase period characterized by increasing levels of manufacturer involvement in long-term logistics support for maintenance and availability; total life-cycle cost becomes increasingly important

Business logistics concerns itself with goods that are not generally characterized by extensive, complex, and costly long-term support requirements. Conversely, the major concern of logistics engineers *is* with long-term considerations of product or system reliability, availability, and maintainability.

Our concern here is with *business logistics* as defined earlier in the chapter, not with logistics engineering. The latter constitutes a major field of study in its own right, with its own analytical disciplines and imperatives, such as extended life-cycle costing; design, manufacturing and maintenance of test and support equipment; extensive and complex spares and repair parts provisioning, and more.* Students interested in the subject of logistics engineering are referred to works by such authors as Benjamin S. Blanchard[18] and Norman E. Hutchinson.[19]

The Scope of Business Logistics

The direct relationship between basic activities of production, distribution, and facilitation in the economy and functions of production, marketing, logistics, and finance in the

---

*For example, the B-52 bomber has been in active service in the U.S. Air Force for more than thirty years. Similarly, many models of commercial jetliners have been in service for more than twenty years.

FIGURE 1–5: Basic product-flow activities in the economy and the firm

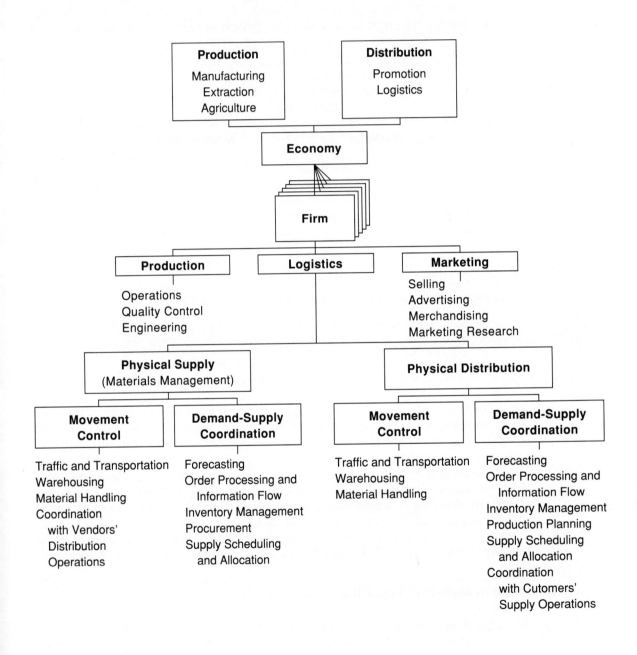

business firm is illustrated in Figure 1–5. Although these activities are omnipresent in the economy, they have varied levels of importance in individual firms.

Figure 1–5 also illustrates how the various managerial and operational functions of business logistics in the firm are grouped and aligned. Familiarity with the diagram will facilitate understanding of the use of terminology throughout the text.

It is important to understand that Figure 1–5 illustrates a situation in which the firm has what may be termed a ''balanced'' or ''two-way'' logistics system. That is, such a firm purchases a substantial amount of inbound raw materials, parts, components, and subassemblies and produces a corresponding volume of finished goods for inventory and subsequent distribution to many customers. Or, the firm may be a wholesaler that purchases from many vendors and then distributes to a large number of customers.

Many firms, however, have what may be termed ''one-way inbound'' or ''one-way outbound'' logistics systems. Examples of such firms are given in Figure 1–6. Firms having primarily one-way inbound logistics systems, such as automobile assembly plants, transportation companies, financial institutions, and independent retail stores that perform no delivery for customers, will view logistics as supporting the production/operations function. Those having primarily one-way outbound logistics systems will tend to view logistics as supporting the marketing function. Either of these situations will likely be reflected in the placement of the logistics function in the organization structure of the firm. This point will be discussed further in Chapter 16, Organization for Logistics Management.

Physical Supply (Materials Management) and Physical Distribution In Figure 1–5, logistics is shown as two related subsets of activity, physical supply, and physical distribution. Each of these, in turn, involves movement control and demand-supply coordination.

Physical supply, or materials management as it is more popularly known, involves the accumulation of materials from various supply points and the coordination of such activity with demand placed on the firm's manufacturing or warehousing facilities. Dean S. Ammer has defined materials management as ''simply the process by which an organization is supplied with the goods and services that it needs to achieve its objectives.''[20]

Once materials are procured, processed, assembled, blended, and refinished, they must be moved either to another facility in a vertically integrated firm or to a customer, again with the attendant coordination of demand and supply. This movement and demand-supply coordination for products outbound is, from the viewpoint of the facility or firm in question, physical distribution. In a logistics channel, a movement of goods from a supplier to a customer is physical distribution to the supplier, but it is physical supply to the customer. Conceptually, physical supply and physical distribution are both accomplished by the supervision of a common set of activities dealing with movement control and demand-supply coordination.

Movement Control Every business firm using, making, or dealing in tangible goods must concern itself with problems of moving goods from one point to another, obviously involving transportation in some form. This includes not only the various forms of long-distance transportation that normally come to mind, but also a second aspect of movement control: the handling of materials over very short distances.

Storage is often necessary to hold goods until the time when they are needed. Thus, storage is the third aspect of movement control. The apparent contradiction between ''storage'' (which implies the absence of physical motion) and ''movement'' can be resolved when

FIGURE 1–6: Examples of primarily inbound, primarily outbound, and balanced logistics systems

Type of Logistics System	Inbound	Outbound
Primarily Inbound Systems		
Automobile assembly plants	Parts, components, subassemblies	Automobiles and light trucks[a]
Transportation companies	Fuel, food (airlines), parts, supplies	Transportation services
Financial institutions	Administrative and office supplies	Financial services
Independent retail stores	Merchandise and supplies	None (store does not deliver)
Primarily Outbound Systems		
Mining companies	Operating supplies	Large quantities of coal, ores
Forest products companies	Operating supplies	Large quantities of lumber, plywood, particle board
Balanced Systems		
Appliance manufacturers	Parts, components, subassemblies, materials	Large quantities of finished goods to many customer destinations
Food processors	Raw foods, cans, bottles, supplies	Large quantities of packaged foods to many customer destinations
Wholesalers	Merchandise	Merchandise

[a] Contrasted with typically as many as 4,000 vendors on the inbound side, the outbound logistics system of an automobile assembly plant is a relatively simple operation: just load the vehicles on rail cars or over-the-road auto carriers and tell the railroad or trucking company the dealer destination(s).

one reasons that storage actually *moves goods closer* to sale or consumption, *in time*, by making goods available *when* as well as where they are needed. It should be noted that, particularly with respect to finished goods, the period of storage may range from hours (some wholesale grocery operations) to months or even years (seldom-ordered repair parts). The trend is to reduce inventories, and this results in faster "throughput" times in storage facilities.*

---

*The word "throughput" is a very important logistics term. It refers to the movement of goods into and later out of a warehouse or other storage facility. It is defined as the quantity of goods "put through" a facility in a given period of time. The quantity can be expressed in terms of value (dollars), weight (tonnage), units (items, cartons of items), and so forth. It is a significant measure of logistics production and productivity.

Demand-Supply Coordination To coordinate demand and supply effectively, one must be able to estimate what the demand will be. This is the goal of forecasting activities, and it allows a firm to anticipate demands from its customers or its production facilities, thereby providing more time to respond to such needs. Demand can be identified through order processing and information flow. The information must be acted upon, and this is the primary function of inventory management, involving the updating of inventories for shipments and receipts; the identification of replenishment needs in terms of quantities, times, and locations; and the preparation of replenishment orders. This, in turn, will trigger the procurement of raw materials or release of goods purchased previously for physical supply, or the planning of the time and place at which production is to take place for physical distribution. Whether for physical supply or distribution, the timing and placement of product to be made available must be determined before such plans are turned over to those in charge of movement control activities for follow-through.

Logistics Management in the Channel of Distribution Unlike manufacturing and marketing responsibilities, logistics management often is beset by problems of varying or overlapping responsibilities for timing, methods, and other considerations in the shipping and storage of goods. Such responsibilities will vary with the terms used in the purchase and sale of goods.

Overlaps of authority regarding matters of logistics are inevitable in distribution channels. What is physical distribution to a producer must by its very nature be physical supply to a customer, whether a wheat grower or wholesaler. Such overlap poses problems in the determination of responsibility for, and control over, logistics activities and in the measurement of their costs and performance effectiveness.

Development of the Logistics Function

The development of the integrated logistics function in the business firm has its origin in traffic management, purchasing, and inventory management activities.

Traffic Management This function gained initial identification and recognition in the United States when the railroad system was developed and the distribution of manufacturing outputs over wide geographic areas began to take place.

Railroad capacity far in excess of need was built and intensive competition was experienced in many geographic areas. In the nineteenth-century era of unregulated rates, the traffic manager able to ''wheel and deal'' in such a manner as to produce a competitive advantage through rate differentials or rebates from the railroads gained an important position in many industrial and commercial organizations.

With the passage of the Interstate Commerce Act in 1887, the role of the traffic manager changed dramatically from that of an entrepreneur to one of a technician charged with the responsibility for translating an increasingly complex set of rate tariffs into management action. The prohibition of rebates and the publication of regulated rates greatly restricted the latitude of the traffic manager to negotiate preferential rates. Increasing emphasis on the technical nature of the task, necessitating the use of a largely ''private'' language and producing somewhat narrow managerial interests, did nothing to enhance the traffic manager's candidacy for top management positions.

Development of Materials Management (Purchasing) The development of the field that has come to be known as materials management was based on interest and support among those managing the procurement function in industry. Its early development occurred primarily among those responsible for procuring and assembling in one place at the right time the various components for highly complex products ranging from civilian aircraft to military defense systems. It was in these companies that the function of procurement was particularly important in relation to other functions, such as traffic and production control, usually identified with materials management. After all, the cost of transportation in relation to the value of the components being received from manufacturer-suppliers often was low. And production control concerned itself largely with the coordination of the assembly process.

It was the design and adoption of two techniques in particular that fostered the reorganization of many other industrial and service firms to achieve closer coordination between procurement, traffic, and production control. The first of these, value analysis, introduced more systematic ways of analyzing the value of functions performed by the components or ingredients used to make up end products. Its adoption resulted in highly publicized cost savings in a number of firms, savings often resulting from the standardization of components or the substitution of less costly components capable of performing (''adding value'') in a comparable manner to more costly ones.

A second major development, that of the technique called materials requirements planning (MRP), resulted in recent years from the availability of large-scale computing facilities. It has allowed firms with coordinated purchasing, traffic, and production control functions to obtain more dependable delivery and reduced inventories by timing purchases according to manufacturing needs and required lead times and tracking the purchases from suppliers to the end of the manufacturing process.

Because of the orientation of this branch of logistics, many materials managers involve themselves in, and relate most closely to, the work of organizations such as the National Association of Purchasing Managers (NAPM), the American Production and Inventory Control Society (APICS), and the Society of Logistics Engineers (SOLE).

Development of Physical Distribution Management Physical distribution management in manufacturing firms was recognized as a separate organizational function or field and developed almost entirely after World War II. At the end of World War II a few industrial firms had integrated departments in charge of all elements of movement control (traffic and transportation, warehousing, and material handling). Grouping of these activities led to the establishment of what are now recognized as the first physical distribution departments.

Early growth of the function occurred in manufacturing firms marketing a wide line of products through retail grocery and drug outlets. In 1954, one of the first physical distribution departments, under the previously stated definition of the term, was created at H. J. Heinz.[21] Here an existing traffic and warehouse division with control over traffic, material handling, privately owned transportation equipment, and warehousing operations was combined with the planning and distribution division. This action added responsibilities for customer order processing, finished goods inventory control, internal order processing, and manufacturing planning, to create a physical distribution department under the former manager of traffic and warehousing reporting to the executive vice president of the firm.

Several physical distribution divisions grew out of cost-cutting investigations initiated during periods of austerity within their respective firms. The timing of early departmental reorganizations coincided closely with periods of recession in the economy. In each of these cases, the initial mission of the new departments was to reduce costs of transportation, storage, and inventory, with only secondary regard for customer service.

In 1956, Lewis, Culliton, and Steele published a milestone study of the use of air freight in physical distribution. It was of particular importance because it crystallized and communicated an idea that a few firms had already begun to implement and that has since dominated thinking in the field of logistics: the total cost concept.[22] In identifying the role that air freight could play in physical distribution, Lewis, Culliton, and Steele concluded, among other things, that (1) a cost identification system breaking out fixed and variable logistics costs and (2) a breadth of system evaluation that included both transportation and inventory-related costs would be necessary to encourage firms to trade higher out-of-pocket costs for air freight to achieve cost savings from inventory reductions.

The total cost concept, in simplified form, is shown in Figure 1–7. The logistics system alternatives at the right of the cost graph are typified by high inventory costs (perhaps resulting from the use of many market-oriented warehouses and inventories), low transportation costs (possibly as a result of using low-cost forms of transportation such as water or rail), and low-cost, mail-speed order processing. Those at the left feature relatively low inventory costs (for relatively small shipments by air or truck), and high-speed order processing (for which costs may be relatively high). However, the lowest total cost system configuration is typified by the use of an intermediate number of inventory locations and a mixture of low- and high-priced transportation services. For many firms operating logistics systems at the right side of the spectrum, the idea that a firm could spend more dollars for transportation services in order to reduce its total logistics costs was pinpointed for the first time.

Identifying the concept was one thing. But, as Lewis, Culliton, and Steele pointed out, implementing it was another. In fact, implementation could be accomplished only by means of (1) revised costing methods to identify relevant costs; (2) coordination of related management functions through improved communication, a revised system of management incentives, or centralized control in one department of all related logistics functions; and (3) a willingness on the part of firms to revise their distribution systems, in some cases closing facilities and in others relocating employees as well as making capital expenditures.

Given the implementation of total cost concepts in a growing number of firms, attention has turned in more recent years to the impact of logistics activities on customer service, inventory availability, and ultimately sales. As a result, the early cost orientation of the field has evolved to a profit orientation, thus drawing the steadily increasing interest of top management.

It is not surprising to find that attention to physical distribution management has been greater in certain types of industries than in others. Among the factors favoring the establishment of separately identified departments to supervise physical distribution activities are (1) multiple sources of raw materials or stocks; (2) a number of manufacturing or storage locations; (3) many consumption points; (4) seasonal or cyclical demand for finished products; (5) problems associated with inventory management arising from the predominance of production to stock rather than to order; (6) product lines comprising many items; and (7) perhaps most important, the need to establish a balance between onerous customer service requirements on the one hand and sizable logistics costs on the other.

There is a considerable exchange of ideas and procedures among firms belonging to industry associations such as the Grocery Manufacturers of America. As a result, changes in management techniques frequently occur on an industry-by-industry basis. Executives of firms in industries where initial growth of physical distribution management has been rapid often have felt compelled to reorganize logistics activities in order to remain competitive in terms of customer service, price, and profit.

FIGURE 1–7: A simplified illustration of the total cost concept, showing hypothetical trade-offs among transportation, inventory, and order-processing costs

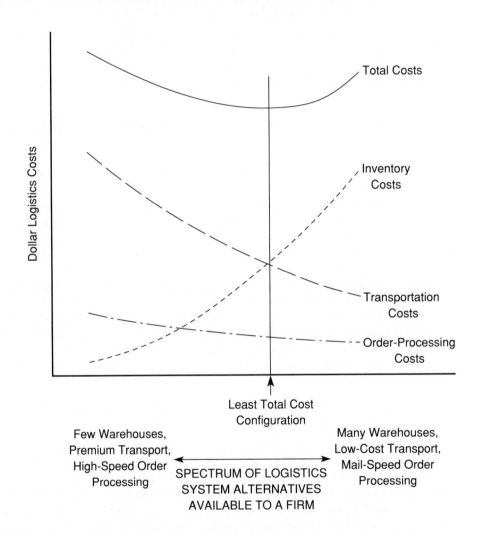

A significant medium for the exchange of such ideas was created in the spring of 1962 with the founding of the National Council of Physical Distribution Management (NCPDM), which became the Council of Logistics Management (CLM) in 1985, by seven representatives from industry and academia sitting around a table in St. Louis.* This organization has grown

---

*The more recent name, Council of Logistics Management (CLM) will be used throughout the remainder of the text, except in formal citations of works originally published under the NCPDM organizational name.

TABLE 1-2: Logistics Executive Compensation
(median salary plus bonus)

Job Title	Highest Third	Middle Third	Lowest Third	Annual Raise
Manager	$ 80,000	$ 57,000	$41,000	6%
Director	95,000	75,000	60,000	7%
Vice President	177,000	122,000	85,000	8%

SOURCE: "The 1988 Ohio State University Survey of Career Patterns in Logistics," *Annual Conference Proceedings of the Council of Logistics Management*, Council of Logistics Management, Oak Brook, Illinois, 1988.

rapidly to a membership of about 6,500, and offers channels of communication across industry categories through its annual meetings, regional roundtables, university seminars, and publications.*

Careers and Compensation The 1988 Ohio State University Survey of Career Patterns in Logistics[23] conducted by Professors Masters and LaLonde furnishes a wealth of up-to-date information about careers and career patterns in the field of logistics. It is clearly a field that offers substantial career opportunity, but it also requires training and education — 46 percent of logistics managers have bachelor's degrees and a further 42 percent hold both bachelor's and master's degrees. Additionally, 17 percent have a professional certification. Compensation ranges are shown in Table 1-2. That logistics management is a field in which career advancement of qualified individuals can be reasonably rapid is evident from the information in Figure 1-8. From the information contained in Table 1-2 and in Figure 1-8, one could reasonably infer that logistics managers have substantial budget responsibility in their organizations, and this is confirmed by the Ohio State study findings that the average logistics budget responsibility for managers is $25,000,000; for directors $35,000,000; and for those holding the title of vice president it is $65,000,000.

In his 1984 survey of compensation trends in distribution, Mahal found that: "Most surveyed [distribution] positions have experienced base salary progression rates that are better than the overall national averages."[24] Careers in distribution and logistics have clearly emerged as a very fertile ground for ambitions and qualified college graduates as noted in *Business Week's* Spring-Summer 1985, *Guide to Careers*.[25]

Relationships of Logistics with Other Functions The subject of the organization of logistics functions within the firm, as well as the relationship of logistics management to other management functions in the firm, will be presented and discussed in detail in Chapter 15.

---

*As described in a CLM brochure, "The Council of Logistics Management is a non-profit organization of people who are interested in improving their knowledge and skill in logistics management. It works in cooperation with private industry and various organizations and institutions to further the development of the logistics and physical distribution concept. It does this through a continuing program of formal and informal activities and discussions designed to (a) develop the theory and understanding of the logistics process, (b) promote the art and science of managing logistics systems, and (c) foster professional dialogue and development in the logistics field."

CLM's current membership numbers about 6,500 managers, executives, and educators in the logistics field. The majority of its members come from business and academia, with a relatively smaller number coming from government or military organizations. The Society of Logistics Engineers (SOLE), discussed briefly later in this chapter, draws its membership largely from the ranks of government, the aerospace industry, and the armed services.

FIGURE 1–8: Logistics respondents' age by job title

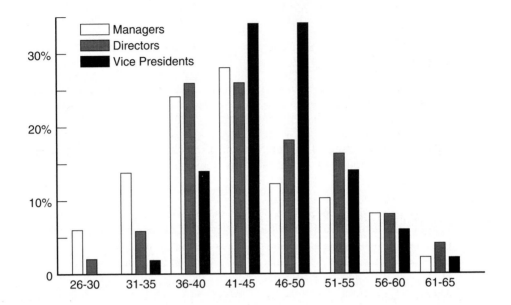

SOURCE: "The 1988 Ohio State University Survey of Career Patterns in Logistics," *Annual Conference Proceedings of the Council of Logistics Management*, Council of Logistics Management, Oak Brook, Illinois, 1988.

However, it is important to be aware that effective management of logistics activities requires coordination and cooperation with other functional areas in the firm.

As noted previously, logistics decisions often involve cost trade-offs. Sometimes these trade-offs conflict with the plans or wishes of production, marketing and finance. For example, production might prefer longer production runs — this would spread setup costs over a greater number of units and thus reduce per-unit manufacturing costs. But, logistics may want shorter production runs of each product to keep inventories in balance. Or, marketing may want to promise unrealistic delivery times or costly rush shipments that would please customers but greatly increase logistics (transportation) costs. Or, finance — always the watchdog of company assets — may complain about the amount of capital invested in inventory or, conversely and perversely, the cost of premium transportation used to minimize inventories.

The purpose of careful management of cost trade-offs — both within the logistics function and among the functional areas of the firm — is to avoid costly sub-optimization at the expense of the whole firm. Doing what is best for the firm overall, regardless of its impact on a particular functional area, is what produces profits and contributes to the firm's survival in a competitive marketplace.

Throughout this book we consider the need to balance the operations of a firm, to avoid suboptimization. It is the task of logistics to facilitate the firm's production and sales efforts, while at the same time helping to reduce production and distribution costs through the careful management of raw-material and finished-goods inventories.

The Increasing Interest in Logistics

A number of explanations have been advanced for the upsurge of interest in, and development of, logistics management. Among them are (1) rapidly escalating costs, particularly for transportation services and the cost of money invested in inventory; (2) the development of mathematical techniques and information processing equipment capable of efficiently handling the mass of data typically required for the analysis of logistics problems; (3) the availability of a wider range of logistics services than ever before, offering both variety and more competition for the shipper's dollar; (4) the deregulation of certain aspects of transport carrier operations, making available services at varying prices; (5) changing markets and channels of distribution, especially for consumer goods; (6) the evolution of the "marketing concept" in many firms; (7) upper management demand for greater asset rationalization; and (8) the increasing globalization of business, including considerations of disruption or discontinuities in the supply of petroleum and other raw materials.

Volatile Costs and Cost Relationships Smart business executives know that costs are *relative*. That is, if a logistics cost increase affects all firms in an industry equally, no firm in that industry will suffer a competitive cost disadvantage. Of course, if an industry's products compete with those of another industry that is not (or is less) affected by a particular cost increase, the former may experience a competitive disadvantage.

However, if there are intraindustry cost differences, the results of cost increases can be substantial and even dramatic. For example, transportation companies, particularly many motor carriers and airlines, have been hard hit by deregulation, which caught many established carriers with relatively higher costs than their competitors. The result has been a large number of bankruptcies among motor carriers and several airline bankruptcies as well.

In respect to rising logistics costs (for example, energy, labor), most industries have been affected more or less equally. Volatility of costs, and changes in cost relationships, are much greater problems for logistics management than are generally rising costs. Executives complain frequently and loudly about rising logistics costs, but volatility of and changes in cost relationships are much greater "villains."

Volatility Interest rates furnish the classic illustration of the effects of volatile costs on logistics management. An inventory decision based on what turns out to be a poor (too low) projection of interest rates can produce moderate or severe financial losses. It can even result in bankruptcies such as have happened to many automobile dealers and discount appliance stores that operate heavily on the basis of bank borrowing, for example, those that "floor finance" their inventory.

Cost Relationships As a consequence of the deregulation of transportation and communications (such as the ruling that brought about the AT&T "breakup") many firms have found themselves stuck with operations that have become high-cost when compared with those of their competitors. For example, some firms had, prior to deregulation, chosen to commit themselves heavily to the use of rail transportation because of its cost advantage to them. They later found themselves badly hurt financially by the combined effects of rail deregulation (increased rates for many firms) and motor carrier deregulation (decreased rates for most firms, especially larger shippers). Plant warehouses and distribution centers designed and located to receive and ship primarily by rail transportation can be converted to heavy use of motor carriers, but usually only at a (substantial) cost. Similar situations have occurred in regard to electronic communications and data transmission costs.

Development of Techniques and Capabilities The development and application of operations research techniques such as linear programming, queuing theory, and simulation, as well as the further development of computer technology, was an important by-product of World War II. It was a short step and an easy transition from the application of techniques for allocating equipment to provide optimum military firepower to the solution of problems of vehicle assignment for the local delivery of consumer products or the allocation of production and shipments between plants and warehouses.

Recently the quality of information for the ongoing operation of a logistics system has been improved with electronic on-line point-of-sale terminals connected to computers, which collect sales and inventory data on a real-time basis. And computing capability has been moved right into many warehouses with the development of minicomputers, microcomputers, and even programmable hand-held calculators capable of handling the day-to-day planning of order processing and work force assignments.

The Application of Quantitative Techniques Logistics offers great opportunity for the application of quantitative techniques. Although research regarding marketing efforts, particularly that concerning consumer behavior, has utilized quantitative techniques, relatively little of it has governed decisions made by marketing managers. Some possible explanations for greater application of quantitative techniques in solving logistics problems are:

1. The human (nonquantitative) factor is great in logistics, but not as important in carrying out logistics as contrasted with marketing activities.

2. Logistics goals often can be more clearly defined than those for marketing efforts.

3. Logistics system alternatives lend themselves more readily to comparative quantification and analysis than do most marketing activities, such as advertising, personal selling, and so on.

Because of basic differences in marketing and logistics activities, it is well to consider them separately while at the same time keeping in mind that, together, they make up a powerful combination that accomplishes a vital task — distribution in the economy.

Expanding Range of Logistics Alternatives In the past three decades, air freight service and intermodal transportation, such as trailer-on-flat-car (TOFC), have become viable alternatives for the transportation of freight. The capabilities of bulk handling methods and bulk transport vehicles have increased greatly in both speed and capacity. Containerized methods of shipment have become available. In addition, a wide variety of mechanized approaches to warehousing and material handling have been developed.

While introducing complexities to the task of logistics system design and management, the development of alternative methods has produced a healthier competitive environment based not only on price competition, but also on more creative ways of accomplishing various tasks.

Reduced Regulation of Transportation Services Recent legislative decisions to reduce regulatory restrictions on the operations of interstate carriers of freight, particularly by air, highway, and rail, have introduced increased levels of price and service competition and reduced the stability in the patterns of both. This has increased pressures on logistics management to build and maintain larger transportation price and service data bases, improve channels of communication with carrier organizations, develop improved analytic capabilities to assess constant price and service changes, and generally review policies for the allocation of freight shipments to carriers. In short, transportation rate and service deregulation has required that logistics be managed better if firms are to meet the challenges of a somewhat turbulent transportation marketplace.

Changing Markets and Channels of Distribution More than half of all Americans now live in suburban areas, according to the 1980 Census of Population. This diffusion of people away from city centers has increased greatly the problem of product distribution, particularly for those types of products the consumer is unwilling to travel great distances to purchase. Although more a problem for retailing organizations than for manufacturers, the diffusion of population has fragmented distribution efforts that depend on large shipment size for efficient operation.

The retailing practice called "scrambled merchandising" has also complicated channels of distribution for convenience goods such as aspirin, writing tablets, soft drinks, and even shopping goods such as small appliances. Gasoline service stations now carry assortments of packaged and frozen goods, soft drinks, bakery goods, and wine. Supermarkets carry proprietary drug items, hand tools, stationery, and many other nonfood items. In many "drugstores," the inventories of proprietary and prescription drugs are small compared with those of household items, paperback books, small appliances, and a host of other nondrug items. The reason for scrambled merchandising is simple: you've got the customer in the store, so why not try to sell the customer more items — and therefore make more profit — than would be possible with a narrower line of goods.

In recent years, retailers and wholesalers, particularly of consumer products, have attempted to improve or at least maintain their profit performance by reducing storage space, maintaining lower inventories, and ordering replacement stocks more frequently in small quantities. The introduction of the computer into retail and wholesale inventory planning and control has had the same effect, with frequent computer review producing orders composed of one or two units of many items, often on a daily basis. These developments have reduced the average sizes of shipments moving from processing and manufacturing facilities, and have also shifted some of the costs of warehousing and inventory maintenance back to primary suppliers who must provide higher levels of logistics services to remain competitive. The inevitable result has been that logistics, especially physical distribution, has become an important element in a manufacturer's marketing strategies.

A further extension of logistics as an element of corporate strategy has also taken place in regard to physical distribution executives having *full international distribution responsibility* within their firms. In 1974 only 9.5 percent of the physical distribution executives surveyed by

LaLonde and Emmelhainz had such responsibility (and authority). By 1984 this number had increased to 25.2 percent.[26] This figure had risen to 69 percent by 1989.[27]

The Marketing Concept   The economies of many of the world's industrialized countries shifted from a seller's to a buyer's market in the late 1940s and early 1950s. As a result, many companies shifted their primary emphasis from production to marketing. The new emphasis was called the "marketing concept," the process of detecting and satisfying customers' needs or wants at a profit. It required the establishment of marketing research efforts charged with the task of finding out what potential customers wanted. Product managers were employed to translate consumer wants into products available to meet them. This led to a proliferation of product offerings among both consumer and industrial product marketers. Consequently, both the number of product-line items (stock-keeping units, or SKUs) and locations (SKULs) for their distribution have been increasing in many industries as a result of the adoption of the marketing concept as a way of business life. Naturally, this has further complicated the task of logistics management.

The Marketing Mix   Closely related to the marketing concept is the marketing mix, which views a product or service as having four characteristics that will determine its appeal to a potential customer. These are often called the "Four P's"; they are product, promotion, price, and place.

Product   This refers to the product or service itself, its intended use, design, quality, convenience of use, and so on.

Promotion   Promotion includes advertising, eye-catching packaging, display, sampling, and other activities that bring the product or service to the attention of the potential buyer.

Price   Price is both *absolute* (a dollar number) and *relative* to the quality or other characteristics of the product or service, and to competing products or services as well. Price is also affected by terms of sale, such as early payment discounts, charges for credit, and shipping charges. Many of these terms of sale affect logistics decisions and costs and will be discussed in Chapter 2.

Place   As noted earlier, a prime task of logistics is to provide *place* utility. Unless a product is where it is needed when it is needed, it is of no use to the potential buyer. However, products do vary as to "customer patience." That is, a consumer expects to find Campbell's Tomato Soup® on a supermarket shelf (convenience goods), will shop around (or wait a few days) to purchase a particular brand of blue jeans (shopping goods), and will be willing to (expect to) wait two or three weeks for a special order at the local bookstore. Such differences affect logistics policies and decisions and will be discussed in Chapters 5 and 6 respectively.

The Globalization of Business

The post–World War II period saw the complete rebuilding of the shattered economies of Western Europe and Japan, as well as the emergence of new "international players" in the production of goods. The latter include Hong Kong, Taiwan, South Korea, Brazil, and Mexico, to list just a few. Today, parts or subassembly components for a product may be manufactured in ten different countries and shipped to another country for assembly with some components made there. The finished goods may then be shipped to markets in a dozen other countries.

Visits to car dealerships or to TV, VCR, and radio stores or even to clothing departments in many stores, reflect the tremendous impact of imports on the American marketplace that has taken place in the past two decades. At the same time, the United States continues to export great quantities of goods to other nations. Coupled with this great growth in international trade in raw materials, components and finished goods are problems arising from political instability in many areas of the world.

In Chapter 13—"International Logistics Operations"—we will discuss the significance of and challenges posed by these international trade developments to logistics managers.

Logistics Costs in the Firm

Estimating logistics costs in an individual firm is an imprecise art, given the current state of accounting for such costs. Inbound transportation costs may be buried in a "cost of materials for manufacturing" account in a manufacturing organization or a "cost of goods sold" account in a retail enterprise. Outbound transportation costs may not be known if a firm sells on a basis requiring customers to arrange for their own transportation away from the plant. Material-handling labor at a plant or warehouse may be charged to "manufacturing labor." Order-processing costs may be a part of "sales service." A portion of inventory carrying costs may be contained in the "interest expense" category. Currently, no functional area of business is more poorly served by accounting practice than logistics.

It was seen earlier that logistics costs are of major importance from a macroeconomic point of view. Naturally, their degree of importance will vary greatly from firm to firm. The following sections explore several basic factors accounting for such variations, including product characteristics, the firm's role in its channel of distribution, and competitive strategies elected by a firm's top management.

Product Characteristics Two characteristics illustrate the comparative differences in products that affect the major logistics costs of transportation and inventory maintenance: (1) dollar density (value per unit of cubic measure) and (2) weight density (weight per cubic measure). This assumes, for the moment, that we hold constant the level of customer logistics service needed to remain competitive.

Figure 1–9 illustrates the relationship between dollar and weight density and the alternative methods and costs of transportation that can be considered in distributing various products. A variety of products are plotted on this graph. Clearly, as one moves to products with higher dollar and weight densities (from the lower left-hand corner toward the middle of the graph), the cost of transportation as a proportion of the total sales value of the product will decline and the number of viable logistics alternatives available to us increases.

The manner in which goods are distributed depends on the way in which transportation and inventory costs (including warehousing) are likely to be altered under different alternatives. For this consideration, look at the various alternative transportation and inventory configurations shown in Figure 1–10(a). Start with configuration X in Figure 1–10(a) involving computing equipment. Clearly, the high value of the product suggests that the firm can spend much more money for faster, more dependable forms of transportation to enable it to reduce the sizes of its individual product inventories, the overall inventory level, and inventory carrying costs. The converse is true for crude oil, as shown in Figure 1–10(b).

FIGURE 1–9: Relationships between dollar and weight densities of products and the alternative methods and costs of transportation that can be considered in distributing them (The graph shows the general nature, not the magnitude, of the relationships.)

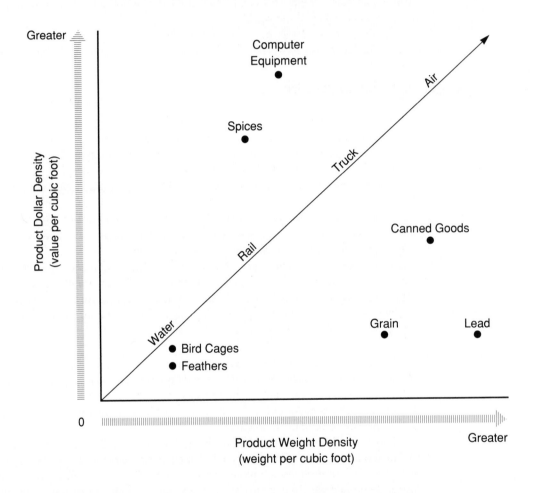

Notice that although total costs are perhaps 3 percent of sales for computing equipment and 37 percent of sales for crude oil, in both cases a redesign of the respective systems resulted in a higher proportion of expense for transportation than for inventory maintenance.

In the case of computing equipment, the firm decided to spend more for transportation in order to reduce inventory carrying costs substantially. From a configuration in which it actually spent more to carry our inventory than to transport goods, we shifted to an alternative requiring about twice the amount of transportation costs as inventory carrying costs. Just the reverse was decided for crude oil.

FIGURE 1–10: The relative costs (hypothetical) of various transportation and inventory alternatives for the distribution of computing equipment (a) and crude oil (b)

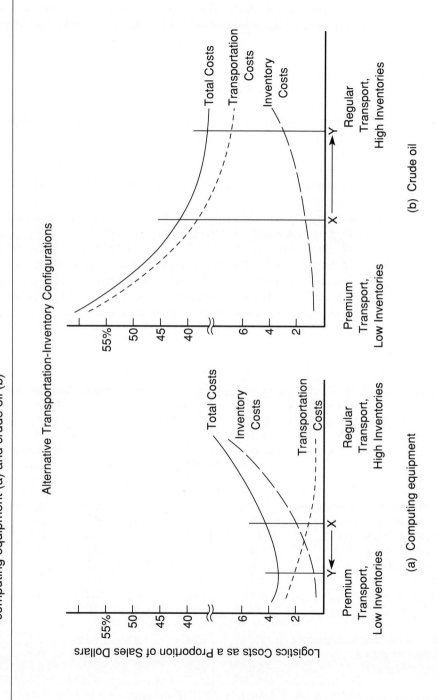

Alternative Transportation-Inventory Configurations

LaLonde and Zinszer, in analyzing customer service policies followed by manufacturing and merchandising firms, compiled the logistics cost information presented in Table 1–3. It indicates that the sum of transportation, warehousing, inventory carrying, order processing, and related costs as a proportion of sales varied in 1975 from 4.4 percent for pharmaceutical manufacturers to 25.9 percent for industrial goods merchandisers. Interestingly, the relative proportions of transportation-related and inventory-related costs do not appear to vary in direct relation to the probable dollar density or weight density of the broad product categories for which information was collected.

In 1988, the CLM published an updated survey of customer service.[28] This publication includes shipper estimates of logistics costs collected in a manner similar to that of the 1976 NCPDM study. Table 1–4 presents the 1988 survey results.

In the opinion of the authors of this text, the significant differences between the cost percentages shown in Table 1–3 and Table 1–4 represent more careful identification, allocation, and internal reporting of logistics costs in 1988 as contrasted with 1976. This is most clearly demonstrated with respect to cost allocation in categories of expense such as "administration" as contrasted with cost categories for which reasonably accurate information has long been recorded, such as transportation costs.

In addition, the 1988 CLM study included two cost categories not specifically identified in the 1976 NCPDM study: (1) interest and (2) taxes, insurance, and so forth. The authors speculate that many expenses in each of these two cost categories have only recently been "broken out" by company accountants to show amounts that should be charged as logistics costs rather than being lumped together in corporate totals under general and administrative expense. The authors further speculate that much, if not most, of the interest cost shown Table 1–4

TABLE 1–3: Logistics Costs as a Percentage of Sales Dollar in Selected Industries

	Inbound and Outbound Transportation	Inventory Carrying	Ware-housing	Admini-stration	Receiving and Shipping	Pack-aging	Order Process-ing	Total
All manufacturing companies	6.2%	3.6%	3.6%	0.5%	0.8%	0.7%	0.5%	13.6%
Chemicals and plastics	6.3	1.6	3.3	0.3	0.7	1.4	0.6	14.1
Food manufacturing	8.1	0.3	3.5	0.4	0.9	a	0.2	13.4
Pharmaceutical	1.4	a	1.2	0.7	0.5	0.1	0.5	4.4
Electronics	3.2	2.5	3.2	1.2	0.9	1.1	1.2	13.3
Paper	5.8	0.1	-4.6	0.2	0.3	a	0.2	11.2
Machinery and tools	4.5	1.0	2.0	0.5	0.5	1.0	0.5	10.0
All Other	6.8	1.0	2.9	1.2	1.4	0.4	0.4	14.1
All merchandising companies	7.4%	10.3%	4.2%	1.2%	0.6%	1.2%	0.7%	25.6%
Consumer goods	8.1	8.5	4.0	1.3	0.9	0.9	0.5	24.2
Industrial goods	5.9	13.7	2.9	0.7	0.2	2.0	1.0	26.4

aThese cost categories were used by less than 30 percent of the firms surveyed.

SOURCE: B. J. LaLonde and P. H. Zinzer, *Customer Service: Meaning and Measurement* (Chicago: National Council of Physical Distribution Management, 1976), Chapter III, pp. 17–79.

TABLE 1-4: Costs as a percentage of sales for each of the following distribution categories, both today and as projected in 1990[a][b]

	Food		Chemical		Pharmaceutical		Auto		Paper	
	Today	1990	Today	1990	Today	1990	Today	1990	Today	1990
Inbound transportation—common carrier	1.8%	1.9%	1.1%	1.4%	.9%	.9%	1.9%	1.8%	2.0%	2.7%
Inbound transportation—private carrier	.9	.9	.9	1.0	.9	.9	c	c	c	c
Outbound transportation—common carrier	2.9	2.9	3.2	3.4	1.2	1.5	2.6	2.3	5.0	5.0
Outbound transportation—private carrier	2.0	1.5	1.0	1.7	.9	.9	c	c	c	c
Administration	.8	.8	1.0	1.0	.9	.6	.9	1.0	2.0	c
Receiving and shipping	.9	.8	.9	1.0	.7	.9	.9	1.0	c	c
Packaging	2.9	1.3	1.9	2.0	1.2	1.1	.9	1.0	1.0	c
Order processing	.4	.5	.8	.9	.6	.6	.9	1.0	1.0	c
Warehousing, in-plant	.9	1.0	1.0	1.0	.8	.9	c	c	2.7	c
Warehousing, field—private	.8	1.0	.6	.8	.5	c	3.0	c	c	c
Warehousing, field—public	.9	1.0	.9	.9	.4	.5	c	c	c	c
Inventory carrying cost	1.0	1.0	1.8	1.0	1.4	1.0	4.0	5.0	3.0	2.0
Interest	1.1	1.0	1.8	1.9	2.0	c	c	c	c	c
Taxes, insurance	.5	.7	.9	.9	.8	.5	.4	.5	1.7	c
TOTAL	17.8%	16.3%	17.8%	18.9%	13.2%	10.3%	15.5%	13.6%	18.4%	9.7%
	d		d		d		d		d	d

(continued)

[a] Median value of responses.
[b] Zero values omitted from calculations.
[c] Fewer than six responses.
[d] These totals are actually larger than shown because data was not included for some categories when there were less than six responses for a category by an industry.

SOURCE: B. LaLonde and M. Cooper, *Customer Service: A Management Perspective*, Council of Logistics Management, 1988, Appendix A, Responses to Shipper Questionnaire, Table III.B.2.

TABLE 1–4 (continued): Costs as a percentage of sales for each of the following distribution categories, both today and as projected in 1990[ab]

	Electronic		Cloth/Textiles		Other Manufacturing		Total Manufacturing		Merchandise		Total Response	
	Today	1990	Today	1990	Today	1990	Today	1990	Today	1990	Today	1990
Inbound transportation— common carrier	1.0%	1.0%	2.0%	1.8%	1.3%	1.0%	1.7%	1.5%	1.3%	1.4%	1.6%	1.5%
Inbound transportation— private carrier	c	c	c	c	.5	.5	1.0	1.0	c	c	1.0	1.0
Outbound transportation— common carrier	1.9	1.8	2.0	2.5	2.3	2.9	2.7	2.8	2.0	3.0	2.8	2.9
Outbound transportation— private carrier	c	c	c	c	1.0	1.0	2.0	2.0	c	c	1.2	1.4
Administration	.3	.6	1.0	c	1.0	.8	1.0	1.0	.8	.7	1.0	1.0
Receiving and shipping	.8	.9	c	c	1.0	1.0	1.0	1.0	.9	.9	1.0	1.0
Packaging	c	c	.9	.9	1.0	1.0	1.0	1.0	c	c	1.1	1.0
Order processing	.8	.9	.9	1.5	1.5	1.0	1.0	1.0	1.5	1.0	1.0	1.0
Warehousing, in-plant	.8	.9	1.4	1.5	1.5	1.3	1.0	1.2	c	c	1.0	1.2
Warehousing, field—private	c	c	c	c	.9	.8	1.0	1.0	c	c	1.0	1.0
Warehousing, field—public	c	c	c	c	.5	.5	1.0	1.0	c	c	1.0	1.0
Inventory carrying cost	c	c	c	c	4.0	4.0	2.0	2.0	6.0	5.0	2.0	2.0
Interest	c	c	c	c	4.0	4.5	2.0	3.0	c	c	2.0	3.0
Taxes, insurance	c	c	c	c	2.0	3.3	1.0	1.3	2.0	3.0	1.0	1.5
TOTAL	5.6%[d]	6.1%[d]	8.2%[d]	7.6%[d]	22.5%	23.6%	19.4%	20.8%	14.5%[d]	15.0%[d]	18.7%	20.5%

[a] Median value of responses.
[b] Zero values omitted from calculations.
[c] Fewer than six responses.
[d] These totals are actually larger than shown because data was not included for some categories when there were less than six responses for a category by an industry.
SOURCE: B. LaLonde and M. Cooper, *Customer Service: A Management Perspective*, Council of Logistics Management, 1988, Appendix A, Responses to Shipper Questionnaire, Table III.B.2.

is imputed interest, a very real cost albeit one not shown in traditional corporate income statements.

The 15 years between 1975 and 1990 have been a period of major advances in logistics cost identification by firms, but the process is not yet complete. However, as the contrast between the percentages in Tables 1–3 and 1–4 shows, much has been done, and many more firms today have a clearer understanding of their logistics costs than they did only 15 years ago.

In his broad annual survey of physical distribution costs Herbert W. Davis computes logistics costs as a percentage of sales *and also* in terms of dollar expenditures per hundredweight of goods shipped.[29] Table 1–5 shows clearly that high value goods such as pharmaceuticals incur very high costs per pound shipped, but have low physical distribution costs as a percentage of the sales dollar, while nearly the reverse is true of lower value goods such as industrial (bulk) chemicals and canned and processed food.

From industry to industry, regardless of the nature of the product involved, economic relationships suggest that the most effective logistics systems do not involve extremely large expenditures for one major category of expense (transportation or inventory maintenance, for example) vis-a-vis the other. Rather, for most products under most circumstances, there is a moderately greater expenditure for transportation than for inventory maintenance.

TABLE 1–5: Average Distribution Cost by Industry[a]

	Percent of Sales	Cost per Hundredweight
All Companies	7.50%	$33.35
Industrial Nondurable	8.10	16.08
Plastics	8.65	4.90
Chemicals	6.40	3.50
Nonchemical	8.82	12.50
Hospital and medical supply	8.15	58.55
Industrial Durable	7.40	37.64
Industrial durable < $10/lb.	8.07	27.49
Consumer Nondurable	7.14	36.58
Food Products		
Dry and packaged food	8.66	6.88
Canned and processed food	8.58	4.79
Temperature-controlled food	7.94	7.03
Nonfood in grocery channel	9.39	9.48
Pharmaceuticals > $10/lb.	3.77	119.35
Pharmaceuticals < $10/lb.	5.59	22.63
Consumer Durable	8.86	44.48
Retail Stores	8.22	29.13

[a]Average distribution costs by industry or trade group show significant variations, underlining importance to individual firms of developing standard cost figures that can be compared with their industry groups rather than overall averages.

SOURCE: "Physical Distribution Costs 1984: In Some Companies, A Profit Contribution, In Others Cost-Price Margins Continue to Dwindle," Herbert W. Davis, *Annual Conference Proceedings, 1984*, The National Council of Physical Distribution Management, Chicago, Ill., p. 37.

Firm's Role in the Channel of Distribution The role that a firm plays in a channel of distribution, including the terms of sale under which it does business, determines not only the relative importance of physical supply and physical distribution costs in its cost structure, but also influences the degree of knowledge and control that the firm's management may have concerning the actual costs of logistics activities in its operation. Consider Figure 1–11, showing four firms in a channel of distribution, all contributing to the ultimate distribution of the same product.

Firm A is a supplier of raw materials to processors in the channel who subsequently distribute finished products. Several things can be said about its logistics costs. First, it is likely that Firm A is located closer to its sources of supply than to its customers. Thus, physical distribution costs probably are much greater than physical supply costs in this firm. Second, its product may have relatively low value, producing logistics cost levels in relation to sales similar to those for crude oil in Figure 1–11. Finally, there are few costs of physical supply obscured in the value of the product stored in Firm A's warehouses at the supply source. Firm A probably has extensive knowledge of the costs of business logistics as a proportion of its sales.

In contrast, Firm D in Figure 1–11 owns its own supply sources, processing plant, warehouses at the processing location, and market-oriented distribution warehouses. Both physical supply and physical distribution activities will constitute important elements of the total cost of doing business in Firm D. Greater control over the channel also provides more complete information in regard to logistics costs incurred at various points in the channel.

Competitive Strategies Competing firms may adopt distinctly different strategies leading to relatively higher or lower costs for a functional activity such as logistics. For example, the conscious adoption of something other than a lowest total logistics cost strategy can influence the relative importance of cost categories. Such strategies include support for speculative purchasing (in advance of price increases, for example) or a high level of customer service.

An increase in logistics expenditures can reduce production costs in a firm by enabling it to expand its geographical marketing territory or its share of the market, or both. The resultant increase in sales volume will result in lower costs of production if economies of scale are present. And, a firm that thus lowers its production costs may be willing to incur greater transportation or inventory costs while being able to realize the same profit margins as its competitors. This process can "feed on itself," for example, growth leads to lower production costs, which can lead to further market expansion, and so on. The Japanese have taught this lesson very well to the rest of the world.

SUMMARY

Logistics in an organization encompasses activities associated with both materials management (for inbound raw materials, supplies, components, and products purchased for resale) and physical distribution (for outbound components and finished products). The president of the Norge Division of Borg-Warner Corporation once gave an excellent rationale for this coordinated approach to the planning and management of physical flows:

> We have a production lead time of 90 days or better and if we stop the line abruptly, material continues to arrive for weeks afterward or we incur very substantial cancellation charges. In our business, and I suspect in many others, an effective system of physical distribution cannot begin at the end of the production line . . . It must also apply at the very beginning of

FIGURE 1–11: A channel of distribution for a single product, indicating the relative logistical role of Firms A, B, C, and D

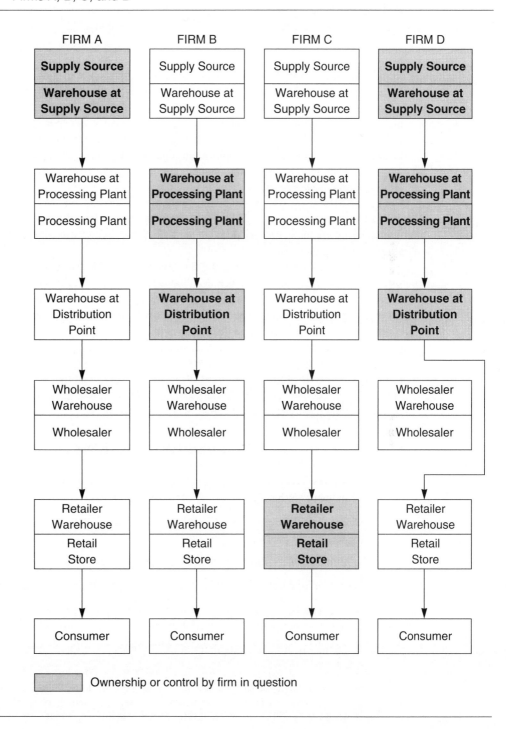

the production process — at the planning, the forecasting and the scheduling stages and not simply from the end of the production line.[30]

Further, coordination must extend beyond corporate boundaries to deal with the inevitable overlap in responsibility and conflicts of logistical goals that arise in a channel of distribution.

The field of logistics management has evolved from specific ideas that can be traced back in the literature at least as far as the early nineteenth century, and in a more general sense back to the earliest recorded history of man. However, forces emerging in the last three decades have accelerated the emphasis on logistics as a previously-neglected area of management. Among such forces are changing cost relationships, the development of new analytical techniques and capabilities, the expanding range of methods for transporting and handling materials, reduced regulation of certain modes of interstate transportation, changes in the marketplace and in channels of distribution through which goods move, pressures created by the widespread adoption of the marketing concept, and recent disruptions in the supply of petroleum and other raw materials.

As the field of logistics has evolved, emphasis has spread from the earlier narrow development of approaches to materials management in defense-oriented firms and physical distribution management in the grocery products manufacturing industry, to a much wider spectrum of commercial organizations.

Costs form an important part of the decision process for logistics management. As we have seen, they vary widely in importance from industry to industry as firms attempt to balance basic costs of transportation and inventory maintenance in such a way that a relatively low total cost results. The relative importance of these costs will depend on such factors as the physical characteristics of the product, a firm's role in its channel of distribution, and the various competitive strategies, including logistics strategies, adopted by a company's top management.

Before turning to the design and operation of logistics systems it will be useful to explore in the next three chapters several areas of business policy making and decisions that impact and sometimes constrain logistics management. These include procurement and purchasing policies, pricing policies, and customer service standards.

DISCUSSION QUESTIONS

1. Why did it take so many years before the logistics concept became widely accepted by industry? What forces brought this about? Explain.

2. Define "marketing activities" and "logistics activities." What is the significance of the differences between them?

3. What economic utilities are created by logistics activities?

4. What is a logistics channel? How does it differ from a marketing channel?

5. Are quantitative techniques more useful for analyzing and managing logistics activities or marketing activities? Why?

6. Trace the historical development of the logistics function. How good a career field is it today?

7. Why are rapidly changing interest rates a problem for logistics management? Explain.

8. How has transportation deregulation affected logistics management? Explain.

9. How are "the marketing concept" and "marketing mix" related to logistics? Explain.

10. Does logistics have a place in the corporate strategic planning process? Explain.

SUGGESTED READINGS

Annual Conference Proceedings, the National Council of Physical Distribution Management, National Council of Physical Distribution Management through 1984 and the Council of Logistics Management, Council of Logistics Management since 1985, Oak Brook, Illinois. The annual volumes in this series present many articles of current interest covering a broad spectrum of physical distribution and logistics topics. Of special interest are Bernard J. LaLonde's annual update articles on careers and compensation in the field.

Corporate Profitability & Logistics, Council of Logistics Management, Oak Brook, Illinois, 1987. The title of this book is a bit misleading in that it treats broadly many aspects of logistics management.

Measuring and Improving Productivity in Physical Distribution, an A. T. Kearney study undertaken for NCPDM, National Council of Physical Distribution Management, Chicago, Illinois, 1984. Probably the best available combination of surveys and summaries of macroeconomic logistics cost information currently available. See especially Section I and Appendix F.

Bowersox, Donald J., *et. al*, *Leading Edge Logistics: Competitive Positioning for the 1990's*, Council of Logistics Management, Oak Brook, Illinois, 1989. This comprehensive survey of 695 North American firms contains a wealth of information on current logistics management practices.

LaLonde, Bernard J. and Paul H. Zinzer, *Customer Service: Meaning and Measurement*, National Council of Physical Distribution Management, Chicago, Illinois, 1976. Chapter 3 of this book contains detailed information about logistics costs in a variety of industries in the 1970s.

LaLonde, Bernard, M. Cooper, and T. Noordewier, *Customer Service: A Management Perspective*, Council of Logistics Management, Oak Brook, Illinois, 1988. Although focused on the topic of customer service, this study contains a wealth of information on current logistics management practices and costs.

LaLonde, Bernard and M. Cooper, *Partnerships in Providing Customer Service: A Third Party Perspective*, Council of Logistics Management, Oak Brook, Illinois, 1989. Building on previous customer service studies, this study addresses the issues from the perspective of third-party providers of logistics services. Similar to the 1976 and 1988 studies cited above, this study also includes extensive information on logistics management practices and costs.

Robeson, James F. and Robert G. House, *The Distribution Handbook*, The Free Press, New York, New York, 1985. This formidable handbook is an excellent reference source and a comprehensive treatment (32 chapters) of physical distribution topics organized into 14 sections.

Shapiro, Roy D., "Get Leverage From Logistics," *Harvard Business Review*, May–June, 1984, pages 119–26. The thrust of this article is that logistics should be viewed as a major source of potential strategic competitive advantage, and that it unqualifiedly deserves strong attention from top management.

Sharman, Graham, "The Rediscovery of Logistics," *Harvard Business Review*, September–October, 1984, pages 71–79. The theme of this article is that "aggressive competitors and demanding customers [are] bring[ing] new prominence to an unglamorous old function [logistics]." Sharman emphasizes the need for strong executive action in the logistics area if a firm wants to stay competitive and profitable.

The following publications are generally regarded as the leading academic journals and trade publications in the field of business logistics. Publication periods vary.

Academic Journals

International Journal of Physical Distribution & Logistics Management (three journals and five monograph issues each year)

Journal of Business Logistics (two issues per year)

Journal of Transportation Management (two issues per year)

The Logistics and Transportation Review (four issues per year)

Transportation Journal (four issues per year)

Trade Publications

Distribution (monthly)

Handling and Shipping Management (monthly)

Inbound Logistics (monthly)

Traffic World (weekly)

Transportation & Distribution (monthly)

ENDNOTES

1. Graham Sharman, ''The Rediscovery of Logistics,'' *Harvard Business Review* (September–October 1984): 71–79.

2. Roy D. Shapiro, ''Get Leverage from Logistics,'' *Harvard Business Review* (May–June 1984): 119.

3. Ralph Borsodi, *The Distribution Age* (New York: D. Appleton & Co., 1929): 3.

4. Edward W. Smykay, Donald J. Bowersox, and Frank H. Mossman, *Physical Distribution Management* (New York: The Macmillan Co., 1961).

5. Peter F. Drucker, ''The Economy's Dark Continent,'' *Fortune*, Vol. 72 (April 1962): 103.

6. J. L. Heskett, Robert M. Ivie, and Nicholas A. Glaskowsky, Jr., *Business Logistics: Management of Physical Supply and Distribution* (New York: The Ronald Press Company, Inc., 1964).

7. National Council of Physical Distribution Management, *Measuring and Improving Productivity in Physical Distribution*, an A. T. Kearney study undertaken for NCPDM (Chicago: NCPDM, 1984).

8. *Ibid.*, 336.

9. *Ibid.*, 2.

10. Paul D. Converse, ''The Other Half of Marketing,'' *Twenty-Sixth Boston Conference on Distribution* (Boston: Boston Trade Board, 1954): 22–25; reprinted in Alfred L. Seelye, ed., *Marketing in Transition* (New York: Harper & Row, 1958): 114–21.

11. A. W. Shaw, *An Approach to Business Problems* (Cambridge: Harvard University Press, 1916): 99–100.

12. Definitions Committee of the American Marketing Association, ''1948 Report,'' *The Journal of Marketing* (October 1948): 202.

13. *Ibid.*

14. Shapiro, "Get Leverage," 126.

15. James L. Quinn, *Logistics Management Concepts and Cases* (Wright-Patterson Air Force Base, Ohio: School of Systems and Logistics, Air Force Institute of Technology, 1971): 8. (Emphasis supplied.)

16. Society of Logistics Engineers (SOLE) (August, 1974).

17. Comprehensive discussions of these and other elements of government and military logistics can be found in Benjamin S. Blanchard, *Logistics Engineering and Management*, 2nd ed. (Englewood Cliffs, N.J.: Prentice-Hall, Inc., 1980).

18. Benjamin S. Blanchard, *Logistics Engineering and Management*, 3d ed. (Englewood Cliffs, N.J.: Prentice-Hall, Inc., 1986).

19. Norman E. Hutchinson, *An Integrated Approach to Logistics Management* (Englewood Cliffs, N.J.: Prentice-Hall, Inc., 1987).

20. Dean S. Ammer, *Materials Management and Purchasing*, 4th ed. (Homewood, Ill.: Richard D. Irwin, Inc., 1980): 2.

21. For a full description of the organization of H. J. Heinz' physical distribution division, see John H. Frederick, *Traffic Department Organization* (Philadelphia: Chilton Co., 1956): 27–32.

22. Howard T. Lewis, James W. Culliton, and Jack D. Steele, *The Role of Air Freight in Physical Distribution* (Boston: Division of Research, Graduate School of Business Administration, Harvard University, 1956).

23. *Annual Conference Proceedings of the Council of Logistics Management*, vol. 1 (Oak Brook, Illinois: Council of Logistics Management, 1988): 23–50.

24. David G. Mahal, "Compensation Trends in Distribution: The 1984 Survey," *Proceedings of the Annual Meeting of the National Council of Physical Distribution Management, 1984*, 25.

25. Nicholas Basta, "Inventory and Distribution," *Business Week's Guide to Careers* (Spring/Summer 1985): 23.

26. Bernard J. LaLonde and Larry W. Emmelhainz, "Distribution Careers: 1984," *Annual Conference Proceedings of the National Council of Physical Distribution Management, 1984*, 13.

27. James M. Masters and Bernard J. LaLonde, "The 1989 Ohio State University Survey of Career Patterns in Logistics," *Annual Conference Proceedings of the Council of Logistics Management, 1989*, 32.

28. B. LaLonde, M. Cooper, and T. Noordewier, *Customer Service: A Management Perspective* (Oak Brook, Illinois: Council of Logistics Management, 1988): Appendix A, Table III.B.2.

29. Herbert W. Davis, "Physical Distribution Costs 1984," *Proceedings of the Annual Meeting of The National Council of Physical Distribution Management, 1984*, 29–40.

30. "From Red to Black," *Handling & Shipping* (September, 1966): 72.

Purchasing decisions trigger the flow of goods in a logistics system.

CHAPTER TWO

Procurement and Purchasing

LEARNING OBJECTIVES

The objectives of this chapter are to:

➤ Distinguish between the broader concept of procurement and the narrower concept of purchasing.

➤ Define and discuss the functions of a purchasing department.

➤ Show the role of the purchasing department in the procurement process.

➤ Explain the effects of various procurement policies on logistics management.

➤ Discuss how buying for resale differs from industrial purchasing for use.

➤ Consider the special purchasing considerations involved in acquiring capital goods.

This chapter discusses procurement and purchasing policies that impact on logistics management, and frequently also act as constraints on logistics decisions. The terms "procurement" and "purchasing" are commonly used interchangeably in practice, although procurement is generally considered to have a broader meaning than purchasing. The discussion in this chapter takes the view that procurement is a process that includes the activity of purchasing.

The act of buying (purchasing) is only the tip of the iceberg representing procurement activities. Purchasing is preceded and followed by many other activities that are part of the overall procurement process. As many firms discovered to their dismay during the 1973–74 period of supply shortages, procurement involves the structuring of supplier relationships to insure the availability of resources vital to a firm's operations.

After considering procurement generally, and particularly the purchasing function, the chapter emphasis shifts to specific procurement policies that impact logistics management. The discussion includes items purchased repeatedly and in some volume (such as raw materials, component parts used in manufacturing, and consumables and supplies used in manufacturing or operations), goods purchased for resale, and capital goods.

THE INDUSTRIAL PURCHASING DEPARTMENT

Most procurement actions are carried out by the purchasing department in an industrial firm. Figure 2–1 indicates the influences exerted upon and by the purchasing department and the relationships between purchasing and other logistics functions.

Within each industry, there are environmental factors that act as constraints on purchasing. These include external influences from competitors, suppliers, and customers; technological change; and general economic conditions, particularly those affecting supplier economic health and the adequacy of supply sources.

As can be seen in Figure 2-2, the purchasing function encompasses only one of the nine steps of the materials cycle. The grouping of these steps into five categories of corporate activities illustrates their interdependency. The purchasing function cannot be activated without first receiving information from several other departments; and once activated, it triggers the activities that complete the materials cycle.

Top management influences — and sometimes directs — procurement policies in the light of environmental constraints and corporate objectives. Procurement policies set guidelines for purchasing department organization, functions, and responsibilities, which in turn define purchasing operations. The output of the purchasing department is the value added to the product through the creation of possession utility. In some firms the major effort of the purchasing department is directed toward the procurement of materials, parts, and components that find their way into the finished goods of the company. However, the opposite is true in some cases. For example, in the case of the Michelin Tire Company, there are only *two* rubber buyers for the entire firm but more than *fifty* people concerned with the purchase of capital goods and maintenance, repair, and operating supplies to keep the production system running.

Due to the extensive contacts that a (wide-awake) purchasing department has with the "outside world" of vendors, the activities of the purchasing department supply feedback to those charged with establishing company objectives and policies. As the President of Allen-Bradley, a machine tool manufacturing firm, put it:

> Purchasing provides feedback on changes that are going to affect key decisions on new product selection, product design, choice of materials and planning . . . especially cash planning.[1]

FIGURE 2–1: Purchasing Department influences and relationships

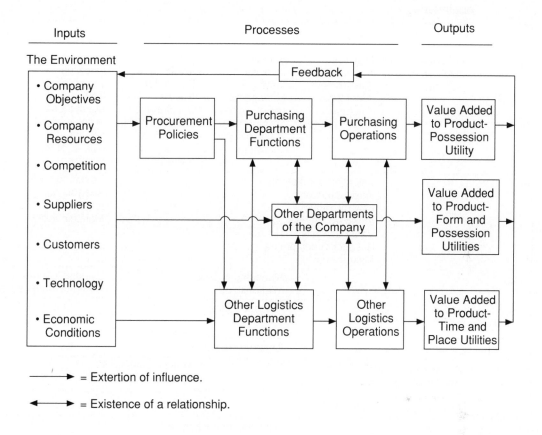

= Extertion of influence.

= Existence of a relationship.

Purchasing Department Functions

Within the guidelines established by company procurement policies, the purchasing department is responsible for conducting procurement functions. The purchasing department has been defined as:

> . . . corporate management's group of professional and expert specialists for the procurement of materials, supplies, tools and services required by all other groups in the enterprise in the over-all process of adding value.[2]

The president (at the time) of a major high-technology manufacturing firm put it more forcefully.

> There is a tendency on the part of many to think that the purchasing mission is to buy things, whereas I think the purchasing mission is to be a part of a larger system creating profits and

FIGURE 2-2: The "materials cycle" in various types of firms, indicating the relationships between purchasing, procurement, materials management, buying for resale, and logistics engineering

Materials Cycle Stage	(1) Activities Involving Purchasing	(2) Activities Involving Procurement (All of those in column (1) plus all of the following:	(3) Activities Involving Materials Management (All of those in columns (1) & (2) plus the following:	(4) Activities Involving Buying for Resale (All of those in columns (1), (2), and (3) plus all of the following:	(5) Activities Involving Logistics Engineering (All of those in columns (1), (2), and (3) plus all of the following:
Design		Selection of materials Introduction of new materials Standardization Value analysis Supplier development Make-or-buy			Design to cost Analysis of reliability Maintainability
Sourcing			Managing supplier relationships		Systems contracting Contract management
Production Planning			Preparing master schedules Calculating requirements Changing schedules		
Ordering		Processing requisitions Selecting alternative sources Preparing purchase orders		Maintenance of "open-to-buy"	
Shipment			Selection of packaging materials Selection of carriers		
Receiving		Inspecting material Preparation of receiving reports Quality control Approval of invoices for payment			
Inventory Control			Determination of order quantities, safety stocks, customer service levels, and reorder points and intervals		
Production					Management of maintenance
Sales				Merchandising Selling department management	

growth. I'm not satisfied to have buyers sit at their desks waiting for paper requisitions to arrive and then converting these into other papers and sending them out to vendors. I want them to become more informed and influential and less simple data transmitters.[3]

Sixteen years later the president of Digital Equipment Corporation said much the same thing in more current terms.

There is a growing expectation that our purchasing people understand broad business strategies. They need to understand such things as materials, distribution, forecasting, quality control, finance, and international markets. They must meet the specific needs and priorities of the company operations they service by participating in the strategic decision-making process.[4]

There is, however, some conflict between what company presidents *say* about their expectations concerning purchasing department performance and how purchasing managers *believe* their performance is actually evaluated. One survey (taken seven months after Digital's president was interviewed) showed that "getting good (low) prices," "getting competitive bids" and "total dollars spent" ranked well ahead of presidentially expressed priorities.[5] Another survey, taken a few months later, produced similar results.[6] This conflict in objectives is understandable, but hard to deal with. When it comes to purchasing, top management seems to want to have it both ways — get the best price *and* get everything else too. This pressure is present in most purchasing departments and purchasing managers must live with it. What top management should keep in mind is Ammer's observation that:

Managements obviously get what they are willing to pay for. Those who want first-rate purchasing can get it by hiring the right executive and giving him the responsibility and authority needed to do his job. Other managements obviously don't care and, from our observations, they also get what they pay for.[7]

Among the general functions of a purchasing department are those of providing purchasing services, obtaining the most effective value in items purchased, controlling financial commitments, conducting negotiations, engaging in supplier development activities to help insure continuity of sources of supply, and providing information to other departments.

Providing Purchasing Services   A purchasing department is an organization of specialists performing company procurement functions on a centralized basis. Other departments that have procurement needs submit purchase requests to the purchasing department. Purchasing must be able to coordinate all of the factors affecting procurement, including those emanating from within the company as well as those external to the company, such as present and potential suppliers. This points up the continuing importance of relationships between purchasing and other departments of the firm.

Obtaining Effective Item Value   Value, as opposed to costs, is a measure of the worth of items to an individual or a firm. Typically, when value equals or exceeds cost, a purchase takes place. A basic function of purchasing is to coordinate the inputs necessary to create the most effective, favorable relationship between value and cost for the firm. As such, the purchasing department is the firm's defense against the person once described by John Ruskin: "There is hardly anything in this world that some man cannot make a little worse and sell a little cheaper, and the people who consider price only are this man's lawful prey."

Any savings that can be accomplished in the procurement process have a direct effect upon profits. Each dollar saved in purchasing typically is equivalent to the profit earned on many sales dollars. However, cost savings should not be overemphasized, because sometimes it is necessary to spend additional purchasing dollars in order to provide proper product availability in terms of timing, quality, or quantity. For example, to produce the best overall product value, it would not be wise to haggle over a few purchasing dollars at the risk of closing down the production line.

Controlling Financial Commitments Purchased materials represent a significant portion of sales dollars in most manufacturing firms, as shown in Table 2–1. This notable financial obligation is a strong reason for centralizing purchasing functions. It requires a purchasing manager to operate within limits defined by a firm's ability to pay, as set by its cash flows. It requires close control over personnel authorized to make procurement commitments on behalf of the firm. Above all, it suggests the need for close coordination between finance and purchasing.

Conducting Negotiations One of the major functions of the purchasing department is to conduct contract negotiations between the firm and its suppliers. In order to bargain effectively over proposal and contract issues, a firm must maintain tight control over the negotiating process and those of its personnel involved. Such control generally is exercised by appointing a purchasing department representative in charge of negotiations with one or more suppliers. All communication with a supplier is performed through, or with the knowledge of, the designated purchasing representative. In this manner, conflicting or otherwise harmful statements can be monitored and adjusted to match overall company strategies prior to communication with a supplier.

Developing Suppliers and Supplier Relations A firm's competitive position can be directly influenced by the character of its vendor relationships. In their article, "Cooperative Buyer/Seller Relationships and a Firm's Competitive Posture," Landeros and Monczka noted that:

> Some purchasing managers . . . have begun to use "cooperative buyer/seller relationships" with a few preferred-suppliers; this approach enhances the purchasing function's ability to support several strategic postures available to a manufacturing firm. Cooperative buyer/seller relationships allow purchasing managers to better manage the interdependent tasks of the buying and selling firms, and to become conduits of information between the manufacturing firm and its preferred-suppliers.[8]

The scope and nature of these relationships are shown in Figures 2–3 and 2–4.

The importance of maintaining supplier relationships was driven home forcefully to managers of many firms when shortages of supplies of many basic raw materials were experienced at the time of the oil embargo in 1973. Those shortages led directly to many suppliers allocat-

TABLE 2–1: Purchased Materials as a Percentage of the Value of Finished Product for Selected Industries, 1982 and 1987[a]

SIC Code	Industry Group	1982 Proportion of Purchased Materials	1987 Proportion of Purchased Materials
291	Petroleum refining	(NA)	88%
201	Meat products	84%	82%
227	Carpets and rugs	71%	68%
371	Motor vehicles and equipment	69%	68%
341	Metal cans and shipping containers	63%	65%
265	Paperboard containers and boxes	61%	62%
242	Sawmills and planing mills	66%	60%
331	Blast furnace and basic steel products	68%	60%
204	Grain mill products	67%	58%
286	Industrial organic chemicals	68%	58%
353	Construction and related machinery	49%	54%
206	Sugar and confectionary products	60%	54%
(X)	**All manufacturing establishments**	**58%**	**53%**
285	Paints and allied products	57%	51%
230	Apparel and other textile products	51%	49%
357	Computer and office equipment	(NA)	47%
301	Tires and inner tubes	50%	47%
316	Luggage	45%	46%
394	Toys and sporting goods	44%	45%
281	Industrial inorganic chemicals	49%	43%
366	Communications equipment	(NA)	41%
321	Flat glass	49%	36%
386	Photographic equipment and supplies	36%	33%
273	Books	34%	31%
283	Drugs	31%	28%
211	Cigarettes	33%	25%
271	Newspapers	28%	24%

[a]These figures assume that purchased materials represent the difference between the value of shipments and the value added by manufacture.

SOURCE: *Annual Survey of Manufactures*, Washington, DC: U.S. Department of Commerce, Bureau of the Census, as shown in Table 1296, *Statistical Abstract of the United States, 1990*.

ing their limited supplies, often giving preference to those firms that had been their most loyal customers. For many firms, this had a major impact on profits and thrust purchasing into the forefront of corporate strategy. This experience also highlighted the importance of programs designed to strengthen suppliers and their position in the industry and to develop alternate sources of supplies. Such programs include engineering assistance, financing involving early payments for purchases, and advance information concerning amounts of product to be purchased to aid suppliers in planning their production.[9]

FIGURE 2–3: Cooperative buyer/seller relationship tactics and the strategic posture of overall cost leadership

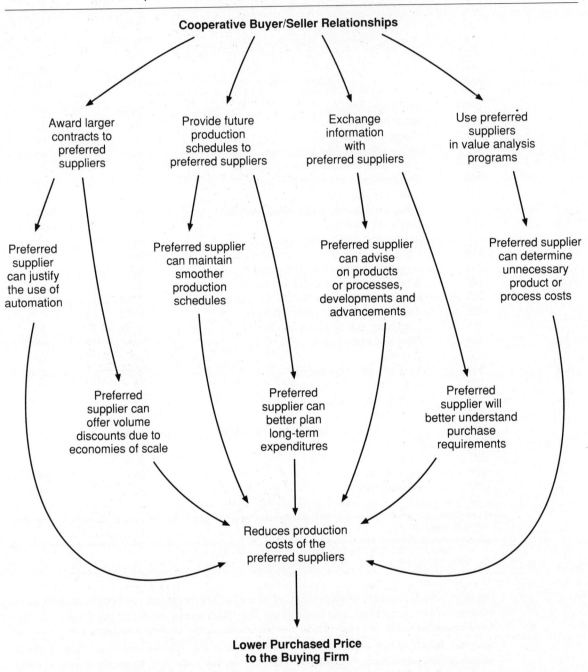

Cooperative Buyer/Seller Relationships

Award larger contracts to preferred suppliers

Provide future production schedules to preferred suppliers

Exchange information with preferred suppliers

Use preferred suppliers in value analysis programs

Preferred supplier can justify the use of automation

Preferred supplier can maintain smoother production schedules

Preferred supplier can advise on products or processes, developments and advancements

Preferred supplier can determine unnecessary product or process costs

Preferred supplier can offer volume discounts due to economies of scale

Preferred supplier can better plan long-term expenditures

Preferred supplier will better understand purchase requirements

Reduces production costs of the preferred suppliers

Lower Purchased Price to the Buying Firm

SOURCE: Robert Landeros, Ph.D. and Robert M. Monczka, Ph.D., C.P.M., "Cooperative Buyer/Seller Relationships and a Firm's Competitive Posture," *Journal of Purchasing and Materials Management* (Fall 1989) 15.

FIGURE 2–4: Cooperative buyer/seller relationship tactics and the strategic posture of product differentiation

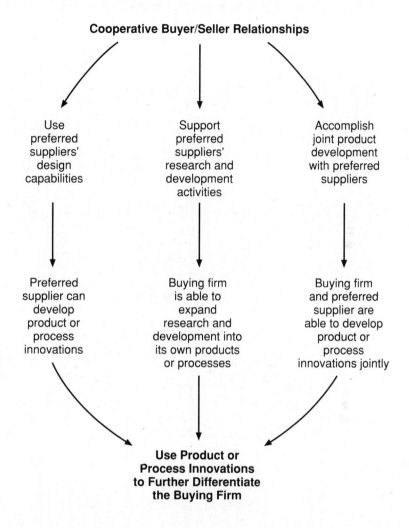

Cooperative Buyer/Seller Relationships

| Use preferred suppliers' design capabilities | Support preferred suppliers' research and development activities | Accomplish joint product development with preferred suppliers |

| Preferred supplier can develop product or process innovations | Buying firm is able to expand research and development into its own products or processes | Buying firm and preferred supplier are able to develop product or process innovations jointly |

Use Product or Process Innovations to Further Differentiate the Buying Firm

SOURCE: Robert Landeros, Ph.D. and Robert M. Monczka, Ph.D., C.P.M., "Cooperative Buyer/Seller Relationships and a Firm's Competitive Posture," *Journal of Purchasing and Materials Management* (Fall 1989) 16.

Providing Information Input As previously indicated, the procurement process involves large amounts of information flowing among a number of departments. It is a function of the purchasing department to obtain the information required to process specific purchases and to provide appropriate information feedback to the departments for whom procurement actions are being accomplished. The nature of information exchanged between purchasing and other departments within a firm is illustrated in Figure 2–5.

FIGURE 2–5: The nature of information exchanged between purchasing and other departments within a firm

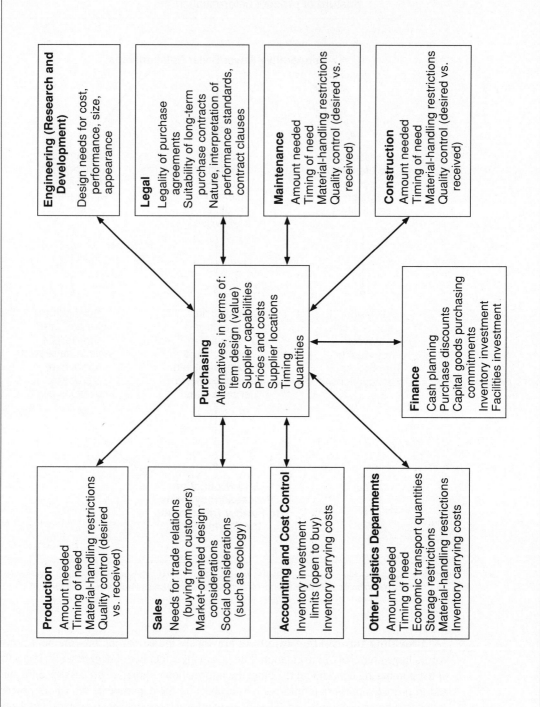

Engineering (Research and Development)
Design needs for cost, performance, size, appearance

Legal
Legality of purchase agreements
Suitability of long-term purchase contracts
Nature, interpretation of performance standards, contract clauses

Maintenance
Amount needed
Timing of need
Material-handling restrictions
Quality control (desired vs. received)

Construction
Amount needed
Timing of need
Material-handling restrictions
Quality control (desired vs. received)

Purchasing
Alternatives, in terms of:
Item design (value)
Supplier capabilities
Prices and costs
Supplier locations
Timing
Quantities

Finance
Cash planning
Purchase discounts
Capital goods purchasing commitments
Inventory investment
Facilities investment

Production
Amount needed
Timing of need
Material-handling restrictions
Quality control (desired vs. received)

Sales
Needs for trade relations (buying from customers)
Market-oriented design considerations
Social considerations (such as ecology)

Accounting and Cost Control
Inventory investment limits (open to buy)
Inventory carrying costs

Other Logistics Departments
Amount needed
Timing of need
Economic transport quantities
Storage restrictions
Material-handling restrictions
Inventory carrying costs

THE ROLE OF THE PURCHASING DEPARTMENT IN THE PROCUREMENT PROCESS

As an illustration of the relationships between purchasing and other functions party to the procurement process in the industrial firm, Figure 2–6 identifies basic procurement questions, significant criteria that help define further the questions, the primary functions that often are responsibile for action, and the other functions with which coordination is required.

As noted in Chapter 1, the management of the logistics function involves cost trade-offs. The nature of these trade-offs is well illustrated by the economic relationships between purchasing and other logistics functions, such as transportation, warehousing, and inventory carrying-costs. For example, a decision to purchase a larger than normal quantity of raw materials because of a very favorable price may or may not be offset by the extra costs of storage, insurance and other inventory holding costs, or risk of obsolescence. Therefore, purchasing decisions should always take into account their impact on the logistics system as a whole.

What to Procure The prerequisite to any procurement action is to define what will be procured. Three different but related criteria are helpful in specifying the "what." These criteria include the purpose, design, and quality of the material to be procured.

Purpose concerns the manner in which material (or services) will fit into, or be utilized in support of, the end product. Because production is responsible for manufacturing the end product, it often has the greatest single voice in determining how the elements of production will be united. Further, production personnel typically are in the best position to determine what is to be purchased from suppliers. However, additional, specialized inputs may be required from engineering, purchasing, accounting, inventory control, and sales.

Design defines the "role" of the material or product to be procured. In an industrial firm, engineering typically develops drawings and specifications, from which a bill of material is prepared. These documents provide information to production (for the planning of production processes), purchasing (for design requirements), and logistics (for inventory definition). Quality assurance assists engineering, production, and purchasing in determining the desired level of quality assurance and quality conformance (inspection and related techniques). Generally, purchasing prefers design documentation that allows flexibility and competition in the procurement process, perhaps using standardized nomenclature or specifications. Sales inputs to engineering may include information about market conditions, competitive products, and customer preferences in design considerations.

Quality characteristics may be planned to conform to the desired image of company products. Within these bounds, many cost and performance combinations may need to be evaluated. In their deliberations regarding product design and quality, engineering and production personnel will receive inputs from sales and purchasing as well. Final quality determinations are incorporated into product design and material choice. This may have an effect on inventory management, particularly if relatively low-quality materials are procured and

FIGURE 2–6: Basic procurement questions and functional relationships in an industrial firm that procures to inventory

Basic Procurement Question	Significant Criteria	Primary Functions	Other Functions With Which Coordination Is Required
What to procure	Purpose:		
	Materials	Production	Engineering, Purchasing, Accounting, Inventory Control, Sales
	Consumables	Using Function	Accounting
	Services	Using Function	Accounting
	Design	Engineering	Production, Purchasing, Quality Control
	Quality	Production	Engineering, Inventory Control, Quality Control, Sales, Purchasing
From whom to procure	Alternative suppliers	Purchasing	Production, Traffic, Engineering, Accounting
	Price negotiation	Purchasing	Production, Traffic, Accounting
	Procurement schedule	Purchasing	Production, Traffic
Where to procure	Alternative supply points	Traffic	Purchasing
	Alternative modes	Traffic	
	Alternative routes	Traffic	
	Receiving & storage	Warehousing	Production, Purchasing, Quality Control
Which item to procure	Replenishment order	Inventory Control	Production, Sales, Purchasing, Accounting
How much to procure	Total dollar investment	Inventory Control	Production, Purchasing, Accounting
	Reorder quantity (EOQ):	Inventory Control	Production, Sales, Purchasing, Accounting
	Customer demand rate	Inventory Control	Sales
	Production requirements rate	Inventory Control	Production
	Quantity discount	Purchasing	Production, Inventory Control, Warehousing
	Ordering costs	Inventory Control	Purchasing, Sales
	Inventory carrying costs	Inventory Control	Purchasing, Production, Sales
	Lead time	Inventory Control	Purchasing, Production, Sales
When to procure	Schedule:		Production, Purchasing
	Delivery requirements	Inventory Control	
	Lead time	Inventory Control	Production, Purchasing
In what form to procure	Characteristics of use	Purchasing	Production, Traffic, Warehousing
	Receiving, handling, and storage capability		

subsequently found to be inadequate, thus creating a supply of unusable material simultaneously with a shortage of proper material.

From Whom to Procure Within the guidelines established by procurement policies concerning "alternative sources of supply" and "reciprocity" (buying from customers on a preferential basis), purchasing has the primary responsibility for identifying, evaluating, and establishing contact with potential suppliers for materials and services required by the firm. Purchasing may establish a "laundry list" of potential suppliers and maintain up-to-date records regarding supplier products, prices, services, and general policies. Purchasing has a responsibility for keeping other departments informed about suppliers and their products. Such information is useful, both in procurement negotiations and as an input to the "what to procure" decisions discussed above.

Where to Procure The location of the procurement source is defined by the designation of a specific supplier. However, in some cases, suppliers may offer alternative origins from which an order may be filled. Based upon an existing pattern of shipments, a more distant point *might* provide either faster or more economical supply or, in some cases, both than a less distant point in view of traffic and transportation charges, transit time, and the pattern of other shipments to or from the firm. This is frequently the case when a firm operates privately owned equipment to meet a portion of its movement needs. Close coordination is required between traffic and purchasing in the selection of transportation mode and routing, the performance of receiving and storage functions upon receipt of the material, and resolution of loss and damage claims against carriers.

Which Items to Procure Once materials and components have been identified and the product has been placed into production, inventory replenishment decisions must be made. Here, the output from the inventory management program for materials and components will provide the necessary inputs to the purchasing action.

How Much to Procure For inventoried purchases, the question of "how much" to order is subject to continual review. Two aspects are the desired investment (in terms of dollars) in inventory and the determination of specific reorder quantities (usually in terms of economic order quantities). Proper reorder quantity size is influenced by such factors as customer demand for the end product, production rates, purchase quantity discounts, ordering costs, inventory carrying costs, and the available lead time for acquiring and receiving materials. The relationship among these factors will be discussed in detail in Chapter 7. Inventory control is the primary function concerned with "how much." Coordination, as indicated in Figure 2–6, is required among production, sales, accounting, and purchasing.

When to Procure "When to procure" is keyed to delivery requirements and the lead time (order cycle), defined as the total time period between the notification to replenish stock and the actual receipt of materials. The length of lead time will be influenced by order cycle times at both the firm initiating the order and its supplier as well as transportation transit time considerations. "When" is a primary function of inventory control, and is coordinated with production (in terms of production needs) and purchasing (in terms of procurement time requirements).

THE PURCHASING MANAGER OF THE 1990S

Jay Gordon

The purchasing manager of the 1990s, believe it or not, is going to be an engineer.

Not an engineer in the vocational sense, necessarily, but an engineer of corporate relationships. No longer is the purchasing manager concerned solely with how to make the next buy; he now is responsible for supplier management.

With this added scope of the function has come a new trend: the scattering of purchasing responsibilities within the firm. Purchasing is no longer the stand-alone function it once was, a fact noted with chagrin by many purchasing pros who have busied themselves building empires over the past several years.

Yet they may turn out to be the big winners. With the shift to supplier management, purchasing is being asked to develop or acquire new skills and make new contributions in a number of areas such as quality, transportation, forecasting, production scheduling and product design. As a result, purchasing will have a level of input into strategic corporate planning and decision making that is unprecedented.

"The smart purchasing people are realizing that this might be the biggest power play of all," says Dr. Joseph Cavinato, associate professor of business logistics at Penn State University. "They are managing commercial relationships."

Jack Barry, a senior consultant in the logistics practice of Arthur D. Little, has a name for this. "The old line approach to purchasing problems is to treat it like a hot potato," he says. "You call up a supplier and dump on him. The new approach is *simultaneous engineering*. Here, you work with the vendor to solve problems and reduce costs for both parties. You take a nickel out and say, 'You get three cents, I get two cents.'

"And there's teeth behind this," Barry adds. "There's money to be made here. Vendors are saying, 'I'm 20 percent higher than the other guy. Let me explain to you why that is a good investment.'"

Organizational Relationships

How will this be played out in the real world of the 1990s? How will purchasing be organized to accomplish this ambitious game plan? A study recently published by the National Association of Purchasing Management's Center for Advanced Purchasing Studies answers some of these questions.

One of the most revealing aspects of the study is that it counters the notion that companies are organizing so that all materials flow functions, both inbound and outbound, report to a logistics manager. While this idea is often discussed in U.S. and European logistics circles, the CAPS study found that it is uncommon in practice: less than one percent of the organizations reported that purchasing reports to logistics.

The study did find that a vast majority of the 297 respondents have opted for some combination of centralized and decentralized purchasing. This enables a company to have some purchasing done locally, close to the actual requirement, and some handled centrally to take advantage of volume buying.

This is exactly the setup at chemical and pharmaceutical manufacturer Hoechst Celanese, which was formed in 1987 when American Hoechst and Celanese Corp. merged. At the time of the merger, says Rich Young, manager, domestic & import distribution, Hoechst was mostly centralized, while Celanese was mostly decentralized. "Now," says Young, "we're at the mean of the two."

Each of Hoechst Celanese's five operating divisions has a centralized purchasing department. For "leverage issues" — goods and services used by all the divisions — there are regional purchasing managers who take advantage of the company's collective clout. "What we have tried to do," says Young, "is to decentralize to get closer to the customer without losing leverage on important items."

On the international side, inbound freight is a function of the distribution department and is well controlled by the company, Young says. Domestically, control of inbound freight depends on the commodity, who's buying it and where they're buying it from. "I might have a microcosm of the world in this company," Young says. "Our purchasing terms range from FOB-shipping point, which is complete abdication, to a situation where the purchasing manager meets with the distribution manager and says, 'I'm buying this; what's the best way to do it from a transportation standpoint?'"

Supporting Corporate Growth

The situation is much the same at Merck Chemical Manufacturing Division (MCMD), a unit of pharmaceutical giant Merck Sharp & Dohme. Materials management is organized on a divisional basis, reporting to the senior vp of manufacturing and technology. This senior corporate executive sets corporate materials management policy and establishes objectives.

According to Allan L. Mysel, executive director, materials management for MCMD, the materials management units are responsible for purchasing, production planning, inventory control and transportation. Based at corporate headquarters in Rahway, N.J., MCMD purchasing serves other groups at that location, including research and various corporate staffs. MCMD is basically a captive manufacturing division. Its eight plants — four in the U.S., one in Puerto Rico and three in western Europe — provide bulk active pharmaceuticals to Merck's other divisions.

At the division level, purchasing is highly centralized. Some purchasing is done at the plants, but major buys are made at division headquarters. A transportation council, made up of representatives from the operating divisions, negotiates company-wide transportation rates and services.

Perhaps the biggest task for Merck is to integrate its international purchasing to help meet some lofty corporate objectives in an increasingly intense competitive environment. Merck, already the largest U.S.-based pharmaceutical company in Europe, has its sights set higher. "Our chairman has made it clear that we expect to rank number one in sales in Europe by 1992," says Mysel. "The challenge to purchasing is to support these growth objectives. We will look at what we are buying, for whom we are buying and *from* whom we are buying. One question we'll be asking is, 'Could we be buying in a country where we're not manufacturing in order to increase our presence in that country and support our sales efforts there?'"

Merck's action plan includes enhancing vendor evaluation and certification programs and reducing the supplier base. While he doesn't embrace single sourcing for the pharmaceuticals business, Mysel feels it would be advantageous to have one major source for an item and a second, viable source that gets enough of Merck's business to remain interested and willing to work with the company. The position of these two prominent sources could shift from year to year, and a small portion of the company's requirements would remain uncommitted to allow development of new sources. Mysel also foresees a continuing commitment on Merck's part to encourage, develop and use minority vendors. "The key to the future," Mysel says, "is strong, close, mutually advantageous partnerships with the best suppliers — those that are high quality, reliable, technically and commercially innovative and competitive."

Hoechst Celanese's Rich Young says his company also is partnershipping with vendors. The biggest part of that is sharing information, which enables both sides to control costs. "We're moving toward the point where we won't need to inspect the vendor's product," he says, "but the responsibility for measuring and monitoring quality is squarely on the vendor."

SOURCE: *Distribution* (January 1989) 46–48. Reprinted by permission of Chilton Company.

In What Form to Procure Purchasing responsibilities include determining (1) alternative forms in which items may be procured; (2) assessing constraints that may dictate the form in which such items must be received; and (3) matching the two. In some cases, the proper form in which to order goods may be suggested by material-handling requirements and the patterns (quantities and frequency) in which an item is used in the production process. In other cases, receiving and storage capabilities may be major constraints. In any event, prior coordination with production, traffic and warehousing can save the purchasing function a great deal of grief.

PROCUREMENT POLICIES

Certain procurement policies have a significant impact on other logistics activities. These policies are typically formulated by top management rather than by purchasing or any other single department. In many companies, a formal management committee may be formed to evaluate and recommend such policies to top management. In any company, it is necessary to obtain inputs from the various functional areas (such as procurement, production, marketing, engineering, traffic, and quality control) in order to develop effective procurement policies that take into account cost/benefit trade-offs.

Procurement policies having the greatest impact on other logistics activities include "make or buy" decisions, the inbound material pricing method, the maintenance of alternate sources of supply, contract or "blanket" ordering, reciprocal agreements, value analysis, standardization, systems contracting, purchase order draft (POD) systems, customer-vendor coordination programs, and the use of computerized buying methods.

Make or Buy Decisions

"Make or buy" refers to a company's decision of the level(s) at which materials (sub-assemblies, components, or parts) will either be manufactured or purchased for incorporation in finished products. The comparative cost to make or buy an item is a primary criterion in the evaluation of such alternatives. Therefore, it is necessary for the purchasing department to obtain supplier prices and for manufacturing, accounting, and other internal company departments to estimate the alternative cost of internal manufacture.

Cost comparisons are not the only criteria for make or buy decisions. The manufacture of an item not only requires investment in equipment, personnel, raw materials, space, and supervision, but also involves various overhead or indirect expenses. In some cases, a company may benefit from such investment in terms of additional control that it can achieve over its own operations, including control over design, schedule, quality, personnel and equipment utilization, and continuity of supply. On the other hand, procuring an item permits lower investment of company resources, thereby permitting investment in the manufacture of those items on which a company enjoys the greatest comparative return on investment. Thus, procurement of specified items from outside sources may permit cost saving resulting from greater specialization on the part of a supplier, lower in-plant inventories, application of competitive bidding, and greater flexibility to change design and quantity requirements.

One further view of make or buy is that, through very careful planning and scheduling, a supplier can be viewed as an extension of a company's manufacturing capacity.[10] This view is incorporated in MRP (Material Requirements Planning) and in more sophisticated MRP II (Manufacturing Resource Planning) systems which provide for highly integrated vendor-purchaser systems.[11] Make or buy may also employ application of "Just-in-Time" inventory planning and management techniques that require close coordination with suppliers. These three inventory management approaches (MRP, MRP II, and Just-in-Time) are discussed in detail in Chapter 6 ("Inventory Management").

Make or buy decisions affect the inventories that must be moved, stored, and coordinated. The specific impact on other logistics activities may depend upon the level of item under consideration for manufacture or purchase.

Assembly (or Subassembly) Level Procurement at this level will require fewer items of greater value and the logistics system will deal with fewer origin points (suppliers) for incoming materials. The inventory carrying cost per unit will be higher because of the value added to the product by the supplier. Logistics scheduling and coordination (including the management information system) may require rapid response times in order to minimize inventory investments while maintaining an adequate supply for the production line. In some cases, such as assembly line production, the latter factor may be extremely critical, for example, the need to avoid a plant shutdown due to the nonavailability of incoming materials.

Higher valued items generally incur higher transportation rates per hundred pounds. However, the higher rates might be offset somewhat by significant weight reductions achieved in the supplier's manufacturing process. Greater value and susceptibility to damage of assembled goods could result in increased damage during transportation and subsequent damage claim activity for purchased items.

Equipment Level Here we assume that equipment signifies a self-contained product that performs a specialized function in the conversion process but does not become a part of the end product. Similar to other materials, equipment involves logistical movement, storage, and coordination of requirements. Unless a firm procures equipment from the same supplier over a long period of time, changing shipment patterns may require special logistics planning for each purchase. Perhaps most important of all, equipment spare parts as well as repair requirements tend to further complicate the logistics task. Spare or repair parts involve small shipments, often from scattered locations, and a relatively high degree of accompanying paperwork. Unless purchased equipment and supporting parts are highly standardized, complex inventory management needs can be created.

Component Level Procurement at this level will tend to result in greater quantities of purchased parts and a greater number of suppliers than the other configuration levels. Unless component purchases are consolidated, the logistics system will have to deal with many origins involving relatively small-sized shipments.

Raw Material Level Procurement at the raw material level may require special transportation and handling equipment and special warehouse facilities to accommodate raw materials. Inventory carrying costs are likely to reflect the generally lower value of raw materials per unit of measure, and transportation costs may play a greater part in a determination of the landed costs of such items. Thus, the geographic locations of sources become increasingly important. Raw material buying may involve speculation (buying in advance of need) to take advantage of price fluctuations or trends. Where this is the case, the major logistics mission may shift from inventory control to the handling and storage of unusually large stocks.

In most industrial companies, conditions are such that some combination of all four design levels is represented in make or buy decisions. Thus, in reality, the logistics system must be able to accommodate multiple procurement objectives.

Inbound Material Pricing Method Up to now, we have assumed that purchases are made on an origin basis (exclusive of freight charges) on inbound shipments. If, in contrast, the purchase price includes transportation (and consequently seller control over carrier selection and routing on inbound shipments), logistics responsibilities in the purchasing firm may be confined only to purchasing, receiving, storing, handling, and inventorying of materials at destination. There are several other vendor pricing policies that fall in between the complete inclusion or exclusion of transportation costs and control, and thereby include varying logistics responsibilities. Further, it should be noted that regardless of the ''legalities'' in respect to who controls inbound transportation (carrier selection and routing), the realities of business give the buyer the real say in the matter, as a vendor disregards a buyer's wishes at its peril.

A vexing aspect of inbound shipments is that while there is usually no question about the contract price of the goods, there is considerable potential for error in respect to carrier charges for inbound transportation. One way or the other, the buyer pays such charges and, as Dillon points out, ''all too frequently shipments are weighed incorrectly (phantom weight), described inaccurately (often a higher rate), aren't consolidated into a bigger shipment (cheaper rate) when this could easily be done, etc.''[12] Either on its own initiative, or by coordination with the traffic department, the purchasing department must do its best to prevent such losses that could easily wipe out a good purchase price advantage. Under no circumstances should a purchase order contain the statement (addressed to the vendor) ''Ship Best Way.'' Whether due to carelessness, laziness or ignorance, this is an invitation to (1) incur unnecessarily high inbound transportation costs or (2) incur delayed receipt of materials because the vendor may choose to ship by ''slow boat'' at a low freight rate.

Alternate Sources of Supply

Top management sets the policy regarding the degree to which alternative sources of supply will be developed, established, and maintained. There are a number of ingredients in this decision. For example, what degree of competition (between alternative suppliers) is desired? What is the risk associated with a single source of supply? Are satisfactory substitute materials available? What is the cost implication of doing business with more than one supplier, thereby reducing economies of scale for any one supplier? As Treleven has said:

> Clearly, there are both positive and negative aspects to single sourcing on both sides of the relationship. Experts in the quality field can be found on each side of the debate. For example, Deming is a strong advocate of single sourcing, while Crosby and Juran have gone on record against it. In general, however, the positives appear to outweigh the negatives for vendors and buyers alike. As is the case with most managerial decision rules, though, there are obviously numerous exceptions to the general rule.[13]

Alternate sources of supply may be maintained at a somewhat higher cost to the purchaser in order to prevent significant material shortages in case of a single-supplier strike, adverse weather, or other unplanned events, such as supplier discontinuance of the product line or bankruptcy. But, alternate sources will also increase the number of origin points in the inbound logistics system. Because purchases are more widely dispersed, individual shipments may be smaller and relatively more expensive to transport, store, handle, and coordinate. Also, if sources are continually added or deleted, the pattern of shipments will be changing continuously, resulting in a premium on flexibility in the planning and management of transportation, warehousing, and inventory requirements.

Contract or ''Blanket'' Ordering

Advance orders for a year's supply (or some other extended time period) of a given item, against which repeated specific releases and shipments may be made without requiring a new order to be prepared, are called blanket orders or contract purchasing. This allows a buyer to reduce paperwork, obtain a more favorable price (for a larger quantity), reduce inventories (by requiring the supplier to hold goods until needed), and saves purchasing time. Consider the experience of a manufacturer buying pipe, valves, and fittings:

> . . . Our blanket order for this category is based on a list of specific items, and estimate of annual quantities, and price guarantees. It also includes a clause requiring the supplier to have enough stock on hand so that he can deliver specified quantities within three days.
>
> As a result of this agreement, we reduced our inventory by two thirds, lowered prices by 15–20%, and we have price protection.[14]

In addition to eliminating repetitive order processing, contract purchasing programs may enable logistics management to preplan movement and storage schedules and requirements, and should reduce the storage capacity required for incoming goods.

Reciprocal Practices

Purchase and sales reciprocity, or "trade relations" as some prefer to call it, refers to purchasing from customers in a manner designed to support sales effort or, conversely, the use of purchasing data to bring buying pressure to bear on a firm's customers.

Reciprocity is probably the most controversial of all practices associated with procurement. While it may assist sales efforts, reciprocity can also hamper a company to the extent that it encourages purchasing on bases other than quality, price, or service. Further, the legality of reciprocal purchasing policies has been questioned.

> In recent years the Federal government . . . charged a number of companies with violating various antitrust provisions of the Sherman and Clayton acts by coercing or attempting to coerce suppliers to purchase their products, or products of subsidiaries, under threat of withdrawing their business from suppliers. . . . The FTC (Federal Trade Commission) attitude has been that reciprocity does not necessarily have to be coercive to be considered in violation of Section 5 of the Federal Trade Commission Act; that is it would be illegal in cases of (1) systematic use by a sales department or purchasing department in communicating with suppliers or (2) a discernible pattern of dealing between supplier and purchaser notwithstanding better price, quality, or service available from competitors.[15]

In practice, only those reciprocal trading practices that tend to restrain trade and competition are likely to attract unfavorable attention from the Justice Department. As Ammer points out:

> . . . Reciprocity, like sin, still exists. But it has largely gone underground. While it is probably perfectly legal—especially when practiced by smaller firms—its image is basically unfavorable.[16]

Reciprocal practices generally occur independently of logistics considerations. All other things being equal, the practice of reciprocity often increases the number of suppliers and supply points served by the logistics network in cases where it is practiced with a large number of customers and suppliers. Also, the average size of shipments will be decreased where purchase quantities are split up among a larger number of vendors, thus increasing ordering and transportation costs.

Value Analysis

Value analysis has been defined as:

> . . . the study of the relationship of design, function, and cost of any product, material or service with the object of reducing its cost through modification of design or material specifications, manufacture by more efficient processes, change in source of supply (external or internal), or possible elimination or incorporation into a related item.[17]

The manner in which value analysis (or value engineering) is carried out is suggested by the following procedure:

The trained VE (value engineering) practitioner, alone or in a team, selects a target, either a high-price-tag item or perhaps some small part that is used in large quantities. Then three basic questions are asked about the item.

1. What does it do? The discipline requires that the answer be reduced to two words, a verb and a noun. A pencil, for example, "makes marks." This breaks habitual patterns, pulls the thinking back to fundamentals, puts the emphasis on function rather than on "the way we've always done it."

2. What does it cost? The answer should already be known but frequently is not. And, the answer is often an eye-opener.

3. What else would do the job, at what cost? This calls for a brain-storming session in which alternatives may be suggested. . . . Value engineering starts from scratch and approaches each product as if it had never existed. . . . "On the average," says Miles (Larry Miles, a General Electric design engineer generally credited with organizing existing techniques into the concept of value analysis in 1949), "one fourth of all manufacturing cost proves unnecessary — or half, if it's a new rush product."[18]

To date, value analysis largely has been applied to the examination of component parts. Value analysis, in the short run, may tend to increase the number of inbound and inventoried items as designs are revised and new part numbers issued. As a result, inventories may have to be very closely monitored to reduce the risk of obsolescence of various inventoried items. However, in the long run, value analysis may contribute to the standardization of parts and other items.[19]

Standardization

There is a natural tendency on the part of design engineers and marketing managers to introduce nonstandard product features. Over time, this can result in an uneconomically large product line, a swollen inventory of components, and a large logistics bill per dollar of sales.

Executives asking themselves the following set of questions have, in may cases, eliminated over half of the raw materials, components, and supplies purchased and inventoried by their companies.

1. Can this item be eliminated from stock?

2. Can an existing item be used in more than one application?

3. Can one item, with capabilities sufficiently high to meet several needs, replace several items with lesser capabilities?

4. Until item usage becomes extensive, can we avoid ordering a specially designed component?

Potential logistics savings from standardization include those resulting from a reduction in the number of inventoried items and from the shipment of larger quantities. In many cases, companies standardizing around more expensive, more versatile items have found that higher per-unit purchase prices have been more than offset by logistics cost savings. In other cases, greater quantity discounts have offset potentially higher prices for the more versatile item.

An example of this occurred at the Bogen Division of Lear Siegler, Inc., a manufacturer of public address systems and high-fidelity home entertainment products.

> . . . [T]he purchase of both transistors and carbon resistors was standardized for greater savings. Transistors were being bought in two grades, but by standardizing on the better grade, better than needed for one particular use, a quantity saving was achieved. Also, by buying 5% 1/2-watt resistors, instead of cheaper 10% resistors, purchasing was able to negotiate a blanket order from one, instead of several, suppliers at a lower unit price for a superior product. In addition, special packaging, which formerly cost 80 cents per thousand, is now supplied free.[20]

However, despite the obvious importance of standardization, which is so often espoused by many senior executives, surveys indicate that in practice standardization actually rates very low as a purchasing priority. Dowst found the "Number of Items Standardized" rated the *lowest* of 13 criteria used by purchasing managers to evaluate the performance of buyers in their departments.[21] On a list of 14 criteria purchasing managers believed their company peers and superiors used to judge them, standardization was not better than 10th.[22] Similar to the "price v. other factors" conflict discussed earlier in this chapter, implementing a policy of standardization obviously remains an unresolved purchasing/logistics problem in many firms.

Purchasing Systems

Systems Contracting Systems contracting involves (1) selecting a single source for the *widest possible* array of supplies; (2) placing the burden of inventory acquisition and availability on the vendor; (3) installing a system by which departments requisition directly from vendors, with purchasing only being "copied;" and (4) selecting the sole source on a "permanent" basis, but subject to periodic audit and review.[23] *Purchasing* lists the claimed advantages of systems purchasing as:

Major reduction of in-plant inventories
Reduced obsolescence
Reduced number of calls by distributor-suppliers

Reduced number of open order files in purchasing
One delivery for all supplies contracted
Reduced or eliminated backorders
Predetermined price structure
Elimination of duplication of effort between supplier and customer
Functions are transferred from buyer to seller when seller can perform same at lower cost
Faster delivery
Purchasing is freed to perform value analysis and negotiating function on higher value items
Frees capital for investment in more profitable items
Promotes better planning between maintenance and operations
Reduced pilferage
Simplified ordering procedure
Reduced paperwork
Improved supplier service
Improved order accuracy
Promotes standardization
Improved profitability through reduced costs of acquisition and possession[24]

The results of Hannaford's survey of users' perceptions of the advantages and disadvantages of systems contracts are shown in Table 2–2 and Table 2–3. The advantages of such systems shown in Table 2–2 appear to be greater than the disadvantages shown in Table 2–3. However, the survey respondents noted three cautions.

1. Proceed slowly at first

2. Have all concerned parties attend final negotiations

3. Provide more education for users — both in-plant and distributor personnel.[25]

On balance, it appears that systems contracting is here to stay and will continue to grow.

POD Systems   Purchase order draft (POD) systems involve (1) the preparation of a purchase order and an accompanying blank check by the customer; (2) the completion and deposit (at the vendor's bank) of the check by the vendor at the time the goods are shipped; and (3) auditing by the customer (often by computer) of receiving reports for vendor error.

A POD system, for example, was initiated at Kaiser Aluminum & Chemical Corporation after it was found that of about 18,000 checks written each month to vendors, those under $200 accounted for about 75 percent of the number of checks but only 4.5 percent of the total cash amount disbursed. A subsequent check indicated that Kaiser had made payments on its first 175,000 POD's without suffering a single loss.[26]

Subsequently, Kaiser announced the success of the latest application of POD in logistics, a method of paying freight carriers with blank checks. Under this program, known as "cash-in-first" (CIF), the check is part of the bill of lading; the carrier simply computes the shipping charges, fills in the correct amount on the check, and deposits it in his bank account.

Other Customer-Vendor Coordination Programs   There are many approaches to the problems of coordinating the logistics of procurement, particularly for the frequent, low-value, often routing, repetitive type of requisition or order. Some of the more imaginative and potentially significant are the following.

TABLE 2–2: Perceived Advantages of Systems Contracts

Statement Content	Percent Agreeing
1. Paperwork has been reduced	93
2. Costs of acquisition and possession have decreased	81
3. Inventory has been reduced	75
4. There is more time to negotiate other items	75
5. Accounting procedures have been simplified	67
6. There is adequate purchasing control	65
7. The purchasing department is now more efficient	64
8. The system provides daily and emergency deliveries	62
9. The system offers price stability	61
10. The system is built on mutual trust	55
11. Ordering errors have been minimized	55
12. Inventory control has been simplified	46
13. Systems offer competitive prices	39
14. There has been a reduction in purchasing and central stores employees	32

SOURCE: William J. Hannaford "How Effective is Systems Purchasing?," *Journal of Purchasing and Materials Management* (Summer, 1979) 16. Reprinted with permission of National Association of Purchasing Management, Inc.

TABLE 2–3: Perceived Disadvantages of Systems Contracts

Statement Content	Percent Agreeing
1. It is very hard to get started	44
2. There is resistance by low level maintenance personnel	24
3. Distributor's inventory is unable to meet unforeseen needs	19
4. It prevents purchasing from shopping the market	18
5. There is resistance by lower level purchasing personnel	13
6. Control over purchasing is inadequate	10
7. Distributors refuse to stock specials	10
8. Deliveries are often not made on time	10
9. Price changes create many problems	9
10. We have requisitioning problems	7
11. You can't depend on other suppliers during emergencies	7
12. Item prices are higher under systems	6
13. Distributors do not meet service level requirements	4
14. Distributors may back out when you need them most	3
15. No safeguards exist against distributors making excessive profits	2

SOURCE: William J. Hannaford "How Effective is Systems Purchasing?," *Journal of Purchasing and Materials Management*, (Summer, 1979) 17. Reprinted with permission of National Association of Purchasing Management, Inc.

Honor-systems Dundee Cement Company passes much of the responsibility for buying to its vendors' salespeople under its "honor system." On visiting Dundee's storeroom, salespersons will take stock, write up a requisition, leave it with purchasing for approval, and send a copy to their company for immediate order pricing and assembly. When the approved requisition (or purchase order) is received from Dundee, shipment is made immediately.

On-premise storerooms One major vendor has established its storeroom on the premises of the Kearfott Division of General Precision's Aerospace Group. Under this arrangement, goods are issued from requisition by Kearfott personnel, the vendor staffs the storeroom and owns the stock in it until it is issued. The vendor bills Kearfott monthly on the basis of the value of requisitions issued.

Flexible price agreements The combination of inflation (at varying rates, but always upward), volatile interest rates and other factors affecting vendor costs has led to the negotiation of flexible price agreements (FPA's) by many firms. FPA's provide for vendor price increases (or decreases) depending on business environment factors that affect the vendor's costs. Sometimes called "escalator clauses," these arrangements are mostly found in longer-term purchasing agreements where the vendor cannot "hedge" against cost increases. In general, purchasing agents are not opposed to FPA's, but most consider them a bit more favorable to vendors than to buyers.[27]

Computerized Buying Buying procedures that utilize computers and electronic data transmission for order initiation and immediate confirmation by the vendor are becoming increasingly popular.

A buyer-oriented computerized system may take on various tasks. For example, a scientific research and development laboratory has an operating EDP purchasing system that (1) is triggered automatically when the reorder point for any one of several thousand stocked items has been reached; (2) automatically and immediately prints out a purchase-order release to be sent to a preselected supplier for a quantity that is determined by the computer; and (3) signals the buyer if the material is not received on time or if other discrepancies occur.

Others now are using systems that will, in addition, (1) store price quotations and other departmental records; (2) calculate economic order quantity and price breaks to determine whether a quantity should be increased over the amount requisitioned; (3) evaluate stored information on price and delivery, then place the order with the supplier offering the best combination for that quantity; (4) print the purchase order to the chosen supplier; (5) check the supplier for order acknowledgement and acceptability; (6) note the receipt of material delivered against the order; and (7) compare invoices with receiving reports and with the order, printing the check to the supplier if they agree.[28]

Computerized buying, pioneered in large part by automobile manufacturers, today is practiced in many firms. It has been facilitated by the development of computer terminals through which orders are placed directly with a supplier. Such systems provide for order placement and verification, recall of sorted information about the cumulative order and credit record, and "conversation" between the order placer and receiver. Once the order is placed, the inventory availability has been checked on computer by the supplier, and credit has been approved (all in a matter of seconds with no use of paper), the order can be entered directly into the supplier's computer for subsequent release, preparation, and shipment.

BUYING FOR RESALE

Thus far the chapter has concentrated on purchasing in the industrial firm. However, purchasing and other logistics activities also play critical roles in a wholesale or retail firm that buys products for resale.

The creation of form utility in a resale firm is usually limited to repackaging, but sometimes includes minor assembly operations. However, a kind of form utility is also created by the particular assortment of items purchased and the assembly and display of assortments that customers find convenient and attractive. A great deal of emphasis is placed also on possession utility (buying of merchandise) and on time and place utilities (such as giving rapid customer response from a local inventory maintained for a number of customers, none of whom could singly afford to hold such inventory).

Role of Buying

Within the wholesale or retail firm, the function of buying (often referred to as mer--chandising) is to purchase goods to be resold without significant change in their physical properties. This differs from the function of purchasing in an industrial firm where the emphasis is on the procurement of materials or services required for the production process. Both buying and industrial purchasing functions are performed by personnel commonly referred to as buyers.

In a retailing organization, a buyer often is responsible for merchandising a department or an entire store. The buyer's decisions and the ways in which individual items purchased relate to one another, may well be the major determinant in establishing the character or ''image'' of the store in the customer's mind. Thus, buying and merchandising represent major functions within the organization.

A number of contrasts can be drawn between the purchasing function in a resale organization as opposed to an industrial firm. In the former, the buyer is more likely to establish product specifications; in purchasing for an industrial firm, production or engineering departments may play major roles in establishing such specifications. In many purchases for resale, there is a much greater need for personal judgment, or feel, on the part of the buyer, particularly for ''style'' merchandise. This judgment may have to be exercised several months in advance of the actual receipt of goods for resale, because many manufacturers of style merchandise base their production runs on the initial orders from respected buyers. Typically, a buyer for resale will have much greater freedom to buy, will be involved in the pricing of the goods purchased, and will be responsible for replenishing depleted stocks. In purchasing for resale, brand names are more important and standardization is less important than in the industrial purchasing situation.

Buying Performance and Control

Goods purchased for resale typically move more quickly through a firm's logistics system than materials purchased for production. The faster movement of goods creates the need for faster information flow and response times. There are no planning buffers such as are created by the production process and the supply inventory in the industrial firm. Thus, the buying function is required to coordinate customer demand with supplier capabilities and to remain ready to respond rapidly to changes in customer demand patterns. This points up the importance of control over buying activities.

The basic method of controlling buying for resale is the "open to buy" figure. This designation of the dollar amount that a buyer may be free to commit in purchases stems directly from a store's sales plan and the amount and mixture of merchandise necessary to support the sales plan. Once merchandise is purchased, a buyer regenerates his or her "open to buy" as the purchased merchandise is sold. Items that prove slow to sell may be "marked down" in order to move them off the shelf and free "open to buy" dollars for merchandise that offers greater promise of faster, more profitable sales.

Two critical measures of a buyer's performance are the dollars of sales generated from items purchased (as compared with the planned amount) and the margin (the difference between the purchase price and the sale price) realized on the goods sold. If sales are achieved at the expense of reduced margins, the net result will be a reduction in dollars available to cover the expenses of the wholesaling or retailing operation.

Given the broad responsibility assigned to buyers in a retailing or wholesaling organization and the special knowledge needed to buy various types of merchandise, it is not surprising that the buying activity may be divided among specialists. For example, a large department store may have 30 to 40 buyers, each responsible for a department within the store featuring a particular kind of merchandise. In many retailing organizations, buyer responsibilities may be extended even further to include sales and profit responsibility for the department for which they buy.

PROCUREMENT OF CAPITAL GOODS: LOGISTICS ENGINEERING

The procurement process for capital goods, ranging from buildings to equipment, contrasts sharply with that for materials, consumables, or goods for resale. While value and performance in relation to price and the task to be accomplished are important in both, the emphasis in the purchase of capital goods often is weighted heavily toward the cost of acquiring, operating, and maintaining the capital good *over its useful life or some number of units of output*. In addition, techniques of negotiating, writing, and enforcing contracts play a large role here.

With a budget of approximately one-fifth of the gross national product of the country, the United States Government is by far the single largest purchaser of capital goods. Within the government, the Department of Defense (DOD) represents the largest purchaser of such goods, typically weapons and related support systems. Practices implemented by the DOD literally have influenced entire industries. For example, when the DOD required the use of program evaluation review technique (PERT) scheduling in the administration of projects for which it had contracted, this requirement guaranteed the widespread use of this scheduling technique and fostered its introduction in other industries not dealing directly with the government.

Among the more important concepts that have been refined in recent years by logistics engineers are those of reliability, maintainability, and life-cycle costing.

Reliability

Reliability is defined as the probability that a given system or product will perform in a satisfactory manner for a given period of time when used under specified operation conditions.[29] Probabilities can be stated in terms of the likelihood, for example, that a light bulb will last for two hundred hours of burning time, given an average of fifteen minutes per use. Thus time is also an important element in the measurement of reliability. It is often defined in terms of mean time between failure, mean time to failure, or mean time between maintenance.

Maintainability

Maintainability is the ability of an item to be maintained, as opposed to the maintenance activity itself. It emphasizes the design of products or systems to make maintenance easier, more accurate, safe, and more economical, something that is not always taken into account by designers. The implication of this, of course, is that the procurement task should include involvement in design, something that actually occurs in much military procurement activity.

Life-Cycle Costing

Life-cycle costing takes into account all of the costs associated with the purchase and operation of a capital good throughout its life. These include research and development, production and construction, operation and maintenance, and system retirement and phase-out costs. As costs of operation have risen faster than the purchase prices of many capital goods, primarily because of rising labor and fuel costs, life-cycle costing has taken on new importance in the purchase of a wide range of items.

Trends in government procurement have influenced strongly the organization of the management of logistics activities in aerospace and other industries supplying the government. They have led to the creation of departments with broad responsibilities for procurement, inventory control, scheduling of raw materials and component parts, and even production scheduling. By their very nature, these organizations have concerned themselves to a great extent with supply rather than distribution logistics, concentrating on the problems of bringing together the many important components for a weapon or other hardware systems, the physical distribution of which is relatively simple. This has led to the creation of organizations that may be regarded as siblings of physical distribution departments, so-called "materials management groups."

SUMMARY

Purchasing is the act of buying, literally signified in most dictionary definitions as the act of paying money for something in the completion of a purchase agreement. Procurement signifies a broader range of activity associated with bringing about the acquisition of a product or service through an assessment of function, quality, price, and service associated with a product. It involves all of the many steps necessary to bring to a close a successful transaction.

Materials management, in addition, deals with that broad portion of the spectrum of logistics activities concerned with supply, including procurement. Buying for resale emphasizes certain merchandising activities generally associated with marketing, including actual sale responsibility. Logistics engineering, associated most frequently with government procurement, in addition concerns itself with product maintainability, reliability, and life-cycle costs. Relationships among these four activity "sets" are shown in the context of the "materials cycle," a specific sequence of activities that were set forth in Figure 2–2.

The importance of procurement activities is underlined by the fact that in many industrial firms, the bill for purchased items is more than half that of the value of products sold.

Purchasing services provided by most purchasing departments include those of obtaining the most effective value in items purchased, controlling financial commitments, conducting negotiations, engaging in supplier development activities, insuring continuity of sources of supply, and providing information input to other departments of the firm. Not only must purchasing managers decide what to procure, they must also devote a great deal of attention to the sourcing, location, quantity, timing, and form of a particular purchase.

Procurement decisions have an impact on logistics activities. In particular, decisions concerning whether to make or buy a product; the pricing terms by which the product might be bought; the selection of sources of supply; the development of contract or "blanket" orders; the use of reciprocal buying practices; and the use of value analysis, standardization, systems contracting, PID systems, customer-vendor coordination programs, and computerized buying all influence logistics costs and plans.

Buying takes on a particular importance in firms trading in goods for resale either at retail or wholesale. In these firms, attention must be paid to the assortment and selection of goods assembled for resale. Buying responsibilities often extend to the actual merchandising of a department, sometimes including responsibilities for sales and profits as well.

Different factors must be considered in the purchase of capital goods to be employed in the business or the performance of a function, such as defense in the military. Here, there is concentration on such concepts as the reliability and maintainability of the product being purchased as well as the costs of designing, buying, operating, maintaining, and disposing of it — its life-cycle costs. These concepts have been pioneered by practitioners of logistics engineering, primarily comprising the defense establishment and those firms marketing to it.

DISCUSSION QUESTIONS

1. Distinguish between the terms "purchasing" and "procurement."

2. What are the functions of an industrial purchasing department?

3. Why is it important to develop good relations with suppliers? Explain.

4. Explain what is *meant* by:
   What to procure?
   From whom to procure?
   Which items to procure?
   How much to procure?
   When to procure?
   In what form to procure?

5. What are ''make or buy'' decisions? At what levels do they occur? Explain.

6. What are the pros and cons of having alternate sources of supply, for example, multiple vendors for the same item?

7. What is contract or blanket ordering? Why is it used? Explain.

8. Is purchase-and-sales reciprocity a good business practice? Explain.

9. What is value analysis? What questions are asked in performing value analysis? What purpose do these questions serve?

10. What are the advantages of standardization? Why can it be difficult to achieve? Explain.

11. What is systems contracting? How does it differ from contract or blanket ordering?

12. What is a POD system? Have such systems been successful? Explain.

13. What are flexible price agreements (FPA's)? Why are they used? Explain.

14. How does buying for resale differ from industrial purchasing? Explain.

15. Define the terms reliability, maintainability and life-cycle costing. What is their relationship to the original purchase price of the item? Explain.

16. What activities in procurement impact logistics, and vice versa?

CASE: **Allied Industrial Products, Inc.***

POLICY ON MULTIPLE VENDORS

The newly appointed assistant vice president for Purchasing and Materials Management of Allied Industrial Products, Inc., Mr. Rosco Turner, was reviewing his company's policies in regard to the purchasing function for which he was responsible. Mr. Turner was aware that Allied had not had a consistent policy with respect to having either single or multiple vendors for purchased raw materials, parts, components, or operating supplies, such as machine lubricants, office supplies, and so forth.

Over the past several years, this lack of a consistent policy had been criticized by a number of persons in the Purchasing Department, including Mr. Turner himself. He believed that the lack of a consistent policy was poor management and that his people — particularly the purchasing staff — needed clear guidance from his office.

There were pros and cons with respect to a single- versus multiple-vendor policy. Mr. Turner believed that the strongest argument in favor of a single vendor policy was ''clout.'' If all of Allied's purchases for a product were from a single vendor, that firm would put a high value on Allied's business. Also, it would simplify the purchasing agent's task.

On the other hand, a policy favoring the use of multiple vendors had some advantages. Chief among them was, as Mr. Turner put it, ''the principle of divide and conquer.'' That is, don't let any vendor think it has a lock on your business. Further, in the event of a strike at one vendor's plant, other vendors would still be able to supply Allied with its needs.

Mr. Turner decided to call a meeting of his six purchasing agents to discuss the problem and try to articulate a policy that would provide decision-making guidance to the purchasing agents.

CASE QUESTIONS

1. What information, or types of information, would be useful to have in order to help the group in its discussion?

2. Other than those already mentioned, what additional arguments might be advanced in favor of one policy or the other?

*This case was prepared as a basis for discussion and is not intended to portray either correct or incorrect approaches to managerial decision making. All names have been disguised.

SUGGESTED READINGS

Purchasing Handbook, 4th ed. New York: McGraw-Hill, 1982. An encyclopaedic coverage of every significant purchasing topic.

ROBESON, JAMES F. and ROBERT G. HOUSE, eds., *The Distribution Handbook*, New York: The Free Press, 1985. Section 7, Chapter 19, "Managing the Purchasing Function" surveys this topic.

The following textbooks are representative of the more useful texts in the field. Each does an excellent job of coverage, with the Ammer and Heinritz books being a bit more oriented to the practitioner. The Blanchard text is oriented toward the acquisition of capital goods having long service lives and therefore requiring consideration of operation, maintenance, and repair costs over the life of the equipment in addition to its original purchase cost. The Banks text is more mathematical treatment of procurement and inventory systems analysis.

AMMER, DEAN S., *Materials Management and Purchasing*, 4th ed., Homewood, Ill.: Richard D. Irwin, 1980.

BANKS, JERRY and W. J. FABRYCKY, *Procurement and Inventory Systems Analysis*, Englewood Cliffs, N.J.: Prentice-Hall, Inc., 1987.

BLANCHARD, BENJAMIN S., *Logistics Engineering and Management*, 3d ed., Englewood Cliffs, N.J.: Prentice-Hall, Inc., 1986.

BROWNING, JOHN M., NOEL B. ZABRISKIE, and ALAN B. HUELLMANTEL, "Strategic Purchasing Planning," *Journal of Purchasing and Materials Management* (Spring 1983) 19–24. An excellent presentation of the reasons for integrating the purchasing function with corporate strategic planning.

HEINRITZ, STUART F. and PAUL V. FARRELL, *Purchasing: Principles and Applications*, 6th ed., Englewood Cliffs, N.J.: Prenctice-Hall, 1981.

LEENDERS, MICHIEL R., HAROLD E. FEARON, and WILBUR B. ENGLAND, *Purchasing and Materials Management*, 7th ed., Homewood, Ill.: Richard D. Irwin, 1980.

LEE, LAMAR, JR., and DONALD W. DOBLER, *Purchasing and Materials Management*, 3d ed., New York: McGraw-Hill, 1977. See page 11.

SPEKMAN, ROBERT E., "A Strategic Approach to Procurement Planning," *Journal of Purchasing and Materials Management* (Winter, 1981) 2–8. In a sort of "predecessor" article to Browning, et. al. (above), Spekman articulates a well presented approach to viewing procurement strategically.

WAGNER, WILLIAM B., " The Role and Relevance of Improved Purchasing for Logistics," *Journal of Business Logistics* 8, no. 1 (1987) 61–78.

Two of the most informative periodicals in this field are *Purchasing* magazine and the *Journal of Purchasing and Materials Management*. *Purchasing* is a bi-weekly trade publication featuring good coverage of a variety of topics of current interest in the field, while the *Journal*, published quarterly, is devoted to more scholarly articles.

ENDNOTES

1. Denise Brootman, "Top Executives Can Add Punch to Purchasing," *Purchasing* (January 21, 1975): 34.

2. George Aljian ed., *Purchasing Handbook*, 2nd ed. (New York: McGraw-Hill Book Co., 1966), 1–3.

3. Mark Shepard, Jr., "Buyers Must be More than Data Transmitters," *Purchasing* (January 11, 1968): 61.

4. "CEO's to Purchasing: Buy Quality, Staying Power," *Purchasing* (January 27, 1983): 57.

5. Somerby Dowst, "Updating the Numbers on Performance Measurement," *Purchasing* (August 2, 1984): 50–53.

6. Somerby Dowst, "What Buyers Want from Distributors," *Purchasing* (October 13, 1983): 69.

7. Dean S. Ammer, "Top Management's View of the Purchasing Function," *Journal of Purchasing and Materials Management* (Spring 1989): 21.

8. Robert Landeros and Robert M. Monczka, "Cooperative Buyer/Seller Relationships and a Firm's Competitive Posture," *Journal of Purchasing and Materials Management* (Fall 1989): 15–16.

9. For the views of six corporate chief executive officers on such programs see, "Vendors Profile Forecast—How Tomorrow's Suppliers Shape Up," *Purchasing* (January 27, 1983): 80–85.

10. Daniel J. Bragg and Chan K. Hahn, "Material Requirements Planning and Purchasing," *Journal of Purchasing and Materials Management* (Summer, 1982): 21.

11. James P. Morgan, "MRP II—That Powerful Tool! Parts I, II and III," *Purchasing* (September 6, 1984): 109–115, (October 4, 1984): 59–64, and (October 18, 1984): 129–132. These three articles present an in-depth analysis of MRP II and its significance to purchasing management.

12. Thomas F. Dillon, "Inbound Transportation: The Shippers' View," *Purchasing* (February 28, 1980): 48–51.

13. Mark Treleven, "Single Sourcing: A Management Tool for the Quality Supplier," *Journal of Purchasing and Materials Management* (Spring, 1987): 23. The reference in the quotation to Deming pertains to Deming's *Quality Productivity*, pages 29–30. The reference to Crosby pertains to Philip B. Crosby, *Quality is Free*, New York: McGraw-Hill, 1979. The reference to J. M. Juran and Frank M. Gryna, Jr., is found on pages 230–31 of *Quality Planning Analysis* (New York: McGraw-Hill, 1980).

14. A. E. Owens, "Blanket Orders Cut Costs, Reduce Your Inventory," *Purchasing* (May 15, 1969): 67.

15. Stuart F. Heinritz and Paul V. Farrell, *Purchasing: Principles and Applications*, 6th ed. (Englewood Cliffs, N.J.: Prentice-Hall, Inc., 1981) 375.

16. Dean S. Ammer, *Materials Management and Purchasing*, 4th ed. (Homewood, Ill.: Richard D. Irwin, Inc., 1980) 549.

17. "What Value Analysis is All About," *Purchasing* (May 1957): 38.

18. Lloyd Stouffer, "Biggest Thing Since Mass Production," *Reader's Digest* (January 1964): 108.

19. For a concise analysis of the use of analytical techniques in purchasing, including price analysis, cost analysis, and value analysis see Leland Batdorf and Jay A. Vora, "Use of Analytical Techniques in Purchasing," *Journal of Purchasing and Materials Management* (Spring 1983): 25–29.

20. Peter Wulff, "It Doesn't Have to be Official . . . ," *Purchasing* (February 8, 1972): 49 ff. See page 53.

21. Somerby Dowst, "Updating the Numbers on Performance Measurement," *Purchasing* (August 2, 1984): 53.

22. *Ibid.*

23. William J. Hannaford, "How Effective is Systems Purchasing?" *Journal of Purchasing and Materials Management* (Summer 1979): 13–19.

24. "How Solid are Systems Contracts?" *Purchasing* (September 13, 1977): 69.

25. Hannaford, "How Effective," 16.

26. Lassor Blumenthal, "How to Cut Purchasing Costs," *Dun's Review* (March, 1964): 53–54 and 66–69. Descriptive data on Dundee Cement Co. and Kearfott Division of General Precision in subsequent sections are also from this source.

27. For an excellent discussion of flexible price agreements and escalator clauses see Jay Roman, "Control of Contract Escalation," *Journal of Purchasing and Materials Management* (Fall 1982): 20–25 and Dale Varble, "Flexible Price Agreements: Purchasing's View," *California Management Review* XXIII, no. 2 (Winter 1980): 44–51.

28. J. William Widing, Jr., and C. Gerald Diamond, ''Buy by Computer,'' *Harvard Business Review* (March–April, 1964): 109–20.

29. Benjamin S. Blanchard, *Logistics Engineering and Management*, 3d ed. (Englewood Cliffs, N.J.: Prentice-Hall, Inc., 1986): 14.

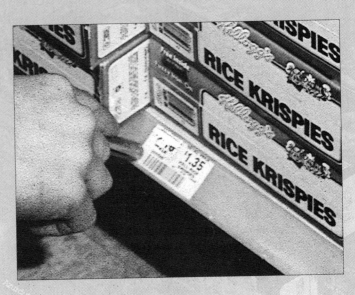

The price of each box of cereal absorbs all costs incurred to produce and distribute to the end user, the cereal consumer.

CHAPTER THREE

3

Product Pricing Policies

LEARNING OBJECTIVES

The objectives of this chapter are to:

➤ Describe the relationship between product pricing policies and logistics costs.

➤ Explain and illustrate a variety of logistics responsibilities and activities that affect pricing decisions.

➤ Show the effects of pricing policies on logistics costs, the legal ramifications of pricing policies, and the use of logistics cost information as legal justification for various pricing policies.

➤ Illustrate the methods and purposes of offering quantity discounts and their effects on logistics costs.

➤ Explain the effects on logistics costs of the use of special sales arrangements involving dating (seasonal) pricing or deals (special lower prices).

As noted in Chapter One, one of the four elements of the marketing mix is pricing.* Pricing decisions made by marketing managers affect, and are affected by, logistics considerations. Below are three situations that illustrate ways in which pricing decisions and logistics are interrelated.

A manufacturer of soaps and detergents, upon analyzing the relevant costs and revenues realized in selling to various customers, found that logistics costs as a proportion of dollar sales dropped rapidly as the size of a given transaction increased. The manufacturer's price structure offered quantity discounts for purchases in quantities of nine cases, twenty-five cases, one hundred cases, and five hundred cases. However, many of its sales were in one- or two-case quantities to small grocery outlets. While its overall costs of logistics in relation to sales were only 12 percent, comparable costs for one- or two-case orders were found to be 150 percent.

A distributor of thirty thousand different mill-supply items, upon analyzing the profitability of product groupings in its line, found that profitability varied directly with dollar sales per order, sales per written line on an order, and gross margin (the difference between purchase price and sales price). The average order size was $80, but ranged from $36 to $250 for various product categories. Orders with sales below the average were found to be unprofitable. The average line item sales value was $32, but varied from $16 to $100. Once again, line item sales below the average were judged unprofitable. Customers typically placed orders containing nonstandard items that required a special order to the manufacturer. As a result, the distributor was rarely able to fill a complete order at the time it was received. Instead, special items on a given order might arrive from the manufacturer in several shipments over a period of up to twelve weeks. This resulted in frequent communication with both the customer and the manufacturer, as well as duplicated delivery charges for a given order. In addition to the basic cost of about $3 for servicing an order, it was estimated that each subsequent shipment for ''back ordered'' goods on that same order involved at least $8 in additional costs, not counting the time spent by the distributor's sales representatives. Although reluctant to change policies because they reflected those of the competition, the president of the distributorship was certain that this type of business could not be producing profits on the basis of the 20 percent margin on sales that the distributor received.

A manufacturer of wearing apparel sold its products under terms of ''2/10, net 30 E.O.M.'' (end of month), meaning that an invoice for products that were received by the customer in July, for example, could be paid for up to August 10 (10 days after the end of the month in which the order was placed) to qualify for a 2 percent discount. If the discount were not taken, the invoice would be due in full on August 30. This produced a large peak in customer orders near the end of each month and a large number of requests from company salesmen to schedule shipments (and billing) to customers early in the month, making goods available before payment on the shipment was due. The practice increased as competition grew, and retail customers exerted pressures on the company's sales force to have goods available further in advance of payment. Unfortunately, this placed an increasing burden on

---

*The ''Four P's'' of marketing are product, place, price, and promotion. This chapter is concerned with the relationships of pricing policies and logistics. The logistics contribution to promotion is treated primarily in Chapter 4, ''Customer Service.'' Chapter 9, ''Location Theory and Practice,'' treats logistics issues relating to place. Product characteristics important to various logistics considerations are treated mainly in Chapters 8, 10, 11, and 13 (''Traffic Management,'' ''Packaging and Materials Handling,'' ''Warehousing Management,'' and ''International Logistics Operations'').

the company's order processing and shipping departments at the beginning of each month. Work scheduling was complicated by the fact that 40 percent of a month's shipments were made during the first four days of each month. The company's operating committee scheduled the matter for discussion at its next meeting.

At the end of the chapter, these three situations will be revisited to see what decision actually was made by the company's management in each case and what happened as a result of their decisions.

NON-ZERO-SUM PRICING AND LOGISTICS COSTS

The way in which customers behave during the purchase of a company's products is a direct result of the nature of incentives that reward or punish certain behavior patterns. Price incentives are probably the strongest (and most effective) of all factors that influence customer behavior, but there are other terms of sale that also affect customer behavior patterns and influence the profitability of sales.

Other things being equal, logistics costs as a percentage of the sales dollar will increase under the following conditions:

1. Orders decrease, either in dollar or physical measures.

2. The average value per order-line item decreases.

3. The number of shipments required to supply all of the items contained in an order increases.

4. There are (severe) peak requirements for processing orders or effecting shipments during various periods of time.

5. The number of points through which an order must be administratively processed increases.

6. The number of points through which an item must pass physically before it reaches the customer increases.

Price reductions that do not influence customers to order or otherwise behave in a desired manner do not produce cost reductions. They merely transfer profits from the seller to the buyer. These are termed zero-sum results by students of game theory. A strong case can be made for instituting only pricing strategies that influence customers to change their behavior in such a way that cost reductions in excess of associated price reductions occur. Such pricing strategies produce genuine economic benefits to both buyer and seller and can be termed non-zero-sum pricing strategies.

Logistics is only one of many elements to be considered in pricing decisions, but it can be an important one. The objectives of this chapter are (1) to acquaint you with terminology as well as a number of alternative approaches to pricing; and (2) to explore the impact of pricing decisions on logistics and vice versa. First, terms of sale and basic types of pricing policies will be discussed as background for a subsequent consideration of more specific matters, such as the determination of quantity discounts.

TERMS OF SALE

Once a price is quoted on a product, a buyer might well ask the following questions: Do I receive a cash discount if I pay for the goods early? Does the quoted price include transportation charges to my warehouse or factory? Am I required to make arrangements to pay the shipping charges, to file claims for damages to goods enroute, or to determine which actual shipping charges apply? Who has control over the selection of the mode of transportation and specific carrier for the shipment of the goods? Various elements of a complete statement of the terms of sale typically answer all of these questions. Omission of one or more of these elements can lead to litigation or embarrassment in buyer-seller relationships.

There are three basic elements in a statement of terms of sale for a given quantity and quality of goods: (1) price, (2) cash discounts and credit terms, if any, and (3) logistics responsibilities.

Price

The most visible term of sale is the stated price. Other terms of sale will determine the "real" price, for example, actual cost to the buyer, and aid in the interpretation of a price quotation.

Cash Discounts and Credit Terms

It is common practice for a manufacturer or distributor to quote terms of sale that include a statement, for example, of "2/10, net 30." This type of statement on the part of the seller makes two stipulations: first, a cash discount of 2 percent off the quoted price will be allowed the buyer if the goods are paid for within ten days from the invoice date; second, the goods must be paid for within thirty days from the date of invoice. These two elements of a statement of mercantile credit are commonly called the cash discount and the net credit period. Although terms of "2/10, net 30" are common in many businesses, there are a great number of variations in statements of trade credit.

The size of the cash discount quoted in a statement of trade credit generally depends upon three factors: (1) the cost of the capital needed to carry the trade "loan"; (2) custom in certain industries; and (3) competitive factors. First, in regard to cost of capital, consider a situation in which a selling firm computes its cost of capital at 14 percent. It may quote terms of sale of "2/10, net 60." Thus, the 2 percent discount offered the buyer on payments for goods within ten days of the date of the shipment or the date of the invoice (whichever applies) roughly corresponds to the amount that it would cost the selling firm to carry the buyer's credit for an additional 50 days. The annual percentage rate (APR) is calculated as 360 days/(net days − discount days) × (discount percentage), or $360/50 \times 2 = 14.0$ percent. (The use of a 360-day year is common commercial practice because it facilitates simple calculations resulting from the easy divisibility of 360 as contrasted with 365 or 366.) In this case, the amount and timing of the discount and net credit period correspond to the savings in the cost of capital on the part of the selling firm. This amounts to the seller offering the buyer 50 days of credit in return for the buyer paying the quoted price for the goods.

The buyer compares its cost of capital to the 14 percent cost of taking the discount and decides whether or not it is worth it. If the APR is greater than the buyer's cost of capital, then the buyer would pay early and take the discount. If the APR is less than the buyer's cost of capital, then the buyer would delay payment and not take the discount.

The discussion above assumes a rational financial decision-making process, but fails to take into account two situations frequently found in business. A seller may badly need cash and would be willing, therefore, to quote more favorable terms to the buyer than would be the case if the seller were in a healthier financial condition. Or, a buyer may be strapped for cash and be unable to take advantage of attractive discounts that may be offered.

Second, other types of businesses and channels of distribution have operated under mercantile credit terms that have not been varied for many years. Custom plays a large part in keeping terms the same even though changes may be warranted on economic grounds.

Third, the intensity of competition has in some cases necessitated the quoting of cash discounts far in excess of the cost of capital. In these cases, it is hard to distinguish a cash discount from an ordinary price reduction for competitive purposes. Consider the previous example, with terms of "2/10, net 30" substituted for "1/10, net 60." From the standpoint of the seller in this situation, the incremental credit period is 20 $(30 - 10)$ days, or 1/18th $(20/360)$ of a year. The cost of capital for 1/18th of a year, at the rate of 14 percent, would be 14/18 percent. And yet, in this example, other considerations apparently make it necessary for a seller to quote a cash discount more than double its cost of capital.

Similar considerations may prevail from the buyer's point of view. A net credit period is commonly designed to correspond roughly to the period of time in which goods bought for resale can reasonably be expected to be resold. In many businesses, goods bought for resale are expected to "pay for themselves." Goods with potential for rapid turnover, such as grocery products, commonly carry a short net credit period. The net credit period for jewelry, however, could be expected to be relatively long.

Logistics Responsibilities

Buyer and seller must determine the appropriate division of responsibility for matters of logistics, including (1) the point at which delivery is to be taken by the buyer; (2) responsibility for the payment of shipping charges; and (3) control of shipping matters. These responsibilities are often summed up in a statement of "free on board" (F.O.B.) terms.

Point of Delivery to Buyer   The quotation of an F.O.B. point in terms of sale generally indicates the point at which the seller turns over the goods, and responsibility for them, to the buyer. This includes responsibilities for paying for transportation and handling charges, determining the appropriate charges to be assessed, selecting the modes and carriers for transportation purposes, and filing any claims for damages which might occur in transit.

An F.O.B. point can be selected for quotation from many alternatives. Four common quotations are illustrated in Figure 3–1. Theoretically, a statement of F.O.B. without specific location is incorrect or incomplete. However, in common parlance, the terms "F.O.B." and "delivered" are often used to signify whether the terms of sale include payment of transportation charges by the seller: in most cases "F.O.B." does not; "delivered" does.

Payment of Shipping Charges   Certain additional stipulations may be attached to a basic F.O.B. statement of terms. By means of these stipulations, a seller or buyer can apportion the payment of transportation charges in a manner other than that indicated by the basic F.O.B.

FIGURE 3–1: Common quotations of F.O.B. points and responsibility for costs of transportation and handling associated with them

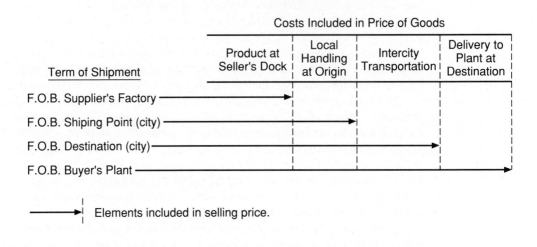

| | Costs Included in Price of Goods | | | |
Term of Shipment	Product at Seller's Dock	Local Handling at Origin	Intercity Transportation	Delivery to Plant at Destination
F.O.B. Supplier's Factory				
F.O.B. Shiping Point (city)				
F.O.B. Destination (city)				
F.O.B. Buyer's Plant				

——————▶| Elements included in selling price.

statement. For example, "F.O.B. origin, freight allowed" signifies that title to and responsibility for the goods passes at the point at which the carrier picks up the shipment, while the transportation charges must be paid by the *seller*. By means of various "freight allowed" statements, a seller may agree to pay none, a part, or all of the transportation charges on a shipment completely independent of the statement transferring title to the goods.

For example, a shipper desiring to quote a delivered price comparable to that of a competitor might quote "freight allowed" terms from the city cited in the competitor's terms of sale, rather than the actual city from which the shipment is made. The amount of freight charges allowed under such terms would result in a delivered cost comparable to that quoted to the buyer by the seller's competition. In other cases, a shipper might wish to limit the transportation charge it would be willing to pay on a given shipment by stating the maximum that it would be willing to bear. A common quotation is "F.O.B. shipping point, carload freight allowed to destination," under which the seller agrees to pay transportation charges up to, but not over, the rail carload rate level on a shipment between the two points.

Routing Control Unless specified to the contrary, F.O.B. terms generally indicate the right of the seller or buyer to route shipments, to the extent that the privilege is granted by carriers of the various modes of transportation. Thus, terms including "F.O.B., origin" designations indicate the right of the buyer to route the shipment. The right of the shipper or receiver to route based on pricing terms has developed largely from custom. Deviations from the general rule occur because of the effectiveness with which one firm is able to route its shipments as contrasted with another. Thus, in the case of a large supplier shipping to a small customer, greater resources for effective routing may exist in the selling firm, thus warranting a stipulation of "F.O.B. shipping point, routing and form of transportation to be selected by shipper."

Regulations governing transportation in the United States place varying emphasis on the right of a shipper to route freight via the various modes (rail, truck, and so on) of transportation. The Revised Interstate Commerce Act specifically designates the shipper's right to route carload traffic by rail. That right is not guaranteed in those sections of the Act pertaining to motor carriers, water carriers, and freight forwarders. As to air freight, the Federal Aviation Act makes no mention of a right to route shipments.

In practice, however, a shipper may have a great deal to say about the route the shipment may take. Under any method of shipment, the shipper of freight has a right to tender the shipment to any originating carrier selected. Conversely, a receiver of freight might designate to the supplier a mode by which and carrier to which the shipment should be tendered. For competitive reasons, a carrier will nearly always honor the routing instructions of a shipper or receiver even when not required to do so.

Maximum control over routing may be very important to a firm. Without it, the best laid plans for optimizing a logistics system can be destroyed by a customer's insistence on the right to receive a shipment by a specified route. A firm that ships all or a portion of its product directly from plants or plant-oriented warehouses is particularly vulnerable when it does not have maximum control over routing through the terms of sale quoted to its customers.

In the situation illustrated in Figure 3–2, plans recently formulated by Alvarez Electric called for less-than-truckload (LTL) shipments to Pittsburgh customers from its Toledo warehouse. In the past, both truckload (TL) and and less-than-truckload (LTL) shipments to Pittsburgh were made from Alvarez's Omaha plant. Terms of sale quoted by Alvarez were F.O.B. Omaha. The Pittsburgh Electric Company had a standing routing request on file with Alvarez's Sales Division: "Ship via Greatway Trucking." Greatway operated between Omaha and Pittsburgh, charging an LTL rate of $4.90 per hundredweight (cwt., or 100 pounds) for its services between the two cities. Alvarez's new system called for rail carload shipment from Omaha to its Toledo warehouse at $1.40 per hundredweight, warehousing and handling at

FIGURE 3–2: Potential conflicts in a supplier's distribution system and a customer's specification of originating carrier

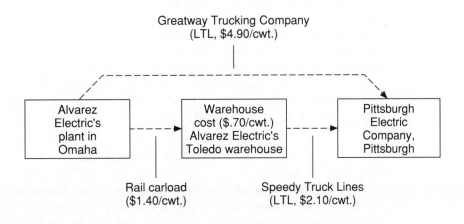

Toledo at an estimated cost of $.70 per hundredweight, and LTL shipment from Toledo to Pittsburgh via Speedy Truck Lines for $2.10 per hundredweight, or a total cost of $4.20 per hundredweight. On receipt of a particular LTL order from Pittsburgh Electric, Alvarez Electric made the shipment from its Toledo warehouse, prepaid the freight from Toledo to Pittsburgh, and billed Pittsburgh Electric for $4.90 per hundredweight, even though the shipment was not made via Greatway. In a situation like this, Pittsburgh Electric might well believe it had the right to specify routing of this shipment, at least in regard to the originating and delivering carrier. If Pittsburgh Electric were to specify delivery of Alvarez's shipments by Greatway Trucking, it would penalize Alvarez in terms of delivery time, increase the cost of delivery, and reduce the opportunities for consolidation of Alvarez's shipments from Omaha to its warehouse at Toledo.

This example illustrates one possible penalty of F.O.B. point-of-origin pricing, particularly from the standpoint of the vendor. Another is the inability of the supplying firm to utilize the carriers believed to be most dependable or most helpful in problems requiring tracing (location of shipments enroute), rate quotations, or other types of service. Carrier willingness to make rate adjustments, such as reduce prices, is often conditioned by the degree to which a firm has control over the routing of its inbound or outbound shipments, and can divert freight from one carrier to another.

Other Responsibilities   F.O.B. terms designate the point at which title to a shipment usually passes from the seller to the buyer. Along with title, other responsibilities pass as well. These include the determination of the appropriate transportation rate under which a product moves and the settlement of claims for any damage to the product during shipment.

Individual supplier policy regarding freight claims often overrides "legal responsibility" for such action. For example, it is common practice for many suppliers quoting F.O.B. point-of-origin prices to "make good" damaged or lost merchandise and file transportation damage claims for customers. A supplier may also issue credit to its customer and collect overpayments of freight charges from carriers when such charges are proven incorrect. These types of services in excess of legal responsibility are often necessitated by competitive considerations.

Comparable Terms in International Logistics   There is a wide array of special terms used to designate logistics responsibilities in terms of sale for international transactions. These are presented in what are now commonly called INCOMTERMS (International Chamber of Commerce Terms of Sale). Among the most important of these is "free along side" (F.A.S.), used in much the same way as F.O.B. "Cost, insurance, freight [charges]" (C.I.F.) is used to designate that the transportation charges for an international shipment will be paid by the seller. Relationships between trade terms and legal responsibilities vary significantly between domestic and international logistics, however. The subject of international logistics operations will be treated in detail in Chapter 13.

PRICING POLICIES

Pricing policies can be divided into two basic categories: delivered and F.O.B. The former are more popular because delivered pricing policies meet the needs of sellers to (1) simplify their price-quoting procedures by maintaining "uniform" prices;[1] (2) meet competition by quoting "identical" prices; and (3) maintain maximum control over physical distribution.

Delivered Pricing

The four basic types of delivered pricing systems are those centered around basing-point, zone, single or national, and individual prices. The latter is really F.O.B. pricing in effect and will be discussed later in connection with F.O.B. pricing systems.

Delivered pricing systems are characterized by their use of "uniform" and "identical" pricing, and the extent to which they are directly or indirectly influenced by transportation and handling costs. The importance of logistics in each of these pricing systems is indicated by the use of the terms "freight absorption," "phantom freight," and "freight allowed or equalized."

Freight absorption refers to the payment of all or a portion of freight charges out of that portion of margin on price reserved for overhead and profit by the seller. It generally occurs when the seller wishes to meet or beat a competitor quoting lower prices. Policies of "freight allowed" or "freight equalized" are more specific means by which a firm practices freight absorption.

Phantom freight is the assessment of freight charges by a seller in excess of those actually incurred for a shipment. It arises when prices are based on freight charges that are higher than those actually incurred by the supplier in accomplishing delivery to the customer and occurs when the seller's competitive position is favorable enough to permit such pricing.

Basing-Point Policies The underlying principle of basing-point pricing systems is that customers are charged prices based on a predetermined manufacturing cost plus the transportation costs from one (single basing point) or more (multiple basing points) designated locations. The actual locations at which goods are manufactured, or from which they are shipped, may not correspond to basing points.

As shown in Figure 3–3, two manufacturers of cornstarch, located at Denver and St. Louis respectively, supply a customer in Louisville, using Kansas City as a basing point. Although the applicable transportation rate from Denver to Louisville is $2.50 per hundredweight, the Denver-based manufacturer charges only $1.75 per hundredweight (the basing-point rate from Kansas City to Louisville) in order to land his goods in Louisville at a price comparable to his competitor's. He thus absorbs $.75 per hundredweight of freight costs. In contrast, the St. Louis-based manufacturer charges the applicable basing-point rate from Kansas City to Louisville of $1.75 per hundredweight, but actually incurs only $1.00 per hundredweight in transportation charges. His price includes $.75 per hundredweight of phantom freight.

The example discussed above uses a single basing-point system. The principle of a multiple basing-point system is precisely the same. The only difference between the two is found in the quotation of the basing-point rate to a destination from the basing point with the lowest freight rate. The basing-point system was developed by the steel industry, primarily as a means of enabling its members to quote identical prices at various points throughout the United States. According to one authority:

> Probably the first group of firms to use it were the members of the Steel Beam Association, a price cartel formed in 1880. The system was only slowly extended to other steel products by various pools and trade associations, until it was more or less generally adopted by the industry under the leadership of the giant United States Steel Corporation.
>
> The next industry to use it was the cement industry. It was probably introduced there by a subsidiary of the United States Steel Corporation, which had become also the largest

FIGURE 3–3: A diagram showing (1) the applicable transportation rate for cornstarch between St. Louis and Louisville; (2) the basing-point rate charged by both Manufacturers A and B; and (3) the applicable transportation rate for cornstarch between Denver and Louisville

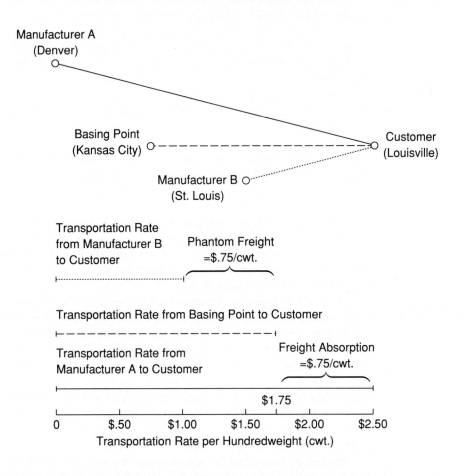

cement producer in the country. While the steel industry was the first to adopt the single basing-point system, cement was the first to adopt the multiple basing-point system.

Little information is available about when the system spread to other industries. Single or multiple basing-point systems are known to have been used, temporarily or permanently, for the following products: iron and steel, welded chain, rigid steel conduit, cast-iron pipe, lead, copper, zinc, muriate of potash, gasoline, cement, fire brick, asphalt roofing materials, maple flooring, oak flooring, other lumber products (cedar, hemlock, cypress, pine, fir), wood pulp, sugar and corn products (corn syrup, corn oil, starch, gluten, feed).[2]

Arguments put forth against basing-point systems, particularly those based on a single-point, were (1) the manner in which they had to be administered led to exchanges of information among competing firms in violation of antitrust laws; (2) single basing-point systems encouraged customers to order from uneconomic sources, which produced a certain amount of uneconomic cross-hauling of goods in opposite directions; and (3) the system did not allow F.O.B. pricing to a customer wishing to purchase on that basis. As a result some specific basing-point systems resulting from industry conspiracy or restraint of trade were ruled unlawful in a series of post-World War II court decisions. These decisions affected the corn products, cement, steel, and chain manufacturing industries, among others. The rulings so restricted industry pricing agreements (usually reached through the medium of a trade association) as to make basing-point systems relatively ineffective in practice. An understanding of the nature of basing-point systems is, however, important because of their relationship to other systems of delivered pricing.

Zone Pricing Policies A seller may establish zone prices based on the varying distances between customer locations and the seller's point of sale. Zones are created to reflect differences in transportation charges to various geographic groups of customers. All customers in a zone pay the same price. This usually results in some customers situated in a zone paying "phantom freight" while others are the beneficiaries of "freight absorption" by the seller.

Zone pricing systems have been under the close scrutiny of the Federal Trade Commission for many years. Some have been considered to be discriminatory between buyers (for example, those that charge different delivered prices to competing customers located short distances from each other), and have been deemed unlawful. For this reason, zone boundaries generally have been designated where wide discrepancies in transportation costs exist between one region and another. For example, firms operating in the eastern United States frequently establish higher prices for the western part of the country, at least until such time as capabilities for producing products on the West Coast are developed by the company or its competitors.

Although zone pricing policies are typical of certain industries, they do not depend upon the organized action of a group of firms. Individual firms can, and many do, quote zone prices.

Single or National Price Policies Under a single price policy, a firm establishes one price for a particular product for all markets in which that product is sold. In cases where the firm markets its product nationally, such a policy has come to be known as a national price policy.

Single or national price policies are particularly popular for those types of products sold for ultimate consumption. They make possible market-wide advertising and packaging based on price as well as other promotional material. This type of promotional effort is thought to be reassuring to the consumer who sees a single price printed on the package wherever it may be found.

Legal Status The current status of delivered pricing systems in the United States is not as clear today as it was even five years ago. It was and is the position of the Federal Trade Commission (FTC) that if a seller offers F.O.B. pricing to competing customers as an alternative to its delivered price, its delivered prices are legal.

However, the former FTC position allowing a uniform national delivered price to all competing customers has been modified, some would say drastically. In the 1983 DuPont/

Ethyl case the FTC ruled, in effect, that manufacturers' prices should be based on price at the plant or warehouse plus actual transportation costs to the customer. Thus, even the classic defense of "meeting competition" has come under scrutiny because " . . . independent, parallel activities that make price coordination easy, even with no agreement at all between the companies, can run afoul of the law."[3]

Further, zone (delivered) pricing may also be subject to similar FTC rulings if it is shown that, as a result of zone pricing, competing customers pay identical prices not based on identical transportation costs.

It is clear that formerly acceptable price discrimination defenses such as "meeting competition" (mentioned above) or "we charge a uniform price to everybody" may no longer suffice. A seller's plant or warehouse price *plus logistics costs* appears to be evolving as a new standard for defensible price differentiation. However, it may be several years before these issues are ultimately resolved by the courts, and there is always the possibility of Congressional action to change the law to either reaffirm previous policy or follow the new lead of the FTC.

Finally, one must always remember that the antitrust laws and related FTC rulings apply to prices charged to *competing customers* of the seller. If competition is not affected, a wide variety of pricing policies will continue to be available to sellers.

Importance for Logistics   Delivered pricing systems result in either phantom freight or freight absorption being present in a majority of sales. The theoretical incidence of phantom freight and freight absorption under a zone pricing system is shown graphically in Figure 3–4; the principle applies to a single or national pricing policy as well.

The implications and problems of delivered pricing systems for logistics should be clearly understood. They have been used as a means of expanding geographical markets and volume of sales for individual products. But, delivered pricing systems are put into effect for other reasons as well. The action may be taken to counteract a delivered pricing policy of a competitor, which may place competing products at a comparable price in a company's "home market." Where one item in a product line is priced on a delivered basis, its companion items are likely to be priced similarly to allow the distribution of a full product line throughout a firm's market area. As firms grow in size and develop nearby markets to a near saturation point, they are forced to expand geographic marketing territories if they wish to increase sales volume. A delivered pricing system is the basic method for this type of expansion.

As the average distance between the point of manufacture and the point of resale increases, physical distribution costs per unit of product sold can also be expected to increase. Under a delivered pricing system, particularly single pricing, the price charged for the product in the long run may have to be increased also, if there are insufficient compensating savings in the manufacturing or selling costs.[4]

If delivered pricing systems result in the lengthening of the average distance between consuming markets and a manufacturer's plant and distribution warehouses (where such exist), they can increase problems of control over matters of logistics. Increased separation of distribution points and markets can lead to increased variability in the level of service offered customers, the dependability of transportation schedules and services, and the precision with which production and supply schedules can be drawn up to meet customer demand.

Under these circumstances, steps can be taken to improve control. New plants or distribution facilities may be established nearer newly developed markets, or the logistics organization may be decentralized to increase effective management in the field.

FIGURE 3–4: Phantom freight and freight absorption under a zone pricing policy

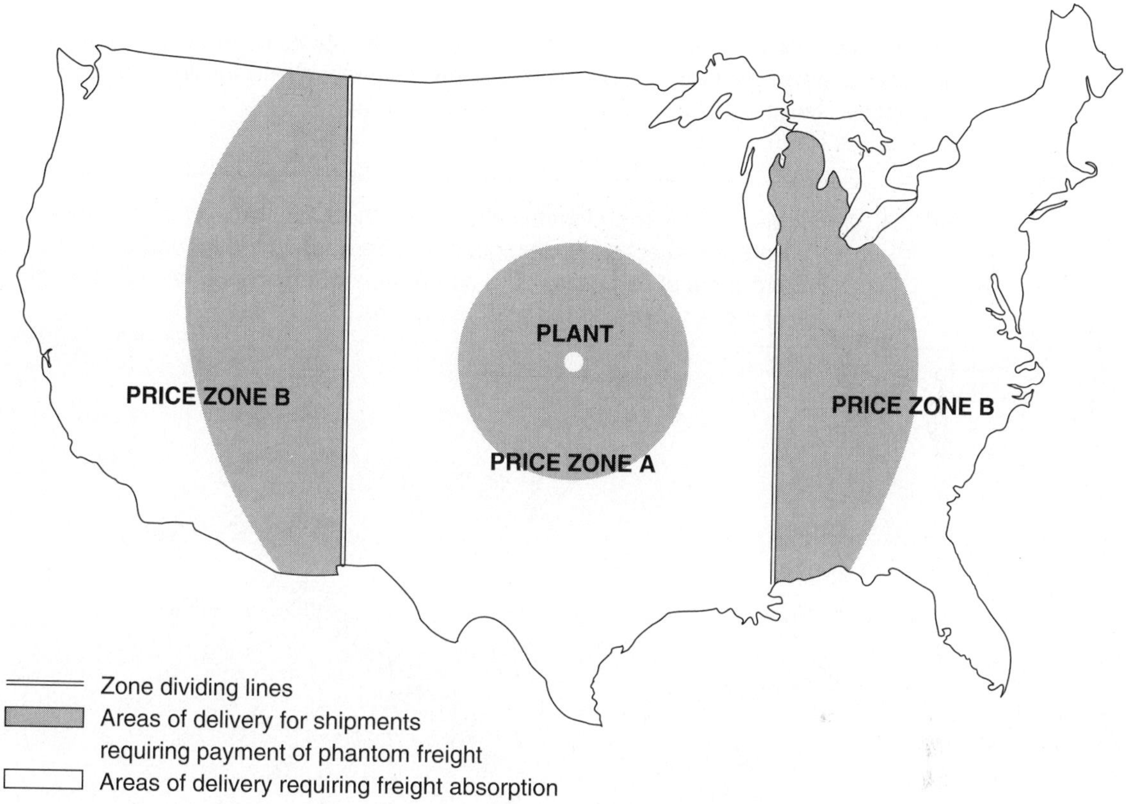
PLANT
PRICE ZONE B
PRICE ZONE A
PRICE ZONE B
Zone dividing lines
Areas of delivery for shipments requiring payment of phantom freight
Areas of delivery requiring freight absorption

Under any system of price averaging, such as that employed in most delivered pricing systems, some customers (usually, but not always, those located nearest manufacturing facilities) will "subsidize" others. The transportation cost component of a zone or single price established for a product, just as other components of cost, must be developed on an *average* basis. That is, dollar amounts of phantom freight and freight absorption must closely approximate each other. Once established, however, imbalance may develop in these logistics cost elements. If more distant markets are developed to a greater extent than closer ones, for example, the amount of phantom freight will not be sufficient to balance out growing increments of freight absorption; or, if the mix of customer locations in a zone is or becomes "unbalanced," the seller could find itself losing money because it would not be recovering much of its shipping (outbound transportation) costs.

F.O.B. and Individual Delivered Pricing Policies

Judicial rulings in support of the Federal Trade Commission in actions against certain types of delivered pricing systems have led many firms to adopt either F.O.B. or individual delivered pricing policies. The underlying principle of these policies is that all goods are priced basically from the point of origin, whether that origin be a manufacturing plant or a company warehouse. In such price systems, physical distribution costs will determine the market area to which a firm can price its goods competitively. This is illustrated by the transport isotims shown in Figure 3–5 for two competing firms.

FIGURE 3–5: Map of transport isotims showing a theoretical line of indifference and actual areas and points of indifference in the landed cost of products of two competing companies operating under F.O.B. origin or individual delivered pricing policies

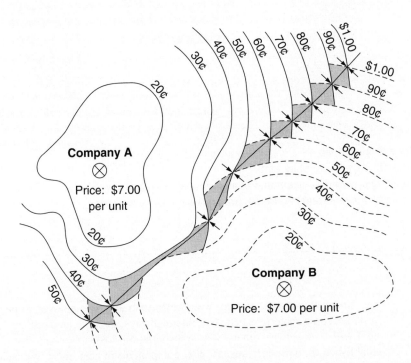

20¢   Shipping distance boundaries at indicated rates per unit (transport isotims).

→←   Points of indifference in landed price.

——   Theoretical line of indifference, or market boundary.

▨   Areas of indifference in landed price.

Edgar M. Hoover has drawn a colorful contrast between market competition under F.O.B. and delivered (with the exception of individual) pricing policies:

> The difference between market competition under F.O.B. pricing (with strictly delineated market areas) and under discriminatory delivered pricing is something like the difference between trench warfare and guerilla warfare. In the former case all the fighting takes place along a definite battle line: in the second case the opposing forces are intermingled over a broad area.[5]

Many firms have tried to cope with the economic limitations imposed by pricing policies and geographic location by decentralizing manufacturing and storage facilities to place them within "competitive range" of major markets.

Quantity Discounts

In 1936 legislation was passed that was to have a profound effect on the importance of physical distribution costs in establishing quantity discounts on goods. An amendment to Section 2 of the Clayton Act, the legislation that has become known as the Robinson-Patman Act, states in part:

> That it is unlawful . . . to discriminate in price between different purchasers for commodities of like grade and quality . . . where the effect of such discrimination may be substantially to lessen competition or tend to create a monopoly in any line of commerce or to injure, destroy, or prevent competition with any person who either grants or knowingly receives the benefit of such discrimination, or with customers of either of them . . . provided that nothing . . . shall prevent differentials which make only due allowance for difference in the cost of manufacture, sale or delivery. . . .

Thus the Robinson-Patman Act specifically mentions three major areas of cost that might be used to justify quantity discounts to customers purchasing commodities of like grade and quality: manufacture, sale, or delivery. In actual practice, however, it has been difficult to prove that items sold in quantities of, say, 1,000 units cost less to manufacture per unit than those same items sold in quantities of 10 units. This leaves "sale and delivery" as justifications. As Kintner points out:

> Differences in distribution or direct-selling costs have been and undoubtedly will continue to be the most fertile source of cost savings. Most cost justification defenses presented to the FTC have been based primarily on distribution costs. Distribution costs encompass a wide variety of expenses including the following specific unit costs of sale and delivery that experience has shown frequently vary with the size of orders: (1) transportation, (2) warehousing and storage, (3) sales promotion and advertising, (4) sales accounting, (5) sales management, (6) sales administration such as clerical work, (7) salesmen's salaries and expenses, and (8) special services for the customer.[6]

Note the order of the items in the quote. For those firms wishing to maintain quantity discount schedules and justify them before the Federal Trade Commission, logistics cost evidence appears to be the best justification. This is due not only to the reduction in the average cost per unit of goods transported in larger quantities, but also to the detailed documentation that usually accompanies transportation activities. Lower rates per unit on shipments of larger quantity are a well-known fact, one that examines and judges cannot ignore. For some firms wishing to maintain quantity discount pricing schedules, it has become common procedure, in considering quantity discounts suggested by pricing executives, to analyze and approve them in terms of relative logistics costs in handling orders of varying quantities.

Determination of Discount Limits If the Robinson-Patman Act dictates the upper limit of quantity discount size, how do we determine the lower limit? Although no rule applies to all situations, a general principle can perhaps be stated as follows: a quantity discount should be at least large enough to compensate the buyer for carrying a larger average inventory resulting from a quantity purchase if it is to achieve its purpose of encouraging purchases of larger quantities at one time. Consider the following example.

The Nashville Stereo Company is interested in establishing a discount schedule that will encourage its distributors of stereophonic phonograph records to buy in quantities larger than their current average order of two cases each. The records are priced to distributors at about $70 per case. What is the minimum discount needed to encourage them to purchase in lots of ten cases, assuming a relatively constant demand for records throughout the year and average annual sales of Nashville's records of ten cases per distributor?

A simple formula provides an approximate solution:

$$D = \frac{r(I_n - I_o)}{vS}$$

where:

r = cost of carrying $1 of inventory for one year.[7]

I_n = the average value of inventory on hand if ten cases are purchased (1/2 the value of the purchase).

I_o = the average value of inventory on hand if two cases are purchased (1/2 the value of the purchase).

vS = the dollar cost of goods sold during a year's time (assumed to be an average of all customers).

D = minimum discount required.

Substituting the appropriate information yields the following results:

$$\frac{.25(\$350 - \$70)}{\$700} = \frac{\$70}{\$700} = 10 \text{ percent}$$

This indicates that the minimum discount necessary to encourage purchases in quantities of ten cases is 10 percent.

Individual firms may deviate widely from "average" performance figures. However, the method provides a rough approximation of the minimum discount needed to encourage an alert distributor to consider increasing his order size.

Setting Quantity Discounts The job of setting discounts requires a supplier to balance the firm's needs and the customer's needs against regulatory requirements. Consider once again the problem of the Nashville Stereo Company.

A minimum discount of 10 percent off distributor list price is required to encourage distributors to purchase in quantities of ten versus two cases of records. Because of the existence of a stiff minimum shipment charge, it costs $10 to ship ten cases (300 pounds) or $8 to ship two cases (60 pounds). This represents a savings of $3.50 per case, or 5 percent of sales value, on shipments of ten as opposed to two cases. Savings in packaging for ten cases versus two cases amount to about $7.00, or roughly 1 percent of the total sale. However, since the combined savings in transportation and packaging amount to only about 6 percent, it would be hard indeed to justify a 10 percent quantity price discount on records to the Federal Trade Commission. Yet, a 6 percent discount would not be enough to induce an alert distributor to buy in larger quantities. Reconciliation of the economic minimum and maximum is impossible in this case.

For other types of goods, reconciliation is possible. The nature of the cost functions involved should be considered for a better understanding of the nature of the decisions that may be reached. The minimum discount function—the statement of the amount of discount needed (stated in percentage of purchase price)—is linear in nature, as shown in Figure 3–6. If one were to compute the discount needed to encourage the purchase of any quantity of a product with the characteristics of Nashville Stereo's records, the results would fall on line D in the figure.

Transportation rate reductions for shipments in larger quantities follow a "sloping stairstep" pattern when graphed in the manner of Figure 3–6. Packing, material handling, and warehousing cost savings may tend to be somewhat more linear. When combined, these factors yield a percentage cost savings function similar to that shown for the two companies in Figure 3–6. Nashville Stereo's cost savings from quantity sales correspond to those for seller B. Because they never exceed the minimum discount requirements (D), no areas of decision are present; no quantity discount schedule (at least no legally defensible one) can be quoted.

Contrast seller B with seller A, whose maximum discount function repeatedly intersects with the minimum function because of the difference in the nature of the product sold. The cross-hatched areas in Figure 3–6 show the two ranges of quotable percentage discounts and quantities within which pricing executives, in consultation with logistics management, might select specific discount schedule points.

At quantities of 5,000 pounds, for example, seller A could quote a defensible discount of up to 8 percent off list price. He would have to offer at least 5 percent to justify economically the discount to his customers. The quantity discount range defining the "decision zone" at 5,000 pounds would be 5 percent to 8 percent. If a quantity discount were desired on orders of 6,000 pounds, the decision zone range would be narrowed to two percentage points, 6½ percent to 8½ percent. At 10,000-pound quantities, the range would be expanded again to from 11.4 percent to 14 percent off quoted unit prices.

Quantity Discounts and Purchase Contracts Discounts can be based on the quantity of goods purchased or sold over a period of time, regardless of the number or size of orders placed during the period. This type of discount system is formalized through the vehicle of a purchase (or sale) contract. It eliminates the problem of establishing quantity discounts large enough to encourage increased sales by basing the discount on something other than individual order size. A variation on this form of pricing is to negotiate a contract for a period of time, usually a year, with a sliding scale of discounts that increase as the customer buys more.

FIGURE 3–6: Comparison of seller cost savings with buyer cost increases with quantities of sale of increasing magnitude

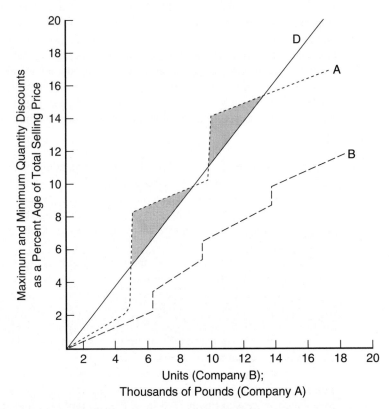

A   Physical distribution cost savings in quantity shipments, Seller A.
B   Physical distribution cost savings in quantity shipments, Seller B.
D   Increased buyer inventory costs with quantity purchases for both
     Sellers A and B.
▨ Area of flexibility within which discounts might be quoted, Seller A.

From the standpoint of logistics considerations, purchase contracts (sometimes called system agreements) are essentially customer-oriented agreements. They require customers to estimate their needs over the period of the contract (usually periods of up to one year) and pay the price per unit corresponding to the estimated total order quantity. Deviations in order quantity from the estimated needs may result in a final additional assessment or a rebate on all goods sold during the period of the contract. Economies of the seller are difficult to assess in regard to purchase contracts. Chief among them are production scheduling economies and associated benefits resulting from a foreknowledge of quantities likely to be sold and shipped to individual customers. However, for reasons previously discussed, price discounts based on the *total* purchase quantity covered by the contract would likely face legal difficulties. The real advantage to purchase contracts lies in the planning benefits to both buyer and seller.

Dating and Deal Pricing

Terms of sale often are designed to encourage speculative buying — buying in advance of normal need — on the part of a customer. Among variations employed for this purpose, price dating and deals are especially important for logistics.

Dating Under a dating plan, a supplier may ship a product to a customer in advance of need, allowing the customer possession of the product with payment delayed until such time as the product is likely to be sold. For example, many manufacturers of lawn care products offer dating plans to their distributors under which products with highly seasonal demand in the spring and early summer are shipped to distributors throughout the winter *with payment delayed* until the beginning of the season. Similar plans are offered by manufacturers of winter-use products (snowblowers, snowmobiles, and such) who will ship to distributors in the summer.

Dating plans allow suppliers to spread the manufacture and shipping of finished products with highly seasonal demand more evenly over time, thereby reducing inefficient peaks in production and logistics activities. They also reduce the need for storage capacity in a supplier's facilities. They further provide an incentive for the early movement of a product closer to the point of eventual need by allowing a customer to build stocks without suffering the financial burden of an investment in inventory. Finally, dating plans often include price discounts for purchases before certain dates, thereby providing an added incentive to the customer to order early and arrange for storing the product in company-owned facilities. Where this is an important factor, the discount must be sufficient to defray additional costs incurred by the customer. For example, for many types of products, the cost of storage, extra handling, and potential obsolescence of the product may approximate 1 percent of the value of the product per month. Therefore a supplier seeking to encourage early orders for a product with seasonal demand beginning in April might wish to establish the following dating plan:

Discount	For Orders for Immediate Shipment Received Before:
3 percent	January 1
2 percent	February 1
1 percent	March 1

Under this arrangement the price might be net end of April.

Deals Deals are special prices quoted on a one-time or limited-period basis. They may be designed to sell obsolete products quickly at the point of ultimate demand, to introduce new products, or to stimulate sales of products whose sales are lagging. Successful deal pricing must take into account buyer economics, particularly in such industries as grocery and drug product manufacture and distribution in which it is used frequently.

A number of food chain organizations have designed guidelines for the consideration of deals by buyers. Features of these models have to be taken into account by vendors (suppliers).

ILLUSTRATIVE PROBLEMS

What about the pricing problems faced by the manufacturer of soaps and detergents, the distributor of mill supply products and the manufacturer of wearing apparel whose situations were presented at the beginning of this chapter?

The manufacturer of soaps and detergents instituted a minimum order level of five cases, below which it would not sell. This action immediately reduced the number of orders processed by 20 percent, *but there was no significant change in sales volume.*

The distributor of mill supply products took several steps to deal with his problem, including (1) the elimination of certain lower value items from inventory; (2) instruction to salesmen to concentrate their sales efforts on higher value items and to attempt to sell lower value items in larger quantities; (3) the preparation of sales material highlighting such higher value items; (4) the negotiation of a lower price for one line of relatively unprofitable items upon the discovery that other distributors were experiencing similarly low profits with the line; and (5) limiting manufacturers allowed to explain new products at meetings of the distributor's sales force to those who manufactured higher value, higher profit items. A check several months after the initiation of these steps indicated that the average sale per line item had risen by about 12 percent for a particularly unprofitable product family and that a greater proportion of higher value items were being sold.

The manufacturer of wearing apparel dropped the "E.O.M." designation from its terms of sale, thereby eliminating any incentive on the part of customers to play the "calendar game." When this failed to produce immediate results, perhaps because of the difficulties of changing customers' long established customary order schedules, the company instituted temporary sales commission incentives for its salesmen on orders placed for shipment at times other than the first week of each month.

SUMMARY

Creative pricing policies, by inducing particular behavior patterns on the part of buyers and sellers alike, can produce savings in logistics costs sufficiently great to enhance the profit performance of both parties to a transaction. Such results are termed non-zero-sum, and should be sought wherever possible as a means of gaining a legitimate competitive advantage.

In industries where logistics costs in relation to sales are great, or at least significant, logistics factors may be *major determinants* of pricing decisions. And, in any industry even modest logistics costs should provide input to pricing policy decisions.

Terms of sale provide a great deal of information about matters other than price. Among these are cash discounts, credit terms, the point of delivery to a buyer, the responsibility for paying shipping charges, the party with control over the routing of the shipment, and the point at which title passes to the buyer.

Firms may elect either delivered or F.O.B. pricing policies. Delivered pricing meets the needs of sellers to (1) maintain uniform prices to different buyers; (2) meet competition by quoting prices identical to theirs; and (3) maintain maximum control over physical distribution. Such practices may involve basing points, zones, or single or national prices. Where there are competing sellers over a wide geographic area, F.O.B. pricing practices tend to restrict sales to geographic areas in closer proximity to manufacturing sites and pass responsibility for transportation and other logistics activities to the buyer.

Quantity discounts can be justified to the Federal Trade Commission on the basis of lower costs per unit associated with larger orders. In practice, it is easier to justify discounts on the basis of logistics cost savings than to claim either sales or manufacturing economies. In addition, customers may be offered delayed billing (dating) or deals as a means of encouraging early acceptance of shipments by the buyer, thus lowering the seller's inventory carrying costs and rewarding the buyer with a purchase price discount.

DISCUSSION QUESTIONS

1. What is the relationship between the concept of non-zero-sum pricing and logistics costs? Explain.

2. *What* terms of sale affect (determine) the *actual* price of a product? Which of these are logistics costs?

3. *How* do various terms of sale affect the *actual* price of a product? Explain.

4. What are the four basic types of delivered pricing?

5. What legal problems exist in regard to delivered pricing?

6. What can happen if the mix of customer locations gets "out of balance" in a zone or single delivered price system? Explain.

7. What is the relationship between an F.O.B. pricing policy and the size of a firm's market area?

8. What is the purpose of quantity discounts? How are they determined? Explain.

9. Define the terms "dating" and "deal" pricing. What is the purpose of each? How do these practices affect logistics costs? Explain.

CASE: PHANTOM FREIGHT OR FREIGHT ABSORPTION — A MATTER OF OPINION?

Nationwide Distributors, Inc. (NDI) manufactured home and industrial fire extinguishers. NDI sold its products to distributors on a "nationwide delivered price" basis from its plant in St. Louis, Missouri, and had done so for the nearly 20 years of the firm's existence. The typical shipment was made by motor carrier, freight prepaid, and weighed between 200 and 500 pounds. NDI's 98 distributors were scattered widely across the United States, each ordinarily receiving a shipment every few weeks. In addition, NDI made a number of sales to exporting firms on both the West and East Coasts. NDI's marketing advantage lay primarily in the quality of its products.

Although the deregulation of interstate motor carrier rates had benefitted many firms who were able to use their "clout" to get lower rates from motor carriers, NDI was not among them because it was not a "megashipper"; its shipments were small in size, and NDI did not have an appreciable volume of shipments from St. Louis to any particular destination. However, NDI's annual motor carrier freight bill did amount to nearly $200,000.

Over the past several years there had been increasing conflict between NDI's logistics manager and marketing manager with respect to NDI's policy of selling its products on a delivered price basis. The marketing manager appeared to be quite satisfied with the *status quo*, while the logistics manager had become increasingly concerned about the situation. The logistics manager argued that NDI did not know whether it was making money on phantom freight or losing money by reason of freight absorption; and further, perhaps NDI should change its policy and sell on an F.O.B. pricing basis.

The marketing manager's view was that the company was making a profit and customers were satisfied with its delivered pricing policy, so why rock the boat? The logistics manager took the position that a national delivered pricing policy might be all right, but it should be based on something other than a "feel" that the company was at least breaking even on phantom freight and freight absorption. The argument surfaced sharply during a meeting of the company's managers, and NDI's president turned to her executive assistant and said, "I agree that this matter is important. But, before any decision is made, I want to know whether we are making or losing money on this. You study the situation and report back to me."

CASE QUESTION

1. Assume you are the president's executive assistant. What information would you attempt to gather in order to answer the president's question and resolve this situation?

SUGGESTED READINGS

BRESSLER, RAYMOND G., JR., and RICHARD A. KING, *Markets, Prices, and Interregional Trade*, New York: John Wiley & Sons, Inc., 1970. A study of the market and pricing system of the U.S. economy, this book offers a comprehensive analysis of the impact of transfer costs on prices in markets separated by space and time. In particular, Chapter 11, pages 205–28, presents an interesting discussion of temporal market-price relationships.

DAGGETT, STUART, *Principles of Inland Transportation*, 4th ed. New York: Harper & Row, 1955. Although it may be hard to find now, this book is a classic, offering an excellent discussion of the early development and use of group and basing-point freight rates.

KINTNER, EARL W., *A Robinson-Patman Primer*, 2d ed. New York: Macmillan Publishing Co., Inc., 1979. In addition to providing an in-depth review of the Robinson-Patman Act and the important cases in which it has been interpreted, this volume offers a particularly useful discussion of cost justification as a defense against charges of price discrimination, particularly prices involving quantity discounts, in Chapter 7, pages 172–92.

MACHLUP, FRITZ, *The Basing-Point System*, Philadelphia: The Blakiston Co., 1949. Also a classic, this book presents a comprehensive economic analysis of basing-point pricing systems.

MONROE, KENT B., *Pricing: Making Profitable Decisions*, New York: McGraw-Hill, 1979. Chapter 16, "Justifying Price Differentials," presents a concise and well organized discussion of both legal and managerial aspects of price differentiation.

OXENFELDT, ALFRED R., *Pricing Strategies*, New York: Amacom, 1975. While this book deals almost not at all with spatial or temporal aspects of pricing strategies, it does present an interesting discussion of organizational responsibilities and structure for managing pricing decisions (in Chapter 1) and the place of price in marketing strategies (in Chapter 2).

PHILIPS, LOUIS, *Spatial Pricing and Competition*, Brussels, Belgium: European Economic Community, 1976. This monograph offers a concise review of spatial pricing systems and their impact on trade, the interpenetration of markets, and regional development.

SCHERE, F. M., *Industrial Pricing: Theory and Evidence*, Chicago: Rand McNally College Publishing Company, 1970. The author presents a comprehensive analysis of geographic price discrimination and the basing-point system in pages 134–144.

ENDNOTES

1. In this discussion, the term "uniform" prices will be used to refer to the prices quoted by one seller to different buyers: the term "identical" prices will be used to refer to the prices quoted by different sellers to one buyer.

2. Fritz Machlup, *The Basing-Point System* (Philadelphia: The Blakiston Co., 1949): 17.

3. "The FTC Redefines Price-Fixing," *Business Week* (April 18, 1983): 37–238.

4. Little evidence exists to support or refute the theory of economies of scale, particularly in manufacturing, beyond some undefined intermediate size of firm in any particular industry. For a discussion of empirical evidence, see Caleb A. Smith, "Survey of Empirical Evidence on Economies of Scale," in *Business Concentration and Price Policy* (Princeton: Princeton University Press, 1955): 213–238.

5. Edgar M. Hoover, *The Location of Economic Activity* (New York: McGraw-Hill Book Co., 1948): 57.

6. Earl W. Kintner, *A Robinson-Patman Primer*, 2d ed. (New York: Macmillan Publishing Co., Inc., 1979): 186.

7. Interest on capital is a major component of the cost of carrying inventory. Prior to the mid 1970s, commercial interest rates were relatively low (6 percent–8 percent) and rather stable. At that time a commonly used inventory carrying cost figure for many products was .25, representing 25 percent of the value of the average annual inventory and including all of the costs associated with carrying inventory, including the interest cost of capital. However, in recent years commercial interest rates have been as high as 24 percent, resulting in a need for many firms to use an inventory carrying cost percentage as high as .40 (40 percent) at times. Firms dealing in perishable or highly seasonal goods use even higher figures. This subject is discussed in detail in Chapters 6 and 7.

Full satisfaction of customer needs and wants is the foundation for lasting business success.

CHAPTER FOUR

4

Customer Logistics Service

LEARNING OBJECTIVES

The objectives of this chapter are to:

➤ Define customer service and, more specifically, to define customer logistics service.

➤ Describe and illustrate the components of the customer service package.

➤ Describe and analyze the component activities of the order cycle.

➤ Explain the importance of and need for actively managing the customer logistics service program.

➤ Discuss the various factors involved in designing a customer logistics service management program.

➤ Point out and discuss problems likely to be encountered in the implementation of customer logistics service programs.

➤ Illustrate ways in which the actual performance of customer logistics service activities can be measured against the customer logistics service standards of a firm.

Different types of businesses sell a multitude of products to customers having widely varied service needs, and a useful definition of customer service must take these many differences into account. In their landmark study of customer service, LaLonde and Zinszer presented a definition that is general enough to accommodate a wide spectrum of business situations and, at the same time, is specific enough to be useful:

> Customer Service constitutes those activities that occur at the interface between the customer and the corporation which enhance or facilitate the sale and use of the corporation's products or services.[1]

The key phrase in that definition is *those activities that occur at the interface*. Many of those activities are logistics activities, and they are the focus of this chapter.

First and foremost, customer service exists in the mind of the customer, and nowhere else. There is no use in a firm telling the world what a wonderful customer service program it has if its (former) customers don't believe it. As Falvey observes:

> You can do almost everything "wrong" in business and still succeed if you serve the customer. You can do just about everything "right" in business and fail if you do not take care of their needs, wants, desires, and emotions.[2]

Full managerial awareness of the need for active management of customer service is vitally important. This is especially true of the logistics service components of a customer service program because logistics service activities cost time, money, and effort, and such costs must be balanced against the benefits management hopes to achieve.

A customer logistics service program can aid sales, especially in cases where the quality and prices of competing products are similar or nearly identical. In effect, logistics service activities can "differentiate" undifferentiated products in the mind of the customer.

The objectives of this chapter are to define customer service; review its components; explore and analyze the nature of the order cycle; and discuss important aspects of the design, implementation, and management of successful customer logistics service programs. The chapter emphasis shifts to a detailed discussion of logistics support activities after first reviewing the total customer service package, the context in which logistical support is carried out.

THE SERVICE PACKAGE

A customer service package can include many different types of financial, marketing, product, and logistical support activities. It should be noted that many of the financial, marketing, and product support activities about to be discussed also have significant logistics effects on the supplier as well as the customer.

Financial Support

A company many find it profitable, or even necessary, to provide various forms of financial support to its customers. Customers may desire direct support in the form of loaned equipment, as when a soft drink bottler places a refrigerated display unit in a retailer's store at no charge. Financing through trade credit not only is desired, it is expected as the norm in most industries. Terms for the payment of goods received by customers may be extended to allow delays in payment that correspond roughly to the time when those goods are likely to be resold.

A special form of extended credit, typically called a dating plan (discussed in Chapter 3), is sometimes quoted on products sold on a highly seasonal basis in order to spread orders and shipments over a longer period of time. This reduces the pressures of seasonal business on order processing, warehousing, and transportation and encourages customers to stock larger quantities of goods in anticipation of the upcoming selling season.

A supplier may place goods on a consignment basis with (some) customers, agreeing to retain title to the goods until they are sold and allowing the customer to return unsold items. This may be done because the customer is short of capital and *unable* to invest in such inventory, or because the customer may view the salability of an untried product with skepticism and be *unwilling* to invest capital to stock it in inventory. Or, the customer may simply have enough "clout" to be able to demand and receive goods on consignment.

Another practice is for a supplier to set up a warehouse close to a customer's plant. For example, strong competition in the container manufacturing business (bottles and cans) often forces competitors to store their products, particularly cans, at the locations where the containers are used by large customers. The container manufacturer retains title to the goods right up until the time they are used, thus relieving the customer of having to finance its own inventory of unfilled containers.

Publishers of books and magazines often agree to accept payment after their publications have been resold by their bookstore or newsstand customers. In addition, publishers often allow the return of unsold items from customers who are unable or unwilling to finance the risk of inventory loss associated with unsold copies.

Logistics-related financial support may be offered by vendors in the form of freight allowances or the payment of all freight charges by the seller on orders exceeding a certain quantity. In effect, these are quantity discounts.

Marketing Support

In simplest terms, customers want to be important to their suppliers and they want the treatment that implies. Aside from the satisfaction provided by feeling wanted, this allows the customer to exert leverage to obtain concessions and vendor assistance, some of which may involve marketing support.

For example, customers may shift the responsibility for all or some of the advertising of a product back to the supplier. Such promotional aids as free samples, point-of-purchase displays, and consultation from the supplier on methods of improving sales operations may be expected by the retailer or wholesaler. The industrial customer may expect technical information and assistance in the training of employees to use or service the product.

Industrial firms, wholesalers, and retailers all like to have information about the market. Information about competitors may also comprise part of the marketing data provided by suppliers. At trade levels, there often is an interest in having information about new products as well as promotional plans of the supplier and the customer's competitors.[3]

A customer prefers a vendor's sales representative to be well informed about the products he or she sells and to take a personal interest in the customer's operating problems. In addition, the customer wants a vendor's salesperson who can do something to help improve the customer's sales and operations, either through direct recommendations (which hopefully turn out to be right) or through concessions obtained from "the head office." The more productive the customer's contact with a vendor's sales representative, the more frequently a customer will want the salesperson to call.

Product Support

Where product maintenance is important, suppliers are judged in part on the quality of their service programs. This includes the warranties offered to ultimate users of the product as well as the quality and convenience of service and repair networks. The more complex the product, the more critical its service and repair network will be to potential buyers. Manufacturers of mechanical, electrical, and electronic products have literally succeeded or failed on the basis of their product support policies and facilities.

Product support also relates to the assortment of products offered by a supplier. Companies not manufacturing a broad enough line of products to suit customers who want to "buy a product family from a single vendor" may have to purchase items for resale at relatively high cost (and low profit) to fill out a product line. Yet, this may be a smart policy if the alternative of manufacturing the purchased products would require the supplier to acquire and operate manufacturing facilities outside of its experience and expertise.

Logistical Support

Logistical support takes on several dimensions to a customer. Included among these are inventory maintenance, order placement, transportation, and material handling.

Inventory Maintenance   Customers may want suppliers to keep quantities of readily accessible inventory on hand and as nearby as possible, thereby reducing the customer's need for warehouse space. In some cases, customers may want to eliminate inventory entirely, getting orders from their customers and having the supplier ship directly (called "drop shipping") to those customers.

At the retail level, a vendor's sales representative may be persuaded to take a retail customer's inventory count, rotate stock, and "dust it."

Above all, a customer is likely to be sensitive to product availability and will remember a stock-out much longer than an in-stock situation. This is especially the case during new product introductions or special promotions, or when a badly needed repair part turns out not to be available quickly.

Assistance to customers in the management of their inventories may be critical if repeated stock-outs are to be avoided. This is important particularly where the task of inventory control is made complex by product lines consisting of hundreds or even thousands of different items. For example, manufacturers of drugs and toiletries have traditionally provided effective inventory control procedures for their distributor-customers. With the increasing capabilities of computers and communications equipment, many suppliers have made available to their customers programs for the automatic control of inventory, including computerized order placement and inventory monitoring.

Order Placement   In attempting to keep inventory at a minimum, the customer will order only as frequently as is reasonable, considering the effect of quantity discounts, ordering costs, and inventory holding costs. Customers may resent limits imposed by minimum order quantities and may wait until inventory is almost depleted before reordering, taking the attitude "I want it yesterday; if I wanted it today, I'd order it tomorrow." The ease and economy with which they can place orders, possibly by no-charge telephone service, preprinted order forms, or even a telecommunications device provided by the supplier can influence customers. Those who are particularly concerned about delivery dates are likely to be impressed by the timeliness and accuracy with which they are informed about the progress of the processing and shipping of their orders, particularly when deviations from expected service standards have occurred or are expected to occur. The ability of the firm to track the status of an order is an increasing expectation of customers—an ability that has been greatly enhanced by modern computer and telecommunications systems. As noted in *Fortune* magazine, the increasing use of direct computer-to-computer ordering by customers is tying firms more closely than ever to one supplier at the expense of that supplier's competitors.[4] A full treatment of developments in this area is presented in Chapter 12, "Data Processing and Communications."

Although knowing the status of their orders and shipments is important to industrial buyers whose purchases are feeding production lines, their principal concern is maintaining a reliable inbound stream of production materials. They are more concerned with reliability of quoted delivery dates than with shipment transit times.

Transportation Customers may wish to control the selection of the carriers moving their shipments. This preference may result from a desire to obtain any "fringe benefits" (either in terms of service concessions or special favors) they may be able to get from a carrier. Or, the customer simply may believe that its traffic department is more capable in this respect than the supplier's. Some customers want the supplier to file all claims with carriers for loss or damage, especially because shipments typically are more easily traced by the originator of a shipment who usually has easier access to documents and information related to the shipment. In some cases, a customer may deduct the costs of loss or damage from payments due the supplier without even bothering to obtain approval for such deductions.

When it is profitable for customers to operate their own private transportation equipment, they may insist on doing so regardless of whether their private transportation operations fit in with the logistics system of the supplier. This most often occurs in respect to private trucking activities.

Material Handling Customers may want to minimize their investment in material-handling equipment. For example, a customer using a system based on 30 inch $\times$ 36 inch pallets will want the supplier to deliver on 30 inch $\times$ 36 inch pallets even if this presents serious problems to the supplier, who uses 40 inch $\times$ 48 inch pallets.* The customer may request that the supplier load specific parts of shipments together in a truck or rail car so they can be reshipped directly with little or no additional sorting. A customer may request that the shipment of pallets be loaded so they will fit the dimensions of the "slots" in the pallet racks in the customer's warehouse, or that the pallets containing more than one product-line item or stock-keeping unit (SKU) be loaded in proportions that reflect the customer's sales patterns.

---

*The 40 inch $\times$ 48 inch (1.0 meter $\times$ 1.2 meters) pallet has been adopted as the standard pallet of the Grocery Manufacturers Association because its dimensions allow efficient loading of rail box cars and truck trailers. A full treatment of materials handling is given in Chapter 10, "Packaging and Materials Handling."

A TEXTBOOK CASE OF ADDING VALUE

Jay Gordon

Pick up just about any study concerning logistics today and what do you read? The future belongs to those companies that differentiate their products based on *value-added* logistics services. Consultants are saying it. Academia is saying it. Shippers are slowly beginning to believe it.

One of the best current examples of this value-added philosophy in practice is that of Betz Laboratories, a provider of specialty water treatment chemicals based in Trevose, Pa. The company has turned to its distribution department to come up with a service that will help sell the product. What the distribution people came up with is a Custom Distribution Service™ (CDS) that makes it particularly easy for a customer to buy its chemicals from Betz.

Betz Entec, one of seven Betz subsidiaries, is responsible for administering CDS. Entec's customers are moderate users of water treatment chemicals: shopping malls, office buildings, hospitals and sports complexes. Robert J. Finley, assistant vice president of distribution, likens Betz's service to that of a physician. "We prescribe treatment for a facility," he says. "One boiler requires something different than another."

Through CDS, Betz is delivering these chemicals in ready-to-use form—sort of an LTL delivery system in bulk. Users previously had to buy the chemicals in powder form and mix them into the proper formula. Then Betz came up with the idea of point-of-feed (POF) systems, which would feed the chemicals into the production line or other process precisely where they were needed.

Finley says the POF system has put Betz on the cutting edge of the water treatment business. "It's quick and you don't have to worry about it," he says. "It's really the point-of-feed system that has made Betz the industry leader." POF also was the forerunner of the Custom Distribution Service.

Drumming Up Business

Several chemical-related tragedies in the 1970s and early 1980s, including Love Canal and the leak at Union Carbide's plant in Bhopal, India, focused attention on the potential hazards of manufacturing, distributing and disposing of chemicals. With these incidents fresh in the public's mind, "the industry got very frightened," says Finley.

The 55-gallon drum, long the most common form of transporting and storing chemicals and other hazardous materials, became a target for eradication. The Environmental Protection Agency and conservation groups pushed hard for strict regulations regarding proper rinsing and storage procedures. Penalties for violations were stiff.

Yet the phaseout of the 55-gallon drum posed a more practical problem for many shippers, particularly small- to medium-sized ones. "Getting rid of drums was no sweat for a big company," says Finley. "They'd make a phone call and say, 'Hey Joe, I've got two truckloads of empty drums here.' And Joe would send two trucks over to pick them up. The operations manager of a shopping mall might call up and say, 'Hey, I've got five empty drums here,' and the guy would say, 'Forget it.'"

According to Finley, the idea for CDS was born when Betz's salespeople came to the distribution department saying, "If you could give us a way to eliminate those drums, we could sell it at any price."

"With drums coming in week after week there's the possibility of human error," says Finley. "'Did I get six drums or seven?' The drums may have to be moved, which is difficult. You may get the wrong drums, and then pump the wrong product into the wrong tank. There's also the hassle of storing them."

Finley's group came up with a delivery system that eliminates drums and makes it almost effortless for customers to receive and use water treatment chemicals. Betz first installs a plastic tank and fills it, then monitors chemical usage until a reliable rate is established. Betz then schedules deliveries automatically based on that usage rate.

The delivery tanks are metered, and when the delivery is finished Betz's driver gives the customer a meter ticket. This ticket lets him know exactly how much product was delivered and ensures accurate billing. The metering system also can help the customer in its accounting, by assigning costs to a specific operation or unit.

The same customer may have another application three stores up the street in which the chemicals are stored on the roof or other limited access area. In these situations the driver will haul a 35-gallon pressure tank to the roof with a hand cart, transfer the chemicals and record the amount. "The same guy that we used to have to interrupt to get this drum up to his roof, we're now making it easy for him to fill up his tank," says Finley. "The only way a customer knows we made a delivery is that he has a meter ticket."

The data from the meter ticket for a customer in, say California, is entered into a Betz computer there, and then downloaded to Entec headquarters. A salesperson will visit the customer's facility once a month for an inventory check, then predict a run-out date.

"The thing that concerns our customers now is, 'Hey, we were down to almost 10 days of inventory. You had me scared to death,'" Finley says. "We say, 'Did you check with us to see whether a delivery was scheduled?' And sure enough, we were scheduled to be there the day after tomorrow." Still, most customers have come to expect and rely on Betz's well-timed service. "Nobody likes to be taken for granted," Finley says, "but it's a backhanded compliment, because they have confidence in us."

That confidence was bestowed without a second thought by Armstrong World Industries, a manufacturer of floor tile. "It was worth it to me to take the chance and not have to worry about those damn drums," says Dan Thimmes, senior technician for finished products and raw materials at Armstrong's South Gate, Calif., plant.

Armstrong uses a number of chemicals in its manufacturing and water treatment processes. Nearly all of them are handled in drums. Thimmes says Armstrong used to pay $5 per drum to have them hauled away. Then the fee went up to $15 per drum, and even at that rate he couldn't get anybody to come and pick them up.

Saving Time and Money

Before Armstrong signed up for CDS, Thimmes would have to send a mechanic out to take inventory of the chemical supply. When it got down to two drums they would call and order five more. This took a lot of time and was subject to error. Now Betz comes out once a week, takes inventory and fills the tanks. The South Gate plant has run out of chemicals on two occasions, both when the company worked several unexpected overtime shifts and used more chemicals than what Betz had predicted they would. Each time Betz rushed in a small replacement tank to tide them over until a delivery could be made.

Armstrong issues a blanket purchase order to cover the cost of the delivery. It pays about the same price for its chem-

icals with CDS as it would if it was still buying them in drums. The difference is, it doesn't have the costs or the headaches associated with drums.

"My plant manager is thrilled that he doesn't have to mess with those drums anymore," says Thimmes. "We use drums for a couple of other chemicals that we use in manufacturing, and if we could get the same type of service for those, we'd be sitting pretty." For example, another chemical Armstrong uses in its production process is manufactured at the company's Lancaster, Pa., plant. From there, drums of the chemical are shipped to California by rail. When they're empty, South Gate ships them back to Lancaster, again by rail, for refilling. That's an expensive way to do business.

It's also expensive for Betz to provide the service. The company has invested considerable sums in all facets of CDS. The company doesn't operate just any old bulk trailer. Betz's sparkling CDS delivery vehicles are equipped with $25,000 worth of hoses, meters and other sophisticated equipment, plus $10,000 cabinets to house it all. So while a competitor may spend about $60,000 on a delivery truck, Betz is spending close to six figures. Neither does the company employ mere drivers; they are *delivery specialists*, highly skilled in regulatory compliance, product safety and basic chemistry.

"Competitors say, 'Betz, you're crazy. All you're doing is transporting a product,'" Finley says. "That's where the difference comes in. We don't see it that way. We see ourselves providing a value-added service. If we sit around because what we have is good enough, when we wake up tomorrow it *won't* be good enough. It's a painless process. We're doing all the things a customer would have to do. But we're *not* building up inventory."

Source: *Distribution* (August 1989): 103–105. Reprinted by permission of Chilton Company.

Logistical Support in Perspective The results of the LaLonde and Zinszer 1976 survey established the relative importance of customer service in relation to other types of marketing effort as well as the relative importance of various elements of customer service and are presented in Table 4–1. The survey showed that customer service ranked right alongside price in perceived importance by sellers of various types of goods. And, product availability was the most important element of customer service for these firms. A follow-up study by LaLonde, Cooper, and Noordewier in 1987 produced the data in Tables 4–2 and 4–3. Table 4–2 shows that by 1987 price competition had become significantly more important than advertising, selling, and promotion as an element of the marketing mix while customer service remained

TABLE 4–1: Importance of Marketing Variables and Major Customer Service Elements by Industry

Relative Importance of Marketing Variables[a]	All Industries	All Manufacturing	Manufacturing Chemicals & Plastics	Manufacturing Food	Manufacturing Pharmaceuticals	Manufacturing Electronics
Product	36	38	38	36	47	48
Price	23	24	26	27	20	14
Customer Service	23	20	18	15	12	22
Sales Efforts	18	18	18	22	21	16
TOTAL	100	100	100	100	100	100

Relative Importance of Major Customer Service Elements[a]						
Product Availability	42.4	42.7	44.5	37.1	39.7	32.7
Order Cycle	20.7	19.4	17.4	21.4	28.0	17.4
Distribution System Flexibility	11.5	11.6	10.6	12.9	10.6	12.9
Distribution System Information	12.6	12.4	11.7	14.8	9.0	16.7
Distribution System Malfunction	7.7	8.0	9.1	10.3	7.8	7.9
Post-Sale Product Support	4.5	5.1	6.2	2.3	2.9	11.7
TOTAL	100	100	100	100	100	100

[a]Respondents were asked to distribute 100 points among the listed categories.

SOURCE: Bernard J. LaLonde and Paul H. Zinszer, *Customer Service: Meaning and Measurement* (Chicago: National Council of Physical Distribution Management, 1976), 116–117.

the same in importance. The shift between price and promotion is attributed to increased domestic and international competition. Table 4–3 shows the expectations of the respondents as to the relative importance of marketing mix variables in 1990. The significant predicted change was in the increased relative importance of customer service, with the other three elements of the marketing mix showing declines.

A complete program of financial, marketing, product, and logistical support will deal with many or most of the problems confronted by a firm's customers. Theodore Levitt has summed up the role and importance of the customer service package in this manner:

> . . . a truly marketing-minded firm tries to create value-satisfying goods and services that consumers will want to buy. What it offers for sale includes not only the generic product or service, but also how it is made available to the customer, in what form, under what conditions, and at what terms of sale.[5]

Logistical support, while only one element of the total customer service package, is usually important, and sometimes decisive, in the realization of product sales. A concept of central importance to an understanding of the role of logistical support as a component of customer service is the order cycle.

TABLE 4–1 (continued): Importance of Marketing Variables and Major Customer Service Elements

Relative Importance of Marketing Variables[a]	Manufacturing Paper	Manufacturing Machine Tools & Machinery	All Other Manufacturing	All Merchandising	Consumer Goods Merchandising	Industrial Goods Merchandising
Product	29	43	38	30	31	28
Price	26	30	25	22	23	17
Customer Service	24	20	22	27	23	39
Sales Efforts	21	7	15	21	23	16
TOTAL	100	100	100	100	100	100

Relative Importance of Major Customer Service Elements[a]						
Product Availability	41.3	56.3	50.5	43.1	40.5	43.9
Order Cycle	12.3	10.7	18.0	25.5	26.2	20.2
Distribution System Flexibility	18.5	17.3	12.4	10.1	9.0	12.9
Distribution System Information	20.1	1.0	9.5	11.8	14.0	8.0
Distribution System Malfunction	4.5	4.0	5.4	7.2	8.2	10.0
Post-Sale Product Support	1.8	10.0	4.1	2.3	2.1	5.0
TOTAL	100	100	100	100	100	100

[a]Respondents were asked to distribute 100 points among the listed categories.

SOURCE: Bernard J. LaLonde and Paul H. Zinszer, *Customer Service: Meaning and Measurement* (Chicago: National Council of Physical Distribution Management, 1976), 116–117.

ORDER AND REPLENISHMENT CYCLES

The order cycle describes the activities carried out and the time elapsed from the placement of an order to the receipt of the goods. As shown in Figure 4–1, it includes the identification of the need for an item; the accumulation of items in, and placement of, the customer's

TABLE 4–2 Elements of the Marketing Mix 1976 versus 1987

Element	1976	1987	% Change
Product	36	33	– 14.9
Price	23	30	+ 30.4
Customer Service	23	23	NC
Advertising, Selling, Promotion	18	14	– 22.2
Total	100	100	–

SOURCE: *Customer Service: A Management Perspective* (Oak Brook, Illinois: Council of Logistics Management 1988), 26.

FIGURE 4–1: A conceptual diagram of the steps in a typical "two-stage" distribution system with an order cycle (- - -►), noted by numbers, and related replenishment cycle (——►), noted by letters, centralized inventory control, and decentralized order processing (- -►)

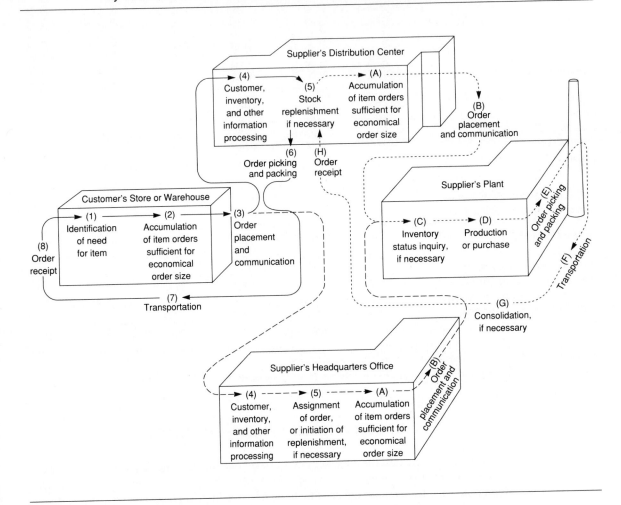

TABLE 4–3: Elements of the Marketing Mix 1987 versus 1990

Element	Today	1990	% Change
Product	33.3	32.7	− 1.8
Price	29.9	28.8	− 3.7
Customer Service	22.4	24.9	+ 11.2
Advertising, Selling, Promotion	14.4	13.6	− 5.5
Total	100.0	100.0	

SOURCE: *Customer Service: A Management Perspective* (Oak Brook, Illinois: Council of Logistics Management 1988), 27.

order; order communication to a supply point; order and information processing activities; stock replenishment where necessary; order picking and packing; shipment; and receipt of the order at its destination point.

A need for stock replenishment initiates a supplier's replenishment cycle. Thus, order and replenishment cycles are interdependent. The volume and regularity (or lack of it) of customer orders will influence the replenishment cycle. Further, the order cycle is dependent on how well the replenishment cycle functions because both the frequency and length of supplier stockout conditions affect order cycle dependability. Simply stated, "You can't ship it if you haven't got it."

In a typical two-stage distribution system, such as that shown in Figure 4–1, an order cycle and an associated replenishment cycle can be thought of as a series of loops with demands communicated through each loop in one direction and goods flowing through each loop in the opposite direction.

Each stage in an order and replenishment cycle can be achieved in a variety of ways. This means that the objectives associated with the performance of the cycle can be achieved through a bewildering number of alternative combinations of methods. Before discussing customer logistics service design problems, it will be useful to consider important alternatives at each step in an order cycle. Because many of the same considerations apply to replenishment cycles, the discussion will focus on the order cycle.

Order Cycle

1.* A customer must first identify the need to place an order for an item. There may be a time lag between the customer needing to place an order and knowing there is a need to do it. If the customer does not maintain a perpetual inventory, manually or by computer, and does not review and update required inventory levels on a continuing basis, an order may be placed days or weeks later than it should have been. As noted earlier in the chapter, this is one of the reasons why suppliers who deal in extensive product lines frequently offer their customers help in setting up effective inventory control systems. In this manner, orders will be placed when they should be placed.

2. Once the need for an item order is identified, it may be thrown into a pool to allow a sufficient quantity of item orders to accumulate to meet some desired order size. This order size might be the minimum quantity needed to qualify for a discount on rates charged for transportation services. Or, more typical at this stage of the distribution system, item needs may be accumulated to qualify for a quantity price discount that a particular supplier may allow for orders consolidated up to a given weight, number of items, or value. The consequent delay can vary considerably, and in many cases can add a week or more to the order cycle time. Items of critical importance to a customer typically are not subjected to the order accumulation process.

3. Customers may communicate their orders to a supply point by means of a supplier's sales representative, direct mail, telephone, or by electronic means, such as a computer-to-computer link (commonly referred to as electronic data interchange,

---

*These numbers correspond to the numbers in Figure 4–1.

EDI). Supplier's salespersons and direct mail provide "hard copy" (information in writing) at the supply point, but they are probably the slowest and least dependable of the methods, requiring up to several days (or in the case of the sales representative who misplaces the order, weeks). Telephone order placement is fast, but mistakes in "taking down the orders" are the source of many errors made in recording order placement information. Electronic "hard copy" systems combining high-speed data transmission with written input and output are now available in many configurations and, while not foolproof, such systems produce very few errors and are being increasingly adopted by many companies for that reason. This subject is treated in detail in Chapter 12, "Data Processing and Communications."

An analysis in *Business Week* of how companies are using new information technologies to gain a competitive edge highlighted the success of American Hospital Supply Corporation's (AHS) efforts in this regard. AHS, the largest firm in its industry with more than 100,000 customers and 8,500 suppliers, set up computer links by which its customers can place and track orders directly through AHS terminals. This has resulted in greatly improving customer service and sales.[6] This experience indicates that emphasis on locating stocks in major markets in order to reduce *shipping time* is a questionable strategy when *order transmittal time* is at least as important as other elements in the order cycle.

Apparently a growing number of suppliers have had the same experience. Many have turned to order takers who are equipped with TV screens connected to information input devices. As the order is called in over the telephone, the order taker types it up, sees it on the screen, makes any necessary corrections, verifies the order with the caller, and finally release the information for order processing. Some firms now operate such order-taking systems on a 24-hour-a-day basis; this costs money, but it is currently the best method in this aspect of customer service.

4. Upon receipt of the customer's order at the supply point, the supplier initiates a series of steps that may include (a) a credit check for customers not previously approved or for customers ordering in excess of a previously approved credit limit; (b) updating inventory records, if this has not been done independent of the receipt of the order, for items contained on the order received; (c) placing an inquiry on the updated inventory records to determine whether the items ordered are in stock; and (d) carrying out any other prescribed information processing activities that do not directly affect order cycle activities, such as the preparation of sales records.

    A supplier with multiple distribution centers may be organized to carry out these steps on a centralized or decentralized basis. If the process is centralized, orders must be communicated to the supplier's central order processing office, and then be sent to an outlying distribution center. In recent years, particularly with the introduction of high-capacity microcomputers, some suppliers have redesigned their procedures to allow for the decentralized processing of orders, typically with the elimination of at least one communication link and a reduction in order processing time. Decentralized order processing is assumed in Figure 4–1.

5. Orders may contain line items for which there is no stock at the supply point. This situation may initiate a rather complex decision process. The supplier may have the options to (a) ship available items and back order the rest, thus creating a "split shipment" situation; (b) hold available items until those items found out of stock can be replenished and the entire order sent in one shipment; (c) order out-of-

stock items from other supply points where they may be found in stock (requiring a decision as to where to direct the first or subsequent inquiries in the system); (d) purchase items found out of stock from other sources, even from competitors; or (e) cancel orders for items found out of stock. In some cases the supplier may have no choice. A number of customers, particularly those in grocery products retailing, will no longer accept back orders. Instead they will place the order for such items again as part of their next order, particularly in cases where weekly (or even more frequent) orders may be placed. Of course, if supplier stockout situations become too frequent, customers may elect to place orders with other suppliers. If stock replenishment is necessary, the range of times required for this stage in the process may be great indeed, from several days (required for the transfer of goods from another supply point) up to months (in cases where production for replenishment must be scheduled long in advance). The in-stock condition at the supply point, and a supplier's ability to respond to stockout situations, are the most important determinants of the quality of customer service in most systems.

6. Order picking may be carried out on a semiautomatic or manual basis. A supplier dealing in products typically ordered in single units—appliances of a given model, such as a refrigerator—may be able to pack for shipment at the time of manufacture. Suppliers dealing with customers whose orders resemble "laundry lists" of items relatively small in size must maintain extensive picking and packing facilities. Picking and packing times are influenced by such factors as (a) the degree of automation and "machine pacing" built into the system; (b) the complexity of customer orders; (c) the size and complexity of the distribution facilities from which orders are filled; and (d) the necessity to palletize, depalletize, or transfer goods from a pallet of one size to one of another because of incompatibilities in methods employed by the supplier and the customer or transportation company. Relatively small delays in the order cycle result from picking and packing operations. Many suppliers maintain "same day" shipping policies for orders received before some cutoff time, usually at noon or before. Firms on the West Coast enjoy a special advantage in respect to a combination of taking telephone orders and "same day" shipping policies because of time-zone differentials with customers located in the Midwest and the East.

7. Transportation times vary in length with (a) the size of the shipment, (b) the mode of transportation, and (c) the distance the shipment must travel. Total transit time for a shipment is usually less dependent on the distance involved than on the method of transportation. Small shipment services, such as the overnight, nationwide, air-movement services provided by Federal Express, Purolator, U.S. Express Mail, and others, are very fast and dependable over long distances, but are relatively costly. United Parcel Service (UPS) costs less but takes a bit longer. Truckload (TL) shipments are usually faster and their schedules are more dependable than rail carload shipments. However, less-than-truckload (LTL) shipments, handled and rehandled through two or more terminals, are much slower than their truckload brethren. The size of a shipment is ordinarily a factor only when contrasting LTL and TL movements.

8. Typically, the receiver of a shipment is highly motivated to process an incoming shipment quickly upon its receipt, leading to a minimum of delay in completing

the order cycle. However, in some cases, the receiver cannot physically handle an unexpected large incoming shipment due to lack of storage space or limited unloading facilities. Thus, the timing of the arrival of a large shipment may be an important customer service factor. There is a growing tendency to schedule delivery of large orders somewhat "by appointment." This creates situations where deliveries tendered before or after the appointed time may be refused. Naturally, only a valued customer can enforce such a policy on a supplier.

One step that is a primary determinant of cycle time and variability — stock replenishment — is within control of the supplier. Order-filling delay can be eliminated if the supplier is willing and able to stock a sufficiently large quantity of goods at a supply point, but in most cases the cost of keeping large "excess" inventories on hand is prohibitive. Typically, timely stock replenishment depends heavily on such factors such as (1) the accuracy of demand forecasting; (2) the volume of goods sold from the supply point; and (3) the speed with which inventories can be replenished after they have reached a replenishment level.

The steps in the replenishment cycle shown in Figure 4–1 have many of the same characteristics as those in the order cycle because each of these cycles is essentially a "mirror image" of the other.

Order Cycle Profile

The various stages in the order and replenishment cycles are listed in Table 4–4, along with example information drawn from general experience about each stage. Information in Table 4–4 illustrates several points.

TABLE 4–4 Sample Characteristics of Various Stages in an Order Cycle and Related Replenishment Cycle

Stage[a]	Range of Variation in Time for Completion (Days) in 99 Percent of all Cases	Under Supplier Control?	Relative Ease of Measurement
1. Identification of need for item	1–7	No	Difficult
2. Order accumulation	1–30	?	Difficult
3. Order placement and communication	1–5	?	?
4. Information processing at supply point	1–3	Yes	Easy
5. Stock replenishment, where necessary (A, B, C, D, E, F, G, H)	1–60	Yes	Easy
6. Order picking and packing by supplier	1–3	Yes	Easy
7. Transportation from supplier to customer	3–7	?	?
8. Order receipt by customer	1–3	?	Difficult
TOTAL	15–90		

[a]Stages are numbered and lettered to conform with the identification scheme used in Figure 4–1.

FIGURE 4–2: A diagrammatic representation of the frequency distributions of times required to complete the stages in the order cycle for which information is presented in Table 4-2

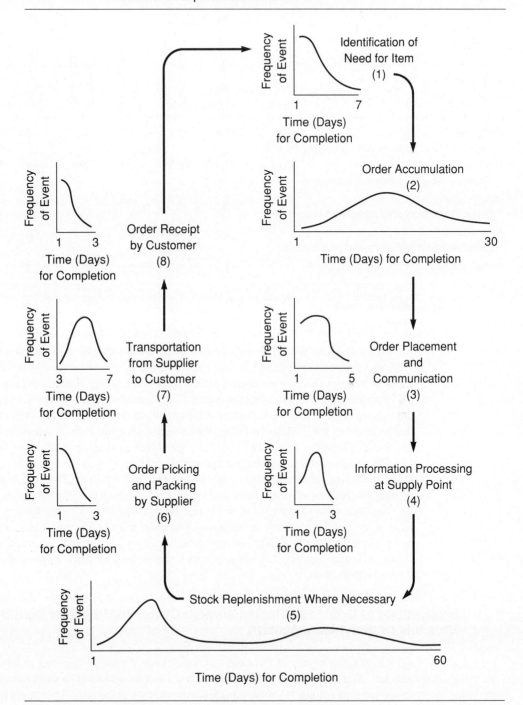

TABLE 4–5: Components of Order Cycle by Industry (Days)

	All Manufacturing	Chemical and Plastics Manufacturing	Food Manufacturing	All Other Manufacturing	All Merchandising	Merchandising Consumer Goods	Merchandising Industrial Goods
Time Frame Customer places order until received by firm	1.9	1.2	2.0	2.3	1.0	0.8	0.8
Time Frame Order received until order processed	2.1	0.8	1.5	2.5	1.1	1.0	1.0
Time Frame Order processed until order shipped	2.2	1.7	0.8	2.7	1.6	0.9	1.5
Time Frame Order shipped until received by customer	4.1	3.0	3.0	5.2	1.8	1.0	3.2
TOTAL ORDER CYCLE TIME (Days)	10.3	6.7	7.3	12.7	5.5	3.7	6.5

SOURCE: Bernard J. LaLonde and Paul H. Zinszer, *Customer Service: Meaning & Measurement* (Chicago: National Council of Physical Distribution Management, 1976), 116–117.

First, when all the stages in an order cycle are taken into consideration, the possible variance in the total cycle time required to fill a customer order may be very large. Second, the supplier may have little or no control over several of the stages. Third, the ease of measuring performance varies roughly with the degree of control which the supplier has over each stage; thus, measurement may be relatively difficult for several stages in the order cycle. Probabilities based on the frequency of times with which each event in the order cycle occurs can be developed. Examples of these probabilities are shown in diagrammatic form in Figure 4–2.

The ranges of times required for individual cycle stages may overlap to the extent that the activities carried out in each stage overlap. For example, transportation may begin before the picking and packing stage has been completed, particularly when multiple loads or shipments are contained within an order. Or, needs may be transmitted on an item-by-item basis as they arise at the customer's place of business. The order may be communicated and much of it processed before the final item demand which triggers a shipment is communicated by the customer to the supplier. Order cycle times experienced by firms in several industries are shown in Table 4–5.

Implications of Order and Replenishment Cycles for Physical Distribution and Materials (Supply) Management

Cycle times represent the extent to which orders must be initiated in advance of need (receipt). The assumption is that stock on hand will be sufficient to meet demands that arise during the time required to obtain a replenishment stock of the item. The longer the anticipated cycle time for an item, the larger the amount of stock required to be on hand at the time a replenishment order is placed. Because of potential variations in cycle times, reorder points have to be higher than would be necessary *if* cycle times could be known with certainty. To the extent that cycle times are uncertain, firms must keep excess inventory, known as "safety stocks," on hand to protect against stockouts. Stocking out of an item may cause disruption of production in a manufacturing firm, or inability of a wholesaler or retailer to serve its customers in a competitive market. In the discussion of inventory control in Chapters 6 and 7 it will be shown how a (sometimes large) reduction in safety stocks can result from customer service standards and controls that reduce variability in order and replenishment cycle times.

MANAGING CUSTOMER LOGISTICS SERVICE

"We provide a 95 percent customer service level in our business." This type of statement is often recited proudly, and usually a bit mechanically, to satisfy a customer's inquiry about a supplier's customer service level or policies. In one case it might mean, "We fill 19 out of every 20 orders for a given item." Or, it might mean, "We fill 19 out of 20 customer orders completely." Or, "We fill 95 percent of the dollar value of all orders received." And so on. None of these statements addresses anything except a supplier's inventory availability, and even then each statement expresses a different aspect of the matter. Typically, when managers from various companies get together at professional association meetings, they often can be heard trading meaningless percentage figures to compare their noncomparable customer service standards and policies.

Customer logistics service must be carefully defined and understood to be managed effectively. Once customer service is defined, standards can be established, implementation carried out, performance monitored, and control exercised.

Importance of Customer Logistics Service Management

A great deal of attention in logistics management is properly devoted to cost control, and this is good management if it is waste that is being eliminated. But simply reducing expenditures for logistics service without considering the benefits being gained from those expenditures is not good management. The bottom line profit figure on a financial statement may be influenced quite markedly by a carefully planned and controlled logistics service program through the impact of logistics service on sales and profits.

An outstanding example of customer logistics service management was featured in the previously cited *Business Week* article on how companies are using new information technologies to gain a competitive edge. Norton Company, a 100-year-old company involved in abrasives, engineering materials, petroleum, and mining businesses, is putting technologically sophisticated managers in line jobs in a effort to give its distributors "the highest service levels in the industry." The company has set up an information network in which distributors can enter new orders and in a matter of seconds obtain details on the status of orders, pricing, and catalog items. Distributors are thus able to promise a delivery date right on the phone when their customers call in an order. Plans call for linking the system to "a larger in-house system, which will take orders, compare them with backlogs and then adjust factory operating schedules to hold down costs." Although this is an expensive network to set up, the company sees it as a definite competitive advantage.[7] Another example, the Steelcase company's commitment to customer service, is shown in Exhibit 4–1.

EXHIBIT 4–1: Red Faces

On a Tuesday evening Mike Gelfand, VP of Sales at Waldner's, the Steelcase dealership in Farmingdale, NY, was having dinner with his family when the phone rang. "Mike, we're in trouble. You're my only hope!"

The caller, the facility manager at one of New York's largest banks, was seeing red. Actually, red-red orange.

His bank had ordered half a million dollars' worth of Steelcase open-office panel systems, but somewhere along the line someone had keyed in the wrong color number.

"When the first 500 panels came in," Mike recalls, "the poor guy at the bank took one look and nearly died. 'Those aren't my panels! I ordered beige!'"

The carpeting was down, the walls were painted, the door bucks were stained. Important clients would be coming to see the installation in a week. Disaster.

Mike called Jane Williamson, his Steelcase rep, and she got on the phone to Dealer Services in Grand Rapids. They authorized the panel factory to do what-

ever was necessary to correct the rest of the order, but the 500 red-red orange panels that were already at the bank had to be fixed on-site.

On Friday, the factory flew in 1,800 yards of beige fabric. Saturday morning, three Steelcase technicians from the Athens, GA, factory arrived and met five of Waldner's installers at the bank. They set up an assembly line, ripped off the old fabric, put on the new. By Sunday evening, working around the clock, they'd completely reupholstered all 500 panels.

The bank was up and running by Wednesday. While the bank's important clients toured the new installation, Jane and Mike took the guys from Athens, who'd never been to New York City, to see the Statue of Liberty.

"Steelcase really came through in a clutch situation," Mike says. "It was an amazing job. No other manufacturer could do that, or would."

No other dealer, either.

SOURCE: Information courtesy Steelcase, Inc.

There is no *essential* difference between firm-to-firm and firm-to-ultimate-consumer customer service. A customer is a customer! The difference between the two types of relationships is in the degree of rationality of the customers involved and their individual importance to the seller. Clearly industrial purchasing decisions involve greater degrees of economic and service support analyses than individual retail purchases. Likewise, relative importance may range from a single purchase relationship to the extreme of being a "captive company" in which, for example, 75 percent or more of one's sales may go to a single customer.

In contrast to the Steelcase example given above, the WordPerfect Corporation features its customer support group in advertisements that note that they answer *more than 10,000 toll-free calls a day* from customers having questions or problems concerning their use of their WordPerfect word processor software. In addition to solving customers' problems, these calls provide the company's development team with valuable suggestions on how to improve their industry-leading product.

A faulty logistics service program may take its toll in costs as well as foregone sales opportunities. For example, an order involving one or more out-of-stock items often costs at least three times as much to process as one that can be filled completely from stocks held at the order-picking location. Excess costs result from duplicated communications, holding information about incomplete orders on file until all items are in stock or received, delays in billing, and extra service demands on a salesperson when a customer receives an incomplete order.

Products found damaged or deteriorated upon delivery may require extra expenses for transportation, reworking, communication and, of course, the time of the field sales force.

Considering its importance, the number of firms that have gone about developing a program for controlling logistics service is relatively small. One can, however, learn a great deal from the work that has been done thus far.

A Management Program

A program for managing logistics service requires the definition of such service for an individual industry, company, product, geographic area, or customer. Once the concept of service is defined, standards can be established, implementation carried out, measurement accomplished, and control exercised.

Service Definition   Various measures of customer logistics service standards, ranked roughly in order of their popularity, are:

1. The elapsed time between the receipt of an order at the supplier's warehouse and the shipment of the order from the warehouse.

2. The minimum size of an order, or limits on the assortment of items in an order that a supplier will accept from its customers.

3. The percentage of items in a supplier's warehouse that might be found to be out-of-stock at any given point in time.

4. The proportion of customer orders filled accurately.

5. The percentage of customers, or volume of customer orders, that describes those who are served (whose orders are delivered) within a certain time period from the receipt of the order at the supplier's warehouse.

6. The percentage of customer orders that can be filled completely upon receipt at a supplier's warehouse.

7. The proportion of goods that arrive at a customer's place of business in salable condition.

8. The elapsed time between the placement of an order by a customer and the delivery of goods ordered to the customer's place of business.

9. The ease and flexibility with which a customer can place an order.

Companies may employ more than one of these measures, although most marketing and logistics executives typically prefer to use one method over the others. Just which one may depend on the orientation of the company.

The definitions near the bottom of the list of measures rarely are employed today on a regular basis, perhaps because they present greater measurement and control problems. And yet, they are customer-oriented definitions in contrast to the supplier-oriented definitions appearing at the top of the list. From this it should be reasonable to conclude that a problem of some importance in the management of customer logistics service will be that of introducing and maintaining customer-oriented rather than supplier-oriented programs.

What is important from the customer's point of view? Is it the immediate availability and shipment of a complete order? Is it merely knowledge of when and if an order will arrive? Is it the flexibility with which the customer can place an order? Or is it the policy that determines whether the customer or the supplier will pay the extra transportation costs of emergency shipments? Many companies don't know the answers to these questions because they have never asked their customers. Those who do, for example, are often surprised by the fact that most customers express a greater need for dependability than for speed in response to their orders.

From the supplier's viewpoint, costs associated with certain types of service failures may suggest which definitions are appropriate to the company's needs. Service definitions should be relevant, offer some basis for continuing measurement, and be as few in number as possible. This will require a manager to rank service matters in terms of their importance and to concentrate on those few that have the most meaning (if everything is important nothing is important).

Establishment of Standards Customer service standards are influenced by many factors: economics, the nature of the product, and environmental considerations, such as competition, to name a few.

Economics Perhaps first and foremost are economic considerations. Some aspects of customer service cost money, such as money spent for more rapid means of communication, greater inventory coverage, or faster and more dependable methods of transportation. However, on a benefits-to-costs basis, such expenditures are usually more than warranted if the system is managed properly. In this sense, one should speak of the *value* of customer service rather than its costs. It is similar to the point of view represented by Philip Crosby in his book *Quality is Free*.[8]

What customers dislike most are bad surprises with respect to delivery delays, an inability on the part of the vendor to advise them of the status of their order, and, in general, a lack of response to the customer's statement "I have a problem." In the vast majority of cases, what the customer wants is responsiveness to his or her problem. For example, "Yes, we understand what your problem is. We'll look into it and get back to you *within ten minutes*." Just as important is the *anticipation* of a problem, for example a delay in delivery, and prompt notification to the customer of the nature of the delay and an expected alternative arrival date. Customers, especially business firms, understand that errors and unanticipated events do occur — no firm is perfect. It is lack of information and being "kept in the dark" that infuriates customers.

Any service standard can be translated either directly or indirectly into a cost. One example of a manufacturer's attempt to translate the coverage of item demands placed on its distributors by their retail customers is shown in Figure 4–3. The table in Figure 4–3 is prepared in advance to allow each distributor-customer to select an automatic replenishment policy that will satisfy item availability standards of that distributor; will produce an acceptable order frequency; and will result in a reasonable cost, reflected indirectly as the level of inventory necessary to support each item availability level and order frequency.

Improved service need not always cost more. The results of one study reflecting this are shown in Table 4–6. By consolidating eight small and incomplete inventories at eight locations into one large and complete inventory at a full-line distribution center, it was found that moderate cost increases associated with outbound transportation to customers could be more than offset by significant reductions in the costs of inbound transportation, warehousing, administration, and inventory carrying cost. Further, the length and variability of order cycle time were reduced.

FIGURE 4–3: Sample printout from a pro forma estimate provided by a manufacturer to its distributor customers contemplating the use of the manufacturer's system for the replenishment of distributor stocks

Percent of Retail Customer Order Fill by Distributor	Annual Inventory Turnover for Distributor (Annual Sales/Average Inventory)	Average Distributor Inventory
If Distributor Orders Every Two Weeks from Corning		
99.50%	6.80x	$24,052
99.20	7.16	22,910
99.00	7.33	22,373
98.00	7.93	20,560
97.00	8.48	19,351
96.00	8.88	18,478
95.00	9.21	17,806
94.00	9.53	17,202
92.00	10.13	16,194
90.00	10.66	15,389
If Distributor Orders Every Three Weeks from Corning		
99.50%	6.26x	$26,208
99.20	6.57	24,957
99.00	6.73	24,369
98.00	7.33	22,382
97.00	7.79	21,058
96.00	8.16	20,102
95.00	8.47	19,386
94.00	8.77	18,704
92.00	9.32	17,600
90.00	9.81	16,717
If Distributor Orders Every Four Weeks from Corning		
99.50%	5.69x	$28,823
99.20	5.97	27,472
99.00	6.11	26,836
98.00	6.64	24,691
97.00	7.05	23,260
96.00	7.38	22,227
95.00	7.65	21,433
94.00	7.92	20,717
92.00	8.40	19,523
90.00	8.83	18,572

(continued)

FIGURE 4–3 (continued): Sample printout from a pro forma estimate

Percent of Retail Customer Order Fill by Distributor	Annual Inventory Turnover for Distributor (Annual Sales/Average Inventory)	Average Distributor Inventory
If Distributor Orders Every Five Weeks from Corning		
99.50%	5.23x	$31,373
99.20	5.48	29,929
99.00	5.61	29,250
98.00	6.08	26,956
97.00	6.45	25,427
96.00	6.74	24,322
95.00	6.99	23,473
94.00	7.22	22,708
92.00	7.65	21,434
90.00	8.03	20,415
If Distributor Orders Every Six Weeks from Corning		
99.50%	4.82x	$34,003
99.20	5.05	32,471
99.00	5.17	31,760
98.00	5.59	29,318
97.00	5.92	27,696
96.00	6.18	26,524
95.00	6.40	25,623
94.00	6.61	24,812
92.00	6.99	23,461
90.00	7.33	22,379

Nature of the Environment Environmental considerations may take into account customer and competitor behavior. What is the impact of customer inventory management policies? Do they allow for adequate replenishment cycle times? Or do they, by accident or design, produce the need for rapid response time, service that must be provided through the decentralization of supplier stocks, the frequent use of premium transportation methods, or some other means?

One firm manufacturing a line of cleaning products found that its industrial customers, largely other manufacturing companies, had storage space sufficient to house sizable inventories and anticipated their demand by means of systematic inventory programs. Institutional accounts, such as restaurants, not only did not have space to store inventories of cleaning products, but also relied typically on informal ordering procedures that often were not initiated until the customer had run out of product. This company's institutional accounts clearly required a higher level of customer logistics service than did its industrial accounts. By the same token, retailers as a group may require higher levels of service than wholesaler customer. And,

TABLE 4–6: Results of an Actual Study Showing the Impact of Inventory Consolidation on Customer Service and Logistics Costs

Distribution Cost Centers	Alternative Inventory Configurations	
	Eight Partial Line DCs	One Full Line DC
Transportation Inbound to DCs	$233,500	$ 79,800
Warehouse Facilities and Equipment	$150,000	$ 84,000
Warehouse Handling and Storage	$187,000	$ 74,600
Order Processing	$108,000	$108,000
Transportation Outbound to Customer	$163,000	$398,200
Administration Overhead	$180,000	$ 80,000
Inventory Carrying Cost at 20 Percent	$234,500	$174,000
TOTAL COST	$1,256,000	$998,600
Customer Service		
Order Cycle	30 days	14 days
Standard Deviation of Order Cycle Time	20 days	4 days

SOURCE: O. Keith Helferich and Lloyd B. Mitchell, "Planning for Customer Service with Computer Simulation," *Transportation & Distribution Management* (formerly *Handling & Shipping Management*) (January/February, 1975), 20. Reprinted with permission of Penton Publishing Co.

those customers whose inventories turn over very rapidly—a high volume of sales from a small retail outlet, for example—will require high standards of service, frequently daily deliveries.

Competitors' service policies, whether they are carefully set or not, can be an important influence on the level of service established as standard. Research shows that competitors' physical distribution service levels can have considerable influence on sales results. A classic experimental study, later supported by field research, indicated that selected wholesalers of convenience goods (1) did not distinguish between differences in logistics service levels that were provided by their competing supplier-manufacturers when the wholesalers planned and executed orders for the replenishment of their stocks; (2) as a result, the wholesalers experienced a higher rate of stockout conditions on line items for which poor service was provided (as measured by the length and variance in cycle times); and (3) when this occurred, the wholesalers sold more than usual of the competing products when a product line was out-of-stock in their warehouses.[9]

Nature of the Product Several product characteristics have a direct effect on the level of customer service that a firm would want or could afford to provide. They include the customer's willingness to substitute one product source or brand for another, physical characteristics of the product itself, and its pattern of demand.

Substitutability Product substitutability at all levels in a channel of distribution will determine the degree of care with which a seller regards his customer service policy.

Results of a survey conducted by *Progressive Grocer* magazine, reported in Figure 4–4, indicate a great deal of variability in customers' tendencies to substitute various competing products for one another.

In industrial goods markets, factors such as standardization of product specifications and the expiration of patent rights to products and processes have greatly increased cross substitution of one brand for another. Similar substitution occurs in consumer products, particularly in replacement parts ranging from phonograph needle cartridges to automobile tires and batteries.

Physical Characteristics   Of primary importance among a product's physical characteristics are (1) its ability to bear the cost of high-priced premium customer logistics service, and (2) the risk of storing it.

In Chapter 1, it was shown that the dollar density of a product largely determines its ability to bear the cost of high-priced transportation. This factor also influences inventory holding costs, but inversely to movement costs. For example, scientific instruments have very high dollar densities and can bear high movement costs. On the other hand, inventory holding costs for such products are very high because of their value. This combination of factors will encourage a wholesaler dealing in such products to maintain low inventories and utilize fast (and costly) methods of transportation for delivery to customers. At the same time, the wholesaler's own order cycle may include a relatively large amount of time for replenishment activities because its supplier — the manufacturer — may store very little of the product in anticipation of orders. In fact, it may produce an expensive item only when an order for it is received ("manufacturing to order").

On the other hand, refined lead used in car batteries, with its moderate dollar density but extremely high weight density, might be stored in quantity at various points in order to conserve movement costs and accommodate the refining schedule. Lead would not likely be moved rapidly from point to point to meet customer service demands. Customer orders for lead may be required to be placed some time in advance of actual need, not so much to provide for production and replenishment activities as to allow for a slow, economical movement and storage pattern.

The characteristics of goods refer not only to weight and value, but also to the financial risk of storage. This has a marked influence on customer service. The distribution of wet yeast, for example, is highly regulated by the government because of its tendency to deteriorate rapidly. To insure supplies of fresh yeast on grocers' shelves, those who deal in this product make daily or thrice-weekly deliveries to their customers.

Pattern of Demand   Customer service standards are much more difficult to comply with during periods of peak customer demand. But, it is precisely during peak demand periods that customer service, as evidenced by the availability of the product, is most important. Supplier stockouts during periods of peak demand can only be avoided if suppliers are aware of such peaks and plan their inventory levels accordingly.

Some products are demanded only during certain seasons. Sales lost because of a stockout of canned cranberry sauce during a Thanksgiving–Christmas holiday period will never be recovered. A line of spring fashions declines dramatically in value if not delivered (and sold) by Easter. In these situations where a stockout can result in a considerable loss of sales, customer service standards will be set at relatively high levels. This is a result not so much of a supplier's desire to provide good customer service, but of its need to do so if it wishes to remain competitive.

FIGURE 4–4: Selected results of the *Progressive Grocer* survey that examined how different types of customers said they would react to stock-outs on favorite brands

Product	Percent of Customers Who Would[a]														
	Buy Elsewhere[b]					Switch Brands[b]					Buy Later at Same Store[b]				
	#1	#2	#3	#4	#5	#1	#2	#3	#4	#5	#1	#2	#3	#4	#5
Margarine	17%	18%	26%	36%	17%	58%	46%	66%	27%	52%	25%	36%	10%	45%	33%
Cigarettes	75	82	81	83	80	10	4	17	17	5	15	14	2	8	15
Gelatin	13	11	27	10	21	61	50	60	40	49	26	42	13	60	32
Liquid starch	6	9	27	11	28	50	39	54	44	53	44	52	19	56	19
Hand soap	30	21	33	45	30	43	43	53	36	49	26	36	15	27	23
Toothpaste	39	36	63	60	43	52	40	28	30	36	9	24	10	20	21
Cereal	30	28	28	20	24	61	59	58	30	57	9	17	15	60	20
Dog food	61	62	39	25	41	39	38	50	50	44	—	—	11	50	19
Baby food	40	60	48	20	59	40	33	46	40	33	20	7	9	60	7
Deodorant	59	54	67	56	58	36	19	25	33	26	5	27	10	22	16
Shampoo	61	54	66	67	57	26	21	27	33	23	13	25	8	17	20
Regular coffee	46	48	36	27	36	32	28	57	18	33	23	28	6	64	33
Catsup	30	7	26	40	19	57	59	67	40	63	13	35	8	30	19
Mayonnaise	52	7	39	22	27	26	55	51	22	59	22	41	13	67	14
Instant coffee	33	14	44	11	29	52	36	53	33	50	14	55	4	67	23
Canned tuna	30	19	22	9	18	52	56	67	46	53	17	26	12	55	29
Canned peaches	9	10	11	9	18	73	52	81	36	55	18	38	8	64	27
Peanut butter	17	18	26	20	27	67	46	61	50	58	17	36	14	40	18
Jam	9	21	15	36	21	77	48	77	27	64	14	31	8	46	16
Tomato juice	27	15	17	11	17	68	56	76	44	66	5	30	7	56	17
Toilet tissue	26	28	24	25	22	65	52	63	33	61	9	21	13	50	18
Facial tissue	22	19	19	—	19	70	52	67	33	64	9	30	14	78	19
Aluminum foil	17	18	13	33	15	78	46	80	33	68	4	36	8	44	19
Salad oil	26	11	24	38	20	57	50	67	38	62	17	39	10	38	20
Solid shortening	13	12	27	18	20	65	35	65	50	56	22	54	8	46	27
Canned soup	32	14	33	25	25	46	45	51	33	50	23	41	17	50	25
Canned milk	20	14	15	30	13	70	43	77	30	68	10	43	8	50	20
Canned corn	27	7	18	9	19	55	65	73	55	57	18	31	10	46	24
Canned green beans	18	11	17	29	19	64	61	78	57	57	18	32	6	29	24
Laundry detergents	46	36	51	50	52	38	29	43	30	23	17	43	9	30	27
Waxed paper	13	12	13	20	14	78	65	74	40	73	9	23	13	50	14

[a]Out-of-stock, a big problem to supermarket operators, is also a big factor in the minds of consumers when selecting a favorite store. In answer to a question about how they would react to an out-of-stock situation on their favorite brands of 31 types of grocery products, they show some interesting unanimity of opinion. A dominant percentage of customers in all neighborhoods say they will go to another store to buy their favorite brands of cigarettes, coffee, deodorant, dog food, laundry detergent, and shampoo. High-income shoppers and blacks show strong brand loyalty to toothpaste. Young marrieds and small-town customers will go out of their way to get their favorite brands of baby foods.

In nearly all but the few categories mentioned above, better than half the customers in all neighborhoods say their reaction to an out-of-stock situation on their favorite brand would be to choose a substitute.

The percentages sometimes add up to more than 100 percent due to the fact that some respondents checked "buy elsewhere" and "buy later at the same store," indicating that they would do one or the other but will not switch brands.

[b]Key to store neighborhood numbers: #1 = young married, #2 = blue collar, #3 = high income, #4 = black, #5 = small town.

SOURCE: *Progressive Grocer: The Magazine of Super Marketing*, vol. 47 (October, 1968).

Demand may take on short-run patterns related to special sales incentives, ultimate consumer demand patterns (daily, weekly, and monthly variations), inventory tax levies, and such. Many firms whose salespersons have monthly sales quotas get 40 percent of their orders in the last week of the month, the result of hard pushing by the sales force to "catch up" by getting enough orders to meet or exceed their sales quotas.

A wholesaler of grocery products is likely to encounter heavy demand from retailers just prior to the weekly bulge of retail sales corresponding to wage payment dates and weekend consumption patterns of consumers. In most communities, this results in a midweek peak of wholesaler deliveries and heavy consumer buying on Friday and Saturday.

To reduce property taxes on inventories, buyers and sellers alike may arrange to have goods in transit — and thereby nontaxable — on certain dates during the year. This reduces the amount of goods "legally" in stock for both the buyer and the seller without interrupting the supply cycle. At the same time, it places a periodic burden on the supplier to meet fluctuations in demands of customers caused by this type of disturbance in the supply process.

In establishing customer service standards, managers often unintentionally overlook the need for differentiated standards for various major groups of items in the product line. For example, high-volume items in the line will, if stocked out, produce many more back-order situations than stockouts on low-volume items. This might result in a supplier having a policy of, say, a 99 percent line-item fill rate for high-volume items versus a 95 percent line-item fill rate for low-volume items.

Nature of Demand   At the level of the ultimate consumer, marketers have distinguished the nature of products on the basis of the manner in which the customer regards them when contemplating a purchase. In this respect, convenience items are those frequently purchased in small quantities at many retail outlets. Shopping goods are those that customers buy only after visiting several stores, comparing qualities and prices, and pondering their decision. Specialty items are bought at exclusive, or widely spaced, outlets; they are purchased at lengthy intervals, without extensive product comparison between stores.

In general, consumers are more willing to substitute one brand of convenience or shipping goods for another (given the absence of the first brand in the market) than they are to substitute one brand of specialty goods for another. This may require an intensive distribution strategy for the manufacturer of convenience or shopping goods, with emphasis on obtaining distribution through as many retail outlets as possible. In contrast, a manufacturer of specialty goods may be able to distribute those products through relatively few retail outlets, possibly under an agreement that provides each with an exclusive sales territory. Thus, there is a strong emphasis on full range of customer logistics services among firms marketing convenience or shopping goods. This is one reason why the grocery products industry has been a leader in emphasizing all forms of customer logistics service.

Customer expectations vary with the type of item ordered. The president of a retail discount department store chain, in discussing his customers' expectations of availability for major household appliances, commented that customers expected standard items such as white, 16-cubic-foot, right-hand-door refrigerators to be delivered to their homes within 48 hours of their purchase. In sharp contrast, most customers were prepared to wait as long as six weeks to get delivery on a coppertone refrigerator, of a non-standard size, and with a left-hand door. Yet, many firms treat all their products alike for purposes of establishing, implementing, measuring, and controlling customer service. It is costly, *and usually unnecessary*, to maintain the same (high) level of customer logistics service at all times, for all products, for all customers, and to all geographic areas.

Once standards are determined, a statement of logistics service policy for customers can be developed. The nature, character, and scope of such a policy varies from firm to firm. A short, simple, and effective statement can be developed that provides the necessary internal decision-making guidance in this critical area of concern. An excellent checklist to assist in developing a suitable statement of customer logistics service policy is illustrated in Figure 4–5.

FIGURE 4–5: Some standards and measures of customer service

Standard	How to State It	Remarks
Order generation and transmittal	"Inbound orders from area X arrive in Y days. (For each area)"	If possible, build in factor to represent customer's internal order generating time from requisition to purchase order.
Processable orders received	"X percent of orders processable upon receipt."	Variances may reflect inadequate product sheets, catalog descriptions, price lists.
Internal order cycle: Mail opening and delivery	"Mail to be delivered (or picked up) at P.O. box at _____ intervals."	A dedicated P.O. box (for orders only) will bypass mail room bottlenecks. But time pick-up to post office distribution schedules.
Order confirmation	"X percent of orders confirmed within Y hours."	Set corollary standard for orders not confirmed timely; follow-up on legal matters.
Exceptions	"Customers (or other departments) contacted about exceptions of all types with X hours."	Include discrepancies on orders, information not supplied; restricted articles, stockouts, delays, etc.
Credit check/reports	"Credit report on existing customers within X hours, on new accounts Y hours (days)."	Excessive divergence from standard would suggest prescreening accounts before selling.
Sales review, edit, etc.	(Time standards as appropriate)	Include elements unique to the company.
Order processing	"X percent of orders processed within Y hours."	Set corollary standard for completion of orders not processed timely.
Subroutines: bill of lading, invoices, etc.	(Time, accuracy standards as appropriate)	Terms of sale (F.O.B. plant, delivered, delivery proof required) may be a major factor.
Plant/warehouse order filling	"X percent of orders to be assembled (produced) within Y working hours (days)."	Include packing, stencilling, strapping, etc., along with order assembly elements.
Staging and shipping	"X percent of shipments to be picked up/shipped within Y hours of availability."	An element often overlooked.

(continued)

FIGURE 4–5 (continued): Some standards and measures of customer service

Standard	How to State It	Remarks
Transit	"X percent of orders delivered within Y days of shipment."	Should allow for differences in location, mode, length of haul.
Order status, inquiries by customer	"Inquiries on order status to be answered within X hours."	Also: tracing and expediting.
Product availability Line item fill	"X percent of line items ordered to be available on presentation of orders."	Can be misleading.
Dollar fill	"X percent of dollars ordered to be filled on presentation of orders."	A measure of inventory investment strategy and its effectiveness.
Complete order fill	"X percent of orders to be shipped complete."	One of the more reliable indices of custormer satisfaction.
Orders accepted as shipped	"X percent of orders accepted as shipped."	Can reflect acceptance of substitutions, minor errors, or intentional overshipping.
Errors and credits	(By dollars, orders, or as percentage of invoices or invoice dollars.)	Also classifiable by source.
Complaints	"X percent of complaints to be resolved in Y days, balance within Z days (weeks)."	Should include provision for regular review of all unresolved complaints.
Customers' target dates met	"X percent of orders to meet customer due dates after acceptance."	Another reliable index of customer satisfaction.
Phone response	"X percent of calls answered on second ring."	Other standards: maximum busy signals per hour, maximum wait by customer, etc.
Courtesy, effectiveness	(Attitude towards customer, ability to handle the situation.)	Rated by monitoring or after-the-fact questionnaires to customers.
Accuracy	"No more than X percent errors in responding to customer inquiries."	Error rate will reflect adequacy of information system.
Timeliness	"X percent of inquiries to be handled while customer is on the phone."	Provision should be made for follow-up on inquiries referred to other departments.
Callbacks	"All callbacks to be made at the promised time, whether or not there is anything new to report."	Very important from the customer's point of view.

Other: above minimum order, damage-free delivery, conformance to marking-labeling-packaging requirements, full palletloads, personnel performance standards, security and other standards as appropriate.

SOURCE: *Practical Handbook of Distribution Customer Service*, (Warren Blanding, Washington, D.C.: The Traffic Service Corporation, 1985), 132–133. Used with permission.

The concern with customer service is receiving increasing top management attention as reflected in the immense popularity of the book *In Search of Excellence*[10] and its sequel, *A Passion for Excellence*.[11] It is noteworthy that the chapter on staying "Close to the Customer" in the former, the most popular management book of all time, became one of three central themes in the sequel.

Measurement

Measurement of logistics service performance must be consistent with definitions used for customer service standards, must be current, and must be carried out at reasonable cost. It varies in difficulty with the scope of the customer service cycle being measured.

Unfortunately, customer service standards are too often defined in terms of what can be *easily measured* rather than what is *relevant* to the performance of a logistics system. For example, it may be convenient to record the percentage of orders picked, packed, and shipped within 24 hours of order receipt at a supply point. However, this measure provides information about only a small and relatively unimportant element in the order cycle. A management deluded into thinking that it has measured customer service adequately with such information perhaps would be better off not collecting it at all.

An excellent example of this problem was a manufacturer of industrial expendables with a policy of filling 95 percent of all individual line items appearing on customer orders from stock. In fact, company executives cited computer-generated information indicating that inventories were being controlled in such a way that the standard was being met. Continued customer complaints led to an investigation and the discovery that an average order contained approximately four line items. Thus, if all items appeared on orders with about the same frequency, one out of every five orders (totaling 20 line items × 95 percent line-item coverage) would contain an out-of-stock item. The resulting 80 percent order-fill rate produced by a 95 percent item-fill policy was not acceptable to many of the company's customers.

Interestingly, in terms of cost to the manufacturer in this case, unfilled orders were a more significant indicator of back-order costs than unfilled line items. From the standpoint of both the supplier and the customer, an order-fill measure was more relevant.

Customer-oriented standards of service are the most relevant aspect of customer service program design. Their measurement requires the cooperation of both customers and carriers in providing information about time in transit, schedule dependability, and the condition in which goods arrived. Realistically, three dates can be found for every order: (1) the date of the order, (2) the date on the bill of lading indicating order shipment, and (3) the date on a dock receipt signed by the customer at the time of delivery. The first two are often available in the supplier's files. The third will be held by the carrier or by the customer receiving the shipment or sometimes by both. While these dates do not fully "time" the order cycle, they provide the most complete readily available information considering the time and effort likely to be expended to get and record them. The "missing" element is whatever time elapsed prior to actual receipt of the customer's order by the supplier — the initial stage of the order cycle — and this is difficult, if not impossible, to determine.

Customer and carrier cooperation can be obtained for measurement purposes, particularly if the effort is well-defined and conducted on a current basis. After all, if such measurement can lead to improved performance, the customer ought to be easily convinced of the value of measurement. If the carrier values the supplier's business — and it should — it will be willing to assist in the monitoring effort as a part of the customer service package it provides to the supplier—the shipper.

The costs of carrying out an audit of many of the stages in an order cycle often require that such work be accomplished with a *sample* of orders pulled from the supplier's files. As in any statistical sampling process, care must be exercised to insure that an adequate and unbiased sample is obtained.

Requested information is much more likely to be obtained if it is solicited on a current basis. Requests for information about shipments tendered to carriers should be made of the carrier's representatives at the time the shipment is initiated. Information requested of customers may be obtained by means of short response forms attached to the shipment or invoice for completion and return to the supplier. Such forms typically are useful only for determining the date of the receipt of the shipment and the condition in which the goods arrive at their destination.

More detailed information may be obtained on a periodic basis by salespersons or other representatives of the supplier's organization. Information pertaining to randomly preselected customer orders, using proper sampling techniques, may be more precise and less biased than that volunteered by the customer on a nonsystematic basis.

An alternative to the sampling of documents for fixing service levels is to survey customers' attitudes toward a company's logistics service compared to those of its competitors. As part of their market research efforts, many firms devote considerable attention to how their customers view the firm's products, yet fail to determine their customers' views on the adequacy of their customer logistics service policies. These views may be critically important, particularly if there is little product differentiation between competing firms. As Martin Christopher points out, "There is . . . a great premium to be placed on gaining an insight into the factors that influence buyer behavior and, in the context of customer service, which particular elements are seen by the customer to be the most important."[12]

Without a systematic collection of information, organizations are prone to manage customer service by the "half-deaf ear to the ground" approach, relying on customer complaints as the measure of service. This approach delegates responsibility for an important element of business to the customer. Customers may not perceive differences in service provided by competing suppliers in sufficiently accurate terms to be reliable sources for control information. Their reactions tend to be based on the most recent good or bad experience or most flagrant violation of expected performance. The systematic collection of information from a sample of customers on a continuing basis can help to avert this problem.

Implementation

Even after considering the elements discussed at some length above, a program of customer service management, no matter how well designed, may founder in implementation because of a tendency to overlook certain obvious elements of an effective program. Several elements that are commonly overlooked are discussed here as representative of a much longer list of possible pitfalls.

Failure to Consider Human Aspects of the System   Customers are human. It is increasingly easy in a machine age to overlook this fact. Several companies have encountered adverse customer reaction to the installation of a central order-processing facility requiring communication by long-distance telephone, even when the calls can be made toll-free. Even though goods continued to be shipped in such cases from the same decentralized supply points, customers were found to prefer dealing with supplier account representatives (order takers) located closer to them. In some cases, suppliers have created telephone switching systems that allow them to make customers feel they are dealing with an account representative "close to home" when in fact their orders are received and processed centrally. However, such a policy can backfire if the customer has a problem requiring "local" knowledge and the order taker is unable to solve the problem or provide helpful information to the customer.

Failure to Establish Procedures for "Nonstandard" Situations Many companies operate as if back orders, for example, never occur, even though few companies are immune from that plague. They fail to establish a routine for dealing with back-order situations. As a result, such matters are handled in nonroutine, expensive ways. The worst problem resulting from back orders, for example, is the costly excess of duplicated stock checking and communication effort that they produce. One manufacturer of automotive parts estimated that 85 percent of the capacity of its phone lines was consumed by communications resulting from back orders, a load that significantly interfered with major functions of the company. Yet, a manufacturer of home and industrial tools generates two back orders (individual items) for every multi-item order received, but is able to handle the resulting back-order load without a major disruption to its order operations. Problems resulting from "nonroutine" occurrences can be dealt with by (1) limiting the alternatives for resolving back-order or other "nonstandard" problems and situations; (2) providing special routing for messages and product involved in back orders; and (3) issuing procedures designed to assign all responsibilities for resolving "nonstandard" situations to a separately identified group of specialists, for example, "troubleshooters" or "expediters."

Failure to Invest Sufficient Time and Effort in Communicating Programs to the Customer Most adverse customer reaction to system innovations can be traced to a failure to orient the customer to the advantage to be received from the innovation and the ease with which the customer's personnel can adapt to it. The time and money required to communicate a change in the logistics service program to customers may represent the most important investment that a supplier can make to insure the success of a well-designed program.

Certainly one of the most important reasons for providing excellent customer service is that holding on to a customer costs far less than acquiring a new one. As an article in *Fortune* magazine pointed out, providing good customer service takes a lot of hard work, but the payoff comes in building loyal repeat buyers. *Fortune* estimates the cost of holding onto a customer to be only one-fifth the cost of acquiring a new one.[13]

One of the more difficult situations facing a company is, as Keiser puts it, "What do you do when your customer turns into Attila the Hun?" Keiser suggests eight ways to save a disintegrating sale:

1. Prepare by knowing your walkaway and by building the number of variables you can work with during the negotiation.*

2. When under attack, listen.

---

*"Walkaway" means the point beyond which you will not go—you will walk away.

3. Keep track of the issues requiring discussion.

4. Assert your company's needs.

5. Commit to a solution only after it's certain to work for both parties.

6. Save the hardest issues for last.

7. Start high and concede slowly.

8. Don't be trapped by emotional blackmail.[14]

Control "We checked transit times several years ago and found them to be satisfactory." "We don't get many service complaints; therefore, we assume we're doing all right." These types of comments are often made in response to inquiries about supplier control efforts. And while customer service may be controlled under the philosophy that it is a by-product of the system, such an approach may overlook opportunities for gaining competitive advantages.

Logistics service control can be incorporated as part of a broader program for controlling all aspects of logistics management. Specifically, once the appropriate measures and standards of performance are established, information about them should be reported up through the organization; they should be taken into account in evaluating performance; and they should form the basis for corrective action, which, when possible, has been planned in advance as part of the program.

At a given distribution center or at the corporate level, a company may employ periodic reports indicating items such as:

1. Proportion of line items shipped versus ordered.

2. Proportion of orders filled completely within a time after their receipt, with a tabulation of reasons for nonperformance.

3. Proportion of emergency orders in the total processed.

4. Proportion of air freight (or other premium transportation) costs in total transportation costs in a warehouse region or on a corporate wide basis.

5. Sampled customer replenishment cycle times.

6. Transit times and their variability between given points, by carrier.

In using such measures to evaluate individual performance, care must be taken to insure that managers so measured have a reasonable amount of control over the activity being measured. Further, it is important that they have continuing knowledge of their performance ratings as well as information about how to improve their performance levels. Finally, the most effective programs involve the individual manager in establishing his or her own standards of performance.

Control detached from corrective action and future planning is like a broken electrical circuit. The mere existence and knowledge of a system of service measurement and control often will influence performance. This, in combination with the development of explicit procedures for coupling the control program with appropriate corrective actions will contribute to an effective program.

SUMMARY

A customer may require financial, marketing, product, and logistical support. This discussion has concentrated on the latter. Logistical support may be measured in terms of product availability at the time, at the place, and in the quantities desired; relative freedom in the manner and timing with which orders can be received from customers for processing; the condition in which ordered goods are delivered to customers; and the speed and dependability with which items ordered can be made available to the customer.

The product availability feature of customer service can be treated in terms of the order cycle. The order cycle is one of the most basic concepts for logistics management, and provides the foundation for an understanding of the role of demand forecasting and inventory theory, to be discussed in Chapter 6.

The effective management of customer logistics service requires that service be defined, standards for its management established, measurement be carried out, and necessary corrective action be taken. In implementing the program, it is important to take note of the human aspects of the system, establish procedures for "nonstandard" situations, and invest sufficient time and effort in communicating the program to customers. Adequate control requires that previously established measurement efforts be used to provide feedback to allow operating managers to compare their performance against standards.

The ultimate test of any customer logistics service program is its relevance to the overall goals of the company, customer needs, and competitive behavior, as well as the manner in which those needs vary by customer, product line, individual products, geographic territory, and point in time.

DISCUSSION QUESTIONS

1. What are the four types of support activities in the customer service package?

2. To what extent and in what ways are logistics considerations involved in the other customer support activities? Give examples from the text or from your own experience.

3. Why are the order cycle and the replenishment cycle so similar? In what respect(s) *do* they differ?

4. Which step in the order cycle commonly offers the greatest opportunity for improvement? Why? Explain.

5. What is a "management program" for customer logistics service? Can you name and explain the significance of all nine of the points to be considered in developing such a program?

6. What is meant by "product substitutability" and what is its significance in regard to customer logistics service? Explain.

7. What is a "back order"? What problem(s) does it create? How can a firm cope with this problem? Explain.

8. What aspects of customer logistics service are easier to measure? Why?

9. What aspects of customer logistics service are difficult to measure? Why?

10. You are the purchasing and materials manager for a firm. You are evaluating two suppliers. One has a relatively short average lead time, but the firm only meets the promised date 80 percent of the time. The other takes about two weeks longer but delivers about 95 percent of the time on the promised date. Which should you select, and why?

CASE: DIFFERING VIEWS ON CUSTOMER SERVICE AND ORDER-FILL RATES

At a Council of Logistics Management Roundtable meeting, a discussion among several logistics managers grew a bit heated. The subject of their discussion was order-fill rates. Their disagreement stemmed from how each viewed the question of the relationship of order-fill rates to customer service levels.

A logistics manager who had been "kibitzing" the discussion, but had not been taking part in it, sought to help by pointing out that each of the three disputants was advocating a different way in which an order-fill rate could be defined: (1) the percentage of line items* partially filled, (2) the percentage of the total of all units of all line items filled, and (3) the percentage of line items in an order not filled at all versus the percentage of line items filled completely.

Although the kibitzer's comments had clarified the matter, they did not clear the air. The argument continued, with each of the logistics managers maintaining that his or her definition was the right one.

Finally, the kibitzer could take it no longer, and asked, "Is it possible that each of you is right? Could it be that a particular definition of order-fill rate and its relationship to customer service is appropriate in one industry, but not in another?"

---

*A "line item" is one of the items on a customer's order. The order for a line item may be for one "unit" of that item or for any larger quantity of that item. For example, a customer order might contain 30 line items, with the quantity of each being ordered ranging from 1 to 50 for a total of, say, 600 units for the whole order.

CASE QUESTION

1. Can you settle the argument? Who is right, or are they all right? If they are all right, for what industry or industries might each of the several definitions be appropriate?

SUGGESTED READINGS

BLANDING, WARREN, *Practical Handbook of Distribution Customer Service*, Washington, D.C.: The Traffic Service Corporation, 1985. This 564-page handbook is a definitive treatment of customer service principles and practices. Written by an outstanding authority in the field, it is extremely well organized and provides a balanced treatment of both theory and practice.

BOWERSOX, DONALD J. (Principal Researcher, Michigan State University), *Leading Edge Logistics: Competitive Positioning for the 1990's*, Oak Brook, Illinois: Council of Logistics Management, 1989. This is a comprehensive survey of "leading edge" firms with respect to their management of the logistics function. It provides an excellent overview of logistics policies, practices, and procedures reported in 909 questionnaires and 100 interviews in a cross section of industry sectors and leading firms within those industries. There is an obvious and strong correlation between being on the "leading edge" of logistics practice and providing a high level of customer service.

CHRISTOPHER, MARTIN, "Creating Effective Policies for Customer Service," *International Journal of Physical Distribution and Materials Management*, 1983, pages 3–24. This 22-page article provides an excellent review of the literature relating to customer service as well as a very well organized six-step guide to the management of the customer service function.

GUSTAFSON, JOHN F., and RAYMOND RICHARD, "Customer Service in Physical Distribution," Parts I through V, appearing in the following issues of *Transportation & Distribution Management*: April, 1964, pages 19–21 and 24; May, 1964, pages 34–37; June, 1964, pages 34–37; July, 1964, pages 35–37; and August, 1964, pages 31–34. Despite its age, this series of articles is still "current" and it presents a comprehensive treatment of various aspects of managing customer service, including the determination of levels of required service, assigning organizational responsibilities for setting customer logistics service standards, and the control of performance.

HESKETT, JAMES L., *Service Breakthroughs: Changing the Rules of the Game*, New York: The Free Press, 1990. Although concerned exclusively with service industries (banking, hospitality, airlines, insurance, retailing), the customer service concepts dealt with offer useful insights to anyone concerned with delivery of customer satisfaction.

LALONDE, BERNARD J., and PAUL H. ZINSZER, *Customer Service: Meaning and Measurement*, Oak Brook, Illinois: Council of Logistics Management, formerly National Council of Physical Distribution Management, 1976. This 492-page volume offers an in-depth comprehensive study of the subject of customer service and presents extensive industry-by-industry data concerning product characteristics and distribution practices, physical distribution costs, and customer service needs. It contains a comprehensive review of the literature on physical aspects of customer service up to the time of the report. This study has emerged as a classic benchmark in the field of customer service. It has subsequently been updated by the two references cited immediately below.

LALONDE, BERNARD J., MARTHA COOPER, and T. NOORDEWIER, *Customer Service: A Management Perspective*, Oak Brook, Illinois: Council of Logistics Management, 1988. A successor study to the LaLonde and Zinszer study cited above. It focuses on the managerial concerns with the implementation, maintenance, and monitoring of customer service strategies. It represents the most comprehensive treatment of customer service from a logistics management point of view. *Appendixes H.1 and H.2 of this study contain more than 100 citations of customer service articles and research studies. The references in Appendix H.1 are annotated.*

LALONDE, BERNARD J., and MARTHA C. COOPER, *Partnerships in Providing Customer Service: A Third-Party Perspective*, Oak Brook, Illinois: Council of Logistics Management, 1989. This landmark study extends the concept of customer service to the provision of logistics services by third parties, such as public warehouses, transportation carriers, and electronic data interchange services. *Appendix G of this study contains 27 pages of annotated references on the topic of customer service through a third-party perspective.*

LEVY, MICHAEL, "Diminishing Returns for Customer Service," *International Journal of Physical Distribution and Materials Management*, 1981, vol. 11, no. 1, pages 14–24. An analysis of what pays off and what does not pay off in providing customer service.

LEVY, MICHAEL, "Customer Service: A Managerial Approach to Controlling Marketing Channel Conflict," *International Journal of Physical Distribution and Materials Management*, 1981, vol. 11, no. 7, pages 38–52. The author focuses on the fact that distribution channel members may have dissimilar or competing goals that may cause channel conflict. This article illustrates how these differences can be identified for conflict management purposes.

MARR, NORMAN E., "Do Managers Really Know what Service their Customers Require?" *International Journal of Physical Distribution and Materials Management*, 1980, vol. 10., no. 7, pages 433–444. The article develops the point that if you want to know what your customers want you have to ask them rather than assume you know.

NOVITSKY, MICHAEL P., and C. RICHARD POLZELLO, "Improving Customer Service: Nine Techniques that Work," *Production and Inventory Management*, Third Quarter, 1984, pages 102–113. The authors describe nine practical techniques for improving customer service without triggering a negative reaction to inventory or efficiency.

PETERS, THOMAS J., and NANCY K. AUSTIN, *A Passion for Excellence*, New York: Random House, Inc., 1985. This sequel to *In Search of Excellence* explores customer-focused activities in more detail. It extends the basic analysis of sources of excellence in more industries and in a wider range of company sizes.

PETERS, THOMAS J., and ROBERT H. WATERMAN, JR., *In Search of Excellence: Lessons from America's Best-Run Companies*, New York: Harper & Row, Publishers, Inc., 1982. This book is an analysis of factors that account for excellence by selected firms in a wide variety of industries. It captured the interest of readers globally and has been translated into 15 different languages. The book sold more than five million copies world-wide. Although one chapter was dedicated to the specific subject of customer relationships, the entire book reflects a central theme of customer satisfaction for the basis of business success and industry leadership.

SCHARY, PHILLIP B., and MARTIN CHRISTOPHER, "The Anatomy of a Stock-Out," *Journal of Retailing*, Summer, 1979, pages 59–70. The article analyzes the frequency with which stockouts trigger various types of buyer behavior and the relative importance of stockouts in influencing customer perceptions of service.

SCHARY, PHILLIP B., "Management Control over Customer Service," *International Journal of Physical Distribution and Materials Management*, 1980, vol. 10. no. 4, pages 147–159. In this article the author develops the theme that firms seldom have complete control over customer service, particularly when one considers that customers may delay in placing an order, transportation carriers may cause delays or damage to shipments, and so forth.

SHYCON, HARVEY N., and CHRISTOPHER R. SPRAGUE, "Put a Price Tag on Your Customer Service Levels," *Harvard Business Review*, July-August, 1975, pages 71–78. The authors quantify, based on two field studies, the current and future costs of a product stockout and offer suggestions concerning ways of assessing the most profitable levels of service.

TUCKER, FRANCES GAITHER, "Creative Customer Service Management," *International Journal of Physical Distribution and Materials Management*, 1983, vol. 13, no. 3, pages 34–50. A major conclusion reached in this article is that a broad marketing orientation to customer service will be concerned with the entire channel of distribution, for example, how the manufacturer is able to service the wholesaler so that the wholesaler can, in turn, service retailers.

ENDNOTES

1. Bernard J. LaLonde and Paul R. Zinszer, *Customer Service: Meaning and Measurement* (Chicago: National Council of Physical Distribution Management, 1976): 116–17.

2. Jack Falvey, "Customer Service: Who Delivers?" *Sky* (March 1985): 67.

3. These are not references to industrial espionage or to stealing trade secrets. For most industries there is usually a wealth of publicly available information concerning the market and one's chief competitors. What is difficult is the task of assembling this information in useful form. Doing so is perfectly ethical conduct — it is simply market research — but it takes time and effort, which is why it is so appreciated by customers.

4. Peter Petre, "How to Keep Customers Happy Captives," *Fortune* (September 2, 1985): 42–48.

5. Theodore Levitt, "Marketing Myopia," *Harvard Business Review* (July–August, 1960): 50.

6. "Information Power: How Companies are Using New Techniques to Gain a Competitive Edge," *Business Week* (October 14, 1985): 109.

7. *Ibid*. 114.

8. Philip Crosby. *Quality is Free: The Art of Making Certain* (New York: McGraw-Hill, 1979).

9. James L. Heskett, "Predictive Value of Classroom Simulation," in William S. Decker, ed., *Emerging Concepts in Marketing* (Chicago: American Marketing Association, 1963): 101–15. A follow-up field study of actual business decisions offered confirmation of laboratory findings. For some results of this work, see John I. Rider, *An Evaluation of the Predictive Value of Observational Gaming*, an unpublished Master's thesis deposited in the library of the Ohio State University, 1963.

10. Thomas J. Peters and Robert H. Waterman, Jr., *In Search of Excellence: Lessons from America's Best-Run Companies* (New York: Harper & Row, Publishers, Inc., 1982).

11. Thomas J. Peters and Nancy K. Austin, *A Passion for Excellence* (New York: Random House, Inc., 1985).

12. Martin Christopher, "Creating Effective Policies for Customer Service," *International Journal of Physical Distribution and Materials Management* (1983): 6–7.

13. "Getting Customers to Love You," *Fortune* (March 13, 1989): 38–49.

14. Thomas C. Keiser, "Negotiating with a Customer You Can't Afford to Lose," *Harvard Business Review* (November–December, 1988): 30–34.

Sound inventory control practices are the heart of a successful business logistics system.

CHAPTER FIVE

5

Principles of Inventory Control

LEARNING OBJECTIVES

The objectives of this chapter are to:

➢ Discuss the reasons for holding inventories of goods in stock.

➢ Note the role of sales forecasting as a prerequisite to inventory control.

➢ Introduce and explain the concept of the economic order quantity model and some of its useful modifications.

➢ Explain the concept of total inventory costs as a basis for inventory management decisions.

➢ Differentiate between approaches to inventory control under conditions of certainty and uncertainty.

➢ Discuss the differences between ''no replenishment'' and ''replenishment available'' inventory situations.

➢ Review the basic inventory models and their characteristics.

Inventory means different things to different managers. To a manufacturing manager, a warehouse full of raw materials is protection against having to shut down the production line, and a large stock of finished goods is a buffer that allows long production runs to be scheduled without irritating interruptions to meet emergency order demands from the sales force. To the sales force, inventory is highly desirable protection against losing sales because of product stockouts or a lack of repair or replacement parts for customers. Enlightened logistics management views inventory as a means to the end objective of meeting customer order service standards efficiently and effectively. A financial manager, however, may regard inventory as a necessary evil, one that should be minimized because of the investment it requires and the costs of carrying it. In today's electronic world, some firms are now investing and lending money on their own for the 16-hour overnight period rather than letting their local bank use these funds during this time. Financial managers in large firms have the opportunity to lend out company funds overnight, first in the Far East and then in Europe, and have it returned before business starts the next morning. Inventory has to compete with this electronic opportunity.

The objectives of this chapter are to explore the several purposes that inventory serves, the nature and limitations of inventory control models, and techniques for controlling inventory under conditions of certainty and uncertainty. This will provide sufficient background to examine practical approaches to inventory management programs in Chapter 6.

REASONS FOR HOLDING INVENTORY

The chairman of a large consumer goods manufacturer once stated that "every management mistake ends up in inventory." While there may be a grain of truth in the statement, there are many positive reasons for creating and maintaining inventories. In practice, stocks of inventory may be planned as:

a way of facilitating more efficient, less costly, longer production runs in excess of the amounts that might be sold immediately;

a buffer against seasonal production or sales patterns;

protection against uncertainties in, or disruptions to, the supply process;

a means of taking advantage of quantity price discounts, dating plans for early delivery, or transport freight rate breaks on larger shipments;

a hedge against future price increases;

part of a strategy of locating dedicated stocks of finished good or repair/replacement parts near valued customers;

a way of protecting against undesired stockouts caused by mistaken sales forecasts or variations in the time required to replenish a depleted stock.

Production Savings

Longer production runs require fewer machine setups and lead to higher productivity and lower costs so far as production operations are concerned. For example, consider a firm operating a plant producing 50 units per hour on an 80-hour-per-week, two-shift basis with setup costs (to change the line to produce wambits instead of ratchets) of $500 per setup in addition to four hours of lost production. With weekly fixed costs of $8,000 and variable costs per unit of $2 (for labor and materials), the plant can produce 4,000 units per week at a total cost of $16,000, or $4 per unit, assuming there are no interruptions to change production from one item to another. The effect on production costs of successively greater numbers of setups per week is shown in Table 5–1.

Long production runs often create inventories in excess of current demand. But, the production cost savings achieved may be worth it. And, the "excess" inventory may also serve other purposes profitably. Finally, in some cases, such as processing ripening crops, there may be no alternative to a long or "full" production run.

A Buffer against Seasonality

Apples ripen once a year. In order to make them available year-round, apple growers store them under climate-controlled conditions. Although costly, this practice produces greater profits (and more satisfied apple eaters) than throwing away apples that could not be consumed in season. Conversely, if snow shovels were produced only as people needed them, everyone would have to go to work in a shovel plant the day of the first winter storm. To avoid this costly practice, a small labor force working through the fall season produces and stocks snow shovels in sufficient quantity to meet peak winter demands.

Protection against Disruptions in Supply Lines

Automobile manufacturers may accumulate inventories of raw materials in anticipation of a pending strike in their suppliers' steel mills. Although expensive, the practice may be less costly than being unable to meet customer demands for automobiles during or immediately

TABLE 5–1: The Effect of Setups (Machine Changeovers) on Production Efficiencies and Costs

Number of Setups per Week	Hours of Production Lost to Setups	Productive Hours per Week	Production for the Week (at 50 Units per Hour)	Setup Costs (at $500 per Setup)	Fixed Costs	Variable Costs (at $2 per Unit)	Total Production Cost	Production Cost per Unit
0	0	80	4,000	0	$8,000	$8,000	$16,000	$4.00
1	4	76	3,800	500	$8,000	$7,600	$16,100	$4.24
2	8	72	3,600	1,000	$8,000	$7,200	$16,200	$4.50
3	12	68	3,400	1,500	$8,000	$6,800	$16,300	$4.80

following such a supplier strike. In recent years, disruptions in the supply lines for many basic raw materials, such as petroleum products and newsprint, have led to the stockpiling of these items by anxious customers. Many governments maintain stockpiles of imported "critical" materials necessary for economic survival in case supplies of these are cut off by international events.

Taking Advantage of Price Breaks

Purchasing managers are sometimes offered "good deals" — incentives to stock in excess of the amount needed to satisfy immediate demand. These may be price discounts on purchases of large quantities in excess of immediate needs. Or they may reflect opportunities for early delivery on goods with the incentive of an extra period of time for payment under so-called "dating plans." Managers in traffic departments may recommend purchases of vehicle loads instead of smaller quantities as a means of obtaining lower transportation cost per unit shipped.

A Hedge against Future Price Increases

Price increases often are announced ahead of time, sometimes to stimulate sales. And it may be a smart move for a purchaser to buy in advance of need in order to insure lower future costs.

A Strategy for Customer-Oriented Stock Locations

Container manufacturers have, on occasion, committed themselves to patronizing suppliers willing to warehouse quantities of raw materials literally next door to their can factories. Charges for these materials, for example, aluminum cans, are levied only as they are used. While such practices result in higher-than-normal inventories for suppliers, they help insure sales in highly competitive industries.

Protection against Unexpected Sales Demands

Nearly all of the reasons for holding inventory discussed thus far warrant building stocks because of known future price changes, seasonal demands, seasonal supply patterns, strikes, and so on. In addition, inventories may be held as protection against uncertainties about sales patterns and the ability of sources of supply to respond to needs to replenish depleted stocks. These are called "safety stocks" or "just-in-case" stocks.

The combined effect of uncertain customer demand and supplier ability to deliver is defined as the total elapsed time between the moment an order is placed and the time the ordered products become available for sale or use by the customer.

These uncertainties suggest that a firm might (1) try to do a better job of forecasting sales demands, (2) attempt to reduce variation in times required for replenishment from suppliers, or (3) build larger buffer or safety stocks as protection. The latter alternative is accomplished by raising the *trigger point* — the level of inventory on hand that indicates that a replenishment order be placed.

Either of the first two alternatives above might be accomplished at relatively little cost by alert and intelligent management. The third alternative, however, will certainly increase capital investment in inventory and the firm's inventory carrying costs. Figure 5–1 illustrates graphically what happens when demand "overcomes" supply.

Figure 5–2 shows the two effects of increasing safety stock: (1) the stockout is avoided, but (2) investment in inventory is heavily increased. This suggests that economical inventory management depends on accurate sales forecasts.

Figure 5–1: Stockout impact of longer than normal replenishment cycle

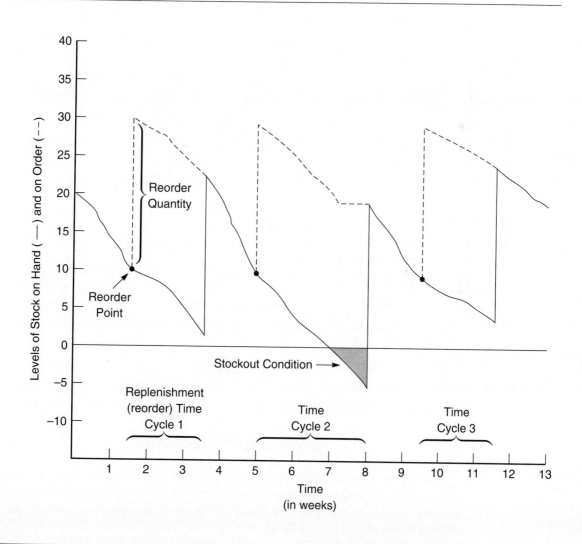

Figure 5–2: Avoidance of stockout resulting from increasing the reorder point and thereby carrying a larger safety stock inventory

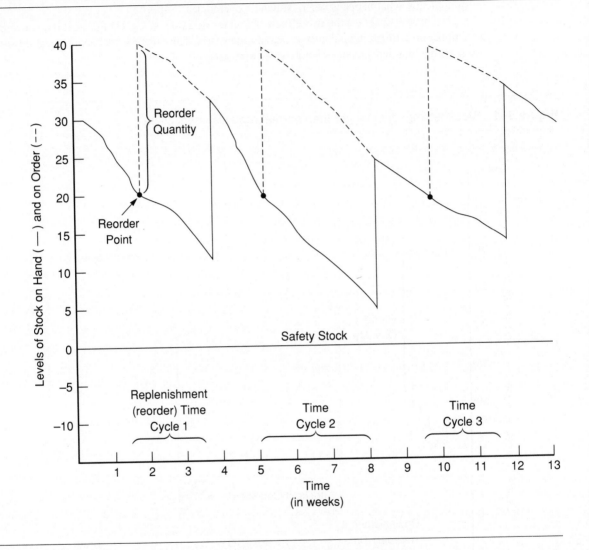

INVENTORY FORECASTING

All businesses must make forecasts in a variety of areas. Financial managers are concerned with forecasting interest rates, inflation rates, general economic conditions, trends in financial markets (both domestic and international), and so on. Personnel managers are concerned with forecasting staffing needs based on employee retirements, attrition, promotions, transfers, and more. Production and operations managers are concerned with forecasting technological developments, equipment life, costs and availability of raw materials, and so forth.

Marketing managers are concerned with forecasting sales demand for the firm's products. Logistics managers are dependent on sales forecasts made by marketing managers. Forecasting sales demand is *not* a logistics management function.

Sales forecasts should be made in terms of both dollars of revenue as well as product units. For purposes of sales management, such forecasts are frequently broken down by sales territory and product lines. However, the sales forecast that satisfies the needs of the marketing manager may fall far short of the needs of the logistics manager.

For example, sales territories may not be congruent with territories served by distribution warehouses. Dollar volume forecasts for the company as a whole, or even by sales territories and broad product lines, are useless to the logistics manager. Inventory planning and control by logistics managers requires that forecasts furnished by the marketing department be expressed in terms that enable the logistics manager to know future requirements for production, storage, and distribution of each individual item produced by the company for sale.

Because the sales forecasting function resides in the marketing department and is *not* a logistics function, forecasting techniques and methodologies will not be treated in this book. The interested reader is referred to any standard marketing or statistics text that treats sales forecasting.

THE ECONOMIC ORDER QUANTITY (EOQ) MODEL

Assuming for the moment that a marketing manager has furnished a sales forecast in terms that meet the needs of a logistics manager, the logistics manager can then concentrate on the task of inventory control. Consider this situation: the task is to determine the purchase quantity that will enable the small appliance department of an electrical goods distributor to replenish its stock of alarm clocks in such a way that the distributor incurs the lowest possible inventory ordering and carrying costs over a period of a year. The firm believes that it will be able to sell 400 alarm clocks, costing $20 each, over the coming year. It will cost 25 percent of the value, or $5, for each alarm clock held in inventory for an entire year.* Each order to replenish stock costs $10 in administrative costs to place. How many alarm clocks should be ordered at a time?

One way to approach the problem is to try several different order quantities and display in tabular form the total annual ordering and holding costs produced by each. The results of such an effort are shown in Table 5–2. Table 5–2 shows that as larger and larger order quantities are tried, the ordering costs decline but the inventory holding costs increase. At some point the *total* of the two costs (ordering and inventory holding) will be at a minimum. In the table, the total cost minimum is at an order quantity of 40 units placed 10 times per year.

Another way to display total inventory cost and the relationship between ordering cost and inventory carrying cost is to graph the costs and quantities involved. Figure 5–3 illustrates this. The lowest total cost can be read as $200 at an economic order quantity of 40 clocks. The

---

*Inventory carrying cost includes interest (actual or imputed) on the capital invested; costs of storage and handling; insurance; obsolescence; and loss through damage, spoilage or pilferage. This cost will vary considerably with the type of goods involved. In the past, a "benchmark figure" commonly used for annual inventory carrying cost was 25 percent of the average investment in inventory, but rising interest rates in recent years have increased this number substantially, and many firms now calculate their annual inventory carrying cost to be as high as 35 percent or even 40 percent. An excellent treatment of inventory costing is found in Zinszer, Paul H. "Inventory Costing: A Return on Inventory Approach to Differentiating Inventory Risk," *Journal of Business Logistics* 4, no. 2 (1983): 20–39.

Figure 5–3: Relationship of ordering costs, inventory carrying costs, total costs, and the economic order quantity (EOQ)

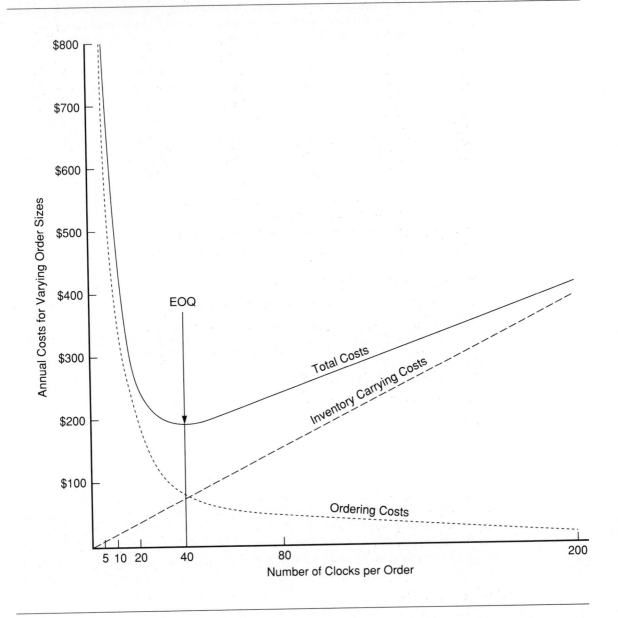

value of a graphic presentation is that one can see the pattern of cost relationships. The draw-backs — and they are substantial — are that graphs are time-consuming to draw and, if very large numbers are involved, they are difficult to graph or read accurately.

The graphic method illustrates the fact that in a zone close to the computed EOQ *the total cost curve is nearly flat*. Because of this, logistics managers are not overly concerned about ordering, or being required to order, a quantity as much as 25 percent more or less than the calculated EOQ. Such action is often necessary when items must be ordered in dozens or some other fixed number. Thus, if alarm clocks could *only* be ordered by the distributor from the manufacturer in *dozens*, either 36 or 48 (not 40) clocks would have to be ordered at a time. Since 36 is closer to 40 than 48, the order quantity would be 36 and the inventory costs would be $201.10, as contrasted with the optimum EOQ cost of $200.

The Basic EOQ Model

There should be some quicker way to relate the components of this problem, and there is. It was discovered late in the nineteenth century by various individuals, but no one knows for sure who developed it first. It has come to be known as the Camp or Wilson Lot Size Model, or more anonymously as the EOQ (economic order quantity) model. Using it, the problem in Table 5–2 can be solved easily by stating total costs in the following manner:[1]

$$C = \frac{Qvr}{2} + \frac{AS}{Q}$$

where:

C = total inventory cost (in dollars)

Q = the quantity ordered (in units)

v = the average cost or value, per unit, of the product (in dollars)

r = the annual inventory carrying cost (as a percentage of the product cost or value)

A = the ordering or setup cost (in dollars per order or setup)

S = the annual demand or usage of the product (in units)

TABLE 5–2: Alternative Quantities for Use in Ordering Alarm Clocks by an Electrical Goods Distributor

(1) Order Quantity	(2) Orders per Year	(3) Average Inventory in Units[a]	(4) Ordering Costs (at $10 per Order)	(5) Inventory Carrying Costs[b]	(6) Total Costs (Columns 4 + 5)
5	80	2.5	$800	$12.50	$812.50
10	40	5	$400	$25.00	$425.00
20	20	10	$200	$50.00	$250.00
40	10	20	$100	$100.00	$200.00
80	5	40	$50	$200.00	$250.00
200	2	100	$20	$500.00	$520.00

[a]Calculated as one-half the order quantity on the assumption that the order arrives just as the last alarm clock is sold from the inventory, once again creating a beginning inventory the size of the order quantity to be sold over time down to zero units in stock.

[b]$5 per year per unit in average inventory.

From the equation for total cost a formula can be derived for the optimum value for Q, designated as Q^*:*

$$Q^* = \sqrt{\frac{2AS}{rv}}$$

Applying this formula to the information used in the intuitive approach to the problem in Table 5–2, one finds that:

$$Q^* = \sqrt{\frac{2(\$10)\,(400)}{.25(\$20)}}$$

$$Q^* = \sqrt{\frac{\$8000}{\$5}}$$

$$Q^* = \sqrt{1,600}$$

$$Q^* = 40 \text{ Units}$$

How does this compare with the lowest total cost order quantity found in Table 5–2?

One minor drawback to the "formula-computed EOQ" is that it yields only a number, with no accompanying "picture" (graph) or table. Thus, an error in computation may well go undetected unless the answer is so large or small as to be "impossible" on its face. For this reason, it is always desirable to check an EOQ formula computation carefully.

Before proceeding, it is useful to check out the model from the standpoint of common sense. The basic relationships in this model provide the foundation on which many inventory control procedures used in business rest. But, the highly restrictive assumptions of certainty about demand, the assumption of one price or cost for the product regardless of quantity, the lack of consideration for other related matters, such as differing transportation costs associated with various quantities ordered, all combine to make this a crude, but nonetheless robust, model. As previously noted, the "flat zone" around each side of the computed EOQ allows for purchase-quantity requirements, some degree of error in estimating demand, setup or purchasing costs, and carrying costs. Therefore, it is fair to say that the EOQ model gives a ballpark indication of the proper quantities to order, and it also gives you a way of testing sensitivities of the variables in the EOQ model equation.

It may be argued that order-placement costs are rarely a factor anymore. This is especially the case with fax machines on the production floor sending shipping releases to the supplier's production floors. Even systems contracts are eliminating cumbersome purchase orders today. However, the degree of order-cost significance depends on what subcosts a firm includes in this category. If, for example, the only cost charged is the preparation of a purchase order, then the argument is valid. If, however, a firm includes such things as processing receipt of the

---

*This is achieved by setting C equal to a minimum value, zero, taking the first derivative of the cost equation, and solving for Q. Throughout the book, so-called optimums will be designated by an asterisk (*) in addition to the regular symbol.

shipment, processing payment to the vendor through the accounting department, placing the items in inventory, and so on, as part of the order-cost, then the argument no longer holds.

Adjustments to the Basic EOQ Model

There is a wide variety of special circumstances that might require a particular firm to adjust its economic order quantity in some special fashion tailored to its needs. However, there are two types of adjustment to the basic EOQ model that occur particularly frequently and merit specific treatment here. The first of these involves adjustments as a result of discounts offered by suppliers. The second involves production operations situations where parts are produced faster than they are used in the production activity. The latter situation is commonly referred to as *noninstantaneous resupply*.

Quantity Discounts Any business person responsible for purchasing products or transportation services will often be faced with the question of whether or not to ''take advantage of a discount.'' The discount may be in the form of a price reduction for purchasing a larger quantity of goods at one time or a lower per unit transportation rate (price) for a larger shipment or both. In each case, the result of a larger purchase quantity will be a larger average inventory on hand with fewer orders being placed. The question for the buyer is whether it will be advantageous to order a larger quantity if offered a discount.

The question can be answered by a relatively simple two-stage calculation. First, calculate the EOQ resulting from ordering at the lowest price (highest discount). If the resulting EOQ is at or above the quantity required to get the lowest price the problem is solved. However, if the resulting EOQ is *less* than the order quantity required for the best price, proceed to ''test'' the next higher price, and continue testing until a discount level is found that ''fits'' the EOQ (the problem is solved), or until all discount levels have been checked out. If no *discount level* results in a feasible EOQ, one must proceed to the second step.

The second step is to calculate the *total annual inventory cost* for each level of discount *and* the nondiscount (highest) price because this is what the ordering decision rests on: *the lowest total cost*.

Business Distributors, Inc. Example Business Distributors, Inc. (BDI) sells office furniture, including standard steel filing cabinets. BDI's supplier has offered a per-order discount schedule to BDI as follows:

Quantity Ordered	Price
One to six	$90 each
Seven to Twelve	$85 each
Thirteen or More	$80 each

BDI calculates its annual inventory carrying cost to be 40 percent, its cost of processing a purchase order to be $21, and BDI sells 30 of this model file cabinet each year. Should BDI order more than 6 of these file cabinets at a time to ''take advantage'' of the proffered discount? Previous to the supplier's offer, the price had been $90 per file cabinet regardless of the quantity ordered at one time by BDI and BDI's ordering quantity (EOQ) was:

$$Q^* = \sqrt{\frac{2AS}{rv}}$$

$$Q^* = \sqrt{\frac{2(30)(\$21)}{.40(\$90)}}$$

$$Q^* = \sqrt{\frac{1,260}{36}}$$

$$Q^* = \sqrt{35}$$

$$Q^* = 5.92 \text{ or } 6$$

BDI's buyer now checks out the lowest price on the supplier's discount schedule, $80:

$$Q^* = \sqrt{\frac{2AS}{rv}}$$

$$Q^* = \sqrt{\frac{2(30)(\$21)}{.40(80)}}$$

$$Q^* = \sqrt{\frac{\$1,260}{\$32}}$$

$$Q^* = \sqrt{39.37}$$

$$Q^* = 6.27 \text{ or } 6$$

An order for 6 file cabinets is not large enough (13 or more) to get the $80 price. BDI's buyer now tries the $85 price:

$$Q^* = \sqrt{\frac{2AS}{rv}}$$

$$Q^* = \sqrt{\frac{2(30)(\$21)}{.40(85)}}$$

$$Q^* = \sqrt{\frac{\$1,260}{\$31.20}}$$

$$Q^* = \sqrt{34}$$

$$Q^* = 5.83 \text{ or } 6$$

An order for 6 file cabinets is not large enough (7 to 12) to get the $85 price. So the EOQ remains at 6 at a price of $90 each.

However, BDI's buyer must now look at the total inventory cost in each case. Table 5–3 presents the situation (price levels) in tabular form, including an example based on ordering only two file cabinets at a time.

TABLE 5–3: Business Distributors, Inc. Total Inventory Cost for Varying Order
Sizes

Price Each	$ 90.00	$ 90.00	$ 85.00	$ 80.00
Order Size (units)	2	6	7	13
Number of Orders per Year	30	5	4.3	2.3
Average on Hand Inventory	1	3.0	3.5	6.5
Carrying Costs[a]	36.00	108.00	119.00	208.00
Purchase Cost ($\times 30$)	2,700.00	2,700.00	2,550.00	2,400.00
Ordering Cost ($21 per order)	315.00	105.00	90.30	48.30
TOTAL COST	$3,051.00	$2,913.00	$2,759.30	$2,656.30

[a].40 $\times$ $90 unit $\times$ one unit average inventory on hand.

The *lowest total cost* is achieved by ordering 13 file cabinets each time. What happens is that the total annual price discount at that level ($300, or 30 $\times$ $10) and the ordering cost saving of $56.70 ($48.30 versus $105.00) are greater than the increased inventory carrying cost of $100 ($208 versus $108). BDI should therefore order 13 filing cabinets each time it places an order for them with its supplier. Tabular analysis (as in Table 5–3) is useful for illustrating "what is going on", but is usually too awkward and time consuming to use in practice. The algebraic method shown below is easier and faster than setting up and filling in a table.

Let:

C = total inventory cost

v = cost (price paid) per unit

S = annual demand (sales)

A = ordering (set-up) cost per order

Q = order quantity required at this price

r = annual inventory carrying cost percentage

2 = a divisor used to obtain average inventory on hand.

The total cost at the $90 (1 to 6 units) price level is:

$$C = vS + A(^S/_Q) + rv(^Q/_2)$$

$$C = \$90(30) + 21(^{30}/_6) + .4(90)(^6/_2)$$

$$C = \$2,700 + \$105 + \$108$$

$$C = \$2,913$$

The total cost at the $85 (7 to 12 units) price level is:

$$C = vS + A(^S/_Q) + rv(^Q/_2)$$

$$C = \$85(30) + \$21(^{30}\!/_7) + .4(85)(^7\!/_2)$$

$$C = \$2,550 + \$90 + \$119$$

$$C = \$2,759.00$$

The total cost at the $80 (13 or more units) price level is:

$$C = vS + A(^S/_Q) + rv(^Q/_2)$$

$$C = \$80(30) + \$21(^{30}\!/_{13}) + .4(80)(^{13}\!/_2)$$

$$C = \$2,400 + \$48.46 + \$208.00$$

$$C = \$2,656.46^*$$

There are, of course, other factors that a manager must consider when contemplating whether to take a quantity discount. For example, is there enough *storage space* to accommodate a larger on-hand inventory? Does the firm have the *capital* to invest in more inventory? Even if the firm has sufficient capital, will the Finance Department tolerate a higher inventory investment when other alternative uses of capital are available. If the answer to one or more such questions is NO, then the discount may have to be foregone.

Noninstantaneous Resupply Another common inventory situation occurs in production operations when parts, components or subassemblies are produced at a higher rate than they are used. For example, a machine in a bicycle factory can turn out handlebars at a rate of 120,000 a year, but only 52,000 are required. Bearing in mind that *some* of the handlebars are *used as they are produced*, how many handlebars should be produced at one time?

This is basically an EOQ problem, but with an added dimension. That is, the full amount of the order (the production run) does not arrive all at one time as is usually the case with purchased goods. It arrives as a "stream" of goods and can be pictured as shown in Figure 5–4.

To determine how many handlebars to machine at one time, all that is necessary is a modification of the EOQ formula to allow for the fact that handlebars are being used while the new supply is being made. The model further assumes that, just as the last handlebar in stock is used, production of handlebars can start again, as shown in Figure 5–4. The EOQ formula is modified by adding a second term, which expresses the fact that some handlebars are being used (S) while the new production supply (P) is being made. The modified EOQ formula is:

$$Q^* = \sqrt{\frac{2AS}{rv}} \ \sqrt{\frac{P}{P - S}}$$

---

*The very slight differences between the table totals and the solved equation totals are due to rounding.

Figure 5–4: Pattern of production and usage under conditions of noninstantaneous resupply. Q* calculated on the basis of the modified EOQ formula

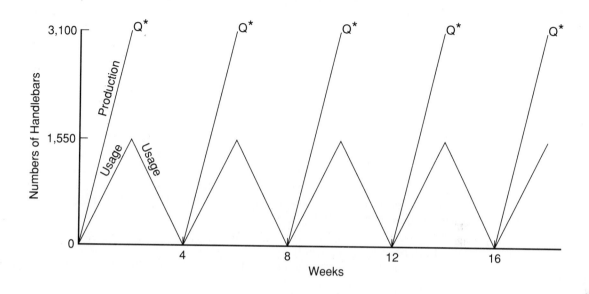

In the handlebar example, assume that the manufactured cost of each handlebar is $4, the annual inventory carrying cost is 36 percent, the setup cost for a production run is $75 and, as noted above, the annual usage is 52,000 (S) and the handlebar forming machine can produce 120,000 (P) a year.* The calculation is:

$$Q^* = \sqrt{\frac{2AS}{rv}} \ \sqrt{\frac{P}{P - S}}$$

$$Q^* = \sqrt{\frac{2(52,000)(\$75)}{.36(\$4)}} \times \sqrt{\frac{120,000}{120,000 - 52,000}}$$

$$Q^* = \sqrt{\frac{\$7,800,000}{\$1.44}} \times \sqrt{\frac{120,000}{68,000}}$$

$$Q^* = \sqrt{5,416,667} \times \sqrt{1.765}$$

$$Q^* = 2,327 \times 1.33$$

$$Q^* = 3,095 \text{ or } 3,100 \text{ (about one production run}$$
$$\text{every three weeks or 17 runs a year}$$
$$\text{for annual usage of 52,000).}$$

---

*Production and usage rates can be stated in terms of any period of time, provided that *both* are stated for the *same* period of time, for example, per day, per week, per month, per year.

INVENTORY CONTROL UNDER UNCERTAINTY

The previous section examined inventory management issues under conditions of *certainty*. In the real world of logistics management the normal situation is one of *uncertainty*, either as to sales demand, time required for replenishment of inventory, or both. Inventory decisions made under conditions of uncertainty vary according to the supplier company's customer service standard for filling customer orders and replenishment time for incoming shipments.

Stock Level Determination without Replenishment

Determination of inventory levels is affected by the circumstances facing the logistics manager. A relatively simple situation occurs when the items to be stocked are ordered only once with no opportunity for replenishment prior to the end of the sales period. This type of situation occurs particularly in the case of seasonal merchandise having limited periods of demand and no opportunity for replenishment, such as that faced in stocking calendars or dated appointment books.

The Stationery Store Problem   The manager of Smedley's Stationery Store must place an order for next year's calendars in October of each year. Only one order can be placed because the supplier (publisher) will not risk a press run in excess of firm advance orders due to the total obsolescence of unsold calendars. The store manager knows that the sales of a particular expensive executive calendar have varied from a minimum of 4 to a maximum of 10 in previous years. Any calendars not sold must be thrown away as the supplier will not accept any returns. The manager knows the cost of these calendars ($9) and the price for which they are to be sold ($15). The question is: How many of these calendars to order this year?

Based on her long-term empirical experience, the manager should not order less than 4 nor more than 10 of these calendars. If the manager does not know what the likelihood of selling 4, 5, 6, 7, 8, 9, or 10 calendars is, she should order 6 calendars, as shown in Table 5–4 because that quantity has the highest expected value" of profit, in this instance $29.57. Alternatively, if she has historical sales information from previous years indicating the various probabilities of how many of these calendars will be sold, she would use these probabilities to calculate the "expected value" associated with various sales levels and order the quantity resulting in the highest expected value. Thus, in the example given in Table 5-5, she would order seven, which has an expected value of $40.25.

Stock Level Determination with Replenishment

Although there are business situations in which sales demand and replenishment times are known with certainty, by far the more common are situations where demand (sales) varies in an irregular and somewhat unpredictable manner, usually within historically known limits. Likewise, replenishment from a supplier will vary in terms of time. That is, actual shipment times will vary from expected "normal" schedules. Logistics managers must take these variations into account when planning inventory levels.

TABLE 5–4: Smedley's Stationery Store Inventory Ordering Decision under Conditions of Equally Probable Outcomes

Number of Calendars Purchased[a]	Demand for Calendars[b] that Could Have Been Sold							EV[e]
	4	5	6	7	8	9	10	
4	$24[c] [0][d]	$24 [1]	$24 [2]	$24 [3]	$24 [4]	$24 [5]	$24 [6]	$24.00
5	$15 [0]	$30 [0]	$30 [1]	$30 [2]	$30 [3]	$30 [4]	$30 [5]	$27.86
6	$6 [0]	$21 [0]	$36 [0]	$36 [1]	$36 [2]	$36 [3]	$36 [4]	$29.57
7	−$3 [0]	$12 [0]	$27 [0]	$42 [0]	$42 [1]	$42 [2]	$42 [3]	$29.14
8	−$12 [0]	$3 [0]	$18 [0]	$33 [0]	$48 [0]	$48 [1]	$48 [2]	$26.57
9	−$21 [0]	−$6 [0]	$9 [0]	$24 [0]	$39 [0]	$54 [0]	$54 [1]	$20.57
10	−$30 [0]	−$15 [0]	$0 [0]	$15 [0]	$30 [0]	$45 [0]	$60 [0]	$15.00

[a]Purchase cost is $9 per calendar.

[b]Sale price is $15 per calendar.

[c]Profit or loss for that number purchased and either sold or thrown away.

[d]Number within the brackets is the number of disappointed potential customers—lost sales.

[e]Expected Value (Profit) with no probability information (assuming equally probable outcomes).

TABLE 5–5: Smedley's Stationery Store Inventory Ordering Decision under Conditions of Historically Determined Probabilities

Number of Calendars Purchased[a]	Demand for Calendars[b] That Could Have Been Sold							EV[e]
	4	5	6	7	8	9	10	
4	$24[c] [0][d]	$24 [1]	$24 [2]	$24 [3]	$24 [4]	$24 [5]	$24 [6]	$24.00
5	$15 [0]	$30 [0]	$30 [1]	$30 [2]	$30 [3]	$30 [4]	$30 [5]	$29.95
6	$6 [0]	$21 [0]	$36 [0]	$36 [1]	$36 [2]	$36 [3]	$36 [4]	$33.00
7	−$3 [0]	$12 [0]	$27 [0]	$42 [0]	$42 [1]	$42 [2]	$42 [3]	$40.25
8	−$12 [0]	$3 [0]	$18 [0]	$33 [0]	$48 [0]	$48 [1]	$48 [2]	$40.25
9	−$21 [0]	−$6 [0]	$9 [0]	$24 [0]	$39 [0]	$54 [0]	$54 [1]	$30.00
10	−$30 [0]	−$15 [0]	$0 [0]	$15 [0]	$30 [0]	$45 [0]	$60 [0]	$23.25
								$15.00
Probability	5%	10%	20%	30%	20%	10%	5%	

[a]Purchase cost is $9 per calendar.

[b]Sale price is $15 per calendar.

[c]Profit or loss for that number purchased and either sold or thrown away.

[d]Number within the brackets is the number of disappointed potential customers—lost sales.

[e]Expected Value (Profit) with known probability information.

In practice, the most important decision to be made is the amount of *safety stock* to be kept on hand to protect against variations in sales volume and replenishment time. The problem is that on the one hand it costs money, both capital investment and inventory carrying cost, to stock inventory. On the other hand, having little or no safety stock results in stockouts for customer orders and possible or probable lost sales, temporary or permanent. To solve this problem it is necessary to make three calculations and one decision.

The Three Calculations

1. The variability of sales demand must be calculated using either historical data or estimates in the absence of such information.

2. The variability in transit times for receipt of stock replenishment from the supplier, again using either historical data or estimates in the absence of such information.

3. A calculation that combines the answers to 1 and 2 to determine the reorder point for the item.

The Decision Given that the company has estimated the variability in sales — if any — for an item, and the variability in lead time — if any — it must now determine the desired level of customer service (stock availability). Depending on the circumstances, particularly the extent

TABLE 5–6: Hardware Wholesalers, Inc. Sales History by Period and Quantity for Quarter-Inch Drills

Period[a]	Unit Sales	Period	Unit Sales
1	120	16	80
2	110	17	90
3	115	18	110
4	120	19	115
5	130	20	120
6	140	21	130
7	120	22	140
8	140	23	130
9	160	24	120
10	150	25	110
11	140	26	100
12	130	27	110
13	110	28	120
14	100	29	130
15	90	30	120
		TOTAL	3,600

$$X = {}^{3600}/_{30} = 120 \text{ average daily sales}$$

[a]Usually operating days, as in this example, but could be calendar days, weeks, or some other period if appropriate.

TABLE 5–7: Hardware Wholesalers, Inc. Frequency Distribution of Daily Sales and Calculation of Standard Deviation

Daily Unit Sales	Frequency of Occurrence (F)	Deviation from X (D)	Deviation Squared (D²)	FD²
80	1	−40	1,600	1,600
90	2	−30	900	1,800
100	2	−20	400	800
110	5	−10	100	500
115	4	−5	25	100
120	7	0	0	0
130	4	10	100	400
140	2	20	400	800
150	2	30	900	1,800
160	1	40	1,600	1,600
	N = 30			Sum of FD² = 9,400

$$\sigma = \sqrt{\frac{\Sigma FD^2}{N-1}}$$

$$\sigma = \sqrt{\frac{9,400}{29}}$$

$$\sigma = \sqrt{324}$$

$$\sigma = 18$$

to which customer service is a critical factor, a company might wish to maintain a 90 percent, 95 percent, 98 percent, or even a 99 + percent level of stock availability to fill customer orders or its own internal needs. The most common situation is one in which both lead time and sales demand are variable. Less common situations are those in which lead time is fixed but demand is variable and those in which lead time is variable but demand is fixed. The following problems illustrate these three types of situations, beginning with the most common.

The Drill Distributor Problem Hardware Wholesalers, Inc. (HWI) sells quarter-inch drills to retailers. HWI's sales history for quarter-inch drills over 30 operating days is shown in Table 5–6. HWI's logistics manager uses business operating days for all logistics planning. Allowing for weekends and holidays there are thus about 250 operating days in a year.

Given the sales history in Table 5–6, the standard deviation σ of the average daily sales figure can be calculated, as shown in Table 5–7, using the standard formula.

The value of σ, rounded to 18, means that about 68 percent of the time the daily sales figure of quarter-inch drills will be 120 ± 18 units. Since HWI only cares about covering orders for *more* than 120 units, they are concerned only about the *upper half* of the "uncovered" 32 percent (100 percent less about 16 percent). Thus, a safety stock calculated using one standard deviation will "protect" HWI about 84 percent of the time. But that may not be an acceptable level of customer logistics service. And, there is still the problem of replenishment time variability to be considered.

TABLE 5–8: Hardware Wholesalers, Inc. Data for Calculation of the Standard Deviation of the Replenishment Cycle Time

Observed Cycle Times for Replenishment	Frequency (F) of Each Observation	Deviation (D) from X	D^2	FD^2
11	1	−4	16	16
12	2	−3	9	18
13	3	−2	4	12
14	4	1	1	4
15	6	0	0	0
16	4	1	1	4
17	5	2	4	20
18	2	3	9	18
X = 15	N = 27			Sum of FD^2 = 92

$$\sigma = \sqrt{\frac{FD^2}{N-1}}$$

$$\sigma = \sqrt{\frac{92}{26}}$$

$$\sigma = \sqrt{3.54}$$

$$\sigma = 1.88$$

Table 5–8 presents an analysis of the variability of replenishment times for quarter-inch drills when ordered by HWI from its supplier. One standard deviation from the average time, 15 days, is 1.88 days. HWI's logistics manager now can combine customer-order variability with its supplier replenishment schedule variability to determine the reorder point and amount of safety stock needed for quarter-inch drills. Assume HWI's manager wants a customer service level of 99 percent for this very popular item. This is a **z** value of .9901 as shown in the appendix for this chapter (Areas Under the Normal Curve) on page 165.

The calculation of the reorder point is as follows:

$$ROP = \bar{d}\,\overline{LT} + z\sqrt{\overline{LT}\,\sigma^2 + \bar{d}^2\,\sigma^2}$$

$$= 120(15) + 2.33\sqrt{(15 \times 18^2) + (120^2 \times 1.88^2)}$$

$$= 1{,}800 + 2.33\sqrt{(15 \times 324) + (14{,}400 \times 3.53)}$$

$$= 1{,}800 + 2.33\sqrt{4{,}860 + 50{,}832}$$

$$= 1{,}800 + 2.33\sqrt{55{,}692}$$

$$= 1{,}800 + (2.33 \times 236)$$

$$= 1{,}800 + 550$$

$$= 2{,}350$$

where:

ROP = reorder point

$\bar{d}$ = average demand

$\overline{LT}$ = average lead time

z = desired customer service level (from Appendix 5-A)

σ_d = standard deviation of demand

σ_{LT} = standard deviation of lead time.

The first term of the above equation ($\bar{d} \times \overline{LT}$) represents the expected demand during the time required for replenishment. The second term of the equation (the z term) is the safety stock.

The next step is to calculate the EOQ for quarter-inch drills. Assuming annual sales of 30,000 (120 × 250 business days), a cost of $10 per drill, a carrying cost of 36 percent, the EOQ is calculated as:

$$Q^\star = \sqrt{\frac{2AS}{rv}}$$

$$Q^\star = \sqrt{\frac{2(30,000)(\$15)}{.36(\$10)}}$$

$$Q^\star = \sqrt{\frac{\$900,000}{\$3.60}}$$

$$Q^\star = \sqrt{250,000}$$

$$Q^\star = 500$$

The average stock on hand will be $Q^\star/2$, or 250 quarter-inch drills. To this must be added the desired level of safety stock. Of course HWI's manager might want to choose a different customer service level. Table 5–9 presents an array of choices for HWI management. The level of customer service (product availability) chosen is a *management decision*, weighing the cost of carrying more safety stock against the cost of lost sales or backorders and the resulting customer dissatisfaction. In the final analysis, the evaluation of such tradeoffs is a matter of *judgment*. One can "assign numbers" to the costs of lost sales, customer dissatisfaction, backorders, and so forth, but these are really only guesstimates; no two cost accountants (working independently and using their own judgment) are going to come up with the same numbers. Figure 5–5 presents the relationships of these trade-offs. Competition will influence the decision, usually in direct proportion to how strong it is.

If customers of HWI (the retailers) keep reasonable stocks of HWI quarter-inch drills themselves and once in a while can more or less conveniently replace an order and are willing to do so, a 95 percent or even a 90 percent service level may be good enough. Note that between the 95 percent and 99+ percent service levels the required HWI safety stock nearly *doubles* (708 versus 378 units). And, at the 90 percent level only 307 units of safety stock are required.

TABLE 5–9: Hardware Wholesalers, Inc. Safety Stock and Total Average Stock Quantities on Hand at Varying Customer Service Levels (Stock Availability)

Number of Standard Deviations	Customer Service Level[a]	Average Stock on Hand Above Safety Stock at this Level $(EOQ/_2)$	Safety Stock Required at this Level	Total Average Stock on Hand at this Level
1.0	84%	250	236	486
1.3	90%	250	307	557
1.6	95%	250	378	628
2.0	98%	250	472	722
3.0	99 + %	250	708	958

[a]These are rounded percentage numbers. The 99+ percent figure approaches, but does not reach, 100 percent.

The Kendall Hardware Store Problem Another type of reorder is the one in which sales demand varies but replenishment time is fixed. For example, the Kendall Hardware Store (KHS) sells quarter-inch drills. Sales of this item average 16 drills per day with a standard deviation of 3. There is no variability in replenishment time of one day because KHS's supplier (Hardware Wholesalers, Inc.) is located in the same city and maintains an ample stock of this item. KHS's problem is to determine its reorder point (ROP) for this item, considering the variability in sales and desired customer service level. The manager of KHS has decided that a customer service level of 98 percent is desirable for this item because it is so popular with the store's do-it-yourself customers. The calculation of the reorder point (including safety stock) is made as follows:

$$ROP = \bar{d}LT + z\sqrt{LT}\sigma_d$$

$$= 16(1) + 2.05\sqrt{1(3)}$$

$$= 16 + 2.05(1)(3)$$

$$= 16 + 2.05(3)$$

$$= 16 + 6.15 \text{ or } 6$$

$$= 22$$

where:

ROP = reorder point

$\bar{d}$ = average demand

LT = lead time

z = desired customer service level (from Appendix)

σ_d = standard deviation of demand

Figure 5–5: Trade-offs associated with inventory control under uncertainty

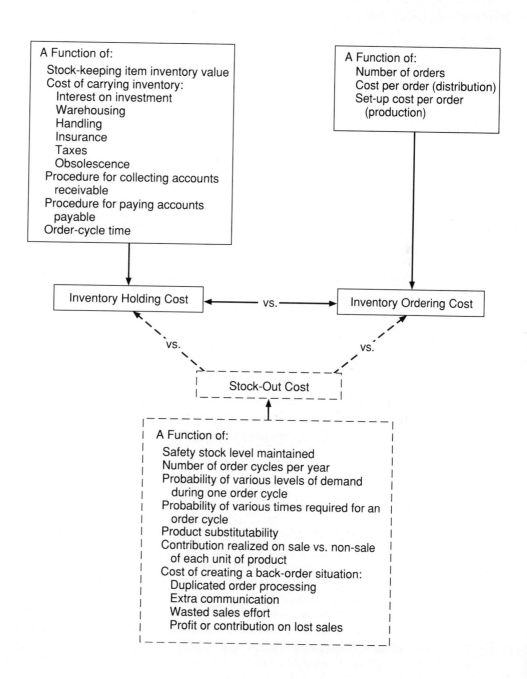

The Commercial Building Services Company Problem The third type of reorder point situation is the one in which the demand is fixed but the replenishment time is variable. For example, the Commercial Building Services Company (CBSC) uses 15 gallons of industrial floor wax each night to polish the floors in the buildings it maintains. The company's supplier is located in a distant city and replenishment lead time averages seven days with a standard deviation of two days. The company has limited storage space and could in an emergency obtain this floor wax locally, but at a much higher price than it pays its regular supplier. CBSC has, therefore, decided upon a service level of 94 percent. The company would calculate its reorder point using the following formula in which demand is fixed and lead time is variable.

$$ROP = d\,\overline{LT} + zd\,(\sigma_{LT})$$
$$= 15(7) = 1.555(15)(2)$$
$$= 105 + 1.555(30)$$
$$= 105 + 46.65 \text{ or } 47$$
$$= 152$$

where:

ROP = reorder point

d = demand

$\overline{LT}$ = average lead time

z = desired customer service level (from Appendix 5-A)

σ_{LT} = standard deviation of lead time

Thus, CBSC's reorder point for floor wax is 152 gallons, which includes a safety stock of 47 gallons.

Basic Inventory Control Models

It is safe to say that no two inventory control models in actual use are alike. If they do not vary in structure, at least they vary in the nature of the inputs used for computational purposes. Differences in terminology and symbolism further confuse anyone attempting to invade the mysterious and often private world of the inventory controller (particularly the green eye-shade variety). Much of the confusion can be credited to academicians and authors, many of whom use private symbols and definitions for a world already redefined many times by their predecessors. For these reasons, it is useful to review the basic structural forms that describe all formal inventory control models.

There are three considerations that all inventory control models must take into account. They are the order point, the order quantity, and the order interval.

Order point This is the moment in time when the uncommitted quantity of inventory on hand has dropped to a specified level.

Order quantity This is the amount to be ordered when an order is placed. It is determined by use of an EOQ (or modified EOQ) calculation.

Order interval This is the time interval between the placement of orders. It is a function of the order quantity (EOQ) and the total usage of the item over a period of time.

The order point (P), order quantity (Q), and order interval (R) may take on fixed or variable values, thereby in combination describing the basic models available for inventory control purposes. These elements are listed in Table 5–10, along with notations indicating elements typically associated with each type of control model.

Inventory control models incorporating features of both P and Q models are perhaps most popular in actual practice for items of low value. The most common of these is called variously the S,s, min-max, or optional replenishment approach.

The S,s Model The S,s model incorporates a fixed order point with a fixed order interval system. If the fixed order point is not reached at the time of the review of stock levels, *no order is placed*. This allows orders to be placed in efficient quantities and reduces costs resulting from the frequent placement of small orders. However, where stockout costs are significant (for example, significant lost sales or a production line shutdown), the amount of safety stock under an S,s model will have to be increased (often substantially) to guard against the possibility that the level on hand and on order at the time of a review may be only slightly above the order point and will be well below it at the time of the next order interval. For this reason, the S,s inventory model is primarily used for "nuts and bolts" inventories, that is, items of relatively low value, consumed at a fairly steady rate, and requiring little storage space. Office supplies (typewriter ribbons, stationery, pencils) are classic examples of S,s inventory items, ordered in routine fashion at the beginning of each week (or month) by the office manager. Quantities ordered are usually "judgmental"—based on usage histories—and take into account the fact that lead time is usually very short as such items are usually purchased locally.

In general, fixed order interval models result in higher average inventory levels than do those involving variable order intervals and fixed order points. However, they may provide savings from more efficient transportation quantities, more efficient ordering, and lower quantity discount prices that more than offset higher inventory carrying costs.

TABLE 5–10: Basic Features of Q, P, and S,s Inventory Models

Inventory Control Model Element	Form Assumed by Model Element in each Type of Model		
	Q Model	P Model	S,s Model
Order Point (P)	Fixed	Variable	Fixed
Order Quantity (Q)	Fixed	Variable	Fixed
Order Interval (R)	Variable	Fixed	Fixed

SUMMARY

Inventory may be accumulated for a number of reasons. Among the more important are its use as a way of facilitating larger, more efficient production runs, as a buffer against seasonal production or sales patterns, as protection against uncertainties in, or disruptions to, the supply process, as a means of taking advantage of price discounts or transportation rate breaks, as a hedge against future price increases, as part of a strategy of locating stocks nearer customers, and as a way of protecting against undesired stockouts resulting from uncertainties in sales or replenishment cycle times.

In order to provide sufficient inventories to accommodate sales expectations, it is necessary for the marketing department to forecast expected sales levels. Forecasts to be used for planning new manufacturing facilities, for example, may be long term in nature. For purposes of inventory control, however, forecasts over much shorter time periods and for individual stockkeeping units (SKUs) are needed.

The EOQ (economic order quantity) model for the control of inventory under conditions of certainty is the ancestor of all inventory models, having been formalized late in the nineteenth century. However, since few inventories have ever been managed under conditions of certainty, various approaches to the management of inventory under uncertain sales and order replenishment conditions have been developed.

Approaches to managing inventories under conditions of uncertainty balance trade-offs between costs of holding and ordering inventory as well as the costs associated with failing to serve customer demands. These approaches, based on properties of probabilities associated with various patterns of customer demands and replenishment times, include those employing fixed order quantities (Q models), fixed order intervals (P models), or both (S,s models). Each has its appropriate use.

Of primary importance to a logistics manager is the *result* produced by the inventory model in actual application, not what it is called or how it is categorized. Having here explored the basic theory of inventory models, Chapter 6 will provide a more detailed examination of how these models are employed in practice.

DISCUSSION QUESTIONS

1. What purposes are served by inventory?

2. What are the advantages of tabular and graphic presentations of EOQ calculations?

3. What are their disadvantages?

4. What are the advantages of the algebraic method of EOQ calculation?

5. How would a logistics manager, having calculated an EOQ of 90 units, deal with the requirement that orders be placed in dozens?

6. What assumptions does the basic EOQ formula make?

7. Differentiate between inventory control under certainty and under uncertainty.

8. What inventory management technique(s) may be used when inventory replenishment is not possible, for example, only one order may be placed for seasonal merchandise?

9. When inventory replenishment is possible, how are variations in customer order patterns and delivery times from suppliers taken into account?

10. What are the three basic characteristics of the Fixed Order Quantity Model? The Fixed Order Interval Model? The Mixed Quantity/Interval Model?

SUGGESTED READINGS

It is difficult if not impossible to draw a clear line between "principles of inventory control" and "inventory management." There is substantial overlap between these two topics, and the suggested readings that follow contain material also applicable in Chapter 6. The two older sources (Brown and Pritchard) among those listed here are included because they are classics in the field.

ADAM, EVERETT E., JR., and RONALD J. EBERT, *Production and Operations Management: Concepts, Models, and Behavior*, 4th ed. Englewood Cliffs, N.J.: Prentice-Hall, Inc. 1989. This book presents a sound treatment of inventory models in Chapters 12 and 13 which include many useful examples and worked-out problems.

BROWN, ROBERT G., *Decision Rules for Inventory Management*, New York: Holt, Rinehart and Winston, 1967. This book, written almost like a novel (complete with a love story), is the result of a wealth of practical experience on the part of the author. Calling upon a number of examples centered around a richly described company case situation, Brown provides a "how-to-do-it" for a wide range of inventory control techniques oriented to procurement and distribution as well as production. This is easily the most readable of all comprehensive treatments of inventory control.

LAMBERT, DOUGLAS M., and MARK L. BENNION, "Establishing a Minimum Order Policy," *Journal of Business Logistics* 7, no. 2 (1986): 91–108. This article addresses the age-old problem of the costs associated with small orders, and includes an interesting case study.

LAU, HON-SHIANG, "Toward an Inventory Control System Under Non-Normal Demand and Lead-Time Uncertainty," *Journal of Business Logistics* 10, no. 1 (1989). A somewhat quantitative treatment of non-normally distributed inventory lead times, daily demands and lead-time-demand interactions.

LEE, HAU L., "A Multi-echelon Inventory Model for Repairable Items with Emergency Lateral Transshipments," *Management Science* 33, no. 10 (October 1987): 1302–1316. This article treats the special case of inventory management concerning stocking of repair parts at successively higher levels in a product-support system.

LEVY, MICHAEL, WILLIAM CRON, and ROBERT NOVACK, "A Decision Support System for Determining a Quantity Discount Pricing Policy," *Journal of Business Logistics* 6, no. 2 (1985): 110–141. An excellent and comprehensive treatment of the strategy and tactics for determining quantity discounts with particular attention to predicted customer ordering behavior for a proposed discount structure.

PRITCHARD, J. W., and R. H. EAGLE, *Modern Inventory Management*, New York: John Wiley & Sons, Inc., 1965. This is a carefully written, well illustrated book that presents its complex subject in a clear manner requiring only a knowledge of algebra. The relationship of inventory models to customer service objectives is covered especially well.

SCHROEDER, ROGER G., *Operations Management: Decision Making in the Operations Function*, 3d ed. New York: McGraw-Hill Book Company, 1989. Part 4 of this text is a very well organized three-chapter treatment of the general subject of inventory management.

TERSINE, RICHARD J., RICHARD A. TOELLE, and ALBERT B. SCHWARZKOPF, "An Analytical Model for Determining Excess Inventory," *Journal of Business Logistics* 7, no. 1 (1986): 122–142. The focus of this article is appropriate liquidation of excess inventory and its positive effects on the firm's cash flow.

VERAL, EMRE A., and R. LAWRENCE LAFORGE, "The Performance of a Simple Incremental Lot-sizing Rule in a Multilevel Inventory Environment," *Decision Sciences* 16 (1985): 57–72. The incremental rule developed in this article generated lower total order/setup and carrying costs than lot for lot (LFL), economic order quantity (EOQ), periodic order quantity (POQ), and several other less well-known decision rules.

ZINSZER, PAUL H., "Inventory Costing: A Return on Inventory Approach to Differentiating Inventory Risk," *Journal of Business Logistics* 4, no. 2 (1983): 20–39. This article focuses on an aspect of inventory carrying cost—risk—that often receives only minimal attention in circumstances where prudent management would indicate the need for greater emphasis.

ENDNOTES

1. Symbols used in this discussion have been selected to correspond to those commonly found in current usage. However, there are no rules for assigning symbols, and only a few can be considered standard usage, such as σ for standard deviation and Σ for "sum of."

APPENDIX

Areas under the
Standardized Normal
Curve from .0 to +**z**

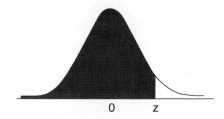

z	.00	.01	.02	.03	.04	.05	.06	.07	.08	.09
.0	.5000	.5040	.5080	.5120	.5160	.5199	.5239	.5279	.5319	.5359
.1	.5398	.5438	.5478	.5517	.5557	.5596	.5636	.5675	.5714	.5753
.2	.5793	.5832	.5871	.5910	.5948	.5987	.6026	.6064	.6103	.6141
.3	.6179	.6217	.6255	.6293	.6331	.6368	.6406	.6443	.6480	.6517
.4	.6554	.6591	.6628	.6664	.6700	.6736	.6772	.6808	.6844	.6879
.5	.6915	.6950	.6985	.7019	.7054	.7088	.7123	.7157	.7190	.7224
.6	.7257	.7291	.7324	.7357	.7389	.7422	.7454	.7486	.7517	.7549
.7	.7580	.7611	.7642	.7673	.7704	.7734	.7764	.7794	.7823	.7852
.8	.7881	.7910	.7939	.7967	.7995	.8023	.8051	.8078	.8106	.8133
.9	.8159	.8186	.8212	.8238	.8264	.8289	.8315	.8340	.8365	.8389
1.0	.8413	.8438	.8461	.8485	.8508	.8531	.8554	.8577	.8599	.8621
1.1	.8643	.8665	.8686	.8708	.8729	.8749	.8770	.8790	.8810	.8830
1.2	.8849	.8869	.8888	.8907	.8925	.8944	.8962	.8980	.8997	.9015
1.3	.9032	.9049	.9066	.9082	.9099	.9115	.9131	.9147	.9162	.9177
1.4	.9192	.9207	.9222	.9236	.9251	.9265	.9279	.9292	.9306	.9319
1.5	.9332	.9345	.9357	.9370	.9382	.9394	.9406	.9418	.9429	.9441
1.6	.9452	.9463	.9474	.9484	.9495	.9505	.9515	.9525	.9535	.9545
1.7	.9554	.9564	.9573	.9582	.9591	.9599	.9608	.9616	.9625	.9633
1.8	.9641	.9649	.9656	.9664	.9671	.9678	.9686	.9693	.9699	.9706
1.9	.9713	.9719	.9726	.9732	.9738	.9744	.9750	.9756	.9761	.9767
2.0	.9772	.9778	.9783	.9788	.9793	.9798	.9803	.9808	.9812	.9817
2.1	.9821	.9826	.9830	.9834	.9838	.9842	.9846	.9850	.9854	.9857
2.2	.9861	.9864	.9868	.9871	.9875	.9878	.9881	.9884	.9887	.9890
2.3	.9893	.9896	.9898	.9901	.9904	.9906	.9909	.9911	.9913	.9916
2.4	.9918	.9920	.9922	.9925	.9927	.9929	.9931	.9932	.9934	.9936
2.5	.9938	.9940	.9941	.9943	.9945	.9946	.9948	.9949	.9951	.9952
2.6	.9953	.9955	.9956	.9957	.9959	.9960	.9961	.9962	.9963	.9964
2.7	.9965	.9966	.9967	.9968	.9969	.9970	.9971	.9972	.9973	.9974
2.8	.9974	.9975	.9976	.9977	.9977	.9978	.9979	.9979	.9980	.9981
2.9	.9981	.9982	.9982	.9983	.9984	.9984	.9985	.9985	.9986	.9986
3.0	.9987	.9987	.9987	.9988	.9988	.9989	.9989	.9989	.9990	.9990
3.1	.9990	.9991	.9991	.9991	.9991	.9992	.9992	.9992	.9993	.9993
3.2	.9993	.9993	.9994	.9994	.9994	.9994	.9994	.9995	.9995	.9995
3.3	.9995	.9995	.9995	.9996	.9996	.9996	.9996	.9996	.9996	.9997
3.4	.9997	.9997	.9997	.9997	.9997	.9997	.9997	.9997	.9997	.9998

CHAPTER SIX

6

Inventory Management

LEARNING OBJECTIVES

The objectives of this chapter are to:

➢ Discuss reasons why inventory may be managed to achieve company goals other than lowest inventory costs.

➢ Present and discuss approaches to managing multi-item and multilocation inventories.

➢ Explain the concept of inventory program design and management, including the need for contingency procedures and progam review.

➢ Discuss problems of inventory management related to production scheduling, sequencing and smoothing, and approaches to handling associated inventory problems.

➢ Review the concepts of Materials Requirements Planning (MRP I), Manufacturing Resources Planning (MRP II), kanban, and Just-in-Time (JIT) scheduling, and the applications of these concepts to inventory management.

➢ Discuss the inventory-scheduling-related concepts of waiting-line (queuing) theory and shipment split-offs.

As discussed in Chapter 5, inventory theorists are primarily interested in finding optimal values for order quantities, reorder points, and order intervals, and rightly so. Solid theory is the necessary foundation for effective practice. However, inventory managers — and those to whom they report — have additional questions on their minds. Questions such as: When we're in a severe cash squeeze, how can we cut inventory by 20 percent? Our production capacity is at its limit; we need longer production runs, but what will this do to inventory levels? Just how "sacred" is an EOQ in the face of limited warehouse capacity? We have 1,350 different stockkeeping units (SKUs); does each one deserve equal attention? How inaccurate does a forecast have to be before it really hurts? Are *kanban** and "Just-in-Time" (JIT) really something new and different, or are they just buzzwords? Are Materials Requirements Planning (MRP I) and Manufacturing Resources Planning (MRP II) concerns of the logistics manager, or the production manager, or both? How does one design an inventory management program that helps the company reach its corporate goals? How does a company evaluate the effectiveness of the inventory management program it is using? With such questions in mind, the objective of this chapter is to review common problems of managing inventory and methods for solving them, or at least mitigating their cost to the firm.

The design of an inventory management program is of major strategic importance to many firms. It requires bridging the gap between inventory theory and inventory management. To this end, the logistics manager should be in a position (1) to encourage his or her staff to think of the inventory management program in broad terms and (2) to represent top management views and objectives in the appraisal and any redesign of the program.

MANAGING TO ACHIEVE GOALS OTHER THAN LOWEST INVENTORY COSTS

There are a number of reasons for managing an inventory to achieve a goal other than that of minimizing order, holding, and stockout costs. In actual practice one or more of these reasons may be controlling at any given time. They include production capacity constraints, warehouse space constraints, inventory investment constraints, managing to a specified customer service level, and decisions based upon external environmental factors of importance to the firm.

Managing within Production Capacity Constraints

Values assigned for use with various inventory models may serve as ways of conforming results to capacity constraints in production. For example, setup costs may be an important element of a production planning decision. Where production capacity constraints are severe, it may be necessary to reduce the number of machine setups in order to increase the use of limited producing capacity, regardless of whether this leads to larger-than-optimum inventories. The quantity of product produced in relation to demand is a direct determinant of the number of times during a given period that setup costs are incurred. Therefore, Q (fixed order quantity) models provide a device for adjusting the number of setups to accommodate production capabilities.

---

*Kanban is a Japanese word meaning "card" or "signboard." It refers to the practice of attaching a card to a bin or other container, with the card specifying the quantity of parts or components to be manufactured at a work station for use by the next work station in the manufacturing process. As noted later in this chapter, the term is often misused by American managers.

For example, consider the basic EOQ model discussed in Chapter 5:

$$Q^* = \sqrt{\frac{2AS}{rv}}$$

In this formula, the letter A represents setup costs. In order to reduce the number of machine setups by, say, one-half, the quantity ordered must be doubled. This can be done by increasing arbitrarily the cost assigned to each setup until it produces the desired result. For example, suppose the setup cost is $51, the annual usage is 2,000 units, the inventory carrying cost is 40 percent, and the unit cost (value) is $20. One need only increase the setup cost fourfold to double the EOQ. The calculation is simple and straightforward:

$$Q^* = \sqrt{\frac{2(\$51)(2,000)}{.40(\$20)}} \qquad\qquad Q^* = \sqrt{\frac{2(\$204)(2,000)}{.40(\$20)}}$$

$$Q^* = 160 \qquad\qquad\qquad Q^* = 320$$

An EOQ of 320 is, of course "invalid." It is merely a temporizing approach to the handling of an operational problem. The problem — a shortage of production capacity — has not been solved.

Managing within Warehouse Capacity or Capital Constraints

The incremental inventory carrying cost at a warehouse that is filled to its "normal" capacity will be high. At such times, the inventory carrying cost factor (the letter r in the basic EOQ equation) provides at least a crude method for reducing all inventories at the facility, assuming that some sales activity is taking place. Using the numbers in the preceding example, arbitrarily increasing r will reduce the EOQ to the desired level, say by 40 percent for example, from 160 units to 96. The same technique may be used when the problem is a shortage of capital to invest in inventory. Again, the calculation is simple and straightforward:

$$Q^* = \sqrt{\frac{2(\$51)(2,000)}{.40(\$20)}} \qquad\qquad Q^* = \sqrt{\frac{2(\$51)(2,000)}{1.10(\$20)}}$$

$$Q^* = 160 \qquad\qquad\qquad Q^* = 96$$

And again — as in the preceding limited production capacity situation — the real problem is not solved. The smaller EOQ is "invalid" and is only a temporary expedient.

Consequences of Overlooking Hidden Costs

Another type of inventory management problem will arise if a cost element is overlooked in computing an EOQ. This is most likely to happen as in the following situation where a less-than-obvious cost element was involved. The warehouse manager of a large grocery chain was confronted continually with incoming grocery product deliveries in partial-pallet quantities. Because the warehouse was equipped with pallet racks permitting the full use of vertical space through the insertion of pallets into a metal framework of slots, partial-pallet quantities greatly reduced the capacity of the warehouse at a time when space was becoming critically short. Upon investigation, it was found that buyers for the chain were buying on the basis of economic order quantities and were not taking account of the handling and storage economies of purchases of pallet-sized quantities. In this case, a calculation of cost implications suggested that when economic order quantities constituted more than 40 percent of a pallet quantity, in most cases the pallet quantity should have been ordered. Obviously, the company could not be short of working capital to invest in inventory if such a policy were to be adopted.

Similarly, many grocery chains have adopted the policy of not restocking store shelves in quantities of less than a full case, even though this results in a larger minimum (about one and one-half cases of merchandise) of shelf space devoted to any one item displayed in the store. The costs of handling quantities of less than one case are considered to be prohibitive. But note, such a policy will reduce the total number of different items the store can display on its shelves.

Managing to a Preset Quantity of Inventory

The management of a company, faced with a working capital squeeze, may decide that it has to reduce inventories. This may occur with or without concern for the impact of such a decision on customer service. Let's consider the latter situation first.

Without Regard for Customer Service Many inventory control systems measure quantities of inventory on hand in terms of weeks of demand. In such a case, order trigger points would also be stated in weeks of demand, reflecting the amount of time required to replenish a depleted item, plus some amount for safety stock (see Chapter 5). Similarly, order quantities would be EOQ-based calculations. If management ordered a reduction of 25 percent in the average level of inventory on hand, this could be accomplished *either* by reducing the order point (and the safety stock) *or* the size of each order. It is easy to adjust gross levels of inventory to respond to top management directives, but this is not accomplished without cost. Something has to give. Either stockouts will increase or the per-unit costs of order processing and transportation will increase due to ordering smaller quantities. There is no free lunch in respect to inventory decisions.

Managing Inventories to Customer Service Levels Managers should think about both customer service and inventory levels concurrently. They may inquire, for example, about the inventory savings resulting from a reduction in customer service from 97 percent to 95 percent of orders or units filled from stock, as previously discussed in Chapter 5. Or, conversely, upon perceiving a deficiency in customer service levels, a perception often gained from customer complaints, a manager might inquire about the inventory increase — and the associated cost — needed to boost the customer service level from 90 percent to 95 percent of line items ordered that can be filled from stock.

MANAGING MULTI-ITEM INVENTORIES

Rarely does a business deal in only one item ordered into or sold out of a single location. Rather, it will have many stock-keeping units (SKUs) and perhaps a number of stock-keeping unit locations (SKULs). Several approaches have been established for the management of multi-item stocks. They include the use of multi-SKU programs, methods for allocating scarce stocks across SKULs, sourcing decisions, and ABC-oriented programs.

Multi-SKU Programs

Multi-SKU programs have been developed to accumulate and expedite orders for families of products being managed at one location. Typically, they are min-max or S,s in form. A computer is programmed to scan a family of SKUs, for example, those bought from the same supplier or the same origin. Daily or more frequently, the "order up to" quantities for all items is totaled. When that total reaches an economic transport or purchase quantity, an order is entered for all line items in the family showing "order up to" amounts in excess of some minimum efficient handling quantity (such as pallet load).

In case an item reaches a minimum level before the economic transport quantity for the family is accumulated, various response rules have to be preprogrammed (1) to do nothing; (2) to expedite a shipment of the one item, as in a multi-trigger point system; (3) to scan the family to determine if other items approaching their minimums should be added to the expedited shipment; or (4) to initiate a full order, including items not approaching their trigger points. In this latter event, most programs of this sort fill up orders so that the resulting quantity of each family item on hand and on order is equal in terms of days of demand.

Given the growing capacity of low-cost computers and available software packages, complex multi-SKU programs can be used to deal with specific circumstances and company needs.

Multi-SKUL Programs

Multi-SKUL programs are used for the management of inventories of the same SKU at several locations (SKULs). These include both allocation and sourcing programs that are especially helpful in dealing with contingencies resulting from depleted stocks, the need to reschedule production to accommodate unusual demands, or delays in order replenishment.

Allocation Programs Where the quantity on hand at a plant warehouse, for example, is not sufficient to meet distribution center orders or potential needs before the next production run at the plant, the least-cost approach to the problem is to allocate the product in such a manner that all distribution centers have their stocks brought up to roughly the same levels, stated in terms of days or weeks of demand. This assumes, however, that no additional shipments (for example, between distribution centers) will be needed as a result of the decision. Further, it assumes a constant estimated cost per stockout. Under circumstances where customers will settle for nothing less than their full order, this may become a determining factor in the final decision.

Sourcing Programs Inadequate stocks at a distribution center and its supply point, a plant warehouse, may create a temptation to reschedule the plant's production. Before rescheduling production, however, it would be desirable to compare the costs of a decision to reschedule with the cost of replenishing one distribution center from another. The latter might be a wise choice if the second distribution center had the desired EOQ in its "excess" stock. Excess can be determined in a variety of ways, but in many companies it represents anything in excess of the amount expected to be sold before receipt of the next scheduled replenishment of the SKU.

The widespread adoption of distributed data processing systems has led to the use of "smart" computer terminals for local inventory control at distribution centers.* Periodically, these local terminals transmit inventory data to a central location using a large-scale unit that processes information on a multi-location basis for an entire network of plants and distribution centers. Inventory information may then be updated and returned to the memory of the outlying computer terminals. Unfortunately, where this is coupled with decentralized responsibility for controlling inventories at each location, distribution center managers, upon being confronted with a stockout, may contact "buddy" distribution center managers rather than those from whom replenishment shipment would produce the lowest transportation cost. Further, in the absence of any definition of what "surplus" is, distribution center managers may tend to help each other out, only to find that they have shorted themselves on the very items they shipped to another distribution center.

ABC Approaches to Inventory Management

The term "ABC inventory policy" is used generically to cover a wide variety of practices involving varying degrees of attention to the management of inventories for various groups of SKUs. Each SKU group receives a different level of attention on the basis of such factors as (1) rates of sale, (2) value per unit, (3) costs of storage, or (4) the strategic value of the item to customers. Most are concerned with the provision of different levels of "coverage," or customer service standards, through the use of safety stocks, for various categories of items.

Concentration on SKUs with High Rates of Sale   This approach employs detailed forecasts with frequent updates of inventory levels and forecast information, and it also involves detailed inventory management programs for inventories of SKUs in the product line with the highest rates of sale. These SKUs usually offer the greatest opportunity for cost savings and sales benefits from the careful application of inventory control techniques. In contrast, SKUs with slow rates of sale typically are stocked in quantities sufficient to reduce the need for reviews of stock levels to relatively infrequent time intervals. ABC inventory control is especially useful when storage space, personnel, or capital is limited.

Overall customer service levels, defined in terms of the proportion of items ordered that are available in a firm's stock, can be affected most directly by the coverage provided for the SKUs with the greatest rates of sale.

As an example, the data shown in Table 6–1 for Mohawk Metal Fabricators, a manufacturer of plumbing fixtures, is reasonably typical. In this case, 20 percent of Mohawk's products represent 81 percent of its sales. Mohawk calls these A items. At the other extreme, 57 percent of Mohawk's SKUs make up only 6 percent of its sales. These are called C items.** By providing a significantly higher level of coverage on **A** items than on others, Mohawk can both increase its overall inventory coverage and reduce its dollar investment (increasing its inventory turns) in relation to the results produced by a nondifferentiated approach.

---

*"Smart" computer terminals have their own memory and data processing capability. In contrast, "dumb" terminals function only as input and output devices for a central computer at some other location.

**Classifying inventory in three levels (A,B,C) is common practice, but there are many situations in which only a dual classification (A and B) or even four levels (A,B,C,D) would be more appropriate.

TABLE 6–1: The Impact of an ABC Inventory Program Based on Sales Volume for Mohawk Metal Fabricators

	SKU Category			
	A	B	C	TOTAL
Number of SKUs	20	23	57	100
Proportion of total SKUs	20%	23%	57%	100%
Proportion of total unit sales	81%	13%	6%	100%
Situation A: Nondifferentiated Inventory Coverage				
Level of coverage	90%	90%	90%	90%
Inventory required (millions)	$1.0	$1.15	$2.85	$5.0
Situation B: ABC Coverage Based on Sales Volume				
Level of coverage	95%	90%	50%	91.6%
Inventory required (millions)	$1.4	$1.15	$1.3	$3.85

Concentration on SKUs with High Values per Unit Where values per unit for SKUs vary greatly, the greatest savings in inventory carrying costs may be effected either by the use of a more careful and exacting inventory program for the management of high-value items or by a reduction in inventory coverage levels for them.

Concentration on SKUs with Extensive Storage Requirements ABC inventory policies may differentiate SKUs on the basis of cubic footage per unit where storage facilities represent a scarce resource with a high opportunity cost per unit of space. Extra attention may be paid to inventory control measures and inventory coverage reductions for SKUs requiring the greatest space per unit for storage.

Concentration on SKUs with Costly Storage Requirements Products such as frozen foods may be singled out for this type of attention because of the high cost of storing them in expensive freezers.

Concentration on SKUs with High Strategic Values to Customers SKUs vary in their strategic values to customers. For example, a replacement water pump or alternator is likely to be a much more critical item than, say, a rear-view mirror to the repair customers of an automotive parts distributor.

ABC-based approaches are a practical recognition of the simple fact that some things would cost more to do than they would be worth. Inventory managers cannot devote significant time, effort, and resources to precise inventory control of items whose total inventory value is low, whether it is low absolute dollar value, low value to customers, or some other measure. It is sufficient to insure that such items are kept on hand in sufficient quantity to avoid unacceptable stockouts.

Figure 6–1: Priority levels in an ABC-based approach to inventory management in the military

Importance of the Using
Organization's Mission

		HIGH	MEDIUM	LOW
Strategic Value of the Item to the Using Organization's Mission	HIGH	1	2	3
	MEDIUM	2	3	4
	LOW	3	4	5

One ABC approach uses a matrix of the sort shown in Figure 6–1 for establishing five levels of priority based on a combination of the strategic value of the item and the importance of the mission being performed by the using organization. Although it is an example drawn from the military, this approach applies to setting business inventory management priorities as well. Those items rated highest on the grid will receive the most attention from inventory managers, and those rated lowest will receive very little.

Finally, it should be kept in mind that modern high-speed, high-capacity, low-cost computers have changed the "cost equation," so to speak, in regard to the costs of data processing associated with inventory control. One of the most common examples of this is seen in the use of bar codes at grocery store checkout stands; the identification of the item is "read" by a holographic device, the item is automatically rung up, and simultaneously the central computer updates the in-stock inventory of that product as well as putting the information into the store's sales records.

In establishing the rationale for an ABC approach to inventory management in any one company, it is important to understand the objectives of the company and the needs of its customers. The design of inventory control systems cannot be accomplished without a great deal of attention to the context in which they are to be used. This attention distinguishes off-the-shelf inventory control systems from custom-designed inventory management programs.

INVENTORY PROGRAM MANAGEMENT

The difference between inventory control and inventory management is embodied in the elements of a broad-based inventory management program outlined in Figure 6–2. They include the maintenance of an awareness of management goals, assessment of business and logistics strategies, design of the inventory control models, design of one or more forecasting models to provide demand inputs, design of a program for other inventory model inputs, establishment of inventory contingency procedures, testing for internal compatibility of program elements, and testing for the compatibility of the program design with business requirements external to the program itself.

Figure 6–2: Elements of an inventory management program

I. Maintaining an awareness of management goals

II. Assessment of business and logistics strategies

III. Design of inventory model, such as:

$$Q^* = \sqrt{\frac{2S\ [A + E(s)]}{rv}}$$

$$p(x)^* = \frac{rvQ}{S} = P$$

$$E(s) = \pi \left[\sum_{x = P + 1}^{x\ max} (x - P)\ p(x) \right]$$

IV. Design of forecasting model (for S, above)
   Trend seasonal

V. Design of program for other inventory model inputs:
   A = order cost (source: accounting)
   π = stock-out cost (source: marketing management)
   r = inventory carrying cost (source: top management)
   v = unit cost of product (source: accounting)
   order interval and order lead time

VI. Establishment of inventory contingency procedures

VII. Design of remaining program elements
   Computational device
   Update cycle
   Program review procedures

VIII. Testing for internal compatibility

IX. Testing for external compatibility

Maintaining an Awareness of Management Goals

It would be presumptuous to assume that inventory managers in large firms participate in corporate goal-setting. But, through lines of communication provided by senior logistics management, inventory managers should be made aware of long-range goals being pursued by top management.

In the shorter term, business trends and aspirations, usually set forth in the annual business plan, often have clear relevance for inventory build-ups or reductions, signaling necessary changes in the inventory management program. Such business plans usually include estimates of available working capital, suggesting a rate of turnover for inventory in the future.

An Assessment of Business and Logistics Strategies

The level and nature of management goals will limit the range of strategies suitable for achieving them. However, several alternative strategies may be developed for meeting a goal. For example, a profit goal may be met by strategies centered around differing levels of customer service and inventory carrying costs. A high level of service probably would imply relatively high inventories (safety stocks), a lower inventory turnover rate, and the use of expedited transportation services. It might carry with it higher prices and margins on sales. A low level of service might be associated with just the opposite strategic elements, but with a price low enough to attract a quantity of business sufficient to attain the same profit level as the high-service strategy.

The number and location of suppliers, plant and warehouse facilities, and major customers and their purchasing patterns will influence the number of SKULs, the magnitude of the inventory management task, and the opportunities for consolidating SKULs and shipments. A company's computer and communications network may influence how inventories are managed. And, organizational attitudes toward centralized or decentralized management can influence the extent to which inventories are managed by means of small stand-alone computers at each inventory location as opposed to being managed centrally through a communication network emanating from a central computing facility.

The Design of the Inventory Model

The selection of an inventory model, whether it features fixed or variable order intervals, order quantities, or order points, depends on a number of operating conditions and constraints. For example: How complex and varied is the product line? How important is shipment consolidation? Will coordination of inventories among several distribution centers be necessary? What are the practical limits on storage capacity? How important and useful is shipment expediting or the occasional use of premium transportation to meet service needs? What do customers expect of the system? How do competitors manage their inventories?

Questions concerning computing capacity and capability used to be included in this list, but these constraints are declining dramatically in importance as factors in inventory model design. Today's computers allow for a great range of latitude in the design and implementation of various inventory models and also permit varying degrees of differentiation in managing individual SKUs or families of SKUs.

The Design of the Forecasting Model

The actual level of demand predicted for a future period will affect the economic order quantity used to replenish an item. The accuracy of the forecasting method will influence the amount of safety stock required to support a specified level of SKUL availability (or customer service), as we saw in Chapter 5.

The effects of inaccurate forecasting on inventory management performance are not always clear. For example, Brown has demonstrated in a general case that when sales are overestimated by 100 percent in an EOQ (Q) model, the resulting EOQ is about 40 percent greater than it should be, producing average cycle stocks about 20 percent greater than they should be. But when inventory carrying cost increases are offset by reduced ordering costs, the *total* annual costs of carrying the inventory increase by only 6 percent over the total obtained by using accurate demand inputs.[1] The best way to assess the impact of a forecasting approach on inventory management results is simply to try it out on recent sales and inventory data.

The Design of the Program for Other Inventory Model Inputs

In addition to demand estimates, inventory models require estimates of order placement or setup costs, stockout costs, inventory carrying costs, the unit costs of the product, and relevant lead times for inventory replenishment. This is where the fun starts, for there are many ways, a great number of them highly subjective and all justifiable on some basis, for measuring these inputs.

Order Placement or Setup Costs Order placement costs occur at a distribution center and in the plant purchasing function. The equivalent type of cost in the production process is the cost of setting up a machine or a production line to produce an item.

Order placement costs for replenishment of a distribution center stock from a plant warehouse may include wages and fringe benefits for time actually spent in order preparation and inventory review, the cost of communicating the order, and wages and fringe benefits in the selection and packing of the order at the plant warehouse.

Purchase orders involve costs of inventory review and order preparation and communication, invoice payment and updating of records. Other costs associated with the order typically are incurred by the supplier and will be reflected in the price of the goods.

Some companies, particularly those where orders containing few line items are the rule, collect all order-processing costs and divide them by the total number of orders placed, to obtain a full average cost per order. Others approach the problem by estimating the cost to prepare standard order information that has to be entered regardless of line item composition, multiplying this by the number of orders processed, and then allocating the remaining costs to the number of line items entered on all orders. This approach produces a base fixed cost per order and an additional variable cost by line item. It is not unusual to find that fixed costs per order placement may range up to $20, while the variable costs per line item amount to several dollars each.

Machine or production line setup costs have a wide range of values, depending on the sequence in which products are made and the need for time-consuming machine shutdowns for changeover. For example, in a soft-drink bottling plant a changeover from bottling cola in one size of bottle to another is done more quickly than changing from bottling cola to bottling

EFFECTIVE INVENTORY PIPELINES

Warren G. Malkerson

Ways in which inventories are valued today in most companies need to change radically. The current undervaluation of inventory has led to the strangulation of U.S. manufacturing systems and allowed overseas competition to take business out from under our noses in our own backyard.

The real impetus behind my concern for inventory levels really began just over three years ago with the formation of the materials management department within Pillsbury U.S. Foods. Previous to that, the various departments that now comprise that group were scattered all over the company.

The transportation group was broken along the lines of rail and truck, with rail reporting into corporate management and truck into U.S. Foods. The purchasing department record into corporate management. The distribution network, including the field located distribution centers (DCs), reported into manufacturing for total U.S. Foods, while the plants themselves reported into five separate business units that then existed within U.S. Foods.

The order entry and customer service departments were split along the three distribution channels of dry products, frozen products and refrigerated products. To say there was confusion and lack of focus would be an understatement. Imagine all the sub-optimizing occurring.

Order from Chaos

So, three years ago all this confusion was organized into what is called "the materials management pipeline." The entire operations and distribution effort now is viewed as one continuous flow of information, communication, product and service to its customers. The total department now consists of:

- *PURCHASING.* (Ingredients, packaging, capital equipment and supplies.) A few maintenance and repair part items are at plant locations—otherwise, it's centralized.

- *TRANSPORTATION.* (Rail and truck for inbound, interplant and outbound.) Finished product from plants to DCs, and from consolidated DCs to customers; raw materials from suppliers to plants.

- *CUSTOMER SERVICE.* (All distribution channels.) All within one department organized geographically by customer.

- *PRODUCTION PLANNING.* (All 44 plants.) Macro-planning with schedule changing but not line or shift assignments, which are done by the plants.

- *INVENTORY MANAGEMENT.* (Total U.S.) By product group or stock-keeping units (SKUs) across total system—plant, DCs, etc.

- *DISTRIBUTION CENTERS.* (Nine owned and 30 + public.) Dry facilities are owned and leased; frozen basically are public designed to consolidate products from various plants and put close to the customer.

- *ORDER ENTRY.* (All customer orders.) From retail grocery stores and food service buyers.

- *INVOICING.* (All customer orders.) Handle the billing on all orders.

A Lot of Shipping

More than 240-million cases of finished product are shipped each year, and about $1 billion of raw materials are handled. Actually, company's industry research indicates that many other food and non-food companies have gone this organizational route in the last couple of years. Some call it "logistics" or "operations." Name makes no difference. The important part is to have all departments interlocked and working on common goals together.

The only two pieces to the pipeline believed to be missing (and that should be part of the organization) are the plants themselves and quality assurance. The plants still report to their individual business units; quality assurance into the research and development (R&D) function. Hopefully, these two will be in the pipeline within the next couple of years.

There have been significant benefits to the company in creating the materials management pipeline organization. These benefits range from less overall general and administrative costs, to more clear customer focus, to better communication within departments, and all the way to a better view of the amount of inventory in the system.

Getting into Inventory

Inventory within Pillsbury really consists of raw materials in the plant at the front end of the pipeline, and finished products ready for the customer at the other end. Unlike some other industries, there is little, if any work-in-progress inventories. Pillsbury has attempted to limit any inventory burden or buildup at suppliers. The inventory ratio between finished goods and raw materials is roughly 70:30.

One of the critical aspects of Pillsbury's finished goods inventory, however, has to do with the fact that it is food. No one should forget that food product integrity and quality deteriorate quickly with time. This is a fact often overlooked when an accounting system puts a value on its inventory. It is called "age of product," and you can bet customers and consumers can tell the difference in eating quality. Over time, aged inventory levels (of course, with the exception of cheese, a good bottle of California wine or a classic scotch) really can negatively impact one's consumer franchise.

And Pillsbury worries about obsolescence, much like any other industry would. Out-of-date packaging materials, ingredients and even finished products occur more often that a firm would like to admit.

Inventory costs can consider of many other factors more tangible than old age and obsolescence. Pillsbury witnesses high inventory levels affecting the costs of warehousing, transportation, general and administrative budgets, R&D, premium raw materials, capital and insurance rates to name a few. And there are other more "hidden" costs throughout the entire food product system that actually could be associated with inventory.

The Associated Costs

Warehousing. This would seem pretty straightforward. The more inventory chosen to hold, the higher the overall costs are to hold it. There are more costs here, however, than meet the eye.

Costs at the warehouse level would include people to watch and count the inventory, to move it from place to place for repositioning needs, to receive it into the facility and later ship it out, extra forklift trucks and, if you have those, then you need a maintenance shop. You also have more shipping docks to handle the trucks or rail cars unloading as well as loading, computer systems to keep track of the product movements, pick lines to differentiate between high-moving items and slow ones, and the list could go on indefinitely.

Transportation. The more inventory you hold . . . the more you have to move it, and the more you have to reposition it within your network. There are a considerable number of moves to make from one DC to another without even going to a customer.

If your distribution network does not include major warehouse capacity at the palnts, even higher transportation costs will be experienced. Also, a least-costed transportation network might have more rail than truck usage. For Pillsbury, customer service requirements and inventory costs associated with higher inventories in a rail mode have driven the company more to truck shipments. Six years ago the rail/truck ratio was 60:40. today it's 15:85.

General and administrative budgets. It comes down to one simple statement: Someone has to count the "stuff," watch the "stuff," and move the "stuff." Therefore, the more "stuff" one has, the more people, systems and reports one will need to manage it. Insurance rates and expense also fluctuate with the amount of inventory one is holding.

R&D. This may be peculiar to the food industry, but large inventory levels drive R&D expense. In order to combat the "old age" issue that one can experience with food products, Pillsbury spends upwards of 10% of the R&D time and effort in trying to extend the shelf life of products to make them seem fresher or still cook properly when the consumer finally brings the product to the kitchen. Large inventory levels tend to create "older" products.

Premium raw materials. This ties into the R&D effort to lengthen the shelf life of products. Usually, only expensive chemicals—the ones with really long names that only a registered pharmacist can spell or pronounce—can help extend product shelf life. Consumers see them on the side of the package and wonder what they are putting in their mouths.

Obviously, smaller inventories with higher turns would eliminate the need for this $5-million expense per year. At least, that's what it costs at Pillsbury.

Overall product quality should be mentioned here, too. Pizza that has been through two or three freeze-thaw cycles as it wanders through a poorly configured, high inventory distribution system will not bring a lot of consumers back for a repeat purchase. And repeat purchases are what build the long-term consumer franchise that Pillsbury is trying so hard to create.

Capital. All of the dollars tied up in these inventory levels do not come free either. The mistake Pillsbury sees many companies make is their idea that this cost is equal to the short-term borrowing rate for their company. For many, this is around 10%.

However, any money tied up in inventory over a long period of time is money that cannot be tied up in either a new piece of equipment, a new product or even an acquisition. If your internal hurdle rate for these investments is 25% or your return on invested capital (RIC) goal is 25%-to-30%, then that's how you should really cost out your investments in inventory. After all, it is using dollars that could be earning higher rates of return someplace else in the company.

Not Necessarily Bad

Inventory is not always an evil. Certain levels of inventory need to be maintained to handle customer or consumer demand. The worst case possible—much worse than a little extra inventory—is to have a customer demand go unfilled due to lack of finished product available. The customer will either go away and possibly come back another day or, worse yet, purchase a similar product of one's competitors.

Continued

Pillsbury is trying very hard to manage this delicate balance of being a preferred supplier to the customer trade while, at the same time, managing low inventory levels. It is necessary to get to the point of having inventory available just-in-time (JIT) vs. just-in-case (JIC).

There are two main focal points to be considered when analyzing the costs of inventory. One must look at the marginal costs of inventory and tackle those issues that surround excessive costs in this area. And one must look at the structural or strategic costs of inventory and deal with those issues that are much broader in scope. The marginal costs can be attacked within the current manufacturing/distribution system and vary with the actual movement of the current level of inventories whether up or down.

But the structural costs must be attacked with a longer term process. They generally are associated with capital investments to either reposition one's manufacturing/distribution network or substantially upgrade the in-plant, on-line manufacturing flexibility to produce shorter, more frequent runs of products vs. the old standard long-run, low-standard costs manufacturing paradigm.

A number of steps must be taken to move one's company in the correct direction in regards to inventory assessment and control. There are four important areas of concentration:

■ *THE DISCOVERY PROCESS.* Find out what the "true cost" of inventory is in the company. It is substantially more than just the current cost of borrowing money.

There are a staggering number of "hidden" costs associated with the burden of inventory.

■ *LOST SALES.* Place a value on lost sales due to poor quality product or obsolescence caused by the inventory pipeline. In the food business, everything produced is "date-coded." Thus, it is a simple matter to walk through the grocery store and find out how old the product on the shelf really is.

Remember, this is the product you expect the consumer to purchase, love the taste and convenience of, and come back for more.

■ *INFORMATION.* Gather accurate and timely data concerning the inventory level and actual movement. Historically, the information systems within companies have been designed with a single purpose in mind. These systems were instituted to eliminate general and administrative expense and report financial data to top people in the company.

In the world of inventory management and operations, not only is this kind of financial information generally irrelevant, but it is also way too late. It is analogous to driving a car while only looking out the rear-view mirror: you certainly can see where you have been, but you have no idea where you are going.

In order to really minimize the level of inventory and maximize customer service, one needs to have on-line, real-time information concerning the actual order flow and product movement within the entire manufacturing/distribution pipeline.

■ *CHANGE.* Major structural change within any corporation requires a significant shift in the culture of an organization. The ability to recognize the importance of inventory control, assess the underlying obstacles to its change, analyze the ensuing cost benefits, and then move in the necessary direction requires a lot of collaboration within the company and guts by someone at the top.

Any time that change is necessary, someone has to let go of the status quo or something that is currently in place. Breaking down old paradigms and exploring new territory is risky business. Individuals must feel comfortable enough to stop doing those things that once were considered successful and step outside their comfort zone as they try on new ideas and organizational formations.

Exploring Inner-Self

The importance of having a corporate culture capable of exploring its inner-self cannot be overestimated. It is the one stumbling block more than any other that has thwarted positive change in many corporate environments. Far too many people are worried about their personal survival than about the growth of their fellow employees and the company. This leadership and cultural change must not only start but also be totally supported at the top levels within the organization.

Empowerment can only come down from the top of an organization. Empowered individuals, down in the organization, are the only ones that can affect the change necessary to create an efficient and effective product pipeline. And this is most evident within a company where inventory is kept at minimal levels and preferred, top-notch customer service is advanced as the battle cry.

orange drink; in the latter case all the lines carrying the product have to be cleaned and flushed out to avoid mixing flavors.

Purchase order placement costs — composed of an allocated portion of the labor, communication, and overhead expenses of the purchasing department — can be divided between contract purchases involving periodic standard shipments and other orders requiring preparation each time an order is placed. Contract purchases may involve a large negotiating expense per contract. Once agreed to, however, shipments under contract purchases are received periodically without the placement of an order. The only incremental expense involved in contract purchasing is a review of stocks to determine whether the shipping schedule or quantities should be changed.

Stockout Costs "Hard" stockout costs that are most easy to measure include the costs of duplicate order processing, extra communication (often at the company's expense), and premium transportation costs where a routine order might have moved at a truckload rate. It is not unusual to find these costs amounting to three times those for the processing of a routine order involving no stocked-out items.

The "soft" costs of stockouts, which are seldom considered and nearly impossible to measure, are those of lost selling time (if a sales representative, as the result of a stockout, must "hand-hold" to maintain customer goodwill) and foregone profit. In many situations, the "soft" costs probably exceed the "hard" ones, particularly for products that have substitutes readily available to the buyer.

Lost sales are often a function of consumer buying behavior. There is some evidence, for example, that consumers are more willing to substitute a popular standard item in one company's product line for a similar item in another's, but are less willing to do this in respect to nonstandard items. They have higher expectations regarding product availability for standard or popular items. This suggests that the number of lost sales resulting from stockouts varies by item substitutability.

An ingenious way has been suggested to estimate costs of lost sales by attaching probabilities and costs to (1) the loss of an item sale, (2) the loss of an order, and (3) the loss of a customer as a result of the repeated inability to supply an item when ordered.[2] This approach tends to produce considerably higher lost sales cost estimates than other methods.

Stockout costs in procurement of items used in a production process are usually severe or even drastic. The cost of being out-of-stock on a component needed in the production process is so great that it usually precludes any stockouts at all. Here, the potential stockout problem is dealt with by increasing safety stock to a level that would suffice against almost any contingency. Taking a chance on having to shut down a production operation for lack of material is simply too costly an alternative for most firms to consider even for a moment. This is not to say that such events never occur, but the circumstances should be essentially unpredictable, such as a tornado destroying a vendor's plant or warehouse.

Inventory Carrying Costs

Major inventory carrying cost categories are those associated with (1) the investment in inventory, (2) warehousing, and (3) spoilage, damage, obsolescence and pilferage.

Investment in Inventory Many executives are surprised by the high cost of carrying inventory. Since the dramatic increase in interest rates in the 1970s, a commonly quoted figure

TABLE 6–2: Inventory Carrying Costs in Six Companies

Carrying Cost Components	Costs, by Company[e]					
	A	B	C	D	E	F
Capital Costs[a]	40.00%	29.00%	25.50%	8.00%	30.00%	26.00%
Inventory Service Costs[b]	1.99	.67	1.77	1.22	.51	4.88
Storage Space Costs[c]	.74		.57	2.89	.46	2.98
Inventory Risk Costs[d]	.23	.40	.50	2.09	2.46	N/A
TOTAL CARRYING COST	42.96%	30.07%	28.84%	14.20%	33.48%	33.87%
Value for carrying cost actually used in inventory management	9.5%	15.00%	20.00%	8.00%	25.00%	15.00%

[a]Interest on money invested in inventory

[b]Property taxes and insurance

[c]Warehousing

[d]Deterioration, spoilage, damage, or pilferage

[e]Stated in terms of percentage of the average value of inventory on hand over a period of a year.

Source: Adapted from Bernard J. LaLonde and Douglas M. Lambert, "A Methodology for Determining Inventory Carrying Costs: Two Case Studies" James F. Robeson and John R. Grabner, eds. *Supplement in Proceedings of the Fifth Annual Transportation and Logistics Educators Conference*, Council of Logistics Management, Chicago (October 12, 1975).

for these costs is approximately 35 percent of the average value of inventory on hand over the course of a year. Carrying cost figures vary from firm to firm and from product to product, so it is not surprising to find the differences exhibited in Table 6–2. Note that firm D in Table 6–2 uses an 8 percent interest cost; this is probably an example of failure to review the cost component aspects of its inventory management program.

The implementation of computer-oriented inventory control programs in many firms, both large and small, has increased knowledge and awareness of inventory carrying costs a great deal in recent years.

Warehousing Relevant warehousing costs associated with inventory holding include storage (facility) costs, property taxes and insurance costs, but not the costs of handling goods into and out of a warehouse facility. Each of these cost elements varies by firm and by location. Table 6–2 reflects such differences and shows that they vary substantially among different firms. Property taxes and insurance are the best documented costs in this category. If public warehousing is used, bills paid for storage services provide the basis for documenting storage costs.

Further, unless capacity limits are being reached, the incremental cost of storing more inventory may be very small. But, when capacity limits are reached, the incremental cost then becomes high.

Inventory Risk Costs of spoilage, damage, obsolescence, or pilferage are elusive to document and vary greatly with the type of product under consideration.

Costs of spoilage or damage range from those associated with the total loss of the product (as with perishable produce) to the reworking of product (as with powdered soap products) to the reallocation of product from one distribution point to another. In the case of total loss, it is not only the product but also the associated transportation and storage "invested" in the product that is lost. In a rework situation, costs incurred are those of extra transportation (two extra shipments, to and from the plant), potential loss in rework, the cost of rework itself, extra storage, and possibly customer badwill. Concealed spoilage or damage may not even be known until an irate customer complains about a defective shipment.

Obsolescence can be difficult to define. When is a product obsolete? When it has been superseded by another item in the product line, even though it continues to sell in reduced quantities? When it has not been sold from a distribution center's inventory for some time, even though it continues to be sold in other distribution center territories? Most firms identify obsolete merchandise, often called "dead stock," in terms of the frequency of orders for such items. For example, an item for which no order has been received at a distribution center for 90 days might be considered "dead" at that center and become a candidate for reallocation to other distribution centers that are still shipping it. Reallocation generally allows "dead stock" to be sold at full price, but it requires above-normal transportation and handling expense. One large firm manufacturing a wide line of products assigns obsolescence factors ranging from 0 percent to 30 percent of the average value of inventory on hand over the year for individual items.

Inventory losses from pilferage have *two* very bad effects. First, they represent a definite financial loss. Second, the pilfered goods will continue to be carried in the firm's records as "available for sale" until the loss is discovered. Unfortunately, the loss frequently is discovered as a result of telling a customer, "It's in stock, we'll ship it to you today," and then discovering it's not in stock because it has "disappeared."

Inventoried Cost per Unit of Product The inventoried cost per unit of products purchased from outside vendors includes the purchase price plus the cost of inbound transportation. For products produced within the company, standard manufacturing costs often are used to establish the inventoried value of finished goods. To this must be added the cost of transportation to subsequent distribution points where other inventories may be located. Thus, item values for a given product at a distribution center will be *greater* than at the plant.

Testing the Sensitivity of Results to Model Inputs

The difficulty of obtaining some types of inventory model inputs and the wealth of equally defensible bases for estimating others may seem discouraging. One encouraging note, however, is that the impact of even large variations in many of the inputs is relatively small, both in terms of resulting inventory carrying and ordering costs, and in terms of the customer service variations caused by the failure to identify inputs accurately. This suggests that the relative importance of the accuracy of each input should be *tested* so that management can concentrate on establishing or updating the one or two inputs that are found to be most critical.

For example, assume a situation in which the variation in order-cycle and order-interval times is underestimated by 50 percent, the inventory carrying cost factor is underestimated by 50 percent, and the order cost is overestimated by 50 percent. It can be shown that variation in total costs from the optimum resulting from these grossly inaccurate inputs range from 0 percent to about 13 percent, depending on the values for true costs and correct cycle times and interval times.

In contrast, in the example above, if demand were to be underestimated by 50 percent, both in terms of its level and variation, the resulting low level of inventory carrying cost would likely be offset several times by the large number of sales lost because of stockout conditions, assuming "normal" negative customer behavior patterns when confronted with a stockout.

Potentially severe penalties from inaccurate demand inputs are a characteristic of fixed order interval inventory models, and this explains the emphasis that has been placed on accurate demand forecasting when using such models. The magnitude of penalties due to inaccurate demand inputs is caused mainly by the long time period for which inventory coverage must be provided (an order cycle and an order interval). The use of a fixed order quantity model, in which demand must be covered only for the length of the order cycle, will produce better (less worse) results when demand forecasts are inaccurate.

ESTABLISHMENT OF INVENTORY CONTINGENCY PROCEDURES

Inventory theory is not very helpful when it comes to dealing with the practical question of what to do when a stockout occurs or is imminent at a distribution center. The assumption often is made that a replenishment order can be expedited from a plant warehouse. When that source is exhausted, under what conditions do we (to the horror of the plant manager) reschedule the production process, or wait for the plant to produce the order according to its previously set schedule (to the horror of the distribution center manager), or replenish the stockout from another distribution center (to the horror of the traffic manager)? The task is the unpleasant one of choosing one from among several possible evils.

These types of problems require that procedures be established in advance for dealing with *routine contingencies*. What is important is that there be established procedures for handling stockouts, delayed shipments, backorders, and more, and that these procedures be known and understood by all concerned, particularly those responsible for communicating the (bad) news to the customer.

THE DESIGN OF REMAINING PROGRAM ELEMENTS

The remaining elements of an inventory management program include the computational device, the update cycle, and the program review procedures.

The Computational Device

Basically, the choice of computation devices these days can be described in terms of the proportion of the task committed to machine (the computer) or human. The most effective systems today are designed to capitalize on the advantages of each.

The computer, of course, offers the basic advantages of low-cost and accurate handling of complex computations. Where model inputs, such as forecasts of demand, must be updated frequently and the size of the product line is large, the computer is the only way to implement the use of a comprehensive inventory model. Complex inventory contingency procedures may also require the use of a computer. Finally, computerized procedures offer the advantage of frequent, low-cost review of all of the inventory records.

Manual inventory control is useful or even necessary in some situations. This is particularly true for newly introduced products with no demand history and for products that fall seasonally into the "dead stock" category, but for which upcoming seasonal demand will occur. In many companies, items stocked only at one warehouse, essentially for the convenience of one or a few customers, are managed manually by the personnel at that warehouse who are in close contact with the customer and sensitive to his or her ordering intentions.

The Inventory Update Cycle

The inventory update cycle is the time difference between the receipt or withdrawal of stock and the actual adjustment of the stock records. "Withdrawal" means any action that reserves stock for any reason that makes it unavailable for sale.

Clearly, the length of the update cycle determines the accuracy of the recorded inventory balance and the decisions based on this figure. The development of computing and communications technology has made it possible for more and more firms to maintain inventory records (for at least the fastest moving SKUs) on a real-time, or constantly up-to-date, basis.

Program Review Procedures

A formal program for management review is an essential element of an effective inventory management program. The frequency of review will depend on the degree to which conditions influencing each element to be reviewed might change. For example, changes in the nature of product demand brought on by changes in the market might warrant changes in forecasting methods. Judgmental inputs required by the inventory model should be reviewed periodically. For example, the cost of money invested in inventory is part of the inventory carrying cost and has varied greatly in recent years. It is now a highly variable input, requiring frequent review.

The most common problem with many inventory management programs is that they are simply out-of-date. Program review must be accomplished and responsibility for doing it must be set forth explicitly. Burr W. Hupp has argued persuasively that such responsibility should be assigned to someone in top management ranks.[3]

TESTING FOR COMPATIBILITY OF PROGRAM ELEMENTS

The elements of an inventory management program must always be checked for compatibility. For example, the forecasting period used by marketing should conform to the time periods in the inventory model. Thus, if the order point is of great concern in the inventory model because it sets the levels of stock coverage during an order cycle, and the typical order cycle is no more than two weeks in length, a forecast of demand for the next two weeks is much more useful than one that produces an estimate based on one-thirteenth of the forecasted demand for the next six months. In contrast, production planning may require a six-month forecast of overall demand be used in the model so that materials to be used in production can be programmed for that period.

To what extent does the inventory management program, regardless of the internal compatibility of its elements, take into account external factors, such as (1) environmental trends and other external determinants of company performance; (2) customer and supplier behavior patterns and needs; (3) objectives and strategies of general and logistics management; (4) company operating characteristics; and (5) the way the company is organized to do business? Environmental factors may range from economic cycles and their affect on demand to weather patterns and other determinants of seasonal usage. Often they may have to be taken into account by manual inputs to a forecasting or inventory model and require considerable judgment.

Customer and supplier behavior patterns and needs in a multistage channel of distribution are often in a state of flux. Independently managed inventories by the firms in a channel of physical distribution often cause "whipsaw" effects in the channel. For example, this will occur if a firm "misreads" a temporary or seasonal increase or decrease in orders as being permanent and proceeds to adjust production or inventory levels accordingly. The result will be either a glut or an extreme shortage of goods in the channel, depending on which type of mistake is made. For this reason, many firms are cautious about adjusting demand forecasts and inventory levels.

We have already discussed the importance of determining management objectives and strategies in advance of designing the inventory management program. However, given changing business conditions, it is important to review an inventory management program in the context of changes that may be desirable such as switching from a strategy of inventory accumulation during times of high inflation to a strategy of inventory minimization during times of high interest rates.*

The number of plants and warehouses, product characteristics, capacity constraints, and economic purchasing and transportation quantities are all examples of company operating characteristics that may influence the design of the program.

Similarly, the program must be compatible with a company's organizational philosophy. This may be indicated by the number and type of profit centers within the company, the nature of incentives and rewards offered to managers, and the emphasis on centralization or decentralization in the management of various functions within the firm.

INVENTORY SCHEDULING

Goods must be at the right location in the right quantity at the right time if a desired level of logistics service is to be achieved. Inventory scheduling involves the timing, sequencing, and grouping of purchases, production runs, and shipments. It is an amorphous topic encompassing a wide variety of techniques and applications. Inventory scheduling decisions typically affect several departments in a firm and often produce interdepartmental conflict as one manager perceives that his or her department's "turf" is being stepped on by another department.

This section of the chapter considers production scheduling and other types of inventory scheduling problems such as priority determination, system loading, and split-shipment planning.

PRODUCTION SCHEDULING

When and in *what quantities* will goods be produced, and when must the needed raw materials be on hand? In many firms, answers to these questions are found in a haphazard manner, particularly in regard to the scheduling of production of finished goods. During the search, there is often pulling and hauling between the production department and other departments of the firm. The reason is natural enough: the production department wishes to produce

---

*In recent years there have been periods when both high inflation and high interest rates prevailed, to the consternation of economists. Business firms typically bowed in the direction of the high interest rates and minimized inventories.

"efficiently," and this is usually interpreted to mean "produce in economic lot quantities." Unfortunately, this seldom provides a solution to the requirements of customer service as reflected in optimum finished goods inventory levels.

Two problems exist here. First, an economic lot quantity as viewed by the production department may not be an economic lot quantity when viewed from the standpoint of the firm as a whole. Second, even if the production runs are scheduled in quantities that are economic lots from the standpoint of the whole firm, there still remains the question of what "lot" of product(s) to produce today, this week, next week, or next month.

Because formulas for the determination of economic lot quantities are sophisticated enough to include costs not directly related to the production process, such as inventory carrying costs, poor customer service penalties (costs of lost sales, back orders, and so on), purchase discounts, transportation rate discounts, and the like, it is possible to determine a true "firm" economic order quantity (FEOQ).

Assuming that an FEOQ can be determined, the next problem concerns determining *when* lots of particular products should be produced. The problem can be broken into two parts: (1) the gross production planning of the items and quantities that should be produced during a given time period, and (2) the detailed scheduling of activities *within* the production process. To a greater and greater extent, gross production scheduling is being placed in the hands of managers responsible for corporate logistics.

Effective coordination of planning of inventory levels and production scheduling imposes certain requirements on several departments in a firm. These requirements include the transmission of information (sales forecasts) and decisions (customer service standards) from the marketing department to logistics. Also, the production department must advise logistics of its production capabilities (capacity) for various products, lead times, and the quantity of raw materials needed to produce a given amount of a product. And, however and by whomever determined, the FEOQ must be known to logistics management. For its part, logistics management must inform the production department of what lots of products are to be produced by what dates, and must see that required supplies of materials are available as needed for production.

Much has been written in recent years about a variety of inventory management practices called MRP I, MRP II, JIT and the Japanese concept called *kanban*. All of these are related to production scheduling, but only two of them (MRP I and *externally oriented* JIT) are true concerns of logistics managers.

Kanban is an in-plant production control technique for minimizing capital invested in in-process parts inventories, a desirable end in itself. Doing this also prevents *accumulation* of parts (or subassemblies) that are defective, and reflects the deep concern of Japanese management with quality control and the cost savings resulting from minimizing rejects. However, kanban is a tool of the production manager; it is not a direct concern of the logistics manager, whose responsibility simply does not extend to the factory floor.

Kanban is sometimes termed JIT, particularly by American managers. When so defined, JIT is *internally* oriented and is not the concern of a logistics manager. The other definition of JIT refers to *external* material movements inbound to a plant; this definition, which *is* of concern to logistics managers, is discussed later in this chapter.

MRP II is the acronym for Manufacturing Resources Planning and addresses the subject of plant capacity. This is of considerable interest to the logistics manager, and his or her input may be sought when such decisions are being made. However, questions of investment in added plant capacity, or the reduction of capacity, are generally top management decisions that result in a "given" plant capacity so far as logistics management is concerned.

It is in respect to MRP I (Materials Requirements Planning) and externally oriented JIT practices that the logistics manager has an active concern. MRP I is treated below, following the discussion of Aggregate Analysis and Planning.

Aggregate Analysis and Planning

Most manufacturing organizations face the need to plan the manufacture of a number of different products during a given day, week, or month. This requires advance planning of production to produce relatively constant plant loads, optimal scheduling of loading to meet changing seasonal needs, and rationing of limited production capacity in times of high (peak) demand levels.

Advance Planning and Master Scheduling   Master schedules are prepared for production operations on the basis of the following criteria:

1. Translation of general sales forecasts into general production loads for up to six months into the future.

2. Development of item-by-item production needs for shorter periods of time.

3. Reconciliation of production needs with intermediate-term production capacities.

4. Development of short-term (90 days or less) plant loadings, including the allocation of needed production among plants with overlapping production capabilities; this often is accomplished with the aid of linear programming techniques, particularly where an attempt is made to relate the production point to the location(s) of expected demand(s).

Typically, master scheduling is seldom done for periods of more than one year. In some industries — especially those not subject to much seasonality and having only moderate lead times for materials purchases — master schedules may cover a period of only six months, or less.

Trade-offs encountered in the master scheduling process are (1) the desire to load to capacity as opposed to retaining some flexibility for last-minute schedule changes; and (2) the desirability, in particular during periods of demand in excess of capacity, of scheduling for maximum output as opposed to more frequent production "cycles" of product groupings (involving more frequent line changes).

Many companies set aside capacity, even in the short-term production schedule, to accommodate unanticipated manufacturing delays or last-minute orders from preferred customers without disrupting the production schedule. An example is found in the manufacture of consumer paper products sold largely under private (retail chain) brands. In this business, unexpected orders, short lead-time demands from customers, and an intense level of competition for retailer orders are the rule. One manufacturer never loads its plants to more than 85 percent of capacity at the time schedules are "locked in." This provides the marketing and physical distribution groups in this firm with a cushion to absorb last-minute orders.

Production Sequencing   Typically, SKUs in product groupings that can be produced in the same facility and on the same equipment are cycled, or produced in turn, several times a year. Internal cycle sequence is often designed to minimize the costs of machine setup in switching from the production of one SKU to another. This means that once an SKU is scratched or omitted from a given cycle, its production must await the production of all other items in the cycle.

During times of heavy demand for a particular SKU or SKUs, it is tempting to increase the production runs (lot sizes) for them. Doing this will reduce the number of cycles that can be produced in a given period of time and increase order-cycle times for the replenishment of company stocks of other SKUs.

The desirability of such a strategy is related directly to the magnitude of setup costs, inventory carrying costs, and the short-term sales and profit implications from the current sale of larger numbers of a particular SKU or group of SKUs. On the other hand, there is no direct link to the long-term sales and profit implications of a deterioration in customer service from a likely upcoming shortage of SKUs whose production has been delayed. Problems that would be caused by disrupting established production plans to achieve short-term profit increases usually rule out making drastic adjustments to production schedules in order to take advantage of short-term opportunities.

Production Smoothing If a firm has enough production capacity to meet its annual demand, but not enough to meet peak demands during the year, inventory stocks must be built up during slack periods in order to meet demand in subsequent peak periods. Thus, inventory levels will vary from period to period, but the rate of production will be level or ''smooth'' throughout the year.

In its most simplified form, the nature of the problem at the Cleveland plant of the hypothetical Norm Manufacturing Company could be described as one in which peak seasonal demands were approximately twice those for slack periods, as shown in Table 6–3.

If the mix of units produced (typically 6 to 12 weeks in advance of an outbound shipment from the distribution center to Norm's customers) varies little from month to month, capacity planning and production smoothing decisions could be made on an aggregate basis for all types of SKUs. The economics on which such decisions would be based include (1) the interest cost on the investment in plant production capacity, (2) a fixed charge per unit of production capacity for maintaining plant facilities and the fixed costs of maintaining the labor force, (3) a monthly inventory carrying cost per unit in stock, (4) the average contribution over variable cost per unit sold, (5) a sales loss (stockout) cost for the quantity of items not produced by the plant during the month they were demanded by the distribution centers, and (6) a one-time production scheduling per-unit cost for increases or decreases in the monthly output. The total number of possible combinations and permutations of alternative numbers assigned to these factors (variables) and those discussed in the next paragraph is extremely large.

To determine what amount of plant capacity and what pattern of month-to-month production should be scheduled so as to maximize company profit, one would have to program an extensive simulation of Norm's production operations. Solving the problem becomes even more complex when matters such as the timing of vacations, the scheduling of overtime or additional production shifts to increase capacity, and possible alternatives of purchasing parts, components, and subassemblies from subcontractors are factored into the simulation. Computers are essential for carrying out such large simulations and thereby facilitating the decision process.

Allocation of Limited Capacity Plans used by manufacturers for allocating limited capacity include (1) first-come, first-served; (2) SKUs with the fastest production rates; (3) SKUs found on the smallest (quickest to fill) orders; (4) the most profitable SKUs, or orders from the most profitable customers; or (5) orders from the oldest, most loyal customers. The

TABLE 6–3: Sales, Production, and Inventory Projections (in Units) for the Coming Year, Norm Manufacturing Company

Month	Customer Orders on DCs	DC orders on Plant	Plant Output[a]	Planned Stocks Beginning of Month
January	40,000	40,000	55,000	154,000
February	35,000	50,000	55,000	169,000
March	40,000	60,000	55,000	174,000
April	50,000	70,000	55,000	169,000
May	60,000	65,000	55,000	159,000
June	70,000	45,000	55,000	169,000
July	65,000	55,000	25,000	139,000
August	45,000	70,000	55,000	124,000
September	55,000	65,000	55,000	114,000
October	70,000	35,000	55,000	134,000
November	65,000	40,000	55,000	149,000
December	35,000	35,000	55,000	169,000
TOTALS	630,000	630,000	630,000	1,823,000
				(or an average of 152,000 units on hand)

[a]Shown as a "leveled production rate" of 55,000 units per month except for July, when the plant closes for three weeks of vacation. Whether or not this is an optimum schedule depends on the relative costs of changing production levels versus the costs of carrying larger amounts of inventory than required during some periods of the year.

policy most frequently followed is probably the latter, particularly when production is scheduled on the basis of individual customer orders rather than forecasts of distribution center replenishment orders.

The experience of a number of companies suggests that an organization's ability to quote accurate, realistic delivery times is a function largely of:

1. The existence of a prearranged plan for allocating and scheduling demand.

2. Adherence to the prearranged plan, even during periods of stress.

3. The degree to which sufficient allowance is made for slack in the loading of plant facilities.

4. The quality of communications among marketing, production, and logistics regarding changes in sales demands or producing capabilities.

Materials Requirements Planning (MRP I)

In simplified form, MRP I consists of (1) the preparation of a master production schedule for some period into the future, (2) the preparation of a bill of materials for each item to be produced, (3) the ''explosion'' of the units on the master production schedule into a component-by-component requirement schedule, both in terms of quantities and dates needed, and

(4) the scheduling of component inventory replenishment according to necessary lead times and economic order, buying, or shipping quantities *to conform with the requirement schedule rather than average demand over time*.

For a multistage manufacturing process, the calculations become overwhelmingly complex. This explains why MRP I is a child of the computer. Although it is a relatively simple concept, MRP I requires massive amounts of data that cannot be processed in timely fashion by manual methods.

MRP I systems can produce significant inventory savings. On the other hand, according to Buffa and Miller:

> The disadvantages of MRP systems are inherent in the cost of developing them, and the demands they create for skilled and astute managers to operate them.[4]

Conflict between EOQ Calculations and Materials Requirements Statistical inventory control of the sort described in Chapter 5 usually works fairly well in marketing-oriented situations where the pattern of demand must be forecasted and is *independent* of the firm's internal operations. But when materials and component parts are procured in response to production needs, demand is said to be *dependent* (on the production schedule); it is known some time in advance. However, in the case of noncontinuous production, particular products are made only at certain times and demand for these materials or parts is *irregular*. Table 6–4 shows such a pattern of material demand (need) for an SKU production schedule.

Laufer's treatment of this problem is concise and lucid.[5] He discusses four approaches to handling it and notes the major limitation(s) of each:

1. Use a calculated EOQ. The limitation of this approach is the cost resulting from the need to carry inventory over periods of nonuse.

2. Order only what is needed for each period. This will lower inventory carrying costs but is likely to result in very high ordering costs.

3. Order periodically on a "judgment" basis. Despite its informality, this intuitive method may well produce reasonably acceptable results. However, the use of this method is quite impractical if large numbers of SKUs are involved; every SKU would have to be monitored manually by persons skilled in applying inventory management principles.

TABLE 6–4: Placement of Orders and Order Size for an SKU Using the Part-Period Method of Order Sizing

	Weeks											
	1	2	3	4	5	6	7	8	9	10	11	12
Requirements	180	0	470	570	780	0	100	200	300	0	150	150
Periods carried	0	0	0	0	0	0	0	1	0	0	0	1
Part period value	0	0	0	0	0	0	0	200	0	0	0	150
Order size	180	0	470	570	780	0	300	0	300	0	300	0

4. Use a technique that roughly balances carrying costs and ordering costs over time and that can be computerized. This technique is called *part-period balancing*. Laufer describes it in this fashion:

> To determine the order quantity with the part-period balancing method, the total cost of placing an order is equated with the total cost of carrying the inventory (or at least come as close as possible to this). A ''part period'' is one part held in inventory one period, and the economic part period is computed by dividing the ordering cost by the inventory carrying cost for one period. There is a carrying cost associated with each part period. Thus the total carrying costs of x units held for n periods or of n units carried for x periods is the product of xn and the period carrying cost. This product is the part-period value.
>
> The part-period values are accumulated to the point where they are still less than or equal to the economic part period. The requirements up through this period are then ordered, and a new calculation begins with the next period.[6]

An Example Table 6–4 shows the weekly requirements for an SKU whose EOQ is 394 units. (The unit value is $65, the annual inventory carrying cost is 36 percent, annual usage is 13,000 units, and the ordering cost is $140.) The weekly carrying cost is calculated as ($65 × .36)/52 = $0.45. This results in 311 part periods, calculated as $140/$0.45 = 311. Orders would be placed for delivery and use as shown across the bottom line of Table 6–4.

To summarize, the basic managerial approaches to inventory control are that:

1. The concept of *independent* demand (and the consequent use of statistical inventory control techniques) applies to marketing-oriented situations, as discussed in Chapter 5, where demand is *unknown* and *irregular*.

2. The concept of *dependent* demand (and the use of MRP I inventory control techniques such as part-period balancing) applies to production operations in which demand is *known*, but *irregular*.

3. When production operations are continuous as to the use of an SKU, demand is *dependent*, *certain*, and *regular*. All that is required here is the use of accurate EOQs and monitoring of the system to adjust EOQs to accommodate any anticipated changes in production output levels.

Just-in-Time (JIT) Scheduling

The concept of ''externally oriented'' JIT is that shipments of inbound materials should arrive at the plant ''just in time'' for use. The objective is to minimize inventories of production materials, either purchased or manufactured in other company plants. This concept has received an indecent amount of attention and management emphasis in the United States in recent times, much of it misplaced and some of it foolishly costly.

If a firm and its suppliers have in the past been ''sloppy'' in respect to management of inventory levels, placement of orders, and control over order-filling and shipment times, the managers responsible deserve to be justly criticized. Further, merely putting one's ''house in order'' with respect to having reasonably intelligent inventory management practices is not particularly deserving of praise, nor should it be confused with JIT.

JIT literally means exercising extremely tight control over suppliers and carriers to produce a continuous flow of small quantities (orders) of inbound materials so as to minimize the amount of such inventory on hand. However, it is one thing to control *internal* company production operations very tightly (such as kanban or internal JIT), and quite another to have suppliers and transportation carriers continuously ship and deliver many orders of small quantities of goods within very narrow time frames.

As noted earlier in this chapter, stockouts of materials required for production are anathema and to be avoided at any cost within reason. JIT requires a very high level of carrier reliability, suppliers preferably located close to one's plant,* frequent deliveries, smaller shipments at higher transportation rates per unit shipped, an increase in order processing costs, quite possibly a single supplier for an item to facilitate coordination, and it is very likely to violate any reasonable EOQ calculations. Any "failure" in the system will result in a stockout and will shut down the production line because no safety stocks are held.

To summarize in respect to JIT, many benefits will be achieved if a firm "tightens" a formerly "loose" inventory management system for incoming materials used in production, but *there is no free lunch*. Some U.S. firms have discovered, to their dismay, that JIT applied in the extreme can be a disaster; it asks for too high a level of performance from vendors and carriers at too great a cost. Other firms have discovered that what they thought would be the application of JIT fortunately turned out simply to be a better program of inventory management—one that did not ask the impossible of suppliers and carriers, did not result in greatly increased costs of transportation, and did not increase the risk of production line shutdowns to an unacceptable level.[7]

SCHEDULING OF OTHER ACTIVITIES

In addition to production scheduling techniques, there are a number of other scheduling techniques that are of importance to logistics management. Most of those discussed in the sections that follow have applications in many functions of business in addition to logistics. For purposes of emphasis, however, all examples of their application will be drawn from logistics. They include system loading, route selection, and shipment splitting.

System Loading: Waiting-Line Theory

The number of waiting-line, or queuing, problems confronting logistics management is usually great. In nature they range from the processing of orders through a monitoring station to the loading and unloading of trucks at a warehouse facility. All pose the common problem of the extent to which facilities or labor should be provided at varying times to hold service and waiting costs to a minimum level. A simple illustration will demonstrate its rationale.

Single Line, Poisson Arrival, and Service Time The most basic use of waiting-line theory is in a facility equipped to handle only one waiting line in which units arrive and are serviced over times described by normal distributions of numbers. As an example, suppose the Altoona Manufacturing Company plant warehouse has one dock and one bay for unloading incoming trucks with shipments of components from a number of vendors located largely

---

*Intercompany or intracompany plant-to-plant movements of parts or components on a kanban or JIT basis may be possible if the plants are relatively close to each other, although the constraints mentioned above will still be present to some degree. It should be kept in mind that Japan is roughly geographically equivalent in size to the state of California, and many Japanese suppliers are located very close to their industrial customers. In contrast, many U.S. suppliers and their domestic customers are as much as 2,000 miles or more apart.

within 100 miles of its plant. Most of the trucks are operated by common carriers. Some are owned by vendor companies. All are making deliveries on a "delivered" basis; that is, the cost of inbound transportation is borne by vendors, who control the deliveries.

An observation of Altoona's plant warehouse dock over a period of time yields the information that the arrival rate of trucks during selected segments of time approximates that shown in Figure 6–3. That is, the range of arrivals per hour is from 2 to 12 trucks, with an average of 6 per hour. This distribution is called a Poisson distribution and is typical for vehicle arrivals in a variety of situations. Its mathematical properties allow it to be used in a number of theoretical formulations, including those pertaining to waiting-line theory. In the latter problem, the following relationships can be proven if arrival times are approximately Poisson and an event (in this case, arrival) can occur in any small interval of time, no matter what has happened in an adjacent time interval.

Figure 6–3: Distribution (Poisson in nature) of arrival rates of trucks during 100 half-hour intervals, Altoona Manufacturing Company plant warehouse

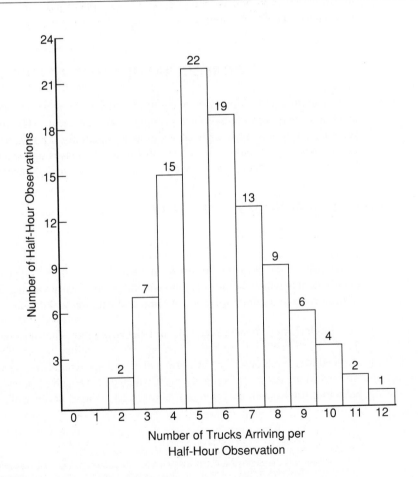

$$\bar{n} = \frac{\lambda}{\mu - \lambda}$$

$$\bar{t} = \frac{1}{\mu - \lambda}$$

$$p_n = p^n (1 - \rho)$$

where:

n = Number in line, including the one being serviced

$\bar{n}$ = average number in line, including the one being serviced

t = time an arrival spends in the system

$\bar{t}$ = average time an arrival spends in the system

λ = rate at which units arrive for service

μ = rate at which units are serviced

p = probability of an event

ρ = load factor = λ/μ.

If the rate for servicing trucks is seven per hour, with a range from 4 to 10, the following results would be obtained for the case at hand.

$$\bar{n} = \frac{6}{(7-6)} = 6 \text{ trucks in line on the average}$$

$$\bar{t} = \frac{1}{(7-6)} = 1 \text{ hour waiting time per truck on the average}$$

$$p_1 = \frac{6}{7}(1 - \frac{6}{7}) = \frac{6}{49} = \text{probability of finding 1 truck in line.}$$

If one worker could service 7 trucks per hour, it might be worthwhile to investigate the additional total cost or saving of adding a second worker, thereby reducing service time to the equivalent of 11 vehicles per hour. Under these conditions:

$$\bar{n} = \frac{6}{(11-6)} = 1.2 \text{ trucks in line.}$$

$$\bar{t} = \frac{1}{(11-6)} = .20 \text{ hour or 12 minutes of waiting time per truck.}$$

If the dock labor cost per worker was $8 per hour, the maximum number that could be used in a single crew was five, and the waiting cost of vehicle and driver was $12 per hour, the economic analysis shown in Table 6–5 could be carried out. It indicates that a dock crew of four workers would provide the lowest total cost for the operation.

One additional factor must be considered in a study of this type. Altoona does not suffer the costs of truck waiting time. Therefore, it might not be willing to increase the cost of labor to service each truck in order to help its suppliers or their hired carriers reduce their trucking costs, *unless* the savings could be shared.

Passage of legislation deregulating much of the transportation industry during 1976–1980 made it possible for shippers and carriers to negotiate rates so as to share in savings of the type

TABLE 6–5: Analysis of Service and Waiting Costs, Inbound Deliveries of Component Parts, Wilton Manufacturing Company, Plant Warehouse Receiving Dock

Number in Crew (L)	Service Rate, Number of Trucks per Hour (μ)	Arrival Rate, Number of Trucks per Hour (λ)	Waiting Time per Truck, in Minutes (t)	Labor Cost per Truck[a] (L_C)	Waiting Time Cost per Truck[b] (t_C)	Total Cost per Truck (C)
1	7	6	60.0	$1.14	$20.00	$21.14
2	11	6	12.0	1.45	4.00	5.45
3	14	6	7.5	1.71	2.50	4.21
4[c]	16	6	6.0	2.00	2.00	4.00[c]
5	17	6	5.5	2.35	1.67	4.21

[a]At the rate of $8 per worker-hour for dock labor.

[b]At the rate of $20 per truck-and-driver hour.

[c]Optimum staffing to produce lowest total cost per truck serviced.

the Altoona example shows are possible.* For this reason, analyses of the kind shown in Table 6–5 are no longer frustrating exercises. Today it would be possible for Altoona to negotiate lower trucking rates (directly or through its vendors) to compensate it for investing in an improved unloading method.

Situations involving multiple service stations require much more complicated calculations than the simple example considered above. Further, Poisson distributions for arrival rates on which most waiting-line theory is based may not be as common as is often assumed. Rarely are arrival rates for adjacent time periods independent and random in nature. More typically, systematic dispatching customs may produce peaks and valleys in arrival rates during the day, creating even worse delays and waiting-line lengths than those suggested by waiting-line theory.

Use of Simulation It is common practice to use simulation to reproduce waiting-line situations under various conditions. In the case described above, it would be desirable to document many days, weeks, or even months of arrival and service times in order to assess the impact of different procedures or facilities on vehicle flow and service times.

Manual simulation can be carried out with the use of random selection of numbers from distributions typifying observations and measurements previously made of the system being analyzed. However, simple computer routines generate random numbers and perform necessary calculations much more quickly than do manual methods for all but the simplest of waiting-line simulations.

Shipment Splitting

So-called ''split-offs'' in order shipment have become more common as the result of growing pressures to make goods available more and more rapidly for sale or further process-

---

*The subjects of transportation and traffic management and the many effects of transportation deregulation are covered in Chapters 7 and 8.

ing. Because the transportation rate per unit generally increases with a decrease in the quantity shipped, the use of split-offs incurs added transportation costs. In addition, where speed is a ruling factor, the transportation cost of a split-off is further increased by the use of faster methods (for example, airfreight) than would be utilized normally. This requires that split-offs be used judiciously and with careful timing.

Routine Split-Offs The Wilton Equipment Company purchases compressors from the Eastern Manufacturing Company. The weight of each compressor is 150 pounds when crated for shipment. Thus an order of 450 compressors would weigh about 67,500 pounds. The minimum weight per shipment, rate per hundredweight, and transit times required to ship compressors from Eastern to Wilton by various methods are shown in Table 6–6.

Several basic alternatives regarding the shipment of compressors would be available to Wilton, assuming that it purchased this item on an "F.O.B. origin" basis and controlled as well as paid for transportation: (1) all compressors could be shipped by air, (2) all by truck, (3) all by rail, (4) enough compressors could be shipped by air to accommodate Wilton's production until the arrival of the main portion of the shipment by truck, and (5) enough compressors could be shipped by truck to accommodate Wilton's production until the arrival of the main portion of the shipment by rail. Other alternatives, such as the use of more than two shipments (involving one split-off) might be considered. This is especially true for air freight, where one day of Wilton's production needs (40 compressors = 6,000 pounds) would exceed the minimum weight requirement for a volume rate.

On the basis of Eastern's setup time and production rate, the fastest that goods could be made available to Wilton would be 5 days ($O_t = 2 + 2 + {}^{50}/_{50} = 5$) if an air freight split-off were used. The slowest possible availability of compressors would be 19 days ($O_t = 2 + 8 + {}^{450}/_{50} = 19$) if all compressors were accumulated into one rail carload shipment. In the latter case, the same transportation cost would be incurred if the shipment were split in the fifth day of production and one-half shipped at that time by carload, thus reducing the availability time to roughly 15 days.

The choice of alternatives would depend upon Wilton's estimate of the penalties of having the goods available before or after they were needed by the production line. In cases where

TABLE 6–6: Transit Times, Rates, and Minimum Weights for Shipments of Compressors (Eastern Manufacturing Company to Wilton Equipment Company)

Method of Shipment	Transit Time (days)	Rate (per hundredweight)	Minimum Weight (pounds)
Rail	8	$1.60	30,000
	8	1.90	20,000
Truck	5	2.00	20,000
	5	2.80	15,000
	8	3.60	10,000
	8	4.50	5,000
Air	2	8.50	5,000
	2	12.80	100

sales might be lost, the penalty of receiving compressors late would be limited only to the profit on the daily sales that would have been realized had the compressors been available. Where delayed arrival might mean "downtime" for the production line, the resulting costs could be tremendous. On the other hand, if Wilton's production line could not begin scheduled work on the compressors until five days after they left Eastern's plant, the early arrival of any compressors utilizing air shipment would not produce any attendant savings. On the contrary, such early arrival would result in a cost penalty in the form of inventory carrying costs over a longer-than-usual period.

Timed Split-Offs Consider an example in which Wilton's production of heavy-duty automatic grinding machines using the same type of compressors could begin eight days from the date of order placement. Growing costs would result if production began one or more days later than that. The problem becomes a question of whether small shipments should be initiated upon completion of the daily production at Eastern's plant or whether compressors ready for shipment should be held until more economical shipping volumes accumulate. Delivery dates, costs of delivery, and costs of nonavailability of compressors under alternative combinations of split shipments are shown in Table 6–7.

TABLE 6–7: Some Alternative Delivery Dates and Costs under Methods of Splitting Compressor Shipments to the Wilton Manufacturing Company

		Costs				
Method of Shipment:	Availability Time[a]	Transportation[b]	Inventory Carrying[c]	Idle Manufacturing Capacity[d]	Lost Sales	Total
1. Five 50-unit shipments by truck; two 100 unit shipments by truck	8 days	$2,527.50	$256.00			$2,783.50
2. One 200-unit shipment by air; one 100-unit and one 150-unit truck shipments	8 days	3,420.00	226.20			3,646.20
3. Three 100-unit shipments and one 150-unit truck shipments	9 days	1,710,00	291.20	$100		2,101.20
4. Three 150-unit shipments by truck	10 days	1,350.00	321.60	600		2,271.60
5. One 200-unit and one 250-unit shipments by truck	11 days	1,350.00	356.80	1,600	$50	3,356.80

[a]For purposes of simplicity, computed on the assumption that shipments on the average would move by rail or truck during two plant nonoperating days (weekend). Thus, in situation 1, the setup time would require two operating days, first day's production, one operating day; and transportation, five operating and two nonoperating days—a total of eight operating days.

[b]Computed on the basis of rates and minimum rates in Table 6–6.

[c]Computed on the basis of inventory carrying costs on the average value of compressors on hand (added at the time of shipment; subtracted at the time the compressors enter Wilton's production line) over the shipping and storage cycle at the rate of .1 percent of the value of inventory on hand at the end of each operating day (36.5 percent annually).

[d]Estimated.

Although some minor costs of logistics and some less feasible combinations of split-offs were omitted from Table 6–7 for the sake of simplicity, it appears that savings in transportation costs would more than outweigh inventory carrying cost increases and costs of idle manufacturing capacity up to an availability time of nine operating days from the time of order placement. With longer availability times, total costs would rise. The most effective split-off in this example would be to allow a 100-unit batch to accumulate before shipment by truck. This would be followed by two 100-unit shipments and one 150-unit shipment by truck.

SUMMARY

Inventory theory deals primarily with ways of managing inventories to achieve the lowest total costs of holding and ordering inventory and servicing customer orders. In practice, inventory models may be used to achieve goals other than the lowest inventory costs. This may be necessary, for example at times when there are warehouse, factory capacity, or capital constraints. Purchasing and shipping costs may be so great that they overshadow other costs featured in many inventory models. And management may be more concerned about cutting inventory investment by a certain amount than it is about the correct application of a lowest total cost inventory model.

In the management of multi-item inventories, problems tend to center around the allocation of available stocks of a given item to several locations, questions of sourcing multiple SKUs, and the sequencing of orders to facilitate production economies. Opportunities arise as well for managing differently items with high rates of sale, high values per unit, expensive or extensive storage requirements, or high strategic values to customers. These differential approaches have come to be known as ABC systems.

The core of an inventory management program is composed of an inventory model, contingency procedures, computational device, update cycle, and program review procedures. In an effective inventory management program, these elements are internally consistent and their design is responsive to management goals, basic needs of the organization, and affairs of the organization external to the program. Further, through periodic appraisal and review, the program must reflect changes in these goals, needs, and external forces. The decision to institute the use of an inventory management program is more important than the choice of the particular program elements or the inputs used in particular inventory models. The questions asked in assembling inputs for the design of any program likely will be of much greater value to the practicing manager than philosophical debates about which of several programs is best.

The scheduling of inventory-related production activities, whether for the purpose of timing, determining priorities, or deciding upon appropriate sequences of actions, employs a wide variety of systems and procedures. Production-oriented scheduling techniques fall into the two basic families: (1) inventory control under conditions of certainty and regularity for use in supplying a continuous flow process; and (2) materials requirements planning (MRP I), for use in supplying production processes in which finished goods demand is dependent, scheduled in production batches, highly uneven, and known in advance.

Waiting line (or queuing) theory has been employed widely in the planning of capacity for facilities through which demand for service is processed. And, various analytic approaches are available for determining when to split off and expedite shipment of a portion of an order.

Experience shows that the causes of so-called scheduling problems are often external to the scheduling operation itself. Common examples are the setting of unrealistic dates for the receipt of incoming supplies and materials for production, or quoting unrealistic dates for the delivery of finished goods to customers or distribution centers. The cause of such problems may be pressure from top management for "impossible" performance. But, more often the cause is the inability of purchasing or sales personnel to divorce whimsy from reality or their inability to exercise willpower in accepting or quoting accurate availability dates. This suggests that in dealing with such problems, a manager of logistics activities should have a basic understanding of human behavior as well as knowledge of analytic techniques for inventory management.

DISCUSSION QUESTIONS

1. Why might a company wish to have its inventory managed to achieve goals other than minimizing inventory costs?

2. Explain the concept of "ABC" inventory policy. What objectives does it serve?

3. What are the principal elements of an inventory management program?

4. What is the most common fault of inventory management programs?

5. What are the relationships between logistics management and production management? and marketing management? Why are these relationships frequently strained?

6. In respect to MRP I, MRP II, kanban, and JIT scheduling, which are concerns of the logistics manager? Explain.

7. What difficulties are likely to be encountered in attempting to apply the concept of JIT scheduling for plant-inbound shipments of materials for production?

8. Explain the technique of "part-period balancing" as applied to ordering supplies of production materials. What problem does it solve, or at least mitigate?

9. What role does shipment splitting play in logistics management? Explain.

CASE: Debate on Implementation of Just-in-Time

The top managers of The Fullmore Corporation (TFC) were considering the implementation of JIT inventory management with respect to the purchased materials, parts, and components used in the company's production processes and products. TFC manufactured industrial floor- and wall-cleaning equipment, including several models of floor scrubbers, waxing machines, and hydraulic pressure cleaners, as well as a variety of specialized attachments used with these machines.

TFC purchased several sizes of electric motors used in its machines, all of the nuts, bolts, and fasteners used, sheet metal, paint, hoses, control cables, and raw materials, such as the fiber used to make scrubbing brushes. The company fabricated its sheet-metal parts, such as engine housings and the exterior coverings of its machines. It also fabricated hose connections, control handles, wheels, and other parts for its machines.

The president had conferred with several company executives including the production manager, the logistics manager, and the controller concerning JIT and the possibility of implementing the JIT concept at TFC.

The president of TFC had read a lot about JIT and believed these principles should be considered for implementation by the company with respect to inbound shipments of materials, parts, and so forth. The president was, however, open-minded on the matter and had invited the comments of TFC's production manager, logistics manager, and controller.

TFC's plant was located in Chicago. Most of the company's purchases of materials, parts, and components were supplied by vendors located within seven hundred miles of the plant, but only a handful were located within fifty miles of Chicago, and none were within the Chicago metropolitan area.

The production manager was lukewarm to the proposal to implement JIT for inbound shipments, pointing out that TFC dealt with about one hundred vendors, the firm had adequate storage space for its preproduction inventories, purchase orders were placed for economic order quantities, and, finally, that JIT posed a grave risk of any foul-up causing a shutdown of one or more of the firm's production operations.

The logistics manager acknowledged the arguments of the production manager. Further, she knew that her neck would be on the line if things went wrong and a production line had to be shut down. She would be held responsible even if a bad situation beyond her control developed. She didn't oppose the idea of JIT, but she knew from reading articles about JIT in trade magazines that it was a lot easier to talk about it than to implement it.

The controller was "all for the idea," commenting further that, "You (looking at the logistics manager) get paid to manage the logistics function in this firm. It looks to me as if the reduction in investment in inventory, plus the space gain in our plant warehouse, would be very desirable for the company."

The president had listened carefully to the discussion among the three executives, and had noted the concern on the logistics manager's face. The president said, "Clearly, the logistics manager is the person who would have to manage an inbound JIT system if we put it into practice. So, what I want you to do (looking at the logistics manager) is to study the matter and write up a feasibility report for us. Then we'll discuss the matter further."

CASE QUESTION

1. Assume you are TFC's logistics manager. How would you go about preparing the feasibility report requested by the president? What information would you need? What factors would you want to consider?

SUGGESTED READINGS

In addition to the references given below, the reader should also refer to the list of Suggested Readings at the end of Chapter 5. There is often substantial overlap in the literature between the topics of "principles of inventory control" and "inventory management."

ADAM, EVERETT E., JR., and RONALD J. EBERT, *Production and Operations Management: Concepts, Models, and Behavior*, 4th ed. Englewood Cliffs, New Jersey: Prentice-Hall, Inc., 1989. This book presents a sound treatment of inventory models and applications in Chapters 12 and 13, which include many useful examples and worked-out problems.

AKAAH, ISHMAEL P., and GEORGE C. JACKSON, "Frequency Distributions of the Weights of Customer Orders in Physical Distribution Systems," *Journal of Business Logistics* 9, no. 2 (1988): 155–164. Based on a study of 40 firms, this article provides guidelines for logistics managers with respect to determining the actual pattern of customer orders rather than depending on an assumed distribution that is likely to be wrong at least two-thirds of the time.

BLUMENFELD, DENNIS E., RANDOLPH W. HALL, and WILLIAM C. JORDAN, "Trade-Off Between Freight Expediting and Safety Stock Inventory Costs," *Journal of Business Logistics* 6, no. 1 (1985): 79–100. This article presents a model for determining the optimal relationship between the cost of holding safety stock and the cost of expediting shipments.

CHASE, RICHARD B., and NICHOLAS J. AQUILANO, *Production and Operations Management: A Life Cycle Approach*, 5th ed., Homewood, Illinois: Richard D. Irwin, Inc., 1989. Chapters 12 and 13 present excellent discussions of the design of inventory systems for independent and dependent demand; material requirements planning and just-in-time production system applications are treated in Chapters 13 and 16.

CLOSS, DAVID J., and WAI-KIN LAW, "Modeling the Impact of Environment and Inventory Management Policy on Materials Management Performance," *Journal of Business Logistics* 5, no. 1 (1984): 57–80. This article examines and discusses the management implications of different environmental conditions upon the performance of various inventory management alternatives and points out that the actions of customers, suppliers, competitors, and even other functions of the firm, such as trade promotion, cause uncertainty in the firm's environment.

GLASKOWSKY, NICHOLAS A., JR., "Kanban/Just-in-Time: Panacea or Plague?," Part I, *Logistics Spectrum, Journal of the Society of Logistics Engineers* 21, no. 4 (Winter, 1987): 15–19; Part II, vol. 22, no. 1 (Spring, 1988): 19–21. As the title of this article suggests, kanban/JIT techniques properly applied may be of great benefit to a firm or, alternatively, may be inappropriate and therefore actually dysfunctional. The article contains an analysis of differences between the Japanese and American business environments, and also summarizes the types of situations in which kanban/JIT practices can be implemented effectively in the American business environment.

GOMES, ROGER, and JOHN T. MENTZER, "A Systems Approach to the Investigation of Just-in-Time," *Journal of Business Logistics* 9, no. 2 (1988): 71–88. This article points out the lack of a consistent definition of the concept of Just-in-Time (JIT), lack of a systems approach to empirical research, and lack of a method of organizing the research area. Proposals for dealing with the absence of these elements are developed.

GREENE, JAMES H., *Operations Management: Productivity and Profit*. Reston, Virginia: Reston Publishing Company, 1984. Chapter 20 presents a very good treatment of dependent-demand inventory management.

HENDRICK, THOMAS E., and FRANKLIN G. MOORE, *Production/Operations Management*, 9th ed. Homewood, Illinois: Richard D. Irwin, Inc., 1985. A good general reference with an excellent treatment of waiting-line (queuing) theory and analysis in Chapter 17.

HERRON, DAVID P., "Integrated Inventory Management," *Journal of Business Logistics* 8, no. 1 (1987): 96–116. This article develops an approach for calculating the best combination of buffer stocks, expediting measures, and replenishment frequencies to deal with the inevitable uncertainties of supplying components and materials to manufacturing and finished goods and spare parts to customers.

LAMBERT, DOUGLAS M., and MARK L. BENNION, "Establishing a Minimum Order Policy," *Journal of Business Logistics* 7, no. 2 (1986): 91–108. This article addresses the age-old problem of the costs associated with small orders and includes an interesting case study.

SCHROEDER, ROGER G., *Operations Management: Decision Making in the Operations Function*, 3rd ed. New York: McGraw-Hill Book Company, 1989. Part 4 of this text is a very well organized four-chapter treatment of the general subject of inventory management. Part 3 treats capacity planning and scheduling and is a useful reference for that topic.

TERSINE, RICHARD J., RICHARD A. TOELLE, and ALBERT B. SCHWARZKOPF, "An Analytical Model of Determining Excess Inventory," *Journal of Business Logistics* 7, no. 1 (1986): 122–142. The focus of this article is oriented toward appropriate liquidation of excess inventory and its positive effects on the firm's cash flow.

ZINN, WALTER, and DONALD J. BOWERSOX, "Planning Physical Distribution with the Principle of Postponement," *Journal of Business Logistics* 9, no. 2 (1988): 117–136. This article deals with the problem of providing effective physical distribution while serving an increased number of delivery destinations and simultaneously supporting a growing number of stock keeping units by postponing labeling, packaging, and assembly.

ZINN, WALTER, MICHAEL LEVY, and DONALD J. BOWERSOX, "Measuring the Effect of Inventory Centralization/Decentralization on Aggregate Safety Stock: The 'Square Root Law' Revisited," *Journal of Business Logistics* 10, no. 1 (1989): 1–14. This article develops a general model which eliminates the need for the restrictive and unrealistic assumptions inherent in the "square root law" approach to inventory centralization.

ENDNOTES

1. Robert G. Brown, *Decision Rules for Inventory Management* (New York: Holt, Rinehart and Winston, 1967), 16.

2. This approach is described in Harvey N. Shycon and Christopher R. Sprague, "Put a Price Tag on Your Customer Servicing Levels," *Harvard Business Review* (July-August, 1975) 71–78.

3. Burr W. Hupp, "Inventory Policy Is a Top Management Responsibility," *Handling & Shipping* (August, 1967) 47–49.

4. Elwood S. Buffa and Jeffrey G. Miller, *Production-Inventory Systems*, 3d ed. (Homewood, Illinois: Richard D. Irwin, Inc. 1979) 367.

5. Arthur C. Laufer, *Production and Operations Management*, 3d ed. (Cincinnati, Ohio: South-Western Publishing Co., 1984) 559–61.

6. *Ibid*.

7. "Survey Shows J-I-T Taking Off," *Inbound Logistics* 5, no. 4 (October, 1985) 27–28. A very careful reading of this article shows that much of the expressed enthusiasm for JIT represents (1) simply the sensible tightening of inventory management systems, and (2) concentration on internal operations. As the article says, "More progress has been made in developing J-I-T uses for internal operations than for those that use outside transportation carriers" and "It is significant that J-I-T is used less as management responsibility changes from purchasing and production to transportation and distribution. This decline is consistent through all three measures of J-I-T use [inventory management; vendor lead-time management; and production, inbound transportation and distribution]."

PART TWO

INTEGRATED LOGISTICS SYSTEM OPERATIONS

Intermodal transportation is playing an increasingly important role in the operations of logistics systems.

CHAPTER SEVEN

Transport Facilities

LEARNING OBJECTIVES

The objectives of this chapter are to:

➤ Explain and discuss the structure of the transportation industry and the role it plays in logistics systems.

➤ Discuss the existence of and reasons for the several legal forms of transportation.

➤ Explain the role of auxiliary users of transportation such as freight forwarders, shippers' cooperatives, and so forth.

➤ Discuss the several forms of intermodal transport and their roles in the transportation industry.

➤ Explain the relative importance of the several modes of transportation in terms of the volume of freight carried by each.

➤ Explain, discuss, and compare the cost characteristics of the several modes of transportation and the relevance of these to logistics management.

➤ Explain, discuss, and compare the various operating characteristics of the several modes of transportation and the relevance of these to logistics management.

Transportation is the vital connecting link among farming, forestry, fishing and mining operations, manufacturing and processing plants, distribution centers, wholesalers, retailers, and ultimate consumers in business logistics systems. And, with few exceptions, the cost of transportation is by far the largest category of expense in logistics activities.

Given the importance and expense of transportation in the operation of logistics systems, it is helpful to understand the structure of the transportation industry as well as the more important trends in the costs and other characteristics of each of the several modes of transportation. That's what this chapter is about.

The better a logistics manager understands the structure of the transportation industry, and particularly the operating and cost characteristics of the several modes and various intermodal services, the more effective that manager will be. To put it another way, it is critically important for a logistics manager to know what carrier performance is possible and at what cost. A favorite saying of economists is that "there is no free lunch," and shippers buying transportation services are no exception to this rule.

The "managerial behavior" of carriers is based on their operating/cost characteristics and traffic patterns and is clearly reflected in their pricing policies, operating practices, and capabilities. Three examples will illustrate this point.

1. Airfreight service via scheduled passenger airlines from Miami to many island destinations in the Caribbean is notoriously delayed (a *week* in many cases) because the limited cargo capacity of the airplanes serving these routes (mostly 727s, 737s and DC9s) is largely absorbed by the great volume of checked luggage of resort-bound vacationers and an incredible amount of checked baggage consisting of Miami shopping purchases of island-country residents returning home. A similar situation occurs *throughout* the airline industry during peak travel periods such as Easter week and the Christmas holiday period when planes are packed with passengers and mountains of luggage in the cargo holds. An alert logistics manager will be aware of such situations. Service that is advertised is sometimes service that is not available.

2. A motor carrier handling a large amount of high-density freight such as canned motor oil might well offer a significant inducement to a shipper who can offer the carrier low-density "balloon" freight the carrier can use to "top out" its trailer loads and thereby stay within gross vehicle-load limits. The motor carrier wants to use both its cubic carrying capacity as well as its weight carrying capacity. However, another motor carrier might well be in the opposite situation, and be seeking high-density freight. Again, an alert logistics manager should seek out such situations.

3. Separable cargo and power units are another factor that accounts for carrier "behavior." Railroad cars, truck trailers, and towed barges can be separated from their costly power units (locomotives, truck tractors, and towboats). But the cargo space of a ship or aircraft is integral to that ship or aircraft; it can't be separated from the power units (engines) and hull. The result is that railroad cars, truck trailers, and barges can be, and often are, left for loading or unloading at origin or destination for some period of time while the power unit (locomotive, tractor, or towboat) goes about its business elsewhere. The opposite is true in the case of ships and aircraft, which must be unloaded and reloaded as fast as possible because the costly hull and engines are out of service as long as the cargo space is being loaded or unloaded.

THE STRUCTURE OF THE TRANSPORTATION INDUSTRY

The five basic modes of transportation are rail, highway, water, air, and pipeline. Two other "modes of transportation," technically speaking, are conveyor and wire. As a mode of transportation, conveyors have experienced very limited growth, except within fixed facilities. Wire generally is not included in this type of discussion as it is limited to carrying only information or energy (electricity).

It is necessary to distinguish between "water" and "ocean" transportation as the terms are used in this book. Water transportation includes and refers to the movement of vessels and barges on inland waterways, the Great Lakes, and in intercoastal and intracoastal traffic. It is, therefore, defined as follows: water transportation consists of freight movements that could alternatively move from origin to destination entirely by land transportation. Ocean transportation is therefore defined as a transportation movement for which the only alternative is air transportation.

Further, one should bear in mind that water, ocean, rail, highway, air, and pipeline transportation may be either domestic or international, as well as the fact that some ocean and overseas air movements are "domestic," for example, mainland U.S. to or from Hawaii, Alaska, Puerto Rico, the American Virgin Islands, or between those "offshore" places.

The transportation industry also includes a number of specialized transport variations and sub-groups comprising (1) several different legal forms, (2) a number of auxiliary users of transportation, and (3) intermodal transportation systems.

The relationships among these groups are shown in Figure 7–1. You may find it helpful to refer to Figure 7–1 now and again as you read this chapter.

Legal Forms

The term "legal form" refers to the manner in which a transportation operation is regarded for regulatory purposes by agencies of federal, state, and local governments. The motor carrier industry illustrates the most complete range of legal forms, and its legal structure is shown in Figure 7–2.

The broadest legal distinction is between trucking companies in the business of providing transportation services to others on a "for hire" basis, and firms in nontransportation businesses operating private truck fleets to facilitate a primary activity such as manufacturing.

A third legal form is the transportation broker who plays a significant role in the motor carrier industry. Brokers match available freight and resultant shipper needs with transport capacity for a fee, but they do not actually operate equipment. They are prominent in facilitating the carriage of agricultural products, particularly fresh fruits and vegetables. They are also starting to play a larger role than formerly — due to deregulation of the motor carrier industry — with respect to less-than-truckload shipments, more of which will be discussed later.

Federal legislation — the Motor Carrier Act of 1980 — and the relaxation of many administrative regulations by the Interstate Commerce Commission (ICC) led to the elimination of nearly all restrictions on routes that may be served by interstate common carriers, commodities that may be carried by exempt carriers, and customers that may be served by private carriers. Many provisions of the Motor Carrier Act reflected what the ICC had already done on its own during the 1970s as the pressure for deregulation gained strength. In addition, common carriers by highway and rail as well as those carrying household goods have been granted

Figure 7–1: The relationship of modes, legal forms, auxiliary users and principal intermodal systems of transportation

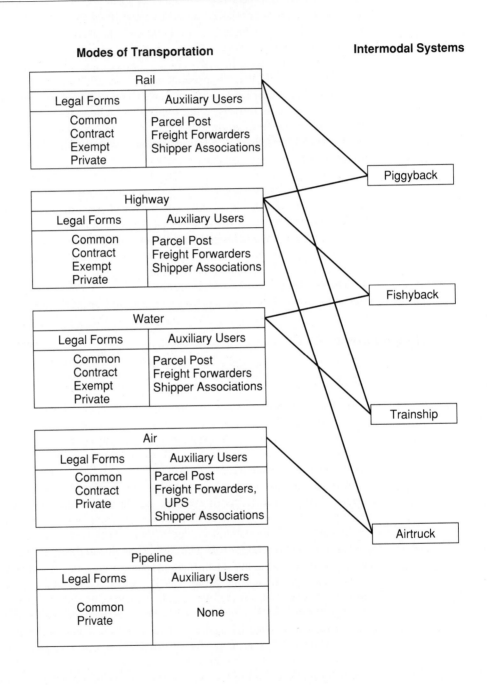

Figure 7–2: ICC classifications of motor carriers of property

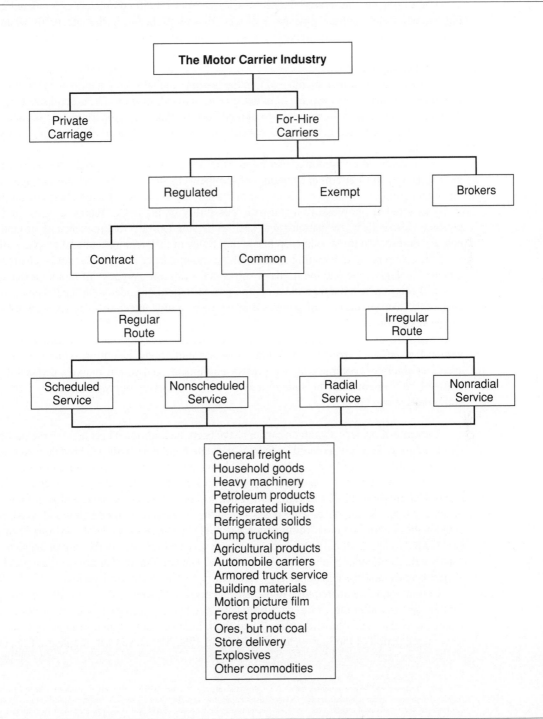

greater pricing and operating freedom. This has blurred the legal forms of transport somewhat. But the five legal forms remain: common, contract, exempt, private, and broker.

For all practical purposes, the Motor Carrier Act of 1980 completely deregulated entry into common and contract carriage, a process that really began in the late 1970s when the Interstate Commerce Commission correctly read the Congressional tea leaves. Simultaneously, most of the legal distinctions among common, contract, and exempt motor carriage were essentially removed.

However, it must be remembered that the historical legal segmentation of the motor carrier industry prior to 1980 was far from being arbitrary in its origins. The several subsectors of the industry developed in response to shipper needs; that very important fact is, and will continue to be, reflected in the functional structure of the motor carrier industry regardless of deregulation.

For example, the common carrier versus contract carrier dichotomy reflects the realities of varying geographic patterns and volumes of shipments by firms, as does private carriage. Even the legal definition of exempt carriage, established in 1935 largely by the efforts of the farm lobby as a defensive measure against the possibility of high ICC-approved rates for farm products, also reflects the nation's real need to be able to shift trucking capacity around the country in response to varying crop harvesting times in different agricultural growing areas.

The economic and operating realities of the motor carrier industry cannot be changed or repealed by legislative fiat; the needs of shippers for different ''types'' of motor carrier services will continue to exist regardless of who provides them or under what legal banner. And, each of these different types of services is provided by a fundamentally different type of motor carrier operation.

Likewise, the need for specialized motor carrier services could not be affected by deregulation legislation. Carriage of bulk liquids, household goods, electronic equipment, explosives, automobiles, commercial steel, heavy equipment, and so on, requires dedicated specialized equipment and the management of motor carrier operations tailored to such commodity movements.

Common Carriers Common carriers have been the traditional backbone of the transportation industry. They are required by federal and state regulatory bodies to hold themselves out to carry goods tendered by all shippers of designated commodities. Common carriers are certified by and required to perform according to rules promulgated by the Interstate Commerce Commission (ICC) regarding rail, truck, domestic water carriers, and also joint rail-ocean and truck-ocean movement rates between the continental United States and Alaska and Hawaii; the Federal Aviation Administration (FAA) to airlines; the Federal Maritime Commission (FMC) to international ocean carriers in liner service,* and also in the case of ocean traffic between the continental United States and Alaska, Hawaii, Guam, Puerto Rico, and the U.S. Virgin Islands; and the Federal Energy Regulatory Commission to pipelines.

Common carriers are required to publish and make available to the public all rates charged for their services after these rates have been approved by the appropriate regulatory body. This is known as the ''filed tariff doctrine,'' and the failure of many motor carriers to observe it since deregulation of the motor carrier industry in 1980 has caused very unpleasant financial

---

*The term ''liner service'' in ocean transportation is roughly equivalent to ''common carrier.'' It means regularly scheduled service, open to all shippers under published tariffs. Ocean transportation also includes ''tramp'' service (roughly equivalent to ''contract'' carriage) as well as private transportation, the latter exemplified by bulk ocean carriers owned and operated by firms as diverse as oil companies and banana growers.

consequences for many shippers. Many motor common carriers went bankrupt in the wake of deregulation and many of them had carried traffic under lower-rate tariffs they had failed to file with the ICC, resulting in "undercharges" to shippers. These shippers are now being held liable for payment — large sums in many cases — of these undercharges by the bankruptcy courts.

In the past, those wishing to attain common carrier status had to prove that "public convenience and necessity" warranted their proposed services. With the passage of the Motor Carrier Act of 1980, common carriers by highway now only have to demonstrate that they are "fit, willing, and able" to perform such services. By eliminating any implied reference to the existing level of competition as a basis for granting new service authority, Congress instructed the Interstate Commerce Commission (ICC) to lower the barriers of entry into the highway transport industry. Similar legislation has freed the carriage of air freight from economic regulation. Railroads have also been granted much greater pricing freedom under deregulation.

Contract Carriers   Contract carriers make themselves available to a limited number of customers on a selective basis defined by individual shipper-carrier contracts. They may charge different rates to different customers for the same service. Permits to operate as a contract carrier are issued by regulatory bodies on a less restrictive basis than for common carriers. Railroads are also now allowed to enter into contract carriage. They are also permitted to keep secret the rates charged contract shipper customers, although these rates must be filed with the ICC on a confidential basis. Fostered by the freedom conferred by deregulation and the increasing customization of their logistics systems by shippers, contract carriage is the fastest growing segment of truck and rail carriage. Under deregulation, both motor and rail carriers may be both common carrier and contract carriers; some of the largest motor common carriers now carry as much, or nearly as much, contract traffic as common carrier traffic.

Exempt Carriers   Exempt carriage is a legal form of transportation that embraces a variety of activities. Exemption may be determined on the basis of the commodities being moved, the organization involved, or the area served.

For example, unprocessed products of agriculture and fishing are largely exempt from economic regulation regardless of mode, although any common carrier transporting such freight must publish its rates. Agricultural cooperatives (farmer-owned marketing organizations) similarly are exempt. Originally established to allow farmers to haul their products over public roads, the agricultural exemption has been extended to a wide range of specifically defined products. Since deregulation, transportation of exempt commodities has been steadily expanded to include intermodal (piggyback) and rail transportation.

Water carriers are exempt if they are transporting liquids in tank vessels or when they are carrying not more than three different bulk commodity shipments in a single ship or barge tow. These provisions effectively remove about 90 percent of water traffic from economic regulation.

A third class of carriers exempt from federal economic regulation and, in all but a few cases, state economic regulation are those engaged in local cartage within municipalities or commercial zones contiguous to municipalities, airports, and harbors. During 1978, the ICC enlarged the commercial zones for 42 major metropolitan areas to account for changing urban patterns and expanded the radius of the "free zone" around airports from 25 to 100 miles.[1]

Private Carriage   Private motor carriage refers to the common ownership of goods being transported and the lease or ownership of the equipment in which they are being moved.

TRUCKING: WHAT'S STILL REGULATED

Daniel J. Sweeney

Many shippers and carriers believe that the Motor Carrier Act of 1980 deregulated the motor carrier industry. Actually, that act left most of the industry's regulatory scheme in place. Following is the current regulatory situation in some areas affecting motor carriage.

Entry: The act left in place much of the entry framework for both common and contract carriers. A certificate or permit to operate is issued only after filing fee, and processing through the Interstate Commerce Commission (ICC).

The act relaxed the entry standards in that prospective diversion of revenue or traffic from an existing carrier cannot be found, in and of itself, to be inconsistent with the public convenience and necessity. A carrier objecting to a new entrant would have to show that the latter would put the former out of business, and that this would be inconsistent with the public interest.

Carriers also were permitted to hold both common and contract carrier authority, and many carriers now hold both types. In addition, the act expanded the types of operation for which any entry certificate or permit is not required, including intercorporate hauling (which requires filing of notice with the ICC and a list of participating subsidiaries), agricultural commodities and livestock, transportation within commercial zones and terminal areas, and casual and emergency transportation.

(It is worth noting that operating certificates and permits remain in effect only if the carrier maintains on file with the ICC adequate proof of security for public liability and property damage.)

Rates: Motor common carriers still must publish their rates and practices in tariffs on file with the Commission. In one of the truly major changes brought about by the act, the ICC, responding to an invitation in the act, relieved contract carriers from filing rates. The act also prescribed a zone of rate freedom within which a carrier can raise or lower its rates within percentage limits set by the ICC, but little use has been made of this provision.

The Commission has been notably disinterested in carrying out its statutory role of assuring reasonable rates, although faced with rate discounts that have been called ''kamikaze.'' In one proceeding, it demurred at limiting reduced

rates; in another, it declined to adopt standards for maximum rates in general increase cases, opining that it would be better to use a case-by-case approach. (General increase cases that would provide the vehicle for the case-by-case approach have been pending before the ICC continuously since 1978, but no decision has been issued.)

In the resulting environment, carriers individually have cut rates sharply and then, acting collectively in rate bureaus, generally increased rates beyond the rate of inflation on the grounds that they have the right to recoup adequate system profits through increases in their rate-bureau-made rates alone.

Rate Bureaus: The act decreed that collective action could not be used to establish single line rates as of July 1, 1984. There are specified exceptions to this provision for general rate increases, changes in classification, and changes in tariff structures. The ICC has rebuffed a series of challenges in which rate bureaus have attempted to construe these exceptions broadly.

Mergers and financial transactions: Pursuant to a special exemption power under the act, the ICC has exempted from its former procedural rules and substantive requirements most mergers, consolidations, and acquisitions involving motor carriers.

In a 1984 decision, the ICC adopted new and shortened procedural rules for processing those prospective exempt transactions. However, approval under these rules is subject to complaint by employees alleging adverse effect or by any party alleging anticompetitive effect.

Of interest here are cases involving acquisition of motor carriers by railroads. The Commission no longer requires a showing of special circumstances to justify acquisition by rail carriers of motor carriers whose operations are not limited to auxiliary-to-rail operation; last year, it approved Norfolk Southern Corp.'s acquisition of North American Van Lines. But the ICC still requires that such acquisitions be consistent with public interest and that they not restrain competition unreasonably.

SOURCE: Reprinted with permission, *Handling & Shipping Management*, August 1986 © Penton Publishing, Inc., Cleveland, OH.

Private carriers must exercise "significant" control over their drivers and equipment, and transportation must be carried on as an activity incidental to the primary purpose of the business. This "not for hire" legal form allows firms to transport their own goods without facing economic regulation at the state or federal level.

During the post–World War II period, the growth of private truck fleets coupled with the increased cost of empty backhauls and other "deadhead" mileage generated pressure for a relaxation of restrictions on private carrier operations. As a result, in its 1978 decision in the "Toto" case, the ICC ruled that private carriers could supplement their operations by obtaining common or contract carrier operating rights.[2] Congress took one step further by allowing, in the Motor Carrier Act of 1980, a private carrier to haul products for all subsidiaries of its parent organization, thus opening new opportunities for motor carrier private transport. Further, private motor carriers may also obtain contract and common carrier authority, although as discussed in more detail later in this chapter, such a "mix" of operations may not be advisable in many situations.

Private carriage is quite limited with respect to rail and air transportation. Water and ocean transportation have many private operations, primarily in the transportation of bulk cargoes such as oil, grain, chemicals, and so forth. Oil pipelines are all common carriers. Natural gas pipelines are generally treated as natural monopolies owned by gas producers and are heavily regulated with respect to service and rates.

Auxiliary Users

Auxiliary users are organizations that purchase a major portion of their transportation service from other carriers. They concentrate their operations on the handling of shipments of a few pounds up to container,[3] less-than-truckload (LTL), or less-than-carload (LCL) quantities.[4] They do not own or operate the equipment used for the line-haul movement of their loads, emphasizing instead the collection of freight at origin and distribution at destination. While many freight movements may involve more than one carrier, auxiliary users assume complete responsibility for the movement of a shipper's freight regardless of the number of carriers or modes involved. Major auxiliary users include the United Parcel Service (for some of its air shipments), the U.S. Postal Service's Parcel Post and Express Mail, freight forwarders, shippers' associations, and freight brokers. Additionally, so-called "third-party" providers of logistics services may be regarded as auxiliary users.

Freight forwarders are considered by some to be a separate legal form of transportation because they are subjected to regulation similar to that for common carriers. Their major function is the consolidation of small shipments into larger ones for long-distance movement. While obtaining lower line-haul rates and faster service for shippers, freight forwarders rely on a portion of the differential between vehicle-load and less-than-vehicle load rates to defray the expenses of their operations and to leave a profit from them.

Shippers' associations perform much the same function as freight forwarders, but they are voluntary organizations composed of members who use the service to take advantage of the economies of consolidation. These associations are the private counterpart of the "for hire" freight forwarders and usually are made up of firms shipping similar items between common origins and destinations.

Third-party providers of logistics services exhibit some of the characteristics of auxiliary users. Such third-party firms are providing an increasing variety of services to their client firms (usually manufacturers), including warehousing, order processing, data transmission, shipping (including purchasing transportation). Most of these firms have evolved from what were formerly traditional public warehousing companies. Where the services provided include arranging for transportation of the client company's goods, such third-party firms may be regarded as auxiliary users. Current and probable future developments in the growth and evolution of third-party providers of logistics services will be treated in greater detail in Chapter 18, ''A Look to the Future.''

Intermodal Transportation

Intermodal systems are joint, point-to-point, through transportation services involving two or more modes on a regular basis. The most well-developed combinations of modes offering intermodal service are truck-rail, truck-water, air-truck, and rail-water. A concept called containerization figures prominently in each of these systems.

Truck-Rail Truck-rail service may be trailer-on-flatcar (TOFC) or container-on-flatcar (COFC), and in either case is called ''piggyback'' service. Between 1960 and 1980, the number of rail cars loaded with highway trailers or containers grew 13 times. Piggyback service now ranks second only to coal in the number of rail car loadings, accounting for 14.5 percent of all rail car loadings in 1985.[5]

Several types of piggyback service are offered by various carriers. These are described briefly in Table 7–1. Not all types or plans are provided by each railroad. The several variations of Plan 2 that utilize rail-owned trailers, containers, and flat cars, are the most popular, accounting for almost 60 percent of all TOFC/COFC movements in recent years.

Truck-Water Intermodal truck and water service, sometimes referred to as ''fishyback,'' is achieved by coordination of truck and water transport movements.

The roll-on, roll-off (Ro-Ro) method allows standard highway trailers to be driven on and off ships via large side or stern doors. Another system uses standard demountable containers and specially-constructed containerships. Although the first container voyage in 1956 was an inter-coastal move from New York to Houston, U.S. domestic service now is concentrated offshore on the routes connecting the West Coast, Alaska, and Hawaii and those connecting East and Gulf Coast ports with those in the Caribbean.

Air-Truck First established in 1957 by a single air carrier in cooperation with a number of trucking firms, this service now is widely available throughout the United States. It provides both feeder and delivery service between major airport ''hubs'' and distant outlying communities having inadequate airfreight service or none at all. It sometimes utilizes containers designed to conform to the configuration of the aircraft fuselage, either main deck or lower deck (''belly''). These may be preloaded, unloaded by shippers and consignees at their plants or warehouses, or both.

Rail-Water Rail-water service has been offered for many years. East Coast and Gulf Coast as well as Seattle-to-Alaska ''hydro-train'' rail-water service involves the use of specially constructed ships or barges on which strings of freight cars are moved over water to the port nearest their ultimate inland destination. In international rail-water services, the rail portion often is regarded as a ''bridge'' connected to one or two water movements. For example, ''landbridge'' is a term used to refer to an overland movement that is preceded and followed by

TABLE 7-1: Summary of TOFC/COFC (Piggyback) Services

Plan I	*Railroads carry trailer or container loads of freight for motor common carriers at a flat charge per unit. The railroad has no direct contact with the shipper and merely substitutes trailer, or container, on flatcar transportation in place of the motor common carrier's transportation by truck. The motor common carrier solicits and bills customers at truck rates, takes trailers or containers to, and picks them up from TOFC terminals.*
Plan II	*This is a total railroad door-to-door transportation service. The railroad furnishes all transportation equipment; delivers the trailers or containers to shipper's loading dock and, in some cases, helps load them; transports them to its loading ramp; loads and transports them to consignee's unloading dock and sometimes helps unload the units.*
Plan II¼	*Same as Plan II, except railroad either picks up or delivers the trailer or container, but not both.*
Plan II½	*Provides for the shipper and receiver to perform pickup and delivery of railroad-owned trailers or containers with railroad performing ramping and deramping and linehaul service between ramps.*
Plan III	*This is a railroad transportation service restricted to ramp operations [sometimes called "ramp-to-ramp"]. The shipper loads his or her own or leased trailer or container and provides for its deliver to loading ramp. The railroad loads the trailer or container on the flatcar at origin piggyback terminal, transports it to destination piggyback terminal, and grounds it.*
Plan III Minibridge	*Containerized shipments having origin or destination from or to an international foreign port and moving by rail to or from originating or final destination U.S. ports. This rail-water service is instead of an all-water move.*
Plan III Landbridge	*Containerized shipments moving by water into U.S. ports for transport by rail to another port for further transport by water to destination.*
Plan IV	*Rail carrier handling of loaded and empty privately owned or leased trailers and flatcars between specific points or areas under charges published in regular rail tariffs. These are flat per car charges to compensate the rail carriers for service in moving the loaded or empty trailers on flatcars and not for the commodity being shipped.*
Plan V	*Railroads and motor common carriers participate in a joint rail-truck transportation service at a published single-factor joint through rate. Each participating carrier gets a division of the through rate.*

Source: Association of American Railroads, *Railroad Ten-Year Trends* 2 (Washington, D.C.: Economics and Finance Department, 1985) Table III-C-14.

water movement, such as Europe to the Pacific basin with a transcontinental rail leg across the United States instead of an all-water voyage. "Mini-bridge" and "micro-bridge" refer to intermodal service for international shipments to and from inland points.[6]

Other Intermodal Services Ship-barge combinations, known traditionally as lightering, are found most frequently in the transshipment of bulk cargos such as coal, grain, wine, petroleum, and lumber when the ship cannot be navigated to the origin or destination of the cargo. Barges are also used to provide feeder service for container shipments between inland waterway points and major ocean terminals. A variation on this alternative is the lighter-aboard-ship (LASH) system, in which specially-constructed lighters (small barges that may be self-propelled or towed) are floated or lifted on and off specially-built vessels for movement into ports unable to accommodate the "mother" ship or to a location where such an operation will save the time required to dock and load or unload. In the latter case the lighter can be picked up when the ship, or a similar ship, next calls at that port.

Modal combinations involving pipelines almost always require bulk storage in transit at a terminal and therefore are not included within the definition of intermodal transportation service. However, the use of the Trans-Alaskan Pipeline in conjunction with very large crude carriers (VLCCs) to provide almost continuous movement of enormous quantities of crude oil (50 to 60 million barrels in 50 or more tankers per month) from Valdez, Alaska, to West Coast refineries demonstrates that combined pipeline-water service can be an efficient solution to logistics needs in particular circumstances.

At first glance, the combination of the fastest mode, air, with one of the slowest, water, seems both impractical and uneconomical. However, sea-air service, using standard 20-foot ocean containers and large cargo aircraft now is available to some international shippers. One such service was developed by Atlantic Container Line, an ocean carrier, in conjunction with Cargolux, a European all-cargo airline, to provide single-bill through service from East Coast ports to destinations in Africa and the Middle East to avoid port delays or problems with inadequate local surface transport to inland destinations from the port.

Containerization Containerization is the placement of goods in standard-size metal (usually steel) containers to eliminate multiple handling of freight in transit, facilitate mechanized intermodal transfer, and provide cargos with increased protection from damage in transit, pilferage, and the environment. Besides reducing handling and damage costs, containers can be reused over a period of several years and do not require specialized crating and bracing of shipments.

Containers currently are used in all modes of transportation except pipeline. They range in size from a small box (airline Type C container) to van-sized containers measuring 8 feet $\times$ 8 feet $\times$ 10 feet, 20 feet or 40 feet in length.[7] Besides dry freight units, a variety of refrigerated, dry bulk, tank, and flat-rack containers capable of handling items as varied as automobiles, whiskey, and unsawed redwood logs have been developed to meet shippers' needs. Several air carriers even offer containers suitable for transporting pigs, cattle, and other livestock.

Even though the advantages of containerization are obvious, several obstacles have hindered the full realization of its potential benefits. Containerization makes transportation less labor-intensive and more capital-intensive. Besides requiring substantial investments in hardware (large gantry cranes) and port facilities, containerization may create considerable labor union resistance. Traditional managerial and regulatory attitudes and practices must also be changed. The growing dominance of containerization in international ocean nonbulk trade demonstrates that these problems can be and are being overcome.

RELATIVE IMPORTANCE OF INDUSTRY COMPONENTS

Significant changes have occurred in the relative roles played by industry components in the transportation of freight in the past two decades. The purpose of this section is to explore the nature of the changes.

Modes

Statistics showing trends in traffic carried by transport modes are presented in Table 7–2. These volumes are stated in ton-miles, a common measure of activity that refers to one ton being carried one mile.

TABLE 7-2: Volume of Domestic Intercity Freight Traffic, by Type of Transport: 1970 to 1987

Type of Transport	1978	1979	1980	1981	1982	1983	1984	1985	1986	1987	1988	1989	1990[b]
Freight Traffic (billion ton-miles[a])													
Total	2,467	2,573	2,487	2,430	2,252	2,337	2,515	2,458	2,501	2,642	2,781	2,805	2,861
Railroads	868	927	932	924	810	841	935	895	889	972	1,028	1,048	1,083
Motor vehicles	599	608	555	527	520	575	606	610	634	663	699	716	736
Inland waterways[c]	409	425	407	410	351	359	399	382	393	411	438	436	433
Oil pipelines	586	608	588	564	566	556	568	564	578	587	607	595	599
Domestic airways[d]	4.8	4.6	4.8	5.1	5.1	5.9	6.5	6.7	7.3	8.7	9.3	9.8	10
Percent Distribution													
Total[e]	100.0	100.0	100.0	100.0	100.0	100.0	100.0	100.0	100.0	100.0	100.0	100.0	100.0
Railroads	35.18	36.03	37.47	38.02	36.00	35.99	37.18	36.41	35.55	36.8	37.0	37.4	37.9
Motor vehicles	24.28	23.64	22.32	21.69	23.11	24.60	24.10	24.82	25.35	25.1	25.1	25.5	25.7
Inland waterways[c]	16.58	16.52	16.37	16.87	15.60	15.36	15.86	15.54	15.71	15.6	15.8	15.5	15.1
Oil pipelines	23.75	23.64	23.64	23.21	25.16	23.79	22.58	22.95	23.11	22.2	21.8	21.2	20.9
Domestic airways[d]	.19	.18	.19	.21	.23	.25	.26	.28	.28	.33	.33	.35	.35

[a] A ton-mile is the movement of 1 ton (2,000 pounds) of freight for the distance of 1 mile. A passenger-mile is the movement of 1 passenger for the distance of 1 mile. Comprises public and private traffic, both revenue and nonrevenue.

[b] Preliminary, based on partial year data.

[c] Includes Great Lakes and inland waterways, but not coastwise traffic.

[d] Revenue service only for scheduled and nonscheduled carriers including small section 418 all-cargo carriers. Includes express, mail, and excess baggage.

[e] Columns may not add exactly due to rounding.

Source: *Transportation in America*, May, 1990, with periodic supplements. © Transportation Policy Associates, Washington, D.C. Reprinted with permission.

Rail Historically, rail carriers have accounted for the largest percentage of freight tonnage moved in the United States. The ability of the railroads to transport efficiently large quantities of freight over long distances is the primary factor behind their leading share of ton-miles. As Table 7–2 shows, the traffic shares of the several modes have been fairly stable over the past 20 years, and particularly since 1982. However, the composition of rail shipments has changed from a broad range of products to a narrower group of generally low value, bulk commodities such as coal, grain, basic chemicals, and metallic ores. Much of the higher value merchandise previously carried by boxcar now moves either by highway or in piggyback service.

Highway During the post–World War II period, the operations of highway carriers grew dramatically. Truck operators established huge fleets and route structures evolved from regional to transcontinental in scope. The speed and flexibility of highway transportation has given motor carriers an inherent competitive advantage over railroads in carrying certain types of freight, particularly higher value freight requiring dependable transport and door-to-door delivery over intermediate distances.

Water Water carriers have achieved a mixed performance in recent years. Inland waterway, coastwise, and intercoastal (Atlantic to Gulf to Pacific) carriers have increased their share of total tonnage, but their share of total revenues has declined. During the same period of time, Great Lakes traffic, largely seasonal because of winter weather effects, has been especially hard hit, declining in both ton-miles carried and revenue share. Much of the decline in Great Lakes traffic reflects the decline in iron ore production in Minnesota and Michigan as well as the decline of the steel industry, particularly those steel mills located on or near the shore of Lake Erie.

Labor union restrictions on maritime automation and large wage increases have adversely affected costs for many water carriers. In addition, unit trains (trains with fixed configurations shuttling back and forth as units between two designated points with full trainloads in one direction and returning empty), have lured traffic away from water carriers by offering better service and equal or lower rates between points where the two modes compete.

Pipeline Pipeline tonnage has been nearly constant over the past 20 years. The Trans-Alaska Pipeline, completed in 1977, once again demonstrated the ability of pipelines to move efficiently massive volumes of fluid over difficult terrain. Pipelines built to move solids in hydraulic suspension (slurry) also can be built and operated. However, it appears that they cannot compete economically with rail or water transportation. Only one coal slurry pipeline, the 273-mile Black Mesa line linking Kayenta, Arizona, to an electrical generating station in southwestern Arizona, was operating commercially in 1985.[8] Due to geography (no navigable river) and terrain (mountainous and rugged) this line has no competing rail or water transportation, which accounts for its success.

Air Air freight has shown the most significant increase in percentage of tonnage during the period of 1978 to 1990. This might be expected for a previously undeveloped mode with important service advantages that has only recently been able to utilize the productive wide-bodied jet freighters capable of massive, long-range air cargo movements. However, airfreight traffic is still only a tiny fraction of total freight movement, only just over a third of one percent of the total in 1990.

COST CHARACTERISTICS

Total transportation cost, like that of any manufacturing or service activity, is a combination of fixed and variable costs. Fixed costs do not vary with the amount of activity or service offered. Examples of fixed costs in transportation include depreciation of facilities and equipment, interest expense, amortization of debt, and property taxes. Variable costs are those that vary directly with the amount of service operated, the two most important being fuel and labor. Some costs have both fixed and variable elements in them. Their nature may alter with significant changes in volume and the time frame over which they are viewed.

At the beginning of the chapter, several examples of carrier operating situations were given; one of them referred to the mixing of high-density and low-density (balloon) freight when loading a vehicle. Truck trailers, boxcars, barges, a ship's hold and deck space, an aircraft fuselage and sometimes belly compartments, and a barge all have a finite amount of cubic space available for cargo as well as a finite cargo weight limit. The carrier is operating at maximum cost efficiency when the cargo to be carried "cubes out at the weight limit" — when both the maximum cubic space and weight limits have been reached. For these reasons, non-bulk carriers seek a mix of cargo that will result in the vehicle being "full and down" when it is dispatched.*

It is more common for vehicles to "cube out" before they "weigh out" due to the trend to lighter weight materials used in manufacturing goods. This is particularly true in the motor carrier industry where balloon freight such as styrofoam cups is increasing in quantity.

Further, to operate safely, cargo must be loaded or stowed so as not to result in an imbalanced load or a shifting of cargo that would run the risk of capsizing the vehicle, barge, or ship, or make an aircraft uncontrollable. Weight and balance is a very serious subject for all carriers except pipelines.

Modes**

The relationships between fixed and variable costs in each of the five transportation modes are shown in Figure 7–3. These graphs, shown in the form of break-even charts, are not intended to portray particular firms or even composites or averages. They are generalizations designed to illustrate the degree of sensitivity of each of the modes to changes in traffic volume. They are based generally on estimates of the relative importance of various operating expenses.

Fixed costs are much more important elements of cost for pipelines and railroads than for other modes. They result from heavy charges for such items as depreciation, taxes, and maintenance of way and equipment. Highway, waterway, and air carriers do not own their own rights-of-way; they pay for the maintenance and depreciation of these facilities largely through user taxes.

The added costs associated with an incremental amount of business may depend in some degree on whether additional equipment or schedules have to be operated by a carrier. This, in

---

*Full and down is actually a nautical term meaning that the vessel's cubic capacity is *fully* used and the vessel's hull is *down* in the water to plimsoll mark level (the vessel's weight limit).

**The comments that follow take a short-run view of costs that do not permit large-scale additions to, or deletions from, facilities that might eliminate or add a fixed cost element.

Figure 7–3: Generalized break-even charts for five modes of carriers

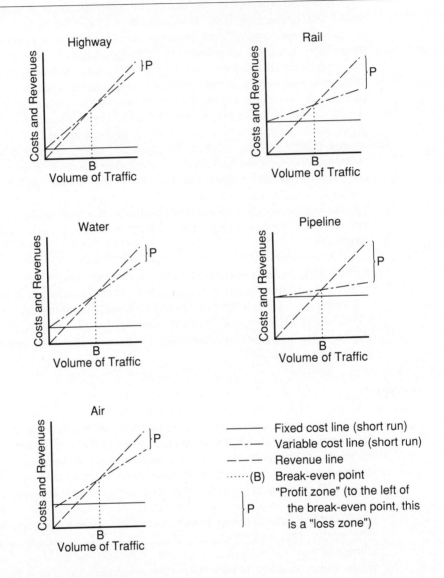

turn, often is a function of the size of the incremental units of equipment that can be added to accommodate added traffic. This may range from the small units of incremental operating capacity that can be added by a motor carrier at relatively low cost to the large units of capacity associated with a pipeline. Longer-term cost trends for various modes may be influenced by the extent to which each is labor and energy intensive.

OPERATING CHARACTERISTICS

The operating characteristics of a mode of transportation include its dependability, speed, frequency, availability, and freight-handling capability. These factors, in combination with the freight rate charged, are the most important factors in the selection of modes and carriers by shippers.

Dependability

Dependability of service is measured most often by the percentage deviation from the normal or promised level of performance. Thus, an airline that frequently is one day late with a shipment scheduled for delivery within 24 hours would be considered much less dependable than a vessel that is often one day late on a twenty-day voyage, even though the absolute deviation is the same (one day) in both cases. Many shippers rate consistency of service higher than all other factors, including cost and speed, in selecting methods of transportation and individual carriers.[9]

Equipment availability often is a factor affecting carrier dependability along with other factors beyond carrier control, such as bad weather and natural disasters. Airlines are the most vulnerable to such factors, pipelines the least.

Some shippers include loss and damage experience when rating carrier dependability. Many shippers maintain more accurate records of carrier loss and damage of shipments than of on-time delivery by various carriers because of the maintenance and availability of company files on loss-and-damage claims.

Speed

Speed refers to the total ''door-to-door'' time required to move goods from origin to destination. The importance of speed is a function of shipper need. Such need may reflect the dollar value or perishability of the freight involved, the customer service standards of the shipper, the requirement for rapid resupply of a fast-moving retail item, a vitally needed repair part, a medical emergency requirement, and so forth.

Frequency

Frequency of service is determined by the number of schedules (trains, trucks, airplanes, ships) moving between a city pair during a given time period. Frequency of service offered by carriers depends on the amount of shipper demand for service between a city pair.

Availability

Availability refers to the geographic scope of a given service. The term can be applied broadly to cities or towns or to a specific type of facility, such as a factory or riverside dock. Intermodal systems play a major role in expanding the availability of various modes.

Capability

The ability to handle out-size, heavy lift, fragile, frozen, liquid, explosive, perishable, or easily-contaminated goods reflects the capability of a particular transportation service. Provision of such specialized services may require a carrier to operate costly, specially designed, shipper-dedicated equipment.

Modal Comparisons

A subjective ranking of the performance relationships of the five basic modes of transportation is presented in Table 7–3. The rankings indicate general relationships only. In any particular situation, details of shipment origin and destination, commodity, volume of movement, terrain, or other factors may change the rankings materially for any one or more of the characteristics.

Pipelines are ranked first in terms of dependability because they run quietly day and night with the only interruption being infrequent repair on a part of the line or to pumping facilities. Though the slowest form of transportation, pipelines are not subject to delays or uncertainties that affect movement by other modes. Even at speeds of two to five miles per hour, large pipelines can transport a stream of as much as a million barrels of product past a given point during a 24-hour period. The small amount of energy expended in pumping activities makes the pipeline far and away the most energy efficient carrier, as shown in Table 7–3.

With the exception of remote locations accessible only by boat or aircraft, highway service is available to practically every shipper. This ability to provide door-to-door service between most points places highway transportation far ahead of all other modes in terms of availability. In addition, the truck offers a relatively small, flexible unit of capacity that can be scheduled on relatively short notice to offer a high frequency of service compared with other modes.

No other mode of transportation even approaches the "block speed" (from one terminal to another) of aircraft that can span the North American continent in five or six hours. Such speed enables air carriers to offer usually dependable overnight delivery of packages anywhere in the United States. However, the *effective door-to-door speed* of air carriers is not superior in all cases, particularly for shorter distances, where they are matched by motor carriers on this measure.

Perhaps because of high expectations held by their users, air freight carriers have some difficulty achieving the level of dependability expected of them. Ground handling delays often play a larger role than aircraft mechanical difficulties or bad weather in causing airfreight dependability problems. Passenger airlines often have limited belly capacity for freight on those routes served by smaller aircraft. Although many significant improvements have been made in the movement of air freight in recent years, schedules designed to capture the line-haul advantages of air service leave a very small margin for error. Only in the small package segment of air transportation have high levels of dependability been achieved by the use of dedicated equipment. This has been the case in such firms as Federal Express, DHL, and United Parcel Service, or by very high-cost "airline express services" where the package is personally checked in at the terminal counter for the next flight out and personally picked up at the destination counter by the recipient.

TABLE 7–3: General Relationships between Operating Characteristics of the Five Modes of Transportation

Rank	Highest 1	2	3	4	Lowest 5
Characteristics					
Dependability	Pipeline	Highway	Rail	Water	Air
Speed	Air	Highway	Rail	Water	Pipeline
Frequency	Highway	Air	Rail	Water	Pipeline
Availability	Highway	Rail	Air	Water	Pipeline
Capability	Water	Rail	Highway	Air	Pipeline
Energy "efficiency"[a]	Pipeline	Water	Rail	Highway	Air

[a]Measured in BTUs consumed per net ton-mile.

Seagoing and inland waterway ships and barges are the most capable transportation units available. Any type or size of shipment that is transportable in any sense can be moved on a barge, from eight-story prefabricated buildings destined for the Alaskan oil fields to the giant rockets used in the national space program. Multiple movements or "tows" of several barges connected together provide great capability to move large volumes of commodities such as grain, petroleum, and coal.

Speed is not the hallmark of water service. Barges headed upstream on a river system sometimes move as slowly as two miles per hour. Many users, in fact, utilize the large capacity and slow speed of barges to provide floating warehouse space for low-value commodities. High capacity and low speed help make barges an energy-efficient form of transportation. A limitation of water movements in the northern United States results from the freezing of the Great Lakes and rivers in wintertime. During the winter, cargoes that would otherwise move over such water routes either do not move or must be moved by rail.

Rail performance ranks near the middle of the pack for all of the characteristics listed in Table 7–3. The service of rail carriers is available only to communities served by main or branch lines. If a user's facility does not have its own siding, a public "team" track must be used. Rail cars have limits on capability because of overhead and side clearance restrictions along rail lines.

Other characteristics of railroads' performance are constrained by organizational attitudes and practices, the inability of some carriers to generate sufficient investment to maintain a modern plant, and route systems designed to meet nineteenth-century needs. The speed, frequency, and dependability of the railroad system as a whole has suffered from poor maintenance of tracks and equipment by "sick" railroads, particularly in the East and Midwest. Other delays are caused by "bottlenecks" at terminals and classification yards, especially those still located in congested urban areas.

Stronger railroads serving growing areas and coal-moving routes, particularly in the South and West, have pointed the way to the future by building modern electronic classification yards in suburban areas, installing sophisticated computer systems to monitor equipment use and trace customer shipments, and generally improving the level of service and performance of their rail systems.

Legal Forms

Because the widest range of operations, described by legal forms, exists in the motor carrier industry (see pages 209–215), the following comparisons are for various types of trucking operations.

Private truck transportation, essentially subject to complete user control, offers the greatest potential in terms of speed, availability, frequency, and dependability of service. In fact, most companies initiating private transportation operations do so to obtain better service rather than marginally lower costs. The extent to which this potential is realized is a function of the financial resources and managerial skill of each particular firm.

By working closely with reputable contract carriers, many shippers are able to achieve ''tailored'' service comparable to that of private transportation without the headaches of daily operational involvement, equipment ownership, and labor negotiations. However, desired performance standards must be clearly specified, and investment in dedicated equipment may be needed to meet special requirements.

The LTL nature of most motor common carrier shipments means more door-to-door transit time because of the amount of terminal handling required. This also presents more opportunities for errors that can affect dependability adversely.

The specialized nature of exempt carriers limits generalizations about their performance. Their capability is sharply defined by the list of cargos they can or cannot haul. Availability is confined to areas where exempt loads, mostly agricultural products, are found. Frequency of service is determined by negotiation with customers, as published schedules are not used. Their speed and reliability may depend to a large extent on the revenue received for the shipment.

Auxiliary Users

Service characteristics of auxiliary users take on the character of the modes used by each type. In many instances, however, they are able to structure schedules and otherwise coordinate operations with the carriers they employ to achieve higher levels of service than an occasional shipper.

Because shippers' cooperatives directly control the freight being shipped, they offer very dependable service. But these services are only available between major metropolitan areas for which such associations have been formed. This can represent a distinct disadvantage, for example, for a candy manufacturer located some distance from Chicago, where nearly 90 percent of all candy is manufactured and operations of the candy shippers' cooperative are centered.

Freight forwarders are able to offer a high degree of frequency and availability of service by taking advantage of different services and schedules offered by various carriers and modes. Speed and dependability are enhanced by advanced block booking of a fixed portion, in terms of volume or tonnage, of each scheduled departure, a common practice among air freight forwards.

Horror stories about the U.S. Postal Service have become part of American folklore. However, the nationwide network of post offices, serving even remote and sparsely populated locations, provides the most readily available service for small package shipments. Parcel Post capability is limited to shipments of less than 40 pounds between major post offices, although less restrictive limits apply to more rural areas. Express mail service offering guaranteed delivery of small package shipments according to a published schedule is now offered by the Postal Service as part of a service improvement program.

Intermodal Systems

The performance characteristics of a successful intermodal transportation service are derived from the performance characteristics of the component modes. The goal is to retain or emphasize the more desirable characteristics of each mode while the less desirable characteristics are reduced or eliminated.

For example, the LASH (lighter-aboard-ship) system previously discussed offers inland shippers the economy and speed of deep water transportation and the availability of ''pick-up and delivery'' service by barge either to a port or into inland waterways. Upgraded and expanded TOFC service is advocated by the U.S. Department of Transportation as an energy-saving measure. The goal of federally-sponsored demonstration projects, such as all-TOFC ''sprint'' service between Chicago and Milwaukee, is to capture the line haul efficiencies of rail movement while providing the availability of motor carrier pick-up and delivery.

SUMMARY

The structure of the transportation industry can be viewed from several perspectives. Among them are modes or methods of transportation, legal forms, auxiliary users, and inter-modal systems.

Each of the five basic modes—rail, highway, water, air, and pipeline—has its own distinctive cost structure and service characteristics. Under most circumstances, the modes with the highest fixed costs, rail and pipeline, achieve the most significant operating economies at high volumes of activity. Modes with high terminal costs but relatively low operating costs have an inherent cost advantage over longer hauls. Pipeline transportation offers the highest level of dependability and energy efficiency, air the fastest terminal-to-terminal speed, highway the greatest frequency and availability of service, and water the widest range of freight hauling capabilities. But it is important to emphasize the words *under most circumstances*. Under specific conditions, the relative characteristics of various modes may be altered.

The widest range of legal forms is found in highway transportation. It includes ''for-hire'' legal forms of common, contract, and exempt carriage as well as private carriage. The former are performed by firms primarily in the business of providing transportation service to others. Private transportation is performed in support of a primary business activity by firms usually engaged in manufacturing. Common, contract, and exempt carriage have been distinguished by the type of operating authority associated with each by regulatory bodies; common carriers are restricted primarily regarding routes serviced, contract carriers are restricted to certain numbers of customer contracts, and exempt carriers are restricted to hauling certain agricultural and unprocessed commodities. In addition, private carriers were prohibited from hauling freight on a for-hire basis. In recent years, regulatory rulings and legislation culminating in the Motor Carrier Act of 1980 have relaxed greatly restrictions on each form, making the distinctions between legal forms less sharp.

Auxiliary users typically consolidate smaller shipments into larger ones, purchasing their line-haul services from other carriers and relying on the difference in transport rates for large and small shipments for their profits. Major auxiliary users are United Parcel Service (especially for air shipments), the U.S. Postal Service for its Parcel Post, freight forwarders, and shippers' associations, composed of members operating a "do-it-yourself" consolidating service. The service characteristics of auxiliary users tend to take on the characteristics of the line-haul mode used in the service.

Intermodal systems of transportation, employing two or more basic modes and often involving the use of containers capable of being transferred from one mode to another without freight rehandling, have grown rapidly in use in the past two decades. The most popular of these include truck-rail (piggyback), truck-water (fishyback), trainship, bargeship, and air-truck.

Transportation facilities have undergone remarkable changes in recent years. These changes have brought with them a greater variety of services offered to shippers and a greater freedom of pricing for these services. This underlines the dynamic nature of logistics and the need for the successful logistics manager to maintain an awareness of changes in transportation rates and services and their possible impact on his or her area of responsibility. In the next chapter, we will concentrate on these transportation rates and services.

DISCUSSION QUESTIONS

1. What is meant by the term "carrier managerial behavior"? Why might this be significant to a logistics manager?

2. As defined in the text, what is the difference between "water" and "ocean" transport?

3. What is meant by a "legal form" of transportation? What are the several legal forms? Are they purely arbitrary, or are there reasons for them?

4. What is a "landbridge"? Why are such services established?

5. What are the advantages of containerization? What are its disadvantages?

6. Looking at Table 7–2, it appears that the percentage distribution of traffic among the modes of transportation has been relatively stable for nearly two decades. In your opinion, what accounts for this?

7. Why would an increase or decrease in traffic volume be more significant for a railroad than a trucking company? Explain your reasoning.

8. Which modes of transportation rank highest with respect to dependability, speed, frequency, availability and capability? Which modes rank lowest with respect to these five operating characteristics? Explain the reasons for these rankings.

SUGGESTED READINGS

Because of the extensive changes that have occurred in the transportation industry as a result of deregulation, the books listed here are recommended as providing a current treatment of the industry in its postderegulation period.

BARRETT, COLIN, *Practical Handbook of Private Trucking*, Washington, D.C.: The Traffic Service Corporation, 1983.

COYLE, JOHN J., EDWARD J. BARDI, and JOSEPH L. CAVINATO, *Transportation*, 2d ed. St. Paul: West Publishing Company, 1986.

KENDALL, CANE C., *The Business of Shipping*, 5th ed. Centreville, Maryland: Cornell Maritime Press, Inc., 1986.

MULLER, GERHARDT, *Intermodal Freight Transportation*, 2nd ed. Westport, Connecticut: The Eno Foundation for Transportation, 1989. Easily the best and most comprehensive treatment of the subject that has been written to date. Highly recommended to those seeking information on all aspects of the subject.

STEPHENSON, FREDERICK J., *Transportation USA*. Reading, Massachusetts: Addison-Wesley Publishing Company, 1987.

TAFF, CHARLES A., *Commercial Motor Transportation*, 7th ed. Cambridge, Md.: Cornell Maritime Press, Inc., 1986.

WELLS, ALEXANDER T., *Air Transportation*, 2d ed. Belmont, California: Wadsworth Publishing Company, 1989.

WOLBERT, GEORGE S., *U.S. Oil Pipelines*, Washington, D.C.: American Petroleum Institute, 1979.

WOOD, DONALD F., and JAMES C. JOHNSON, *Contemporary Transportation*, 3d ed. New York: Macmillan Publishing Company, 1989.

ENDNOTES

1. *1978 Annual Report* (Washington, D.C.: Interstate Commerce Commission, 1979): 61, 69.

2. *Ex Parte No. MC-118*, 43 Fed. Reg. 33945 (1978). For a discussion of the aftermath of the "Toto" decision, see *Traffic World* (June 4, 1979): 41–45.

3. Containers are reusable boxes of various shapes and sizes, capable of being transferred from mode to mode and used to provide door-to-door service.

4. The abbreviations, LTL and LCL, stand for "less than truckload" and "less than carload", respectively. What is considered a truckload or carload varies with the commodity involved. For example, for rate-making purposes, a truckload of hanging garments might be 5,000 pounds while the minimum quantity considered to be a truckload of canned goods might be 30,000 pounds or more.

5. Association of American Railroads, *Cars of Revenue Freight Loaded*.

6. For a more detailed discussion of these concepts, see R. K. Miller, "Land-Bridge, Mini-Bridge, and Micro-Bridge: A Question of Getting it Together," *Transportation Journal* (Fall, 1977): 64–66.

7. The most common container lengths are 20 feet and 40 feet. However, increased allowable truck-trailer length (48 feet) has already caused some intermodal operators to introduce 48 feet containers.

8. As reported by Frederick J. Stephenson, Jr. in his text *Transportation USA*, Addison-Wesley Publishing Company, Inc., Reading, Massachusetts (1987): 275–76.

9. See, for example, "Carrier Evaluation in Physical Distribution Management," by Edward R. Bruning and Peter M. Lynagh, *Journal of Business Logistics* 5, No. 2 (1984): 40.

CHAPTER EIGHT

8

Transportation Rates and Services

LEARNING OBJECTIVES

The objectives of this chapter are to:

➤ Review the history and effects of economic regulation and subsequent deregulation of the transportation industry.

➤ Describe the several types of transportation rates (prices), geographic rate systems, and rates based routes, quantities, and miscellaneous factors.

➤ Explain the types of and reasons for a variety of accessorial and terminal charges made to shippers.

➤ Explain the application of the concepts of carrier cost-of-service and shipper value-of-service to the process of rate making (transportation pricing).

➤ Discuss various factors (including direction of movement, size, and regularity of movement, intramodal and intermodal competition, and the alternative of private transportation) that influence carrier competition and rate levels.

➤ Review the rate-making process and the negotiation of rates by carriers and shippers.

The logistics manager is the ''customer'' of transportation carriers. This is true even if the firm transports some or all of its goods by private carriage. An informed customer should be fully aware of the array of services and prices (or costs in the case of private carriage) available in the market place in order to make informed decisions with respect to choice of mode and choice of carrier and with respect to any special carrier services that may be required. Making such judgments depends on having a clear and comprehensive understanding of a rather complex subject: the nature, scope, and variety of transportation rates and services.

TRANSPORTATION RATES AND SERVICES

The task of evaluating the myriad of common-carrier rates and services is so complex that many shippers aren't sure when they've achieved their goal: finding the best rate or service to meet a particular need. This problem has been further compounded by the effects of rate and service deregulation.

The purpose of this section of the chapter is to present the what's, how's, and why's of transportation rates, the prices that shippers pay. To accomplish this objective, there is a brief discussion of what remains of rate regulation after deregulation, a description of different types of rates and services, and a discussion of rate level determinants.

The Regulation of Transportation Activity

A brief review of the history of regulation in the transportation industries provides a feel for the environment in which transport services have been managed, sold, and bought. The dates of the major pieces of legislation described below correspond to the moments when the major modes of transportation developed a significant role in the economy.

The 1887 Act to Regulate Commerce*   The Interstate Commerce Act of 1887 was the first federal regulation of interstate commerce in the United States.[1] U.S. Supreme Court cases had established that individual states could regulate transportation within their borders, but the Court decided in 1886 that states could not regulate interstate transportation, particularly with regard to rates.

Pipeline Regulation   The Hepburn Act of 1906 (an amendment to the Interstate Commerce Act) brought all interstate oil pipelines under regulation as common carriers. Interstate natural gas pipelines came under regulation at a later date with the passage of the Natural Gas Act of 1938. Both oil and gas pipelines are now regulated by the Federal Energy Regulatory Commission, although the Natural Gas Policy Act of 1978 exempts a number of categories of natural gas from price regulation.

Maritime Regulation   The Merchant Marine Act of 1920, known as the Jones Act, established a Federal Maritime Commission (FMC) and required that all U.S. domestic ocean (inter- and intracoastal), Great Lakes, and inland waterway trade be carried in ships owned,

---

*The 1887 act was titled ''An Act to Regulate Commerce.'' The name was changed to the ''Interstate Commerce Act'' in 1920. In 1978 the name was changed again to ''Revised Interstate Commerce Act.'' For convenience to the reader, future references to this Act will simply be referred to as the Interstate Commerce Act (ICA).

registered, and staffed by U.S. firms. The Intercoastal shipping Act of 1933 provided for the regulation of rates, services, practices, agreements, and discriminatory actions of common carrier lines and conferences engaged in intercoastal commerce. Although much of this authority was later transferred to the ICC, the Federal Maritime Commission retains jurisdiction today over off-shore shipping to and from Alaska, Hawaii, Puerto Rico, and the U.S. Virgin Islands.

The Motor Carrier Act of 1935 In 1935, the regulation of motor carriers involved in interstate commerce was placed under the jurisdiction of the ICC. The law prescribed for motor carriers the same general rules of rate making that were applicable to rail carriers, with two important exceptions: for-hire motor carriers were subject only to minimum rate regulation, and the hauling of certain agricultural commodities was exempted from rate regulation. The latter created a class of "exempt" motor carriers completely free from economic regulation.

The Civil Aeronautics Act of 1938 The Civil Aeronautics Act of 1938 established the Civil Aeronautics Authority with general powers and duties similar to those of the ICC as well as a Congressional mandate to develop and actively promote the growth of the fledgling airline industry.

In 1940, the functions of the Authority were reorganized by an executive order that established an independent Civil Aeronautics Board (CAB). A sister agency, the Civil Aeronautics Administration (CAA), was created to oversee technical and safety matters. In 1958, all functions of the CAA were transferred to the Federal Aviation Administration (FAA). The CAB was abolished in 1985, and its remaining regulatory functions were transferred to the FAA.

The Transportation Act of 1940 Full regulatory control over interstate surface transportation under the Interstate Commerce Act (ICA) was completed by the Transportation Act of 1940 when the Motor Carrier Act was made Part II of the ICA, regulation of domestic water transportation was enacted and made Part III of the ICA, and surface freight forwarders were brought under regulation by Part IV of the ICA.

The Reed-Bulwinkle Act of 1948 This act legalized carrier rate associations (rate bureaus) formed for rate-making purposes. The Act provided for exemption of carriers from antitrust law, thereby distinguishing transportation from most other economic activity, and created a specific system by which the ICC could control the operating procedures of such associations.

The Department of Transportation Act of 1966 This law created a new cabinet level Department of Transportation (DOT) by bringing together research, safety, promotional, and administrative activities previously housed in other agencies, such as the Federal Aviation Administration, the U.S. Coast Guard, the Bureau of Public Roads, and the St. Lawrence Seaway Development Corp. It authorized the creation of the Federal Highway Administration (FHA) and the Federal Railway Administration (FRA) on the model of the Federal Aviation Administration to manage programs concerning their respective modes.

During the ten-year period from 1966 to 1976 the growing groundswell in favor of deregulation of the transportation industry took firm hold. In the short space of five years, 1976 to 1980, Congress undid most of the economic regulation of transportation that had been gradually built up over the previous ninety years. Deregulation has had profound effects on the railroad, motor carrier, and airline industries and has greatly changed the decision-making environment of logistics managers.

The Railroad Revitalization and Regulatory Reform Act of 1976 Commonly known as the "4R Act," the purpose of this law, as set forth in Section 101, was to "provide the means to rehabilitate and maintain the physical facilities, improve the operations and structure, and restore the financial stability of the railway system of the United States."

The Air Cargo Deregulation Act of 1977 This law provided the first comprehensive reduction of federal regulation of any transportation mode. Existing carriers were given authority to fly cargo anywhere, anytime, except within Alaska and Hawaii. After November 1978, new carriers were allowed to apply for similar authority. While new carriers are required to meet standards of "fitness, willingness, and ability" to provide service, they are no longer required to demonstrate that the "public convenience and necessity" would be served. In addition, airfreight rates were completely deregulated.

The CAB retained authority to change rates that might be found to be predatory or discriminatory. It subsequently ruled that tariffs no longer had to be published (although many carriers continue to do so as a service to customers) and that carriers were required to provide common carriage of only those commodities that they held themselves out to transport, not all types of freight as before.

The Motor Carrier Act of 1980 Continuing the trend of deregulation, The Motor Carrier Act of 1980 contained major revisions of The Motor Carrier Act of 1935 that have had a considerable impact on the highway transportation industry and the shippers who use its services. Among the more important provisions of the Act are those requiring that new applicants for operating authority need only show that they are "fit, willing, and able" to serve as opposed to the previous requirement that they prove that "public convenience and necessity" required their presence in the marketplace.

Other notable provisions were designed to encourage more energy efficient operations by relaxing route restrictions. Contract carriers no longer are required to identify specific origins and destinations in their contracts with shippers. And corporate-subsidiary private carriers were allowed to haul freight for all companies owned by their respective parent organizations and could carry freight as common or contract carriers.

Perhaps most significant of all, the Motor Carrier Act of 1980 instructed the ICC to encourage pricing competition by establishing a "zone of reasonableness" within which rates could be raised or lowered without prior approval, required that carriers publish their own tariffs, and phased out much of the role of rate bureaus in rate-making by common carriers. Congress thus removed its protective umbrella over routes served and prices charged by motor carriers for interstate traffic.

The result of the enactment of the Motor Carrier Act of 1980 has been intense price competition on the part of common carriers, accompanied by the bankruptcy of thousands of common and contract carriers. The structure of the motor carrier industry has also been greatly affected by deregulation. There has been a very substantial concentration of interstate LTL traffic in the hands of half a dozen major motor carriers while, due to lack of barriers to entry, more than fifteen thousand new truckload carriers (most of them having only one or a few tractors) have entered the industry.[2]

The federal Motor Carrier Act of 1980 does not apply to *intrastate* traffic, a matter for regulation by those States that choose to regulate it as to entry or rates or both. Whether this is significant to a logistics manager depends on where the firm's plants and distribution centers are located. For example, the State of Florida completely deregulated intrastate motor carrier transportation in 1980, while the State of Michigan continues to regulate both entry and rates of motor carriers. Thus, a firm with a distribution center in Jacksonville that serves all of Florida is free to negotiate rates and services for Florida intrastate traffic with motor carriers, while a firm in Michigan cannot negotiate rates for intrastate traffic; it must pay regulated TL and LTL rates unless it is able to negotiate motor-carrier contracts for such traffic.

The Staggers Act of 1980 In 1980 Congress further deregulated the railroad industry by passing the Staggers Act, named after its sponsor, Senator Harley O. Staggers of West Virginia. It is no pun to say that several provisions of the act were staggering, given the historically tight regulation of the railroad industry. The provisions of the act that are of major concern to logistics managers include:

1. *Railroad rates* Railroads were given nearly complete ratemaking freedom except with respect to traffic over which they have "market dominance." Where market dominance exists, the ICC is empowered to set a maximum rate within a zone of 170 percent to 180 percent of the railroad's variable costs. A railroad rate below that ICC-set figure cannot be found by the ICC to show a situation of market dominance. Market dominance is difficult both to define and to determine in many situations, and this provision of the act has led to many cases and arguments before the ICC. So far as logistics managers are concerned, there are now three general types of rail rate and service situations.

   a. Where the shipper is a "captive" of the railroad, as occurs, for example, in coal traffic where there is no competing barge transportation, the ICC can and will protect the shipper from excessive rail rates.

   b. Where the railroad is subject to meaningful competition from barge lines or motor carriers for the traffic, competition will prevent the railroad from charging noncompetitive rates.

   c. In between the extremes of (a) and (b), above, the shipper may have a problem if market dominance cannot be proved. Since passage of the Staggers Act railroad rates have increased substantially for noncontract traffic, and it must be kept in mind that a railroad is under no obligation to enter into a contract (discussed below) with a shipper. It will do so only if it is to the railroad's advantage as well as to the shipper's.

2. *Railroad-shipper contracts* The Act permits railroads and shippers to enter into contracts containing contract rates for the services to be provided by the railroad. These contracts must be filed with the ICC, but the rates are confidential and cannot be disclosed to third parties: other shippers, railroads, or the general public. Many a logistics manager is frustrated by being unable to find out what competing firms are paying for rail transportation service due to this contract confidentiality.

3. *Abandonment of service* The Staggers Act further eased the process of abandonment of branch lines by railroads. The chief significance of this provision is the possible elimination of direct rail service to present or potential distribution center and plant locations, a possibility of which a logistics manager whose firm might be affected should be aware.

Transportation Rates

Transportation rates derived from myriads of freight classifications, tariffs, archaic rules, and exceptions, are one of the most complex topics that confront a logistics manager's staff. Ongoing efforts to simplify and computerize tariffs and classifications have made the task more manageable. But, given the millions of possible origin-destination pairs, the different physical characteristics of the thousands of commodities that are transported, the effect of deregulation, and the many specialized transportation services available, the existence of literally trillions of different rates becomes more understandable.

Fortunately, practicing logistics managers are not concerned with all rates on all commodities to and from all places. Rather, they are interested primarily in the rates that they and their competitors must pay for transporting the commodities bought and sold by their firms.

Accordingly, our discussion of transportation rates will not be comprehensive. We will focus instead on the two principal classes of carrier charges, line haul rates, and accessorial charges. Our emphasis will be on defining and explaining the relationships of the most common types of rates and charges. If you are interested in more detailed discussions of various rates and services, see the suggested readings at the end of this chapter.

LINE HAUL RATES

A line haul rate is the charge for transporting a shipper's goods to points that are not in the same local pickup and delivery zone or railroad switching district. All other payments made by shippers to carriers in connection with the movement, handling, and servicing of their shipments are defined here as accessorial charges.

FIGURE 8–1: General structure of transportation rates

Legal Basis	Rate Type	Rate System	Carrier Routing	Construction of Rate	Quantity Rates	Miscellaneous Rate Provisions
Interstate	Class	Distance	Local	Through	Minimum Quantity	Value
Intrastate	Exception	Blanket	Joint	Combination	Weight Breaks	Measurement
	Commodity			Proportional	In-Excess	Agreed
	All Commodity (FAK)			Arbitrary	Multiple Vehicle	Section 10721
						Space Available
						Guaranteed Schedule
						Intermodal

The terminology of line haul rates is especially confusing because the total price that applies in a specific situation may be composed of several rates based on different criteria. Thus, every line haul rate (1) has a legal basis (interstate, intrastate, or exempt); (2) is a certain type (class, commodity, or exception); (3) is based on one of two systems (distance or blanket); (4) involves one or more carriers (local or joint); (5) is quoted as a single rate or is created by combining two or more rates (through or combination); and (6) will reflect the quantity involved. To complicate matters further, the basic rate may be modified by one or more miscellaneous provisions. Figure 8–1 depicts the general structure of transportation rates.

Types of Rates

All rates are either class, exception, or commodity rates, the latter including a variety of "special" types of rates.

Classification or Class Rates Classification is a method of relating products to one another for transportation pricing purposes. It gives weighted consideration to the factors shown in Table 8–1, which compares the three major freight classifications. The National

TABLE 8–1: Motor Carrier and Railroad Classifications: Number of Classes, Range of Classes, and Classification Factors

	Motor Carrier		Rail
	National Motor Freight Classification (NMFC)	New England Classification (Coordinated Freight Classification)[a]	Uniform Freight Classification (UFC)
Number of classes	23	9	31
Range of classes	35-500	[b]	13-400
Classification factors	Density Stowability Handling[d] Liability Value per pound Fragility Theft risk Flammable Explosive Environment Perishable	Density[c]	Density Stowability Handling[d] Liability Value per pound Fragility Theft risk Flammable Explosive Environment Perishable

[a]The official name is Coordinated Freight Classification (CFC), but in practice it is called the New England Classification.

[b]The nine classes range from 1 (high) to 5 (low), plus higher multiples of Class 1 (3, 2.5, 2 and 1.5 times Class 1).

[c]Although the New England Classification does consider other factors, such as those shown under the NMFC and the UFC, above, the factor of density is given the primary consideration. The objective is to produce the same revenue per truckload regardless of the type (density) of freight being carried.

[d]Handling factors include excessive weight, excessive length, and excessive or awkward size of items.

KEEPING TARIFFS UPDATED

In the fast-paced transportation business, carriers continually must modify their railway, truck, barge and air freight rates in order to stay competitive. The printed rate lists, or "tariffs," which go to customers, must reflect the latest conditions in the often volatile transportation and distribution services market.

Until recently, keeping freight rate lists current was a continual struggle at CSX Transportation. A 12-person tariff production group manually tracked rates received by mail or telephone from sales and marketing, and used conventional production procedures — typesetting and paste-up — to create camera-ready lists that were sent to an outside printer. But today, CSX is speeding tariff production by using electronic publishing systems and laser printers from Xerox Corp., in conjunction with a host computer database management system, to quickly turn out the tariffs in-house.

"Rate changes can occur literally overnight, and we need to be able to update the tariffs on the spot so that we can get them into the public's hands fast," says Gerald Davies, CSX vice president of marketing services. "To that end, we are incorporating our rates into our corporate database, which feeds our publishing systems and also our customer billing system. There's no need for any manual tracking or keying of rate data in order to create the tariff tariffs.

"Although servicing our customers promptly was our main aim in automating our tariff production, there is another not-so-incidental benefit. We're saving about $2 million a year in production costs."

Compatibility Essential

To produce its tariffs, CSX uses two Xerox XPS 701 publishing systems and the Xerox Integrated Composition Systems (XICS), a host-based software package. And because both are fully compatible, CSX can use both together.

Portions of the tariffs that draw extensively from a corporate database are batch processed through XICS on the host mainframe. Then the tariff is routed to an XPS 701, where the remaining composition work is done interactively.

The software is a system for incorporating "copymarks" into test and data. These copymarks direct a printer or photo-typesetter in how to format a document. They also indicate which type of fonts to use and determine the placement of graphics within the text.

The dedicated hardware/software publishing system runs on a 32-bit super-microcomputer and can display all ele-

ments of a document essentially as they will appear on the printed page. When the layout is complete, the user can scroll through the composed pages and see exactly how the copy will flow. Text and data may be added or cut, and the layout will accommodate the change instantly.

Each system at CSX includes a design/pagination terminal with a high resolution screen and digital mouse, five megabytes of memory, a 70-megabyte hard disk, and a 95-megabyte quarter-in. streaming tape cartridge drive. The two systems can exchange documents with one another via "Ethernet."

Meeting All Criteria

Recognizing the need for automated tariff production, CSX management created a task force in September 1985 to evaluate electronic publishing systems. Headed by Davies, the group included CSX technology assistant vice president Mark Jankowski and representatives of the company's sales, marketing and accounting units.

According to Jankowski, CSX used five criteria in evaluating publishing systems from Xerox, IBM, Interleaf and other vendors:

- high-volume, high-quality production capacity

- compatibility with the IMS database environment

- ability to merge text and data into a single document

- ease of use

- graphics capabilities.

"Xerox was the only vendor whose systems met all five criteria," notes Jankowski.

Creating a Tariff

Tariffs give the prices for the handling of specific commodities between two points — origin and destination. Associated with each price are terms and conditions under which the price applies. A tariff can be from one to several hundred pages long.

To generate a tariff, a CSX tariff compiler uses an IBM PC/XT with an IBM 3270 emulation capability to access the host computer. The tariff system residing on the host provides a menu-driven facility that allows the compiler to create the five standard components of most tariffs: a cover page, a table of contents, a list of participating carriers, the shipping conditions, and the price list.

The price list is derived from the latest pricing data, which is stored in the host computer's database. This data automatically is run through a batch program that applies XICS copymarks. As a result, there is no need for the tariff compiler to interactively apply copymarks to the price list after the tariff has been downloaded to the XPS 701.

The downloading is done via a remote job entry (RJE) interface unit from KMW Systems. Once the tariff data is on the XPS 701, the tariff compiler adds XICS copymarks to all portions of the tariff except for the price list, and then does a

"soft proofing" in the "what you see is what you get" mode on the design/pagination terminal's screen. A hard-copy proof of the tariff can be printed out on a printer, when desired.

After the tariff is approved, it is routed back to the host computer via the RJE link. There, it is merged with a mailing list of customers and other recipients, and sent to a high-speed laser printer for production printing.

SOURCE: Reprinted with permission. *Transportation and Distribution*, © December 1988, Penton Publishing Co., Cleveland, OH.

Motor Freight Classification and the railroads' Uniform Freight Classification parallel each other closely. The Coordinated Freight Classification (known colloquially as the New England Classification and used for motor carrier shipments within that area) strongly emphasizes commodity weight density so that a full truckload will produce the same revenue regardless of the commodity's weight per cubic foot.

The classification does *not* establish the rate to be charged for the movement of a product between two points. The rate itself is set forth in a carrier tariff. Products are classified by percentage relationships.[3]

Any product that moves by common carrier *can* be governed by a class rate. If there is not a specific category into which a product fits, then it can be classified within the group of items with which it is most closely associated according to the criteria discussed above.

Once the appropriate classification is determined, reference is then made to the applicable carrier rate tariff showing the rate per hundred-weight for movement between origins and destinations covered by the tariff.

Many carriers of all modes have computerized their tariffs and, instead of place names, use three-digit zip codes to denote origins and destinations. Thus, a rate from Miami to Minneapolis would now be quoted as from 331 to 554. Shippers can access a carrier's computer to determine the rate for a shipment by specifying the zip codes, the classification, commodity number, and the weight of the shipment.

Exception Rates Under certain circumstances (usually including the volume or specialized nature of a shipment), exceptions to the classification are established. The objective is to provide a special privilege, usually in terms of a lower classification, and therefore a lower rate, for a specific type of commodity and movement.

The trend is to restrict the number of exceptions to the classification. Nowadays commodity rates are usually established instead of exceptions to the classification when the volume of individual shipments is in excess of 10,000 pounds.

Commodity Rates Commodity rates are established in cases where a sufficient volume of a product is transported between two points or areas with enough regularity to result in some economies of scale for the carrier(s) handling it. They supercede and frequently are much lower than the class or exception rates for the same item. Commodity rates result from shipper requests for lower rates, from carrier efforts to provide rate concessions for particular commodities or geographical areas in order to develop traffic in those products and areas, or to meet intermodal competition.

Most pipeline, water, and rail carrier shipments are made on commodity rates. They are also widely used by the airlines as a means of generating volumes of air cargo traffic. In the motor carrier industry most LTL traffic moves on class rates and TL traffic moves on commodity rates.

All-Commodity Rates Commonly called ''freight-all-kinds'' or FAK rates, the number of all-commodity rates in effect has increased greatly since deregulation. Under FAK rate provisions, the carrier specifies the rate per shipment, whether in dollars per hundredweight, in total dollars for a specified maximum shipment weight, or in dollars for a specified amount of space, regardless of the items that might be included in the shipment. FAK rates are based on transportation costs rather than the value of service provided to the shipper. Such rates frequently are quoted by freight forwarders and are also used by shippers who send mixed commodity shipments to single destinations. FAK rates are commonly used in shipper-carrier contracts.

FAK rates, as ''convenient'' and ''simplifying'' as they may be, can pose a potentially serious problem to a shipper or a carrier. If the ''mix'' of freight being shipped under an FAK rate changes to any significant degree with respect to density, value, or fragility, the FAK rate may no longer reflect the carrier's cost of transporting the goods. Shippers and carriers alike must be alert to this potential problem, and if the mix of FAK freight changes, the rate should also be changed; if the rate is not changed, one party or the other will get the short end of the stick until it is changed.

Rate Systems

There are two types of rate systems that govern most of the transportation in the United States. These are distance and blanket rate systems.

Distance Rate Systems Distance rates are mileage rates and are based on the tapering rate principle in which rates increase at a slower rate than distance. This reflects the effect of fixed terminal costs associated with a shipment.

Blanket Rate Systems Blanket rate systems involve the grouping of points, either at origin or destination or both, into the same rate group. Figure 8–2 illustrates the Transcontinental Freight Bureau (TCFB) rate groups for shipments originating in the ''North Coast'' and ''South Coast'' territories of the TCFB to destination territories east of the line shown running through North and South Dakota, Wyoming, Colorado, and New Mexico. In Figure 8–2, shipments from the origin territories to points in the ''no man's land'' (shaded areas) are not governed by Transcontinental Freight Bureau rate tariffs.

Rates Based on Route

In addition to being a class or a commodity rate, and a distance or a blanket rate, every rate is also either a joint or local rate and a combination or through rate. In addition, it may be an arbitrary or differential rate.

FIGURE 8–2: Transcontinental Freight Bureau rate groups

TRANSCONTINENTAL FREIGHT BUREAU
RATE GROUPS

(S) Indicates south coast territories
(N) Indicates north coast territories
⊗   Many stations in Group M take Group C-2 or C-3
    rates via certain routes
*   Except as specifically provided,
    Transcontinental Group rates do not apply.

Joint and Local Rates When only one carrier participates in the line haul movement of a shipment, the rate quoted is a local rate. Thus, the word "local" does not mean movements only within local areas or for short distances.[4]

Whether a movement between two points can be made under a local rate, a joint rate, or both often is critical because it can affect competition and rate levels. Under joint rates, two or more carriers band together to match or better a rate quoted by a competitor offering a local rate. While this offers the opportunity for competition, the possibility of the reversal of roles in other situations often constrains competitive pricing and leads to an umbrella created by the higher-cost joint movement through an interchange point. As a result, intermodal competition has perhaps led to more rate competition than the establishment of joint rates.

Through and Combination Rates   A through rate is a rate from one point to another that is stated specifically in a tariff as applying between the points involved. It can be either a joint through rate or a local through rate. A combination rate is one that is made up of two or more existing rates to cover a shipment between two points.

There are two types of combination rates, "aggregate of intermediates" and "proportional" rates. An aggregate of intermediates rate occurs when two or more rates are added to apply from origin to destination. If an aggregate of intermediates rate results in lower charges than the through rate, the former may sometimes be used as a substitute. A combination rate that is lower than the through rate will apply only if the applicable tariff has a rule protecting such combinations. This requires careful checking of a tariff.

The complexity of the rate structure causes situations in which the aggregate of intermediates rate is lower than a through rate. This complexity frequently makes it necessary to determine both a through rate and an aggregate of intermediates rate. When there is a sufficient volume of movement to justify altering the rate structure, carriers usually are willing to adjust the through rate down to the aggregate of intermediates rate level.

A proportional rate is a separately established local or joint rate that creates a through rate by combining one rate with a portion of another. Proportional rates usually are established for competitive reasons by two or more carriers.[5]

Rates Based on Quantity

Quantities shipped are an important determinant of any rate. Rates based on quantity include minimum, any quantity, in-excess, and multiple-vehicle rates.

Minimum and Any-Quantity Rates   Carrier rates are based on specified minimum quantities ranging from "any quantity," on which the minimum charge typically is for 100 pounds, to the capacity of a transport vehicle. Railroads no longer accept less-than-carload shipments.

Rules governing shipments in excess of vehicle capacity are sometimes made a part of carrier tariffs. In some cases, the overflow is moved at the same rate as the quantity loaded in the vehicle. In others, the excess is treated as a separate shipment.

In-Excess Rates   These are a type of incentive rate, designed to improve carrier equipment utilization by encouraging heavier loading of individual vehicles. The term "in excess rate" signifies that one rate is charged up to a minimum weight qualifying as a "vehicle load," and a lower rate is charged for any amount in excess of the stated minimum.

Multiple-Vehicle Rates   Incentives may be offered to shippers who ship more than a single vehicle load of a commodity at one time to a particular destination. There are several reasons for the existence of such rates. A rail car generally has significantly greater capacity than a truck trailer. To overcome this competitive disadvantage, some motor carriers have established multiple-vehicle (in this case, multiple-truckload) rates. For example, where rail carriers might establish carload rates for 80,000-pound shipments, a motor carrier might match this by quoting a competitive 80,000-pound rate and transporting the shipment in two 40,000-pound truckloads.

Railroads also offer multiple-vehicle rates to meet competition from barges for the volume movement of bulk commodities. They take the form of multiple-car or even trainload rates for coal, ore, grain, molasses, and petroleum products. Rail carriers have justified these lower "unit train" rates on the basis of the economy and efficiency of handling multiple-vehicle loads from one origin to one destination, bypassing intermediate terminals and yards, and achieving greater utilization of equipment.

The rent-a-train concept is a variation of the unit train idea that has the effect of creating private carriage in the rail mode. Here, the rail carrier furnishes only the right of way, motive power, and crew. The shipper buys or leases its own cars and is responsible for their utilization.

Miscellaneous Rate Modifications

A rate may be modified in a variety of ways. We have grouped these under the heading of miscellaneous rate modifications. Deregulation has brought about increased use of these types of rates, particularly with respect to shipper-carrier contracts written to provide a full range of carrier services for a particular shipper's traffic.

Value Rates The general rule of carrier liability is that the carrier is liable for the value of goods lost or damaged while in its custody.[6] Value may be specified in several ways. Released value rates are, as the term suggests, rates that are based on carriers assuming a certain fixed liability, usually stated in dollars and cents per pound, for goods transported by them. This liability ordinarily is substantially less than the actual value of the goods and results in a lower rate.

Guaranteed Schedule Rates Carriers and shippers may agree on a guaranteed schedule for the movement of a shipment. Livestock and perishables are examples of commodities for which guaranteed schedules are useful. If the carrier fails to meet the schedule and a loss is incurred, the carrier may be held liable for the resulting loss. Ordinarily, a carrier is responsible only for exercising "reasonable dispatch," which provides greater delivery latitude than a guaranteed schedule.

Space Availability Rates Shippers who can tolerate delay in delivery of their freight may take advantage of lower space available rates. These rates are used widely by air and water carriers because they provide them with a discretionary means of achieving higher capacity utilization after regular cargoes have been loaded.

Measurement Rates Rates reflecting very close attention to weight-density ratios are used in ocean transportation, in airfreight rates, and on certain bulk shipments by rail.[7] Ocean rates commonly are quoted at so much per long ton (2,240 pounds), *or* per 40 cubic feet, *whichever produces the higher charge*. The loading of ships requires extremely careful attention to considerations of weight and balance. If the cargo weight-density ratio is light, maintaining the ship's stability will require taking on non-revenue ballast (usually seawater admitted to ballast tanks below the water line). Generally, heavy cargo is not a problem provided it is properly stowed at the appropriate deck level. In the case of aircraft, there are absolute weight limits and the primary consideration then becomes a matter of fore-and-aft balance.

Rail measurement rates, such as those used for pulpwood, are on a per-cord basis, which assumes an average cubic volume, not weight, per cord.

Agreed Rates Agreed rates are loyalty incentive rates, granted in return for the shipment of a specific percentage share of total annual shipments. When made available by common carriers to all shippers *without reference to specific volumes*, they have been acceptable to the Interstate Commerce Commission. Contract and exempt carrier rates of a similar nature are established through direct shipper-carrier agreement.

Although the volume discount is a common business practice, agreed rates between shippers and common carriers are not as widely used in the United States as they are in Canada and the United Kingdom. The ICC generally has held that loyalty incentive rates, where a shipper agrees to ship a specified tonnage by a certain carrier or group of carriers in return for lower rates, are discriminatory.

Section 10721 Rates The Interstate Commerce Act provides that the general rules of rate-making need not apply to shipments made by or to or from government agencies. Section 10721 of the act (formerly Section 22) provides that carriers may furnish transportation for government agencies and related parties ''free or at reduced rates.'' A thorough understanding of Section 10721 rate-making procedures is essential for logistics managers making shipments to or from military and government installations.

Multi-Modal Rates The growth of intermodal transportation services has produced a variety of multi-modal rates designed to make the pricing for these services more competitive and understandable, as well as to simplify the paperwork and billing for such shipments. Most multi-modal rates are quoted by the originating carrier on a single, joint, through rate basis, usually for door-to-door service. Generally, multi-modal rates are based on carrier costs.

Rates and Deregulation

What was once a stable and orderly marketplace with respect to transportation rates has, since deregulation, become what some have called ''an economic jungle.'' Rate wars have become rampant in the motor carrier industry. Railroads can sign secret contracts with shippers. Larger shippers can bargain for rate discounts, while smaller shippers have to pay ''retail.'' All this has posed a challenge to logistics managers: how to manage the traffic function effectively in a new and changed environment.

ACCESSORIAL SERVICE AND TERMINAL CHARGES

In addition to line-haul rates, carriers also charge for special services as well as assessing certain types of terminal charges.

Services

Carriers provide a wide variety of services to shippers. Such services, often regarded as ''privileges'' by carriers offering them, have resulted from shipper needs and carrier competition. Only the most significant of such services are outlined below.

Diversion and Reconsignment Technically, diversion means a change in the routing of a shipment and reconsignment means a change of consignee (receiver) for a particular shipment. But in practice, the words are used interchangeably. Diversion is used most frequently in connection with the movement of perishables, grain, and lumber. The purpose is to permit the delivery of shipments to one of several possible alternate points, depending upon changes in market conditions or in the terms of sale, some time after the shipment has been originated, but before it has reached its originally specified destination. A charge is assessed by carriers for diversion and reconsignment services.

Diversion also has been used as a method of using the carrier as a warehouse. Through diversion, a shipper can route a shipment circuitously so that transit time will be longer than usual and the need for warehousing at the destination will be reduced. Extreme abuses of this practice have been scrutinized closely by rail carriers because of the costs involved and by the ICC because of possibilities for discrimination resulting from the practice.

Protective Service Carriers provide protective service for goods that are affected by the environment. The services include ventilation, refrigeration, and heater service. In some situations, carriers render these services without charge as a necessary element in the transportation of a commodity. In other instances, where the shipper specifies the type of service to be given to a particular shipment, charges are assessed for the additional service.

Special Equipment Carriers sometimes assess extra charges for the use of equipment furnished to meet special shipper needs. Enclosed, tri-deck rail cars used only to transport new automobiles are an example of this type of equipment. However, railroads are increasingly requiring shippers to purchase (invest in) special types of rail cars. This shifts both the capital investment and the risk involved — traffic using this equipment may decline — from the railroad to the shipper. With respect to ocean carriage, almost all special-purpose vessels are shipper-owned, with only general cargo vessels (including containerships) being owned by marine transportation companies.

Transit Privileges Generally, transit privileges were established to facilitate the flow of goods requiring some handling or processing at an intermediate point between origin and ultimate destination. Several types of transit privileges and the commodities for which they were designed are milling (grain), compressing (cotton), planing (lumber), fabrication (steel), blending (wine), and storage (for commodities produced seasonally and consumed nonseasonally).

Figure 8–3 illustrates the transit privilege. Assuming an inbound movement of raw materials from point A to B at a rate of $.90 per hundredweight, the transit operator would pay the inbound $.90 rate, record tonnage for transit with the carrier, perform the transit operation, and then file with the carrier for the refund ($.80 per hundredweight) of the difference between the $.90 inbound rate and the transit charge ($.10 per hundredweight). Therefore, the cost of a movement from A to C via a transit point B would be $2.10 per hundredweight, compared with that of a direct movement from A to C or from B to C without a transit stop of $2.00 per hundredweight. Where the transit point is not in a direct line to the destination, additional out-of-line charges could be assessed.

Due to rate deregulation in the railroad industry, the use of in-transit rates has declined sharply, and they have largely been replaced with simple point-to-point rates. However, the historical situations that caused the establishment of in-transit rates have not changed, and that is a problem for shippers who have used them. With railroads more and more basing their rates

FIGURE 8–3: Illustration of the processing-in-transit privilege (with points A and B in the same origin-rate group for destination point C)

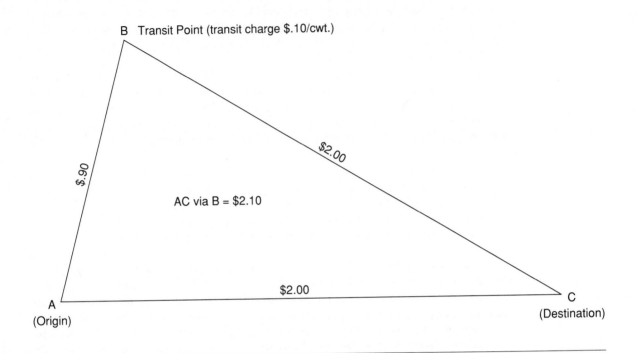

on cost of service, many processing locations that once benefited from in-transit rates are now at a disadvantage compared with competing locations that are either raw-material-source or market oriented.

Stop-Off Privileges Another common type of transit privilege permits the shipper or receiver to stop a shipment at an intermediate point to partially load or unload. Assume that a customer to whom a truckload shipment is directed has warehouses located at three points and wants to unload part of the shipment at each of them. The rate from the origin to the final destination would apply to the total weight of the shipment plus two stop-off charges (with no added charge for the delivery at final destination). Savings between these charges and the cost of three separate LTL shipments could be substantial. Commonly, under such privileges, shippers are limited to one stop to complete loading and three stops to partially unload.

A problem with stop-off shipments is the delay incurred when moving trucks or rail cars to several points that are not in a reasonably direct line with each other. To help solve this problem and to accomplish better car utilization, several rail carriers have established transloading stations. Where a transloading station is available, a car containing goods for three points can be moved to the station where the contents will be unloaded and reloaded into separate cars for direct movement to each destination. The charges for transloading often are the same as stop-off charges in specific tariffs.

TABLE 8–2: An Example of Split Delivery Charges[a]

Weight of Individual Split Deliveries (in pounds)		Split Delivery Charge for Each Individual Delivery
Over	But Not Over	
0	100	$ 4.05
100	250	4.70
250	500	4.95
500	1,000	6.50
1,000	2,000	9.50
2,000	4,000	10.90
4,000	10,000	12.55
10,000		14.45

[a]Assessed in addition to the regular transportation rate on the full weight of the entire shipment.

Split Delivery Both rail and highway carriers offer stop-off services. Split delivery is an additional service provided by highway carriers. It permits an unlimited number of segments of a larger shipment to be delivered *within the limits of a specific split-delivery area*. Special split-delivery charges are made for each partial shipment delivered to a different point. Split-delivery charges are the same regardless of the total weight of the shipment. Table 8–2 shows examples of split delivery charges.

Assembly and distribution services typically are offered by freight forwarders. If rate structure provides the forwarder the necessary profit margin, the forwarder will arrange for transportation of the consolidated shipment (for example, a 20,000-pound shipment made up of twenty 1,000-pound parcels) to a break-bulk point and subsequent movement of the twenty parcels separately to their ultimate destinations.

Pickup and Delivery Air carriers commonly quote rates on an airport-to-airport basis. Additional charges usually apply for pickup and delivery service. These charges must be noted and included when comparing air freight rates with those of "door-to-door" services.

Terminal Charges

Special services often are associated with terminal activities, giving rise to added charges. Among the most important of these are demurrage, detention, and switching charges.

Demurrage and Detention The words demurrage and detention both refer to charges paid carriers by shippers or consignees for the delay of a car, vessel, or vehicle beyond a specified "free-time" allowed for loading or unloading. The term demurrage is used in rail, water, and pipeline transportation. Detention is assessed on highway vehicles and on trailers used in TOFC service.

Rail car demurrage is supervised by railroad rate bureaus. Most rail users enter into "average" demurrage agreements with the various bureaus. Under an average demurrage agreement, monthly demurrage debits (charges for detaining cars beyond the "free time" period) may be offset by demurrage credits (credit for loading and unloading cars in less than the full "free time" period), within limits.

Pipeline demurrage is charged when the receiver is unable (usually because of insufficient storage space) to receive the quantity delivered to it by a pipeline. For water movement, charges for vessel demurrage are based on the size of the vessel and are usually specified in the applicable tariffs or contracts. Free time is based on the volume and characteristics of the cargo to be unloaded.

Detention charges vary widely, depending on the legal form of carriage and the type of equipment involved. They may begin as soon as three hours after arrival for trailers accompanied by a driver and a tractor, or as late as two or three days for vans, containers, and TOFC trailers spotted on a customer's premises.

Switching Charges   Line-haul rail rates usually include switching service to the consignee's point of unloading. Carriers frequently establish reciprocal switching arrangements. Reciprocal switching means that the switching carrier will deliver to destination (within certain switching limits) a car that it did not handle in line-haul movement, and settlement of switching charges is made directly between the line-haul and switching carriers. When the line-haul carrier does not have access to the destination point (for example, railroad siding) and the destination is "closed" to reciprocal switching, the shipper or consignee must pay for the switching, charged on a per-car basis.

RATE LEVEL DETERMINANTS

Value and cost of service are major determinants of the range in which a transportation rate may fall. The value of service to the shipper establishes the upper level that a rate might seek, while carrier out-of-pocket cost tends to define the lower level. Factors that tend to produce actual rate levels *within this range* include the physical characteristics of the product shipped, distance and direction of movement, the quantity and regularity of shipments, and competition.

Value of Service

The value-of-service concept in rate making is based on an assessment of the ability of a product to bear a given transportation rate burden. For example, high-value items can bear higher per-unit, per-hundredweight, or per-cubic-foot rates than items of lower value.

Items of very low value, on the other hand, may be given very low rates, based on the value-of-service concept. Locklin has suggested that preferential (low) rates based on the value-of-service concept are not a burden on other traffic if the rates cover carrier direct or out-of-pocket cost *and* the traffic will not command higher rates.[8] If these two conditions actually were met in making low value-of-service rates, there would be little objection to this approach. However, low value-of-service rates do not always cover out-of-pocket carrier costs, carriers are seldom precise in their determination of whether the same volume of traffic would move at higher rates, and—above all—a carrier must have "excess" capacity available to move such traffic to avoid being unable to move more profitable traffic.

Cost of Service

Transportation cost concepts do not differ significantly from cost concepts generally used in manufacturing and service industries. They include fully distributed costs, fixed costs, variable costs, out-of-pocket costs, and joint or common costs.

Fully Distributed Costs   These are *all* of the costs that can be associated with a particular shipment or movement. Some analysts include profit (return on investment) in their definition of fully distributed costs.

Fixed Costs   These are costs that will be incurred even if the carrier is not operating. They include such items as interest on debt, property taxes, rental payments, mortgage or other periodic fixed payments (for example, on equipment purchases), and so forth.

Variable Costs   These are the costs incurred by carrier operations. Their relationship to total carrier revenue is often referred to as the ''operating ratio,'' frequently used as a measure of carrier operating efficiency.

Out-of-Pocket Costs   These are the added costs incurred to provide an additional increment of operation, such as adding the 100th car to a 99-car freight train.

Joint and Common Costs   These are costs incurred by different shipments moved over the same route, or in the same vehicle at the same time. Items such as driver or crew wages and fuel costs must be apportioned to shipments or services along with common costs, such as railroad maintenance of way, which, for example, must be allocated to both freight and passenger services. The line drawn between joint and common costs is extremely fine and often subject to debate. Both joint and common costs may be present simultaneously and may be either fixed or variable in nature.

Cost-of-service pricing reflects contemporary economic theory that marginal prices should equal marginal costs at a point where maximum short-run profits are realized. Cost-of-service pricing tends to shift freight to lower cost carriers and modes *provided* other shipper requirements (such as time in transit) are met.

Direction of Movement

Freight hauled between two points is rarely balanced in terms of volume in both directions. When a shipment moves in a heavy-haul direction, the rate tends to be higher than for a comparable shipment in the light-haul (or ''backhaul'') direction, for which the carrier will quote lower rates to obtain traffic.

Changes in the direction of heavy movement have presented serious problems to both carriers and shippers. If, for example, backhaul rates, designed to fill unused capacity, create so much demand that the directional imbalance is reversed, a carrier's revenue structure can be upset. Such situations *may* lead to inadequate service by a carrier as it attempts to adjust operations to a new movement pattern.

Size and Regularity of Shipments

Both the volume shipped in an individual shipment and the quantity and regularity of shipments over a period of time affect rate levels. The elements of time and regularity are significant because of the carriers' desire for sustained utilization of equipment, thus avoiding "peaks and valleys" in operations.

Restrictions on Discrimination

Historically, the ICC and CAB went to great lengths to discourage service or price discrimination by common carriers with respect to commodities, origins, destinations, regions, individuals, and shipment distances. However, deregulation has dramatically changed the picture with respect to discrimination by common carriers. It is scarcely an exaggeration to say that, with respect to interstate traffic, a carrier today can charge what it pleases, to whom it pleases, when it pleases, and where it pleases, with few exceptions. That this poses a problem for shippers is a gross understatement. Discrimination is rampant in the transportation marketplace; a century of antidiscriminatory transportation legislation and public policy has been turned upside down by the deregulation of rates and services. This point is discussed further in a later section of this chapter, Rate Negotiation.

Competition

Both intermodal and intramodal competition as well as the private transport alternative influence rate levels. Until recently, intermodal competition was the most important factor in the determination of rate levels. With the passage of The Motor Carrier Act of 1980, the importance of intramodal competition among motor carriers has increased dramatically.

Intermodal Competition   The struggle by the various modes of transportation for increases in volume (and in some cases survival) has been intense at times. Only if a shipper has no reasonable alternative for the movement of its products, will the rate levels at which its products move tend toward the higher limits of the range and be based to a larger extent on the value-of-service concept.

Intramodal Competition   Prior to deregulation, common carriers within the same mode of transportation tended to compete on services rendered rather than price. Since deregulation, the transportation industry has witnessed intense price competition, particularly in the motor carrier sector. Price competition for truckload traffic — for which there have been more than 10,000 new entrant carriers, albeit most of them small — has been very intense, to the point where few truckload carriers have been able to earn a reasonable profit. In the less-than-truckload sector, there have been very few entrants — due to economy of scale barriers to entry — but competition to survive has been keen. All of this has lowered rates, particularly for larger shippers who have been able to extract substantial rate concessions from carriers. Smaller firms have had to pay higher rates, not having the negotiating position to get rate discounts.

Private Transportation   Private transportation developed for two basic reasons. First, private transportation is an attractive alternative to for-hire service when a shipper's traffic has volume and movement characteristics that make it difficult to obtain adequate common carrier service *or* permit it to operate at lower cost than possible under the rates charged by common or contract carriers.

Second, private transportation can be used as a lever to obtain rate concessions from for-hire carriers. When a shipper is unable to obtain a rate concession that it believes reasonable (or unreasonable) and private transportation is a feasible alternative, the shipper can threaten to install a private transportation system in order to encourage the rate adjustment. In addition, the threat of private transportation has, on occasion, been used in the same manner as a "bluff" in a poker game; shippers have been known to develop and make known plans for private transportation as a means of threatening carriers with that alternative if requested rate concessions are not granted.

THE RATE-MAKING PROCESS

Rate Bureaus

Prior to deregulation most rail and motor carrier rates were set by collective action of carriers belonging to a carrier rate bureau which published the rates in bureau tariffs. These tariffs were then filed with the ICC. Carriers were not bound by these rates; they had the option of taking independent action, and by the late 1970s the number of such independently set rates was increasing.

Deregulation legislation effectively removed the antitrust immunity that had been conferred on rate bureaus by the Reed-Bulwinkle Act of 1948 and thereby prohibited any future collective ratemaking by motor carriers and railroads except for joint rates.

Despite the loss of most of their collective ratemaking role, the motor-carrier bureaus do continue to act as publishers of tariffs submitted to them for printing by motor carriers, but can take no part in ratemaking. Several motor carriers may subscribe to the same tariff because they choose to charge the same rates as their competitors.

What is left for the motor carrier rate bureaus? They still can and do perform a number of useful functions for their carrier members. As furnished to the authors by the Middle Atlantic Conference, a major rate bureau, these currently include:

1. Continuing Traffic Study (providing the basis for determining the impact of proposed rate changes);

2. Continuing Financial Analysis (carrier operating results and statistics, payroll studies, nonlabor expense index and special studies);

3. Cost Development and Analysis (industry costs and individual carrier costs — also development of computer costing systems for individual carriers);

4. Economic Analysis of the Motor Carrier Industry, Trends, and so forth;

5. Tariffs: Revenue need adjustments on a collective basis;

   a. Rate structure adjustments to relate rates, weight brackets, and distance factors more closely to costs;

   b. Zip code grouping plans to facilitate computer rating;

   c. Formularization of rate structures to facilitate computer rating;

   d. Publication and distribution of rate tariffs to carriers and shippers;

   e. Compilation of Individual and Special Need Tariffs;

   f. Assist carriers, shippers, and consultants in rate finding, analysis, and audit by making available computer tapes, diskettes, and such, of the bureau rate system;

   g. Providing assistance to carrier and shippers in classifying freight and complying with federal and state regulations;

   h. Providing rate analysis and research to member carriers as requested;

   i. Disseminating information and analysis of rate changes by competing carriers or modes;

   j. Providing a forum for the carriers to meet and discuss mutual problems within the confines of approved rate bureau agreement.

These activities are obviously extremely useful to bureau carrier members, and shippers as well, if they are well carried out. Rate bureaus offer economies of scale to their members, and they have undeniably legitimate functions of value to the industry—both carriers and shippers. Viewed as regional trade associations, they have a very useful role to play in the future.

The New Era in Rates and Rate Making

As much of the preceding discussion with respect to rates indicates, the consequences of deregulation have left carriers and logistics managers alike confronted by a bewildering array of rates and possible rate modifications. What was formerly an orderly and stable system of rates and rate making is now "anything goes." Given the wide range of alternatives facing the logistics manager today, it is now, more than ever before, necessary to "know one's carriers" and to know what is possible with respect to negotiating rates, particularly in the case of shipper-carrier contracts.

SUMMARY

The passage of the Interstate Commerce Act in 1887 was the first of many efforts to regulate interstate commerce in the United States. Although opposition increased from those favoring a "free market" for transportation prices and services, the extent of regulation grew steadily for ninety years. Beginning with the 4R Act in 1976, interstate rail, air, and motor carrier rates and services have been almost completely deregulated. This has had profound consequences for both carriers and shippers, who have had to cope with a truly competitive transportation environment for the first time in nearly a century.

Freight rates may be based on classifications indicating the relative characteristics of products for purposes of transportation or may be commodity rates based on volume, regularity of movement, or both. Rates themselves are found in tariffs published by common carriers and in contracts between shippers and the contract or exempt carriers they might employ. All rates can be categorized in terms of whether they are local or joint, their type, the system employed in quoting them, the type of route they refer to, the quantity of freight they require, and various miscellaneous provisions.

In addition to line haul rates, shippers may also pay a variety of accessorial charges for the handling and servicing of freight at origin, destination, or in transit. Among the more important of these services, often called privileges, are diversion and reconsignment; protective services; the provision of special equipment; transit, stop-off, and split delivery privileges; and pickup and delivery. Terminal charges may be assessed for demurrage, detention, and switching.

The range of rates that might be quoted tends to reflect the value of service near the top and cost of service near the bottom. Other factors that tend to produce actual rate levels somewhere in this range include the physical characteristics of the product shipped, the distance and direction of movement, the quantity and regularity of shipments, restrictions on discrimination, and competition.

Due to the effects of economic deregulation of the transportation industry, it is quite certain that many opportunities exist in the pricing and design of transportation service for a logistics manager able to understand the structure of rates and services and to use that knowledge to the advantage of his or her firm.

The major task of traffic management is that of compiling, analyzing, and using information effectively to plan and control the movement of a firm's supplies and products. In some cases, the traffic function may also have responsibility for the management of privately-owned and operated transportation.

Deregulation has permitted more innovative and creative transportation system design than was possible in the past. It will require more astute traffic managers to meet the new challenges brought about by deregulation.

The importance of transportation costs in the logistics system has been noted. But of more significance than transportation costs is the effective use of transportation in a manner compatible with a firm's overall logistics strategy and patterns. It is this latter characteristic that distinguishes the forward looking traffic manager from his or her predecessors.

DISCUSSION QUESTIONS

1. Nearly a century of transportation regulation, beginning with the Interstate Commerce Act in 1887, was undone by Congress in the space of five years (1976–1980). What do you believe caused this turn of events?

2. What is the difference between a joint rate and a local rate? How did these terms originate?

3. What are FAK rates? What is the reason for such rates? Can problems arise from the use of such rates? If so, what?

4. Under what circumstances, or for what reasons, are commodity rates established?

5. What is a distance rate system? How does it differ from a blanket rate system?

6. What is the difference between in-excess rates and multiple-vehicle rates?

7. Why do ocean carriers use measurement rates? Do other modes of transportation use this principle of ratemaking?

8. What is the difference between diversion and reconsignment? What purpose(s) do they serve?

9. Explain the concept of in-transit rates? What purpose(s) do they serve? What types of commodities are typically shipped under such rates?

10. Do demurrage and detention mean the same thing? Why do carriers assess such charges to shippers?

11. Define the terms value of service and cost of service. What categories of cost are included in a carrier's cost of service?

12. Why is ''directional traffic balance'' an important consideration for transportation carrier managements?

13. After deregulation, what services can rate bureaus still perform for their members?

14. What are the ''implicit'' costs of transportation?

CASE: Industrial Suppliers, Inc.*
Deregulation Temptation

The shouting match between Bill Harrison and Marge Edmonds had started a few minutes earlier as a quiet conversation, but their discussion had escalated rapidly into almost violent disagreement over whether to employ the services of Donnick's Transport, a motor carrier with which their company, Industrial Suppliers, Inc., had not previously done business.

''He's a fly-by-night!'' yelled Harrison. ''At those rates he'd have to hi-jack our shipments to make any money!''

''No way!,'' retorted Edmonds, ''all he wants is to get some of our traffic away from the 'big boys' and he's willing to give us good rates to get into this market.''

''You're crazy,'' snorted Harrison, ''you give him any of our inbound traffic and it will never get here!''

''Look,'' said Edmonds in a calmer tone of voice, ''you've got to get used to a new ball game, Bill. Since deregulation we've had to do a lot of things we didn't used to have to do. One of them is taking a careful look and giving consideration to truckers who are willing to quote us lower rates. Some of them may be new, and maybe we've never heard of them, but there's no reason to think they won't or can't do the job. We're just getting used to real price competition from motor common carriers.''

''Okay,'' muttered Harrison, ''but, it seems to me that we can get in a lot of trouble if we just 'take the lowest bidder' so to speak. You know we don't do that with our product vendors. We do want the lowest price, but only if the vendor is good in other respects like quality and delivery time.''

Bill Harrison was Materials Manager for Industrial Suppliers, Inc. (I.S.I.), a manufacturer of office and factory floor cleaning equipment. He worked closely with Marge Edmonds who was I.S.I.'s Traffic Manager. In the I.S.I. organization Harrison reported to the vice president of manufacturing and Edmonds reported to the vice president of marketing and distribution. However,

---

*This case has been prepared as the basis for a seminar or classroom discussion and is not intended to portray either correct or incorrect approaches to managerial decision making. All names have been disguised.

their managerial responsibilities required them to cooperate closely in matters affecting the inbound transportation of purchased parts, components, subassemblies and other manufacturing materials required by I.S.I.

A small portion, less than 10 percent, of I.S.I.'s inbound traffic was received by rail. There was also an occasional ''emergency'' air freight shipment from a vendor. But, about 90 percent of all inbound shipments from vendors to I.S.I. were handled by motor carriers. I.S.I.'s outbound physical distribution traffic pattern was much more complex than the inbound materials patterns, which accounted for Marge Edmonds' position being under marketing.

Bill Harrison and Marge Edmonds had cooperated very effectively in ''calling the shots'' on motor carrier selection for inbound movements, despite some vendor resistance. Nearly all of I.S.I.'s materials were purchased F.O.B. vendor, and I.S.I. had made it clear to vendors that they were to ship by motor carriers designated by I.S.I. From time to time a vendor would balk at this I.S.I. policy, but Harrison jarred the vendor into complying by, as he put it, ''making him an offer he couldn't refuse,'' such as simply threatening to cut the vendor off immediately and completely as a supplier of I.S.I if the vendor didn't ship via I.S.I.-designated motor carriers.

Marge Edmonds had kept a careful eye on the ''deregulation issue'' hearings and debates in Congress and had not been at all surprised by passage of the Motor Carrier Act of 1980 and the accompanying shifts in ICC deregulatory policies, procedures, and actions. For all practical purposes she considered that the motor carrier industry had been nearly completely deregulated in fact, if not in name.

Edmonds realized that the ''rose bush'' of deregulation also had some ''thorns'' on it, as she put it, and that motor carrier deregulation meant that shippers and receivers now had to make some types of decisions they hadn't been accustomed to making in the past. In the case of I.S.I. this included negotiating with motor carriers in an ''open-market environment'' over rates on inbound interstate TL and LTL traffic. However, Edmonds realized that lower rates were only one side of the coin. The flip side involved the question of *who* was offering the lower rates. That question was what led to her heated discussion with Bill Harrison.

Many shippers and shipper organizations had opposed ''deregulation'' of motor common carriers. Accustomed to stability in rates and services, they were reluctant to trade that stability for the claimed ''benefits of competition'' within the motor carrier marketplace. Reluctant or not, mused Edmonds, we'd better get used to it. It's here and it won't go away.

Bill Harrison's concerns were taken very seriously by Marge Edmonds. Both managers understood the decision-making problem posed by ''a stranger who offers a better deal.'' Harrison admitted freely that Marge Edmonds ''knew her carriers'' and Harrison had consistently deferred to Edmonds' judgement in the past. But, as Harrison put it, ''That was before deregulation. You were familiar with most of the carriers, and if you hadn't done much (or any) business with a particular carrier you could always call a traffic manager friend in another company and get a line on the guy.'' Deregulation had changed the picture, however.

Mr. James Lawrence, whose business card proclaimed him to be vice president of sales of Donnick's Transport, had approached Edmonds with an offer of an 8 percent rate reduction on inbound loads of 5,000 pounds or more from points in Ohio to I.S.I.'s plant in St. Louis. Mr. Lawrence had said Donnick's was in the market to stay. Edmonds had been able to find out only that Donnick's Transport was headquartered in Cleveland, was owner-managed, had previously been a contract carrier in the Ohio-Illinois area, and apparently used a number of owner-operators in its operations. Edmonds had checked with more than a dozen other traffic mangers, but she could find no one who had had any shipping or receiving experience with Donnick's Transport. A sparse credit agency report had told her very little more.

Marge Edmonds knew that although Donnick's Transport was the first "new kid on the block" to show up at her door, it wouldn't be the last. Other truckers, perhaps many others, would appear, and probably sooner rather than later. Many would offer lower rates in one form or another. "What we need is a policy," Edmonds said to Bill Harrison. Harrison nodded at her and replied, "No question about *that*. The question is: What should our policy *be*?"

SUGGESTED READINGS

BOWERSOX, DONALD J., *et al. Leading Edge Logistics: Competitive Positioning for the 1990's*, Oak Brook, Illinois: Council of Logistics Management, 1989.

COYLE, JOHN J., EDWARD J. BARDI, and JOSEPH L. CAVINATO. *Transportation*, 2d ed. St. Paul: West Publishing Company, 1986.

KENDALL, LANE C. *The Business of Shipping*, 5th ed. Centreville, Maryland: Cornell Maritime Press, 1986.

LOCKLIN, D. PHILIP. *Economics of Transportation*. 7th ed. Homewood, Illinois: Richard D. Irwin, Inc., 1972. Locklin's work, although dated in some respects, remains a classic and valuable treatment of the economics of transportation and transportation rates.

SAMPSON, ROY J., MARTIN T. FARRIS and DAVID L. SCHROCK. *Domestic Transportation: Practice, Theory and Policy*. Boston: Houghton Miflin Company, 1985.

SHAPIRO, ROY D., and JAMES L. HESKETT. *Logistics Strategy: Cases and Concepts*. St. Paul: West Publishing Company, 1985.

STEPHENSON, FREDERICK J., Jr. *Transportation USA*. Reading, Massachusetts: Addison-Wesley Publishing Company, 1987.

TAFF, CHARLES A. *Commercial Motor Transportation*, 7th ed. Centreville, Maryland: Cornell Maritime Press, 1986.

TYWORTH, JOHN E., JOSEPH L. CAVINATO, and C. JOHN LANGLEY, Jr. *Traffic Management*. Reading, Massachusetts: Addison-Wesley Publishing Company, 1987.

WELLS, ALEXANDER T. *Air Transportation: A Management Perspective*, 2d ed. Belmont, California: Wadsworth Publishing Company, 1989.

ENDNOTES

1. Actually, the original act in 1887 was titled the "Act to Regulate Commerce." The change in name was made in the Transportation Act of 1920.

2. For a comprehensive treatment of the effects of motor carrier deregulation see Nicholas A. Glaskowsky, *Effects of Deregulation on Motor Carriers*, 2d ed. (Westport, Conn.: Eno Foundation for Transportation, 1990).

3. Products can be classified in one of two ways: (1) by percentage variations from 100 percent (Class I) and (2) by alphanumeric categories.

4. The terms "local rate" and "joint rate" originated in the nineteenth century in the early days of the railroad industry. Railroads were small and their routes covered relatively short distances. Thus, a shipment over only one railroad *was* "local."

Longer-distance shipments had to travel over two or more railroads' lines and were thus "joint" rate shipments.

5. For a more extensive discussion of the nature and use of proportional and other types of rates, see Kenneth V. Flood, *Traffic Management*, 3d ed. (Dubuque: W. C. Brown Co., 1975): 162–163.

6. This is not the case with respect to ocean carriage for which shippers must obtain their own insurance.

7. As noted in Chapter 7, weight density is a primary factor in ratemaking in all modes except pipeline because of the carriers' wish to use both cubic and weight capacity.

8. Locklin, D. Philip, *Economics of Transportation*, 7th ed. (Homewood, Ill.: Richard D. Irwin, 1972): 163.

The loading dock of a busy distributor keeps pace with customer needs for goods to be delivered on time and in good condition.

CHAPTER NINE

Traffic Management

LEARNING OBJECTIVES

The objectives of this chapter are to:

➤ Present and discuss the task shippers face in evaluating carrier performance.

➤ Show the difficulties and methods of dealing with the problem of determining the true cost of transportation.

➤ Explain the nature of transportation documentation, including the multiple roles of the bill of lading.

➤ Explain the problems involved with shipper claims for over, short, and damaged shipments.

➤ Note the importance of gathering and analyzing traffic information by shippers.

➤ Explain the significance and importance of freight-bill auditing by shippers, including the problems of overcharges and undercharges.

➤ Present and discuss the factors involved in rate-making, such as pricing of carrier services.

➤ Explain the changed nature of rate negotiation between carriers and shippers as a result of deregulation.

➤ Consider the need for shipper evaluation of carrier performance and means for accomplishing this.

➤ Point out and explain the causes of the great increase in the amount of freight traffic being moved under shipper-carrier contracts.

➤ Note the advantages and disadvantages of the use of private transportation by shippers.

➤ Point out the factors determining the place of the traffic function in the logistics organization.

In most firms, the cost of transportation is the largest component of total logistics costs. According to one source, manufacturing companies' transportation costs (inbound plus outbound) amounted to, on average, 45 percent of all logistics expenses in 1979.[1] Put another way, the average cost of transportation was $7.73 per hundred-weight of product moved, or 4.4 percent of sales.[2] The data cited above were gathered at a time when many logistics costs were typically aggregated in corporate charts of accounts that did not allow identification of costs that should have been allocated to the logistics function. The results of the 1988 LaLonde and Cooper study presented in Table 1–4 on page 31 show transportation costs to be more in the neighborhood of one-third of total logistics costs. Even with the measurement difficulties involved in accurately determining logistics costs, it is clear that the cost of transportation is the major single component of total logistics costs.

For this reason, in many firms traffic management deserves and demands a major share of the time and effort devoted to overall logistics management. Moreover, traffic can be managed effectively only when it is viewed as an integral part of the overall logistics system. Our discussion considers management of the transportation of a firm's physical inputs and outputs (raw materials, supplies and finished goods), whether the transportation is purchased from carriers or provided by the firm itself, or both.

For purposes of discussion, we have divided our material into two general areas of responsibility: traffic analysis and traffic control. Traffic analysis deals with the evaluation of the effect of carrier service and rates on the logistics system of a firm, and a critical evaluation of carrier rates to ensure that (1) the rates charged for the movement of raw materials, supplies, and finished products are reasonable when related to the movement of related and nonrelated products; (2) the overall logistics system is designed to take advantage of existing carrier rate structures; and (3) the adjustment of the rate structure is sought and obtained when it does not meet the requirements of the logistics system. Traffic control is defined as the management of a firm's transportation activities and resources to achieve optimum productivity, utilization, and performance. This involves the selection of carriers, documentation of shipments, generation of information about carrier services and rates, measurement of carrier performance, correct payment of carrier charges, and taking corrective action when a transportation system does not function as planned.

The management of "in-house" or private transportation is a subject of sufficient importance to warrant separate attention later in this chapter.

TRAFFIC ANALYSIS

Traffic management decisions regarding the selection of carriers, the negotiation of rates, or the implementation of private transportation must be preceded by a comprehensive analysis of transportation costs *and* related costs. In addition to explicit rates and accessorial charges, the following implicit costs of transportation must also be considered: (1) transit time, (2) loading and unloading, (3) packaging and dunnage, (4) unsecured loss or damage in-transit, and (5) transportation service consistency.

Evaluation of Carrier Performance

Evaluation of carrier performance is necessarily based on shipper needs and expectations. The old shipper joke, "I want the best service at the lowest rate," contains more than a grain of truth. However, as Figure 9–1 indicates, Bruning and Lynagh found that some considerations

FIGURE 9–1: Ranking[a] and Grouping[b] of Important Factors in Evaluating Carriers

Factor	Consumer Perishables Rank	Consumer Perishables Grouping	Consumer Nonperishables Rank	Consumer Nonperishables Grouping	Raw Materials Rank	Raw Materials Grouping	Major Equipment Rank	Major Equipment Grouping	Accessories and Equipment Rank	Accessories and Equipment Grouping	Parts and Supplies Rank	Parts and Supplies Grouping
Pickup and Delivery	1	A	1	A	1	A	1	A	2	A	1	A
Rates and Charges	2	A	2	A	2	A	2	A	1	A	2	A
Line Haul	3	A	3	B	3	A	3	A	3	A	3	B
Tracing and Expediting	4	B	5	C	4	B	6	C	6	B	4	C
Loss and Damage	5	B	4	C	5	B	4	B	4	B	5	C
Special Services and Equipment	6	B	7	D	6	B	5	B	5	B	6	C
Sales Staff Support	7	B	6	D	7	B	7	C	7	B	7	C

[a]Rank based on mean scores with 1 being most important.
[b]Factors grouped using Duncan's Multiple Range test with Group A being the most important.

Source: "Carrier Evaluation in Physical Distribution Management," by Edward R. Bruning and Peter M. Lynagh, *Journal of Business Logistics* 5, no. 2 (1984) 40.

are more important than others to traffic managers in different industries when assessing carrier performance. Interestingly, pickup and delivery performance appear to be rated just slightly ahead of rates and charges and line haul performance by traffic managers from *all* traffic groups. This likely reflects a belief (probably true) that carrier pickup and delivery activities have a high potential for delay and error that would denigrate otherwise satisfactory service. Pickup and delivery delays can make a mockery of dependable line haul schedules. Also, a high percentage of damage is incurred in pickup and delivery, which involve a great deal of handling.

Two other findings shown in Figure 9–1 may be noted. First, with one exception (consumer nonperishables) all traffic groups *do* want good, fast service *and* good rates (A ratings). This is normal buyer behavior, and carriers must respond to it if they want the traffic. Second, shippers of consumer nonperishables are not quite as concerned about line haul performance (B rated) as they are about rates and charges (A rated). Consumer nonperishables are finished goods and typically pay higher rates than agricultural perishables, raw materials, and such. Competition among competing brands of finished goods is strong, and manufacturers and distributors of such goods are often more concerned about saving money on transportation costs than on the speed or dependability of line haul service.

A study of the measurement of quality and the transportation purchase decision was made by Chow and Poist whose research included the 22 modal and carrier selection criteria shown in Figure 9–2. Each criterion was categorized as a rate-related factor, a claims-related factor, an equipment-related factor, a people-related factor, an operations-related factor, or a miscellaneous factor. Similar to the Bruning and Lynagh study, the research of Chow and Poist shows the strongest shipper concern to be with rates and line haul (Maximum Importance, columns 1 and 4). Modal selection factors generally parallel carrier selection factors for most of the 22 criteria.

Determination of the True Cost of Transportation

An evaluation of the factors discussed below together with stated carrier rates are required for determination of the true cost of transportation.

Transit Time Transit time can result in two types of costs, those resulting from product deterioration or obsolescence and in-transit inventory carrying charges. The first type is relevant only for products such as perishable food items or highly seasonal merchandise. The second, of course, applies to all products. As transit time increases, inventory-in-transit carrying costs increase.

The burden of transit-time cost nearly always falls on the consignee. In practice, the supplier's credit period often begins with the day of shipment. Assuming a 30-day net credit period and a 15-day transit time, the consignee loses 15 days of "free" credit because of transit time.

Loading and Unloading Some carriers offer more loading and unloading assistance than others. Specifically, most motor common carriers make provision for loading and unloading assistance. Typically, however, this assistance is limited to handling cargo in or out of the truck or trailer and in the area immediately adjacent to its rear door. In nearly all cases, no service of this type is included in the rates of carriers by other modes.

Demurrage and detention charges, penalties for failure to load or unload a railcar, truck trailer, or container within the prescribed time limitations, may be only partially chargeable to loading or unloading procedures or procedural failures. However, in selecting a mode of transportation, it is important to consider the "free time" provided by the carrier for loading and unloading and the contribution this "free time" can make to total system flexibility.

It is important to develop loading methods that are compatible to the greatest extent possible with origin and destination warehouse material handling systems and the type of carrier equipment employed. When incompatibility exists, such as the use of different size pallets by supplier and customer, loading and unloading cost penalties occur.

Typically, loading and unloading costs are charged to warehousing operations. When these costs are not separated and distinguished from warehousing costs, the alternate modes of transportation are not charged with the full costs that should be assigned to them. This incomplete information potentially can lead to costly logistics decisions.

Packaging and Dunnage The term dunnage refers to bracing and other protective devices used for the packing of products in transportation vehicles or warehouse areas. A classification rating, for purposes of pricing transportation service, is partially formulated on the basis of the amount of packaging or dunnage provided by the shipper. Typically, the more packaging provided, the lower the rating and the rate.

FIGURE 9–2: Importance of Quality of Service Factors in Transportation Selection

Quality of Service Factor	Category Designation[a]	Percent of Respondents Indicating Factor in Mode Selection as:			Percent of Respondents Indicating Factor in Carrier Selection as:		
		Maximum Importance (1)	Maximum or Great Importance (2)	Maximum, Great or Some Importance (3)	Maximum Importance (4)	Maximum or Great Importance (5)	Maximum, Great or Some Importance (6)
1. Door-to-Door Transportation Rates or Costs	R	42.0	77.1	95.2	43.8	80.9	97.9
2. Freight Loss and Damage Experience	C	22.0	56.4	82.2	28.6	63.4	68.0
3. Claims Processing Experience	C	15.5	43.3	78.6	19.7	51.8	82.9
4. Transit Time Reliability or Consistency	T	37.0	80.4	94.2	45.9	91.3	96.9
5. Experience with Carrier in Negotiating Rate Changes	R	22.6	55.4	59.7	27.8	68.9	90.7
6. Shipment Tracing	O	16.8	57.6	80.4	22.8	62.7	88.6
7. Total Door-to-Door Transit Time	T	37.1	78.5	93.0	38.9	85.0	95.9
8. Quality of Pick-up and Delivery Service	O	31.0	70.7	84.6	35.6	82.5	93.8
9. Availability of Single-Line Service to Key Points in Shipper's Market Area	O	30.8	67.6	85.4	39.9	76.1	93.7
10. Equipment Availability at Shipment Date	E	40.3	77.4	92.5	42.2	84.9	94.8
11. Shipment Expediting	O	23.6	65.9	86.2	28.0	68.7	89.3
12. Experience with Carrier in Negotiating Service Changes	O	12.2	43.6	77.1	14.9	52.8	82.5
13. Specialized Equipment to Meet Shipper Needs	E	26.1	54.4	71.2	23.4	51.1	72.4
14. Frequency of Service to Key Points in Shipper's Market Area	O	24.9	63.6	87.4	30.9	72.4	91.0
15. Physical Condition of Equipment	E	17.1	50.8	81.3	19.1	55.2	87.2
16. In-Transit Privileges	O	7.2	19.9	37.0	6.0	18.6	36.6
17. Diversion/Reconsignment Privileges	O	3.8	11.5	29.0	6.5	11.9	30.9
18. Quality of Operating Personnel	P	19.4	56.0	81.3	23.1	66.2	90.8
19. Carrier Image or Reputation	M	10.6	38.6	69.3	13.3	48.0	78.1
20. Quality of Carrier Salesmanship	P	3.8	19.4	53.3	4.1	25.2	63.3
21. Reciprocity	M	1.7	9.1	29.0	2.7	10.4	31.2
22. Gifts/Gratuities Offered by the Carrier	M	.5	1.6	2.1	.5	1.5	3.0

[a]R = Rate-related factor; T = Time-related factor; C = Claims-related factor; E = Equipment-related factor; P = People-related factor; O = Operations-related factor and M = Miscellaneous factor.

Source: Chow, Garland, and Richard F. Poist, "The Measurement of Quality of Service and the Transportation Purchase Decision," *The Logistics and Transportation Review* 20, no. 1 (March 1984): 31.

On items shipped in containers or packages, carriers prescribe minimum specifications for packaging in an attempt to limit shippers' claims for loss or damage. One of the factors in determining rate levels is the susceptibility of the product to damage. If the carrier did not specify minimum packaging standards, some shippers would be inclined to ship in less costly substandard packages and thereby place an added potential for liability on the carrier. Figure 9–3 contains an excerpt from the National Motor Freight Classification that gives an example of the type of extreme specificity of packaging requirements established by carriers.

The so-called "damage free" (DF) railcar provides dunnage as part of the equipment of the car. In this case, the dunnage is in the form of metal cross braces built into the car to

---

FIGURE 9–3: Packaging Requirements for Shipments Made in Fiberboard or Corrugated Boxes and Containers

---

"Item 222-4, Specification for fiberboard Boxes, Bag-in-a-Box:
. . .Containers of three gallon capacity or larger will be considered as 'in bulk' in barrels or boxes. When containers have capacity of less than three gallons the bag will be considered an inner container.

Plastic Bag.
Bags must be of a single or multi-ply plastic film having a minimum total wall thickness of not less than three mills (.003 inch). Closure of the bag must be effected by snap-locking plastic fittings or by adequate heat sealing or crimping together the top and twisting, then folding over on itself and finally tieing with pressure sensitive tape or a wire tie. When wire tie is not plastic coated, ends of wire must be looped. Discharge and dispensing tubes must be securely plugged, or heat sealed. The filled bag must be in corrugated or solid fiberboard boxes as follows:

(1) Maximum Void Permitted.
The void between the top of the filled closed bag and the inside of the top of the box must not exceed 1-1/2 inches. The bag must not be adhered to the container at any point.

(2) Box for up to 20 lb. Gross Weight. Boxes having gross weight not exceeding 20 lbs., must be constructed of fiberboard having a bursting strength of not less than 200 lbs. Except as to boxes constructed with full overlap inner flaps, boxes must have the top and bottom pads made of corrugated fiberboard having a bursting strength of not less than 125 lbs. Manufacturers joint of boxes must be taped or glued.

(3) Box for up to 40 lbs. Gross Weight. Boxes having gross weights exceeding 20 lbs. but not exceeding 40 lbs., must be made of fiberboard having a bursting strength of not less than 200 lbs. Boxes must have a joined tube or liner made of fiberboard having a bursting strength of not less than 200 lbs. The joint of the tube or liner must be tapped or glued. Also, except as to boxes constructed as to full overlap inner flaps, boxes must have top and bottom pads made of corrugated fiberboard having a bursting strength of not less than 125 lbs."

Source: National Motor Freight Classification.

compartmentalize it and reduce the possibilities of damage. In the damage free car, the dunnage is supplied by the carrier; in the more conventional car, it must be supplied by the shipper.

In deciding whether to dunnage nonspecialized cars, the shipper must relate the cost of dunnaging to the necessity of providing damage-free goods to customers. The carrier generally does not vary rates according to the type of equipment supplied.

Nonsecured In-Transit Loss or Damage The publication of released value rates allows a shipper to declare a maximum value on a given shipment for purposes of loss or damage liability determination. By limiting the carrier's liability, shippers are offered a lower rate to transport a given commodity.

When shipping goods at released value rates, a shipper must either obtain additional insurance to cover losses in excess of the released value or be prepared to absorb such losses as a cost of transportation.

Transportation Service Consistency LaLonde and Zinszer have observed that product availability and order cycle times are the most frequently-used measures of customer service in most manufacturing firms.[3] Failure to maintain a standard transit time consistently between two points can have at least three adverse effects on logistics systems and customer service: (1) maintenance of excess safety stock at the delivery point, (2) excess labor costs, and (3) lost sales.

Excess Safety Stock at Delivery Points The importance of safety stocks and the determination of optimum safety stock levels were discussed in earlier chapters. In most cases, safety stocks are required as much for protection against inconsistency in the reorder cycle as they are as a hedge against fluctuations in customer demand. A major objective of traffic management is to seek consistent transit time from carriers. When transit time is regularized, one of the difficult variables of inventory planning is eliminated, or at least reduced.

The interdependency of traffic, other elements of logistics, and other functional areas within a firm is illustrated by the risk involved in encouraging customers to take advantage of more dependable service. The risk is that if there is inconsistency or other malfunction, logistics management must be prepared to accept responsibility for the consequences.

A number of manufacturing firms have instituted, or attempted to institute, the practice of ''just-in-time'' (JIT) for their inbound shipments in order to minimize inventories of parts or raw materials, particularly the former. JIT requires that inbound shipments arrive just in time to enter the production process, and thereby puts great pressure on carriers and traffic departments alike. Although JIT can be an advantageous practice, it has its disadvantages, including the high cost of minimum (small) inbound shipments. Much has been written on the subject of JIT by its proponents and its detractors. One of the more balanced treatments of JIT has been written by one of the authors of this book.[4]

Excess Labor Costs Motor carriers typically make local deliveries in the morning and pickups in the afternoon. In addition, consignees sometimes establish standard times for receiving shipments. Violation of these industry or customer practices often results in customer dissatisfaction and excess labor costs. For example, a wholesaler might request truckload deliveries at 6:00 a.m. in order to complete unloading before 8:00 a.m. when warehouse personnel could be shifted to the loading of local retail delivery trucks. Assuming that three truckloads scheduled for arrival at 6:00 a.m. did not arrive until 8:00 a.m., and that a six-person crew waited for two hours with no work to do, what would be the cost to the wholesaler? Of course, the six employees would have to be paid for the two idle hours. If the trucks were held until the afternoon before unloading, the cost of idle time for the drivers and equipment would have to be absorbed by the carrier or shipper (depending on whether private transportation was involved), while the wholesaler might have to pay warehouse people overtime rates to complete the job. Any attempt to try and "fit" unplanned loading or unloading into an otherwise well-planned warehouse operating day could cause confusion and disruptions that would have tangible, albeit hard to measure, costs.

Lost Sales When transportation service reaches a level of inconsistency that safety stocks cannot absorb, the results at the delivery point are customer dissatisfaction, back-order costs, fill-in transportation (often at premium rates), and lost sales. If the product involved has a high degree of substitutability, sales lost due to transportation service inconsistency may never be recovered.

TRAFFIC CONTROL

Effective control of transportation activities requires a system to capture and organize information for purposes of decision making and performance evaluation. Our discussion here will emphasize the managerial aspects and implications of traffic documentation and information. More detailed descriptions of specific tasks and operating procedures are presented in several of the readings listed at the end of this chapter.

Transportation Documentation

The basic documents of transportation are bill of lading, freight bill, and the freight claim. These documents are designed for the purpose of providing identification of shipments, facilitating the flow of goods between carriers and shippers, billing of freight charges, adjustment of freight charges incorrectly billed, and settlement between shipper and carrier of claims resulting from loss or damage to products during movement.

Bill of Lading The bill of lading provides (1) a contract for the movement of a shipment, (2) a receipt for goods itemized on it, and (3) in some cases, a certificate of title of goods.

The bill of lading indicates where the shipment originated, terminated, the volume shipped, and the parties involved at the time of shipping. This document represents a valuable source of data for supply and distribution planning even though it may not contain information about freight charges. The responsibility for preparing bills of lading rests with the shipper. Complete descriptions of the items being shipped on the bill are vital. Items only partially described often carry a higher classification, and consequently, a higher rate, than those more completely described. For example, note the differences in rate levels assessed on items only partially described in Table 9–1.

There are two types of bills of lading, the uniform straight bill and uniform order bill. Each may take several forms such as those of the ocean bill of lading, or airwaybill, depending on the mode of carriage.

Uniform Straight Bill of Lading The straight bill of lading is a non-negotiable instrument and may serve as evidence of title to the goods. Goods may be delivered only to the consignee named on the straight bill of lading. An example of a straight bill of lading is shown in Figure 9–4.

TABLE 9–1: Differences in Transportation Classifications and Rate Levels Assessed on Variously Described Products

Incomplete Description	Classification	Complete Description	Classification	Cost Reduction from Complete Description
Millinery goods	200	Sunbonnets	100	50.0%
Golf balls	85	Golf balls, used	55	35.3%
Dry goods	100	Cotton cheesecloth	77.5	22.5%
Optical goods or instruments	200	Optical glass	100	50.0%
Fishing tackle	125	Fishing line	92.5	26.0%
Dental goods	100	Dental plaster in bulk	55	45.0%

Source: National Motor Freight Classification.

Uniform Order Bill of Lading An order bill of lading is a negotiable instrument used for the purpose of allowing a supplier to obtain payment for goods before they are delivered at destination or for providing a consignee with flexibility in the transfer of title of goods sold while in transit. With regard to this second use, a shipment made on an order bill of lading is often consigned to the account of the shipper and later transferred to the account of the receiver, when they are not the same organization. The negotiable feature of an order bill of lading makes it also a document of finance. It is used extensively in international trade in conjunction with letters of credit.

Freight Bill

The freight bill is the carrier's invoice for freight charges. *Prepaid* freight bills are presented by the delivering carrier to consignors for payment. *Collect* freight bills are paid by consignees. Freight bills for all ICC-regulated carriers must be paid within 15 days of presentation. Similar to other trade terms, carriers may offer discounts for early payment and assess interest charges on late payments. On prepaid shipments, the credit period extends from the time of shipment; on collect shipments it begins when the shipment is delivered. This may appear to be an insignificant factor for individual shipments, however, the opportunity to delay payment of freight bills until after incoming shipments have been delivered (by shipping on a collect basis) may be quite significant when related to a firm's annual freight bill.[5]

Freight Claims

Freight claims are documents providing information about loss or damage to products in transit, unreasonable delay in the movement of freight, and freight charges improperly assessed by a carrier. Claims are prepared by shippers for carrier consideration and must be filed within nine months of the delivery date or the date of discovery of concealed damage against an ICC-regulated carrier.

FIGURE 9–4: Uniform straight bill of lading

UNIFORM MOTOR CARRIER BILL OF LADING
Original – Not Negotiable – Domestic

1

Shipper's No. _____

I.C.C. # MC107107

ALTERMAN TRANSPORT LINES, INC. ALTT

GENERAL OFFICE
12805 N.W. 42nd AVE.
OPA-LOCKA (MIAMI), FL 33054

| DATE | ATL CUSTOMER NO. | | | | | | | ATL CUSTOMER NO. | | | | | |

FROM:

Shipper _____

Street _____

Origin
City _____ ST. _____ ZIP _____

TO:

Consignee _____

Street _____

City _____ ST. _____ ZIP _____

FOR PAYMENT SEND FREIGHT BILL TO:

ATL CUSTOMER NO.

Name _____

Street _____

P.O. Box _____

City _____ ST. _____ ZIP _____

On Collect on Delivery shipments the letters "COD" must appear before consignee's name or as otherwise provided in item 430 Sec 1

COLLECT ON DELIVERY $ _____

☐ CUSTOMER CHECK IS ACCEPTABLE

☐ CASH OR CASHIER CHECK ONLY

REMIT TO: _____

ADDRESS: _____

COD FEE TO BE PAID BY

Shipper ☐

Consignee ☐

NO. PACKAGES	HM	DESCRIPTION OF ARTICLES, SPECIAL MARKS, AND EXCEPTIONS	*Weight (Subject to Corr.)	Class or Rate	Check Col.

I hereby certify that the following described meat or meat food products, which are offered for shipment in interstate or foreign commerce have been U.S. inspected and passed by Dept. of Agriculture, are so marked, and at this date are sound, healthful, wholesome, and fit for human food.

NOTE - Where the rate is dependent on value, shippers are required to state specifically in writing the agreed or declared value of the property
The agreed or declared value of the property is hereby specifically stated by the Shipper to be not exceeding _____ Per _____

Subject to Section 7 of Conditions, if this shipment is to be delivered to the consignee without recourse on the consignor, the consignor shall sign the following statement:
The carrier shall not make delivery of this shipment without payment of freight and all other lawful charges

_____
(Signature of Consignor.)

FREIGHT CHARGES

NOTE IF A BOX IS <u>NOT</u> CHECKED, THIS SHIPMENT WILL BE DEEMED ON A COL– **LECT** BASIS

CHECK BOX IF **PREPAID** ☐

CHECK BOX IF **COLLECT** ☐

RECEIVED, subject to the classifications and lawfully filed tariffs in effect on the date of the issue of this Bill of Lading, the property described above in apparent good order, except as noted (contents and condition of contents of packages unknown), marked, consigned, and destined as indicated above which said carrier (the word carrier being understood throughout this contract as meaning any person or corporation in possession of the property under the contract) agrees to carry to its usual place of delivery at said destination, if on its route, otherwise to deliver to another carrier on the route to said destination. It is mutually agreed, as to each carrier of all or any of said property over all or any portion of said route to destination, and as to each party at any time interested in all or any of said property, that every service to be performed hereunder shall be subject to all the bill of lading terms and conditions in the governing classification on the date of shipment.

Shipper hereby certifies that he is familiar with all the bill of lading terms and conditions in the governing classification and the said terms and conditions are hereby agreed to by the shipper and accepted for himself and his assigns.

This is to certify that the above named materials are properly classified, described, packaged, marked, and labeled and are in proper condition for transportation, according to the applicable regulations of the Department of Transportation.

SHIPPER (Company Name)	CARRIER
	ALTERMAN TRANSPORT LINES, INC.

AUTHORIZED SIGNATURE	PER	PIECES	DATE

Mark with "X" to designate Hazardous Materials as defined in the Department of Transportation Regulations governing the transportation of hazardous materials. The use of this column is an optional method for identifying hazardous materials on bills of lading per Section 172.201(a)(1)(iii) of Title 49, Code of Federal Regulations. Also, when shipping hazardous materials, the shipper's certification statement prescribed in section 172.204(a) of the Federal Regulations must be indicated on the bill of lading, unless a specific exception from this requirement is provided in the Regulations for a particular material.

Source: Courtesy Alterman Transport Lines, Inc.

Traffic Information

The maintenance of timely, usable rate information is vital to the task of planning, controlling, and managing transportation costs. However, the sheer number and inherent complexity of freight tariffs creates a difficult operating environment. There are literally millions of rates on file with various regulatory bodies, and as various factors and percentages are considered for commodity, class, and multiple-carrier or multiple-mode movements, the number of possible rates that may apply to domestic shipments alone grows into the trillions.

Computerized Rates Although the commitment of entire tariffs to computers has long been feasible from a hardware standpoint, the development of reliable software packages to store, update, and generate appropriate rates has been a long and costly process. One distribution information services company invested more than $3 million over a ten-year period to create a comprehensive[6] computerized tariff data base.

Lack of appreciation for the magnitude and complexity of the job has been cited as a roadblock to implementation of sound automated systems by another source.[7] Specifically, problems have occurred in several areas:

1. Input requirements are not totally recognized. All variables must be supplied in order to meet the precise demand of tariff provisions. Stop-offs, consolidations, and specific routes are examples of items that may need to be considered.

2. System design must take place against moving targets. Definitions and methodology for pricing services are changing; inflation and deregulation exacerbate the problem.

3. Systems that rate shipments automatically require consistent maintenance due to constant changes in tariff publishing practices. Fuel and other surcharges and entry of new carriers with nonstandard rates are two examples.

4. The need for a variety of support systems often is underestimated. For example, as errors are identified or rate supplements are received, files must be corrected or updated, as appropriate.

5. Companies underestimate the number of people and resources needed to maintain a tariff base. In a changing economic and regulatory environment, this task becomes even more important. If the system is not regularly updated, errors and costs increase, and investment in the basic information and software is jeopardized.[8]

Generally, only large industrial companies can afford to establish and maintain this capability in-house. Other large firms, with a wide range of products, locations, customers, and suppliers, recently were paying $20,000 to $30,000 annually to access data bases maintained by service firms.[9]

Company Tariffs Smaller shippers, on the other hand, have found that they can simplify the process and save costs by maintaining ''company tariffs'' containing only rates applicable to methods, routes, and commodities significant to company operations. Company tariffs or ''rate ponies'' have long been compiled by traffic organizations. More recently, company tariffs based on computer data bases can be purchased from independent service firms on tape, microfilm, or in hardcopy form. These can be standard packages based on motor carrier class rates for selected origins and destination or zip code areas, or they may be custom systems tailored specifically to a firm's commodity and distribution network. An advantage of most outside services is their ability, for a reasonable charge, to update and maintain company tariffs.

WHO'S IN CONTROL?

E. J. Muller, Senior Editor

Control has always been a key issue in the transportation and distribution field. Who has it? Who should have it? How should it be delegated? When you float these questions in many companies, they often sink in the moat of ignorance and indifference that exists between top management and the traffic department. That moat is what can often lead to harmful power struggles for ultimate control of the department.

What's even harder to accept is that the same type of moat can exist between a corporate Transportation and Distribution staff and its field managers. Too often, the regional managers who control traffic in and out of plants or distribution centers aren't on the same wavelength as the "brass back at headquarters." Sometimes corporate staff is too aloof. Or maybe there's a power-crazed manager loose in the field, building his own empire at the expense of corporate goals. In some cases power is hoarded at headquarters and, as a result, division chiefs grow lazy from the lack of challenge. Perhaps the folks at the very top have stretched resources so thin that control — along with money and uniform service standards — has slipped through the cracks.

The issue of control is usually dealt with in one of two ways — by either centralizing or decentralizing key areas of responsibility. Critics of centralized operations say it stifles market responsiveness and discourages innovation. Decentralization, its detractors claim, is a blueprint for wasteful spending and redundancy. Here's a look, then, at how some companies are successfully dealing with the issue of control by combining the best of both philosophies.

The Square D Solution

In 1985, Square D Co., a major electrical equipment manufacturer based in Florence, Ky., realized it needed greater control of the 40 receiving locations in its decentralized domestic operation. It formed a Transportation Users Group, comprised of corporate transportation staff, marketing and purchasing executives, and plant traffic managers. The result was far more than an acronym everyone remembers (TUG).

"Up until that time, the plants were pretty much doing their own thing," recalls Square D's Manager of Transportation and International Logistics Services, Chuck Gerardi. The company used in excess of 1200 carriers. One major carrier was operating under 16 different pricing programs. "When we formed TUG, we told all the divisions that we'd

have more negotiating clout, and as a result, we'd get better rates and service."

Internally, Gerardi was hoping that TUG would foster greater communication and education among disparate divisions, without stifling the plants' and DCs' sense of autonomy. "It was critical not to force directions down anybody's throat," he says. In setting up the group, corporate headquarters asked the vice president of each division to select the most knowledgeable transportation person in their business unit to serve in TUG.

Bear in mind that TUG was devised and executed by Gerardi and his supervisor, Director of Distribution Services George Berry, without a mandate. Convincing top management of TUG's value (flying 'warehousemen' around for meetings can get expensive, you know) wasn't easy. "They thought transportation was like turning on a light," Gerardi says. "When you wanted it you turned it on, and when you didn't you turned it off."

Fortunately, TUG was given a chance to prove itself, and by 1987 the company had trimmed its carrier roster to 50, with 80 percent of its freight consolidated within that core group. Later, when there was a change in top management, each corporate group had to justify its strategic plans. "The president was so excited by our presentation," recalls Gerardi, "that he said, 'What if you had even more clout?'" With a benediction bestowed from above, Square D's "decentralized" transportation operation now has 98 percent conformance to an agreed-upon carrier selection program.

"Until then we'd never had a corporate mandate," Gerardi notes, "and to be honest, I never thought we'd reach this point — not a company that has 40,000 truck shipments a month."

A similar approach was developed at Kendall Healthcare, which in the early 1980s had five regional DCs and 18 plant sites around the nation. A consultant's study commissioned at that time, however, concluded that these were some critical control issues that needed to be addressed through better strategic planning.

Kendall's Controlled Approach

Kendall ended up forming its own traffic program, similar to TUG, called Transportation Partners in Quality (TPIQ). Its goal is to improve the overall quality of Kendall's national transportation service (and control freight costs in the process). The key is getting corporate staff and field managers pulling in the same direction.

Corporate wanted to drastically consolidate its carrier roster — down to one longhaul and two regionals. After convincing plant and DC managers that the concept was sound, each field manager was told to solicit a bid package from the carriers it preferred. "The smaller locations gained leverage, the larger ones gained volume," says Bob Hansen, Kendall's corporate manager of customer service and inventory deployment. A central analysis of all the bids was performed by a group of six plant managers and three corporate staffers. Pros and cons were hashed out, and the TPIQ program was born.

The key, says Hansen, "is having the right people in the right position, making decisions." On the surface, Kendall has a loose reporting structure. Managers at distribution and plant locations report to corporate staff in four areas: DRP planning, strategic planning, customer service and inventory, and integrated logistics. All of those functions report to the director of distribution, who reports to the vice president of sales and marketing.

"Our emphasis is more on people, not structure," says Hansen. "Really, no one planned the reporting structure this way. The people who need to talk to each other, do — no middlemen, no gate-keepers. And the channels are very strong."

Back to Square D

Communication is also vital at Square D. "We don't have a corporate director of transportation," notes Gerardi. "I'm certainly not it." But he quickly adds: "My role is to lead this group in a decentralized mode."

To gain better control of decentralized transportation decisions, Square D formed a Preferred Carrier Program, similar to Kendall's TPIQ program. TUG members bring their preferred carrier selections to a roundtable meeting. Each person makes a case for why their carrier should be one of only three TL and three LTL vendors to which Square D dedicates most of its freight.

The mix of functions represented in the group was critical, Gerardi notes. It enabled people previously isolated in their own function to learn what others in the company expected of transportation and distribution. "We were able to get away from the idea of just a 'discount list' of carriers," Gerardi says.

The group was also smartly structured. A new group leader is assigned for each round of negotiations, and it will be a field distribution manager as often as it's someone from corporate staff. Jeff Reade, the Dallas DC manager, heads up the current negotiations for Square D's Southwest committee.

"The user's group concept, and the Preferred Carrier Program, have really elevated transportation to a higher status in the company," says Reade. When TUG was created, he notes, its goal was to determine a corporate transportation

policy. "But little by little, it's evolved to where more control is allowed regionally. For the corporate strategy to work, you've got to have a tremendous amount of buy-in at the regional level."

The underlying corporate goal of both TPIQ and TUG was to rein in scattershot spending. Square D, for instance, wanted to funnel those 16 different pricing programs for one major carrier into one national tariff. But the field managers needed to know that service, not cost, was the main issue. "We try not to be price shippers," notes Jeff Reade. So in the group's carrier selection process, service is always given first consideration. "We look at the service figures, operating ratios, and claims performance of the 100 primary candidates," says Gerardi, "and that cuts the list by half. Then we talk price." Eventually, each region draws its own preferred list from a pool of 35 carriers who've made the final cut.

"We'll end up with four to six carriers," says Reade. He doesn't think such a small group limits his options. "For the advantages this process provides the company, I don't see many drawbacks. It can provide some headaches with our customers, when they think we should be using a carrier that has a good reputation within a specific area. But with the four carriers we choose, chances are slim you won't have everything covered."

This is pretty much Kendall's strategy, too, with one significant difference. While Square D hones its preferred carrier list to 35, and lets each region create a six-carrier pool from that group, Kendall's corporate staff dictates an "all or nothing" policy. "We told the carriers that they were bidding on 100 percent of the freight out of a plant location," says Hansen. "We didn't want to do an 80/20 type thing. We told them that all the longhaul business was at stake; there wouldn't be any backup carrier."

Weren't plant managers miffed by the lack of options? "This plan enabled them to get a much better 'shippers allowance' for loading and counting," says Hansen. "And that compensation goes directly to the plant's warehouse budget. They couldn't achieve this level of allowance on their own, without the consolidated volume."

Differences for DCs, Plants

Kendall's strategic planners realized that greater results could be attained by granting distribution center managers more responsibility for budgeting and carrier selection. Corporate staff, however, needed to exert more influence over those areas at the plants.

"The DCs have greater regional responsibility," explains Bob Hansen. "They know their territory, and we realize that carriers which work well in Atlanta, won't necessarily work well in New England, Texas or California." As for the plants,

Continued

most of their transportation needs involve large orders that are longhaul in nature — letting corporate consolidate freight volume and distribute it to a select few carriers results in greater pricing leverage and uniform service standards.

Avoiding "Big Brother" Syndrome

Says Hansen: "We try to convince the plant warehouse managers that what's good for the company is good for the plant. That's sometimes hard to swallow at first. They'll argue that their plant has special needs. But we've found that when you get down to it, transportation requirements among the plants are very similar — and you've got to go with the carriers that can meet all the requirements of a number of plants." The field locations also enjoy newfound clout. "If they're not getting a response from a carrier, they can ask us to exert pressure at a national level. They've got a big stick they didn't have in the past."

The biggest challenge in getting corporate control over decentralized operations is avoiding the Big Brother Syndrome. "When we first started TUG," says Chuck Gerardi, "a lot of people said, 'We don't need Big Brother looking over our shoulder.'"

"We realized we couldn't just direct the plant warehouses to do anything," agrees Hansen. "We had to develop a system that proved joint decisions were beneficial to everybody." There is no place in the process for an authoritarian attitude, both men assert. "You've got to treat your people like customers, not subordinates," Hansen states.

Not that you won't have power struggles. It can happen when new people are brought in to run a facility, or an entirely new division is brought into the corporate fold. "We've purchased some companies that use carriers not on our preferred list," says Gerardi, "and we expect them to want to stick with those carriers. But when we show them the pricing program we've negotiated, they usually agree that it's better than anything they could negotiate on their own."

For an independent assessment of these programs, we turn to Clifford Daugherty, warehouse manager for Broan Manufacturing Co., in Dallas. Broan also has a centralized carrier selection process. "I think it's a pretty good setup," says Daugherty. He notes that distribution, traffic and warehouse managers from 12 Broan locations have input into the selection process before the carrier list is trimmed to five finalists. Because he's had input to the process, Daugherty doesn't feel constricted by his limited options. "I still get to choose who I want to use among the carriers we've agreed upon," he says, "and if I want to change carriers in my region, I just have to prove my case."

Education is Essential

Chuck Gerardi believes the most important ingredient in maintaining control of decentralized decision making is education. A major objective in Square D's mission statement is education; it stresses that all employees have at least 80 hours of outside education. This year, Square D is presenting four two-day seminars for the distribution people in its various regions, to discuss the Preferred Carrier Program and other issues. "Once people understand what we're trying to do, they don't feel like we're dictating to them," Gerardi says.

Hansen concludes that any successful sharing of control between headquarters and the field requires the following:

- A direct commitment to teamwork

- Identifying requirements of individual locations

- Meeting the identified requirements

- Regular communication

- Involving people in the decisions that affect them

- Field visits by corporate staff, not just to oversee. "Get in there and help load," Hansen stresses.

The Results

Both companies have reaped benefits from this approach to decision making. Improved logistics at Kendall has enabled the company to increase its early 1980s level of business while cutting the number of plants it operates from 18 down to five. Square D's Gerardi also notes that his company has closed several DCs due to improvements in transportation service, and that transportation costs as a percentage of sales is much lower.

This month, Square D will bring its entire international operation under the Preferred Carrier Program, starting with Europe. Gerardi doesn't think the expansiveness of global operations will make the process any more difficult. "It will work as long as you set up a program everyone can see the benefits of, and you let the people affected by the decisions participate in the process. When you do that, everyone has a better sense of how transportation is a usable, manageable resource."

SOURCE: *Distribution* (February 1990): 26–30. © Chilton Company. Reprinted with permission.

FREIGHT BILL AUDITING AND PAYMENT

The complexity of rates and tariffs, coupled with the volume of shipments handled and the normal tendency for human error, results in frequent misapplication and miscalculation of rates and overcharges, on freight bills. Not surprisingly, there are over two thousand independent freight audit agencies in the United States that review freight bills before or after payment to detect errors. Some sources indicate that overpayments can amount to three to five percent of a firm's annual freight charges, so opportunities for savings through auditing are significant even after the bills are checked internally.[10]

Post- and Prepayment Auditing

Since the time allowed for the payment of freight bills is short, many companies audit the amounts paid after payment. However, the cost associated with recovery of overcharges on freight bills has encouraged the auditing of bills before payment. In many cases, auditing is performed only for bills over some economic amount, such as $50 or $100. In other cases, bills of lading are rated when they are created so that the charges can be compared with those on matching freight bills, and claims initiated promptly. The ability to perform this service quickly and efficiently is a major selling point of computerized tariff services. Otherwise, this is a time consuming, labor-intensive procedure.

Internal and External Auditing

The auditing of freight bills can be done internally or externally. Each offers different advantages. Internal auditing may (1) perform the task quicker, assuming the availability of personnel; (2) be more familiar with the specific rates and shipments under review; and (3) be easier to control. On the other hand, external auditors (1) typically work on an incentive basis, such as 50 percent of the claims dollars recovered as a result of their efforts, and (2) carry a higher degree of objectivity as independent, third parties.

Most firms can benefit from, and many employ, one or more external auditors as well as at least one in the traffic department. The economies of scale offered by fully computerized services have led many firms to contract out all payment and audit activity to these organizations.

Bank Payment Plans

Many companies use bank payment plans in which carriers submit bills directly to a bank designated by the shipper, with the bank automatically crediting and debiting their respective accounts and preparing periodic reports on activities and balances. These plans are designed primarily to facilitate the timely payment of freight bills. Although bank systems can detect arithmetic errors and provide accounting control, they are not designed to provide rigorous audits of rate applications.

FREIGHT CLAIMS

Freight claims result from the auditing of freight bills as well as other events. The two major types of freight claims are for loss and damage and for overcharges. In addition, in some industries claims resulting from delays in "guaranteed shipments" can be important. And, recently a problem of motor carrier *undercharges* has surfaced for some shippers due to carrier bankruptcies caused by motor carrier deregulation.

Loss and Damage Claims

The carrier has liability for loss and damage that occur during the period of transportation. Common carriers are subject to bill-of-lading, common-law, and the warehouse's liabilities. Bill-of-lading liability specifies that the carrier is liable for loss or damage, without proof of carrier negligence, with the following exceptions: (1) acts of God, (2) acts of a public enemy, (3) acts of negligence of the shipper, (4) inherent nature of the goods, and (5) removal of goods from the carrier's possession by legal action against the shipper or by action of the state or federal governments exercising their police powers (for example, where the federal or state authorities might impound freight that did not comply with pure food and drug standards).

Under common law, the only exceptions to carrier liability are losses resulting from acts of God or an act of a public enemy. To enforce common-law liability on a carrier, a shipper must note on the bill of lading that it does not accept the liability limitations of the bill of lading. An additional charge must be paid by the shipper to extend the carrier's liability. This type of protection against loss and damage rarely is used because of the expense relative to the added protection obtained.

The carrier's bill-of-lading liability changes to that of a warehouseman after the "free-time," provided in the carrier's tariff for removal of goods from a transportation vehicle, has expired. This free-time period may range from several hours to several days, depending on the mode of transportation and the tariff provisions.

As a warehouseman, the carrier is required to take the same degree of care as a prudent person would exercise in protecting his own property. The carrier is responsible for loss or damage only when the shipper can prove that the carrier was negligent by not providing ordinary care for the freight during the period of warehouseman's liability.

Loss and damage claims fall into two categories, those for damage visible at the time of delivery and those for damage that may be concealed, either by packaging or by the nature of the products, at the time of delivery. Claims for visible damage must be filed within nine months of the date of delivery. Claims for concealed damage must be filed within 15 days of delivery.

A claim can be filed by consignor or consignee irrespective of whether freight charges are prepaid or collect. Where customer service considerations are important, a supplier will often handle the detail connected with the filing and settlement of freight claims. This provides an opportunity to relieve some of the customer dissatisfaction that results from receiving merchandise in a damaged condition.

Overcharge Claims

An overcharge is a collection by a carrier of an amount in excess of the published rate or charge. When an overcharge is discovered before payment of a bill and within the prescribed time for the payment of bills, the shipper can return the bill to the carrier for correction before payment.

Overcharge claims result from a variety of errors, such as (1) the use of an incorrect rate, (2) errors in description, (3) errors in weight, (4) incorrect tariff interpretation, (5) duplicate billing by origin, destination, or intermediate carrier, and (6) clerical and arithmetic errors.

The Undercharge Claims Problem

One of the more irritating and frustrating consequences of deregulation is the widespread undercharge problem that has occurred with respect to bankrupt motor carriers. Even though rates were deregulated, motor common carriers carrying interstate traffic were and still are required to file their tariffs with the ICC. After passage of the Motor Carrier Act of 1980, many motor carriers offered lower rates to shippers *but failed to file these tariffs with the ICC*, and thus the quoted lower rates were not official and therefore, illegal. Many of these motor carriers subsequently went bankrupt. The trustees in bankruptcy for these carriers are legally bound to try to recover these "undercharges" from firms who had made shipments under such unfiled tariffs. Shippers protested violently that they were victims of deregulation and strongly resisted payment. Some federal District Courts of Appeal had ruled in favor of the shippers while others ruled in favor of the carriers. This split brought the issue before the U.S. Supreme Court. In June of 1990 the Supreme Court ruled in favor of the bankrupt motor carriers (and their trustees in bankruptcy) in the *Maislin* case [*Maislin Industries, U.S. v. Primary Steel, Inc.*, 110 S.Ct. 2759 (1990)]. As a result of the *Maislin* decision, shippers will have to pay the undercharges, which may amount to several hundreds of millions of dollars, the exact amount collectible being unknown.

TRANSPORTATION RATE MAKING

Transportation rates are determined by the costs of providing a service as well as the value of the service to the shipper (another way of saying "what the traffic will bear"). Every transportation rate is based on these two concepts. The topic of rate making is difficult to handle objectively because of the wide range of opinions and interests of shippers, carriers, regulatory authorities, legislators, and other interested parties. During the 1980s, the effects of deregulation have become the major focus in the transportation sector of the economy.

Deregulation has caused a major shift from emphasis on legal actions before regulatory bodies to accomplish a shipper's wish for lower freight charges to greater effort expended on planning and analysis of methods to optimize the utilization of the various transportation network alternatives.

Factors Influencing the Negotiation of Rates

Among factors influencing the negotiation of rates are the cost and value of the service provided, the extent of intra- and intermodal competition, geography, government regulation, and competition. The relationships between carrier cost of service and shipper value of service are shown in Figure 9–5. In Case A, the value of the service exceeds the carrier cost. Such

FIGURE 9–5: Generalized carrier cost-of-service and shipper value-of-service relationships and resulting zones of rate negotiation

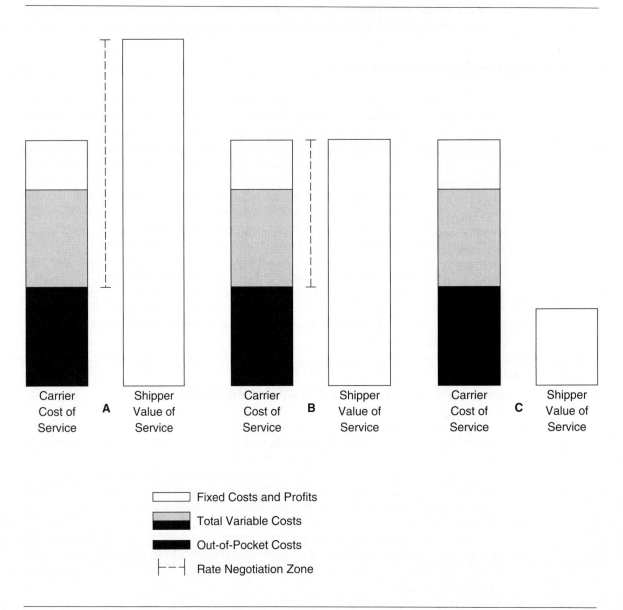

| Carrier Cost of Service | A | Shipper Value of Service | Carrier Cost of Service | B | Shipper Value of Service | Carrier Cost of Service | C | Shipper Value of Service |

Fixed Costs and Profits

Total Variable Costs

Out-of-Pocket Costs

Rate Negotiation Zone

traffic will move and the rate will fall somewhere in the zone between the carrier's out-of-pocket cost and the full value of the service to the shipper. Carriers call this ''good traffic'' for obvious reasons.

In Case B, the carrier's fully distributed costs and the shipper's value of service are shown to be the same. This traffic will also move, but likely at a lower rate than in Case A. The carrier might or might not have to make some rate concession below its fully distributed costs to get the traffic.

Case C illustrates a situation in which the traffic will not ordinarily move because the shipper's value of service is less than the cost of the service to the carrier. Only an inter-carrier "rate war" would offer rates that would move such traffic because the carrier would not even recover its out-of-pocket costs. Deregulation has witnessed several such rate wars in the motor carrier industry that have bankrupted some carriers.

Cost of Service Although carrier cost information is available in a general sense, such information is based on industry averages and is of little value to one concerned with the question of determining whether the rates charged for the movement of particular commodities between selected points are reasonably based on costs. Due to the limited amount of available statistical information, shippers must resign themselves to the fact that they must work with arbitrary or loosely defined carrier costs. Such costs provide a basis for determining only whether the charges assessed for the movement of one firm's commodities are higher than those assessed for commodities with similar characteristics, or for commodities in general. The problem of estimating carrier cost is complex enough for the individual who is faced with the problem of transporting one commodity between two destinations. This complexity may tend toward chaos as the number of commodities, origins, and destinations increases.

However, it should be noted that ascertaining motor carrier costs for *truckload* shipments, is an easier task than is the case with LTL, rail, air, or ocean shipments. This reflects the very high percentage of easily identified costs associated with a motor carrier truckload movement and the knowledge of motor carrier costs possessed by operators of private truck fleets.

Value of Service Value of service, the ability of a product to bear a given transportation rate burden, can place either an upper or lower limit on rate levels, depending upon the nature of the product and the service.

For example, it is assumed under this philosophy that not only are products of higher value less sensitive to transportation rate increases, but they should bear them to support lower rates for products of lower value moving comparable distances and with comparable carrier costs.

The concept can work in reverse too. It suggests that, regardless of carrier costs, certain carriers should price slower, less dependable services lower because they are worth less to shippers than faster, more dependable services provided by their competitors.

The problem is that carriers are not sufficiently sophisticated in their rate making to determine the elasticity of demand for transportation service. This results in rates based on "value of service" that do not include a valid determination of what the "value" is.

In their definitive work on competition in the transportation industries, Meyer, et al. have stated:

> Although the proponents of such a policy (value-of-service rate making) never put their case explicitly, it is generally argued that value-of-service rate making is desirable for the entire economy and necessity for the financial stability of transportation industries. The preponderance of the evidence, however, would appear to point to exactly a contrary conclusion; namely, that value-of-service rate making as now practiced is both undesirable and unnecessary.[11]

Intermodal Competition

Competition between the modes of transportation furnishes significant benefits to the transportation industry and to the traffic manager. Intermodal competition has a profound influence on the establishment of reasonable rates and services and encourages innovation in the management of the various modes as they attempt to develop new methods of competing with each other. For example, for many years rail carriers transported new automobiles in box cars. However, the railroads lost much of this traffic to highway carriers who had developed "truck-away" open rack trailers to carry automobiles. Recognizing the competition of the highway "truck-away" units, the rail carriers then developed a tri-level "auto-car" capable of carrying as many as thirty automobiles with little damage, and with rapid loading and unloading; they thereby recaptured much of this traffic.

A firm must use caution in taking advantage of intermodal or intramodal competition. When a carrier offers some incentive to divert traffic to its service, often it does so in contemplation of the movement of an increased volume of traffic that may or may not materialize.

Somewhat similar to the cost-of-service and value-of-service relationships depicted in Figure 9–5, the relative costs of competing modes of transportation heavily influence intermodal competition, as shown in Figure 9–6. As noted previously, there is today a strong tendency toward cost-of-service carrier pricing and the low-cost mode will get the traffic *if*, but only if, it can meet the shipper's service needs. Intermodal competition thus occurs when (1) two or more modes could each physically move the traffic and (2) the combination of rates and services offered by each poses a choice for the traffic manager evaluating the situation.

Sometimes there is no practical choice: for example, a repair part needed to put a costly production line back into operation will be shipped via one of the overnight air express companies at a premium rate; long-distance overland coal movements will be made by rail; and so forth. But, shipments of canned vegetables or air conditioners from Kansas City to Boston might move either by rail or truck; shipments of fashion clothing from New York to Dallas might move by truck or airfreight; grain or petroleum products might move along the Mississippi on barges or in rail cars, again depending on rates and services.

Intermodal competition can reverse the traditional pricing maxim of "what the traffic will bear," making it instead "how deep into *its* pocket a competing mode will have to go if it wants to compete for the traffic." An alert traffic manager will not hesitate to bargain for as low a rate as can be obtained when given a feasible service choice between competing modes.

Geographic Factors

Geographic factors, such as the traffic density at origin and destination and the terrain between origin and destination, are considered by carriers in determining rate levels. Volume can work in a shipper's favor when the area produces enough volume of freight to justify frequent and varied carrier service. The opposite may occur when the volume of freight potential in a particular area is not adequate to justify the level of service that a firm believes is necessary for the movement of its products. If a shipment moves in the "heavy haul" direction, service may be good, but rates will be higher than for comparable movements in the "light-haul" direction.

To develop volume, carriers sometimes will establish rates that will permit commodities to compete in markets for which the shippers are not as well located geographically as other

FIGURE 9–6: Generalized zones of possible intermodal rate competition among air, motor carrier, rail, and water modes of transportation

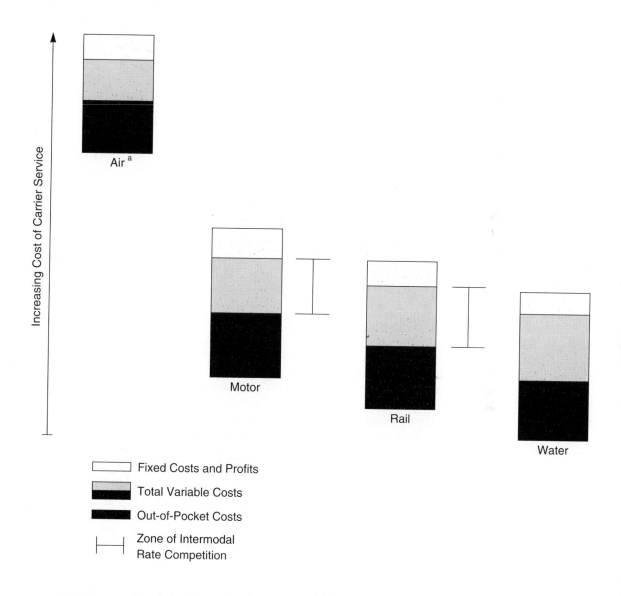

Air transportation can compete with motor, rail or water only on the basis of speed and related values such as lower inventory levels, less loss and damage, etc.

sources of supply. Although carrier costs often do not justify this type of rate making, it exists nevertheless. Frequently, carriers are forced into this practice to maintain the movement of certain commodities and gain some contribution to their fixed costs. This may be an advantage to products that would otherwise be eliminated from certain markets by reason of geography. On the other hand, such rate making may make it necessary for the carrier to transfer some cost burden to other shippers and commodities that are located more favorably with respect to their markets.

Government Regulation

The regulatory limitations on rate making were discussed earlier in this chapter. It is important to keep in mind that rates must be established within the framework of existing regulations. Given all that has transpired since deregulation of the motor carrier industry, one may wonder to what extent any regulations remain in effect. A concise summary of what is still regulated in the trucking industry is set forth on page 214 in Chapter 7.

Competitors

A firm must at least partially define its transportation requirements and objectives in relation to its competitors. Much of the effort expended by a firm to negotiate rates or services will be wasted if its competitors immediately receive the same or corresponding benefits. It is important for a company to try to discover logistical advantages it may have over its competitors and proceed to obtain rate and service adjustments that will be unavailable to competitors by reason of volume, geographical location, fixed facility limitations, or general distribution policy.

With only a limited amount of investigation, one can determine the location and function of fixed facilities used by competitors and the channels they employ to secure and distribute goods. Sources of information on competitors' sales in various markets, often developed by the marketing research function, provide the basis for estimates of the cost of competitors' logistics based on the relative volume moving between origins and destinations. If information concerning competitors' warehousing practices and inventory procedures is not available, a firm can develop estimates for these costs based on its own experience. To these pieces of information, a firm need only add the competitors' costs of transportation to have a relatively accurate "fix" on their logistics activity.

Figure 9–7 illustrates one type of situation where knowledge of competitors' logistics patterns might enable a firm to improve its position relative to competitors in a particular market. Assume that firm A and competitor C have an equal monthly sales volume of 40,000 units in the same market and both serve it from a point where the transportation rates are equal. Assume that A sells through one distributor (A_1) while C ships directly to four large retail chains $(C_1, C_2, C_3,$ and $C_4)$. If the product weighs 50 pounds per unit, then each has 200,000 pounds of freight to move monthly from the supply point to the market.

In this case, for example, it might be possible and economical for A to decrease A_1's reorder cycle to two times per month and negotiate a 100,000 pound rate to the market. This might be an attractive alternative for A that does not appear feasible for C. If a rate of $.75 per hundredweight pounds at 100,000 pounds could be obtained, A's transportation advantage over C to this market (exclusive of the added inventory warehousing costs that might be incurred by both A and A_1) would be increased by $500 to $2,800.

FIGURE 9–7: An illustration of the effective use of comparative transportation advantages in plotting rate and service negotiation strategy

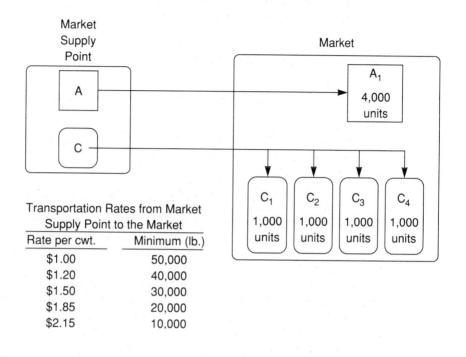

Transportation Rates from Market Supply Point to the Market	
Rate per cwt.	Minimum (lb.)
$1.00	50,000
$1.20	40,000
$1.50	30,000
$1.85	20,000
$2.15	10,000

Recognizing its competitive advantage in particular markets may enable a firm to increase its sales in that market by applying some or all of its savings from transportation to increase sales or promotional activity. This, in turn, could make it more difficult for competitors to build market volume to the point where they could take advantage of transportation rate discounts.

RATE NEGOTIATION

The favorable adjustment of rates, contrary to the belief of some, is not the answer to all problems of shippers. If rate adjustment does appear necessary and feasible, however, it should be approached with caution.

Effective rate negotiation requires *shipper control* over the movements for which rate adjustment is sought. Carriers often are understandably reluctant to adjust rates for one who, in the past, had negotiated lower rates but had not been able to tender to the carrier the volume of traffic that was supposed to have moved when the requested rates became effective.

Before entering into negotiation with a carrier, it is the function of traffic management to determine the rate or rates believed to be reasonable and necessary to continue or create specific movements. The type of information required will depend on whether a shipper seeks an adjustment of a present rate or the establishment of a new rate for new market areas or products.

The bases on which an existing rate is usually adjusted are (1) its current unreasonableness, (2) additional volume that will move after the rate adjustment, or (3) increased carrier revenue per shipment, usually as a result of increasing the minimum weight of shipments with less than a corresponding reduction in the actual rate level. Information must be developed that will overcome a carrier's objection to a rate adjustment that may have the effect of causing reduction on other related or nonrelated commodities.

In negotiating rates for new market areas or new products, the shipper must determine as accurately as possible the ability of the product to withstand a given level of transportation charges. In addition, carrier costs for the specific movement should be estimated as closely as possible.

Since deregulation, the negotiation of motor carrier rates between carriers and shippers has reflected what Hoover terms a "power-based cross subsidy" in which lower rates negotiated by large, "powerful" shippers are compensated by higher rates for smaller, "weaker" shippers.[12] Hoover also found that those motor carriers who were able to "walk away" from major shipper pressures for preferentially lower rates were those who for one reason or another had lower operating costs *and* an overall profitable customer base — one that neither needed nor wanted to take on marginally profitable or unprofitable traffic.[13]

With respect to individual shipper pressure for preferential rates, one must bear in mind that Robinson-Patman Act provisions against price discrimination apply to goods, but not to services, and transportation is a service. In a deregulated environment, price discrimination among shippers by carriers is legal *unless* its purpose is found to be anticompetitive among carriers; for example, predatory conduct designed to drive other carrier(s) out of business. In the latter case the provisions of the antitrust laws (Sherman Act, and so forth) might be invoked.

CONTROL OF CARRIER PERFORMANCE

In addition to the auditing of freight bills, traffic management can influence carrier performance by means of such devices as freight allocation, damage, and transit-time reports.

Freight Allocation Report

Freight allocation reports indicate the volume of business tendered by a shipper to various carriers. This is an important record, because a certain level of carrier performance often can be exacted on the basis of promised and tendered freight.

Damage Reports

Freight claims for loss and damage cover the direct expenses of replacing the items lost or damaged, but they do not cover the intangible costs of claims processing, nor do they cover economic loss that results from lost sales because of inadequate inventory or customer dissatisfaction. A wise logistics manager will insure that an instant-print camera is available for use at the receiving dock to photograph damaged goods immediately on discovery of the damage, and will promptly file a loss or damage claim.

When evaluating carrier performance with respect to loss and damage, the "best" carrier might be said to be one that pays any reasonable claim promptly. Some carriers are hard-nosed about claims that they will pay, but will pay honored claims promptly. Other carriers will pay any reasonable claim, but only after seemingly interminable documentation and correspondence. Finally, a few carriers will do almost anything to avoid paying a claim. Which of these four "scenarios" is actually best for a shipper, however, will likely depend on the actual amount of loss and damage incurred over time. A carrier that pays claims easily and promptly, but loses or damages a lot of shipments, may be a less desirable choice than one that is a bit hard-nosed about claims but rarely damages a shipment and never loses one.

Transit-Time Report

A shipper may be interested in the time that a carrier requires to accomplish a given delivery, but is likely to be more concerned about the consistency with which the carrier can provide a standard level of service. Carriers can be requested to report on their transit-time performance. Another source of this information is a form such as that shown in Figure 9–8. This "service report card" is sent to the customer along with other shipping documents. When the number of customers limits the feasibility of using this type of form for everyone, spot checks may be used as a substitute for total coverage.

CONTRACTING AND THIRD-PARTY LOGISTICS SERVICES PROVIDERS

By far the most significant development in the field of logistics management from the mid-1970s to the present time has been the development and evolution of third-party providers of logistics services. The extent of this development has been directly influenced by (1) the consequences of transportation deregulation; (2) advances in computer technology; and (3) advances in the technology of electronic communications. In this chapter we focus on the provision of third-party services by carriers, and reserve consideration of thirdparty warehousing services to Chapter 12, "Warehousing Management," and consideration of third-party electronic data interchange services to Chapter 13, "Data Processing and Communications."

The Changing Shipper-Carrier Relationship

As reported in the 1989 Council of Logistics Management (CLM) study of third-party logistics services providers, the relationships of shippers and carriers are changing in a number of respects:

1. Shippers are shifting more of their business from common to contract carriage.

2. Individual shippers are dealing with fewer carriers.

3. Just-in-Time systems of shippers and consignees create additional pressures on the performance standards of carriers.

4. A broad base of customer service elements is important to shippers in selecting and evaluating carriers. Carriers agree with shippers on the most and least important factors.

5. Carriers are providing value-added services to be competitive.

Gentlemen:

Please complete the attached business reply postcard, and mail it as soon as possible.

If the card does not provide sufficient space, please return the card with a letter. We would appreciate receiving a letter from you whenever a short, incorrect, or over shipment occurs. Your help will be greatly appreciated. The information requested will help to improve loading methods and improve our service to you.

To _____ Location _____ Cust. Order No. _____ UV Order No. _____

Car No. _____ Route _____

Date: Shipped ___/___/___ Arrived ___/___/___ Unloaded ___/___/___ Reefer ☐ Box ☐ DF ☐ Tank ☐

Seal Nos. _____ Cases _____ Weight _____

☐ No Breakage, Damage, or Loss   ☐ Over Shipment (Qts.)   ☐ Short Shipment (1/2 Gals.)   ☐ Incorrect Shipment (Gals.) _____ (Other)

REPORT DAMAGE OR BREAKAGE IN SPACE PROVIDED } → No. of Bottles Broken _____

LOCATION OF DAMAGE
☐ ENDS
☐ DOOR
☐ MIXED

No. of Cases Damaged _____

Amount of Loss (Tank Car Only) _____ gals. Compartment _____

Comments _____ Signature _____

6. Increased uses of technology are bringing the shipper's and carrier's operations closer together and improving the operations of each individually.

7. A multimodal, worldwide perspective is emerging for both carriers and shippers.

8. There are differences among responses of carriers based on mode and kind of product handled for the core customer.

9. Longer term shipper-carrier relationships are emerging.[14]

Probably the most significant of the nine points listed above is the first: *shippers are shifting more of their business from common to contract carriage*. Arguably, each of the other eight trends above is related to the first — there is more contracting *because* of the other eight trends, *and* the other eight trends each favor more contracting.

Shipper-Carrier Contracting

Shipper-carrier contracts vary widely in their specific provisions because of differences in commodities carried, origins and destinations, traffic volumes, carrier performance specified (such as just-in-time), the mode(s) of transportation involved, carrier-shipper electronic data interchange, and so on.

Tables 9–2 and 9–3 illustrate the trends in shipper-carrier contracting with respect to motor carriage (TL, LTL, and contract) and all other modes of transportation. The shifts are dramatic.

The meaning of the shift to contract carriage for shippers and carriers alike is obvious: adapt to the trend toward contract carriage or suffer any competitive consequences that may arise. In particular, it is larger shippers that must adjust to the new contracting environment;

TABLE 9–2: Shippers' Allocation of Tonnage among Common LTL, Common TL, and Contract Motor Carriage

Primary Mode of Shipper	Shipment Mode	1987	1990	Percent Change
Common LTL	LTL	76.0%	68.3%	− 10.1%
	TL	7.8	7.8	0
	Contract	5.3	11.9	+ 124.5
Common TL	LTL	14.6%	12.2%	− 16.4%
	TL	73.1	71.7	− 1.9
	Contract	3.8	5.5	+ 44.7
Contract	LTL	8.0%	7.4%	− 7.5%
	TL	2.8	2.0	− 40.0
	Contract	74.2	75.9	+ 2.3
All Shippers	LTL	29.1%	26.3%	− 9.6%
	TL	17.6	17.2	− 2.3
	Contract	16.8	20.4	+ 21.4

Source: *Partnerships in Providing Customer Service: A Third Party Perspective* Oak Brook, Illinois, Council of Logistics Management (1989) 19.

TABLE 9–3: Percentage of Carriers' Revenue from Common LTL, Contract TL Motor Carriage, and Other Modes

	1987	1990	Percent Change
Mode 1 (Contract TL)			
Common LTL	*1.5%*	*0.0%*	*– 100.0%*
Common TL	*28.5*	*15.4*	*– 46.0*
Contract TL	*67.4*	*75.8*	*+ 12.5*
Mode 2 (Common LTL)			
Common LTL	*75.2%*	*70.1%*	*– 6.8%*
Common TL	*8.4*	*6.5*	*– 22.6*
Contract TL	*3.9*	*4.6*	*+ 17.9*
Mode 3 (All Other)			
Common LTL	*6.3%*	*3.3%*	*– 47.6%*
Common TL	*21.6*	*18.4*	*– 15.7*
Contract TL	*12.4*	*15.8*	*+ 27.4*
All Carriers			
Common LTL	*25.0%*	*21.9%*	*– 3.1%*
Common TL	*19.9*	*14.0*	*– 5.9*
Contract TL	*26.9*	*31.1*	*+ 4.2*

Source: *Partnerships in Providing Customer Service: A Third Party Perspective* Oak Brook, Illinois, Council of Logistics Management (1989) 20.

smaller shippers cannot offer traffic volumes that would ordinarily justify contracts and contract rates with carriers, so they will continue to "pay retail."

As to carriers, they must be prepared to offer competitive contract services to any shipper who could negotiate contracts with competing carriers. The alternative will be the loss of some or all of that shipper's traffic.

PRIVATE TRANSPORTATION

The private transportation alternative is limited primarily to movements by truck, although there are examples of privately-owned railroad operations that move heavy volumes for short distances, some private airfreight operations, and numerous situations where privately-owned ships are used for waterway, inter-coastal, and ocean shipments. The same principles are applicable to selecting private versus public transportation for each of the modes. Because the private transportation alternative is so frequently used for truck transportation, this review will concentrate on that aspect of private transportation.

Advantages

The predominant reasons for using private transportation are better service, transportation cost improvement, reduction in freight loss and damage, the need for specialized transportation equipment, and the lack of adequate for-hire carrier service.

Any set of factors that leads a shipper to believe that transportation can be provided with a lower *true cost* than that resulting from for-hire carriers favors private transportation. These factors include (1) greater control over movements resulting in more dependable arrivals and departures; (2) flexibility in adapting the service to the shipper's specific needs, such as loading and unloading during regular business hours and the design of specialized equipment; (3) reduction in paperwork connected with bills of lading, freight bills, claims, and delivery reports; and (4) more efficient use of equipment and fixed facilities than that obtained by for-hire carriers.

In addition, the use of privately-owned vehicles serves to create a cost yardstick against which for-hire costs can be compared. It also serves as a lever that can be used to obtain for-hire carrier rate adjustments or service.

Disadvantages

On the other hand, the use of private transportation can subject its user to (1) increased administrative/supervisory costs of scheduling, planning, and staffing that can generally be spread over a larger base by for-hire carriers, (2) greater vulnerability to fluctuations in demand for transportation service resulting in insufficient equipment some of the time, and idle equipment at other times, (3) increased labor-management problems, especially if it adds an additional union to the list of those with which the firm must negotiate, and (4) use of debt capacity to support the investment requirements of private transportation.

The underestimation of administrative costs associated with private transportation is often the greatest mistake made in the appraisal of this transportation alternative. Equipment ownership or lease may involve firms in new problems related to taxes, insurance, maintenance, procurement, and personnel. These can be extremely costly. Nevertheless, there are certain circumstances in which private transportation can be less costly than for-hire transport. These arise when a shipper (1) makes little use of terminal facilities because he or she ships primarily in vehicle-load lots; (2) has a balanced traffic pattern allowing a two-directional haul of goods to fill equipment moving out from and back to a certain point, or over several legs of a route; and (3) has a stable pattern and volume of shipments throughout the year to support privately-owned equipment. In addition, private transportation is attractive for those products that bear unusually heavy for-hire rates, particularly cases that result from the tendency of common-carrier rates to be based on cost averages for many shippers rather than the individual characteristics of one.

TRAFFIC IN THE LOGISTICS ORGANIZATION

While the areas of responsibility assigned to the traffic manager within the logistics organization will vary significantly depending on the importance and magnitude of transportation in the total logistics activities of the firm.

Within the logistics organization, the traffic function communicates to and coordinates its activities with other functions within the firm. For example, it will coordinate its appraisal of current and proposed service with marketing and sales to determine alternative methods of servicing various market territories with varying transportation economics and service needs. Traffic coordinates shipping schedules with purchasing and production to assure the proper arrival times for incoming raw materials. As another example, traffic coordinates with accounting to insure that freight invoices are correct before payment or are carefully audited after payment, and that such invoices are not paid *before it is necessary to do so*. There are a myriad of other coordinations and communication responsibilities.

SUMMARY

The passage of the Interstate Commerce Act in 1887 was the first of many efforts to regulate interstate commerce in the United States and the extent of regulation grew steadily for 90 years, although with increasing opposition from those favoring a "free market" for transportation prices and services. Beginning with the 4R Act in 1976, interstate rail, air, and motor carrier rates and services have been almost completely deregulated. This has had profound consequences for both carriers and shippers alike, who have had to cope with a truly competitive transportation environment for the first time in nearly a century.

Freight rates may be based on classifications indicating the relative characteristics of products for purposes of transportation or may be commodity rates based on volume and/or regularity of movement. Rates themselves are found in tariffs published by common carriers and in contracts between shippers and the contract or exempt carriers they might employ. All rates can be categorized in terms of whether they are local or joint, their type, the system employed in quoting them, the type of route they refer to, the quantity of freight they require, and various miscellaneous provisions.

In addition to line-haul rates, shippers may also pay a variety of accessorial charges for the handling and servicing of freight at origin, destination, or in transit. Among the more important of these services, often called privileges, are diversion and reconsignment; protective services; the provision of special equipment; transit, stop-off, and split delivery privileges; and pickup and delivery. Terminal charges may be assessed for demurrage, detention, and switching.

The range of rates that might be quoted tends to reflect the value of service near the top and cost of service near the bottom. Other factors that tend to produce actual rate levels somewhere in this range include the physical characteristics of the product shipped, the distance and direction of movement, the quantity and regularity of shipments, restrictions on discrimination, and competition.

Due to the effects of economic deregulation of the transportation industry, it is quite certain that many opportunities exist in the pricing and design of transportation service for a logistics manager able to understand the structure of rates and services and to use that knowledge to the advantage of his or her firm.

The major task of traffic management is that of compiling, analyzing, and using information effectively to plan and control the movement of a firm's supplies and products. In some cases, the traffic function may also have responsibility for the management of privately-owned and operated transportation.

Deregulation has permitted more innovative and creative transportation system design than was possible in the past. It will require more astute traffic managers to meet the new challenges brought about by deregulation.

The combination of the effects of deregulation and advances in technology and communications have provided an opportunity for carriers and many shippers to enter into contracts that provide for a negotiated set of carrier services.

The importance of transportation costs in the logistics system has been noted. But of more significance than transportation costs is the effective use of transportation in a manner compatible with a firm's overall logistics strategy and patterns. It is this latter characteristic that distinguishes the forward looking traffic manager from his or her predecessors.

DISCUSSION QUESTIONS

1. When evaluating carrier performance, what factors do shippers consider most important? Why?

2. What is the relationship between safety stock and the consistency of carrier performance?

3. What is the difference between a nonnegotiable and a negotiable bill of lading? In what respects are they similar?

4. Why is it important to have an accurate and complete description of the goods on a bill of lading?

5. Why do shippers audit their freight bills?

6. Undercharges have become a major problem since the motor carrier industry was deregulated. What are undercharges, and why and how did this problem arise?

7. What is the relationship between a shipper's value of a transportation service and a carrier's cost of providing that service in determining whether traffic will move?

8. Carrier costs are hard for shippers (and carriers) to estimate accurately, with one general exception. What is that exception and what accounts for it?

9. What carrier cost considerations tend to set limits on intermodal rate competition?

10. How has deregulation affected the process of rate negotiation between carriers and shippers?

11. What types of reports might shippers use in order to evaluate carrier performance?

12. What factors account for the increase in contract carriage?

13. What are the principal advantages and disadvantages of private transportation as contrasted with the use of for-hire transportation?

CASE: Lambert Products Company*

CHOICE OF MOTOR CARRIER(S)

Ed Robinson was the recently hired Purchasing Manager for Lambert Products Company in Atlanta. The Company manufactured a wide line of aluminum products, including window frames, screen doors, screens, patio and lawn furniture, and a variety of small aluminum hardware items.

---

*This case has been prepared as the basis for a seminar or classroom discussion and is not intended to portray either correct or incorrect approaches to managerial decision making. All names have been disguised.

Ed Robinson's predecessor, Sam Walters, had just retired. Mr. Walters' "heir apparent" as Purchasing Manager had recently been lured away by a competitor, leaving a gap that Robinson had been hired to fill. Robinson was 34 years old and had completed an A.A. business degree prior to three years of military service. After his military service he was employed by the Elliott Sash & Door Company of Louisville and had worked his way up to the position of assistant purchasing manager at Elliott. During that time, he completed a four-year undergraduate business degree at night and was working on his professional purchasing agent certification when the opportunity at Lambert Products Company developed.

During his last day in the office Walters briefed Robinson on various aspects of Lambert's purchasing operations. It was apparent that most matters were going well. However, there was one matter that needed to be resolved: motor carrier LTL service from a number of Lambert's materials vendors in the Chicago area to Lambert's manufacturing plant in Atlanta.

Walters handed Robinson a copy of a report that had recently been prepared by the shipping and receiving supervisor, saying, "You'll have to make a decision about this, and I'd suggest you think it out pretty carefully before you call the shot. Good luck in the job. So long."

Memorandum

January 12, 1990

TO: Samuel Walters, Purchasing Manager
FROM: Barbara Wingate, Shipping and Receiving Supervisor
SUBJECT: Chicago-Atlanta LTL Service

For the past six months, since June when we changed our aluminum materials vendor sources to the Chicago area instead of the East Coast, we have been monitoring LTL services from Chicago to Atlanta by the four motor carriers we've been using. The results have been mixed.

You will recall that these four carriers are the only ones whose operations each completely fit our needs for single-carrier direct service from our vendors in Milwaukee, Chicago, Gary, and South Bend to Atlanta. Use of any other carriers would require interlining and it is company policy to avoid that if at all possible.

The problem is that each of these carriers is "good news and bad news." We are concerned with carrier O.S. & D.,* schedule reliability, claims handling, and some occasional special services such as tracing. There is a lot of variation among these carriers in regard to these criteria.

I've prepared a summary of how each carrier stacks up. We want good service, and it would be desirable to use only the one or two best carriers and cut off the others. Doing business with four of them is too much. Also, if we concentrate our business with one or two we will have more clout with them. Here is what we've learned about them over these past six months. Each carrier has handled about 25 percent of our traffic from the Chicago area.

ALBERT EXPRESS

<u>O.S. & D.</u>   They have a nearly perfect record on O.S. & D. They've never been short, and over the six months there has only been one damage experience. (One of their terminal forklift drivers apparently ran his fork tines through a carton of screening and didn't tell anyone about it.) We

---

*O.S. & D.   Common acronym for "over, short, or damaged."

caught it on inbound inspection. They were very apologetic and sent us a check the next week. They are very good on paying attention to FRAGILE markings.

<u>Schedule Reliability</u> Miserable. Either their drivers can't find Atlanta, or their dispatchers don't know where it is. We never know when a shipment will arrive. LTL time has been as little as 24 hours from South Bend and as much as two *weeks* from Milwaukee. There has been a bit of improvement over time, but nothing worth talking about. According to their drivers, their terminals in Chicago and Gary are too small and the terminal docks are badly crowded.

<u>Claims Processing</u> Practically nothing to process, as noted under O.S. & D., above. The one time they damaged a shipment they paid the claim immediately.

<u>Special Services</u> No tracing capability at all. They are as courteous and polite as can be, but trying to find out where our stuff is hung up is like punching a balloon.

BAKER MOTORWAYS

<u>O.S. & D.</u> So-so performance. A few cartons lost and a few damaged over six months. They may not understand that aluminum is not steel. The shortages have been irritating because Baker seems to lose "all of something" instead of "one of each" and this has shut down production assembly of some of our products a few times for a day or two.

<u>Schedule Reliability</u> Close to clockwork. Baker has a solid reputation for reliability in maintaining their schedules. If they say a Chicago vendor's shipment will be here in 48 hours you can bet on it unless, of course, as in a few cases, it never arrives at all.

<u>Claims Processing</u> Not so good. A combination of a very hard-nosed attitude and delay. Sometimes they try to push off concealed damage as the vendor's responsibility. Most of our claims are eventually paid; but the hassle index is pretty high, and it takes a lot of time, phone calls, and correspondence to settle a claim.

<u>Special Services</u> Tracing has been excellent on the few occasions we've needed it. Also, they are really good on not holding up on delivery to us when their peddle* schedule is light; they deliver whatever has come in.

CAREY TRUCKING

<u>O.S. & D.</u> Our experience has been pretty good, with only a few problems. They don't do too well on large multiple carton shipments; we'll get 16 out of 18 at one time in 72 hours, but the other two cartons will arrive sometime over the next week. There have been only a few slightly damaged shipments.

<u>Schedule Reliability</u> Much more reliable than Albert Express, but not quite as reliable as Baker Motorways. The only time there seems to be a consistent problem is in vendor shipments originating on Fridays; for some reason these tend to get delayed and will often arrive later than a shipment picked up the following Monday.

<u>Claims Processing</u> Very hard-nosed on the few claims we've had. A couple are still unpaid. One of their people told us, "Since you guys are manufacturers you ought to be able to repair some of this stuff instead of claiming the whole value and giving it back to us."

<u>Special Services</u> They are "willing" to trace, but it's the old story. They don't do a good job: they just go through the motions. However, they are generally good on delivery, even late in the day.

DONALDSON HIGHWAY SERVICE

<u>O.S. & D.</u> Almost as good as Albert Express. Very little damage and only one short shipment over the six months, and all of this was in the first three months. There has been *no* O.S. & D. with Donaldson in the last 90 days.

---

*"Peddle" is an industry term (contraction) for peddling—pickup and delivery.

Schedule Reliability   They are *consistent*, but they are very slow. On the average they are by far the slowest of the four trucking companies in regard to shipment transit time, and there has been no noticeable improvement. Our guess is that they do a lot of LTL "accumulating" to raise their average trip dispatch weight. Their slowness is enough to cause an occasional problem with materials availability in our plant.

Claims Processing   Excellent in the several claim cases we've had with them. The best of the four carriers (except perhaps for Albert where we've only *had* one claim). They have a good reputation for fast and reasonable claims processing.

Special Services   Tracing and expediting with Donaldson is like walking through a swamp with a very accurate compass. They will tell us exactly where our shipment is, but then they don't move it any faster than they were moving it in the first place.

CASE QUESTIONS

1. Which carrier(s) of these four should Ed Robinson choose for carrying most or all of Lambert's inbound materials traffic. Why?

2. Is there any other information you would want to have (and likely could get) before making a decision? What information?

3. What motor carrier performance criteria other than O.S. & D., reliability, claims, and services might Ed Robinson want to consider? Why?

SUGGESTED READINGS

BOWERSOX, DONALD J., *et al, Leading Edge Logistics: Competitive Positioning for the 1990's*, Oak Brook, Illinois: Council of Logistics Management, 1989.

COYLE, JOHN J., EDWARD J. BARDI, and JOSEPH L. CAVINATO, *Transportation*, 2d ed. St. Paul, Minnesota: West Publishing Company, 1986.

KENDALL, LANE C., *The Business of Shipping*, 5th ed. Centreville, Maryland: Cornell Maritime Press, 1986.

LALONDE, BERNARD J., and MARTHA C. COOPER, *Partnerships in Providing Customer Service: A Third-Party Perspective*, Oak Brook, Illinois: Council of Logistics Management, 1989.

LOCKLIN, D. PHILIP, *Economics of Transportation*, 7th ed. Homewood, Illinois: Richard D. Irwin, Inc., 1972. Locklin's work, although dated in some respects, remains a classic and valuable treatment of the economics of transportation and transportation rates.

SAMPSON, ROY J., MARTIN T. FARRIS, and DAVID L. SCHROCK, *Domestic Transportation: Practice, Theory and Policy*, Boston, Massachusetts: Houghton Miflin Company, 1985.

SHAPIRO, ROY D., and JAMES L. HESKETT, *Logistics Strategy: Cases and Concepts*, St. Paul, Minnesota: West Publishing Company, 1985.

STEPHENSON, FREDERICK J., JR., *Transportation USA*, Reading, Massachusetts: Addison-Wesley Publishing Company, 1987.

TAFF, CHARLES A., *Commercial Motor Transportation*, 7th ed. Centreville, Maryland: Cornell Maritime Press, 1986.

TYWORTH, JOHN E., JOSEPH L. CAVINATO, and C. JOHN LANGLEY, JR., *Traffic Management*, Reading, Massachusetts: Addison-Wesley Publishing Company, 1987.

ENDNOTES

1. Herbert W. Davis, "Physical Distribution Costs: A Current Look at Performance in Selected Industries," in *Proceedings, 1979 Annual Conference*, Chicago: National Council of Physical Distribution Management (1979): 4.

2. *Ibid.*

3. Bernard J. LaLonde and Paul Zinzer, *Customer Service: Measuring and Measurement* (Chicago: National Council of Physical Distribution Management, 1976).

4. Nicholas A. Glaskowsky, Jr., "Kanban/Just-In-Time — Panacea or Plague?," Part I, *Logistics Spectrum*. Journal of the Society of Logistics Engineers, 23, no. 1 (Spring, 1989): 11–15.

5. For an excellent, concise treatment of this topic see Tyworth, John E., Joseph L. Cavinato, and C. John Langley, Jr. *Traffic Management*. Reading, Mass.: Addison-Wesley Publishing Company (1987).

6. "Saving Money When Freight Rates Are Computerized," *Business Week* (February 25, 1980): 111.

7. David Grumhaus, "The Computer And Transportation: A Difficult Marriage," in *Traffic World* (January 21, 1980): 44–46.

8. *Ibid.*

9. "Saving Money When Freight Rates Are Computerized," *Business Week* (February 25, 1980): 111.

10. J. J. Miner, "The Timely Emergence of the Distribution Audit," *Handling and Shipping* (April 1971): 57 and G. L. Stern, "Traffic: Clear Signals for Higher Profits," *Harvard Business Review* (May-June 1972): 74.

11. John R. Meyer, Merton J. Peck, John Stenason, and Charles Zwick, *The Economics of Competition in the Transportation Industries* (Cambridge: Harvard University Press, 1959): 181.

12. Harwood Hoover, Jr., "Pricing Behavior of Deregulated Motor Common Carriers," *Transportation Journal* 25, no. 2 (Winter, 1985): 55–61.

13. Harwood Hoover, Jr., "Pricing Behavior and Profitability in the Initial Phase of Deregulation: The Case of Motor Common Carriers," *Journal of Business Logistics* 7, no. 2 (1986): 47–63.

14. LaLonde, Bernard J., and Martha C. Cooper, *Partnerships in Providing Customer Service: A Third Party Perspective* (Oak View, Illinois: Council of Logistics Management, 1989): 13–15.

The shrink-wrap machine has improved materials handling and helped reduce logistics costs.

CHAPTER TEN

10

Packaging and Material Handling

LEARNING OBJECTIVES

The objectives of this chapter are to:

➢ Describe and explain the importance and role of packaging in the operation of logistics systems.

➢ Explain and discuss the importance of storage, handling, and transportation considerations in package design.

➢ Explain and discuss engineering, purchasing, production, and marketing considerations in package design.

➢ Describe and explain the role of material handling in the operation of a logistics system.

➢ Describe and explain the uses of devices for the unitization of freight.

➢ Describe and explain the uses of various types of material-handling equipment.

➢ Present and discuss problems caused by differences in intercompany material handling systems.

➢ Discuss the handling of materials in bulk.

We have combined our discussion of packaging and material handling because of their close relationship. Along with computer and electronic communications applications, packaging and material handling are the areas of logistics operations in which the greatest technological advances have been made in recent years. Today, these innovations provide the logistics manager with a wide array of alternatives in terms of capabilities and cost. These alternatives must be understood, selected, and managed effectively in order to deliver the desired level of customer service at the lowest total cost.

First, we will discuss the economic and operational significance of packaging and package design. This will be followed by our discussion of material handling, which is centered around packaged freight and bulk freight, the technologies and management problems associated with each, and factors influencing the point in the flow of material where it is converted from bulk to packaged form.

PACKAGING

Packaging Concepts

The words "package" and "packaging" mean different things to different people. To the supermarket shopper, a package is the box containing 12 ounces of cereal or a plastic bottle holding a liter of a soft drink. To a motor-carrier dispatcher, concern with packaging may relate to the bursting strength of a carton containing an air-conditioning unit being handled across the carrier's dock. The packaging for premixed concrete being transported to a job site is the large rotating drum mounted on a specialized heavy truck designed to haul concrete.

Packaging contains liquids, solids, and gasses and, as discussed later in this chapter, performs many functions, ranging from product protection to advertising. The terms package and packaging can be understood in terms of a "hierarchy of containers." Consider toothpaste, for example.

1. First, the toothpaste has to be put into some kind of container so it can be handled easily by the consumer. So, it is put into a tube.

2. The tube is handy to use, but it's soft and fragile, so it is put into an oblong box to protect it on the store shelf and in a shopping cart.

3. Since tubes of toothpaste are ordered by stores in multiples of ten or a dozen, or more, the manufacturer packs that number of boxed tubes of toothpaste in a small carton.

4. To facilitate economical handling by distributors, some number of such small cartons will be packed in a larger carton.

5. Fifteen or twenty of those larger cartons may then be placed on a pallet for handling by a forklift truck as the pallet is loaded on and later unloaded from a truck or rail car.

6. Even a closed truck, trailer, container or rail car is "packaging" as its role is protection—from theft, rain, extreme temperatures, damage, and so on.

Similar packaging hierarchies could be developed for most items that are transported, handled, and stored. "Package" and "packaging" are very broad terms and require careful definition when used in a logistics context.

ECONOMIC SIGNIFICANCE OF PACKAGING

Based on Department of Commerce and industry estimates, $42.7 billion was spent on packaging materials in 1978. Table 10–1 shows estimates of the amount spent and relative shares represented by various packing materials and components. Corrugated boxes, metal cans, and glass jars and bottles continue to be the most widely used, reflecting the food and beverage industry's role as the dominant end user. Wood use continues to decline while the use of plastic continues to grow. Packaging accounts for about 6 percent of the total value of all manufactured goods. For a packaged product valued at $1.00 retail this breaks down to about $.05 for consumer packaging and labeling, with an additional $.01 as the individual consumer package's pro rata share of the cost of the distribution container that brought it from the factory and distribution center to the retail store. Marketing strategies designed to segment the marketplace by relying on product differentiation have resulted in wider product assortments and brand proliferation. This has greatly increased packaging and other logistical requirements. As new products and new sizes in new packages are added, additional storage, handling, and transport capabilities are necessary to provide the desired level of service for each stock keeping unit (SKU). For example, one Northern California bottler offers its cola for sale in fourteen ways: in five sizes of returnable glass bottles, two sizes of no-deposit, no-return glass bottles, four sizes of aluminum cans, and three large sizes in blow-molded plastic bottles.

TABLE 10–1: Packaging Expenditures

Material	Expenditures (billions of dollars)	Share of Total Packaging Expenditures (percent)
Paper and Paperboards:		
Corrugated	$ 7.7	18.0
Folding cartons	4.5	10.6
Paper bags	1.9	4.4
Other	2.8	6.6
Total paper and paperboards	16.9	39.6
Metal		
Cans	8.6	20.1
Drums and other	2.9	6.8
Total metal	11.5	26.9
Plastic	5.2	12.2
Glass	4.2	9.8
Wood and Textiles	1.5	3.5
Other Materials	3.4	8.0
TOTAL PACKAGING	$42.7	100.0

SOURCES: *United States Industrial Outlook, 1979*, (Washington: Department of Commerce, 1979) 57, 75–76; *Glass Packaging Institute 1979 Annual Report*, (Washington: Glass Packaging Institute) 11–15; and *Fibre Box Association 1978 Annual Report*, (Chicago: Fibre Box Association, 1979).

PACKAGE DESIGN

Management of the packaging function is a complex process. Several considerations that must be taken into account in package design are set forth in Figure 10–1. These considerations vary widely and are often contradictory. The importance of each will vary from situation to situation depending on the characteristics of the product, the market(s) in which it is sold, the channels of distribution through which it is passed, and the cost and performance trade-offs of various packaging alternatives.

The eight sublists in Figure 10–1 contain both logistics and nonlogistics considerations. Strictly speaking, the logistics manager is not concerned with the advertising effectiveness of the package, instructions for the product's use printed on the package, and the like. Other matters, such as those listed under Material Handling, Order Picking, and Traffic-Transportation, *are* primary logistics considerations.

Logistics Considerations[1]

The *shipping package*, often a master container for smaller, end-user packages, is the focus of interest in the logistics system. Besides providing protection, this package is what must be handled, stored, and transported through the distribution chain. Effective packaging may contribute to improved customer service, lower freight rates, and reduced loss and damage with a resulting reduction in freight damage claims and wasted inventory carrying costs.

Protection   A package must protect its contents from a variety of hazards. These can be divided into two types, environmental and physical. Environmental hazards are presented by the elements. A product with wide distribution might encounter great temperature extremes. Protection from moisture, rain, snow, or humidity must also be provided. Physical hazards are closely related to the handling a package receives. The contents must be cushioned so that vibration from transportation and material handling equipment, rough roads, and other sources does not cause damage. Protection from the impact of railroad switching and sudden starts and stops of transportation vehicles must also be provided. The package must also protect its contents from punctures and compression that may result from improper storage, handling or loading, and sudden impacts.

Other hazards are related to specific products. High value items, for example, may be packaged to provide some degree of protection against pilferage. The packaging of toxic products must meet increasingly stringent environmental protection requirements. Food items also present special packaging needs against such hazards as rodents, insects, and bacterial contamination. Protection from contamination caused by uncomplimentary characteristics of products that may be shipped or stored in the same vehicle or building is also a function of packages used with food-grade materials.

Marking and Identification   Efficient distribution methods require that the contents and destinations of containers be clearly and rapidly identifiable if inventory mix-ups and misrouting are to be minimized. In addition, packages are carrying an increasing variety and volume of information. Some, such as hazardous material symbols and codes, are required by government regulations. Others, such as special handling requirements, pallet patterns, and loading instructions are there to improve handling efficiency. These must be clearly visible under a

FIGURE 10–1: The many faces of package design: a sampling of the more important considerations in the design of product packages

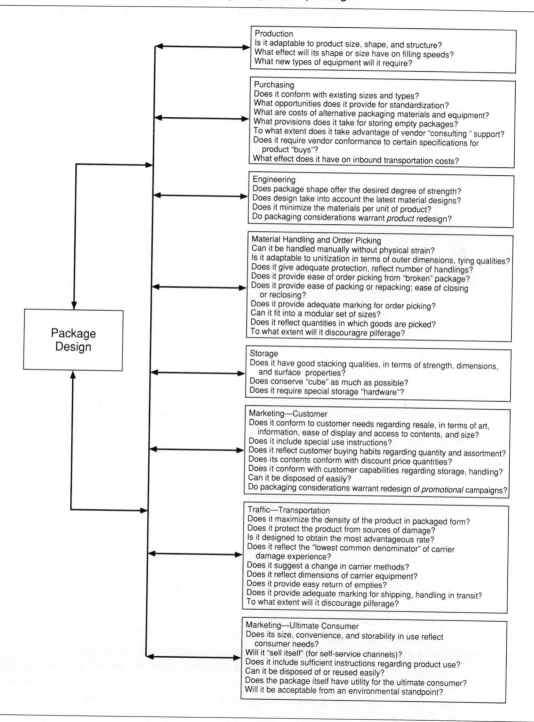

FIGURE 10–2: Percentages of inbound shipments barcoded in 1987, 1990, and estimated for 1995 for the pharmaceutical industry, shippers of general merchandise to receivers, and total for all industries

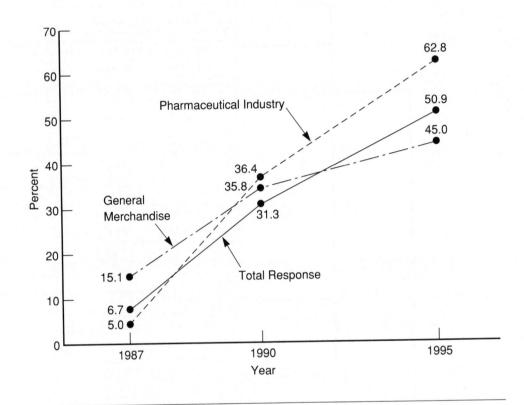

Inbound Shipments Barcoded

SOURCE: *Customer Service: A Management Perspective* (Oak Brook, Illinois: Council of Logistics Management, 1988): 161.

variety of lighting and other conditions in order to be of any use. With the introduction of bar codes, light pens, laser scanners, and other computer-assisted, machine-readable technologies, packages are required to carry an even greater amount of data for stock control and other processing purposes.

The rapid evolution and adoption of bar code technology is illustrated in Figures 10–2 and 10–3. Books such as *Reading Between the Lines: An Introduction to Bar Code Technology* by Harmon and Adams have become "must reading" for logistics managers.[2]

Figure 10–4 contains two examples of a Universal Product Code (UPC). The top figure in Figure 10–4 is a *standard* UPC Version A symbol. Because a standard size UPC symbol may not fit on some products, manufacturers often solve that problem by reducing, or truncating,

FIGURE 10–3: Percentages of outbound shipments barcoded in 1987, 1990, and estimated for 1995 for the electronics industry, shippers of general merchandise, and total for all industries

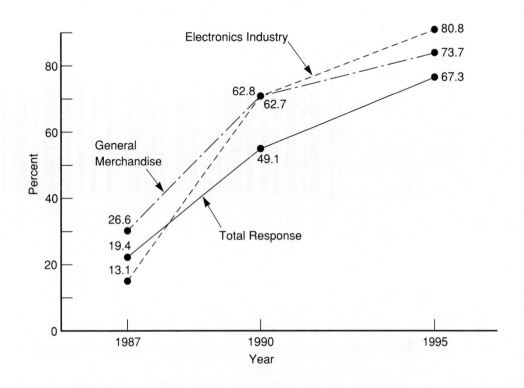

Outbound Shipments Barcoded

SOURCE: *Customer Service: A Management Perspective* (Oak Brook, Illinois: Council of Logistics Management, 1988): 162.

the overall height of the symbol. An example of a truncated UPC symbol appears in the lower figure of Figure 10–4.

Storage The strength of a package, its shape, and the way it is stacked are critical factors in determining the amount and utilization of storage space. For example, by using stronger packages and limiting the proliferation of odd shapes and sizes, the height to which packages may be stacked is increased. By adopting stronger and standard-size packages, many companies have found that they can stack products 50 percent higher or more than before, thus increasing the weight and quantity of products stored per-square foot of warehouse space. Similarly, the shape of a package will determine cubic storage requirements. A case of six rectangular cans, for example, occupies only 76 percent of a cube containing the same amount

FIGURE 10–4: A Universal Product Code version A symbol encoding the data "01234567890." Note that the use of the check digit (5 in this example) helps detect incorrect scans.

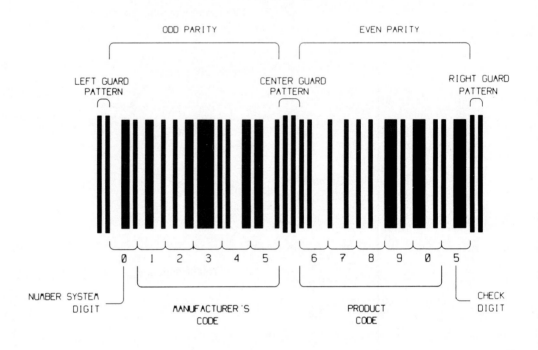

SOURCE: Roger Palmer, *The Bar Code Book*, Reading, Printing, and Specification of Bar Code Symbols, Second Edition (Peterborough, New Hampshire: Helmers Publishing, Inc., 1991), page 21. © 1991 Helmers Publishing, Inc. Reproduced with permission.

of product in round cans. However, the savings from improved space utilization have to be traded for the cost of engineering and producing new package designs. Impacts on other functions, such as production and transportation, must also be considered.

Material Handling and Order Picking The ease and economy with which packages can be handled and picked has become increasingly important. Typically, a package is handled several times, by a combination of manual and mechanical means, as it moves through the distribution cycle. Thus, it must be strong enough to withstand the stress at the roughest point in that cycle, yet be of a size, shape, and weight that can be handled quickly and efficiently by hand. Many packages (cartons, crates, and such) are marked to indicate a need for special handling or that they contain hazardous cargo. Some examples of such markings are shown in Figure 10–5.

Of particular interest for material handling is the potential for unitizing the package by handling it simultaneously with a number of units of the same or other products such as in

FIGURE 10–5: Cargo markings indicating need for care in handling

Sling here

Fragile—handle with care

Use no hooks

This way up

Keep away from heat

Center of gravity

uniform pallet loads. Here, package dimensions as well as strength are important. Perfect cubes do not lend themselves to palletization without the introduction of some means of "tying" the stack together. Differences in the two horizontal dimensions of a package permit interlocking of items in a pallet load. However, unless these dimensions are proportionally correct, they may lead to an overlap of packages at the edge of the pallet, often a source of subsequent damage or the creation of "dead space" in the center of the load. Heavier and larger cartons require less overlap in unitized loading to achieve a given level of load stability.

Modular packaging has been explored by many organizations and adopted by a few for material handling and transportation. This concept is closely related to unitization for it allows the combination of packages of different modular dimensions in the same handling unit, in the case of Figure 10–6, a pallet quantity. But the complexities of product line-item sizes, the need to adjust traditional shipping quantities to the number that fit into the package module, and the need to convince customers that it is feasible to sell a product in such "odd" lots has

FIGURE 10–6: An example of a modular system of packaging

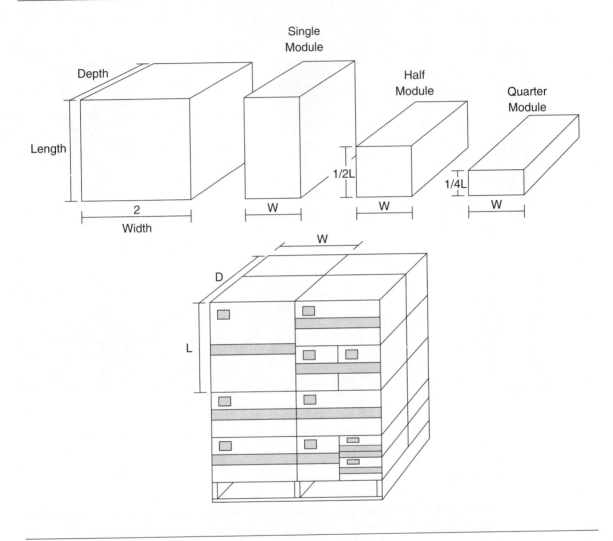

SOURCE: Walter F. Friedman, "The Role of Packaging in Physical Distribution," *Transportation & Distribution Management* (February 1968): 34–39.

limited the implementation of modular packaging to a few uniformly shaped products, such as phonograph records.

Order picking efficiency, in terms of speed, cost, and accuracy, is a function of the adequacy and clarity of marking, the ease with which a package can be opened and items removed in "broken case" quantities, and the ease with which a package can be repacked, closed, and reused for handling and shipping.

Many organizations have achieved significant savings in order picking by adapting the package to quantities in which goods are ordered. For example, many toiletry and sundry items are shipped in cases of 24 or 48 units with the contents prepacked in six- or twelve-packs to speed up and simplify picking and repacking of orders from distribution centers to retail outlets.

Traffic and Transportation Costs for transporting various products, as determined by carrier rate structures, often reflect the density (weight per cubic measure) of the packaged product, the quantity that can be carried in a vehicle load, and the degree to which the package affords protection from damage and pilferage. Additional costs, not generally reflected in such rates, are those for the return of empty packages in separate shipments and carrier costs arising from inadequate package markings. Rising energy costs and associated freight rate increases have given new impetus to increasing product payload and utilizing both the weight and volume capacity of transport units to the greatest extent possible.

Air and highway carriers are often more constrained by cubic capacity than by weight restrictions. Their rates reflect this in lower per-unit prices for the transportation of higher density shipments. In particular, shippers of pallet quantities have found that if the dimensions of the pallet are reduced so that two can be fitted side by side in a standard truck trailer body with an interior width of 92 inches, the resulting load size can nearly double. There is something of a trend toward 48 inches $\times$ 40 inches (1.2 meters $\times$ 1.0 meter) to enable "side-by-side" pallet loading in truck trailers and containers.

A package typically undergoes the greatest stress during the transportation phase of the distribution cycle. This is particularly true if packages or palletized unit loads are stacked to utilize the full cubic capacity of the transportation vehicle. A basic consideration in packaging design is the degree to which packaging costs should be traded against both basic transportation costs and those for loss, damage, and resulting claims. Carrier tariffs, as well as Interstate Commerce Commission regulations, specify package strengths. The task of the logistics manager is to determine whether to accept these specified standards as acceptable minimums or to require greater protection at higher packaging costs.

However, trade-offs may generate a "negative psychology." Packaging engineers sometimes feel that more protective packages lead to more careless handling, while some carriers believe that special safety and care in handling by them encourages manufacturers to lighten and cheapen their packaging. Clearly, there are few products of a value or character that warrant complete protection from all potential damage or theft. However, the case of *Eastern Motor Express v. A. Maschmeijer, Jr.*[3] confirmed the shipper's responsibility and liability for damages caused by latent defects in the container. At the same time, the Interstate Commerce Commission has granted released rates that limit carrier liability in exchange for lower transportation rates.

Of particular interest in recent years has been the cost of returning reusable pallets or containers used for unitized shipments. In some cases, this has led to the negotiation of special rates with carriers interested in promoting the use of the concept for transporting such items. In others it has led to the establishment of exchange agreements whereby organizations trading with one another and using common sizes of pallets, containers, or other reusable packages keep track of the balance owed one organization by the other. Problems with establishing an effective, on-going program for exchange of like-quality pallets was cited as a principal cause of the failure of the Grocery Manufacturers of America's grocery pallet standardization efforts.[4]

Finally, packages that are well-marked for handling in transit will typically move with greater speed in LTL quantities or in situations where carriers or freight forwarders are responsible for assembling or distributing full loads.

Engineering Considerations

Perhaps the most important role of package engineering is in providing a screen for the many packaging alternatives available. This includes a consideration of package strength, the effect of the package on production processes and costs, the amount and cost of materials per unit of packaged product, and the degree to which special product characteristics are accommodated. During the early engineering and design stage, the possibility of redesigning the product to accommodate more desirable packaging alternatives should not be ruled out.

Without slighting the importance of the technical and engineering aspects of package management, package improvements and laboratory testing are beneficial only insofar as they enhance the package's performance as it proceeds through the production and distribution cycle and meets the demands of end users. Package engineers must insist on effective feedback, such as actual loss and damage histories, in order to maximize their contribution to a cost-effective package management program.

Purchasing Considerations

Since packaging is viewed only as a cost item by many organizations, there is strong pressure on buyers to select the lowest cost alternative. However, if the cheapest package is not compatible with all the other elements in the production, marketing, and distribution chain, the "savings" may be wiped out by the cost of damaged goods or lost sales at a later stage. Instead, purchasing should focus on the costs of providing a specified level of performance.

Purchasing will also be interested in the possibility of standardizing package sizes around a few basic dimensions, especially if the per-unit price of the materials is a function of the number of units of a given size purchased. The shape of the package will also influence its cost. For example, the cost of a slotted corrugated box is roughly proportional to the amount of box board it requires. The most economical box, from a materials standpoint, should have greater depth than length or width, because an overlap is required on the top and bottom of a top-opening box. Manufacturers of packaging materials and equipment are sources of a great amount of free, if potentially biased, consulting advice on packaging applications. This information is usually channeled through purchasing or engineering personnel.

Production Considerations

The design of the package and its size, shape, access, and closure characteristics, may affect both the need for investment in new packaging equipment and the unit cost of filling packages on the production line. Production often plays a major role by preparing the product for subsequent handling and shipping by packing, sealing, reinforcing, bundling, or unitizing the product during the production process. This work is now highly automated in organizations where the volume of production is large enough to spread the cost of equipment investment over enough units to produce unit costs below those for labor intensive means.

Marketing Considerations

For many products, the package is sometimes as important, or even more important, than the contents in influencing the ultimate consumer's purchasing decision. Thus, in addition to the ability of the package to deliver the product in good condition, manufacturers and merchants are interested in artistic design, providing information to aid in resale, ease of unpacking and display, and the size of the package itself. The latter is particularly important for goods to be sold through retailers. Supermarket sales, for example, are influenced by the relative proportion of shelf "facing" (linear footage of shelf space facing shoppers) that a product occupies. Manufacturers compete vigorously in attempting to design packages that will effectively utilize available space, encourage retailers to allocate additional shelf space, and attract shoppers.

Shipping cartons must also reflect buying habits regarding quantity and assortment. Oversized cartons with their contents half-sold consume customer space, while undersized cartons require unnecessary packaging and handling. Also, if products traditionally are priced by the dozen, gross, or similar units, this factor should also be taken into consideration.

The "Bag-in-a-Box" is an example of how both manufacturers and intermediaries benefit from package innovation. This combination of a plastic bag within a corrugated box creates a shatter-proof, easy-to-warehouse-and-handle container capable of handling and dispensing large institutional volumes of liquids such as milk, fruit juices, vegetable oil, and ketchup.

Shipping containers also are frequently designed to be convertible into point-of-purchase display units. Other promotions, particularly those involving premiums sold with the basic product, may also alter logistical handling requirements. The costs and benefits of these promotions must be carefully weighed. The winner in such situations, however, will typically be the marketing department, no matter what problems handling such promotional items may cause the logistics manager.

Ease of opening, reclosing, storing, and dispensing are also major consumer concerns. While many consumers are interested only in convenience, environmental concerns have led others to demand packages that can be reused, recycled, or disposed of with a minimum of difficulty. As recycling increases, particularly when required by mandatory deposit "bottle bills" and other laws, new handling, storage, and transportation demands are made on the distribution system.

Metrification[5]

More than 90 percent of the world's population uses the metric system of measurement. In the United States, a voluntary conversion program is underway under the educational and planning guidance of the U.S. Metric Board that will require changes in packaging designs and practices. Several large U.S.-based multinational firms, such as General Motors, IBM, and Hewlett-Packard, have already "gone metric." The wine and distilled spirits industries have also completed industry wide metrification programs.

While the details will vary according to the industry involved, the experience of the wine industry illustrates some of the advantages and pitfalls of metric conversion that may be helpful to other organizations contemplating conversion. By carefully planning the transition in detail, production and logistics problems were handled smoothly and at less extra cost (5 percent versus 10 percent) than anticipated. The number of bottle sizes was reduced, thereby streamlining packaging, logistics, and inventory requirements. Further, by switching to internationally standard metric units, domestic producers are now in a better position to compete in world markets.

Problems did occur, however, in the areas of marketing and public relations. Even though four years were allowed for a conversion, there was insufficient attention given to public education. Because each wine producer followed its own timetable, the public was doubly confused by the changes made. Further, most of the metric sizes adopted contain a bit less product than their English measure "counterparts." As a result, many disenchanted consumers construed metrification as a size "rip-off," not as a simple transition to a new system.

Waste Management and Recycling

Environmental considerations have become a matter of increasing concern in our society. This may be regarded as a permanent trend that affects every party concerned with package design. Garbage and disposal costs are now forcing firms into considering environmental issues in their packaging. Some states have passed laws taxing nonreturnable soft-drink bottles, thus favoring "returnables" that can be reused many times. Many chemical firms that ship toxic chemicals in drums and on pallets now require that these possibly (or probably) contaminated drums and pallets be returned. These firms do not want to have subsequent users throwing away containers with toxic residue in them, thereby causing a possible future liability for the original manufacturer-shipper.

There are two aspects of this emerging environmental situation: (1) the extent of biodegradability of packages and containers, and (2) the depletion of nonreplenishable resources of this planet being consumed rather than being recycled.

Biodegradability Public awareness, coupled with legislation in many states, has resulted in increasing demands that waste materials be biodegradable. Materials of concern are as diverse as disposable diapers and automobile tires. With respect to such refuse, there are three alternatives: (1) incineration, which is costly and uses energy; (2) sanitary land-fills, which have proliferated as many older sites have become saturated; and (3) recycling, if possible and economically feasible. The first two alternatives are generally considered undesirable by the public because of air pollution effects, costs, subterranean water pollution, and the limited number of acceptable landfill locations.

Recyclability To the extent possible, environmental considerations require that packaging be recyclable. Today, in many communities, waste collection requires the business firm or householder to separate refuse into categories of recyclable versus nonrecyclable refuse. The former includes cans, glass containers, certain types of plastic containers, newspapers, cartons, and other paper products. Much of what remains after such items have been separated is truly "garbage" and represents a difficult disposal problem — nonbiodegradable and nonrecyclable items.

Clearly the combination of public pressure and legislation imposes requirements on manufactures to design packages that not only provide the traditional package design considerations discussed in the "Package Design" sections above, but also to take into account the ever-increasing demands of society for protection of the environment.

A Packaging Example from Union Carbide

We will conclude our discussion of packaging with a classic case example of packaging design provided by Carmody:

> Union Carbide moves a considerable amount of plastic resin materials in multi-wall bags. For years they relied chiefly on sewn open-mouth and sewn valve types of bags with all bags designed to carry 50 pounds of product regardless of product density.
>
> The company's distribution and handling system was based on the use of pallet loads of materials: each pallet carried 40 bags or 2,000 pounds of net product. To accomplish this with the sewn bag required a bag pattern of four bags per tier placed in pinwheel fashion on a 48 inch pallet, with ten tiers of bags per pallet. With bag overhang, overall dimension of the loaded pallet were approximately $50'' \times 50''$. Because the pinwheel arrangement left an empty space in the center of the pallet, some instability resulted and it was generally not possible to stack these pallets more than two high in the warehouse.
>
> There were two basic problems with this. First, since the overall width of the pallet in either direction was 50 inches, two pallet loads could not be loaded side by side in a truck (interior truck widths ranged from 88 inches to 92 inches). Therefore, when truck shipments of palletized resin had to be made, the company was not able to meet the minimum truckload weight required by the common carrier; this resulted in higher transportation rates per pound of product. Second, since they could store these pallet loads no more than two high in the warehouse, they could only get about 230 pounds of product per net square foot of warehouse space.
>
> In experiments with the use of more costly pasted valve bags, it was found that for a slight increase in multi-wall bag costs, 50 pounds of product could now be packed in a bag that would stack on a $42'' \times 48''$ pallet, five bags per tier, eight tiers high. The resulting load was quite stable and pallets could easily be stacked three high, provided the warehouse had the necessary overhead clearance and forklift capacity. This system provided an overall package that could be loaded into railcars and trucks, two pallets wide across. Truck freight costs were reduced substantially. Further, with the ability to stack pallets three high, the company was able to store approximately 380 pounds per square foot of net warehouse space. This made it possible for Union Carbide to reduce warehouse space for the same quantity of product to about 60% of previous requirements.[6]

MATERIAL HANDLING

Our intent here is to provide some structure to aid thinking about material handling systems. It is not practical to attempt a discussion of all the various types of equipment currently available to system designers. Specific problems regarding material handling systems are included in the references cited at the end of this chapter.

Equipment for Material Handling

Equipment used in material handling systems can be categorized into five groups: devices for the unitization of freight, individually powered vehicles, conveyors, storage aids, and automated storage and retrieval systems.

In the overall design of a material handling system, we want to emphasize that efficient *individual components* do not necessarily guarantee an efficient *system*. Efficiency is influenced by such factors as the level of and periodic fluctuations in the volume handled, local wage rates for material handling labor, and the relative cost of space, as well as the manner in which the various components are fitted together to form an integrated system.

Devices for the Unitization of Freight

This classification embodies a number of devices used primarily for storage and handling. For the purposes of this discussion, the term is limited to the types of platforms or enclosures used primarily for the accumulation of commodities into units for easy storage, order selection, and transportation. Among the more important are pallets; slipsheets; strapping, tying, or wrapping devices; and containers.

Pallets Pallets are constructed of wood (most common), steel, aluminum, plastic, corrugated cardboard, and even kraft paper, in a variety of designs to accommodate fork lift equipment.

Utilization of pallets is an integral part of the operations of many logistics systems. Depending on circumstances, pallets may be designed to be reusable for many "trips," for only limited reuse, or as one-way, disposable pallets constructed of low-cost materials such as several layers of strong corrugated cardboard.

Pallets may be designed with sideboards to hold materials impossible to stack, or may have an overhead frame to facilitate stacking without the use of pallet racks. If strength and durability are major factors, and pallet weight is not a major consideration, metal pallets may be used, particularly for handling very heavy items, including heavy items with odd-shaped bases for which metal pallets may be specially fabricated.

An important consideration for the logistics manager is whether or not the pallet leaves the firm's control (and ownership) or circulates within the logistics system of the firm, for example, from plant to distribution center and back to the plant. Pallets that "exit the system" should be as inexpensive as possible and durable enough to do their intended job. Pallets that stay within the firm's system (or are returned by customers) should have their cost balanced against their projected useful life. For example, wooden pallets can be made cheaply, using rough, thin, relatively weak unfinished boards "slapped together with a few nails" or, alternatively, can be made quite durable by using high-grade, thick, knot-free finished boards carefully assembled using counter-sunk screws as shown in Figure 10–7.

A number of ways of constructing palletized units of different dimensions and characteristics from packages of the same size developed by the U.S. Navy are shown in Figure 10–8.

One computer software company has developed a computerized Pallet Pattern Calculator® that optimizes the utilization of the pallet cube for any given carton dimension. Examples of the hard copy output of this microcomputer program are shown in Table 10–2 and Figure 10–9.[7] Ideally, unit design, handling systems, and packaging dimensions should be determined concurrently if the unit package system is to be most effectively designed.

Slipsheets A variation of the pallet for unitized handling of freight is the pallet sheet or slipsheet. Used in the warehouse in conjunction with lift trucks fitted with six or more polished, long chisel forks and a "push-pull" attachment, the slipsheet is simply a piece of cardboard the area of a pallet with a five-inch flange turned up along one side. Pallet load

FIGURE 10–7: Wooden pallet constructed to high standards

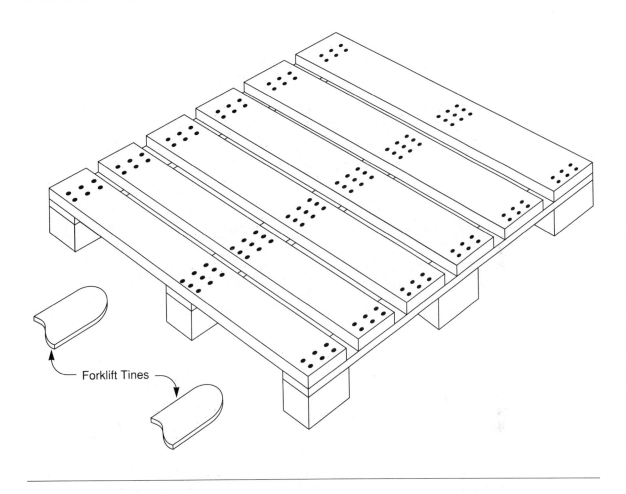

Forklift Tines

quantities can be picked up on slipsheets by running the tines of the fork lift trucks under the cardboard flange and the load. Slipsheets are positioned in a railcar by pushing a load off the tines by means of the mechanical pusher device on the truck. Slipsheets allow unitized freight transportation without the weight and cubic space consumption of pallets and the pallet return problem.

Tying Devices[8] Products such as lumber, bricks, cinder blocks, and steel bars are often banded together with steel strapping to form unit loads without pallets. Lightweight, non-metallic strapping (nylon, polypropoleyne, and such) is also frequently used to band boxes or barrels of common or varying descriptions together to form movable units. Products of similar cubic dimensions or physical characteristics can also be unitized by gluing them together.

Shrink and stretch wrapping are now used extensively to secure unit loads. Shrink wrapping uses heat to securely wrap polyethylene films around loads. Because the resulting wrap

FIGURE 10–8: Examples of possible pallet patterns

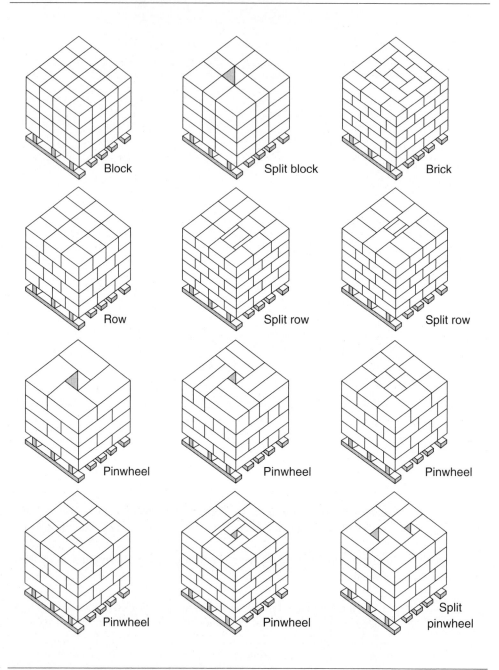

Block

Split block

Brick

Row

Split row

Split row

Pinwheel

Pinwheel

Pinwheel

Pinwheel

Pinwheel

Split pinwheel

SOURCE: U.S. Navy Bureau of Supplies and Accounts, Washington, D.C.

TABLE 10–2: Possible pallet configurations obtained by using the Pallet Pattern
Calculator®

Pallet Number	Pattern Type	Pallet Pattern Configurations				
		Total on Course	Number of Courses	Total on Pallet	Total Weight	Space Utilized
1	Unitblock	18	9	162	972	90%
2	Unitblock	20	9	180	1080	100%
3	Multiblock	20	9	180	1080	100%
4	Multiblock	18	9	162	972	90%
5	Multiblock	18	9	162	972	90%
6	Multiblock	19	9	171	1026	95%
7	Multiblock	17	9	153	918	85%
8	Pinwheel	18	9	162	972	90%
9	Pinwheel	18	9	162	972	90%
10	Pinwheel	18	9	162	972	90%
11	Pinwheel	20	9	180	1080	100%
12	Irregular	18	9	162	972	90%
13	Irregular	17	9	153	918	85%
14	Irregular	19	9	171	1026	95%
15	Irregular	19	9	171	1026	95%
16	Irregular	20	9	180	1080	100%
17	Irregular	19	9	171	1026	95%
18	Irregular	19	9	171	1026	95%
19	Irregular	18	9	162	972	90%
20	Irregular	19	9	171	1026	95%
21	Irregular	20	9	180	1080	100%
22	Irregular	19	9	171	1026	95%
23	Irregular	19	9	171	1026	95%
24	Irregular	17	9	153	918	85%
25	Irregular	19	9	171	1026	95%
26	Irregular	18	9	162	972	90%
27	Irregular	18	9	162	972	90%
28	Irregular	17	9	153	918	85%

These Are All Possible Pallet Solutions

SOURCE: Proprietary product of Professional Micro Systems, Ltd., 4001 West Green Tree Rd., Milwaukee, WI 53209

conforms to load contours, irregular shapes can be accommodated. Stretch wrapping employs tension to encase unit loads in high elasticity plastic film. These techniques provide cleaner, more secure shipments, add a measure of security, and save weight and space by facilitating handling on pallets or slipsheets. Both shrink and stretch wrapping are used widely, but stretch has an advantage in terms of lower material costs and energy use in many applications.

A wide variety of hardware is available to help build and secure unit loads. These items range from simple hand tools for tensioning and sealing strapping to mechanical palletizers and automatic strapping and wrapping machines that have become the last stop on the manufacturing line in many high-volume applications.

FIGURE 10–9: Computer printout of pallet layout using the Pallet Pattern Calculator®

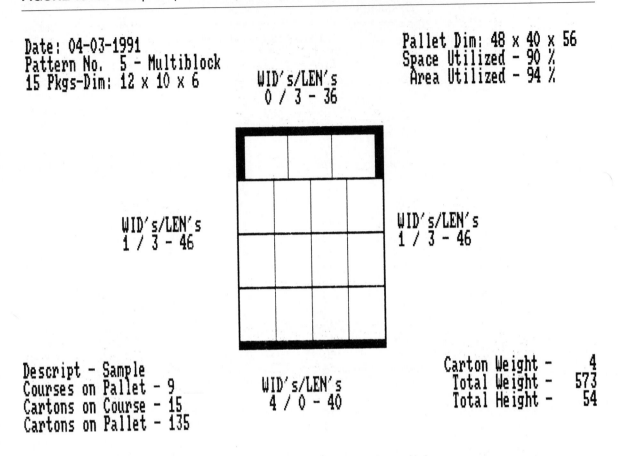

Date: 04-03-1991
Pattern No. 5 - Multiblock
15 Pkgs-Dim: 12 x 10 x 6

WID's/LEN's
0 / 3 - 36

Pallet Dim: 48 x 40 x 56
Space Utilized - 90 %
Area Utilized - 94 %

WID's/LEN's
1 / 3 - 46

WID's/LEN's
1 / 3 - 46

Descript - Sample
Courses on Pallet - 9
Cartons on Course - 15
Cartons on Pallet - 135

WID's/LEN's
4 / 0 - 40

Carton Weight -   4
Total Weight -   573
Total Height -   54

Press ⟨Esc⟩ to return to selection screen,   ^PrtSc for printout

SOURCE: Proprietary product of Professional Micro Systems, Ltd., 4001 West Green Tree Rd., Milwaukee, WI 53209

Containerization[9] Containerization has special significance for our discussion. In a few short years, the adoption of containerization for the ocean shipping of general cargo has exceeded all estimates of growth. Examples of several types of containers are shown in Figure 10–10. In 1968, 13 percent of "containerizable" cargo moving in the North Atlantic was shipped in containers; by 1970, the amount was 60 percent. By 1990 this figure will likely exceed 90 percent. In 1988 Sea-Land purchased and placed into operation the world's 12 largest container vessels, called Econships, each of which can theoretically carry *4,400* twenty-foot equivalent (TEU) containers. For commercial and operational reasons, these vessels normally carry "only" 3,400 TEUs on a voyage.[10]

FIGURE 10–10: Examples of 20-foot containers designed for specialized cargo handling

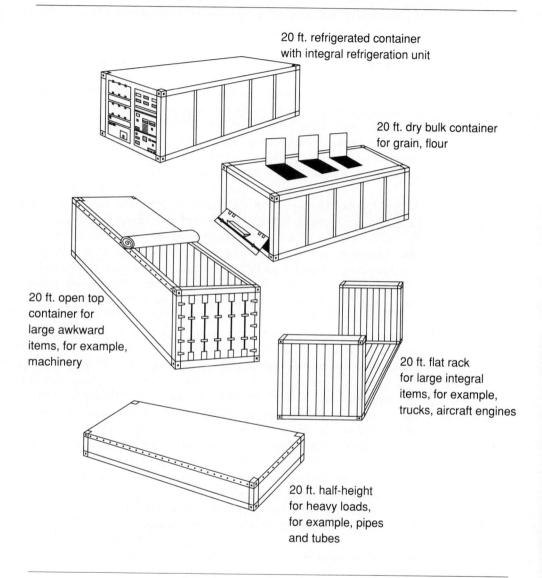

20 ft. refrigerated container with integral refrigeration unit

20 ft. dry bulk container for grain, flour

20 ft. open top container for large awkward items, for example, machinery

20 ft. flat rack for large integral items, for example, trucks, aircraft engines

20 ft. half-height for heavy loads, for example, pipes and tubes

Companies shipping containers ''door-to-door'' (from origin to ultimate destination) have reduced expenses for labeling (with one label per container), plant space for packaging materials, pilferage, damage, inventory carrying (because of faster handling and transit time), and paperwork (with one set of papers for the entire container). In the matter of pilferage alone, it is estimated that before containerization, roughly 10 percent of the Scotch whiskey passing through the Port of New York as regular cargo disappeared.[11]

Transit time savings have been significant with containerization. A container ship requires one day each for loading and discharging cargo and five days for crossing the North Atlantic between the United States and Europe, for example. Container service has been provided on a weekly basis by most competing lines, allowing containerized freight to be accumulated at the port. A typical routing includes two ports of call on each side of the Atlantic, and results in actual transit times of two weeks from first port of origin to second destination port. This is still a significant reduction from transit times via traditional methods of at least three weeks and usually longer.

The irrefutable economic advantages of containerization will continue to support its rapid growth. But ironically, carrier management and labor alike have viewed this growth with great misgivings. With it, the former have seen profits decline, the latter the disappearance of jobs.

Ocean carriers have converted old ships and built new ones rapidly to accommodate the growth of containerization. Port managements similarly have spent large sums on very expensive cranes to accommodate containerization.

These investments have not been matched by inland motor and rail carriers. Nor has sufficient money been spent for information systems necessary for container control. As a result, the use of containers for "door-to-door" shipments has increased only slowly, the type for which maximum advantages for containerization can be claimed. Also, inland turnaround time because of poor control has been much slower than expected, which has raised the investment in containers required to keep ships moving with an economical payload.

Container sizes have been standardized internationally at 8-foot widths, 8-foot heights, and 10-, 20-, 30-, and 40-foot lengths. However, as noted in Chapter 8, the change in permissible trailer length in the United States to 48 feet has led to the introduction of some 48-foot containers, and this different-size "module" causes a problem in containership loading.

Finally, restrictive labor union policies have delayed the realization of the full potential economies of containerization for material handling. This potential was demonstrated in the West Coast-Okinawa service operated for the Defense Department, in which 40,000 tons of containerized cargo can be "offloaded or onloaded" in 750 man-hours as opposed to 24,000 man-hours for break-bulk cargo in old-style ships.[12] Little wonder that labor agreements have included provisions for carrier-funded pensions for the early retirement of displaced union members on the West Coast. The East Coast settlements have reflected a different pattern, including per-ton payments to the International Longshoreman's Association and the union privilege of unloading and loading again at the port any container loaded at an inland terminal by workers outside the ILA's jurisdiction.

In spite of these temporary obstructions, containerization will continue to represent one of the most important developments in logistics. Shippers cannot ignore its savings. Regardless of whether carriers believe they can afford to be in the business, the fact remains that they can't afford to stay out of it.

Individually Powered Vehicles

A fleet of individually powered vehicles in a material handling system is likely to be composed of one or more of the following: forklift trucks, towing tractors, cranes, hand-powered equipment, and miscellaneous vehicles. Power vehicles use electricity, diesel fuel, gasoline, or compressed gas. Except for outdoor or well-ventilated operations, gasoline- or diesel-powered vehicles are not widely used. Rechargeable batteries provide the power source for electrically-operated vehicle fleets. The relative cost to operate with each method of power varies widely between different applications.

Lift Trucks The fork lift truck came into popular use with the advent of pallets and containers designed to accommodate fork tines (blades) that could lift them. More recently, some lift trucks have been designed for use without pallets. The clamp truck is capable of picking up and moving unit loads that are not palletized or strapped. Other units, equipped with chisel forks and push-pull attachments, are designed to handle slip sheet loads. Lift trucks come in a variety of configurations, depending on whether: (1) high lifting or only low lifting is required, (2) load capacity is small (commonly 2,000 pounds), medium (6,000 to 10,000 pounds), or large (up to 120,000 pounds for handling loaded intermodal trailers or containers), (3) fast (driver-rider) or slow ("walkie") movement is needed, and (4) equipment will be used indoors or outdoors (with the latter requiring the use of larger, pneumatic tires and sensitive components being protected against the elements). Figure 10–11 illustrates the wide variety of forklift trucks in use.

The aisle width required for maneuvering different types of equipment involves a critical trade-off between equipment and space cost. Less expensive counterbalanced trucks require wider aisles than "straddle" or "reach-fork" models. "Deep-reach" trucks, capable of stacking pallet loads two-deep, require wider aisles than conventional "reach fork" models, but fewer aisles overall. By eliminating turning, more costly side-loaders and "swing-reach" lift trucks require the least amount of "dead" aisle space.

On-board microprocessors that automatically position loads and equipment, and on-board video display terminals equipped with light pens and other input/output devices for providing inventory and order picking data, have enhanced the productivity of lift truck applications.

Tow Tractors Towing tractors are used in situations where relatively long hauls of large volumes of goods are required. They pull a number of tracking trailers loaded with either palletized or nonpalletized items. They can be used either in combination with fork lift trucks or moved by hand labor.

Cranes Cranes for handling objects of considerable weight may be ceiling mounted on fixed tracks, or they may be portable, self-powered units. The use of the latter requires relatively large, open spaces within a structure, so they are most often used only for lifting and transporting items with handling characteristics that make the use of fork lift trucks unsuitable or unfeasible.

Hand-Powered Equipment Even in an age of mechanization, hand-powered equipment still has a wide range of uses. It is particularly adaptable to situations in which weights are small, the available space is limited, or it is not economically feasible to employ mechanically powered equipment. Hand-powered equipment includes the familiar hand truck, rolling ladders and carts, rolling cages and load buggies, hand pallet trucks or "pallet jacks," and hand hooks for grabbing and lifting.

Miscellaneous Equipment Additional equipment may be needed to compliment that already described. A tiering truck or "order picker," for example, can serve as a substitute for fork lift trucks. These units provide a platform that is equipped with operator controls, is capable of being transported and elevated, and can carry either palletized or nonpalletized

FIGURE 10–11: Forklift truck designs for specialized material-handling operations

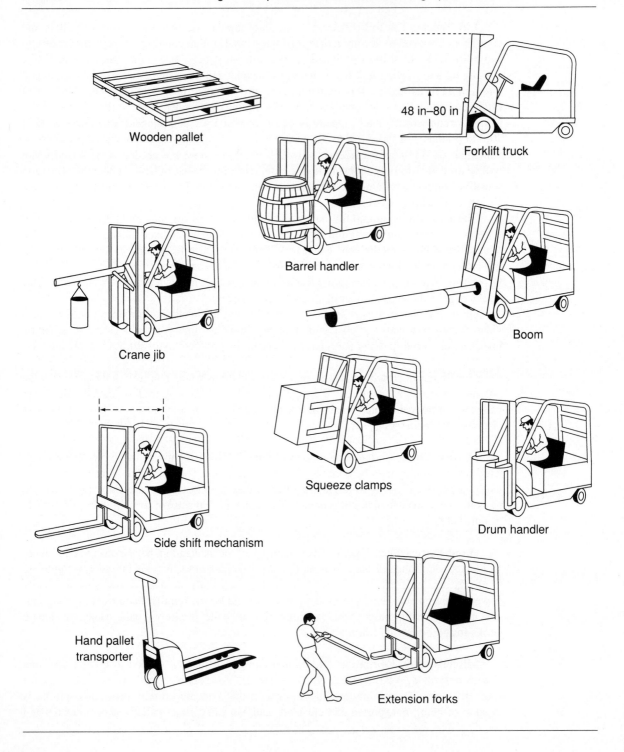

Wooden pallet

48 in–80 in

Forklift truck

Barrel handler

Crane jib

Boom

Side shift mechanism

Squeeze clamps

Drum handler

Hand pallet transporter

Extension forks

material. They are most often used when less-than-pallet-load quantities must be picked from highrise storage racks. A familiar application is their use in "furniture warehouse" outlets, where large pieces of furniture are "filed" in vertical racks with seven or eight levels. A common sight in storage yards and on city streets is the straddle carry truck, capable of hauling great weights and volumes of materials, such as lumber, steel, and other structural materials, in a bay located under the operating cab of the vehicle and between its wheels. Very large, specialized versions of the straddle carry truck are also used to stack and position freight containers at ocean terminals.

A common error in the selection of powered material-handling equipment is the selection of equipment of excess capacity, either as to size or weight-lifting capacity. Extra capacity may be desirable to provide a safety factor for heavy or large loads, but if constantly unused it becomes burdensome in terms of (1) higher initial cost, (2) generally greater floor load requirements to support equipment of greater capacity, (3) extra vehicle operating costs, and (4) extra width required in aisles where freight must be transported and stacked.

Conveyors

Conveyors can be powered by mechanical, gravity, and hand methods. Gravity power is much less expensive than mechanical power, but it is limited by the end-height difference required by a conveyor or given slope (generally 1/4 to 3/4 inch per foot of running length). Mechanically-powered conveyors are referred to as belt, live-roll, chain, or trolley conveyors. Generally, the first two are associated with conveyor systems capable of being relocated. The live-roll conveyor is named after the primary feature of rollers in series powered from a central source. The chain conveyor, usually located in the floor of a terminal or warehouse, is the most "fixed" of all types. It cannot be shifted without considerable expense. Trolley conveyors are often mounted on the ceiling with rolling hooks to which individual vehicles are attached. As such, they can be altered more easily than the chain conveyor, but they are still expensive to move.

Gravity conveyors and hand-powered level conveyors are made up of the same equipment positioned in different ways. Both use either rollers or wheels. As a rule, gravity and hand powered conveyors are highly portable. The portable feature facilitates their use in facilities with varying flows of materials.

The decision to employ fixed conveyor systems in a warehouse must be weighed carefully. A production line, because of its fixed nature, is readily adaptable to the use of fixed conveyors. Generally speaking, a warehouse is not. Even though many highly efficient materials handling systems have been designed around fixed conveyors, those firms subsequently requiring changes in the system have paid a penalty cost to get it. In addition to doing a particular job in terms of carrying freight of certain dimensions and weight, a conveyor system must be selected on the basis of all of the material handling it may be called upon to perform in the foreseeable future.

Storage Aids

Various storage aids in use today include pallet racks, flow racks, bins and drawers, and dunnage.

Pallet Racks The pallet rack is the most common type of storage aid. It is, as its name implies, a tiered rack built of pipe, structural metals, or wood that accommodates stacking two

PALLETIZING IS NO LONGER THE BACK END OF OUR BUSINESS

Karen A. Auguston

For Polaroid's Al Donaghy, the past year has been a lot like running the hurdles. As the principal engineer responsible for the design and implementation of a new robotic palletizer, Donaghy has had to overcome planning, designing, and debugging obstacles while at same time sprinting to meet project deadlines for this major new system.

But now, after many months of long nights and hard work, the system is 90% operational and handling product. That system is a sophisticated cell, which includes a robotic palletizer, 12 pallet loading stations, an overhead conveyor delivery system, bar code scanners, an automatic stretch wrapper, and an accumulating unit load conveyor. Once fully operational, the system will automatically sort, stack, and wrap pallet loads of photographic negative film.

The cell itself is part of the Finishing Automation Project, a plan to upgrade and integrate materials handling practices at Polaroid's Negative Film Manufacturing Division, New Bedford, Mass.

Polaroid has come a long way since the days when palletizing was one of the support functions known as the *back end* of the business. "That description pretty much sums up how people at the plant perceived materials handling," confesses Matt Cohen, engineering manager.

A Need for Change

Cohen describes the old, less-than-efficient palletizing operation as a "virtual army of people scurrying around moving boxes of finished product." All that activity meant excessive handling of the sensitive film, resulting in an unacceptable level of product damage.

Once Polaroid took notice of the dent labor costs and damage were putting in company profits, it began to rethink its entire palletizing operation. "One of our goals," Cohen recalls, "was to eliminate all manual handling of the product after the coating process.

"We basically wanted to automatically sort and palletize up to 12 different types of product at one time," explains Donaghy. "But we also wanted the capability to change parts of our process such as product mix or box size."

To meet the need for flexibility and automation, the design team focused on robotics early on in the project. Two of the alternatives considered involved stationary robots. One option consisted of two huge index tables bringing pallets to a stationary robot. The other option included a carton diverter and several robots, each serving a series of stationary pallet stations. But because of the need for 12 separate loading stations, neither alternative fit into the available space.

"Then we said, 'why not turn the process around,' says Donaghy, 'and move the robot to the pallet?' " In this case, moving the robot to the pallet, which involved mounting a robotic palletizer on a custom-built transporter, turned out to be the best alternative, in terms of time, space, and dollars. "As far as we know," notes Donaghy, "We're the first to use a mobile robot in a palletizing application."

As Easy as One-Two-Three

Now, palletizing is an integral part of the business. And the operation is as easy as one-two-three, or in this case, sort-palletize-wrap.

At the start of the sequence, incoming cartons arrive on one of two accumulation delivery conveyors and pass a stationary scanner. The scanner, linked to a programmable controller (*PIC*) that directs the cell, reads product identification information on a bar code label affixed to the carton. The *PIC* matches this scanned data to production information (downloaded earlier from a central computer) and transmits a pallet location to the robot's internal computer.

The robot, equipped with a four-cup vacuum gripper, then picks up the scanned carton (one of five box types). In the case of a bad read, the robot places the carton on a reject conveyor for checkout by an employee later. If the read is good, the robot places the carton on the appropriate pallet, in one of two stacking patterns, depending on product type.

In a stationary position, the 4-axis robot can reach four pallet stations. If a destination is outside of this primary zone, the robot will stack the carton on a shelf attached to the transporter. When the shelf is full (16 cartons) or there are no more incoming boxes, the robot travels on the transporter to access the other 8 stations.

Internal controls keep tight tabs on inventory. As the robot stacks, the *PIC* assigns a load number to each carton and maintains a load manifest. As the robot palletizes, the *PIC* also tallies the number of cartons per pallet. When a predetermined number is reached, the *PIC* uploads the manifest to a central computer and signals the transporter to pick up the pallet.

The transporter is actually a *precision rail system*. Powered by an on-board, variable frequency AC drive, the transporter moves on a pair of 60-ft-long, floor-mounted steel rails. The drive's controlled acceleration and deceleration eliminate physical shifting of the column-stacked product.

A drive section of roller conveyor, mounted on the transporter, handles the palletized goods. For pallet transfer, the slave drive roller unit powers a roller conveyor at the pallet station, moving the pallet from the transporter to the station, or vice versa. This feature eliminates the need for motors and controllers at each of the 12 pallet loading stations and two pallet dispensing stations.

The transporter delivers a complete pallet load to a live roller conveyor take away station and replenishes the loading station with another pallet. The pallet load travels down the conveyor to an automated stretch wrapper and then on to a live roller accumulation conveyor to await pickup by an AGV.

The Four Laws of Robotics

Polaroid learned several noteworthy lessons about robots in the course of bringing the system on-line. "First, you have to think about the operation," says Donaghy, "from the robot's perspective."

In the early days of robots, Isaac Asimov proposed certain laws governing the behavior of robots. Like these staples of science fiction, today's robots also conform to certain laws. They are:

Law #1: A robot will do just what you tell it to do. That includes dropping a box on the floor or trying to place one box where another already is. "Setting up the coordinates was tricky at first," says Donaghy.

Law #2: A robot is strong. Polaroid's robot lifts 75 lb in a 9-ft reach — and comes down with as much force as it lifts up. To insure against potential product damage, Donaghy installed a special, hinged pickup on the robot's vacuum gripper. The device is designed to provide a smooth set-down every time.

Law #3: A robot is exact. Because a robot is so exact, even small inconsistencies in the interfaces will be magnified. Pallet positioning, for example, is critical. Each time a pallet is offloaded onto a loading zone in this system, a series of cylinders fire, activating a set of clamped pads. These pads orient the pallet and hold it in a precise location while the robot stacks the cartons.

Law #4: A robot is flexible. To meet changing needs and take advantage of a robot's flexibility, Donaghy stresses training both a skilled trades person and a programmer early in the project. In Donaghy's case, he skipped a robot programming class — a big mistake.

"Another mistake," Cohen says, "was underestimating the complexity of integrating the palletizing cell with our central computer." Asked if he had the chance to do it over again, Cohen says he would involve the computer group earlier in the specification stage and build in PC local control as an intermediate step. "Our schedules slipped six months," Cohen asserts, "but we're back on track now."

SOURCE: *Modern Materials Handling* (November 1989). Copyright 1989 by Cahners Publishing Division, Reed Publishing, USA.

or more loaded pallets by providing a stabilizing effect on the stack. Racks also allow removal of a pallet from within the tier without disturbing those above or below it. This is an essential feature of an operation in which pallet loads of items are picked in the selection area of a warehouse or in which items are stored on and picked from pallets in the order filling process. The pallet rack can also be used to increase the warehousing capacity of a given area by permitting the location of dissimilar products on top of each other within the pallet rack.

An important consideration in the installation of pallet racks is the flexible nature of this type of equipment. It may be necessary to alter the design and layout of the material handling operation so often that the use of detachable, knockdown, or otherwise flexible pallet and container racks may be well worth the extra expense for such equipment. A side consideration in the use of pallet racks is the rigidity that permanent pallet racks build into the material handling system in the form of either 90-degree or angular pallet placement. Slip sheet loads and pallet rack systems are somewhat incompatible in that slip sheet loads must be placed on a conventional pallet before being stored in pallet racks.

Flow Racks Flow racks are banks of short gravity conveyors designed to feed streams of items to order picking stations. In grocery distribution centers, for example, flow racks are used to position hundreds of SKUs of drug, toiletry, and sundry items so that they can be easily picked and repacked in smaller quantities for individual retail locations. Because each lane typically holds 10 to 15 cases of product and may regularly be replenished from the back, order picker productivity is improved by eliminating time spent locating, moving, or reaching for backup stocks.

Bins and Drawers Bins and drawers often are placed in frames to serve as ready containers of small or valuable items for order picking purposes. Generally, this type of equipment is used for storage purposes when the item cannot be, or is not, packaged or unitized.

Dunnage Dunnage is a term applied to all objects used to brace, steady, or otherwise protect freight being stored, handled, or transported. Horizontal dunnage, for example, may consist simply of sheets of fiberboard placed between layers of a product to tie a load together and steady it. Vertical dunnage, on the other hand, generally is used to help support the weight of products that are stacked vertically. Besides traditional timber bracing, a dunnaging technique currently used by several shippers involves inflatable rubber or plastic bags that are placed between items or groups of items to cushion impacts during transportation vehicle movement.

Automatic Storage/Retrieval (AS/R) Systems

AS/R systems vary in sophistication depending on the products and quantities involved. One of the most advanced systems installed to date was installed by a grocery wholesaling organization, and is composed of several pieces of equipment. Product arriving at the distribution center in nonpalletized form is moved by conveyor into a palletizing machine, where unit loads are constructed before being moved into a high-rise stacker crane. One or more radio-controlled robot pallet movers are used for lateral movement in conjunction with one or more stacker cranes operating on fixed tracks between facing banks of storage racks 67 feet high. When needed in the order selection areas, pallet loads are moved from this ''giant filing cabinet'' into depalletizers, from which individual cases are moved on a preprogrammed basis into order picking chutes. Electronically controlled gates on each shute disgorge cases onto a conveyor as computerized information is fed into the system for each outgoing order. Only at the point where orders comprising boxes of different shapes are consolidated is manual labor used to palletize orders for subsequent shipment by truck to retailers.

Fully automated (real-time, computer-controlled, unmanned) systems may be employed for random access handling of a large number of SKUs with a low number of pallets per SKU. Semiautomated systems (man aboard, electronically assisted) have been used effectively in deep-lane or high-density applications where handling of large pallet volumes of a few SKUs is involved.

While these systems can provide operating benefits such as improved cube utilization, lower manpower requirements, faster response time, and greater system through-put, the costs in terms of investment in facilities, hardware, and operating software are high. Not surprisingly, a significant percentage of AS/R systems installed to date have been in frozen food and refrigerated warehouses, where construction and operating costs are highest. AS/R system advantages are muted by their inherent lack of flexibility, and the need for manual backups during inevitable equipment and computer breakdowns. Benefits are also lost when through-put volume drops or fails to materialize.[13]

COMPATIBILITY WITH INTERCOMPANY HANDLING METHODS

All too often, the types of packages, pallet sizes, and materials handling systems employed by one firm in a channel of distribution are not compatible with those employed by another. Where possible, not only should the packages and unit load and their supporting system components be designed for easy accommodation in over-the-road transportation vehicles, but they should also be designed to fit in the material handling systems of suppliers and customers.

The latter can only be achieved to a limited extent in the absence of control over the planning of suppliers and customers. However, a firm exercising some degree of economic persuasion over another may be able to influence material handling system design to the mutual benefit of both firms. In any event, a complete disregard for the systems of major suppliers and customers in the design of a material handling system may unduly limit its benefits.

Many material handling systems, particularly in distribution centers, handle combinations of orders moving to several destinations in the same vehicle. To facilitate delivery, orders are placed in the vehicle in the reverse order in which they are to be unloaded. Many shippers have taken a cue from carriers and "build" a truckload or railcar load on the floor of the warehouse before the arrival of the vehicle. This (1) expedites loading, decreasing the required number of truck and rail bays and detention and demurrage charges, (2) helps insure more effective and accurate carrier delivery performance, and (3) improves customer service and carrier relations. This action can be planned only in situations in which the carriers will deliver all shipments directly from the vehicle being loaded, situations usually relevant only to short hauls and local deliveries or to private and contract carriage operations.

According to one 1979 survey, approximately 70 percent of total dry and refrigerated freight tonnage was handled manually at some point in truck dock operations in the United States.[14] About 29 percent was loaded and unloaded by unitized methods, but only 1 percent was handled by rapid turn-around methods that utilize air pressure, power chains, and floor and trailer rollers, to inject or extract unitized truck loads in a manner of minutes. Rapid turn-around methods, as just described, involve considerable costs and are likely to be limited to firms having private trucking operations handling their own goods within the firm's own internal logistics system. Common carriers typically will not make such investments unless a long-term contract with a major shipper is involved.

PRODUCT IN BULK

Up to this point, we have focused on handling packaged freight. However, perhaps the greatest logistical economies have been achieved by handling products in bulk form. Besides reducing or eliminating packaging costs, bulk movements provide economies of scale in handling and generally enjoy lower transportation rates.

The movement to bulk has been encouraged by technological advances that allow faster, more efficient handling of a wider range of products and larger volumes in bulk form. Examples of the improvements in bulk handling systems are provided by the growing acceptance and use of such transport equipment as tankers of 400,000 deadweight tons, 250,000-deadweight-ton ore carriers, and pneumatic/vacuum rail cars. Bulk materials handling advances include pneumatic loading and unloading systems for handling powered, dry bulk commodities such as cement, flour, and granulated plastic; disposable polyethylene liners for ISO standard intermodal containers; 15-stories-tall, 200-foot boom stacker and reclaimer cranes capable of handling 5,000 tons per hour, and weighing systems using advanced digital electronics.

The ability to handle massive volumes of traditional bulk commodities, such as coal, ore, and grain, continues to expand. The Santa Clara ore terminal in Gabon, West Africa, provides a spectacular example of how imaginative engineering and state-of-the-art technology can be blended together to achieve bulk movements on this scale. Iron and manganese ores arrive at the port in 130-car, 13,000 ton unit-trains on the new Trans-Gabon Railroad. An automated car indexer moves the cars through a rotary car dumper, transferring the ores to conveyors that distribute various grades to stockpiles in a 4-million-ton capacity storage yard, blending or segregating them as needed. For loading arriving vessels, a reclaiming crane feeds two belt conveyors, each equipped with automatic weighing and sampling devices, that travel along a breakwater and then a pile-supported causeway to deep-water ship loading berths located in the open sea, three to five miles from shore. There, a surge-bin-equipped, conveyor boom shiploader is capable of continuously loading the largest ore carriers afloat (up to 250,000 tons) at the rate of 10,000 tons per hour. Average vessel turn-around time is projected to be only 34 hours, 14 hours waiting and 20 hours loading.[15]

Domestically, bulk facilities with comparable handling rates and throughput capabilities are under construction. Most of these will employ unit trains and river barges or Great Lakes ships to handle Canadian and Western coal.

CONVERSION FROM PACKAGED TO BULK HANDLING

Greater operating efficiency and significant cost savings can also be achieved by switching products formerly handled in bags or drums to bulk. Hawaiian sugar, which was shipped in bags until the 1950s, provides an example of the economies involved. At the port of Sacramento, the cost of handling a ton of sugar in bulk is $.77 compared with an estimated $20 for handling the same quantity of sugar bagged.[16]

Other conversions have been even more sophisticated. At Hercafina, a joint venture between Hercules Chemical and American Petrofina, a chemical intermediate, DMT, was initially palletized and shipped in bags or drums like many other chemical and plastic compounds. However, since the product was produced and used by customers in molten form, the cooling, palletizing, and bagging by Hercafina and unbagging and remelting by customers constituted a needless and costly intermediate step in product flow. The solution, developed in conjunction with equipment manufacturers and the producer's most frequently used common carriers, uses specially designed railcars and stainless steel tank trailers designed to keep the product in the molten state at over 300 degrees while being transported. Even though customers were required to invest in special equipment to receive the molten shipments, the savings in handling and energy costs they realized more than offset this added expense.[17]

Since large capital investments and alteration of traditional product flows are involved, customer response is often a critical variable in evaluating bulk conversion plans. For example, in order to use single-trip plastic liners (costing about $150) to transform dry-freight intermodal containers into bulk carriers, shippers must acquire loading equipment costing from $14,000 to $30,000 or more depending on the commodity. However, in order to realize the handling economies that this method offers, the receiver must invest in a tilting device to empty the lined containers. Tilt chassis, tilt platforms, and similar devices range in price from

$15,000 to over $25,000. Thus shippers must employ a total system approach to planning bulk conversion programs and must effectively communicate long range savings in handling costs, lower transportation rates, and other benefits to customers if operating economies and improved customer service are to be achieved.

DETERMINING THE CONVERSION POINT FROM BULK TO PACKAGED FORM

There are strong arguments for delaying the conversion of product moving in a channel of distribution from bulk to packaged form as long as possible. This can be achieved more successfully when conversion costs are low or the volume of product moving to any one market is very high. The process required for the analysis involves an estimate of the trade-off in savings on transport and handling costs against the increasing costs of conversion from bulk to packaged form as one approaches the point of end use.

Recent developments in the handling and transportation of bulk freight have led companies and entire industries to reassess points in their logistics systems at which products are converted from bulk to packaged form. These phenomena hold the promise of obsolescence for the location and continuance of certain practices, and will provide the rationale for entirely new packaging activities in new locations.

Bucklin provides us with a useful theoretic framework for reviewing the structure of traditional distribution channels.[18] His is a further development of the principle of postponement articulated by Alderson, which holds that an organization should "... postpone changes in form and identity to the latest point in the marketing flow; postpone changes in inventory location to the latest possible points in time."[19] Bucklin later formulated the converse of this, the principle of speculation, which suggests that:

> ... changes in form, and the movement of goods to forward inventories, should be made at the earliest possible time in the marketing flow in order to reduce the costs of the marketing system.[20]

The combined principle of postponement and speculation is stated as follows: a speculative inventory will appear at each point in a distribution channel whenever its costs are less than net savings to both buyer and seller from postponement.[21] In a sense, this is the total cost concept being given interorganizational scope, a logical extension of the concept. For example, a company that inventories products only at its plant and produces many items to order may maximize postponement and minimize speculation. If, however, it loses sales by increasing speculation and making postponement difficult for customers, it may be advised to establish a market-oriented inventory. If the combined benefits of reduced speculation and increased postponement for the supplier are greater than increased costs of establishing for extra inventory, increasing speculation and reducing postponement for the supplier, then according to the theory a market-oriented inventory will be established.

Clearly, extending the transportation and handling of a product in bulk as opposed to packaged form allows a manufacturer to postpone commitment of that product to specific, possibly differentiated, and often more costly packages, thus reducing speculation at very little cost to the customer.

REVERSING THE POSTPONEMENT PRINCIPLE

Blind obedience to ''rules'' or ''principles'' is seldom a wise idea in business, and logistics management is no exception to this. There can be times when packaging early in the processing cycle as opposed to postponement by shipping in bulk may be a wise idea. The story of the lowly banana furnishes an excellent example of this type of situation.

Individual bananas come in an attractive, airtight, appealing, yellow package. It is even equipped with an easy tear strip opener. However, full stalks of bananas have no regular dimension that permits efficient use of storage and transportation cube. Too, the ultimate consumer usually purchases one or two ''hands,'' rather than a single banana or the entire stalk. Thus, we have identified two problem areas in terms of distribution costs: inefficient use of transportation and storage cube, and a shipping size which is not acceptable to the final customer.

The disposal of the stalk itself presents some interesting problems. It defies the most cunning destruction devices. It cannot economically be burned, smashed, ground, or eaten. Many city dumps refuse to accept stalks. Also, while the banana skin is easy to open, appealing, and fits the product it offers little protection from handling damage. So, stalk disposal and product damage must be added to the list of problem areas.

Previously, bananas were moved from Central America to a produce or chain warehouse where they were ripened, cut from the stalk, weighed, packed in returnable boxes, and delivered to the stores. Each stalk was moved to the seaport individually carried on and off the ship, in and out of the rail car, and in and out of the ripening rooms. The expense of these individual handlings materially reduced the profit from this low-cost fruit.[22]

The banana companies decided to do something about this. They analyzed the elements of their distribution cycle, then made a few simple, but very important changes. First, they developed a properly ventilated container into which the ''hands'' of bananas were to be packed. Then, they took the container right into the grove and cut, weighed, and packed the ''hands'' there. The boxes are designed to fit standard pallet quantities throughout the distribution cycle. The bananas are weighed only once, except for random checks by the purchasers.

The effect on the entire distribution system was dramatic!

1. The banana stalk had been eliminated from the picture.
2. The package now had uniform dimensions, resulting in better use of cube.
3. The shipping unit was now compatible with the consumer's buying habit.
4. Damage was drastically reduced. Packaging now protects the fruit from grove to produce counter.
5. Handling costs were greatly reduced by palletization.

Major alterations of vast systems invariably bring with them some new problems which must be overcome. For example, bananas on the stalk are easier to ripen than those packed in boxes. Each ripening room operator had to be taught how to stack the new boxes so the gas used in the ripening process would reach all the bananas. Also, because of spoilage problems, some strains could not be boxed at all.

One of the toughest jobs was to convince the buyers (and their bosses) that a small price increase was justified to recover the cost of cutting and packing at the grove. Usually, any increase in purchase price results in a corresponding jump in selling price. The buyers had to be assured that they were actually paying less because of the elimination of labor in the ripening rooms and reduced losses from product damage. Evidence of such savings, plus the knowledge that the customer would be offered an unblemished product were the clinchers. All resistance has now been eliminated and boxed bananas are accepted as the standard method of distribution.[23]

SUMMARY

Packaging and material handling considerations intersect at the point where packaging helps determine the way goods may be handled and the condition and manner they arrive at their destination. Among the more important aspects of package design for logistics are the protection that package provides, the marking and identification it carries, and its characteristics for storage, material handling, and transportation. These considerations must be placed in the context of sometimes conflicting needs of engineering, purchasing, production, and marketing management. In addition, important environmental trends, such as metrification, may both offer opportunities and pose problems for future package designers.

There is a wide variety of equipment available for materials handling. it includes devices for the unitization of freight such as pallets, slipsheets, tying devices, and perhaps most important of all, containers. Many types of individually powered vehicles are available to provide motive power. Storage aids such as pallet racks, flow racks, bins and drawers, and dunnage complete the basic elements of a materials handling system. In recent years, more and more of the process of receiving and storing product and picking orders from it has been automated.

Various elements of the material handling system, and the question of automation itself, must be evaluated on the basis of not only their relative economics, but the degree of flexibility they allow in the operation of the system. Based on this analysis, many firms have elected to automate only certain steps in the process.

Many of the economies of an efficient materials handling system may be lost if a firm fails to coordinate its methods with those of its suppliers and customers. In particular, standard pallet sizes, package weights, and package sizes are important to the effective coordination of materials handling methods in a channel of distribution.

Impressive achievements have been made in the handling of product in bulk in recent years. These have made it more important than ever for a firm's management to appraise that point in its channel of distribution, if ever, at which its product should be converted from bulk to packaged form. Principles of postponement and speculation have been useful in thinking about the problem.

DISCUSSION QUESTIONS

1. What is meant by a "hierarchy of containers"? What is the significance of this concept to a logistics manager?

2. What are the logistics considerations in package design?

3. What is the role of the "shipping package" and why is it the focus of interest of logistics managers?

4. What factors could enter into package design? How might their significance vary by product or circumstance?

5. How does packaging affect transportation costs? Why do carriers define packaging requirements so specifically?

6. What is meant by the term biodegradable? What does recyclable mean? What problems do these pose for the environment? What significance do they have for business firms and logistics managers?

7. How can one categorize equipment for material handling?

8. Why is a package that is a perfect cube ''bad news'' with respect to palletization?

9. What are the advantages of stretch and shrink wrapping?

10. What are the advantages of containerization. What are its limitations?

11. Under what circumstances is the use of hand-powered handling equipment (such as ''two wheelers'') advantageous as compared with powered equipment?

12. When is it necessary to use powered conveyors instead of gravity conveyors?

13. What are the advantages of using pallet racks?

14. What are flow racks and what function do they serve?

15. What are the advantages and disadvantages of Automatic Storage and Retrieval (AS/R) systems?

16. What is the relationship between bulk handling and the ''principle of postponement''?

17. What lessons can be learned from the ''banana story'' told in this chapter? *Why wasn't the present method of handling bananas adopted much earlier, especially since there were no technological barriers to doing it years earlier?*

CASE: Problems of Incompatibility

Alexandra Leavell, the manager of Megapaper Corporation's distribution center in Atlanta, Georgia, was frustrated by a pair of related nagging problems that she had thus far been unable to solve. Megapaper Corporation used 40″ × 48″ pallets in its distribution center, and the pallet racks in the center were set for that size of pallet. All but one of Megapaper's vendors used 40″ × 48″ pallets, and all but one of Megapaper's customers also used that size. These exceptions were very annoying, and worse, they were costly.

Megapaper Corporation was a very large wholesaler of office and art supplies and all grades of paper except newsprint. The company dealt with other smaller wholesalers and retail office supply and art supply chains. Most of the distribution center's inbound shipments came by motor carrier, but a few shipments, such as large shipments of copy machine paper, came by rail. All outbound shipments were made by motor carrier. Outbound pallets of varying sizes of cartons of mixed goods were shrink wrapped; pallet loads of a single product of identical cartons were not shrink wrapped.

Alexandra was a very capable manager, but she also had a bit of a temper, not unlike the heroine of the motion picture *Gone with The Wind*. Thus, she had earned the nickname ''Scarlett.'' She was exhibiting some of that temper in a discussion with the center's warehouse operations manager Ben Hardy.

"Ben, have you got any suggestions as to how we could get that vendor and that customer both to use forty by forty-eights instead of the misbegotten sizes they use? Why in the world does that fool distribution manager at Curtis use forty-two by forty-twos? Who ever heard of such dimensions?"

"I think these are two different situations, Scarlett. Curtis would not be an easy vendor to replace. Sales told me Curtis gives us high quality merchandise at very good prices, and we both know that they are very good on delivery schedules. We never run out of their stuff and we never seem to have too much of it on hand."

"What about Office Executive Company and their lousy thirty-six by thirty-sixes?"

"Scarlett, OEC is a CUSTOMER! You just can't mess with a customer! At least you shouldn't mess with one."

"Ben, our costs of warehouse handling are much higher with both Curtis and OEC on account of their incompatible pallet sizes. Both of them are out of step with the industry. And we — the center, that is — incur those rehandling costs and this hurts our cost performance, and that hurts us at bonus time. We've got to do something about this!"

"Scarlett, it really isn't too bad. Curtis picks up their pallets from us every month or so by having a truck from another Curtis corporate division come by and get them and take them back to St. Louis to the Curtis plant. OEC does the same thing to get their own pallets to us from their central warehouse in Jacksonville. So, we don't have any costs for returning or getting these oddball pallets."

"Maybe not, Ben, but they do cause us to have a lot of extra rehandling costs here in our warehouse. We have to reload Curtis' incoming goods on our forty by forty-eights to put them into storage in our pallet racks, and we have to load OEC's pallet-quantity shipments on their stupid thirty-six by thirty-sixes for shipments to them. The only time OEC isn't a costly handling problem for us is when we load one or more pallets of mixed goods for them and for that we can use their pallets as well as ours.

"And, the figures our office accountant prepared show that between them, Curtis and OEC are costing us at least $7,000 a year in extra handling costs, not to mention the wasted warehouse space and the bother of stacking up Curtis' pallets until one of their trucks eventually comes by to pick them up and the inconvenience of keeping OEC's pallets stashed around until we use some of them."

"Well now, Scarlett, I can't disagree about those handling costs. But it seems to me we're stuck between a rock and a hard place. Curtis is a first-rate vendor and OEC is a big customer. We mess with Curtis and purchasing will get all upset, and sales will be on us like a duck on a june bug if we mess with OEC."

"Ben, there's got to be something we can do about Curtis and OEC. We just haven't thought of it yet."

"Well, Scarlett, your namesake always said she'd think about a problem tomorrow."

"Forget it, Ben. We're going to think about this one today."

CASE QUESTION

1. What could be done in an attempt to solve these two problems? What would you do? Explain.

SUGGESTED READINGS

ACKERMAN, KENNETH B. "Packaging and Identification," Chapter 7 in *Practical Handbook of Warehousing*, 2d ed. (Washington, D.C.: The Traffic Service Corporation, 1986) 55–66.

COX, RALPH M., and KENNETH C. VAN TASSEL, "The Role of Packaging in Physical Distribution," Chapter 27 in James F. Robeson and Robert G. House, eds. *The Distribution Handbook*, (New York: The Free Press, A Division of Macmillan, Inc., 1985) 737–773.

HARMON, CRAIG K., and RUSS ADAMS, *Reading Between the Lines: An Introduction to Bar Code Technology*, (Peterborough, NH: Helmers Publishing, Inc., 1989).

MORSE, LEON WM. *Practical Handbook of Industrial Traffic Management*, 6th ed. (Washington, D.C.: The Traffic Service Corporation, 1980) 157–181.

Timely and informative articles concerning packaging and materials handling are to be found in virtually every issue of the following trade journals: *Modern Materials Handling* (monthly), *Transportation and Distribution* (monthly), *Distribution* (monthly), and *Grocery Distribution* (bimonthly).

ENDNOTES

1. Some of the material in this discussion is adapted from Walter F. Friedman and Jerome J. Kipnees, *Distribution Packaging*, (Huntington, New York: Frieger Publishing, 1977), Chapter 1.

2. Craig K. Harmon and Russ Adams, *Reading Between the Lines: An Introduction to Bar Code Technology* (Peterborough, NH: Helmers Publishing, Inc., 1989). This book is an excellent primer for the student or executive seeking basic knowledge and understanding of bar coding and bar code technology.

3. *Eastern Motor Express vs. A. Maschmeijer, Jr.*, 247 F.2d 826, cert. den. 78 S. Ct. 535 (1958).

4. "Pallet Interchange: Troubled Progress," *Traffic Management*, May 1978.

5. This material is based on "The Wine Industry's Report Card on Metrics," an address by Robert M. Ivie before the United States Metric Board, San Francisco, CA, August 16, 1979.

6. D. B. Carmody, "The Impact of Packaging on Physical Distribution," in *Packaging's Role in Physical Distribution*, (New York: American Management Association, 1966): 2–3. This represents a classic case of thinking through a problem, evaluating low-technology alternatives, avoidance of higher-cost solutions, and in the process achieving a superior solution to the problem. Pallet size and arrangement were the overriding considerations in this case, not the packaging of the product itself.

7. The program is a proprietary product of Professional Micro Systems, Ltd., 4001 West Green Tree Rd., Milwaukee, WI 53209.

8. For a more complete discussion of this topic, see "Know the Choices in Load Unitization," *Handling and Shipping Management*, (April 1979): 48–53.

9. As background for this section, see Chapter 3.

10. Federal Maritime Commission, *27th Annual Report* (1988): 17.

11. Harold B. Meyers, "The Maritime Industry's Expensive New Box," *Fortune* (November 1967): 151ff.

12. *Ibid.*

13. For a more detailed discussion of the advantages and disadvantages of AS/R systems see: "The Productivity Improver," *Handling & Shipping Management* (June 1979): 43–47. See also E. Ralph Sims, Jr., "Materials Handling — A Common Denominator," in James R. Robeson and Robert G. House, *The Distribution Handbook* (New York: The Free Press, 1985): 600–612. See also Kenneth B. Ackerman, Section VIII, "Handling of Materials," in *Practical Handbook of Warehousing*, 2nd ed. (Washington, D.C.: The Traffic Service Corporation, 1986): 443–528.

14. "Fast Freight Transfer — A Moveable Feast," *Handling & Shipping Management* (June 1979): 60–66.

15. "Bulk Cargo," *Marine Engineering Log* (September 1979): 45–52.

16. "Bulk Squeezes Shipping Cost," *Distribution Worldwide* (August 1979): 25.

17. *Ibid.*

18. Much of this section draws upon Louis P. Bucklin, "Postponement, Speculation, and the Structure of Distribution Channels," *Journal of Marketing Research* (January 1965): 26–31.

19. Wroe Alderson, *Marketing Behavior and Executive Action* (Homewood, Ill.: Richard D. Irwin, Inc., 1957): 424.

20. Bucklin, "Postponement," 27.

21. *Ibid.*, 28.

22. Michael O. Able, "Packaging for Total Advantages in Physical Distribution," *Handling & Shipping* (December 1965): 36.

23. *Ibid.*, 38–39.

CHAPTER ELEVEN

11

Warehousing Management

LEARNING OBJECTIVES

The objectives of this chapter are to:

➢ Explain the role of warehousing (storage) in a logistics system.

➢ Explain the differences among storage warehouses, materials-handling warehouses, combination warehouses, and specialized storage facilities.

➢ Define and explain the legal terms "field warehousing" and "bonded warehouse."

➢ Explain and discuss the use of public warehousing, including its several advantages and disadvantages.

➢ Explain and discuss the use of private warehousing, including its several advantages and disadvantages.

➢ Present and discuss the methodology for determining warehouse inside requirements, outside requirements, equipment requirements, and loading/unloading dock requirements.

➢ Present and discuss factors to be considered with respect to warehouse design, including the purpose of the facility, site selection, layout, and stock location.

➢ Discuss measures of performance, both physical and cost.

➢ Highlight and discuss other types of "warehousing," including freight terminals, container terminals, bulk commodity terminals, and carrier equipment transfer facilities.

Warehousing facilities are gathering and dispersing points where goods are added to or taken from inventory on a regular basis without any change in the *form* of the goods.* The goods may be raw materials, parts, components, semifinished goods, finished goods, repair parts, operating supplies, or any other item used or sold by a firm.

Warehousing activities may be performed in a company-owned or leased facility. Or, these tasks may be carried out by public warehousing firms specializing in such service. Additionally, the transfer facilities (for example, the terminals) of transportation companies also function as in-transit handling and storage (warehouse) facilities.

It is in warehouse and transfer facilities that most of the "grunt work" associated with the logistics function is carried out. The objectives of this chapter are to examine and discuss the several basic types of warehousing and transfer facilities and to assess the managerial tasks associated with their operation.

CHARACTERISTICS OF WAREHOUSING OPERATIONS

From the point of view of logistics management, there are four significant bases for the classification of a warehouse operation, and all must be included in order to describe the operation completely. They are (1) its role in the logistics system, (2) the commodities it handles, (3) whether it is privately or publicly operated, and (4) its legal status.

Role in the Logistics System

Warehousing facilities may be used for the storage of materials awaiting processing or manufacture, the holding of finished products at a manufacturing site or at some point intermediate to plants and markets, or the holding of finished goods near their points of sale in support of a customer service policy. At the most basic level of operational classification a warehouse is operated primarily as a storage facility or a materials-handling facility.

Storage Warehouses The primary use of storage warehouses occurs in relation to, and usually in advance of, various production processes. It is unusual for finished goods in condition to be delivered to customers of a firm to be stored for any length of time. This may occur, however, in situations where the firm has, for one reason or another, produced or purchased an extremely large amount of a particular product at one time and must store some portion of this amount for later sale or use. Examples are industries in which production is seasonal but sales are not, where sales are seasonal but production is not, where both production and sales are seasonal at times that do not coincide, or where large quantities of product are purchased on a speculative basis to take advantage of favorable prices or anticipated shortages.

Storage warehouses may be located at any point in a logistics system, but usually have some type of strong locational relationship to production facilities. Operations of storage warehouses are all closely related to problems of demand-supply coordination. Industries with seasonal supply or demand patterns frequently use storage warehouses to level out production activities. Storage warehousing is used for maturing, ripening, or aging products of various kinds, such as tobacco, cheese, and wine. Other uses include stockpiling strategic materials,

---

*In some warehouses "change in form" activities *are* carried out, such as simple product assembly, adding or removing one or more components in order to "customize" a product, converting bulk quantities into market-size packages, and so on. Obviously, these are not warehousing activities, so one may say that where such activities are carried out, the facility houses both warehousing and (light) manufacturing activities.

supplies resulting from speculative purchasing decisions, or materials accumulated in anticipation of possible labor disputes, inclement weather, or cyclical production patterns. A typical layout of a storage warehouse is shown in Figure 11–1.

Materials Handling Warehouses The major mission of a materials handling warehouse is to receive, hold (temporarily), assemble, mix, and segment quantities of goods for outbound shipment.

Assembly warehouses are often used by firms purchasing large quantities of processed agricultural goods from a large number of sources spread over a wide region. They also may be used by industrial firms and marketing institutions that normally purchase a great quantity or wide variety of goods from suppliers in a particular region.

Distribution warehouses, sometimes referred to as market warehouses, are used for the mixing and transshipment of carload and truckload shipments moving from one or more producing points to a number of destinations.

FIGURE 11–1: Layout of a typical storage warehouse

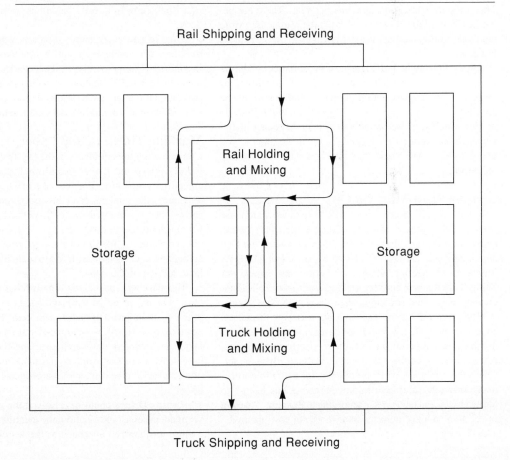

BEHIND THE MAGIC KINGDOM

E. J. Muller

This past summer, as in previous summers, millions of people streamed into Disneyland, the self-proclaimed "Happiest Place on Earth." Not a single one of them, it's safe to assume, wondered how every retail shop and fast food stand kept their shelves fully stocked. You just don't think about such things in The Magic Kingdom.

But in the Disneyland warehouse, that's all they think about. How to supply "The Show." That's the workers' term for the almost non-stop carnival of attractions that is America's premier tourist destination. The main warehouse, 128,000 nondescript square feet nudging the back of Fantasyland, supplies all the retail merchandise and much of the foodstuffs that are ravenously consumed within the park. That's about 20 million line items per year. There are between 150 and 180 deliveries per day at the warehouse. More than one million cartons of merchandise crossed the docks last year.

On a single night at the height of the summer crush, the warehouse staff must deliver up to 2,500 line items to as many as 110 locations within the park. And it must all be done between 1 and 7 A.M., when the park is closed. They do it, quite frankly, with a warehouse system that is very labor intensive and very old-fashioned. Most of the money, you see, goes into "The Show," not into The Show's warehousing needs.

And the Show Must Go On

"We are a totally reactive operation," explained warehouse manager Milo Rainey, who has worked in the Disney warehouse since the park first opened. When we visited the Disney warehouse last year as part of a Council of Logistics Management meeting, Rainey and warehouse supervisor Philip Schmitz were actively seeking input from colleagues on ways they could streamline their distribution operation.

The issue for Rainey and his staff was how to make a contribution to efficiency and cost savings without ever having the time to regroup and institute more effective systems. At the time, bar coding was being considered. Because service is the warehouse's highest priority, the usual solution to many inventory and distribution problems has been "to throw money and labor at it," according to Schmitz. "We are forced to do a lot of things we know are not cost-justified," adds Rainey.

Retail outlets in the park reorder through a centralized department at Disney Studios which handles all order entry and purchasing. The decision by Disney Studios to buy the majority of its apparel and plush items in Korea, rather than North Carolina, as it used to, has put extra pressure on the warehouse, which must contend with more inventory and fewer deliveries.

On average, the warehouse has about 60 employees working at any given time. The number swells to around 140 at peak periods. Estimating the proper staffing levels is the most difficult aspect of the warehouse operation, according to Schmitz. It's a major concern for a top-dollar, all-union shop like Disney. "We are totally dependent on other people for determining our workload," said Schmitz. "If we had adequate lead time going into the heavy season we'd be all right, but we're frequently behind as soon as stuff hits the dock."

"We've had emergency situations where people were back here demanding their stuff before we could even get it inventoried," Schmitz related. This can lead to a "negative quantity on hand" situation, in which items get out to the park, are purchased and reordered before they've even been entered into the warehouse's data management system.

Marking Time . . . and Labor

Compounding the bottleneck is the fact that all merchandise must be priced and marked in uniform fashion before it even enters the warehouse. For the sake of Disneyland's idyllic ambiance, the retailers can't just price merchandise themselves once it's in the stores. "Something you purchase in Frontierland has to cost the same in Tomorrowland," explained Rainey. "We can't have it looking like retailers are competing with each other. It has to seem like it's all Disneyland, all part of The Show."

The marking process is extremely labor intensive. Goods have to be unpacked, unwrapped, and price stickers applied in the most unobtrusive place on an item. Because the merchandise is so varied, no automated system can handle it. So merchandise enters the warehouse, and the inventory data base, only as fast as workers can mark and move it. This often creates a huge backup of merchandise on the receiving docks.

Perhaps Disney could have solved the problem with investment in some type of automatic identification system and a more mechanized approach to the warehouse. But with most of the money allocated to the park going to operations and maintenance, it was people power, not technology, that had to get the job done.

And what if Disney decides to raise the price of a particular item? "Re-marking," sighed Rainey, indicating that this was obviously the biggest boondoggle in the warehouse operation. Merchandise has to be collected from the park, again funneled through the marking system, and redistributed. Manually. Fast. There is no slick system, just long hours and manual labor. Very expensive. Last year Rainey's staff spent an incredible 17,000 man-hours re-marking merchandise.

Rainey attempted to set performance standards for the markers, but the merchandise mix was so varied that it was impossible to determine realistic goals for how many items a marker should be able to process in an hour.

Attempt at Auto ID

A year ago, Rainey talked enthusiastically about getting bar coding, real time inventory and item tracking systems into the warehouse. He especially wanted to bar code the marking process to speed up the product flow. Yet he was incredibly frustrated at how difficult it was to actually find companies in the Southern California area that could demonstrate the successes and failures they had had with auto ID technology. "It all seems to be lip service so far," he told us. "We even considered radio frequency, but we couldn't find anybody that had done anything with it."

Now, a year later, some bar coding has made its way into the warehouse. Ironically, however, it is being done for three new Disney stores in Southern California and San Francisco. These retail outlets, the latest branches of the Disney empire, are supplied by the warehouse in addition to its daily task of stocking the park. It uses a stand alone bar coding system, in no way connected to park operations. The warehouse charges the retail outlets for the service.

Milo Rainey had been hoping to bring in a bar code expert last year that would "turn on the whole company in one shot." That turned out to be Craig Harmon, the well-known Auto ID expert from QED Systems in Cedar Rapids, Iowa. According to warehouse staffers who contracted bar code fever, it wasn't contagious.

"What he was talking about went over the heads of most of the people in Park Operations," related Steve Hill, warehouse supervisor. "Everybody in the warehouse thought it was great, but the people in the park just didn't get it." The lack of consensus enthusiasm has prevented any significant changes in the marking process. Hill wonders if even bar coding could solve the Disney warehouse's particular bottleneck: "One way or the other, you still have to apply the ticket manually. It will always be a lot of work and take a lot of time."

A Frantic Graveyard Shift

Delivery of merchandise presents another problem peculiar to Disneyland. Replenishing small stockrooms within the park must be done in the graveyard shift, because no delivery people are allowed on the grounds during operating hours. It's another aspect of The Show — preservation of the fantasy. Reorders by magic.

"We think of it as our own version of Just-in-Time," laughed Rainey. "Same day delivery. We pick around the clock, sometimes 24 hours straight." The goods are stacked on carts outside the warehouse and, when the carts are full, the whole lot is wrapped in cellophane for the ride into the park. It's exactly like a *kanban* train in a manufacturing plant. However much merchandise is accumulated, it's the third shift of the day, from 11:15 P.M. to 7:15 A.M., that has to make sure it's all delivered. Again, it's a very labor intensive and very expensive way of doing business.

"We get the job done," said Rainey, "even if it's not the optimum way of doing things." When Disneyworld was built, Rainey pointed out, designers took a good look at some of the things in the original park that needed improvement. One of the first decisions they made was to construct a network of tunnels beneath the new park, so that shops and restaurants could be serviced, invisibly, at any time.

"If we had the luxury of delayed picks and larger stock locations in the park, things would be a lot easier," said Rainey. "But this isn't a Thrifty Drug store, it's Disneyland."

SOURCE: *Distribution* (January 1988): 62–64. Reprinted by permission of Chilton Company.

As shown in Figure 11–2, the principal activities carried on in a material handling warehouse are receiving, holding or storing, consolidation, selecting or order picking, and shipping.

The dominant characteristic of an assembly or distribution warehouse is movement. As the diagram in Figure 11–2 indicates, there is likely to be limited space for semipermanent storage in a material handling warehouse. Both carload and truckload shipments commonly are found entering and leaving the same facility. When located between a supply area and a

FIGURE 11–2: Layout of a typical material-handling warehouse

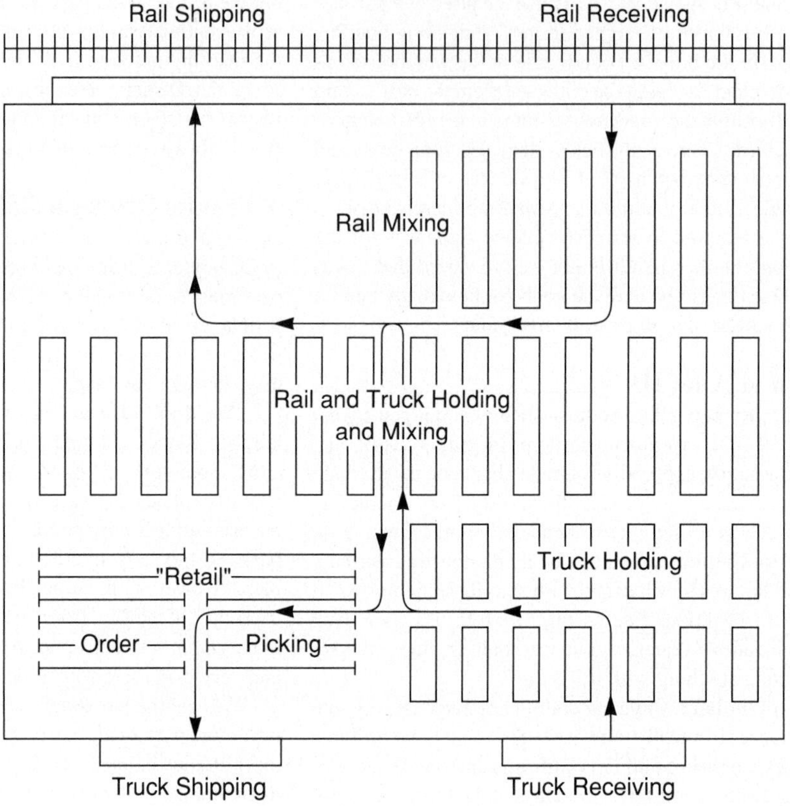

production point or between a production point and a market, a material handling warehouse serves primarily as a storage-in-transit or mixing point. This type of warehouse is operated both by carriers and shippers to provide better service to industrial and trade customers or to take advantage of volume transportation rates.

Distribution warehouses are used to maintain and adjust finished product inventories in the day-to-day coordination of demand requirements and the movement to ultimate customers. Functionally, the distribution warehouse is very different from the storage warehouse, and it must be designed somewhat differently to meet different operational requirements.

The distribution warehouse, often called a distribution center or DC, is characterized by the rapidity with which goods flow through it. Many goods are actually ''stored'' less than a day within its walls. For example, this is often the case in the operation of receiving and marking departments in retail stores. A distribution warehouse therefore will require more in the way of flexible and high-speed material handling equipment and facilities than will a storage warehouse. It follows that, unless the facility is highly mechanized, there will ordinarily be more employees in a distribution warehouse operation than in one primarily designed for storage for a given level of inventory on hand.

Consolidation is a term used to describe the use of a warehouse as a gathering point to achieve lower cost for outbound freight charges to the ultimate destination. Selection, on the other hand, refers to break-bulk operations where incoming vehicle loads are broken down for subsequent reshipment in smaller quantities.

Sale-site warehousing is a term used to describe the holding of goods next to the point of sale. It includes such operations as department store receiving and marking departments, the "back rooms" of supermarkets, ceiling-rack storage of new tires at automobile service stations, and similar other near-to-customer inventory holding points.

Combination Warehouses There is no sharp dividing line between the material handling operations and the storage operations of warehouses; a warehouse may serve as both a storage and a distribution facility. Many, whether plant-oriented warehouses or regional or national distribution centers, are designed to accommodate both types of activity.

For example, a dairy food distributor may utilize a portion of the warehouse for the aging of cheese (storage) and utilize the remainder of the warehouse for maintaining an inventory of products ready for shipment to customers (distribution). In this case, the portion of the warehouse used for distribution will be characterized by easily accessible inventory locations to allow rapid picking and packing in the filling of customer orders and specialized material handling equipment for rapid movement and accumulation of customer orders in preparation for shipment.

In addition, storage and material handling frequently are combined with operations such as the conversion of bulk commodities into packaged stock price marking and labeling. An example of this type of warehouse is shown in Figure 11–3, a diagram of the layout of the warehouse operated by a manufacturer of metal fasteners.

Specialized Storage Facilities The term "warehousing" includes a wide range of activities and facilities. We have summarized the nature of the activities, but it is important to note that an enclosed building is only one of many types of facilities used in warehousing. Tank farms, underground caverns, semienclosed sheds or bunkers, and even open storage piles are used to "warehouse" various commodities. Material handling and combination warehousing are likely to take place primarily in enclosed structures; storage warehousing utilizes all types of facilities. There are additional facility contrasts as well. Material handling and combination warehousing are typified by lateral movement, often carried out in a one-story structure with mechanized material handling techniques. In contrast, storage warehouses may be multistoried facilities, requiring less flexible and less rapid methods for handling materials.

Commodities Handled

A warehouse may be designed to handle frozen products that must be kept at a temperature of 5 degrees above zero, or "cooled" items, such as fresh fruit, at 40 degrees above zero. There also are many types of specialized bulk storage facilities for such commodities as grain (elevators), oil (tank farms), aging wine (steel-lined or redwood tanks), and many others. Coal frequently is stored in the open in very large piles; this is, in effect, "outside warehousing." Some warehouse facilities are specially designed and operated for the storage of household goods. The variety of possible examples is nearly limitless.

FIGURE 11–3: Layout of a warehouse combining volume storage and material-handling activities with picking activities. In this facility packaged goods are stocked on shelves and grouped according to kind. A powered conveyor moves orders, as they are picked, from stock to final packing for shipment. The powered conveyor, with unpowered switch-off rails at each stock section, loops through the stock area. Reserve shelves replenish stock shelves and are refilled when a minimum level is reached. Computerized information captured from customers' orders signals for warehouse stock replenishment when bulk storage gets low (for example, when it reaches a reorder point).

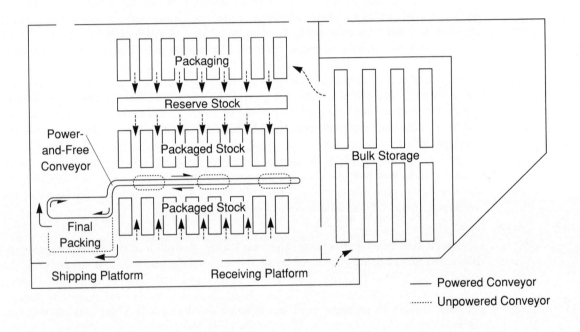

Private and Public Warehousing

Warehouse facilities operated by and owned or leased by a company handling its own goods are classified as *private* warehouse facilities. These contrast with *public warehousing* operated by a public warehousing firm to provide storage and handling facilities to the public for hire on an as-needed basis.

Leased private facilities and public warehouse facilities together form a classification characterized as "rented" in contrast to user-owned facilities. This may be a very important consideration, because a company's capital is not tied up when it leases warehousing space or uses public warehouse facilities, whereas a substantial amount of invested capital may be required to acquire ownership of warehouse facilities. An excellent study of the financial evaluation of warehouse ownership/operation options has been prepared by the Warehousing Education and Research Council.[1] The full range of possible alternatives is shown in Figure 11–4.

FIGURE 11–4: Warehousing ownership/operation matrix

The matrix shows all the possible combinations of warehouse "ownership" and "operations" alternatives. Consider, for example, the first cell in the lower left corner: "Own-Public". Here, the company owns the facility, but the warehouse is operated by a public warehousing company.

The numbers in the cells of the matrix indicate the number of companies in the sample who preferred that particular combination of ownership/operation. The numbers in the margins of the matrix show the total number of firms that prefer that particular ownership option or operation option. For example, eight (8) firms prefer to lease the facility, and of the eight, six (6) privately operate the facility and two have public/contract warehouse companies operate the leased facility.

Operation	OWN (6)	Combination OWN/LEASE (4)	LEASE (8)	3RD PARTY (3)	MIX: ALL TYPES (10)
MIX: ALL TYPES (10)					10
PRIVATE (16)	6	4	6		
CONTRACT					
Combination PUBLIC/ CONTRACT (5)			2	3	
PUBLIC					

Facility Ownership

SOURCE: *The Financial Evaluation of Warehousing Options: An Examination and Appraisal of Contemporary Practices*. The Warehousing Research Center, Warehousing Education and Research Council (Oak Brook, Illinois, 1988) 16.

Legal Status

A warehouse facility may have a special legal status for the purpose of legally securing custody of goods for which money is owed, or goods that are serving as collateral for a loan, or goods on which taxes or import duties are yet to be paid. Facilities having such special legal status include field warehouses and bonded warehouses.

The term "field warehouse" refers to the legal status of a warehouse rather than to any physical aspect or location of such a facility. It describes a situation in which the goods or materials stored are under the actual supervision of a designated public warehouse worker legally responsible for their custody. When a company's goods are stored in its own or a leased facility, all or part of which has been designated as a "field warehouse," the public warehouse worker, in accordance with the provisions of the Uniform Commercial Code, may issue a "warehouse receipt" for the goods. This receipt, which may be either negotiable or nonnegotiable, can be used by the owner of the goods as an instrument of credit for the purpose of obtaining loans on the goods so stored.[2]

The term "bonded warehouse" is applied to both public and private warehouse facilities in which goods are stored under bonding arrangements made with the government. Goods cannot be removed from such warehouses until the required taxes or duties have been paid on them, unless they are being moved to another bonded warehouse by a bonded common carrier. The result is that the owner of the goods need not tie up funds in paid duties or taxes until such time as goods are removed from the bonded warehouse for sale or other disposition.

It is possible for goods to be stored in a bonded warehouse and also to be field-warehoused in the same facility.

THE PUBLIC WAREHOUSING INDUSTRY

The public warehousing industry is composed of small and medium size companies, with no dominant firm. The largest firm in the industry in 1980 operated perhaps 15 million square feet of space in about 60 cities, or about 5 percent of general warehouse space, and no more than 2 percent of all types of public warehousing space in the United States.

Public warehousing businesses were categorized by the 1982 Census of Business in four ways: farm products, refrigerated goods, household goods, and all other (mostly general) goods. General goods warehousing and refrigerated warehousing dominate the industry as shown in Table 11–1.

There has been a dramatic shift in the proportion of public warehousing revenues received by the household goods and general goods sectors. The reason may be that many more firms dealing in general goods are making use of public warehousing. There has also been a significant increase in the sector size of refrigerated goods public warehousing, which reflects the growing use of frozen foods in the economy. The numbers of public warehouses, their receipts (revenues), and numbers of employees in 1982 are shown in Table 11–2.

Most public warehouse businesses serve limited geographic areas. According to a 1970 McKinsey and Company survey of 120 larger firms in the industry, over 80 percent of general goods public warehouse companies did business in only one city. However, that picture has changed markedly over the past 20 years due to two trends in the industry: (1) the growth of public warehouse chains under common ownership and (2) the formation of groups of "cooperating" or "associated" public warehouses not under common ownership. These trends are

TABLE 11–1: Proportion of Total Public Warehousing Revenues, by Industry Sector, 1967 and 1982

Category of Operation		Proportion of Total Revenue in 1967	Proportion of Total Revenue in 1982
Farm products		12.3%	4.4%
Refrigerated goods	14.1 }	20.0	26.7[a]
Food lockers	5.9 }		
Household goods		39.6	5.3
General goods	23.4 }	28.1	52.0[b]
Special warehousing	4.7 }		
		100.0%	100.0%

[a]The 1982 Census of Business combined the data for refrigerated goods warehousing and food lockers.
[b]The 1982 Census of Business combined the data for general goods and special warehousing.
SOURCE: U.S. Department of Commerce, 1967 and 1982 Censuses of Business, Industry Series, Public Warehousing.

TABLE 11–2: U.S. Public Warehousing Industry, 1982: Number of Establishments, Gross Receipts, and Number of Employees

	Number of Establishments	Gross Receipts ($1,000s)	Number of Employees
United States totals	5,148	$3,033,794	61,729
Farm products[a]	723	486,078	10,296
Refrigerated[b]	1,014	811,135	14,434
Household goods[c]	748	160,353	3,414
General warehousing[d]	2,665	1,576,228	33,585

[a]Establishments primarily engaged in the storage of farm products. Does not include refrigerated warehousing.
[b]Includes rented food locker space.
[c]Establishments primarily engaged in the storage of household goods but not engaged in local trucking.
[d]Includes special warehousing other than farm, refrigerated, or household goods.
SOURCE: U.S. Department of Commerce, 1982 Census of Business, Industry Series, Public Warehousing.

likely to continue as more firms make use of extensive third-party warehouse relationships, as discussed later in this chapter.

In contrast to its public warehousing data base, the Bureau of the Census has published information about private warehousing only in conjunction with wholesale trade data. In total, wholesalers reported the use of over one billion square feet of space in 1977, of which about two-thirds was in single-story buildings. Merchant wholesalers, who provide a full range of services including the holding of inventory, were by far the largest users of warehouse space.

Because of the relative importance of public warehousing services in the logistics strategies of some firms, it is useful to look at the structure of costs, rates, services, and regulation experienced by the industry.

FIGURE 11–5: The cost structure of public warehousing operations

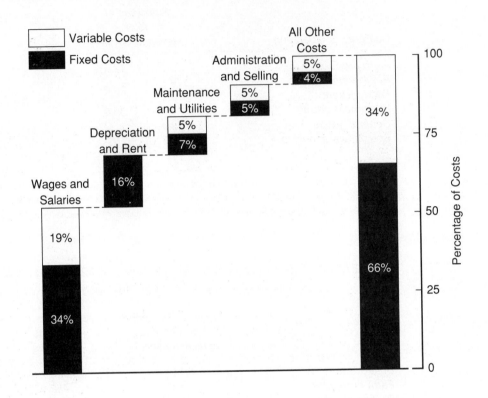

SOURCE: McKinsey & Co., Inc.; survey of public warehousing industry conducted in 1970.

Costs

Roughly two-thirds of all costs of public warehouse operations are thought to be fixed, at least over the short term. Important elements of these fixed costs, as shown in Figure 11–5, include a significant proportion of wages and salaries, all depreciation and rent, and lesser amounts of maintenance and utilities as well as administration and selling. The data in Figure 11–5 are industry averages. One would expect, for example, that facility costs (depreciation or rent, electricity, and so on) would be a greater percentage of costs in the case of a frozen foods warehouse than in the case of a general goods warehouse.

Differences in the fixed versus variable cost structure for major types of services, such as storage, handling, and office services, are great. For example, nearly all costs of storage (depreciation, taxes, insurance, and so forth) are fixed, while significant elements of handling and office services are variable in nature.

Rates and Services

Rates are prices charged by public warehouses for the performance of specified functions or services. Unlike common and contract transportation carriers, public warehouse firms have encountered little rate regulation over the years. However, they are not exempt from antitrust laws in the pricing of their services.

Costs can be allocated in various ways to basic warehousing activities of storage and handling, even by close competitors handling the same product. Costs can also vary for operators in various communities. Further, with such a high proportion of relatively fixed costs in the price structure, the public warehouse worker's performance varies significantly and directly with the proportion of capacity utilized.

Generally, public warehousing charges are based on rates for each of the following categories: storage, handling, and a variety of special services. The latter include rates for services such as preparation of bills of lading, repairing or recoopering cartons and barrels, making cash collections from customers, handling returned deliveries, processing small lot receipts or withdrawals, and setting up "will call" shipments.

Factors of greatest importance in the pricing of basic public warehousing services for a specific commodity and customer are:

1. The cubic dimensions per case, pallet, or other unit of the product;

2. Whether the product will be palletized (allowing a number of cases or packages to be handled as a unit);

3. The height to which the product can be stacked;

4. The square footage under the stack that the product will require;

5. The rate at which the product will move through the warehouse during a given period of time;

6. Special handling, packaging, or other requirements associated with the product.

On the basis of this and other information that the shipper often is asked to provide, the square footage, cubic footage, and handling rate and labor that a given type of product will require can be estimated.

Storage rates typically are assessed on the basis of square feet, cubic feet, weight, or number of units of product. The rate assessed may also vary with the value, fragility, or degree of hazard represented by the product in question. Time storage charges are assessed in many different ways, but most of the differences are matters of detail inasmuch as nearly all methods of assessment are based on periods of a month or half-month. The following provisions, quoted from a Minnesota public warehousing tariff, are reasonably typical of industry practice:

Storage Period and Charges
(a) All charges for storage are per package or other agreed unit per month.
(b) Storage charges become applicable upon the date that warehouseman accepts care, custody and control of the goods, regardless of unloading date or date of issue of warehouse receipt.
(c) Except as provided in paragraph (d) of this section, a full month's storage charge will apply on all goods received between the first and 15th, inclusive, of a calendar month; one-half month's storage charge will apply on all goods received between the 16th and last day of a calendar month, and a full month's storage charge will apply to all goods in

storage the first day of storage for the initial month and thereafter on the first day of the calendar month.

(d) When mutually agreed by the warehouseman and the depositor, a storage month shall extend from a date in one calendar month to, but not including, the same date the next and all succeeding months. All storage charges are due and payable on the first day of the storage month.[3]

"Space rental" rates provide for a specified amount of space to be set aside for the exclusive storage of the renter's goods. These rates are assessed on a square footage basis and are charged even if the space is not fully utilized.

The application of standard costs (including an allowance for profit) to estimated storage and handling volumes will produce a price per case or price per pallet for such services. Such standards will, of course, vary with time and location.

Handling rates too are usually based on the volume, weight, or number of units (often cases) of goods handled. Specialized handling may be quoted as a special rate or on the basis of a man-hour charge.

What do these factors suggest about the range of prices that you, as a logistics manager for your firm, might expect to encounter in purchasing public warehousing services? As you might expect, it can be large. The experience of a manufacturer of low-density paper products is summarized in Table 11–3. Here we see that storage costs, in cents per case per month, were

TABLE 11–3: Public Warehousing Charges a Paper Products Manufacturer Would Expect to Pay at Various Locations

Warehouse Location	Case per Month[a]	Handling In, in Cents per Case[b]	Handling Out, in Cents per Case[b]	Preparation of Bill of Lading[c]	Annual Charge for a Standard Set of Services[d]
Pittsburgh, PA[a]	$.45	$.36	$.36	$1.50	$10,020
New Orleans, LA[a]	.30	.36	.51	1.05	9,030
Kansas City, KS[a]	.282	.435	.45	1.50	9,000
Dallas, TX	.27	.405	.405	1.50	8,400
Chicago, IL[a]	.30	.36	.36	2.10	8,340
Charlotte, NC[a]	.198	.24	.66	1.35	8,040
Atlanta, GA[a]	.303	.324	.324	1.35	7,770
Worcester, MA	.27	.42	.27	1.50	7,680
Bayonne, NJ[a]	.30	.30	.30	1.50	7,500
Milwaukee, WI	.255	.33	.33	1.05	7,230
Denver, CO[a]	.18	.21	.57	1.20	7,080
Des Moines, IA[a]	.24	.33	.30	1.50	6,960
Syracuse, NY	.27	.33	.27	1.20	6,720
Minneapolis, MN	.09	.45	.45	1.05	6,690
Pennsauken, NJ[a]	.18	.285	.285	2.25	6,030

[a]Designates warehouses that assess one-half month versus full month charges on cases in inventory 15 days or less.

[b]Rates assume that shipments in and out exceed minimum quantities established by some warehouses.

[c]For shipments outbound from the warehouse.

[d]Charges shown are based on the assumption of a 6,000-case throughput with an average inventory of 1,000 cases and an average shipment size out of 30 cases (1,000 pounds).

five times as high in the Pittsburgh public warehouse as in the Minneapolis warehouse used by this manufacturer. Handling costs, on the other hand, were higher in Minneapolis. The overall bill in Pittsburgh for a standard set of services under these pricing arrangements would be about 50 percent higher than in Minneapolis.

In addition to handling and storage charges, a wide variety of accessorial charges for special services may make up a smaller proportion of the total public warehousing bill.

Regulation

The public warehousing industry is regulated primarily by the Uniform Commercial Code (UCC). The UCC defines the legal relationship between public warehousing firms and their customers; it also specifies the procedures to be followed by public warehousing firms in contracting with their customers. There is no federal economic regulation of public warehousing; rather, the UCC has been adopted as state law by every state except Louisiana, which has passed generally equivalent legislation in this area. However, one state, Minnesota, does require that the tariffs of public warehousing firms be filed with the state, and a competing public warehousing firm has the right to protest a tariff if the filed rates are so low as to appear predatory to the competitor.

Private warehousing is subject to state and local municipality laws concerning such matters as zoning, safety, and pollution. Laws administered by federal agencies may be applied to the storage of food and drugs, whether stored in private or public warehouses. In one landmark case involving allegations that a food retailing chain failed to correct conditions that contributed to infestation of the food stored in its warehouse, one senior executive of the firm was sentenced to jail.

MANAGING WAREHOUSING ACTIVITIES

Along with traffic and transportation, warehousing is the function that logistics management controls most often in the majority of organizations. Table 11–4 shows the relative importance of warehousing costs in selected industries.

TABLE 11–4: Warehousing Costs as a Percent of Sales and Total Distribution Costs by Selected Manufacturing Industry Groups, 1975

Warehousing Cost as:	Industry Groups						
	Pharmaceuticals, Medical, Health	*Consumer Durables*	*Chemicals, Plastics, Glass*	*Consumer Nondurables*	*Food and Kindred Products*	*Industrial Nondurables*	*Total*
Percent of sales	*1.4*	*2.1*	*1.1*	*1.6*	*1.9*	*1.7*	*1.9*
Percent of distribution costs	*25*	*23*	*12*	*16*	*19*	*14*	*19*

SOURCE: Herbert W. Davis, "Physical Distribution Costs: A Current Look at Performance in Selected Industries," in *Proceedings, 1979 Annual Conference*, (Chicago: National Council of Physical Distribution Management, 1979) 1–13.

Although logistics costs vary by industry and from firm to firm within an industry, Table 11–4 suggests that warehousing costs are a significant element in the physical distribution cost structure of most firms. Translated into dollars, it is estimated that about $33 billion was spent on warehousing activities in 1982.

PUBLIC OR PRIVATE WAREHOUSING?

A firm has four basic warehousing alternatives. It may own *or* lease private facilities, or it may use public facilities on a short-term *or* long-term contract basis. In order to make an informed choice, a firm must evaluate each option in terms of its operating needs and its financial policies and capabilities.

Except for financial considerations, especially those having to do with corporate income tax considerations and the timing of cash flows, leased and owned facilities have much in common and may be grouped in the category of private warehousing. Contract warehousing differs from traditional public warehousing in that services are provided on an extended term basis instead of month to month. Also, since a longer commitment is involved, more supplementary services, such as packaging and assembly, often are included in addition to the usual storage and handling activities.

The important distinction for logistics management is between public and private warehousing. However, since most firms are confronted with varied and changing sets of conditions, public and private warehousing should *not* be viewed as mutually exclusive choices.

Managerial Considerations: Private versus Public Warehousing

Private Warehousing Particular advantages to the user of private warehousing include (1) the flexibility to design and implement specialized or unique operations not generally available from public warehouses; (2) greater direct control of warehousing operations and response time in filling customer orders; (3) housing of local sales, purchasing, or customer service offices; (4) lower per-unit costs in situations where there is a large, constant flow of product or need for space; and (5) possible financial advantages in the case of owned facilities.

The construction, purchase, or lease of private warehousing offers a firm advantages comparable to the operation of privately-owned or leased transportation equipment. First, private warehousing allows greater design flexibility to meet the specific needs of the owner. This is especially important if storage of a firm's products involves special needs, such as temperature control, provision for handling delicate or fragile products, handling and storage of very large items, or other requirements not likely to be provided by public warehouses.

Second, private warehousing may provide a firm with greater control over its activities, enhancing management's ability to conduct operations in the most efficient manner while ensuring that customer service standards are maintained. Private warehousing also facilitates control over the flow of information, giving the organization that closely monitors its operations earlier indications of changes in warehousing costs and market, product, and customer trends.

Owned or leased warehousing may also be advantageous if the facility also is used to house local sales, purchasing, or customer service offices. However, the location of sales, technical service, or other activities at warehouse locations may, in some instances create supervisory and organizational problems (Who's in charge?) that offset any savings that may be achieved by combining these activities.

Generally, larger warehouses can provide greater economies of scale in operations. If a product moves through at a constant high volume, per-unit handling costs are lower. In addition, high volumes provide: (1) a greater opportunity to take advantage of lower, vehicle-load transportation rates; (2) a larger operating base for amortizing capital investments required to mechanize and automate material-handling functions; and (3) a data base large enough to justify installation of more sophisticated and responsive stand-alone mini-computer or distributed data processing systems. Having a few large warehouses instead of many smaller ones will also result in having fewer links in the chain, which will reduce the need for costly data and communication linkages between regional facilities and main offices.

However, beyond a certain point, diseconomies of scale begin to occur. If a facility is too large, internal transit times create operational problems, including difficulties in maintaining effective supervision and internal communication. Also, if the market area served by the warehouse becomes overextended, per-unit outbound transportation costs may exceed the saving in warehouse costs traded for it, and customer service may suffer.

There may also be financial advantages associated with ownership of warehouse facilities. These include cash flow from depreciation, possible long-term appreciation in property value, possible local real estate tax benefits granted to firms investing in the community or state, and so on. The extent to which any of the foregoing might be realized, and their value to a firm, will depend on the circumstances of a particular situation.

Yet, despite the many advantages of private warehousing just discussed, logistically "leading edge"—the most progressive—firms anticipate increasing use of public warehousing as contrasted with less progressive firms.[4] This is likely accounted for by two factors: (1) the flexibility of public warehousing arrangements and (2) the desire of these progressive firms to concentrate their efforts on manufacturing.

Public Warehousing Public warehousing offers space and services on a "for-hire, as needed" basis for industrial and commercial firms in need of storage, collection, and distribution services and facilities. In addition to performing the basic functions of storage and handling, public warehouses offer many services, as indicated in Table 11–5.

The most important feature of public warehousing is that the cost per unit of goods handled varies with the volume of business done by the user. Other important advantages are that public warehousing (1) may be used to accommodate peak needs; (2) can be obtained in hundreds of locations, perhaps on a basis that reflects changing costs, transportation rate patterns, and other factors placing a premium on the flexibility of a user's operations; (3) can provide specialized storage and handling facilities on a short-term basis; (4) in some states offers preferential property tax treatment in comparison with goods stored in privately owned warehouse space; and (5) provides a more definitive documentation of warehousing costs than the operation of owned space. As a result, public warehousing occupies an important position in the logistics systems of many companies.

The services of the public warehouse worker in the warehousing industry are somewhat comparable to those of the common carrier in the transportation industries. Although not required by law to serve all comers, the public warehouseman does provide space and services to a great variety of customers to meet a wide range of user needs.

TABLE 11–5: Public Warehousing Services Offered by 120 Larger Public Warehousing Companies

Service	Proportion of Firms Surveyed Offering Service
Inventory records	100%
Warehouse receipts	100
Storage	100
Break bulk handling	100
Marking and tagging	100
Over, short, damage reports	93
Prepaying freight (on behalf of warehouse users)	88
Local pickup and delivery	72
Accredited customer lists (for credit and other purposes)	72
Recoopering and repairing (for broken and damaged packages)	68
Packaging	52
Field warehousing	32
Make bulk handling	28
Loans on goods in storage	23

SOURCE: McKinsey & Co., Inc. survey of public warehousing industry conducted in 1970. Authors' comments are in parentheses.

Public warehousing does not require any investment in facilities and equipment by the customer. In addition, operating responsibilities assumed by public warehouse operators free executive talent for other activities. Public warehouse operators deal with the problems of labor, insurance, equipment selection and operation, safety, sanitation, security, and other matters related to warehouse design and operation.

When the volume of a firm's operations is low, or the level of operations fluctuates widely, per-unit cost of public warehousing services may be less than those of private or leased facilities. Because public warehousing is a purchased service, the cost per unit handled is a known factor when public warehousing is used. This simplifies cost estimation and budgeting for users, because similar documentation for private operators involves allocation of fixed costs. In addition to exemptions for "goods in transit", some states do not assess personal property taxes on inventories stored in public warehouses. Thus, potential tax savings in various states must be considered along with transportation and storage savings in distribution system design. However, because state and local governments frequently change their tax policies, a choice of location *or* type of facility used based on favorable tax considerations existing at the time may be based on a fleeting advantage at best.

Perhaps the greatest advantage in using public warehousing facilities is the flexibility allowed in inventory location. This is especially important when markets served are thin or shifting, demand is volatile, transportation rate relationships are subject to change, or any combination of elements occurs. In addition, because it is available on a short-term basis, public warehousing lends itself to test marketing, special promotions, and product recall activities, where the need for warehousing support is temporary and perhaps uncertain.

Table 11–6 depicts some of the conditions that may favor private or public warehousing as opposed to the other.

TABLE 11–6: Factors Affecting Choice of Public versus Private Warehousing

Factor	Public	Private
Product flow	Irregular; highly seasonal flows, or promotional or speculative inventories	Stable; seldom subject to significant variations
Specialized product environment requirements	a	a
Market	New and uncertain; changing in volume or geographically	Stable market; little change in volume or area served
Charges/Costs	If market is very competitive and charges are relatively low	If public warehousing charges are high
Capital investment	Capital not tied up	Capital is tied up unless the facilities are leased or rented

aSpecialized product environment requirements—freezer facilities, humidity control, cooling or other temperature control (except freezer), and so on—may favor either public or private warehousing, depending on availability of such public warehousing facilities in the desired location. Ownership of such facilities—private warehousing—involves the risk of difficulty in selling such a specialized facility if it is no longer needed and there is little or no market for it.

Cost Comparisons

The previous section dealt with managerial considerations with respect to the private versus public warehousing decision. A fundamental aspect of the choice, obviously, must take into account comparative cost elements. All other considerations being equal, one would expect to choose the lower cost alternative. The quoted charges (whether standard or negotiated) of a public warehouse are straightforward in the sense that the quoted charges will be the amount billed and paid. In order to compare the quoted public warehouse charges to the alternative costs of private warehousing, it is necessary to do a careful and thorough cost analysis of the private warehousing alternative.

Because of the possibility (even probability) of overlooking some cost items, it is desirable to use a structured worksheet, either manual or computerized. Appendix A of this chapter is a ''Warehousing Cost Calculation Form (Annual Expense),'' which provides detailed step-by-step procedures to be followed in developing private warehousing costs. A computerized version of this calculation form is also available, as noted in the appendix.

Once it has been determined that all relevant private warehousing costs have been fully accounted for, the choice between public or private alternatives becomes a managerial decision that may include other than economic issues, as discussed in the preceding section.

THIRD-PARTY WAREHOUSING SERVICES

The previous sections of this chapter have provided a foundation understanding of the nature and scope of warehousing activity, both public and private. However, significant developments are occurring that are affecting traditional warehousing roles and relationships in logistics systems. A 1989 Council of Logistics Management study investigated this growing phenomenon. Chapter 3 of the CLM study, titled "The Public/Contract Warehouse as a Third-Party Logistics Agent" presents the findings and assesses the implications of the development and growth of third-party warehousing services.[5]

The principal feature of this evolving type of third-party relationship is that it is increasingly a negotiated contractual relationship. In place of the traditional client-public warehouse "boiler-plate" contract for standard services, more and more firms are negotiating tailored contracts for a wide variety of services to be furnished by the warehousing firm. In many cases this results in the third-party provider taking over all, or nearly all, of the client firm's distribution activities. It is fast becoming an industry custom to refer to this new type of relationship as *contract warehousing* rather than public warehousing. The dimensions of this new type of relationship were summarized in the CLM study as follows:

1. Warehousers are very optimistic about the future of both public and contract warehousing.

2. More than half of shippers' raw materials and finished product are privately warehoused, but the trend toward outsourcing and cost reduction analyses suggests the use of nonprivate warehousing and customer direct shipments.

3. Most shippers do not intend to change the combined percent of volume flowing through public and contract warehouses. However, some shippers are increasing and some are decreasing the number of warehouses used.

4. A broad base of customer service elements is critical to the shipper-warehouser relationship.

5. Value-added services are necessary to increase margins and continue to attract and retain customers.

6. Technological advances, particularly those related to information exchange, are key to the shipper-warehouser relationship.

7. There are some differences in responses among warehousers across the kinds of product warehoused and by scope of operation.

8. There is a move toward even longer term relationships between shippers and warehousers.[6]

The trends mentioned above with respect to contract warehousing (third-party) are clearly illustrated in Table 11-7. The trend toward contract warehousing is probably underestimated because many firms that have not signed formally negotiated individual contracts for warehousing services are making use of increased numbers of these services under the provisions of standard contract clauses. Examples of value-added services that may be negotiated or purchased on a standard-rate basis are shown in Table 11-8.

A further factor encouraging the growth of third-party relationships between larger firms and public warehouses is the growing number of public warehouse "chains"; this makes possible the negotiating and signing of national contracts for such third-party services.

TABLE 11–7: Type of Warehouse Used for Shippers' Product or Raw Material

Type of Warehouse	1987	1990	Percent Change
Private warehouse—plant	41.7%	40.9%	−1.9%
Private warehouse—field	26.1	25.8	−1.1
Public warehouse	13.7	13.0	−5.1
Contract warehouse	6.8	7.5	+10.3
Customer direct	11.7	12.8	+9.4
TOTAL	100.0%	100.0%	

SOURCE: LaLonde, Bernard J. and Martha C. Cooper, *Partnerships in Providing Customer Service: A Third-Party Perspective* (Oak Brook, Illinois: Council of Logistics Management, 1989) 57.

TABLE 11–8: Value-Added Services Provided by Warehousers

Assembly
Repair
Testing
Packaging
Labeling and coding
Freezing/refrigeration/special storage conditions
Local delivery
Interstate and intrastate delivery
Recooperage
Import/export assistance
EDI (Electronic Data Interchange)

SOURCE: LaLonde, Bernard J. and Martha C. Cooper, *Partnerships in Providing Customer Service: A Third-Party Perspective* (Oak Brook, Illinois: Council of Logistics Management, 1989) 67.

DETERMINATION OF WAREHOUSE REQUIREMENTS

Determination of needed warehouse capacity requires at least two steps. The first, a determination of the supply or market area to be served, was covered in the discussion of inventory location in Chapter 9. The second is concerned with the capacity of the facility designated to serve a specified territory.

Our discussion will focus on the second issue. It will make use of an example, that of OKI Industries, a Chicago-based manufacturer. By means of this somewhat detailed example, we will trace the steps involved in planning warehouse capacity and the space required for shipping and receiving, storage, and order picking activities. Outside requirements, space for loading docks, and vehicle positioning will also be considered.

Information Required

Information on the level and variability of each type of warehousing activity is necessary to determine facility capacities. Different measures are necessary for each.

The sales estimate (or the purchasing schedule prepared from it) for the territory to be served by the warehouse facility is the basic document necessary to plan for the volume of movement likely to flow through the facility. Table 11–9 presents a sales forecast for a company planning to locate a privately owned distribution facility in Cincinnati.

This type of estimate is typical of those prepared by many firms. In OKI Industries' sales organization, representatives are assigned by states, hence the state-by-state forecast. Assuming it has been determined that the optimum geographic area to be served by the Cincinnati warehouse is bounded roughly by a circle with a radius of 100 miles with Cincinnati at its center, then sales statistics must be recast to reflect the difference in sales and logistics territories. This is shown in Table 11–10, along with a breakdown of additional information needed to complete an appraisal of capacity requirements.

The additional information required can be provided by (1) a sampling of bills of lading for shipments sent into the designated warehouse territory to determine the order-cycle time required for moving product from manufacturing facilities by the warehouse, as well as to determine the relationship of incoming to outgoing volume to be scheduled to the warehouse; and (2) longer-term estimates of trends and demands to be placed upon the warehouse operation.

Inside Requirements

When considering indoor space, planners must think in terms of cubic feet as well as square feet. Since indoor space is expensive to provide and operate, the relative cube utilization that can be obtained at a given ceiling height is important. The determinants of an efficient ceiling height include the ease with which goods can be stacked, the speed and frequency with which they must be moved through the storage area, and the size of the storage area in relation to shipping, receiving, and order picking areas of the warehouse.

Excess ceiling height leaves unused space between the tops of storage racks and the ceiling beyond the minimum clearance needed for ventilation, fire sprinklers, and lighting systems. Since this space still must be heated and cooled, rising energy prices have increased the cost penalty for excessive ceiling height. In the following example, a ceiling height of 20 feet, with goods stacked to 16 feet, has been assumed for OKI's planned warehouse.

Order Picking Space Order picking must be carried out within physical reaching distance from the floor unless the picking is done with mechanical equipment. The constant movement that takes place in an order picking area precludes extensive handling of materials at great heights because of the inefficiency of repeated lifting and lowering of stock. The area must also be more open in nature in order to accommodate the heavy traffic flow required for order assembly activity. Thus, it is not uncommon to find only about 20 percent of the available cubic space occupied by stock in an order picking area, as indicated in Table 11–10. Attempts have been made to make better use of order picking areas by using space over the area for more permanent storage.

Generally, stock is moved into an order picking area just prior to the demand for it. Space requirements will increase just before an anticipated increase in order demand. Order demand

TABLE 11–9: Sales Forecast, Ohio, Indiana and Kentucky Territories for OKI Industries

| State | By Month | | | Year's Total[a] |
	January	February	....	
Ohio	$1,600,000	$1,700,000	....	$23,000,000
Kentucky	900,000	1,100,000	....	16,000,000
Indiana	1,100,00	1,100,000	....	17,000,000
TOTAL	$3,600,000	$3,900,000	....	$56,000,000

[a]If available, a longer-range forecast should be used.

can be estimated by first deducting from estimated sales those shipments that will travel directly to customers from plants, probably in large quantities. The remainder is the amount of sales volume that will move through the planned warehousing facilities. This can be converted to tonnage by applying a dollar-density measure for the company's product mix to the sales volume expected to be delivered from the area warehouse facility.

Some amount of stock will be moved to the order picking area in anticipation of sales over the following few days. In Table 11–10, it has been assumed that a quantity comparable to four days of sales will be kept on hand in the order picking area. The actual quantity in any individual case can be determined by comparing the cost of restocking the order selection area from the storage area at varying intervals with the cost of space needed to maintain stocks of varying amounts in the order selection area, plus the cost of selection (measured in distance and time required to select orders while maintaining various quantities of stock in the area). Individual quantities may be computed for each item in stock, especially if particular items move through the area in widely varying quantities.

Having determined the quantity to be maintained in the area for each stock-keeping unit, this quantity can be converted to cubic feet by application of the ratio of cubic footage actually occupied by product to the total. This is one to five in the example shown in Table 11–10. From the pattern of sales, it appears that these products are highly seasonal. The seasonal demand for OKI's product requires an order picking cube of from 60,000 cubic feet at the end of December to 420,000 cubic feet at the end of November.

Storage and Receiving Space The space required for storage and receiving can be computed in much the same way as that for order picking. However, cube utilization will be higher because less access to the product is needed, reducing the number of space consuming aisleways and allowing higher and deeper stacks.

Quantities placed in storage depend on (1) the nature of the product, (2) the pattern of production in relation to sales, (3) the length of the order cycle required to replenish supplies, and (4) the desired level of customer service.

Goods for which the customer is willing to wait and for which price may be a secondary consideration, such as some industrial items and consumer specialty goods, can be produced to order. Even if produced for stock, often only a minimum stock is maintained. However, most industrial products and supplies and consumer convenience and shopping goods require the maintenance of inventories and warehouses.

TABLE 11–10: Information (and Its Organization) Required for Analysis of Capacity Requirements, by Month (OKI Industries' Cincinnati Warehouse)

	(1)	(2)	(3)	(4)	(5)	(6)	(7)
Month	Sales (millions)	Sales Direct from Plant to Customer (millions)	Sales through Cincinnati Warehouse (millions)	Sales through Cincinnati Warehouse (thousands of pounds)[a]	Number of Shipments Dispatched[b]	Number of Pickups[c] (all truck)	Receipts from Factory (thousands of pounds)
January	$ .8	$ .2	$ .6	300	6,000	120	700
February	1.2	.2	1.0	500	10,000	200	700
March	2.7	.5	2.2	1,100	22,000	220	700
April	3.1	.6	2.5	1,250	25,000	250	700
May	1.6	.3	1.3	650	13,000	260	700
June	1.8	.3	1.5	750	15,000	300	1,200
July	1.7	.4	1.3	650	13,000	260	1,200
August	1.5	.3	1.2	600	12,000	240	1,200
September	2.0	4	1.6	800	16,000	320	1,200
October	3.7	.9	2.8	1,400	28,000	280	1,200
November	4.2	1.0	3.2	1,600	32,000	320	1,200
December	5.1	.9	4.2	2,100	42,000	420	700
TOTAL	$29.4	$6.0	$23.4	11,700	234,000	3,190	

[a]Computed on the basis of an average dollar density of $2 per pound.

[b]Computed on the basis of an average order size of $100 or 50 pounds.

[c]Based on an analysis of orders originating in various parts of the service territory, resulting in computation of 50 shipments per pickup in all months except March, April, October, November, and December, when greater overall volume allows consolidation of 100 shipments per pickup.

[d]Obtained by assuming a 500,000 pound year-beginning inventory and adding Column 7 to Column 8 (for previous month), then subtracting Column 4.

Regulating production levels from day to day to accommodate changing demand is costly, even if sufficient capacity exists to meet demand. First, the excess capacity that must be maintained is expensive. Second, fluctuations in the size of the production labor force are costly and can cause industrial relations problems. Warehousing absorbs much of the shock caused by fluctuations in supply and demand.

The length of the order cycle required to replenish supplies becomes important in the planning of warehouse requirements only if (1) production levels can be easily adjusted to sales levels, (2) a stock can be maintained equivalent to that required to meet demand during one order cycle, with the minimum base or safety stock for contingencies, and (3) customers cannot be persuaded to wait for a given item. In addition, restrictions imposed by order cycle length can be overcome by an overlapping of orders, that is, the placement of orders so that several might be in transit at once, each to arrive at a different time.

In the illustration, the manufacturing facilities appear to be run on a seasonal basis, with production at a higher constant rate from June through November than from December through May. Goods placed in intermediate term storage (30 days or more) may be organized to occupy up to 70 percent of the available cubic footage in the storage area, provided that the

TABLE 11–10 CONTINUED: Information (and Its Organization) Required for Analysis of Capacity Requirements, by Month (OKI Industries' Cincinnati Warehouse)

(8)	(9)	(10)	(11)	(12)	(13)	(14)
Month-End Inventory (thousands of pounds)d	Month-End Inventory in Order-Picking Area (thousands of pounds)e	Month-End Inventory in Storage and Receiving Area (thousands of pounds)	Cubic Feet Needed for Order Picking, Storage, and Receiving Stocksf			Capacity Requirement, End-of-Month (square footage)i
			Order Pickingg	Storage and Receivingh	Total	
900	100	800	100,000	320,000	420,000	21,000
1,100	220	880	220,000	352,000	572,000	28,600
700	250	450	250,000	200,000	450,000	22,500
150	130	20	130,000	8,000	138,000	6,900
200	150	50	150,000	20,000	170,000	8,500
650	130	520	130,000	208,000	338,000	16,900
1,200	120	1,080	120,000	432,000	552,000	27,600
1,800	160	1,640	160,000	656,000	816,000	40,800
2,200	280	1,920	280,000	768,000	1,048,000	52,400
2,000	320	1,680	320,000	672,000	992,000	49,600
1,600	420	1,180	420,000	472,000	892,000	44,600
200	60	140	60,000	56,000	116,000	5,800

eAssumes that a supply sufficient for four business days' (1/5 month) sales is kept on hand.

fAverage product weight density is 5 pounds per cubic foot.

gCubic footage displaced by product is 1/5 of the total cubage required in the order-picking area, assuming a 20-foot-high ceiling.

hCubic footage displaced by product is 1/2 of the total cubage required in the storage and receiving area, assuming a 20-foot-high ceiling and average height of 16-foot storage stacks.

iAssuming a uniform 20-foot-high ceiling.

product can be stacked or otherwise stored with the aid of pallets and racks or other unitizing devices.

In the example, all items not in the order picking area are assumed to be in storage. But, after making an allowance for receiving activities, goods in storage occupy only about 50 percent of the available cubic space. Total storage space requirements thus range from a low of 8,000 cubic feet at the end of April to 768,000 cubic feet at the end of September. In all cases, cubic footage is converted to square footage by dividing by the proposed height of the building, assuming a constant ceiling height.

Interchange of Space The value of flexibility in storage and handling equipment is illustrated by the OKI situation. If permanent facilities were to be established for each separate operation, the amount of space needed to accommodate the inside activity would be 1,188,000 cubic feet or a floor area of 59,400 square feet. Because the amount of space needed for one activity does not vary directly with the other, the peak order picking period falls at a different time than the peak storage time. Therefore, the use of flexible equipment permitting the conversion of space would allow OKI to build a warehouse of 1,048,000 cubic feet (52,400 square feet) capacity to meet its needs. Assuming a cost of $18 per square foot for a warehouse with a usable height of 20 feet, cost savings would amount to $126,000 with the use of movable storage aids and handling equipment.

Only monthly sales and material handling volume have been shown in Table 11–10. If shipments fluctuated extensively over short periods of time, it would be necessary to make sales and activity estimates on a week-by-week or even daily basis.

When possible, some firms encourage customers to order certain products in anticipation of demand so they can accommodate other demands when they occur. In grocery products distribution, for example, nonperishable items are sent to retail stores early in the week so that the peak demand for fresh produce and other perishables on Friday can be met. This type of planning improves productivity and space utilization by leveling the work load.

Use of Supplementary Public Warehousing Before deciding on the amount of private warehouse space required in a given situation, the possibility of meeting some or all of the demand through a public warehouse should be considered, assuming that acceptable alternative facilities exist in the community involved. As mentioned earlier, public and private warehousing have different cost structures. With the former, the user avoids the heavy fixed costs of the latter. Thus, if public warehousing facilities can be used to meet short-run peaks in activity, the same amount of warehousing effort can be provided with a smaller private facility and a lower total cost of warehousing.

The results in Table 11–11 are typical of many warehousing situations. Based on current estimates of demand, the lowest cost method for meeting the warehousing requirements for OKI in Cincinnati is to build or lease private capacity of 21,000 square feet and utilize the public warehousing facilities for handling over one-third of OKI's volume through Cincinnati.

Outside Requirements

Unless a firm stores materials in outside piles, outside warehouse space requirements will be determined by loading dock and vehicle positioning needs. Both are a function of (1) traffic fluctuations of inbound and outbound goods at the warehouse, (2) the degree of effectiveness with which equipment is scheduled, and (3) the degree to which other warehouse facilities are utilized.

Positioning of Equipment

Traffic fluctuations at the proposed warehouse can be measured roughly by the information in Table 11–12. A private warehouse with 21,000 square feet probably will be required to handle a peak of about 16,000 outgoing shipments per months. Equated to pickups, this amounts to 320 truck pickups per month. Under the assumption that pickups are limited to 10 hours a day during each of the 20 working days in a month, and that the pickup of 50 shipments requires about 2 hours, one truck stall (spot) for shipping would accommodate 100 pickups per month. Four shipping stalls would be required to accommodate 100 percent of pickups at the average level of volume during peak months.

Averages cover up peaks and valleys, especially in the pickup and delivery of freight. Thus, eight dock doors might be needed to accommodate all trucks without waiting at a 21,000 square foot OKI facility. The number could be reduced by (1) the use of waiting line theory in

TABLE 11–11: Warehousing Costs under Varying Proportions of Use of Private and Public Warehouse Facilities of OKI Industries' Cincinnati Distribution Point

	(1)	(2)	(3)	(4)	(5)	(6)	(7)
Size of Owned Facilities (square feet)	Average Percentage of Private Warehouse Capacity Used	Annual Volume Moving through Private Warehouse (hundred-weight)[a]	Annual Volume Moving through Public Warehouse (hundred-weight)	Fixed Private Ware-housing Costs[b]	Variable Private Ware-housing Costs[c]	Public Ware-housing Costs[d]	Total Ware-housing Costs
52,400	51.7%	117,000	—	$157,200	$117,000	—	$274,200
49,600	54.2	114,620	2,380	148,800	114,620	$ 4,760	268,180
44,600	59.1	110,880[e]	6,120	133,800	110,800	12,240	256,840
40,800	61.5	110,880[e]	6,120	122,400	110,880	12,240	245,520
28,600	73.8	90,640[e]	26,360	85,800	90,640	52,720	229,160
27,600	74.7	90,640[e]	26,360	82,800	90,640	52,720	226,160
22,500	80.2	75,130[e]	41,870	67,500	75,130	83,740	226,370
21,000	81.8	75,130[e]	41,870	63,000	75,130	83,740	221,870[f]
16,900	85.5	58,630	59,070	50,700	58,630	118,140	227,470
8,500	95.7	21,560[e]	95,440	25,500	21,560	190,880	237,940
6,900	98.6	21,560[e]	95,440	20,700	21,560	190,880	233,140
5,800	100.0	21,560[e]	95,440	17,400	21,560	190,880	229,840
0	—	—	117,000	—	—	234,000	234,000

[a]Computed on the basis of an annual inventory turn of 11.0 through the private warehouse facilities.
[b]Computed on the basis of $3 per square foot of floor space per year.
[c]Computed on the basis of $1 per hundredweight moved through the warehouse.
[d]Computed on the basis of $2 per hundredweight moved through the warehouse.
[e]Due to the relative needs of order picking and storage and receiving space in various months of minimum usage, there is only a negligible difference in the relative usage of each of these warehouse capacities; the same utilization could probably be obtained by using the smaller size of owned facilities in each case by adjusting the timing of the build-up of stocks in the order picking area.
[f]Lowest total cost alternative.

TABLE 11–12: Space Required for Warehouse for OKI Industries, Cincinnati

		Square Feet
Indoor space:		
Building requirements (100 ft. × 210 ft.)		21,000
Outdoor space:		
Truck positioning	14,400	
Rail positioning (12 ft. × 100 ft.)[a]	1,200	
Truck and rail dock	2,680	18,280
TOTAL		39,280

[a]Based on the assumption that a rail spur would be brought in flush with the short side of the building.

the planning of the facility, (2) a strong effort to schedule pickups and to hold carriers to a prearranged schedule, (3) the off-peak scheduling of some shipments, and (4) the spotting of equipment to be loaded by second- or third-shift warehouse labor.

However, because the truck driver helps load and unload the vehicle during regular pickup and delivery hours (unless an empty trailer is dropped off to accommodate a vehicle load shipment), off-peak scheduling is a less desirable practice if common motor carriers handle a large part of the traffic and delivery hours. A railcar, on the other hand, would have to be loaded or unloaded by warehouse personnel in any event, because loading and unloading assistance is not part of the service offered by railroads.

Space must also be provided for "spotting" (backing) highway vehicles at loading or unloading positions. A space at least 12 feet wide and with a depth of 4 times the length of the vehicle is recommended. Thus, a facility built to accommodate six vehicles of up to 50 feet in length would require an area of 72 feet × 200 feet or 14,400 square feet. This figure could be reduced by a third if sawtooth docks that permit diagonal parking of vehicles are used.

The same type of analysis can be made for inbound freight movements. Data in Table 11–10 indicate that these are received on a more constant basis. However, the critical question is: How does the freight arrive? At distribution warehouses, rail transportation is much more likely to be used for inbound freight than for outbound.

Assume that the peak volume of freight (all low intensity) incoming to the proposed 21,000 square foot facility will be about 700,000 pounds, roughly equivalent to 35 20,000-pound railcar loads or 70 10,000-pound truckloads. If approximately four hours are required to unload a truck and eight hours to unload a railcar, the capacity of one unloading spot for each would be 20 railcars and 40 trucks per month (assuming 20 working days per month).

If both rail and truck transportation are used for incoming freight and shipments are scheduled effectively, no more than one spot for a railcar and one spot for a truck trailer would be required on the receiving side of the warehouse. In this case, it would be more efficient to place the inbound truck stalls along-side those planned for outbound trucks, limiting vehicle positioning requirements to only one side of the building.

Rail facilities needed to serve a warehouse consist of a spur-line onto the property. All loading and unloading must be done while the car is situated parallel to the platform. A common distance to the middle of the car floor and the edge of the freight dock is 68 inches. Therefore, at least 12 feet of clearance between the building and the property line should be provided for each spur.

Dock Requirements

When assessing dock requirements, provision must be made for the temporary placement of freight, the storage of dock equipment (such as dock plates similar to gang planks used on a ship), and the two-way traffic typical in most loading and unloading operations. Although it will vary from case to case, 20-foot depths for freight docks are quite common.

The amount of running feet of dock in the illustration would be determined by allowing 12 feet for each of 7 truck bays, or 84 feet, and at least 50 feet to accommodate a railcar. This would amount to a requirement of 134 running feet of dock space, or 2,680 square feet for outdoor shipping and receiving. If the shipping and receiving areas are to be entirely inside the building, as in many installations, then this figure must be included in the estimate of indoor space requirements.

Based on an overall appraisal of the demand to be placed on the Cincinnati warehouse of OKI, the amount of indoor and outdoor space required for the facility is shown in Table 11–12. This is roughly in accordance with an industry rule of thumb that a warehouse building should not cover more than half of the land area. In addition, municipal zoning ordinances and building code specifications tend to reinforce such a rule of thumb guideline.

WAREHOUSE DESIGN

Design is a major determinant of the cost and service levels that can be obtained from a warehouse. A poorly designed facility builds in an operating penalty that may take years to overcome, if ever.

Steps in warehouse design include a determination of the purpose for which the facility is to be used, agreement on the general characteristics of the facility, specific development of the layout, and an appraisal of the overall compatibility between the building and the materials handling system that it will house. This all assumes, of course, that capacity planning has preceded design.

Purpose of the Facility

The intended purpose of the facility will determine such matters as the size of the building module to be employed, the number of storage levels that it might contain, its ceiling height, and its length-to-width ratio. Table 11–13 suggests how these dimensions might vary, depending on whether the facility is to be used primarily for materials handling or storage purposes.

While characteristics set forth in Table 11–13 do not hold for all facilities of each type, they are intended to indicate tendencies. For materials handling purposes, a smaller building module may make it possible to reduce distances over which materials and material handling equipment might have to move to prepare goods for shipment. Similarly, horizontal movement is regarded as more efficient than vertical movement for such purposes, suggesting the need for a single-story facility. Ceiling height is determined by the capabilities of efficient materials handling equipment. The building may be designed in an oblong shape, with anywhere from a

TABLE 11–13: Contrasts in Design Characteristics for Materials Handling and Storage Warehouses

Design Characteristics	Type of Warehouse	
	Materials Handling	Storage
Module (building) size	Smaller	Larger
Number of storage levels	One	More than one
Ceiling height	24–30 feet	Any height
Building length-to-width ratio	More than 1:1	About 1:1
Floor load capacities	Lower	Higher
Level of lighting	Higher	Lower

2 to 1 to a 5 to 1 length-to-width ratio to facilitate the flow of material from one side of the building to the other. This is an important consideration in a typical flow-through operation in which material is received on one side of the building and shipped from the other. And while floor load capacities for materials handling facilities may not have to be as great as those for storage facilities, the level of lighting may have to be higher to facilitate order picking and accurate placement of stocks for subsequent shipment.

Layout of the Facility

Techniques that facilitate plant layout are transferable to the layout problem. The preparation of route sheets, operating schedules, movable templates drawn to scale to represent freight and equipment, and other devices are all effective and too numerous to discuss in detail. We will dwell briefly on some of the problems of layout that have special importance for warehouses.

Constraints   In layout planning, much time can be saved by first determining alternatives that cannot be considered for reasons of physical limitations of a facility. Windows, fire doors, receiving and shipping doors, elevators, and supporting columns all present problems for the layout planner. The more of these limiting factors that can be avoided by eliminating them from consideration in the planning or redesign of a warehouse, the better.

Severe restrictions imposed by supporting pillars have been avoided by the growing number of firms switching to single-story warehouse buildings. This has allowed elimination of elevators as well. Windows have been replaced with adequate overhead artificial lighting. The savings resulting from the more efficient use of space near outside warehouse walls has more than compensated for the extra cost of lighting. Receiving and shipping doors can be planned in relation to one another so that material will flow through a facility essentially in one direction. Fire door requirements may be reduced in some areas by the installation of sprinkler fire devices in the warehouse.

Materials Flow   In laying out the receiving, storage, order selection (sometimes including packaging or repackaging), and shipping areas within a warehouse, it is important to keep several points in mind.

First, to the extent possible, materials should move in one general direction through the warehouse. An effective layout discourages deviations from the flow pattern determined to be most efficient for a facility. Fixed conveyor facilities, for example, discourage a deviation from material-handling flow intended by the layout planner.

Second, provision should be made, where possible or necessary, for the circumvention of one or more stages in the warehousing process. Where turnover of stocks is rapid, layout should facilitate the movement of stock directly from incoming transportation vehicles to the order selection area.

Third, the cross-hauling of freight within areas of the warehouse should be avoided. Layout planning must take into account the traffic volume and patterns at various levels of operation to provide adequate space for movements, especially where individually powered warehouse vehicles are used. It must also consider the efficiencies to be gained by the use of one-way corridors and other devices to route internal traffic in such a manner as to eliminate crossing traffic.

Fourth, the greatest amount of stock possible should be located close to its point of greatest need. Further, if a one-directional flow of material is the objective, the greatest possible amount of stock should be placed at each stage of the warehousing process in such a manner that it will be easy to locate and secure for the next stage. These are truisms, but the analysis needed to accomplish the goals is much more complex than the goals. The goals themselves are rarely reached.

Storage and Aisle Layout

The storage area of a warehouse consists of storage locations and a surrounding network of aisleways. Pallet placement and aisle width often are the most important storage layout considerations.

Pallet Placement There is some argument about the most efficient pattern for pallet placement. Some advocate ''on the square'' layout, while others prefer angular placement of varying degrees. Both types are shown in Figure 11–6. Basically, the first of these methods requires less space for the actual placement of pallets; all of the space within the dotted line in example A of Figure 11–6 is utilized. But square pallet placement requires more surrounding aisle space for the servicing of the actual pallet area.

Of great importance in determining the relative efficiency of pallet placement designs is the amount of access to material that is required. Lower access requirements allow a smaller proportion of pallets to be placed with aisle ''facings'' or exposures. Where less access is required, aisle space savings become less important and on-the-square placement may be relatively efficient. However, at the same time, space losses due to angular placement are reduced in proportion to the total space occupied by the pallet area. Also, angular placement of pallets becomes more attractive as the length of motive pallet-handling equipment increases.

A strong argument for the comparative efficiency of angular placement, under conditions of long aisle length, was advanced by Ballou in a classic study of alternative layout designs.[7] Although Ballou demonstrated that angular pallet placement required less square footage, industry practitioners have ignored his analysis, presumably on the basis of traffic flow patterns rather than simple square-footage considerations. As is clear in Figure 11–6, the on-the-square placement permits the forklift truck to make easy right or left turns in the aisle, whereas the angular placement inhibits maneuvering the forklift truck except in a one-way traffic flow pattern.

Aisle Width Aisle width requirements vary, of course, with the size of material-handling equipment used and freight moved. If the latter is unitized, pallet or container dimensions and the size of forklift equipment will determine aisle dimensions.

Generally, main warehouse aisles are designed to allow two-way traffic of loaded forklifts. With extra allowances, this requires 10- to 12-foot-wide corridors for material handling systems using 48-inch-wide pallets.

Pallet access aisles, on the other hand, need be wide enough for only one vehicle in low traffic areas. The exact width will be determined by (1) the length of motive equipment with pallet, (2) the turning radius of the loaded motive equipment, and (3) the width of the loaded equipment.

FIGURE 11–6: On-the-square and angular pallet placement

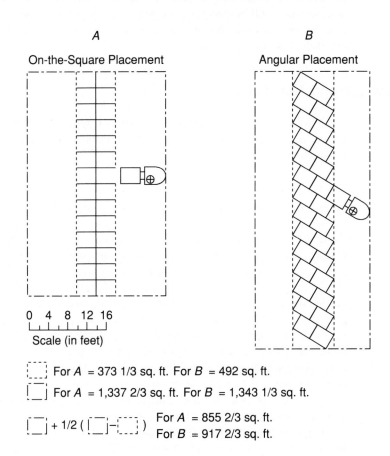

A

On-the-Square Placement

B

Angular Placement

0 4 8 12 16
Scale (in feet)

For *A* = 373 1/3 sq. ft. For *B* = 492 sq. ft.

For *A* = 1,337 2/3 sq. ft. For *B* = 1,343 1/3 sq. ft.

+ 1/2 (−)   For *A* = 855 2/3 sq. ft.
              For *B* = 917 2/3 sq. ft.

To reduce aisle requirements, some firms group or centralize products that require heavy-duty forklift equipment to limit the number of wide access aisles required. At the same time, the handling of less bulky or heavy freight has been accomplished by straddle-type forklifts capable of operating in access aisles as narrow as seven feet in width.

The recent development of forklift trucks with side-loading attachments and stacker cranes guided by tracks has reduced aisle-width requirements in some warehouses to a few inches more than the width of the widest load handled.

Stock Location

There are four basic elements in the determination of the placement of stock, especially in order selection areas where the quantities involved warrant picking by hand. They are: popularity per item, size per unit, traffic patterns resulting from various arrangements of stock, and characteristics of compatibility.

The element of compatibility is little more than a guiding principle in that it must be honored as a starting point in the stock location problem. Generally, petroleum and food products are incompatible because the former may "flavor" the latter; a nut and bolt of a given size ordered at the same time in exactly the same quantity are totally compatible items. The former must be separated; the latter must be adjacent on the stock floor.

The relative emphasis on each of the factors of stock location depends on the system of order selection under consideration. Systems can be based on principles of (1) out-and-back selection of each item; (2) picker routing, whereby several items are picked on a single trip through the selection area; (3) picking stations, where each station is marked and all stations are served by a fixed or portable conveyor system; and (4) random stock location.

Out-and-Back Selection This system is most often used where order items are picked in large quantities, or where the entire job is carried out with the use of forklifts picking only one item on one pallet during one trip out and back. When this type of operation is assumed, a great deal of emphasis may be placed on the positioning of the most popular items and of sets of highly compatible items near the order assembly point. However, it appears that even in this type of situation, some attempt must be made to base location on both popularity and the relative size of stock required in an order selection area.

Order-Picker System Generally, order pickers are employed in the selection of small items from stock. However, in this type of situation more than any other, the stock location planner must lay out items within a zone in a sequence that will provide a logical traffic flow through the zone. He may redesign the shape of order selection zones or create subzones to group items associated more closely with each other, not necessarily in relation to some focal point such as the order assembly point.

When the layout for an order-picker system has been determined, a dispatcher may be required to (1) arrange items on an incoming order in such a fashion that they can be picked in sequence, (2) route conveyorized baskets to various picker posts placed in sequence, or (3) instruct pickers located at picking points to place onto a conveyor line specific items to be consolidated into an order.

Conveyorized System This type of selection is adaptable to stock items of a wide range of volume and size up to the capacity of the conveyor. However, imbalance in conveyor loading produces fluctuating activity at the end of the line, causes inequities in work levels at various stations on the conveyor, and can create traffic jams on the conveyor system itself. In a conveyorized system, order pickers should be stationed at irregular intervals along the line, depending on the cubic volume of items picked that must be moved from their station and the average time required to place a cubic foot of product on the conveyor.

Random Stock Location With the advent of improved, often computerized information systems, many warehousing operations are now turning to random stock location methods, whereby incoming stock is placed in any empty, identifiable slot in the warehouse. A memory system can then provide necessary information for finding items on demand, including the most efficient sequence in which to pick the order. This approach has the basic advantage of saving warehouse space and increasing capacity, because it does not allow any space to be reserved and remain unused. It is particularly suited to picking full pallet loads by forklift. It can, however, result in slower order picking times if order pickers have to pick individual cartons or items, especially if they must do so with location instructions rather than from memory or reflex.

Cube-per-Order Index[8] In designing stock location methods, the objective may be to minimize the distance traveled by order pickers in a system utilizing either out-and-back selection or order-picking routing. Or it may be to minimize the distance traveled by product, measured in cubic footage, on a conveyorized order selection system. Given such objectives, a cube-per-order index method of stock location may prove most efficient. This index is defined as the required cubic footage of stock space per order filled during a given period of time. Required cubic footage in the order selection area is the product of the cube-per-item, average order size in units, number of orders per day, and the number of days demand on hand. Picking cost per order includes the cost of restocking the item, the cost of storage space, and the cost of labor and equipment time for picking the item.

Table 11-14 shows the data on item characteristics needed to perform a stock placement analysis for a hypothetical warehouse stocking six different items.

The cube-per-order index has been computed for each item and appears in column 7 of this table. Figure 11-7 depicts the capacity of each "zone" emanating from the order assembly point in the example warehouse.

Assuming all six items are compatible, how would assignment priority, zone assignment, and total order selection cost vary under each of the stock placement methods suggested? Table 11-15 compares the results of locating the six items on the basis of popularity, unit size, total cubic footage requirements, and the cube-per-order index.

The use of the cube-per-order index results in order selection costs of $265 per day below that achieved by the item popularity criteria, $325 per day below that provided by arrangement of items by unit size, and $88 below that obtained under an item stock cube arrangement.

Even if the calculations in Table 11-15 could be refined to reflect more accurately a continuous spectrum of cost and distance relationships, the results would still favor an integration of size and popularity measurements in determining stock locations.

TABLE 11-14: Item Characteristics for Stock Placement

(1) Item Number	(2) Cube per Item (cubic feet)	(3) Average Order Size (Units)	(4) Number of Orders per Day	(5) Number of Days' Demand on Hand	(6) Required Cubic Footage	(7) Cube per Order Index (6 ÷ 4)
1	2	10	100	3	6,000	60
2	10	6	300	2	36,000	120
3	16	1	900	1	14,400	16
4	1	4	350	3	4,200	12
5	16	3	1,200	1	57,600	48
6	4	20	300	3	72,000	240
TOTALS			3,150		190,000	

FIGURE 11–7: Stock placement zones in the order selection area of a warehouse

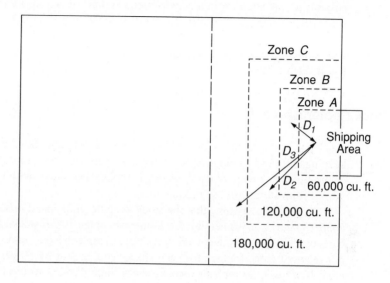

TABLE 11–15: Comparison of Assignment Priority, Zone Assignments, and Daily Order Selection Cost Using Various Stock Placement Criteria

Item	Popularity Priority	Popularity Zone	Popularity Cost[a]	Unit Size Priority	Unit Size Zone	Unit Size Cost[a]	Cubic Footage Required Priority	Cubic Footage Required Zone	Cubic Footage Required Cost[a]	Cube-per-Order Index Priority	Cube-per-Order Index Zone	Cube-per-Order Index Cost[a]
1	6	C	$ 60	2	A	$ 20	2	A	$ 20	4	B	$ 40
2	4	B	120	4	B	120	4	A	60	5	B	120
3	2	A–B[b]	433	6	B	360	3	A	180	2	A	180
4	3	B	140	1	A	70	1	A	70	1	A	70
5	1	A	240	3	B–C[d]	528	5	B	480	3	A–B[g]	312
6	5	B–C[c]	123	5	A–B[e]	78	6	B–C[f]	129	6	B–C[h]	120
TOTAL COST			$1,116			$1,176			$939			$851

[a]Based on measurement of D1, D2, and D3 in Figure 11-6. Cost estimates assume that all units of an item in an order can be picked in one trip out and back. Picking costs per order are: Zone "A" = $.20; Zone "B" = $.40; and Zone "C" = $.60. When stock must be located in each of two order selection zones, picking costs are adjusted proportionally (costs per order appear in footnotes b–h below).
[b]Cost = $.37
[c]Cost = $.41
[d]Cost = $.44
[e]Cost = $.26
[f]Cost = $.43
[g]Cost = $.26
[h]Cost = $.43

The example suggests the applicability of the cube-per-order index method of stock location to out-and-back order selection systems. In an order-picker routing system, the cube-per-order system can facilitate the placement of items making up complete orders as close as possible to one another. In a conveyorized system, it can insure that the greatest amount of cube will travel the shortest distance in order selection. Even in a system operated with random stock location, the cube-per-order index can be implemented if families of product-line items with similar characteristics are treated as groupings and random stock location is practiced within each family.

Stock Replenishment

Up to now, we have assumed that the amount of cubic footage devoted to any one stock-keeping unit (SKU) held in a picking area is fixed. However, more realistically it is a function of the frequency with which the stock is replenished either with incoming goods or product moved from storage to the picking area.

For example, assume that the stock-keeping units listed in Table 11–14 are replenished approximately every other day. Each time we replenish our stocks in the order-picking area, it costs us $300. On the other hand, if we were to replenish our stocks every day, it would reduce our required cubic footage for each stock-keeping unit by 50 percent in the stock selection area. If we were to replenish stocks every three days, it would increase our required cubic footage for each SKU by 50 percent.

Based on this analysis, we are reminded again of the cost trade-offs between inventory ordering and carrying costs and those of handling and order selection.

Stock Relocation

As the cube-per-order index changes for various stock items, or as stock zone capacity changes, or other adjustments occur in the warehousing operation, stock location must be audited and, if necessary, changed. The computed daily savings for a period of time (depending on the audit cycle), when compared with the cost of relocating items, will provide information for the relocation decision.

Compatibility with the Materials Handling System

Before proceeding with subsequent steps in the actual siting and construction of a facility, it is important to check the compatibility of the warehouse design with the materials handling system that it is to house.

Examples of such compatibility are legion. The lifting limits of lift trucks, for example, may determine efficient ceiling heights. Or the use of fixed conveyors may lead to a desire for warehouse dimensions that will allow for the least amount of fixed equipment to be installed.

The most extreme examples of the need to adjust warehouse design to reflect the needs of materials handling systems occurs in those facilities employing high-rise stacker cranes for temporary storage and automated order selection equipment.

Site Selection[9]

Many factors will influence the selection of a site for a warehouse within a community. Among the general factors are (1) the quality and variety of transportation carriers serving the site, (2) the quantity and quality of labor available in the vicinity, (3) labor rates, (4) the cost and quality of industrial land, (5) taxes, (6) the nature of the community government, and (7) the cost and availability of energy and other utilities. Types and sources of information useful for this stage of decision process are shown in Table 11–16.

Other site considerations include location risks, community services, and vehicle access. Potential location risks include unsuitable soil conditions for construction and the threat of flood or nearby hazardous industry. At this point, it is appropriate to seek engineering advice regarding the cost of site preparation, which can in some cases exceed the cost of the land itself. Community services, such as fire and police protection, are also important to the warehouse operator. Finally, site access and traffic congestion that may influence carrier service to a particular location may be reviewed.

In some cases, it may be necessary or desirable to reconcile the design to a site that is especially attractive in all aspects but its dimensions. This problem arises especially in cases of potential sites that are smaller than planned for or that have odd dimensions. The matter must be analyzed carefully, with emphasis perhaps on the impact of a restrictive site on construction

TABLE 11–16: Types and Potential Sources of Information for Warehouse Site Selection

Type of Information	*Potential Sources*
General Factors	
Quality and variety of transportation service	Common carrier executives
Quantity and quality of available labor	Personnel departments of local companies
Labor wage rates	
Cost and quality of industrial land	Industrial development department of utilities
Taxes	
Nature of community government	
Cost and availability of utilities	
Specific Factors	
Zoning for transportation rate	Common carrier executives
Site preparation	Consulting engineers
Flood risk	Industrial development department of utilities
Risk from adjacent hazardous industry	
Community services	Other warehouse operators in area
Local taxing practices	
Traffic congestion problems	Common carrier personnel

SOURCE: Adapted from Kenneth B. Ackerman, *Warehousing: A Guide for Both Users and Operators* (Washington: Traffic Serivce Corporation, 1977) 116–122. Copyright © Van Nostrand Reinhold. Reprinted by permission.

costs for storage-oriented facilities and on yearly operating costs for facilities intended for rapid turnover and extensive material-handling activities.

The above considerations as to site selection and location reflect traditional factors weighed in the choice of location. Recent developments involving Just-in-Time (JIT) inventory procedures may produce overriding imperatives. One effect of JIT has been the absolute requirement by some purchasers that suppliers locate inventories very close to the purchasers' plants. For example, a number of suppliers to automobile assembly plants in Flint, Pontiac, Lansing, and Detroit, Michigan, whose plants and warehouses were located in the northern part of Michigan's lower peninsula, have had to relocate their finished goods warehouses (and their plants in a few cases) close to the automobile assembly plants in order to provide JIT service to their automotive industry customers. They were given no choice in the matter.

WAREHOUSE OPERATIONS

After the opening ceremonies, if any, are over and the top executives, consulting engineers, and visiting fire fighters have left, a private or perhaps a leased warehouse must be operated. Problems of warehouse operation cover the whole range of those associated with line management. The importance of this matter is suggested by the results of a 1972 poll in which public warehousemen cited labor relations and costs overwhelmingly as the most important problems confronting them currently.[10] There is no evidence to suggest that there has been any change in the importance of labor relations and costs. Recent personal experiences of the authors in talking with warehouse managers further confirm their convictions in this regard. It would be impossible to discuss the human elements of management here. Instead, we will concentrate on the peculiar aspects of performance measurement identified with warehousing management.

Physical Measures of Performance

Included among the physical measures are (1) tons moved in and out per 24-hour period, (2) the number of orders picked in a 24-hour period, and (3) labor disputes or momentary work stoppages per period of time.

All of these measures are related to the volume of work available at any point in time. *They are meaningless unless compared to some factor that will yield a ratio indicative of efficiency.* In almost all cases, the required factor is manpower on hand. Thus, measures of tons moved per person, orders processed per person, and number of labor disputes per average labor force all provide measures of value. During periods of extremely low volume, even these measures may become distorted by the necessity of keeping a minimum work force on hand regardless of the volume.

Cost Measures of Performance

To account for the variation in costs per unit of activity at different levels of activity it is important that some attempt be made to identify separately costs that are primarily fixed or variable. Those generally falling into the former category are costs of rental or depreciation on building and equipment, utilities, insurance, fixed property taxes, maintenance, and minimum management. Costs more variable in nature are those of warehouse labor, equipment maintenance, inventory property tax, penalty charges due to delay of carrier equipment, supplies, and depreciation of containers, pallets, and other devices used in the unitization of freight.

This separate identification of fixed and variable costs will provide more accurate information regarding the effect of volume fluctuation on costs. Those units moving through the warehouse at low levels of overall volume should not be charged an excessive unit cost because of high short-run overhead burden. Nor should the warehouse management and labor be penalized with total (fixed plus variable) cost figures during periods of low volume.

TRANSFER FACILITIES

A second major class of material handling facilities are those concerned with the transfer of goods or logistics equipment. The various major types of transfer facilities can be characterized best by the nature of the freight or item they are designed to accommodate. They include terminals for assembling, sorting, transferring, or distributing packaged freight; terminals for handling and transferring containers used in coordinated transportation service; specialized bulk commodity terminals dedicated to particular commodities ranging from grain to oil; and carrier yards, terminals, and ports for combining or separating carrier equipment.

Packaged Freight

Carriers engaging in small shipment transportation (anything less than a vehicle load) may utilize terminals for the consolidation, mixing, or deconsolidation of packaged freight shipments. This is especially typical of highway and air carrier operations.

Shipping and receiving docks operated by individual shippers to serve as staging points for the shipment or receipt of packaged freight shipments also fall into this category.

Typical packaged freight transfer facilities often involve transfer between vehicles of the same mode of transportation.

Small shipment or package sorting facilities operated by carriers such as the U.S. Postal Service, Federal Express, and United Parcel Service have been able to employ mechanical devices and computer-controlled sorting mechanisms. All of these firms impose strict limitations on the sizes and weights of packages they will accept, thus simultaneously (1) facilitating the introduction of labor-saving mechanical devices and (2) limiting their freight to packages that can be lifted and hauled by people when necessary. Further, they concentrate sorting equipment at facilities called hubs located at central points on their route systems in order to gain maximum productivity from their investments in automation. Perhaps the most striking example of this is the policy of Federal Express to fly most of its nightly domestic shipments to its sorting facility at Memphis, Tennessee, for sorting and delivery the next morning by plane and truck to destinations located throughout the United States.

Container Terminals

With the growth of coordinated transport, characterized by the use of two or more modes in the transportation of a single shipment, large containers compatible with two or more modes are in common use. The transfer of a standard 20 foot $\times$ 8 foot $\times$ 8 foot container from one mode to another typically requires the use of a crane capable of lifting 85 tons at one time. Perhaps the world's largest container terminal is located at Port Elizabeth, New Jersey, for the transfer of containers from truck to ship and vice versa.

Bulk Commodity Terminals

The transportation of commodities in unpackaged form has a great economic attraction. It requires the construction of facilities for assembling, transferring, and breaking bulk commodity shipments. Such facilities typically are designed to handle one or a limited number of bulk commodities in great quantities at speeds ranging up to 20,000 tons or 2 million gallons per hour. Often they offer the capability of transferring such commodities between vehicles of two cooperative transportation modes.

Bulk commodity terminals may be owned and operated by carriers, shippers, or public organizations, such as port authorities.

Carrier Equipment Transfer Facilities

Rail, highway, and water carriers operate terminals for the transfer of cars, trailers, and barges, respectively. The sorting of railroad cars at "yard" terminal facilities has long been a feature of railroad freight transportation. With the advent of the Interstate Highway System and other superhighways, motor carriers have been permitted to haul heavier loads and more trailers per powered vehicle between terminals. It is at these terminals where such trailer combinations are assembled and disassembled for handling over more closely restricted highways. The LASH system of water transportation, involving the use of a "motor ship" capable of carrying a number of barges, may or may not require terminals for the handling of such barges.

SUMMARY

Firms have a number of reasons for warehousing their goods, including: stock spotting for customer service, break-bulk operations, inbound and outbound freight consolidation, sorting and mixing goods for outbound shipment, balancing supply with seasonal demand, balancing demand with seasonal supply, storage to facilitate production economies from long production runs, and providing buffer stocks against uncertainties in supply, demand, transportation, labor disruptions, and such.

Warehouses and warehousing operations play a major role in the logistics systems of many firms. Warehouses may function primarily as storage warehouses or as materials handling warehouses, or may combine these two activities. A warehouse facility may also house light manufacturing activities, such as simple assembly operations, customizing of products, and so forth.

In addition to its function as a storage or materials handling warehouse, a warehouse may also be described in terms of the commodities it handles, whether it is privately or publicly operated, and its legal status with respect to being a bonded warehouse or a field warehouse.

A large number of alternatives and decisions concerning warehousing and transfer facilities await the logistics manager, even after decisions have been reached concerning the amount and location of product to be stored or transferred. They include decisions about whether the facility should be leased or owned or whether a public warehousing organization should be employed to provide the service. Regardless of the ownership and operating arrangements, further decisions must be made concerning the extent to which labor-saving devices and procedures are to be employed in the facility. To the extent that the cost structures associated with various alternatives may differ, they in turn may influence decisions concerning the amount and location of storage or transfer activities to be used, suggesting the interrelated nature of these decisions.

Transportation terminals (transfer facilities) also function as materials handling or transit warehouses. As mentioned in Chapter 9, many transportation carriers now contract with shippers for services beyond traditional transportation carriage. These additional services include freight consolidation, mixing, temporary storage, and other "warehouse type" activities agreed upon by the parties.

The most significant development in the warehousing industry is the shift from a limited number of traditional warehousing services to third-party contractual relationships that include provisions tailored to the needs and logistics strategy of the client firm.

DISCUSSION QUESTIONS

1. What is the role of storage warehouses in logistics systems?

2. What is the role of materials handling warehouses in logistics systems? How do these differ from storage warehouses?

3. Under what circumstances would a logistics system require the use of combination warehouses?

4. As examples of specialized storage facilities, the text mentions tank farms, underground caverns, bunkers, and open-storage piles. Can you think of some other examples of specialized storage facilities?

5. What meanings does the phrase "legal status" have with respect to warehousing activities?

6. What are the advantages and disadvantages of public warehousing as compared to private warehousing?

7. What is the difference between "warehouse requirements" and "warehouse design"? Which comes first? Why?

8. What systems can be used to determine stock location within a warehouse? Is any one system superior to the others? Why or why not?

9. Why is manpower utilization such an important factor in assessing the efficiency of warehouse operations?

10. Why is it appropriate to consider transfer facilities as being a form of warehousing?

CASE: The Farwell Corporation—A Warehousing Decision

The president of the Farwell Corporation was considering whether the company should make use of public warehousing or, alternatively, buy or lease existing warehouse space in Orlando, Florida. Farwell's manufacturing plant and finished goods warehouse were located in Birmingham, Alabama, and the company sold its products throughout the southeastern states.

Farwell Corporation manufactured and distributed a wide line of orthopedic equipment: crutches, wheelchairs, walkers, canes, specialized physical therapy exercise machines, knee braces, shoulder braces, back braces, elastic bandages, ice packs, heating pads, and so forth.

Farwell Corporation was a young company and had experienced rapid growth in the six years since its founding by Ms. Kimberly Farwell. Ms. Farwell had a bachelor's degree in physical therapy, and had worked in several orthopedic clinics over a period of 10 years before starting her own firm. Aside from good management, Farwell Corporation had benefitted from two sources of "business": (1) the increasing number of sports-related accidents and injuries resulting from the upsurge in skiing, tennis, and other recreational sports, and (2) the growing number of elderly people in the population who had orthopedic problems.

Warehousing in the Florida market was "a natural," as Ms. Farwell put it, due to the large number of elderly retired persons living in the area and also because the climate was so conducive to outdoor sports. Farwell had been supplying its Florida dealers—mostly retail stores specializing in sales of orthopedic items—from its Birmingham plant warehouse, but Ms. Farwell realized that the firm's customers wanted quick response to their orders since most of them carried only very limited inventories of Farwell's products. This was primarily due to the fact that most Farwell products came in a variety of styles, sizes, and shapes. Stocking even a moderate number of each would bloat a retailer's inventory.

Ms. Farwell had engaged the services of a logistics consultant in Orlando, and his report indicated that the Florida market would support the placement of Farwell product inventory in the Orlando area. The key points of the consultant's report were:

1. Warehouse space was available for either purchase or lease in the Orlando area. The consultant noted that a lease for less than three years could not likely be negotiated at a "reasonable" price; any lease for a shorter period than three years would require significantly higher monthly payments than a lease for three years or longer. The cost of purchasing a suitable warehouse facility was estimated by the consultant to be about $300,000 (a 25 percent down payment and a $225,000 mortgage).

2. There were a number of public warehousing firms in the Orlando area that had good reputations for serving their clients, and several of them were willing and able to provide full third-party services for shipments throughout Florida.

3. The cost analysis of the alternatives (own, lease, or use public warehousing) showed that the figures were so close as to suggest that the decision should be made on factors other than cost of operations.

4. Savings in the operation of Farwell's finished goods warehouse operation in Birmingham resulting from establishment of warehousing in the Orlando area were included in the consultant's cost calculations. Also included were the

costs of the net increase in inventory required as well as the transportation savings resulting from large shipments to an Orlando area warehouse for distribution in Florida.

5. The direct (mortgage) and imputed (on the cash down payment) interest cost on owned facilities had been incorporated in the analysis, but the purchase cost would require the company to invest about $75,000 of its funds in a property.

6. If Farwell operated its own facility it would need, at least initially, a staff of three people: a manager, an order clerk, and a warehouse person.

Ms. Farwell had hoped the consultant's report would produce a clear case in favor of one or another of the alternatives, but from her conversations with executives in other companies with whom she was acquainted she knew that the decision her company faced was a common one, and she would have to make it.

CASE QUESTIONS

1. What decision would you recommend to Ms. Farwell?

2. What factors did you consider in making your recommendation? Explain.

SUGGESTED READINGS

The limited data available concerning the extent of public warehousing activity in the United States is published by the Bureau of the Census. Cost data and standards are published from time to time in *Warehousing Cost Digest*, a publication of Customer Service Institute, Silver Spring, Maryland.

ACKERMAN, KENNETH B., *Practical Handbook of Warehousing*, 3d ed. Van Nostrand Reinhold, New York, 1990. This 640-page book is a comprehensive treatment of the subject of warehousing written by an internationally respected authority in the field.

American Public Warehouse Register, published annually by Distribution Services of America, Foxboro, Massachusetts. A directory of public warehousing with listings in the United States, Canada, the United Kingdom, and other principal trading areas.

Measuring Productivity in Physical Distribution, Council of Logistics Management, Oak Brook, Illinois, 1978. Appendix C (pages 91–142) discusses warehousing productivity measurement.

NELSON, RAYMOND A., *Computerizing Warehouse Operations*, Prentice-Hall, Inc., New York, 1985. An in-depth treatment of methodology that may be employed to integrate warehouse operations with computerized control and record keeping.

ROBESON, JAMES F. and ROBERT G. HOUSE, *The Distribution Handbook*, The Free Press, New York, 1985. Chapters 23, 24, and 25 treat the subjects of warehouse productivity, warehouse design and construction, and materials handling.

SPEH, THOMAS W. and JAMES A. BLOMQUIST, *The Financial Evaluation of Warehousing Options: An Examination and Appraisal of Contemporary Practices*, Warehousing Education and Research

Council (Oxford, Ohio: The Warehousing Research Center, Miami University, 1988). An excellent treatment of the topic of financial analysis as applied to warehousing ownership and operation options.

Warehouse Accounting and Control, Council of Logistics Management, Oak Brook, Illinois, 1985. Prepared by the accounting firm of Ernst & Whinney, this book is a comprehensive treatment of the subject and includes a sample warehousing chart of accounts.

Trade Journals

Many issues of these monthly magazines contain articles on various aspects of warehousing. And, as noted, several publish annual directories. They are a very good source of current information on many warehousing topics and include:

Distribution, Chilton Company, Radnor, Pennsylvania (including "Warehouse Marketplace." An annual supplement to *Distribution* that contains a very comprehensive listing of public warehouses, including special sections on contract warehousing and warehousing sales associations).

Modern Materials Handling, Cahners Publishing Company, Newton, Massachusetts. Especially valuable for its coverage of warehouse materials handling systems (including an annual supplement, titled Casebook Directory, which is a comprehensive source of information on material-handling equipment).

Transportation & Distribution, Penton Publishing, Inc., Cleveland, Ohio. This publication contains many articles on warehousing management and operations.

ENDNOTES

1. Thomas W. Speh and James A. Blomquist, *The Financial Evaluation of Warehousing Options: An Examination and Appraisal of Contemporary Practices*, Warehousing Education and Research Council (Oxford, Ohio: The Warehousing Research Center, Miami University, 1988.)

2. See the Uniform Commercial Code, Article 7—Warehouse Receipts, Bills of Lading and Other Documents of Title. A copy of this section of the UCC appears as Appendix 1 in Kenneth B. Ackerman, *Practical Handbook of Warehousing*, 2d ed. (Washington, D.C.: The Traffic Service Corporation, 1986).

3. Minnesota-Northwest Warehousemen's Association Merchandise Tariff 23M.

4. See *Leading Edge Logistics Competitive Positioning for the 1990's* (Oak Brook, Illinois: Council of Logistics Management, 1989): 200 (Table 7–2).

5. Bernard J. LaLonde and Martha C. Cooper, *Partnerships in Providing Customer Service: A Third-Party Perspective* (Oak Brook, Illinois: Council of Logistics Management, 1989) 47–77.

6. *Ibid.*, 49–50.

7. Ronald H. Ballou, "Pallet Layout for Optimum Space Utilization," *Transportation and Distribution Management* (February 1964): 24–33.

8. Material for this section is adapted from James L. Heskett, "Cube-per-Order Index—A Key to Warehouse Stock Location," *Transportation and Distribution*

Management (April 1963): 27–31. Although the concepts developed in this article are almost thirty years old, there have been no significant modifications or improvements in the technique as it was originally developed. The material truly deserves its reputation as a classic in the field.

9. Much of this section is based on Kenneth B. Ackerman, *Practical Handbook of Warehousing*, 3d ed. (New York: Van Nostrand Reinhold, 1990): 123–133.

10. J. Richard Jones, "Public Warehousing: Today and Tomorrow," *Transportation and Distribution Management* (May 1972): 19–24.

APPENDIX

Part 3 • Section F
WAREHOUSING COST CALCULATION FORM (ANNUAL EXPENSE)

WAREHOUSING COST CALCULATION FORM
(Annual Expenses)

I. DIRECT HANDLING EXPENSE
A. Warehouse Labor
1. Direct Payment to Employees
   a. Wages ....$_____
   b. Bonuses ....$_____
   c. Overtime ....$_____
   d. Other ....$_____
   TOTAL..$_____

2. Compensated Fringe Benefits
   a. Health and Welfare ....$_____
   b. Pension ....$_____
   c. Life Insurance ....$_____
   d. Uniforms ....$_____
   e. Other ....$_____
   TOTAL..$_____

3. Compensated Time-Off
   a. Vacation ....$_____
   b. Holidays ....$_____
   c. Funeral ....$_____
   d. Sick Pay ....$_____
   e. Personal Leave ....$_____
   f. Jury Duty ....$_____
   g. Other ....$_____
   TOTAL..$_____

4. Statutory Payroll Taxes
   a. FICA...$_____
   b. Federal Unemployment ....$_____
   c. State Unemployment ....$_____
   d. Workers' Compensation ....$_____
   e. State Long-Term Disability ....$_____
   f. Other Payroll Taxes ....$_____
   TOTAL..$_____

5. Purchased Labor ....$_____

6. Fees and Compensated Time
   a. Training ....$_____
   b. Education ....$_____
   c. Other ....$_____
   TOTAL..$_____

TOTAL WAREHOUSE LABOR. ....$_____

WAREHOUSING COST CALCULATION FORM
(Annual Expenses)

B. Handling Equipment

1. Lift Trucks and Attachments
   a. Rental or Depreciation
      and Interest ....$_____
   b. Fuel/Chargers and Batteries/
      Lubrication ....$_____
   c. Maintenance
      1) Labor ....$_____
      2) Parts ....$_____
      3) Equipment ....$_____
      TOTAL...$_____
   d. Tires..$_____
   e. Other ....$_____
   TOTAL...$_____

2. Special Purpose Handling Equipment
   a. Rental or Depreciation and
      Interest ....$_____
   b. Power/Fuel ....$_____
   c. Maintenance
      1) Labor ....$_____
      2) Parts ....$_____
      3) Equipment ....$_____
      4) Contract ....$_____
      TOTAL...$_____
   d. Other ....$_____
   TOTAL ....$_____

TOTAL HANDLING EQUIPMENT. ....$_____

C. Other Handling Expense

l. Pallets
   a. Expense ....$_____
   b. Repair ....$_____
   TOTAL...$_____
2. Supplies ....$_____
3. Detention/Demurrage.....................................$_____
4. Recouping Warehouse Damage ....$_____
5. Trash Hauling ....$_____
6. Other ....$_____

TOTAL OTHER HANDLING EXPENSE..$_____

TOTAL DIRECT HANDLING EXPENSE...$_____

WAREHOUSING COST CALCULATION FORM
(Annual Expenses)

II. DIRECT STORAGE EXPENSE

A. Facility

1. Rent or Depreciation
   and Interest .... $_____
2. Real Estate Taxes .... $_____
3. Insurance .... $_____
4. Exterior Maintenance .... $_____
5. Other .... $_____
TOTAL .... $_____

B. Grounds

1. Mowing .... $_____
2. Snow Blowing .... $_____
3. Parking Lot .... $_____
4. Other .... $_____
TOTAL .... $_____

C. Storage Equipment

1. Depreciation and Interest .... $_____
2. Maintenance .... $_____
   a. Labor .... $_____
   b. Parts .... $_____
   c. Equipment .... $_____
   d. Contract .... $_____
   TOTAL .... $_____
TOTAL .... $_____

D. Facility Modification

1. Labor .... $_____
2. Equipment .... $_____
3. Materials .... $_____
4. Contract .... $_____
5. Other .... $_____
TOTAL .... $_____

E. Utilities. .... $_____

F. Interior Maintenance

1. Labor .... $_____
2. Materials/Parts .... $_____
3. Equipment .... $_____
4. Contract .... $_____
5. Other .... $_____
TOTAL .... $_____

WAREHOUSING COST CALCULATION FORM
(Annual Expenses)

G. Security

1. Installation ....$_____
2. Operations ....$_____
3. Guard Service ....$_____
4. Other ....$_____

TOTAL..$_____

H. Pest Control. ....$_____

I. Other Facility Expense

1. _____ ....$_____
2. _____ ....$_____
3. _____ ....$_____
4. _____ ....$_____

TOTAL..$_____

TOTAL DIRECT STORAGE EXPENSE. ....$_____

WAREHOUSING COST CALCULATION FORM
(Annual Expenses)

III. OPERATING ADMINISTRATIVE EXPENSE

A. Supervisory Salaries. ....$_____

B. Clerical Salaries. ....$_____

C. Purchased Labor. ....$_____

D. Office Equipment (major)
1. Rental or
   Depreciation and Interest ....$_____
2. Maintenance ....$_____
3. Other ....$_____
   TOTAL. ....$_____

E. Office Equipment (minor). ....$_____

F. Office Maintenance
1. Repair
   a. Labor ....$_____
   b. Material ....$_____
   c. Equipment ....$_____
   d. Contract ....$_____
   TOTAL. ....$_____
2. Janitorial ....$_____
3. Other ....$_____
TOTAL. ....$_____

G. Telephone/Facsimile. ....$_____

H. Postage. ....$_____

I. Printing. ....$_____

J. Office Supplies. ....$_____

WAREHOUSING COST CALCULATION FORM
(Annual Expenses)

K. Data Processing

1. Rental or
   Depreciation and Interest .... $_____
2. Dedicated Telephone Lines .... $_____
3. Supplies .... $_____
4. Software .... $_____
5. Maintenance
   a. Labor .... $_____
   b. Parts .... $_____
   c. Equipment .... $_____
   d. Contract .... $_____
   TOTAL .... $_____
6. Training .... $_____
7. Contracted Data .... $_____
8. Other .... $_____
TOTAL .... $_____

L. Legal and Professional. .... $_____

M. Taxes and Licenses. .... $_____

N. Travel. .... $_____

O. Personal Property Tax. .... $_____

P. Insurance and Claims. .... $_____

Q. Losses Due to Damage,
   Shortages, and Errors. .... $_____

R. Other. .... $_____

TOTAL OPERATING ADMINISTRATIVE EXPENSE. .... $_____

**WAREHOUSING COST
CALCULATION FORM**
(Annual Expenses)

IV. GENERAL ADMINISTRATIVE EXPENSE

A. Executive Salaries. ....$_____

B. Marketing Salaries. ....$_____

C. Support Salaries. ....$_____

D. Office
1. Space ....$_____
2. Equipment
   a. Rental or Depreciation ....$_____
   b. Maintenance ....$_____
   TOTAL...$_____
3. Maintenance
   a. Repair ....$_____
   b. Janitorial ....$_____
   TOTAL...$_____
TOTAL..$_____

E. Automobile Expense
1. Operating Expense ....$_____
2. Rental or Depreciation ....$_____
3. Other ....$_____
TOTAL...$_____

F. General Office Operations
1. Telephone ....$_____
2. Security ....$_____
3. Postage ....$_____
4. Printing ....$_____
5. Utilities ....$_____
6. Courier Services ....$_____
7. Supplies ....$_____
8. Other ....$_____
TOTAL...$_____

G. Data Processing....$_____

H. Taxes. ....$_____

I. Legal and Professional. ....$_____

J. Selling and Advertising. ....$_____

K. Travel Expense. ....$_____

WAREHOUSING COST CALCULATION FORM
(Annual Expenses)

L. Dues, Subscriptions,
and Educational Expense. ....$_____

M. Donations. ....$_____

N. Personnel. ....$_____

O. Bad Debt Expense. ....$_____

P. Other Non-Operating Expense

1. _____ ....$_____
2. _____ ....$_____
3. _____ ....$_____
4. _____ ....$_____
5. _____ ....$_____

TOTAL. ....$_____

TOTAL GENERAL ADMINISTRATIVE EXPENSE. ....$_____

WAREHOUSING COST CALCULATION FORM
(Annual Expenses)

V. HANDLING EXPENSE PER MAN HOUR

STEP A. Total Direct Handling Expense, from page F-3 .... $_____

STEP B. Proportion of Operating Administrative Expense (OA) and General Administrative Expense (GA) allocated to Handling Expense:

    1. Total Operating Administrative Expense, from page F-7 ....$_____

    2. Total General Administrative Expense, from page F-9 ....$_____

    3. Total OA and GA Expense .... $_____

    4. Percentage of OA and GA Expense to apply to Handling; percentage for Storage:

       _____% for Handling

       _____% for Storage
       100%

    5. OA and GA Expense allocated to Handling

    $_____   X   _____   = $_____
    Total OA and GA   times   Handling %,   Total OA and GA
    Expense, STEP B-3   STEP B-4   Expense, allocated
                                                           to Handling

STEP C. Total Handling Expense. Add:

    1. Total Direct Handling Expense, STEP A ....$_____

    2. Total OA and GA Expense allocated to Handling, STEP B-5 ....$_____

    Total Handling Expense ....$_____

**WAREHOUSING COST
CALCULATION FORM**
(Annual Expenses)

VIII. STORAGE "RATE" PER UNIT

STEP A. Monthly Storage Expense Per Gross Square Foot

1. Total Storage Expense Per Gross Square Foot, from Storage Expense Calculations (including Profit, if applicable); page F-12, STEP F .... $_____

   per Gross
   Square Foot

2. Divide Total Storage Expense Per Gross Square Foot by 12

   $_____   ÷   12   = $_____

   Total Storage Expense   divided by   Monthly Storage
   per Gross Square Foot,   Expense per Gross
   STEP A-1   Square Foot

STEP B. Determine Units Stored Per Gross Square Foot During a Month

   $_____   ÷   _____   =   _____

   Estimate of Peak   divided by   Gross Square Feet,   Units Stored per
   Inventory During   Page F-12, STEP E   Gross Square Foot
   a Month   During a Month
                                                                      where Units are

                                                                      _____

STEP C. Storage "Rate" Per Unit

   $_____   ÷   _____   = $_____

   Monthly Storage   divided by   Units Stored per   Monthly Storage
   Expense per Gross   Gross Square Foot   "Rate" per Unit
   Square Foot, STEP A-2   During a Month,
                                           STEP B

WAREHOUSING COST CALCULATION FORM
(Annual Expenses)

VI. STORAGE EXPENSE PER GROSS SQUARE FOOT

STEP A. Total Direct Storage Expense, from page F-5: ....$_____

STEP B. Proportion of OA and GA Expense allocated to Storage Expense:

    1. Total OA and GA Expense, page F-10, STEP B-3. ....$_____

    2. Storage percentage of OA and GA Expense
       from Handling Expense calculations,
       page F-10, STEP B-4. .... _____ %

    3. OA and GA Expense allocated to Storage:

$_____	X	_____	=	$_____
Total OA and GA Expense, from STEP B-1 above	times	Storage %, from STEP B-2 above		Total OA and GA Expense allocated to Storage

STEP C. Total Storage Expense. Add:

    1. Total Direct Storage Expense, STEP A = ...$_____

    2. Total OA and GA Expense allocated to Storage,
       STEP B-3 =...$_____

    Total Storage Expense ....$_____

STEP D. Public Warehouse Profit Margin

    1. Total Storage Expense (STEP C) times Profit Percentage = Profit Dollars.

$_____	X	_____	=	$_____
Total Storage Expense, STEP C	times	Desired Profit Percentage		Profit Dollars

    2. Profit Dollars + Total Storage Expense = Total Storage Expense plus Profit

$_____	+	_____	=	$_____
Profit Dollars, STEP D-1	plus	Total Storage Expense, STEP C		Total Storage Expense plus Profit

STEP E. Total Warehouse Gross Square Footage = ..._____ Gross Square Feet

STEP F. Storage Expense Per Gross Square Foot

$_____	÷	_____	=	$_____
Total Storage Expense, STEP C (STEP D for public warehouse)	divided by	Total Warehouse Gross Square Feet, STEP E.		Total Storage Expense per Gross Square Foot

**WAREHOUSING COST
CALCULATION FORM**
(Annual Expenses)

VII. HANDLING "RATE" PER UNIT

STEP A. Total Handling Expense Per Man-Hour (including Profit, if applicable)
from Handling Expense Calculations, from page F-11,
STEP F .... $ _____
   Per Man-Hour

STEP B. Estimated Throughput Units Per Man-Hour:

    1. Total Annual Throughput Units   = _____
    (Total annual receipts plus total annual shipments divided by 2)

    2. Total Annual Warehouse Man-Hours,
    from Step E, page F-11   = _____

    3. _____ ÷ _____   = _____
    Throughput Units,   divided by   Total Man-Hours,   Throughput Units
    STEP B-1   STEP B-2   Per Man-Hour

STEP C. Handling "Rate" Per Unit

    $ _____ ÷ _____   = $ _____
    Total Handling   divided by   Throughput Units   Handling "Rate"
    Expense per   per Man-Hour,   per Unit
    Man-Hour,   STEP B-3
    STEP A

WAREHOUSING COST CALCULATION FORM
(Annual Expenses)

VIII. STORAGE "RATE" PER UNIT

STEP A. Monthly Storage Expense Per Gross Square Foot

1. Total Storage Expense Per Gross Square Foot, from Storage Expense Calculations (including Profit, if applicable); page F-12, STEP F .... $_____

   per Gross
   Square Foot

2. Divide Total Storage Expense Per Gross Square Foot by 12

$_____   ÷   12   = $_____

Total Storage Expense   divided by   Monthly Storage
per Gross Square Foot,   Expense per Gross
STEP A-1   Square Foot

STEP B. Determine Units Stored Per Gross Square Foot During a Month

$_____   ÷   _____   =   _____

Estimate of Peak   divided by   Gross Square Feet,   Units Stored per
Inventory During   Page F-12, STEP E   Gross Square Foot
a Month   During a Month
                                                                                      where Units are

                                                                                      _____

STEP C. Storage "Rate" Per Unit

$_____   ÷   _____   = $_____

Monthly Storage   divided by   Units Stored per   Monthly Storage
Expense per Gross   Gross Square Foot   "Rate" per Unit
Square Foot, STEP A-2   During a Month,
                                             STEP B

SOURCE: Dr. Thomas W. Speh, *How to Determine Total Warehouse Costs*, copyright © 1990 by DCW-USA, Inc. Reprinted with permission.

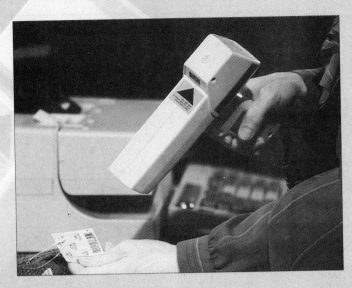

Barcode scanning equipment is revolutionizing the processing of logistics system information in terms of both cost reduction and improved accuracy.

CHAPTER TWELVE

Information Processing and Communication Services

LEARNING OBJECTIVES

The objectives of this chapter are to:

➢ Define the scope of the field of information processing and communication services with respect to suppliers and point out important trends in costs, capabilities, and regulation.

➢ Present and discuss the nature of data communication systems, their role in logistics systems, and the process of determining and evaluating the direct and indirect costs of data communication systems and their capabilities.

➢ Point out the role and limitations of voice communication systems (telephones, car telephones, beepers, and radios) in logistics operations.

➢ Present information concerning current computer applications in the field of business logistics, currently available commercial logistics software packages, and advantages and disadvantages of developing in-house software versus purchasing software packages from vendors.

➢ Present and discuss current trends with respect to the use of electronic data interchange (EDI) in the logistics field, the role of third-party EDI suppliers, and projections of the growth of EDI's role in logistics systems.

➢ Point out the wide variety of information technologies being applied in the field of business logistics.

➢ Discuss several aspects of managing an information processing system, including computer/communications security, errors and error control, and the need to insure the system is operating the way it was intended to operate.

Information processing and communication services are critically important components of logistics systems, in which they parallel the functions of the brain and nervous system of the human body. The extraordinarily rapid growth of computer capability and the sharp decline in computer costs have combined with spectacular advances in communication technology to produce a set of tools for logistics management that one could only dream of just a decade ago. The speed of technological change in these areas continues to be so fast, that just keeping up with what is currently available is today a time-consuming task for logistics managers.

In some circumstances, information (inventory records) and communication links even function as alternatives to the use of transportation to accomplish product "movement" or demand-supply coordination. Consider, for example, the practice of many oil and chemical companies having an extensive communication system and a data base showing available surplus products. This enables such firms to trade a quantity of a commodity representing a surplus to one firm and a shortage to another firm at a particular location. In a sense, this practice reduces the "movement" cost of the product to almost nothing. In a less dramatic but nevertheless important way, a chain retailer may use a communication network and inventory data base to coordinate and minimize reshipments of stocks among stores in the chain.

As a nation develops, its primary strategic resource evolves from agriculture to factory production and financial capital and then to knowledge. Many writers have characterized the latter half of the twentieth century as marking the entrance of the industrial nations into "the information age." Today, the importance of information processing and communication for all functions of a firm competing in our post-industrial society can scarcely be overstated.

SCOPE OF THE FIELD

Information processing and communication services encompass two very large industries, computers and communication facilities. Our concern here is not with these industries as such, but rather with the uses and applications of the many varied products and services they offer to the logistics manager.

The Suppliers

Computing and communication activities increasingly have come to share electronic technology in recent years. These developments have blurred the previous distinction between the two activities and thrown formerly noncompeting firms into the same competitive arena. The most dramatic example of this has been the increasing competition between computer manufacturers such as IBM and telephone companies such as AT&T.

This competition has involved the private and unregulated data processing suppliers against the private but regulated communications suppliers. The likelihood that this competition will increase was assured by two historic court decisions early in 1982. On the same day that an antitrust suit against IBM was dropped, an accord was reached by the courts and AT&T allowing it to spin off its regulated regional telephone companies, while retaining its largely unregulated and more profitable manufacturing facilities and its long distance telephone network. This facilitated a move by AT&T into related information processing and communication industries. It also made possible the entrance of new firms, such as MCI and US Sprint, into the long distance telephone industry. This move toward increased competition in the communication industry in the United States is in distinct contrast to policies in most nations, where the telephone system is a monopoly operated by the government. The shape of the future in communications in the United States is complicated further by the possibility that a third major player, the U.S. Postal Service, will develop electronic mail services to complement its regular and express letter mail services.

International communications and data processing services are provided by a somewhat different set of competitors. Among the leaders in international communications is RCA, while General Electric's MARK III teleprocessing network uses more than 100 computers and satellite communications to serve over 100,000 users in 20 countries, on four continents; and the Telex service has become a widely-used form of communication between many thousands of users of common sending and receiving terminals installed throughout the world. In total, there are perhaps 20 international networks linking computers by means of undersea cables, microwave stations, and satellites.

Important Trends

Many trends occurring in the rapidly evolving technologies of the communication and data processing industries are remarkable, at least to laypersons. However, three specific "business" trends in these industries are most relevant for our purposes: (1) rapidly declining costs, (2) vastly increasing operational capabilities, and (3) changing government regulation.

Cost The costs of transmitting, sorting, and otherwise manipulating information have declined dramatically in recent years. In 1919 a three-minute station-to-station telephone call from New York to San Francisco cost $16.50. By 1946 the charge was $2.50. By 1990, bulk long-distance telephone services, such as AT&T, MCI, and Sprint, have reduced the cost of such a call to less than one dollar. When one takes the effects of inflation into account, this dramatic cost decline is all the more remarkable.

Given the relatively great reductions in the cost of electronic means of communication, an ever increasing proportion of messages involving business transactions is moving by that medium. This has caused a great deal of concern to the U.S. Postal Service, for which the proportion of mailed business checks, bills, statements of account, purchase orders, and other records of transactions have been declining. The fact that this type of mail is one of the least costly and most profitable for the Postal Service to handle helps explain the Service's interest in developing an electronic mail service.

However, the Postal Service may well have been preempted by telephone facsimile document transmission (FAX), which has grown with enormous rapidity in the past few years, with 181,000 FAX machines having been produced in the United States in 1986, and 228,000 in 1987.[1] Unless an original document (such as a check) is required, FAX machines are suitable for the transmission of any document printed (or written) on standard-size paper, such as purchase orders, bills of lading, freight bills, inventory reports, and freight manifests. FAX machines have two very desirable characteristics: (1) they are relatively inexpensive, many models costing less than $1,000, and (2) they make use of regular telephone lines. All that is necessary is that the sender and receiver each have a FAX machine.[2]

The most dramatic cost reductions in the information field have been achieved in the storage and manipulation of data. Computers are now so fast, and computer memory relatively so inexpensive, that the cost of data processing is now much more a matter of the human resources employed (operators, programmers, and such) than the hardware itself. A computer costing more than a million dollars in 1970 can today be outperformed by a computer costing less than $10,000.

Capabilities Advances in communication speeds and capacities — as great as they continue to be — have not kept pace with the sharply declining costs of computer data storage and the speed of data manipulation by computers.

The chief determinant of the capabilities of communication facilities is the speed at which information can be transmitted. Current services provide basically three different ranges of speeds. The first of these is the narrow-band line designed for telegraph and similar machines transmitting at speeds ranging from 45 to 150 bits per second.* Communications facilities that have this speed capability include Telex (offered by Western Union) and the teletypewriter. The second range of speeds is provided by telephone channels transmitting at speeds ranging generally from 600 to 2,400 bits per second. Wide-band services are high-speed data transmission facilities with speeds up to 500,000 bits per second.

Although satellites, microwave relay stations, and fiber optic cable have added to the available alternatives for long distance communication, the field awaits exploitation of even more advanced technologies such as those associated with lasers and related concepts.

Regulation For the most part, the data processing industries have not faced economic regulation. In distinct contrast to this, rates for interstate communication services are regulated by the Federal Communications Commission and intrastate rates are subject to state regulation. Different states frequently have different rates for the same types of services.

The Federal Communications Commission (FCC) is an independent federal agency that regulates radio, television, telephone, telegraph, and other electronic transmissions by wire or other means. The powers of the FCC are defined in the Communications Act of 1934. The FCC's overall goal is ''. . . to make available, so far as possible, to all the people of the United States a rapid, efficient, nation-wide, and world-wide wire and radio communications service with adequate facilities at reasonable charges. . .''[3] The provisions of the Act require that regulated communications common carriers furnish services at reasonable charges upon reasonable request. Every common carrier subject to FCC regulation must have its plans for facilities approved by the FCC before they become effective. To do this, carriers must file tariffs (or concur with existing tariffs) showing all services and charges offered to the public. A tariff, unless suspended or explicitly disapproved by the FCC, automatically becomes effective.

Lines of demarcation between the data processing and communication industries have become blurred as companies in both industries increasingly offer distributed data processing networks. For example, several years ago a company with sizable financial resources, Satellite Business Systems (SBS), was formed to compete with AT&T in the communication of data. SBS is the property of IBM, AETNA Life and Casualty Company, and Communication Satellite Corporation. Instead of the traditional communication by wire, SBS offers its customers the option of communication by way of sending and receiving rooftop ''dishes'' tuned in to a space satellite.

---

*A bit is a unit of information content. A contraction for ''binary digit,'' a bit is the smallest unit of information in the binary system of notation. It is the choice between two possible states, usually designated one and zero. Eight bits make up a byte, referred to in Table 12–2.

Evaluation of Alternatives

A rapidly-increasing array of options for both data processing and data communication has increased the need for evaluating available alternatives. Invariably, this involves the analysis of cost/benefit trade-offs between speed, capacity, and other capabilities and costs associated with each alternative.

Capabilities and Costs   Most computers manufactured through the mid-1970s were large units designed for centralized data processing. In recent years, by far the largest proportion manufactured has been of the microcomputer and minicomputer types, much smaller in size than their early mainframe predecessors. At the same time, miniaturization of computer components has made today's micro- and minicomputers more powerful than the large central processing units produced just a decade ago.

Two types of costs make up the total costs of a data processing system. Direct costs include those incurred in operating the equipment, particularly salaries and equipment depreciation and maintenance. Indirect costs are those associated with system design, such as defining and designing data bases, establishing output formats, designing the reporting system, evaluating and specifying computer systems and selecting equipment. Other indirect costs include selecting and training personnel, management involvement, and other general overhead items such as electrical power for machine operation, lighting, and air conditioning.

Further, costs of computer hardware represent a rapidly shrinking proportion of the total cost of a data processing system. At the same time, the costs of software have risen as a proportion of total system costs. As a result, hardware costs, as a rule of thumb, may make up only about 15 percent of the total cost of an information system, and even this percentage will likely continue to decline.*

Basic Alternatives   The development of minicomputers capable of accommodating a large volume of data processing activities on a "stand alone" basis (unconnected to a large central computer) has opened the way both for increased decentralization of computing activities and the development of what has come to be known as distributed processing. Both of these developments have significant implications for logistics management.

The minicomputer is of particular importance for controlling logistics functions carried out at many locations. For example, a minicomputer may be used to manage centralized inventory control and also to handle order-processing activities at outlying distribution centers. Such a computer can provide a distribution center manager with more complete control of information needed to run the facility, often more rapid system response time, and the flexibility of having available computing capacity without having to rely on a central computing facility shared with other managers of various functional activities. While minicomputers may not be able to handle large-scale problem-solving, they are especially effective when used in the management of day-to-day logistics operations.

The flexibility of the micro- and minicomputers can be wedded to the capacity of a large-scale central computing unit through what has come to be called *distributed data processing*, a strategy in which data processing tasks are parcelled out to smaller computers at several locations linked by a communication network. When data processing and communication

---

*Authors' estimate, based on various industry estimates.

COMPUTERS OF THE WORLD, UNITE!

Jeremy Main

I don't know what you're talking about, but keep talking," said Edson Gaylord, chairman of Ingersoll Milling Machine Co. of Rockford, Illinois. George Hess, his vice president for systems and planning, kept talking. When Hess finished, he had persuaded Gaylord to launch Ingersoll, an extremely competitive machine tool producer, on a complex, risky venture: turning itself into what is becoming known as a computer-integrated business. That was in 1979. Today a lot of CEOs want to do the same.

The computer-integrated business is a hot concept. The phrase describes an enterprise whose major functions—for example, sales, finance, distribution, manufacturing—exchange operating information quickly and constantly via computer. Product designers can send specifications straight to machines on the factory floor. Salesmen—or even customers—can find out which products are in stock and when they can be delivered, and can place orders, which automatically cause new units to be manufactured. Accounting receives on-line all information about sales, purchases, and prices. And high executives can get any of this information, and much more, immediately. The computer system parallels the whole process of producing and selling goods or services and makes it move faster—much faster.

Speed is the compelling reason for computer integration. Old methods of deploying a lot of different computer systems that couldn't talk to each other, or could talk only through expensive translation programs, aren't good enough anymore. Says John Rockart, head of the Center for Information Systems Research at MIT's Sloan School: "The buffers of space, time, people, and inventory are gone, so you have to have the lubrication of information to get the flow going." To react fast enough to customers' demands, corporations need a fast, seamless information network throughout the company. For example, Sony aims to use integration to cut the time it takes to make and distribute products from 50 days to 20.

It isn't easy. No large company is yet fully computer integrated. One company's network started in manufacturing and then grew to encompass management and sales. Another began on the sales side and is just now reaching into the factories. But even if a system falls short of the scale its planners envisaged, it can still dramatically improve performance.

Ingersoll's system, put in place by 1982 at a cost of $5 million and much elaborated since, has helped considerably.

While half of America's machine tool companies have folded since the 1970s, Ingersoll's shipments of large tools multiplied tenfold to nearly $500 million last year. The company is just finishing what it believes to be the largest custom-built machine tool ever made, a monster the size of a three-story house to make large turbines and other parts for hydroelectric generators. The customer is Impsa, a maker of hydroelectric equipment in Argentina.

Companies much bigger than Ingersoll are following its example. Frito-Lay, PepsiCo's most profitable division, has a new network that joins the hand-held computers used by every one of its 10,000 route salespeople to the office of President Robert Beeby, with connections to area and division offices and to company plants. Saturn Corp., the new General Motors small-car subsidiary, starts off fully computer integrated. Du Pont is committed to tying all its 80 businesses in 50 countries into a uniform information network. The effort will take at least five years, swallowing up about $200 million of Du Pont's $900 million annual spending on information systems.

If you're thinking of computer-integrating your operation, brace yourself: It won't be easy. No computer company sells a ready-made integrated system. Because of any large enterprise's vast complexity, each system must be specially created, a fact that provides fertile ground for consultants, business professors, and software and hardware firms.

Digital Equipment Corp. not only is turning itself into a computer-integrated enterprise, but is also showing others how to do it. The large Tokyo office of Andersen Consulting (part of Arthur Andersen) works almost entirely on helping clients such as Sony create networks. The job is big enough that pessimistic experts, such as Brandt Allen of the University of Virginia business school, argue that big companies can never integrate themselves completely. Says he: "The effort is so gargantuan and takes so long that by the time you have finished, everything has changed and the champions of the project have long gone."

Giant conglomerates probably don't need to be fully integrated: The lawn equipment division doesn't require intimate communication with the life insurance division. In any case, argues MIT's Rockart, "total integration is not the issue—integration with the customer is the issue." He says that companies with distinct sets of clients might use a separate network for each, rather than try to tie the whole corporation into one giant network. Johnson & Johnson might have a network for hospitals, another for pharmacies, and a third for other retail stores. Competition to give the customer better and faster service will keep up the pressure to put more business on-line.

In achieving integration on any scale, the key obstacles are no longer technological; they are in management and organization. "Integration was inhibited in the past by cost and lack of technology, but that has changed in the past two or three years," says David Mengden, director of Du Pont's computing and networking services. Unit computing costs have dropped by a factor of 100,000 in 20 years, and telecommunications costs are falling by 10% to 15% a year. Fiber-optic cables can furnish the vast capacity that companies need when transmitting engineering drawings and other graphic material. Two such cables span the Atlantic, another crosses the Pacific, and two more will reach the Orient in the next two years.

So the machines are up to the job. The trouble comes from complicated, sometimes irrational, corporate organizations and procedures. For example, each division in a company often counts sales or profits differently. A computer network can't cope until they are counted the same way. Every process, whether in accounting or design or the CEO's office, needs to be rethought and simplified.

Small companies are easier to integrate than big ones, new companies easier than old ones. Lynda Applegate, a Harvard business school professor, says the companies having the hardest time integrating are the large ones that set up massive back-room computer systems in the 1960s and 1970s, such as banks and insurance companies. The systems are obsolete, but replacing them is difficult and costly. It's easier to computerize the operations of a brand-new company or of an existing company that wasn't heavily computerized, like Frito-Lay.

Ex-CEO Michael Jordan relates that Frito-Lay decided to reorganize its sales system in the mid-1980s because processing 100,000 sales documents a week by hand had become too cumbersome. Besides that, the business was getting more complex and fragmented. As a national company competing mostly with strong regional companies that are close to their markets, Frito-Lay was handicapped because news of competitive incursions took months to drift up to headquarters in Dallas. Says Jordan: "We needed instant actuals."

Frito-Lay anchored its new system to the hand-held Fujitsu computers issued to all its salespeople in 1987 and 1988. The computers are about as big and tough as a long brick. A salesman carries one into the store, punching in the code numbers and quantity of Fritos, Cheetos, Tostitos, and other snacks that need replacing, and the number of "stales" he removes because they have reached the end of their 35-day shelf life. When he attaches his hand-held, as Frito-Lay peo-

ple call it, to a printer in his truck, it spits out an invoice for the day's deliveries to that store, which he hands over with the snacks.

At day's end, the 10,000 Frito-Lay salespeople hook their hand-helds to telephones and the sales information pours into the company's IBM 3090 mainframes in Dallas. They pull it all together and then redistribute it in appropriate chunks to the area and division offices; to marketing, purchasing, and transportation offices, and to top management.

For salesmen, the hand-helds eliminate four to five hours of paperwork a week. To a division sales manager like Paul Davis in Dallas they mean that every Monday he gets a summary of sales, crisp and clear, on his computer screen. He can break down the sales any way he wants — by product, type of store, or district — and he can get the results daily if he wants to follow a critical campaign closely. Bad news shows up in red. Davis recalls that he used to get sales figures six weeks after the fact, in a hard-to-analyze two-foot pile of computer printouts.

When Frito-Lay and Von's, a Los Angeles supermarket chain, recently ran a joint promotion, the daily report showed that sales were up, but more important, that some stores in the chain were doing a lot better than others. A quick trip through the chain revealed a big variance in the displays. Then a call to the chain's headquarters — which didn't know that not all stores were cooperating — got the laggards revved up. The reaction time was two days. The old Frito-Lay would have noticed a slight increase in Los Angeles sales weeks later, and probably would never have known why the promotion didn't do better.

Frito-Lay keeps a product-by-product, store-by-store watch on competitors through its integrated system, although the information comes more slowly. Monthly reports from a market research firm, Information Resources, go into the database with the internal information. Competitors can buy the same information about Frito-Lay, but they can't pass it around the company in the same accessible and friendly graphic fashion. Frito-Lay finds that this use of competitive information has helped persuade store owners to give its products more shelf space. If you can show them that Frito-Lay's snacks move faster or produce a higher margin than the snacks of another brand that is getting bigger displays, says Jordan, you have a powerful argument for winning more space.

Integration certainly has produced results. Since 1988 Frito-Lay has added 400 routes without increasing its sales force of 10,000 and pushed revenues up by almost $1 billion, to $4.2 billion. Jordan, now CEO of PepsiCo World Wide Foods, says, "We couldn't manage the company today without this system." PepsiCo's soft-drink division is going to

Continued

COMPUTERS OF THE WORLD, UNITE! CONTINUED

hand-held computers, and the restaurant division is considering a similar network tied to the cash registers.

How fast can a computer-integrated company move? Take a look at Mayday, a sophisticated $5-million-a-year machine tool shop in Lewisville, Texas. Mayday manufactures bushings, the metal sleeves that protect some moving parts on aircraft, such as the wheel struts. They are often made of exotic metals to fine tolerances.

Jim Nelson, Mayday's president, says every company in the business uses the same type of production equipment. "What we need is time management," he says. "I'm selling time on the machines." He began by buying big automated Japanese lathes for the plant. But as the plant became more productive, he realized he needed to computerize the office to process more orders faster to keep up with the machines. Nelson bought some elements of the integrated system, like the bookkeeping software, off the shelf, which helped keep costs down. Others had to be designed by his own programmer.

Today, Nelson has an automated system for quoting prices when a customer calls in for an order. When the customer gives his specifications, Nelson's computers can figure the costs of materials and machine time and quote a delivery date and suggested prices within 30 seconds, even if the part has never been made before. If the client places the order, then the system itself sends him a confirmation by fax or mail, or both, and takes other steps to make the product, such as ordering materials and scheduling machine time. As the order flows through the plant, Nelson's computers can report its progress. At the end, the system produces the shipping labels and invoices.

Mighty Du Pont is far behind Mayday, but the imperatives are the same. Du Pont needs to develop, sell, and deliver products faster to remain competitive. If a Du Pont salesman in West Germany wants to sell O rings to an auto company today, he can look up the parts available in Germany in a catalogue. But when Du Pont becomes computer integrated in the mid-1990s, he will be able to look into a worldwide database and find not only what O rings are available, but also what products are being developed and when they should be ready for delivery.

Du Pont has a head start on building its system. Ten years ago the company told all divisions to standardize equipment, using IBM mainframes with Hewlett-Packard and DEC minicomputers. Du Pont also has a worldwide electronic mail network linking 80,000 of its 146,000 employees. And last year it installed an executive information system that supplies some 300 top executives with key numbers and charts that can be updated daily.

Over the next five or six years, each of these Du Pont systems will be meshed into a much expanded network with the same basic hardware and software throughout. The system will grow and bend to accommodate new technologies and business needs, says Ray Cairns, vice president for information technology. The effort to simplify and rationalize the corporation to give integration a chance to work has already caused major changes at Du Pont. For example, there used to be more than 40 kinds of distributed control systems corporate-wide. They are the computer brains that run continuous processes like refining oil by manipulating valves, sensing pressures, and so forth. Du Pont cut the 40 types to seven and then to two.

In contrast to Du Pont, GM's Saturn started with a clean sheet since the division is brand new and was conceived as a computer-integrated enterprise. EDS, the data-processing company that GM acquired from Ross Perot, supplies much of the expertise and equipment to tie all of Saturn into a single database. Michael Reed, the EDS group manager for Saturn, uses the slogan FROM ART TO PART, meaning that the pieces that make up a Saturn car are designed on computers, which tell purchasing, manufacturing, and other departments what they must do for that part to be made and then schedule production.

Saturn's system actually goes well beyond art to part. Top suppliers will link electronically with Saturn, so that the orders they get from GM, bills they send, and payments they receive will all move electronically. Once a car is built, a computer record will follow it to the dealer and through its life until it is scrapped, so long as the owners keep going to Saturn dealers anywhere for service. Each service visit or repair will go into the car's record. With this system plus good service at reasonable prices, Saturn hopes to hang on to two-thirds of its customers for regular service and repairs after the warranty period instead of the usual one-third.

By tracking sales and customer preferences closely and fine-tuning production, Saturn also hopes to run on slimmer inventories. Says Saturn vice president Donald Hudler: "Conventional wisdom holds that everybody should have a 60-day supply of cars. We want to operate on a 30- to 45-day supply. Nothing good happens to a car sitting in inventory." How well all this will work, of course, remains to be seen.

Creating the computer-integrated corporation remains chancy. How can you put into a computer the subtleties and intricacies of relationships in a big corporation? Even if you succeed, won't you create an overbearing centralized management at a time when business theorists are calling for more decision-making power down the line? Supporters of integration argue that if the new networks give CEOs better knowledge of what even distant managers are doing, the CEOs will feel comfortable allowing the managers a freer hand—and the managers will have the knowledge to make good decisions.

At least, that is the goal. Reaching it is sure to be difficult. But like a number of other elusive goals, just pursuing it can make a company a lot stronger.

systems are designed in this fashion, a network of computers becomes involved in accomplishing an operation.[4]

The extent to which stand-alone computers and distributed data processing are used rather than large, centralized computers depends to a large degree on the nature of the operation to be managed, the capability of middle managers at outlying locations, the complexity of the data processing task, and the degree to which decentralized management is to be encouraged.

DATA COMMUNICATION

A data communication system is a combination of people and machines whose primary purpose is to transfer digital data between two or more terminals in a reliable manner. As discussed later in this chapter, it is what enables electronic data interchange to take place among a company's multiple logistics facilities, or between one company's logistics system and the data processing facilities of other companies.

Data communication is a rapidly expanding field that has grown because of rapid advances in data processing technologies. In order to utilize effectively the data processing facilities that are available, it is necessary to have high-speed communication links to transmit data to these processing facilities. They are so vital to an effective data system that business corporations have imposed strong pressures upon both communication common carriers and computer manufacturers to develop the necessary techniques and equipment for efficient and economical data transmission.

The functions, structure, and complexity of data communication systems vary widely. For example, some systems transfer messages between remote terminals; other systems may transmit from remote terminals to a central processing facility. Figure 12–1 illustrates several patterns of data transmission that may occur in communications systems.

Electrical data communication systems first became possible when Samuel Morse invented the telegraph in 1844. However, only recently have data communication systems been able to meet industry requirements effectively. As a result, computer users in increasing numbers are taking advantage of company-wide data communication networks and of the closely related concept of integrated management information systems.

For many years, nearly all data communication equipment and transmission channels were leased by users, thus focusing attention on a combination of rates and services offered by communication companies. However, a growing proportion of equipment has become available for sale, thereby requiring evaluation on the basis of return on investment as an alternative to leasing costs.

FIGURE 12–1: Examples of data transmission patterns between or among locations in a communication system

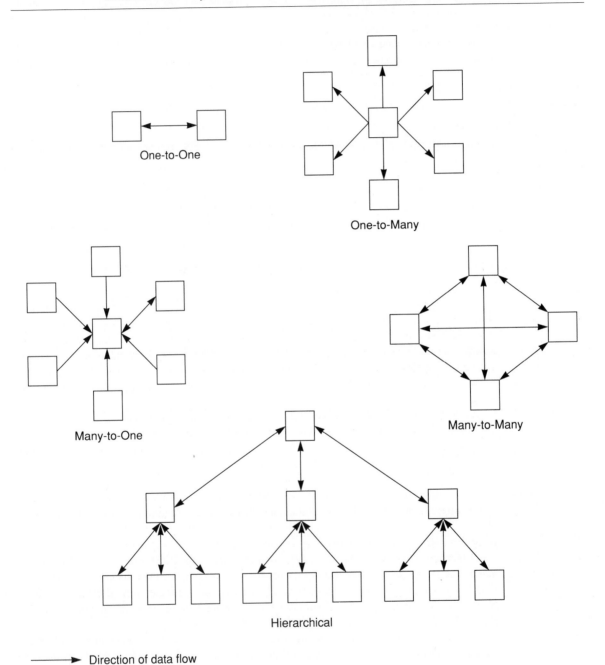

One-to-One

One-to-Many

Many-to-One

Many-to-Many

Hierarchical

Direction of data flow

Assessing Performance Capabilities

Performance capabilities of a communication system are best assessed in the context of the objectives of a company's particular logistics system. Some of these may include (1) improvement of customer service, (2) shortening of the time required to determine stock availability in order to quote delivery dates more rapidly to customers, (3) reduction of inventories without delaying order shipments, and (4) reduction of costs of order processing, inventory management, and related data processing tasks.

Once objectives have been developed, the performance capabilities of the different data communication methods and service should be evaluated in terms of volume, speed, and accuracy of information to be transmitted. For example, *Data-phone* has more capability in terms of speed and volume than the Telex or the Teletypewriter, but the Telex (offering a hard or typed copy of information as it is entered into the system) has more capability in terms of transmitting information accurately than does *Data-phone*. Further, Telpak service has greater capabilities in all areas than any other type of communication facility, but at a higher cost for small volumes of information. The steps for planning a data communication system are shown in Figure 12–2.

FIGURE 12–2: Steps involved in the planning and implementation of a logistics communication system

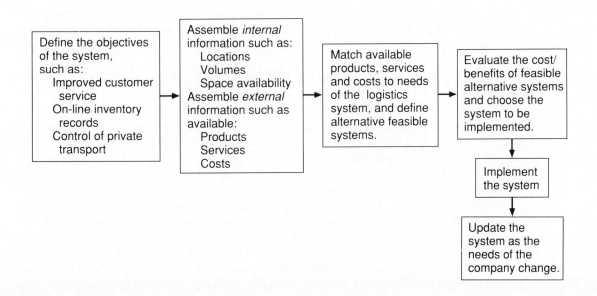

Comparing Rates

Costs of purchased data communication services are based on rates published by communication common carriers and approved by either the Federal Communication Commission or state regulatory agencies.

It should be noted that the rate structures of communication common carriers are very complicated. They comprise many types of transmissions, for example full-duplex lines capable of transmitting in both directions at the same time, half-duplex lines capable of transmitting in both directions but in only one direction at a time, and simplex lines capable of transmitting in only one direction.

Evaluating Costs

When determining the overall cost of communication facilities, various costs must be examined. These include the costs of:

1. Leased or purchased equipment;

2. Leased or purchased communication channels;

3. Salaries (including all benefits) of the employees who operate the facility;

4. Supplies, including printed forms and paper;

5. Building space for housing data communication equipment.

When calculating the overall costs of a system, all of the various cost elements must be combined to yield the total cost for a specific time period for a specified workload.

VOICE COMMUNICATION

In the operation of business logistics systems, much information is transmitted by voice (telephone and radio), with no hard copy of the information being made. Telephone and radio conversations can be tape recorded to retain a record of what is said, but this is very rarely done in most business operations.

The value of voice communication in the operation of logistics systems is its "immediacy" (assuming the party being called can be reached). Its weakness is the lack of a formal written record, even though the party called may make notes of the conversation. Therefore, voice communication should not be used when a written record is needed; *or* if "hard copy" is needed or advisable, voice transmission should immediately be followed up by a written transmission, for example, "This FAX confirms our phone conversation of this afternoon and your request that we ship your order of table china via Easy Handling Transport instead of Rockem Sockem Trucking. As we informed you, Easy Handling's rates are 10 percent higher than Rockem Sockem's, and you agree to these higher freight charges."

Telephones, Mobile Telephones, and Beepers

Many logistics activities involve the need for quick (and sound) decisions, such as "The Atlanta Distribution Center just called. They're out of an item wanted by an important customer. Can we fill the order for them although this would wipe out our safety stock completely?" Such questions should not wait hours for an answer.

From the standpoint of value to many business logistics operations, the greatest recent technological advances in telephone applications are the car telephone and the beeper. Both of these help solve the age-old problem of "Leslie isn't here right now, can I take a message?" Leslie may be out in the warehouse, on the road, visiting a nearby carrier terminal — anywhere but in the office. If she is in a car equipped with a car telephone, Leslie can be reached and the call put right through. If she is out in the warehouse or visiting a carrier terminal, the beeper comes to the rescue.

Radio

Radio is used primarily to communicate within building and yard complexes, and as a method of communication with vehicle drivers. In large warehouses, hand-held walkie-talkies are very useful instruments for communication, and have come to be nearly indispensable for voice communication beyond "yelling distance."

The chief limitation of radio communication with vehicle drivers is transmission distance. Regulations of the Federal Communication Commission (FCC) sharply limit the reception distance of company radio transmission, generally not more than a metropolitan area. However, the radius of most urban pickup and delivery operations is within FCC limitations. If a company does not use radio communication with its drivers, it still has the choices of car telephones (expensive), beepers (less expensive), or having the driver call in from customers' or public telephones at more or less regular intervals for any new instructions.

The installation of an office-to-vehicles radio system involves a modest original capital expenditure, often less than $10,000, depending on the number of vehicles to be equipped. However, its operating costs are very low, and such a radio system can generate substantial savings in driver and vehicle time by minimizing "backtracking" and improving customer service in local operations by prompt response to last-minute customer pickup or other service requests.

APPLICATIONS FOR LOGISTICS

Data Processing

Logistics is a data-intensive management function performed at many locations. It is not surprising, therefore, that a Council of Logistics Management survey of existing and planned logistical computer applications yielded the results shown in Table 12–1. Some highly operational applications, such as order entry and order processing, are approaching 100 percent. Others, more related to planning, such as distribution modeling, have yet to reach 50 percent. The differences with respect to the rates of growth of various applications among the business types shown in Table 12–1 likely reflect differing priorities for development of particular applications.

Software

An information processing system depends on its computer programs, generally termed "software." An enormous amount of software has been developed for use in logistics information management systems. Some companies have developed their own logistics software, while many others have purchased logistics software packages from vendors.

Arthur Andersen & Co. publishes a comprehensive annual directory of commercially available logistics software (the *Directory*). The *Directory* has four sections: U.S. Mainframe Vendors and Packages, U.S. Minicomputer Vendors and Packages, U.S. Microcomputer Vendors and Packages, and International Packages. Each of these sections contains detailed data sheets showing, by vendor name and package, the information presented in Table 12–2. For all packages from U.S. vendors, the *Directory* lists in table form the name of the vendor, the name of the package, an identifying reference number, a logistics function matrix and a hardware matrix. A sample page of this matrix for U.S. logistics software vendors is shown in Figure 12–3.

The three 1988 *Directory* sections of U.S. vendors list a total of 765 logistics software packages, including 150 mainframe packages, 281 minicomputer packages, and 334 microcomputer packages. The number of logistics software packages available from U.S. vendors continues to increase and may soon exceed one thousand.

The question of whether a firm should develop its own logistics software or purchase a software package from a vendor is a classic "make or buy" problem and decision. Considerations include:

It is generally more costly to develop software than to purchase it.

Development in house requires system analysis and programming skills that may not be present in the company.

Software developed in house will be tailored to the company's logistics system information processing needs.

Purchased logistics software must often be modified to meet the particular needs of a firm's information system, and this can be expensive, time-consuming and frustrating. With respect to cost, purchased software requiring *extensive* modification can easily wind up ultimately costing more than in-house developed software.

Vendors of logistics software packages vary greatly in their ability and willingness to help with installation and maintenance of their packages.

As the above considerations suggest, a logistics manager contemplating the need for new or additional software may face a difficult decision even after reviewing the available commercial software packages and surveying the firm's internal analytical and programming skills. The authors posed this type of problem to several logistics managers and all gave more or less this sort of response: "Ask several logistics managers in noncompeting firms that operate logistics systems similar to yours what they have done and are doing with respect to acquiring

TABLE 12–1: Existing and Planned Logistical Computer Applications by Business Type

Application	Manufacturer		Wholesaler		Retailer		Hybrid	
	Existing	Planned	Existing	Planned	Existing	Planned	Existing	Planned
Freight audit/payment	63.9%	16.9%	46.8%	19.2%	58.0%	17.3%	43.1%	20.8%
Purchasing	73.1	20.3	81.6	8.5	81.9	13.3	83.6	8.2
Sales forecasting	77.8	14.2	64.9	14.1	71.9	17.1	64.8	15.5
Inventory control	a	a	92.4	2.8	87.5	10.2	89.5	5.3
Warehouse order selection	70.6	13.6	71.2	9.4	81.5	7.4	68.5	9.6
Warehouse on-line receiving	60.7	24.2	61.2	23.7	69.0	19.1	52.1	23.3
Warehouse merchandise locator	59.9	18.6	56.8	18.7	76.5	9.4	59.7	15.3
Warehouse workload balancing	31.8	23.3	27.0	22.6	38.0	29.1	26.4	26.4
Warehouse short interval schedule	31.7	17.6	23.1	14.9	29.5	23.1	21.4	21.4
Order processing	96.1	3.3	91.6	4.2	90.7	9.3	89.3	6.7
Order entry	96.2	3.8	92.0	5.5	92.0	6.9	89.2	6.8
Vehicle routing and scheduling	32.7	23.9	28.6	27.9	34.2	22.8	28.2	28.2
Inbound freight consolidation	39.8	27.1	25.2	20.0	35.4	24.4	24.0	12.7
Outbound freight consolidation	53.8	17.6	36.8	19.1	45.7	14.8	43.1	18.1
Supporting financials	82.9	10.3	76.6	9.9	83.6	7.6	85.3	6.7
Performance measurement	71.0	17.5	57.8	23.2	67.1	18.3	66.7	16.7
Distribution modeling	46.3	23.7	21.8	22.6	42.5	23.8	30.0	21.4
Direct product profitability	48.3	19.0	49.6	27.5	24.4	23.1	40.0	27.1
Direct store delivery	31.7	9.4	30.5	10.2	45.1	11.0	34.9	12.1
Shelf management	26.5	11.1	28.5	13.1	26.0	15.6	22.6	12.9
MRP	60.9	15.9	—	—	—	—	—	—
DRP	37.6	26.1	—	—	—	—	—	—
Raw material inventory control	79.4	14.3	—	—	—	—	—	—
In-process inventory control	80.3	11.3	—	—	—	—	—	—
Finished goods inventory control	92.8	5.0	—	—	—	—	—	—

aWith respect to the entry "Inventory control for manufacturers," data was broken down into the last five headings shown in this table. These five inventory subcategories do not apply to the other business types.

SOURCE: Donald J. Bowersox, Principal Researcher, *Leading Edge Logistics Positioning for the 1990's*, (Oak Brook, Illinois: Council of Logistics Management, 1989) 156 and 158.

TABLE 12–2: Content of Arthur Andersen & Co. Detailed Data Sheets for Logistics Software Packages

Price	*The one-time purchase price or recurring long-term lease price per time period is shown. In some cases, price is shown as a range, dependent on modules chosen and the types of maintenance and warranty support given with the package.*
Warranty Period	*The number of days for which maintenance will be provided at no extra charge is listed.*
Maintenance Fee	*Maintenance fees are required by some vendors, are optional at other vendors, and may not be provided for some of the packages in the study. The maintenance price per time period is shown along with a brief description of the type of maintenance support provided.*
Installation History	*This shows the number of different companies where the software is installed as well as the year of the first installation.*
Frequency of Major Updates and New Releases	*This lists the time between major software updates and the date of the last update.*
Documentation	*This lists the types of material available and whether or not it is included in the purchase price.*
Training	*Vendors supplied the number of days of training included in the software purchase price; types of training, additional training provided at an extra charge, and the location of the training are also included, where applicable.*
Installation Assistance	*There is a large variation in the amount of vendor installation assistance included in the software purchase price. Many vendors supply additional days for an extra charge, which is noted in this section.*
Hardware	*This lists the type of hardware on which the package will run. In some cases, a package will run on only one type of computer. Other packages have been adapted to several hardware vendors' computers. Packages with extensive interactive features are more difficult to move from one computer type to another.*
Language	*This is the primary language used for the software package (e.g., COBOL, RPG, PL/1).*
Data Bases	*These are the primary data bases which are supported by the software (e.g., IMS/DB, DBII, IDMS).*
Processing Mode	*This specifies the primary mode of operation, either batch, on-line or both.*
Code Provided	*Some vendors provide only object code for their software, making modifications impossible. When source code and object code are provided it is indicated.*
Functions Provided	*Packages are classified at a high level based on the functional areas addressed. These functions are cross referenced in the matrixes. [see Figure 12-3]*
Comments	*Vendor comments include specialized features of the software and other areas for consideration.*

SOURCE: "Logistics Software — 1988 Edition," Richard C. Haverly, Douglas McW. Smith and Deborah P. Steele, *Annual Conference Proceedings, 1988* Volume I, (Oak Brook, Illinois: Council of Logistics Management) 270–71.

FIGURE 12–3: Sample data sheet for selected software packages that support various business logistics functions.

Microcomputer Matrix of Functional Classification and Hardware

Column legend — FUNCTION MATRIX: (1) Order Processing; (2) Inventory Control; (3) Inventory Planning and Forecasting; (4) Distribution Requirements Planning; (5) Materials Requirements Planning; (6) Purchasing; (7) Stock/Pallet Location; (8) Labor Performance; (9) Material Handling; (10) Transportation Analysis; (11) Traffic Routing and Scheduling; (12) Freight Rate Maintenance and Audit; (13) Vehicle Maintenance; (14) Physical Distrib. System Modeling; (15) Special Services. HARDWARE MATRIX: (16) Unisys; (17) Data General; (18) D.E.C.; (19) Honeywell; (20) H.P.; (21) IBM; (22) Other.

Vendor	Package Name	Reference Number	1	2	3	4	5	6	7	8	9	10	11	12	13	14	15	16	17	18	19	20	21	22
Parameter Driven Software, 30800 N. Telegraph Rd. #3820, Birmingham, MI 48010	Inventory Control	3.201	X	X														X					X	26.
	Order Entry/Invoicing	3.202																X					X	26.
	Purchase Orders	3.203						X										X					X	26.
Peachtree Software, Inc., 4355 Shackleford Rd., Norcross, GA 30093	PEACHTREE COMPLETE II: THE BUSINESS ACCOUNTING SYSTEM	3.204		X																			X	
P*I*E NATIONWIDE, 4814 Phillips Hwy., Jacksonville, FL 32207	SHIPMASTER	3.205															X						X	
PMIS, 1965 S.W. Airport Ave., Corvallis, OR 97333	Petroleum Marketers Information System (PMIS)	3.206	X	X	X						X	X	X	X	X								X	26.
Fotter Moving & Storage, 306 S. Castell, Rochester, MI 48063	Fleet Log Analysis Program (FLAP Version 2.0)	3.207										X				X							X	
Process Data Corporation, P.O. Box 795666, Dallas, TX 75379	AFLA (Air Freight Loading Analysis)	3.208										X	X										X	26.
	CUBE-IT (Product Cube Sizing Analysis)	3.209							X													X	X	26.
	DPC/DPP Direct Product Costing/Direct Product Profitability	3.210			X					X	X		X			X			X				X	26.
	FIT-IT (Product Loading Selection Analysis)	3.211										X										X	X	26.
	LOAD-IT #3 (Shipping Vehicle Loading Analysis)	3.212										X							X			X	X	26.

26. Various

SOURCE: "Logistics Software—1988 Edition," Richard C. Haverly, Douglas McW. Smith and Deborah P. Steele, *Annual Conference Proceedings, 1988 Volume I* (Oak Brook, Illinois: Council of Logistics Management) 337.

or developing logistics software, and do likewise. At least you'll have company." The dual thrust of such advice is clear: (1) don't reinvent the wheel, and (2) settle for a well written software package that works rather than attempting to advance the state of the art and quite likely getting into trouble. This is a very conservative view, but industry experience bears it out.

Electronic Data Interchange

One of the most significant developments in electronic data interchange (EDI) is the extent to which shippers, carriers and public warehouse workers have implemented (or plan to implement) applications of EDI systems, as shown in Table 12–3. It is probably fair to say that

TABLE 12–3: Electronic Data Interchange

	Shipper	Carrier	Public Warehouse
1. Does your organization currently participate in an electronic data interchange (EDI) project?			
Yes	66.2	79.8	69.2
No	33.8	20.2	30.8
TOTAL	100.0%	100.0%	100.0%
a. If yes, is the project . . .			
In planning stage	17.9	15.2	16.3
Experimental	20.9	31.8	12.4
Fully Operational	61.2	53.0	71.3
TOTAL	100.0%	100.0%	100.0%
b. If yes, what percentage of the following are transmitted via EDI?			
Orders	34.3%	17.9%	40.5%
Bill of lading and freight bills	57.2	21.5	30.8
Invoices	39.8	20.7	12.1
WINS	47.5	2.4	10.0
Other	—	22.3	13.7
2. Does your organization belong to an industry-wide action group that has as its objective the setting of standards for electronic data interchange?			
Yes	39.4	43.4	51.4
No	60.6	56.6	48.6
TOTAL	100.0%	100.0%	100.0%

SOURCE: *Customer Service: A Management Perspective*, Bernard J. LaLonde, Martha C. Cooper and Thomas G. Noordewier (Oak Brook, Illinois: Council of Logistics Management, 1988) 84.

it will soon be essential for a firm in a channel of distribution to have a compatible (hardware and software) EDI logistics system in place if it wishes to do business with other firms in the channel that have such systems in place.

The existence of incompatible systems among buyers, sellers, transportation firms, and public warehouses results in the opportunity for third-party EDI vendors to solve such incompatibility problems. The third-party EDI vendor supplies the capability of translating the codes and terms of the parties on each side of the transaction who would otherwise be unable to interface their information systems.

In terms of general business relationships, EDI applications by business groups are shown in Table 12–4. As would be expected, wholesalers have little EDI with public warehouses because most have their own warehouse facilities. The same is true for all business groups listed with respect to EDI with copackers and contractors with whom specific arrangements usually have been made; FAX is probably sufficient for communicating with these parties.

Clearly EDI is more a matter of here and now, rather than the future. For example, Figure 12–4 shows projections of the percent of orders transmitted by EDI for the chemical and

TABLE 12–4: Currently Installed and Planned Electronic Data Interchange Applications by Business Group

EDI Application	Manufacturer		Wholesaler	
	Existing	Planned	Existing	Planned
Manufacturers/Vendors	23.2%	30.5%	33.3%	29.0%
Wholesalers	24.6	27.4	16.4	12.7
Public warehouses	21.0	26.7	1.6	3.9
Carriers	25.4	41.4	13.6	16.7
Financial Institutions	28.5	21.8	26.0	13.0
Retailers	17.2	19.0	22.1	14.5
Customers	27.5	42.1	39.6	23.0
Copackers/Contractors	6.0	19.2	4.0	5.6

EDI Application	Retailer		Hybrid	
	Existing	Planned	Existing	Planned
Manufacturers/Vendors	38.0%	32.9%	31.5%	26.0%
Wholesalers	17.6	17.6	17.7	26.5
Public warehouses	10.8	8.1	10.5	7.5
Carriers	30.4	34.2	22.1	16.2
Financial Institutions	38.7	17.3	30.3	10.6
Retailers	23.2	12.2	26.5	13.2
Customers	21.9	11.0	37.0	23.3
Copackers/Contractors	4.1	9.5	6.2	3.1

SOURCE: *Leading Edge Logistics Positioning for the 1990's*, Donald J. Bowersox, Principal Researcher (Oak Brook, Illinois: Council of Logistics Management, 1989) 165 and 167.

FIGURE 12–4: Projected percent of orders transmitted by electronic data interchange for the chemical industry, pharmaceutical industry, and all industries through 1995

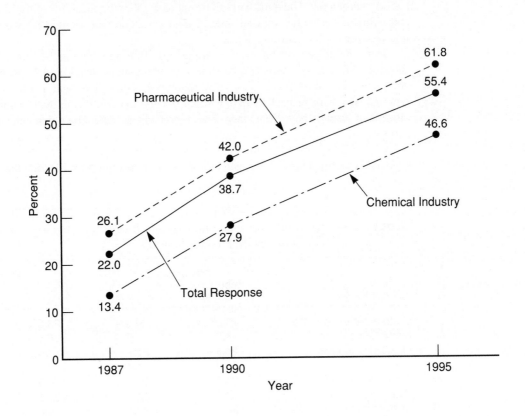

SOURCE: *Partnerships in Providing Customer Service: A Third-Party Perspective*. Bernard J. LaLonde and Martha C. Cooper; (Oak Brook, Illinois, Council of Logistics Management, 1989) 98.

pharmaceutical industries as well as for all industries. The authors believe these projections are somewhat conservative.

Another aspect of EDI is that it can either be produced "in house" or can make use, wholly or in part, of outside (third-party) vendors. Table 12–5 shows a significant degree of use of third-party vendors of EDI services.

Electronic data interchange logistics applications include such activities as transmission of:

Purchase orders and purchase order confirmation;

Inventory availability queries from customers and replies;

TABLE 12–5: Current Situation with Regard to Outside Party Information Vendors (Percent of Respondents Checking Item)

	Total Response
Our firm does virtually everything related to EDI in house.	*33.6%*
We are part of a larger "clearing house" EDI system consisting of many buyers and sellers.	*9.7*
We selectively use certain EDI suppliers.	*16.8*
We use outside EDI suppliers only with transportation and warehousing customers.	*2.7*
Some of our large customers have required us to develop EDI systems for electronic transmission.	*28.5*
Not applicable	*33.6*

SOURCE: *Customer Service: A Management Perspective*, Bernard J. LaLonde, Martha C. Cooper and Thomas G. Noordewier (Oak Brook, Illinois: Council of Logistics Management, 1988) 84.

Bills of lading, freight bills, and other shipment documentation;

Shipment damage claims;

Shipping orders to public warehouses;

Order processing confirmations to customers;

Invoices;

Shipment tracing inquiries and replies;

Shipping instructions to vendors;

Internal exchanges of information among facilities in a firm's logistics system.

Information Technologies

As shown in Table 12–6, there is a quite a wide variety of information technologies currently in use. The leaders are microcomputers and electronic order transmission, with bar coding and optical scanning moving up fast. This is not surprising because these technologies are the major support systems for inventory control and order processing, key activities in the operations of logistics systems.

Bar Coding

Chapter 10 presented bar coding as a method of package identification and illustrated the format and applications involved in this increasingly important component of information technology. Although bar coding is shown as a separate type of existing and planned information

TABLE 12–6: Existing and Planned Information Technologies by Business Type

Technology	Manufacturer		Wholesaler		Retailer		Hybrid	
	Existing	Planned	Existing	Planned	Existing	Planned	Existing	Planned
Bar coding	26.9%	41.4%	22.5%	38.7%	47.2%	27.0%	28.0%	34.7%
Optical scanning	16.2	25.1	18.3	30.7	41.4	16.1	20.6	34.3
Robotics	8.3	6.1	2.9	4.4	3.5	5.8	5.4	9.5
AI/Knowledge Systems	4.0	21.5	3.0	5.9	3.5	15.1	4.3	11.4
ASRS	18.0	7.9	11.0	13.1	18.4	12.6	8.2	11.0
Automated material handling	24.6	17.9	25.7	15.0	42.5	19.5	18.9	17.6
Local area networks	25.1	21.1	14.1	18.5	23.5	24.7	15.5	12.7
CAD warehouse design	17.3	12.8	15.3	15.3	26.7	17.4	16.4	13.7
Handheld data entry devices	19.4	33.3	28.8	35.3	31.8	30.7	31.5	23.3
Electronic order transmission	54.9	23.1	56.1	19.4	54.5	19.3	53.4	23.3
On board computers – delivery vehicles	16.3	15.7	14.8	14.1	4.8	20.2	9.5	16.2
On board computers – lift trucks	12.4	16.9	4.3	14.4	2.4	22.6	5.4	17.6
Voice data capture	6.4	9.2	8.1	5.2	2.4	7.3	5.5	5.5
PC or PC XT compatible	82.8	7.5	70.1	9.7	77.8	3.3	71.2	13.7
80286 Micros (AT or compatible)	47.7	9.1	45.1	5.3	53.7	6.1	44.9	7.3
80386 Microcomputers	26.0	6.5	26.8	9.8	24.1	11.4	33.3	10.6
CD-ROM (read only memory)	7.4	5.6	8.9	6.5	6.7	2.7	8.9	7.1
WORM (write once, read many)	9.0	3.0	4.0	4.0	4.0	1.3	6.4	4.8
68020 – based micros	8.4	3.0	10.4	3.2	6.5	1.3	7.8	0.0
Fiber optics	6.7	2.4	4.2	3.4	5.3	4.0	4.6	1.5

SOURCE: *Leading Edge Logistics Positioning for the 1990's*, Donald J. Bowersox, Principal Researcher (Oak Brook, Illinois: Council of Logistics Management, 1989) 156 and 158.

technology in Table 12–6, it should be emphasized that a number of the other technological applications listed in Table 12–6 use the bar code display as a basic data source.

In order to capture the information contained in the bar code, the code must be read by a scanning device. As the information is scanned into the firm's information system, a number of actions or events may take place. These include updating of inventory records, preparation of shipment routing instructions, preparation of shipping receiving reports, validation of order picking assignments, preparation of invoices, and en route tracking and tracing of shipments by carriers.

The benefits of bar coding are quite pervasive. Historically, data entry—the initial accurate capturing of information—has been the major stumbling block with respect to logistics information systems. Bar coding has largely solved this problem. It provides fast, accurate, and cost-effective data capture and input. The scanning devices can be used by relatively unskilled employees who require only minimal training to be proficient users of the technology. It is safe to say that bar coding has become the core of many firms' logistics information system and its use will be nearly universal by the end of this century.

MANAGING THE SYSTEM

It is fair to say that the dawn of the information age has been accompanied by an information explosion. That is, one can (and some firms do) generate great volumes of computer printouts in indigestible quantities. The real need is to produce that information—and only that information—that is truly required by a logistics manager for the planning, operation and control of a logistics system. That topic is discussed in Chapter 16, "System Performance Measurement and Control." Here, our discussion will be limited to several *caveats* that should be observed with respect to the careful management of information processing and communication services. These include computer security, errors and error control, and the sometimes interesting question, "Who is running the company, programmers or managers?"

Computer Security

There are two aspects to computer security: (1) physical security of the hardware, software and data files (protecting them from physical harm, whether deliberate or accidental), and (2) limiting access to data files and software to those individuals authorized to enter, copy, delete, or alter information in the data files or to alter or copy the software. Computer security has become big business in recent years because of the great value of the information contained in data files *and* the dependence of firms on their computer systems and files for conducting business. Many consulting firms now offer computer security advice to their clients with respect to both physical security and methods of limiting access to authorized personnel.

Protection of computer hardware and data files from power outages is most easily accomplished by having an "uninterrupted power supply" (UPS). The most common form of UPS consists of the interposition of a strong battery (or set of batteries) between the incoming power line and the computer system.

Protection from such risks as anticompany demonstrators, vandals, and such who might destroy or damage computer facilities, depends on sheer physical security. Many firms have spent considerable sums to protect their large, centralized computer facilities by means ranging from armed guards to physically secure, vault-like rooms.

The risk of loss of data and software files arising from system failure or any other cause, is generally dealt with by creating archive copies of original data files. Such archive files should be stored in a different location than the originals.

While most logistics information systems may contain few "secrets," it is necessary to limit access to such systems in order to protect the accuracy and integrity of the information contained and being processed. Fortunately, it is possible, for example, to allow what is known as "read only" access to data; this allows a person to "see what's there," but not to change it. An example would be inventory figures for all SKUs. Many persons in an organization might legitimately need access to such numbers for a variety of reasons (for example, someone might need gross sales this month and year-to-date, sales by customer, value or quantity of inventory on hand). However, only order-entry, production-accounting or receiving personnel, for examples, would be able to actually *change* inventory figures.

Errors and Error Control

One often hears the statement, "It must have been a computer error." In fact, the odds against this statement being true are enormous. As a practical proposition, computers do not make errors; people who use computers make errors. Errors can never be completely eliminated, but they can be minimized. First, computer access must be restricted to authorized personnel. Second, managers must insist on thorough training of those persons whose work can affect the accuracy of the information in the data files. And, third, there should be frequent sampling and spot checks of the accuracy of data entry. The value of accurate data can hardly be overstated, and time and effort expended to insure accuracy generally pays good dividends. It would be upsetting, to say the least, to have told an important hospital customer that there are fifty cartons of gauze bandages on hand to fill the hospital's order, only to find out when the order was being picked that someone had forgotten to enter a notification from the warehouse that twenty-three of those cartons were ruined last week when a sprinkler head broke and soaked their contents.

Who's Running the Company, Programmers or Managers?

A mistake frequently made by managers is failure to insure that the company's information system is what management wants it to be, rather than what a computer programmer has made it. One of the authors who had been doing a lot of traveling received a very nasty "overdue" notice from a major credit card company because he had underpaid the previous month's bill of $1,819.17 by $1.98; he had paid $1,817.19 by mistake. The computer notice said:

> YOU HAVE FAILED TO PAY YOUR ACCOUNT ON TIME, YOUR
> ACCOUNT IS OVERDUE AND YOUR CREDIT IS IN JEOPARDY!
> REMIT IMMEDIATELY!

An overly enthusiastic programmer, apparently having a strong sense of fiscal responsibility, had programmed these phrases into the company's billing statement printout procedures. When the author personally brought the matter to the attention of a senior executive of the major credit card company, the reaction was, ''Good God! I am *very* sorry. Something like this should *never* happen! In the old days an accounts-receivable clerk would *never* have sent out a notice like that for a $1.98 balance due on a bill for nearly two thousand dollars.'' The executive concerned quickly saw to it that the computer program was changed to provide for only a gentle reminder when most of a currently due bill due was paid, and a reasonably phrased reminder when only part—but less than half—of a currently due bill was paid.

The foregoing example illustrates the point that unless properly informed and directed, system analysts and computer programmers may have the last (wrong) word. It is very important that logistics managers monitor the establishment and programming of such things as computer-generated inventory reorder points, degrees of aggregation of data in reports prepared for management use,[5] decisions as to proper item classification in an A-B-C inventory classification system, password controls over data entry, and so on. Simply put, a logistics manager must manage the information system rather than be managed by it.

SUMMARY

Information processing and communications services encompass two very large industries, those associated with communications and computing. Both of these industries are characterized by rapid growth, increasing competition, rapidly declining costs, and greatly increasing capabilities. In recent years, reduced government regulation of these industries has set the stage for an era of potentially greater competition between communications and computing firms.

The number of options available for both data processing and data communications has increased, suggesting the need for systematic methods of evaluating alternative system costs and capabilities against the needs of a particular operation. Although many firms still maintain a centralized data processing strategy utilizing a large mainframe computer, a growing number are making use of distributed data processing in which smaller, decentralized computers are used both for stand-alone computing and communication with a large central computer. Similarly, the communication of data requires an assessment of needs for various capabilities between different points on a network and the evaluation of service costs associated with alternatives.

Companies are, to an increasing extent, connecting their central computers with those of their outlying sales offices and distribution centers, retail stores, suppliers, and customers. This suggests that electronic data communication will soon exceed the volume of business voice communication in the U.S. This has given rise to a number of competing networks (third parties) designed to provide varying data communication capacities and costs.

Because of its data-intensive and communications-dependent character, logistics management requires a heavy use of both computers and communication services. Among larger firms, surveys have shown that nearly all have computerized traffic and distribution systems. The most extensive use is made of computers for order processing, inventory control, the preparation of bills of lading, and the routing of shipments. Further, a majority of such firms have direct lines of communication to their plants and warehouses from their central computers. In addition, a growing number have established on-line or off-line communication with computers operated by their transportation carriers, customers, and public warehouses.

The growth of third-party EDI vendors is based upon two considerations. First, many firms prefer to contract out activities not central to their own operations. Second, incompatibility of hardware and software among buyers, sellers, transportation firms, and public warehouses creates a market for firms that can solve the multitude of system incompatibility problems.

The importance of information processing and communication for logistics management is underlined by the likelihood that already low costs of computing and communication will continue to fall in relation to those of transportation and inventory maintenance. As a result, logistics system design and operation will increasingly assume — and depend on — accurate, high-speed information processing and transmission.

DISCUSSION QUESTIONS

1. How can a logistics information system aid in accomplishing demand-supply coordination?

2. What is meant by the phrase "the previous distinction between communication services and computers has become blurred?"

3. What has happened to the cost of long distance telephone calls? What accounts for this?

4. What are the principal advantages of FAX machines?

5. What has happened to the cost of computers? What is the significance of this?

6. Why is distributed data processing likely to be important for the logistics function in firms with a number of plant and warehouse facilities?

7. What would be a logistics example of each of the five forms of data transmission patterns shown in Figure 12–1?

8. What are the advantages and disadvantages of voice communication in a logistics system? Under what circumstances would a follow-up with "hard copy" be advisable?

9. Reference Table 12–1. What would you say accounts for those areas of application that are presently below 50 percent? Explain.

10. What are the advantages and disadvantages of developing logistics software in house as compared with purchase of commercially available logistics software packages?

11. Reference Table 12–4. What would explain the very low extent of electronic data interchange applications by all business groups with copackers and contractors?

12. The authors state that they consider the projections shown in Figure 12–4 to be conservative. Do you agree or not? Explain.

13. Table 12–6 shows that bar coding and hand-held data entry devices are widely used information technologies *and* even greater use of these technologies is planned. Why? Explain your answer.

14. Why might many people in a company be allowed access to logistics information, but only a few be allowed to change it? Explain.

15. Why should a (logistics) manager exercise care and control over computer programming in his or her firm? Explain.

SUGGESTED READINGS

Annual Conference Proceedings — Council of Logistics Management

BANACH, ROBERT, "Information Technology Makes a Public Warehouse More Competitive," vol. II (1989): 173–177.

DEREWECKI, DONALD J., ROBERT B. SILVERMAN, and ALEX DONNAN, "Warehouse Planning: Computer Aided Design," vol. I (1988): 427–458.

EMMELHAINZ, MARGARET A., "Electronic Data Interchange: A Tutorial," vol. II (1989): 115–123.

FERGUSON, DANIEL M., "The State of US EDI: 1989," vol. I (1989): 417–441.

GREGORY, WILLIAM D., "Planning the Distribution Center for the Nineties," vol. I (1989): 177–214.

HAVERLY, RICHARD C., DOUGLAS McW. SMITH, and DEBORAH P. STEELE, "Logistics Software — 1989 Edition," vol. I (1988): 263–425.

KAWA, JOHN N., "Automated Receiving Using Bar Code, Microcomputers, and Radio Frequency Portable Data Entry Terminals," vol. II (1989): 179–198.

LAVERY, HANK, and G. A. LONG, "EDI in Transportation," vol. II (1989): 261–277.

MALTZ, ARNOLD, and JAMES M. MASTERS, "Strategies for the Successful Implementation of New Information Technology in Logistics: The DRP Experience," vol. II (1989): 13–49.

MARIEN, EDWARD J., JOHN SATEJA, ANN E. SELTZ, and GARY WILSON, "Gaining Logistics Advice Through Electronic Conferencing (EC)," vol. II (1988): 173–193.

NELSON, RAYMOND A., "Integrating the Computer with Warehousing Operations," vol. II (1988): 347–356.

RAUCH, THOMAS J. and JAMES RUST, "The PC Model: A Strategic Planning Tool," vol. II (1987): 159–181.

SEASE, GARY J., "Innovative Use of Information Management Models in Distribution," vol. II (1987): 149–166.

ZEMKE, DOUGLAS E. and DOUGLAS M. LAMBERT, "Utilizing Information Technology to Manage Inventory," vol. I (1987): 119–139.

Journal of Business Logistics

BOOKBINDER, JAMES H. and DAVID M. DILTS, "Logistics Information Systems in a Just-in-Time Environment," vol. 10, no. 1 (1989): 50–67.

EMMELHAINZ, MARGARET A., "Strategic Issues of EDI Implementation," vol. 9, no. 2 (1988): 55–70.

KLING, JAMES A. and CURTIS M. GRIMM, "Microcomputer Use in Transportation and Logistics: A Literature Review with Implications for Educators," vol. 9, no. 1 (1988): 1–18. (Note: This article contains an excellent bibliography of articles pertaining to this subject area.)

Books and Other Articles

Leading Edge Logistics Competitive Positioning for the 1990's, Oak Brook, Illinois: Council of Logistics Management, 1989. This landmark study contains results of several surveys on information management practices and plans of leading edge firms.

BARRETT, COLIN, *Practical Handbook of Computerization for Distribution Managers*, Washington, D.C.: The Traffic Service Corporation, 1987. Expanding upon various issues of the author's column, "Computer Software for Transportation" in *Traffic World* magazine, this book provides helpful tips for transportation/distribution users and would-be users of computers.

LALONDE, BERNARD J., MARTHA C. COOPER, and THOMAS G. NOORDEWIER, *Customer Service: A Management Perspective*, Oak Brook, Illinois: Council of Logistics Management, 1988. Pages 83–86 in Chapter 6 and Table II.C.4. in Appendix A contain interesting and useful information with respect to third-party vendors of EDI services.

LALONDE, BERNARD J., and MARTHA C. COOPER, *Partnerships in Providing Customer Service: A Third-Party Perspective*, Oak Brook, Illinois: Council of Logistics Management, 1989. This up-to-date study considers transportation carriers, public/contract warehouses, and electronic data interchange as the principal partners in newly emerging logistics system modification and development.

NELSON, RAYMOND A., *Computerizing Warehouse Operations*, Englewood Cliffs, New Jersey: Prentice-Hall, Inc., 1985. A superior and quite thorough "nuts and bolts" treatment of the subject.

O'NEIL, BRIAN F., "Information—A Viable Substitute for Inventory," *Logistics and Transportation Review*, vol. 22, no. 1 (March 1986): 83–89.

ROBESON, JAMES F., and ROBERT G. HOUSE, *The Distribution Handbook*, New York: The Free Press, 1985. Section Five, "The Computer and Quantitative Analysis," contains three chapters on quantitative methods in distribution, computer methods in physical distribution management, and computer-assisted freight bill rating.

SUGRUE, PAUL, MANFRED H. LEDFORD, and NICHOLAS A. GLASKOWSKY, Jr., "Computer Applications in the U.S. Trucking Industry," *Logistics and Transportation Review*, vol. 18, no. 2 (June 1982).

WATERS, W. G., ed., "Microcomputers in Transportation and Logistics," *Logistics and Transportation Review*, Berkeley, California, vol. 20, no. 4 (December 1984). This special 262-page issue of the *Logistics and Transportation Review* contains 22 articles on the role and uses of microcomputers in transportation and logistics. It is a particularly valuable single source of broad coverage of this topic.

ENDNOTES

1. Source: Statistical Abstract of the United States, 1989, Table 1321, 748.

2. One annoying aspect of FAX machines is that many enterprising businesses use them to advertise their products or services, thus tying up the receivers' machines *and* using up the receivers' paper supply. Some annoyed receivers of such advertisements fax back a message to the effect, "If you fax me an ad again, I will never do business with you."

3. *The Communications Act of 1934, With Amendments and Index Thereto* (Washington, D.C.: Government Printing Office, 1961), Title 1, Sec. 1.

4. For a more comprehensive review of distributed data processing, see two articles by Jack R. Buchanan and Richard G. Linowes, "Understanding Distributed Data Processing," *Harvard Business Review*, July-August, 1980, pp. 143–153; and

''Making Distributed Data Processing Work,'' *Harvard Business Review*, September-October, 1980, pp. 143–161.

5. For example, in order to be useful to the logistics manager, data concerning *every individual customer's orders* at *each* of a number of distribution centers may be necessary. If such information is combined (aggregated) to produce *only grand totals* for customers whose orders may be processed at four or five distribution centers, the information will be inadequate.

CHAPTER THIRTEEN

Multinational Logistics Strategy and Operations

LEARNING OBJECTIVES

The objectives of this chapter are to:

➤ Point out the increasing globalization of business, particularly the continuing increases in U.S. imports and exports and the consequent increasing involvement of logistics managers with international movements of goods.

➤ Emphasize the complexity of mulitinational logistics operations as contrasted with domestic logistics operations.

➤ Discuss the multinational logistics environment with respect to differing cultures, problems of governmental stability in some countries, differing legal systems affecting business transactions, and differences in national economies.

➤ Consider the factors involved in the formulation of a multinational physical distribution strategy, including the significance of regional economic integration alliances, such as the European Common Market; distribution channel strategies and options; and policies of host countries that may affect logistics operations.

Continued

➤ Discuss the operational considerations involved in multinational physical distribution, including terms of sale, customer service, the use of bonded warehouses and free trade zones, transportation, documentation of shipments, payment for shipments, insurance considerations, and packaging and packing for export.

➤ Discuss financial considerations involved in exporting goods, including currency exchange and fluctuation, country risk and country credit ratings.

➤ Discuss the operational considerations involved in importing goods (physical supply), including vendor relations, host country policies with respect to exports, U.S. government policies with respect to imports, import documentation, imported item availability, and transportation and delivery times.

There are many significant differences between domestic and multinational logistics management. With minor exceptions, a manager concerned only with domestic logistics operations deals with a single legal system, one currency, one language, one economy, and one culture. Managing multinational logistics operations is quite another matter. It will likely involve exasperatingly different legal systems, a number of different—and sometimes very unstable—currencies, several languages, a bewildering variety of customs regulations and duties, and different cultures and ways of doing business.

Multinational logistics operations also commonly require transportation movements over greater distances than domestic movements, usually involving both domestic and foreign carriers in intermodal movements requiring complex shipment documentation. It may involve operations to, from, or within unstable foreign political environments where on-site inventories or facilities are at risk as to confiscation or destruction. All in all, the management of multinational logistics operations poses the type of challenge that many logistics managers might prefer not to face, but must as an increasing number of U.S. business firms become involved in multinational activities.

It is a truism that most American managers "do not think international," while their counterparts in other countries do. This is largely a function of the physical size and population of the United States, the size and wealth of its economy, and the consequent size of the U.S. domestic market. Few American firms need to produce primarily for export, but in many countries, such as Switzerland, Japan, and the Netherlands, many firms depend on exports for their basic economic well being, if not survival.

But, this picture is changing for U.S. firms with respect to both exports and imports as U.S. involvement in the globalization of business continues to increase. This also includes the establishment of distribution and manufacturing operations in other countries. The tables in this section of the chapter vividly illustrate the magnitude of export and import activity with which logistics managers must be concerned. It has been estimated that at least 70 percent of the products manufactured in the United States are subject to direct foreign competition. And, despite the alleged (and probable) discrimination against American exports by other countries, U.S. exports continue to increase.[1] The conclusion that can be drawn is that logistics managers must broaden their outlook beyond domestic operations and be aware of the rapidly changing multinational environment.

Tables 13–1, 13–2, 13–3, and 13–4 show the extent of increase in U.S. imports and exports of manufactured goods during the period 1970–1987. Imports more than doubled (from 6.1 percent to 12.9 percent) as a percentage of manufactured goods for consumption from 1970 to 1987. Exports as a percentage of total production increased at a slower rate than imports (from 5.6 percent to 8.2 percent) over the same period, but that still represented a 46.4 percent increase in exports over an 18-year period.

A survey conducted by the Council of Logistics Management in 1987, produced the data shown in Tables 13–5, 13–6, 13–7, and 13–8. Table 13–5 shows projections by nine industry groups of the percentages of the raw materials and semifinished goods that they imported in 1987 and expect to import in 1990 and 1995. As Table 13–5 shows, figures for the food and chemical industries are fairly stable, but the other seven industries project significant increases in the near future.

Table 13–6 shows projections by the same industries for the importation of finished goods. The slight declines forecast for importation of automobiles may be based on one of two possible scenarios: (1) that U.S. manufacturers will respond with needed quality improvements to be able to compete more effectively with foreign manufacturers, or (2) that more automobiles will be manufactured in the United States by subsidiaries of foreign manufacturers as is already being done by Honda, Nissan, and Toyota. All other categories show projected increases.

Tables 13–7 and 13–8 present projections for nine industries of expected percentages of raw materials and semifinished goods (Table 13–7) and finished goods (Table 13–8) to be exported in the future. With the exception of paper, increased exports are forecasted for the other eight industries.

Total (average) projections of imports and exports for raw materials and semifinished goods for the nine industries listed in Tables 13–5, 13–6, 13–7, and 13–8 are shown in Figure 13–1. Corresponding projections for finished goods are shown in Figure 13–2. Figures 13–1 and 13–2 show clearly the upward trends in imports and exports of raw materials, semifinished goods, and finished goods.

The data in Tables 13–1 through 13–8 and Figures 13–1 and 13–2 show clearly the increasing globalization of business, which shows few signs of leveling off in the near future. A growing number of logistics managers will, directly or indirectly, become involved in the process of either importing or exporting goods, or both. Even if a logistics manager's own firm does not directly export or import, it will be increasingly likely that a firm's vendors or customers will be so involved that the firm will therefore be involved to some degree in an export or import channel of distribution.

COMPLEXITY OF MULTINATIONAL LOGISTICS OPERATIONS

Figure 13–3 illustrates the complex set of vendor-customer relationships that would arise if, for example, a U.S. firm were to import raw materials, parts, subassemblies, or supplies from six countries and export finished goods to 12 countries. In the situation portrayed in Figure 13–3, the logistics manager might have to deal with 16 different currencies, several fundamentally different legal systems, a bewildering variety of differing national customs and

TABLE 13–1: U.S. Imports of Manufactured Goods (Nondurables and Durables), 1970–1987, for Selected Two-digit SIC Codes, by Dollar Value, Growth Rate, and Extent of Import Penetration[a]

SIC[d] code	Product	1987 Value (millions of dollars)	1987 Per-cent distribution	Growth Rate[e] (percent) 1970–1987	Growth Rate[e] (percent) 1980–1987	Growth Rate[e] (percent) 1986–1987	Import Penetration Ratio[f] (percent) 1972	Import Penetration Ratio[f] (percent) 1977	Import Penetration Ratio[f] (percent) 1982	Import Penetration Ratio[f] (percent) 1987
(x)[c]	**Manufacturing**	**340,089**	**100.0**	**15.0**	**12.6**	**10.0**	**6.1**	**7.0**	**8.5**	**12.9**
(x)	Nondurables	94,298	27.7	13.0	9.0	11.6	4.7	5.4	5.8	8.0
20	Food and kindred products	13,180	3.9	8.0	3.4	5.3	3.9	3.8	3.6	4.2
21	Tobacco manufactures	90	–[b]	10.5	–.4	10.2	.6	.7	1.8	.5
22	Textile mill products	4,780	1.4	9.3	13.0	13.1	5.6	4.2	5.4	8.4
23	Apparel and other mill products	21,503	6.3	18.0	18.6	18.3	7.0	10.3	14.3	24.5
26	Paper and allied products	9,715	2.9	11.3	8.7	18.0	5.6	6.3	6.1	7.3
27	Printing and publishing	1,329	.4	13.7	14.6	7.5	1.0	.9	.9	1.4
28	Chemicals and allied products	14,318	4.2	15.3	10.8	8.5	3.2	3.9	4.5	6.7
29	Petroleum and coal products	13,123	3.9	13.3	–.3	2.2	7.1	8.5	7.3	9.8
30	Rubber and plastics products	6,331	1.9	14.2	12.7	17.7	4.7	5.4	5.1	6.9
31	Leather and leather products	9,930	2.9	16.9	16.6	14.8	15.9	21.2	33.9	54.8
(x)	Durables	245,791	72.3	16.0	14.3	9.4	7.2	8.3	11.2	16.8
24	Lumber and wood products	5,959	1.8	11.2	7.3	10.9	9.4	9.3	8.2	10.2
25	Furniture and fixtures	4,575	1.3	19.6	22.9	14.5	2.6	3.6	5.3	10.6
32	Stone, clay, and glass products	5,560	1.6	14.7	13.7	13.2	3.7	4.0	5.3	8.3
33	Primary metal industries	19,108	5.6	9.9	2.9	4.2	8.9	10.0	14.7	16.8
34	Fabricated metal products	9,617	2.8	14.4	11.8	12.7	2.5	3.2	4.3	6.0
35	Machinery, except electrical	42,319	12.4	18.7	18.1	18.4	5.4	6.3	8.4	16.9
36	Electrical and electronic equipment	45,782	13.5	18.2	16.7	8.5	7.6	10.4	12.4	18.5
37	Transportation equipment	86,658	25.5	16.6	16.0	5.6	9.8	10.2	15.4	20.9
38	Instruments and related products	11,547	3.4	17.5	13.7	8.5	6.7	9.2	10.1	16.0
39	Miscellaneous manufacturing industries	14,666	4.3	15.9	15.2	14.8	13.3	17.2	24.0	37.5

[a] Import data for 1974–81 are valued on an f.a.s. basis. Data for 1970–73 and 1982–86 are valued on a customs basis. Data for all years have been adjusted to include comparable commodities in each group. Minus sign (—) indicates decrease.

[b] — Represents zero.

[c] X Not applicable.

[d] Standard Industrial Classification.

[e] 1970–87 and 1980–87 rates are compound annual growth rates.

[f] Ratio of imports to new supply (product shipments plus imports).

SOURCE: *Industrial Outlook* (annual), U.S. International Trade Administration, as published in *Statistical Abstract of the United States – 1989*, U.S. Department of Commerce, Bureau of the Census, 734.

TABLE 13-2: U.S. Imports for Consumption for 28 Leading Three-Digit SIC Product Groups, 1970–1987, by Dollar Value, Growth Rate, and Extent of Import Penetration

1977 SIC[b] code	Product Group	1987 Value (millions of dollars)	Per-cent distribution	Growth Rate[c] (percent) 1970–1987	1980–1987	1986–1987	Import Penetration Ratio[d] (percent) 1972	1977	1982	1987
314	Footwear, except rubber	6,862	2.0	17.6	17.4	11.1	17.1	24.0	38.2	62.4
365	Radio and TV receiving equipment	11,763	3.5	14.1	16.3	-7.2	31.9	37.4	43.1	59.2
387	Watches, clocks, and watchcases	1,613	.5	14.0	6.4	11.2	21.1	34.0	45.9	58.1
375	Motorcycles, bicycles, and parts	1,343	.4	7.6	-1.9	-10.8	65.1	51.2	53.8	57.5
317	Handbags and personal leather goods	1,128	.3	15.8	13.0	22.3	18.1	26.9	37.4	56.5
391	Jewelry, silverware, and plated ware	5,832	1.7	18.7	14.1	3.1	22.0	31.1	41.9	56.3
237	Fur goods	515	.2	28.8	28.4	17.1	3.7	9.6	25.0	55.6
316	Luggage	870	.3	22.1	19.4	23.7	15.4	19.7	34.8	55.4
313	Boot, shoe cut stock, and findings	251	.1	29.5	17.6	14.4	2.2	10.5	24.7	48.8
393	Musical instruments	790	.2	16.0	24.6	35.3	15.0	14.2	21.5	46.0
394	Toys and sporting goods	5,749	1.7	17.3	17.4	27.1	13.0	17.3	25.6	41.8
326	Pottery and related products	1,492	.4	14.3	10.8	17.4	21.3	27.0	30.9	41.3
236	Children's outerwear	6,425	1.9	17.3	20.9	14.7	16.3	18.6	20.2	40.5
238	Miscellaneous apparel and accessories	1,453	.4	14.7	15.6	36.1	16.1	27.7	25.0	38.1
315	Leather gloves and mittens	90	—a	5.6	7.0	10.7	22.3	24.3	27.2	36.5
385	Ophthalmic goods	830	.2	18.3	16.9	13.8	12.4	19.7	24.0	36.4
302	Rubber and plastics footwear	348	.1	3.9	-4.5	27.9	33.9	61.3	33.6	35.8
328	Cut stone and stone products	430	.1	17.7	26.2	15.4	10.6	8.2	23.6	35.6
333	Primary nonferrous metals	6,647	2.0	9.1	-1.1	1.8	17.7	20.3	23.6	33.7
319	Leather goods, n.e.c.	168	—	14.1	15.0	18.7	15.1	13.6	16.1	31.9
381	Engineering and scientific instruments	245	.1	17.1	13.0	15.3	12.5	16.2	32.4	30.6
355	Special industry machinery	4,559	1.3	14.1	14.1	13.9	14.7	13.6	18.4	29.6
261	Pulpmills	2,069	.6	8.9	2.5	29.2	30.4	33.1	29.1	27.7
371	Motor vehicles and equipment	78,113	23.0	16.9	17.1	6.3	11.6	12.4	20.6	26.4
233	Women's and misses' outerwear	4,573	1.3	19.3	20.1	13.0	4.9	8.0	14.4	26.2
396	Costume jewelry and notions	985	.3	14.2	10.4	16.7	13.8	17.5	17.7	25.9
235	Hats, caps, and millinery	210	.1	14.2	9.5	8.9	11.0	12.6	18.8	24.8
232	Men's and boys' furnishings	5,176	1.5	19.3	16.0	26.8	7.2	11.1	16.3	24.0

a– Represents zero.
[b] Standard Industrial Classification.
[c] 1970–87 and 1980–87 rates are compound annual growth rates.
[d] Ratio of imports to new supply (product shipments plus imports).

SOURCE: *Industrial Outlook* (annual), U.S. International Trade Administration, as published in *Statistical Abstract of the United States – 1989,* U.S. Department of Commerce, Bureau of the Census, 734.

TABLE 13–3: Domestic Exports of Manufactured Goods (Nondurables and Durables), 1970–1987, by Dollar Value, Growth Rate, and Ratio of Exports to Total Product Shipments[a]

SIC[c] code	Product	1987 Value (millions of dollars)	1987 Percent distribution	Growth Rate (percent) 1970–1987	Growth Rate (percent) 1980–1987	Growth Rate (percent) 1986–1987	Ratio of Exports to Product Shipments (percent) 1972	1977	1982	1987
(x)[b]	**Manufacturing**	**198,355**	**100.0**	**10.9**	**2.5**	**15.3**	**5.6**	**7.4**	**9.1**	**8.2**
(x)	Nondurables	60,148	30.3	11.3	2.5	16.6	3.5	4.5	5.4	5.2
20	Food and kindred products	12,320	6.2	9.8	.2	9.5	2.9	4.1	4.3	3.9
21	Tobacco manufactures	2,278	1.1	15.7	11.2	53.9	5.7	9.4	10.3	9.1
22	Textile mill products	1,891	1.0	8.9	–3.8	14.4	2.9	4.3	4.9	3.9
23	Apparel and other mill products	1,490	.8	11.8	–1.0	26.5	1.2	2.2	2.4	2.1
26	Paper and allied products	5,676	2.9	10.1	2.8	26.7	4.1	4.9	5.5	4.7
27	Printing and publishing	1,525	.8	9.4	4.6	17.5	1.3	1.5	1.7	1.2
28	Chemicals and allied products	26,090	13.2	11.8	2.7	15.6	7.6	9.7	12.5	11.9
29	Petroleum and coal products	4,479	2.3	13.3	6.7	5.9	1.9	1.4	3.2	3.6
30	Rubber and plastics products	3,710	1.9	12.6	4.8	26.1	3.1	4.0	4.8	4.1
31	Leather and leather products	688	.3	15.0	4.4	32.2	1.8	3.8	5.7	7.3
(x)	Durables	138,207	69.7	10.7	2.5	14.8	7.4	10.0	13.0	10.8
24	Lumber and wood products	3,961	2.0	10.8	1.0	31.2	4.1	5.8	7.2	5.5
25	Furniture and fixtures	550	.3	15.5	2.8	18.1	.6	1.5	2.5	1.5
32	Stone, clay, and glass products	2,045	1.0	9.3	.9	18.7	2.4	3.4	4.3	3.2
33	Primary metal industries	4,772	2.4	4.5	–8.3	32.7	2.8	3.0	5.0	3.6
34	Fabricated metal products	6,185	3.1	8.1	–1.3	11.6	3.9	5.6	6.6	4.5
35	Machinery, except electrical	41,054	20.7	10.2	1.1	12.9	14.9	19.5	23.3	20.1
36	Electrical and electronic equipment	24,359	12.3	13.7	5.8	19.3	6.7	10.6	12.7	10.8
37	Transportation equipment	42,371	21.4	11.5	5.4	11.6	9.2	11.6	15.6	12.5
38	Instruments and related products	10,191	5.1	11.7	4.1	10.3	12.6	16.6	17.4	16.5
39	Miscellaneous manufacturing industries	2,719	1.4	10.4	–.9	30.7	7.6	9.4	9.5	9.3

[a]Data are valued on a f.a.s. basis. Data for all years have been adjusted to include comparable commodities in each group. Minus sign (–) indicates decrease.

[b]X Not applicable.

[c]Standard Industrial Classification.

SOURCE: Industrial Outlook (annual), U.S. International Trade Administration, as published in Statistical Abstract of the United States—1989, U.S. Department of Commerce, Bureau of the Census, 734.

TABLE 13–4: Domestic Exports for 28 Leading Three-Digit SIC Product Groups, 1970–1987, by Dollar Value, Growth Rate, and Ratio of Exports to Total Product Shipments

1977 SIC code[b]	Product Group	1987 Value (millions of dollars)	1987 Percent distribution	Growth Rate (percent) 1970–1987	Growth Rate (percent) 1980–1987	Growth Rate (percent) 1986–1987	Export/Shipments Ratio (percent) 1972	Export/Shipments Ratio (percent) 1977	Export/Shipments Ratio (percent) 1982	Export/Shipments Ratio (percent) 1987
299	Petroleum and coal products	358	.2	11.3	-4.9	-5.6	47.0	48.5	59.3	55.5
261	Pulpmills	2,345	1.2	9.8	4.3	35.0	33.4	37.5	40.9	41.5
357	Office and computing machines	18,342	9.2	15.5	11.6	21.1	20.9	23.8	24.6	28.2
353	Construction and related machinery	5,796	2.9	5.9	-9.0	-7.7	24.0	28.5	38.8	26.6
372	Aircraft and parts	20,618	10.4	11.9	5.2	13.3	24.9	29.1	29.9	25.5
374	Railroad equipment	331	.2	8.5	-3.9	-36.4	9.0	7.3	14.7	24.7
355	Special industry machinery	2,324	1.2	7.5	.2	21.5	19.5	24.6	27.7	22.6
382	Measuring and controlling devices	4,074	2.1	11.2	4.4	10.7	19.4	24.0	24.6	22.4
311	Leather tanning and finishing	391	.2	14.9	5.4	24.9	7.1	11.8	19.0	21.5
383	Optical instruments and lenses	1,121	.6	18.3	7.2	7.3	12.0	10.3	18.8	21.3
287	Agricultural chemicals	3,020	1.5	14.9	-2.6	15.2	9.8	12.1	21.0	21.2
281	Industrial inorganic chemicals	3,609	1.8	11.2	3.2	4.5	12.4	14.7	19.3	20.9
369	Miscellaneous electrical equipment	4,097	2.1	17.6	9.9	21.6	8.5	13.5	21.7	20.3
359	Machinery, except electrical	1,516	.8	26.3	9.7	21.1	1.5	2.2	16.3	20.3
351	Engines and turbines	2,960	1.5	9.9	-2.7	9.3	13.8	20.7	28.3	19.8
367	Electronic components and accessories	10,082	5.1	15.4	8.0	23.4	11.6	17.8	19.8	19.0
286	Industrial organic chemicals	8,195	4.1	12.3	3.6	18.8	11.2	11.6	17.0	19.0
241	Logging camps, log contractors	1,653	.8	9.2	.5	33.3	20.4	20.4	19.1	18.2
391	Jewelry, silverware, and plated ware	1,021	.5	11.3	.2	29.1	14.2	15.3	12.9	18.1
213	Chewing and smoking tobacco	223	.1	12.6	45.1	26.3	13.7	4.2	5.8	17.5
393	Musical instruments	171	.1	11.5	-3.3	49.2	8.2	14.6	16.7	16.7
381	Engineering and scientific instruments	715	.4	9.3	7.8	13.1	11.2	12.1	16.9	15.5
356	General industrial machinery	4,859	2.4	8.1	-.8	7.8	15.0	19.6	18.4	15.4
386	Photographic equipment and supplies	2,333	1.2	10.3	-.4	4.5	11.8	15.6	15.9	15.3
207	Fats and oils	2,240	1.1	5.6	-7.1	-1.5	15.0	17.2	18.6	15.2
348	Ordnance and accessories, n.e.c.	641	.3	5.7	—	-13.3	11.4	25.1	17.9	14.8
306	Fabricated rubber products, n.e.c.	96	—[a]	19.6	17.3	12.3	2.4	3.6	8.1	12.7
352	Farm and garden machinery	1,343	.7	7.9	-6.3	11.9	9.6	14.4	15.3	12.5

[a] – Represents zero.

[b] Standard Industrial Classification.

SOURCE: *Industrial Outlook* (annual), U.S. International Trade Administration, as published in *Statistical Abstract of the United States – 1989*. U.S. Department of Commerce. Bureau of the Census, 735.

TABLE 13–5: Percent of Raw Materials and Semifinished Goods Imported by Industries Shown

Industry	1987	1990	1995
Food	15.5%	16.3%	16.7%
Chemical	11.2	11.1	11.7
Pharmaceutical	12.6	15.9	20.7
Automotive	10.7	13.4	19.3
Paper	3.7	6.3	8.0
Electronic	13.9	17.8	17.2
Clothing/Textile	15.8	20.7	20.0
Other manufacturing	15.8	19.6	21.8
Merchandise	16.9	18.8	19.4
TOTAL	13.8	16.2	18.0

SOURCE: Bernard J. LaLonde, Martha C. Cooper, and Thomas G. Noordewier, *Customer Service: A Management Perspective*, Oak Brook, Illinois: Council of Logistics Management, 1988. Adapted from Appendix A, "Responses to Shipper Questionnaire (Question III.C.1)."

TABLE 13–6: Percent of Finished Goods Imported by Industries Shown

Industry	1987	1990	1995
Food	8.6%	9.6%	10.7%
Chemical	3.0	3.5	4.3
Pharmaceutical	19.0	21.3	25.0
Automotive	27.9	25.1	22.4
Paper	1.8[a]	7.2[a]	11.2[a]
Electronic	28.3	31.0	31.0
Clothing/Textile	37.8	42.5	45.6
Other manufacturing	12.6	15.7	17.8
Merchandise	25.7	29.4	32.1
TOTAL	15.2	17.1	18.6

[a]Less than 50 percent responded to this question.

SOURCE: Bernard J. LaLonde, Martha C. Cooper, and Thomas G. Noordewier, *Customer Service: A Management Perspective*, Oak Brook, Illinois: Council of Logistics Management, 1988. Adapted from Appendix A, "Responses to Shipper Questionnaire (Question III.C.1)."

cultures, and as many as 19 languages.[2] Even within a single country there may be several *official* languages which may be used for doing business. (Switzerland and Spain each have four languages, and Canada and Belgium each have two.) And, the "same" language may be "different" in two countries, as is the case with English in Great Britain and the United States, for example, depot versus warehouse, lorry versus truck, goods wagon versus rail car, and so on.

TABLE 13–7: Percent of Raw Materials and Semifinished Goods Exported by Industries Shown

Industry	1987	1990	1995
Food	4.7%	5.7%	7.6%
Chemical	4.5[a]	5.4[a]	6.2[a]
Pharmaceutical	8.1	9.4	11.3
Automotive	7.1	9.7	13.7
Paper	[b]	[b]	[b]
Electronic	5.3	6.4	7.5
Clothing/Textile	4.3	7.1	10.7
Other manufacturing	9.1	10.9	12.7
Merchandise	1.1	2.1	2.8
TOTAL	6.8	8.2	10.1

[a]Less than 50% responded to this question.

[b]Fewer than six responses.

SOURCE: Bernard J. LaLonde, Martha C. Cooper, and Thomas G. Noordewier, *Customer Service: A Management Perspective*, Oak Brook, Illinois: Council of Logistics Management, 1988. Adapted from Appendix A, "Responses to Shipper Questionnaire (Question III.C.1)."

TABLE 13–8: Percent of Finished Goods Exported by Industries Shown

Industry	1987	1990	1995
Food	7.4%	8.4%	9.7%
Chemical	15.6	17.1	19.3
Pharmaceutical	22.6	24.5	24.2
Automotive	10.9	14.5	17.4
Paper	11.1	10.1	10.7
Electronic	9.8	14.6	14.8
Clothing/Textile	14.8	15.8	17.6
Other manufacturing	9.6	11.8	13.8
Merchandise	2.2	3.5	5.1
TOTAL	11.1	12.9	14.4

SOURCE: Bernard J. LaLonde, Martha C. Cooper, and Thomas G. Noordewier, *Customer Service: A Management Perspective*, Oak Brook, Illinois: Council of Logistics Management, 1988. Adapted from Appendix A, "Responses to Shipper Questionnaire (Question III.C.1)."

MULTINATIONAL CORPORATE STRATEGY AND LOGISTICS

The decision to engage in multinational business is a top management decision, although sometimes it is less a decision than a necessity. There are firms that must import certain materials for their manufacturing processes because they are not available domestically; this is true of items as diverse as chromium (from Africa) and a variety of cooking spices (mostly from tropical countries).

FIGURE 13–1: Import/export patterns for raw materials and semifinished goods

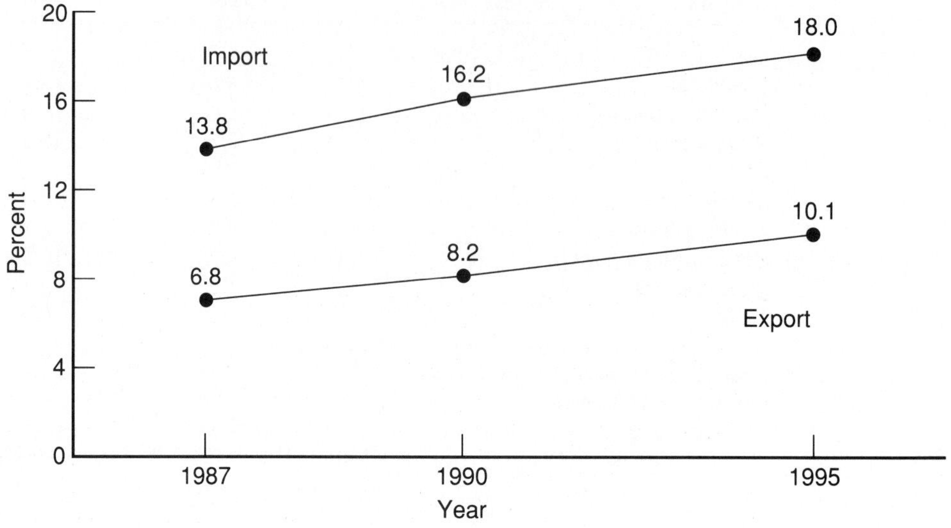

SOURCE: Bernard J. LaLonde, Martha C. Cooper, and Thomas G. Noordewier, *Customer Service: A Management Perspective* (Oak Brook, Illinois: Council of Logistics Management, 1988) 151.

Logistics functions and operations are involved when a firm imports or exports. As noted above, some imports may be absolutely required, but others may not, newsprint or certain textiles for examples. However, a decision to export is a deliberate decision, as would be the establishment of foreign distributorships, whether company-owned or independent. Engaging in manufacturing or extractive activity in a foreign country would certainly be a top management decision requiring approval of the Board of Directors.

The logistics manager has two principal tasks when company strategy calls for engaging in multinational business. The first, and most obvious, is the obligation to arrange for the multinational logistics services required by the firm. A second, and perhaps more difficult task, is to communicate the nature and possible consequences of the many differences between domestic and multinational logistics operations to those managers in the firm who need to be aware of them.

THE MULTINATIONAL LOGISTICS ENVIRONMENT

Cultures

Of all the differences between what a logistics manager must deal with at home as contrasted with other countries, the most profound are those arising from cultural differences. Culture permeates the conduct of business. Cultural factors affecting logistics operations in-

FIGURE 13–2: Import/export patterns for finished goods

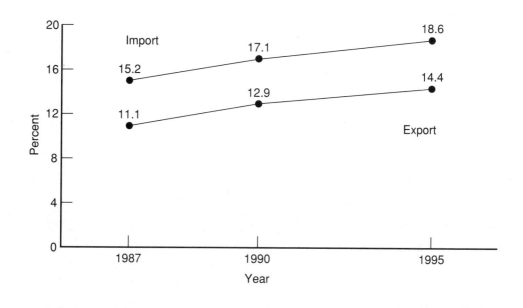

SOURCE: Bernard J. LaLonde, Martha C. Cooper, and Thomas G. Noordewier, *Customer Service: A Management Perspective* (Oak Brook, Illinois: Council of Logistics Management, 1988) 152.

clude sense of time, attitudes toward customs and other government regulations, and approaches to business negotiation.

Sense of Time Americans have an international reputation for "being in a hurry." Although managers in many countries are prompt in their actions, the attitude that "the world won't end if it isn't done immediately" is common in Latin America, the Caribbean, the Middle East, Africa, and much of the Far East. An American logistics manager should understand cultural differences, accept them, and take them into account when meeting and dealing with managers and government officials in other parts of the world.

Customs and Government Regulations In many countries local officials — often woefully underpaid — will *expect* modest personal payments for clearing goods for import or export or for the performance of other ministerial (clerkly) duties. Such payments (variously termed grease, squeeze, cumshaw) are permitted under U.S. law.[3] Attempts to circumvent or ignore such practices are likely to result in shipment delays lasting days, weeks, or longer. Local managers or agents of the firm must be authorized to make such "facilitating" payments and be reimbursed for them.

Business Negotiations On the whole, American business executives are accustomed to negotiating on a "let's get right down to business and make a deal" basis. Such an approach is totally out of place in the Middle East, in the Far East and, for the most part, in Latin America.

FIGURE 13–3: Illustration of the complexity of multinational import/export relationships with respect to languages, currency units, and basic legal systems

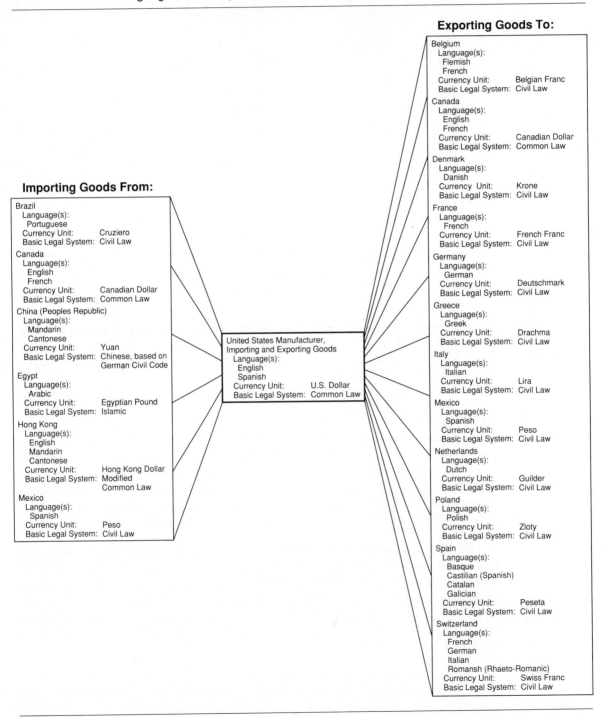

Exporting Goods To:

Belgium
  Language(s):
    Flemish
    French
  Currency Unit: Belgian Franc
  Basic Legal System: Civil Law
Canada
  Language(s):
    English
    French
  Currency Unit: Canadian Dollar
  Basic Legal System: Common Law
Denmark
  Language(s):
    Danish
  Currency Unit: Krone
  Basic Legal System: Civil Law
France
  Language(s):
    French
  Currency Unit: French Franc
  Basic Legal System: Civil Law
Germany
  Language(s):
    German
  Currency Unit: Deutschmark
  Basic Legal System: Civil Law
Greece
  Language(s):
    Greek
  Currency Unit: Drachma
  Basic Legal System: Civil Law
Italy
  Language(s):
    Italian
  Currency Unit: Lira
  Basic Legal System: Civil Law
Mexico
  Language(s):
    Spanish
  Currency Unit: Peso
  Basic Legal System: Civil Law
Netherlands
  Language(s):
    Dutch
  Currency Unit: Guilder
  Basic Legal System: Civil Law
Poland
  Language(s):
    Polish
  Currency Unit: Zloty
  Basic Legal System: Civil Law
Spain
  Language(s):
    Basque
    Castilian (Spanish)
    Catalan
    Galician
  Currency Unit: Peseta
  Basic Legal System: Civil Law
Switzerland
  Language(s):
    French
    German
    Italian
    Romansh (Rhaeto-Romanic)
  Currency Unit: Swiss Franc
  Basic Legal System: Civil Law

Importing Goods From:

Brazil
  Language(s):
    Portuguese
  Currency Unit: Cruziero
  Basic Legal System: Civil Law
Canada
  Language(s):
    English
    French
  Currency Unit: Canadian Dollar
  Basic Legal System: Common Law
China (Peoples Republic)
  Language(s):
    Mandarin
    Cantonese
  Currency Unit: Yuan
  Basic Legal System: Chinese, based on
                       German Civil Code
Egypt
  Language(s):
    Arabic
  Currency Unit: Egyptian Pound
  Basic Legal System: Islamic
Hong Kong
  Language(s):
    English
    Mandarin
    Cantonese
  Currency Unit: Hong Kong Dollar
  Basic Legal System: Modified
                       Common Law
Mexico
  Language(s):
    Spanish
  Currency Unit: Peso
  Basic Legal System: Civil Law

United States Manufacturer,
Importing and Exporting Goods
  Language(s):
    English
    Spanish
  Currency Unit: U.S. Dollar
  Basic Legal System: Common Law

And, it is not much appreciated even in European countries. In many parts of the world, such as the Orient, Middle East, and Latin America, business negotiations are preceded by the observance of social amenities. In addition, social gatherings are not considered appropriate for the discussion of business matters. A logistics manager negotiating agreements or wishing to establish an operating relationship with executives from other countries must understand the culture with which he or she is dealing.[4]

Government Stability

Logistics managers are necessarily concerned with the political stability of foreign governments and political systems. Political instability raises such dangers as the abrogation of contracts, confiscation of goods, and even the possibility of acts of war, revolution, or rebellion that may result in damage to or destruction of goods stored in or en route to such a country. The only complete protection in a situation judged to be risky is to have received payment prior to shipment of the goods. Even a confirmed irrevocable letter of credit (discussed later in this chapter) would not offer protection in the extreme circumstances just mentioned.

Legal Systems

Legal systems differ markedly among the nations of the world with respect to procedures and certain concepts, and this can affect important logistics considerations, such as business contracts, employment of sales agents, distributor relationships, title to goods, and payment for goods. Obviously, however, goods are constantly and successfully bought, sold, traded, and financed throughout the world. It is the procedures accompanying and governing these transactions that can cause delays and problems not anticipated by a logistics manager who is not familiar with different legal systems.

Basically, there are two classifications of legal systems of which the logistics manager should be aware. They are the English or Common Law system and the Civil Law System, and they dominate world trade. Additionally, there are a number of conventions relating to international business that have been ratified (adopted) by many countries and have something of the status of "international business law." Further, there are legal systems that are peculiar to a single country, although they usually possess some of the characteristics of the common law or civil law systems, and sometimes both.

English or Common Law This is the legal system of the British Commonwealth countries and, with a few modifications and much codification, this is the legal system American managers are accustomed to dealing with. In the United States many logistics legal concerns are addressed by the Uniform Commercial Code, which has been adopted in full by all U.S. States except Louisiana.[5] With respect to business matters, an American logistics manager should not find it difficult or unfamiliar to deal with British Commonwealth countries.

The Civil Law System Sometimes called the Continental System, this legal system based on Roman Law is found in all continental European countries, South America, and in the former colonies of continental European countries. It is markedly different in techniques and procedures from the common law system, and a logistics manager should be aware that such differences exist if his or her firm is going to do business with or within a country having the civil law system.

Other Legal Systems Many nations have legal systems that fit neither the common law nor civil law model. This is true of much of the Far East and the communist bloc nations. Doing business with firms in these areas requires expert assistance from knowledgeable legal counsel. However, in their international business dealings these countries do tend to use a common law approach because the common law system has become the international legal *lingua franca* of business when the parties to a transaction do not share the same legal system.

A Unified International System Internationally, great effort has been expended to achieve unification of business law, particularly as it applies to goods, and some progress has been made. English judgments can, under most circumstances, be enforced in the Commonwealth states such as Australia and Canada. American and English Admiralty Courts routinely cite each other's decisions. European Common Market countries, in accordance with Article 220 of the European Economic Community, concluded a convention on Jurisdiction and the Enforcement of Judgments in Civil and Commercial Matters. Other international agreements affecting goods and ratified by many countries, but by no means all, include:

Carriage of Goods by Sea Act

Convention on the Execution of Foreign Arbitral Awards

Convention on the Recognition and Enforcement of Foreign Arbitral Awards

Geneva Protocol on Arbitration Clauses

Convention on Contracts for the International Sale of Goods

The Convention on Contracts for the International Sale of Goods (CISG) and the several arbitration conventions are particularly important to logistics management because so much potential international litigation has to do with matters arising out of shipping, storing, sale, and financing of goods. By early 1990 the CISG had been ratified by the 17 countries shown in Table 13–9, and it is expected that this number will increase significantly in the future.

Arbitration clauses are increasingly found in international contracts concerning goods in order to avoid costly legal proceedings that might go on for years. Arbitration is particularly advantageous in so-called *quality arbitration* disputes dealing with questions of fact, such as whether the goods are of the stipulated quality or description, are in accordance with samples,

---

TABLE 13–9: Nations Now Bound by the Convention on International Sale of Goods (CISG)

Region	Countries
Europe	Austria, Finland, France, Hungary, Italy, Norway, Sweden, Yugoslavia
North America	Mexico, United States of America
South America	Argentina
Middle East	Syria
Africa	Egypt, Lesotho, Zambia
Oceania	Australia
Orient	China

and so on. However, arbitration clauses are not the ''cure all'' that they are sometimes claimed to be. If a dispute involves only the construction of a document or a purely legal question — a so-called *technical arbitration* — it is often cheaper and more expeditious for the parties to submit their dispute to the court where such a question will likely be resolved very quickly.[6]

Economies

Infrastructure In much of the nonindustrial world, the availability of physical facilities, such as warehouses, is limited. Goods may be stored outside or in relatively flimsy structures, with the result that protection from the elements or pilferage is either minimal or nonexistent. Transportation and communication networks may be quite limited. Quite the opposite is true in the industrialized nations where logistics infrastructures match or exceed those of the United States.

Inflation and Nonconvertible Currencies Although primarily a concern of financial managers, the problems posed by very high rates of inflation in areas with weak economies, such as Latin America, may adversely affect planned logistics budgets. And, if a nation's currency is nonconvertible to U.S. dollars without government approval, problems may arise regarding payment for goods despite previous assurances that U.S. funds will be available to meet the buyer's obligations.

MULTINATIONAL PHYSICAL DISTRIBUTION STRATEGY

Top Management and Logistics Management Involvement

As noted earlier in this chapter, a voluntary decision to engage in multinational business is, or at least should be, a top management or even a Board of Directors decision. And, such a decision must be made keeping in mind that the company will be doing business in a different environment than it has been accustomed to in the past. In addition, logistics considerations must be taken into account when such a decision is contemplated. Together with other functional managers, the logistics manager is concerned with channel strategies and the laws, regulations, and policies of both the U.S. Government and the host nations. A further consideration, of increasing importance to international trade, is the continuing growth of regional economic integration alliances.

Regional Economic Integration Alliances[7]

Since World War II, economic integration has been pursued by groups of countries wanting to expand the size of their markets, increase their economic and political power, and realize the economic gains of greater intragroup trade. These developments are important to logistics managers because they result in multinational areas having some or all of the following characteristics:

1. An area free of internal tariff barriers and possibly the erection of higher import barriers for goods originating outside the associated countries;

2. Common tax policies that may affect taxes applied to on-site inventories and repatriation of profits;

3. A common currency or a fixed exchange rate among the member country currencies;

4. Cooperative political agreements affecting freedom of movement of labor and capital among the member nations;

5. Varying degrees of industry sectoral programming affecting location and type of manufacturing and processing facilities within the area encompassed by the member nations.

Given the accelerating pace of regional economic integration occurring, particularly in Europe, a logistics manager must be aware of the significance and logistics ramifications of these developments and must continually monitor the further evolution of laws, regulation, and policies that will impact logistics operations. Logistics is concerned with the movement of goods, and the expansion of an area within which goods may freely move can have a profound effect on inventory location decisions, allow the centralization of previously decentralized inventories, eliminate the costs associated with a former need to process shipments through customs barriers, and so on.

Examples of integration groups are shown in Table 13–10. Four increasing levels of regional economic integration can be distinguished. Each succeeding level of integration involves greater cooperation among the bloc's member countries.

TABLE 13–10: Levels of Economic Integration

Level	Examples	Members
Free-Trade Area	European Free Trade Area (EFTA)	Austria, Norway, Sweden, Switzerland
	Latin American Free Trade Area (ALADI)	Argentina, Bolivia, Brazil, Chile, Colombia, Costa Rica, Ecuador, El Salvador, Guatemala, Honduras, Mexico, Panama, Paraguay, Uruguay, Venezuela
Customs Union	Andean Pact	Bolivia, Colombia, Ecuador, Peru, Venezuela
	Caricom	Antigua and Barbuda, Bahamas, Barbados, Belize, Dominica, Grenada, Guyana, Jamaica, Monserrat, St. Kitts-Nevis, St. Lucia, St. Vincent, Trinidad and Tobago
Common Market	European Community	Belgium, Denmark, France, Greece, Ireland, Italy, Luxembourg, Netherlands, Portugal, Spain, United Kingdom, West Germany
Economic Union	Belgium-Luxembourg Economic Union	Belgium, Luxembourg

SOURCE: Robert Grosse and Duane Kujawa, *International Business: Theory and Managerial Applications*, Richard D. Irwin © 1988, page 255.

Free-Trade Area The first level of economic integration, the free-trade area, involves the elimination of tariffs on trade among the countries in the regional group.

Among the free-trade areas is the European Free Trade Area (EFTA), formed at about the same time as the Common Market (in 1960) and comprising those Western European countries that did not become Common Market members. Today, the members of the EFTA are Austria, Norway, Sweden, and Switzerland. (The United Kingdom and Denmark left EFTA to join the Common Market in 1973.)

The Latin American Free Trade Association (LAFTA), originally composed of the Spanish-speaking countries in South America plus Brazil and Mexico, has evolved into a group called ALADI (Associación Latinoamericana de Integración), which includes the same countries. Even after 25 years of existence, this group has *not* been able to eliminate tariffs or all trade barriers among its members. It has, however achieved a reduction of some trade barriers and an increase in economic cooperation.

Customs Union The second level of regional economic integration, the customs union, involves the elimination of tariffs among member countries *plus* the establishment of a common external tariff structure toward nonmember countries. The Caribbean Common Market (CARICOM) is one such group, and the Andean Pact is another. The former group includes 12 of the English-speaking island countries of the Caribbean (all former British colonies), and the latter includes Bolivia, Colombia, Ecuador, Peru, and Venezuela. In both of these groups, efforts are under way to reduce trade barriers and increase intragroup business, but thus far neither has achieved the regulatory harmonization of a common market.

Another example of such a union is the Association of Southeast Asian Nations (ASEAN) which is composed of Indonesia, Malaysia, the Philippines, Singapore, and Thailand. ASEAN has reduced intragroup tariffs and eliminated some nontariff barriers to trade.

Common Market This third level of economic integration, the common market, is characterized by the same tariff policy as the customs union *plus* freedom of movement for factors of production—labor and capital—among member countries. The largest, and by far most successful, example of regional economic integration is the alliance of European countries variously referred to as the European Economic Community (EEC), European Community (EC), or as the European Common Market (ECM), which now numbers 12 nations. Full integration of the EEC is due to take place on December 31, 1992. From that time onward, the EEC will represent a unified market of 335 million people, the largest single market in the western world having no internal trade barriers.

Economic Union An economic union is characterized by harmonization of economic policy beyond that of a common market. Specifically, an economic union seeks to unify monetary and fiscal policy among its member countries. A common currency, or a permanently fixed exchange rate, is one aspect of an economic union. Harmonized tax rates and tax rate structures are other aspects. At present, only the Belgium-Luxembourg Economic Union (BLEU) fits into this category. Belgium and Luxembourg maintain a fixed exchange rate (1 Belgian franc = 1 Luxembourg franc) and a highly coordinated set of monetary policies. These two countries are the smallest in the ECC, and they have allied themselves with each other primarily to gain a larger voice in EEC affairs.

Channel Strategies — Options and Choices

The channel strategy chosen will determine the logistics manager's responsibility for international inventory management, storage, order processing, and transportation. There are a great many approaches and variations to engaging in multinational business — far too many to discuss here — but all fit into one of three basic classifications: direct export sales, foreign distributorships, and direct foreign investment (manufacturing, extractive operations, and such).

Direct Export Sales In the case of direct export sales, the logistics manager must observe any necessary export packaging and packing rules and any required government export documentation, and he or she must arrange for international transportation. Depending on the terms of sale and the shipping agreement made with the customer, arrangements may also have to be made for customs clearance at the foreign port of entry, payment for the goods, and onward transport of the goods to destination. Direct export sales may be made by the company's own sales force or by appointed sales agents in the foreign country.

Distributors Distributors may be independent operators providing full marketing and logistics services in their respective sales territories under contract with the U.S. firm that they represent, or they may be partially or wholly-owned subsidiaries of that U.S. firm. Regardless of the nature of the relationship with the distributor, the U.S. logistics manager is responsible for all international arrangements for shipping goods to the distributor and the monitoring of inventory levels at the foreign location. Clearly, a key factor in successful management of the these logistics activities is the international communication capability of the firm. Chapter 12 contains extensive information about telecommunications services.

Direct Foreign Investment Logistics concerns with respect to direct foreign investment (DFI) involve the management of shipments to DFI locations or shipments from DFI locations back to the firm's U.S. plants or distribution centers. While it is obvious that ''off-shore'' operations are increasing, and any company undertaking such activity needs considerable expertise to deal with the multitude of political and regulatory factors involved in operating in another country, the focus here is on the international operations tasks of the U.S. logistics manager. The logistics management challenges are essentially the same whether a logistics manager is dealing with a foreign subsidiary owned by a U.S. parent firm or is a manager in a U.S. firm that happens to be a subsidiary of a foreign parent.

Host Country Policies

Import Constraints Most countries limit or prohibit the importation of certain goods. The motives for such limitations are political, economic, or any combination of the two. Import quotas are usually intended to protect part of the domestic market from foreign competition and are essentially economic in nature. Prohibiting the import of certain goods may be political in nature, or its purpose may be to protect an entire market for domestic producers. Logistics managers must keep up to date with specific import constraints, including *components* of finished goods that may be prohibited or under quota.

Tariff Considerations Import tariffs fall into two general classifications: (1) "reasonable" or "financially tolerable" customs duties intended to produce revenue for the host country, and (2) what are known as "prohibitive tariffs," customs duties set so high that for all practical purposes they exclude the goods from entry.

U.S. Government Policies The U.S. Government, like most governments, strongly favors exports of most goods to help with the balance of trade. However, the U.S. Government prohibits or limits the export of many kinds of goods, such as helium (nearly absolute prohibition), and many types of high technology goods to communist bloc countries. It may impose an absolute embargo on trade with certain countries, such as Cuba. Again, the logistics manager must be aware of these export constraints.

MULTINATIONAL PHYSICAL DISTRIBUTION

This section of the chapter describes the nature of the basic logistics activities and special documentation requirements involved in multinational physical distribution. Some of these occur at the point when the goods are ready to leave the United States for export or have arrived from abroad at a port of entry. It is at this point in the movement of the goods that the roles of international freight forwarders and customhouse brokers are of great importance. Although this section of the chapter treats exports (handled by international freight forwarders), for the sake of convenience the roles of both international freight forwarders and customhouse brokers (who handle imports) are noted here.

Only a firm having a very large volume of its goods moving through a particular export location or port of entry could possibly afford to employ its own specialist import/export staff at that location. The necessary alternative for even large firms is the use of international freight forwarders for export shipments and customhouse brokers for goods being imported. The employees of these firms are experienced specialists in handling international shipments, and their assistance in processing export and import shipments is nearly indispensable. They are intimately familiar with shipment documentation requirements, ocean cargo and international airfreight insurance, labeling and marking of goods for export, the personnel, capabilities and schedules of the carriers involved, free trade zone rules and regulations, port rules and regulations, export and import licenses (when required), customs regulations, tariffs and duties, which customs officials handle what matters, and more. Based on several personal experiences of the authors, for amateurs to attempt to find their way through this maze at a port of export or entry is a task that is usually frustrating, invariably time consuming, and often unsuccessful. A logistics manager is well advised to leave these matters in the hands of the field experts. The forms reproduced in the appendix show this to be wise advice.

THIRD PARTIES: YOUR PASSPORT TO PROFITS

Thomas A. Foster and E. J. Muller

The phrase *global third party logistics vendor* doesn't exactly roll off the tongue, but it is a term that has produced a great deal of talk among U.S. shippers in recent years.

Faced with fierce competition from Japan, Germany and other nations, U.S. companies are under severe pressure to become global competitors themselves by rapidly increasing exports, foreign sourcing and overseas manufacturing. At the same time, these U.S. companies find themselves constrained by limited international expertise, lack of investment capital and prohibitive costs of entry into many international business activities.

The obvious solution is to find reliable outside contractors that have global logistics networks and the necessary international expertise to make their clients instant global competitors.

Enter the global third party logistics vendor. In the U.S. alone there are about 60 firms that call themselves third party logistics vendors, according to the consulting firm of A. T. Kearney. But the capabilities of these companies vary.

A. T. Kearney Vice President Pat Byrne notes that about 45 firms are well-known companies, but that many are really involved in only one component of transportation. Only a handful of these have significant international involvement.

The majority of global third party logistics vendors, however, are based overseas where the concept of outsourcing has been widely accepted for decades. That might explain why foreign companies such as Australia's TNT, Britain's National Freight Consortium and Switzerland-based Danzas Corporation have been making far greater inroads in this country than their U.S. competitors.

Given the obvious need for such service, it is surprising that the use of global third party logistics vendors by U.S. shippers remains modest.

One reason for all the fence sitting, most experts agree, is that many U.S. businesses are being inundated with rapid changes such as downsizing, globalization, mergers, LBO's, recessionary forecasts, etc. Reeling executives are hesitant to make the long-term commitment that outsourcing requires, even though these services may solve their problems.

"We represent a major change to the way most companies operate," states Steve Wunning, vice president of Morton, Il-based CAT Logistics, one of the original third party trailblazers. "Although we can document a reduction in our clients' distribution costs and an increase in service levels," he says, "a lot of potential users still sit on the fence because they are resistant to change."

Adding to the confusion is competitive sales talk between the so-called "pure players" and "asset leveragers."

Pure players are companies, typically having sophisticated information systems, which assume the duties of an international traffic department—helping plan distribution strategy, arranging transportation, handling documentation, etc.

A good example of a pure player is C. H. Robinson, a non asset-based third party transportation company headquartered in Eden Prairie, Minn. It has 18 full-time computer programmers on staff and handles 125,000 transactions daily with its homegrown logistics software. "We now want to make a global impression," says vice president, transportation, Mike Musacchio. In Mexico, for example, the company has founded C. H. Robinson de Mexico SA, employed a completely Mexican staff, and is tying those Mexican offices into its information system network. Its transportation will be provided through arrangements with existing truck and rail services.

An asset leverager may end up providing many of the same services, but they typically are a subsidiary of a transportation or distribution company. Such a company would be CSX/Sea-Land Logistics, which is part of huge transportation conglomerate CSX Corp., that offers domestic truck, intermodal and rail services along with its ocean shipping subsidiary Sea-Land Services, as well as European operations through Transport Logistics Services.

Like the pure players, it customizes logistics systems for individual companies, but a significant portion of the freight is handled by sister operating divisions of CSX Corp.

Somewhere in between are companies like TNT Contract Logistics, which according to its European Managing Director Brian Bolam "offers dedicated systems, not systems based on company assets."

Other TNT operating companies have huge fleets of trucks throughout Europe, along with airplanes, distribution facilities and other assets. According to Bolam, however, these assets are not his operation.

"For our contract customers, these are just one resource available," says Bolam. "We generally lease warehouses, trucks, and any other logistics resources needed by the customer."

In marketing their services, these distinct types often engage potential clients in a game of "Who Do You Trust?"

Asset leveragers only want to secure more cargo for their (fill in mode of your choice: trucks, trains, planes, etc.), argue the "pure" players. Consistency of service and long-term stability are not possible when you subcontract transportation services, the asset leveragers argue back.

Once third party firms do gain entry to the corporate boardroom, the sales pitch usually hinges on three key points, deemed to be of the most vital importance to chief executives: cost reduction, asset displacement (facilities, equipment and staff), and a chance for the client to reinvest solely in its core business.

U.S. companies that are likely to use a third party for overseas business typically fit one of several profiles, according to marketing executives for contract vendors. These are either fast growth firms that are breaking into new markets too quickly to develop an in-house logistics network; companies faced with shareholder pressure to immediately improve return on assets and investment, and companies disrupted by takeovers or leveraged buyouts.

"If a company is going into a new overseas market and it has uncertain sales forecasts," explains Wunning, "rather than operate its own DC and perhaps get stuck with an underutilized asset should sales not take off — or get caught short if sales boom — a company can use a third party to handle all the logistics and only pay for the services provided."

TNT's Brian Bolam agrees. "We aim our efforts at companies undergoing strategic change, such as being acquired or acquiring other companies," he says. "That is what is happening in a big way in Europe as it prepares itself for 1992."

Bolam says he uses the "key and core" concept in his sales efforts. "We sincerely believe that logistics is a key part of every company's strategy in Europe," says Bolam. "But we also believe that the companies must concentrate on their core business, whatever that may be, and use the expertise of third parties for their logistics needs."

Bolam says that in Europe, where third parties have had their greatest development, many other arguments for using third parties have been used. These reasons often vary from country to country.

"In Spain right now, the cost of money makes owning logistics assets an expensive luxury," says Bolam. "Just in the last year or so, land costs are up 100 percent. Interest rates are up 50 percent. It makes little sense for companies marketing here to tie funds up in land and assets."

In the U.K., labor relations problems often make outsourcing very attractive, says Bolam. "We can offer most companies in the U.K. considerably better labor productivity than they can get on their own."

In the U.S., companies are beginning to consider the many possible advantages of outsourcing significant parts of their logistics operations, possibly because they have seen the success their foreign competitors have enjoyed.

The interest so far has been among the very large U.S. companies, whose motivation seems to be minimizing fixed costs and head count.

CAT Logistics' Wunning admits that when his company started out several years ago, they thought they would be dealing with the second-tier companies lacking sophisticated resources. So far it hasn't worked out that way. "It's the leaders who are making the move toward outsourcing," he says. However, he does expect that to change in the coming months.

"It is our belief that international third parties will assume far greater significance in the next few years as companies seek innovative and cost efficient ways to develop new global markets," says Wunning, "and as the abilities of logistics contractors catch up with shippers' requirements."

SOURCE: *Distribution* (October 1990): 30–32. Reprinted with permission of Chilton Company.

Terms of Sale

Although international terms of sale are similar to domestic terms, their definitions are more extensive. The checklist below contains the usual definitions for surface transportation.[8] When a shipment is made by air, the process is less complex because there are likely fewer parties involved in moving and handling the goods.

1. *Ex (point of origin)*
   Domestic selling price at factory, warehouse, mine, and so on, less export discounts, if any.

2. *F.O.B. transport vehicle*
   Ex (point of origin) price plus cost of:
   Export packing and marking
   Pickup by carrier or loading on carrier vehicle
   Freight charge, if the point specified is other than the beginning of the journey.

3. *F.A.S. vessel*
   F.O.B. price at point of loading, plus charges for:
   Switching, if any (rail)
   Unloading
   Lighterage, if any
   Wharfage
   Handling and trucking
   Checking (quality, quantity, and so on), if any
   Transit duties, if any
   Forwarder's commission
   Clean dock receipt

4. *F.O.B. vessel*
   F.A.S price, plus costs of:
   Loading on board vessel
   Heavy lift, if any
   Clean ship's receipt or clean on-board bill of lading (depending on country)

5. *C. & F.*
   F.O.B. vessel price, plus costs of:
   Ocean freight
   Export license
   Export duties and taxes

6. *C.I.F.*
   C. & F. price, plus cost of:
   Marine insurance or air cargo insurance

7. *Ex dock*
   C.I.F. price, plus costs of:
   Consular invoice
   Certificate of origin
   Lighterage (if the vessel cannot be wharfed)
   Unloading
   Import licenses
   Import tariffs and taxes
   Customs clearance
   Additional marine and war risk coverage, if applicable

Customer Service

The U.S. firm exercises management responsibility for customer service in the case of direct export sales and for company-managed distributorships. And, of course, independent distributors should be required to adhere to the U.S. firm's customer service policies. However, this is easier said than done because of the lack of direct control over independent distributors. The customer service challenge is perhaps greatest in the case of direct export sales, whether made by company sales representatives or sales agents. This is because there is no on-the-scene inventory backup if goods must be replaced or orders must be filled very quickly. This may require granting greater discretionary authority to the field sales force involved in international sales than is ordinarily delegated to the domestic salesforce members. For example, the sales representative or agent may be given discretionary authority to replace goods or fill an order by air transportation rather than by slower means.

Bonded Warehouses and Free Trade Zones

One of the most valuable tools available to the logistics manager engaged in international operations is the use of bonded warehouses, which were discussed in Chapter 11. An equally valuable tool when available is the use of free trade zones. These may be viewed as large-scale concentrations of bonded warehouses situated in areas designated by a government in which goods are landed and held for distribution or transhipment to other foreign destinations. Storage as well as assembly and manufacturing activities may take place in such zones. A major advantage is the ability to delay payment of customs duties for goods ultimately destined for distribution in the country where the free trade zone is located. In addition, payment of customs duties on goods that are merely in transit to other countries can be avoided entirely.[9] A further advantage of free trade zones is that they allow for the inspection of goods prior to the payment of customs duties, thus allowing the rejection of defective goods before payment of duties.

There are now over 100 free trade zones authorized in the United States. There are free trade zones at all major U.S. seaports and most international airports. There are also many located at interior points such as Tulsa, Oklahoma, and Toledo, Ohio, to which imported goods may be shipped in bond from ports of entry. Additionally, there are free trade zones in cities convenient to the U.S. borders with Mexico and Canada, such as El Paso, Texas, and Buffalo, New York. The number of free trade zones in the United States and abroad continues to increase, reflecting the growing amount of international trade.[10]

Transportation

International transportation movements are in almost all respects more complex than domestic movements. They:

Typically involve longer distances than domestic movements;

Typically involve transportation charges that are a higher percentage of the value of the goods;

Require extensive documentation;

Require special insurance in the case of ocean and air transportation;

Require special packaging, packing, marking, and labeling;

Involve more intermodal movements;

Require using specialized contractors—international freight forwarders for exports and customshouse brokers for imports—to assist in completing shipments through customs and subsequent delivery to carrier for ongoing movement.

An unwelcome surprise may await a shipper when *ad valorem* customs duties include not only the value (cost) of the goods, but also transportation charges and even insurance—the duty is based on the total of cost, insurance, and freight (C.I.F.). This is a possibility that should be checked out prior to a decision to use air freight, given the high cost of that mode of transportation for international shipments. Savings on packing and other costs associated with surface movement may be exceeded by a C.I.F-based customs duty if air freight is used in such circumstances.

Documentation and Payment

Export Documents The many kinds of documentation that are a necessary part of engaging in international trade have traditionally discouraged many companies from expanding into this area. In the last decade, however, great strides have been made to simplify documentation. These changes are discussed later in the chapter.

The major types of documents involved in export and import shipments are:[11]

1. *Bill of Lading* constitutes both a receipt for cargo accepted by the carrier and a contract for transportation between the carrier and the shipper. The bill of lading may be used as an instrument of ownership; it can be bought, sold, or traded while the goods are in transit. For it to be negotiable in this form, it must be a so-called negotiable order bill of lading. Bills of lading can be classified according to the type of carrier: ocean or air bills of lading, waybills for railroads, and pro forma bills of lading for trucking.

   Other types of bills of lading are defined as follows: a *clean bill of lading* is issued when a shipment is received in good condition; it is not issued when shortages or damages are claimed. An *on board bill of lading* certifies that the cargo has been placed aboard a given vessel and is required by the shipper to obtain payment from a bank.

2. *Dock receipt* used to transfer responsibility for cargo between the domestic and international carriers involved. The dock receipt is issued at the terminal where physical transfer takes place.

3. *Delivery instructions* provide the inland carrier with detailed instructions about the arrangements made by the shipper or forwarder to deliver the cargo to a given pier, gate, or carrier.

4. *Consular invoice* required by some countries to identify and control goods shipped to them. It is prepared on special forms available from each consulate.

5. *Commercial invoice* a common invoice sent by the seller to the buyer. It is usually used by customs authorities to assess duties.

6. *Certificate of origin* a document used to prove to the importing country the country of origin of the goods being exported. It is commonly issued by a recognized chamber of commerce.

7. *Insurance certificate*   provides assurance to the consignee that insurance has been obtained covering loss or damage for in-transit cargo.

8. *Transmittal letter*   a list of details of a shipment and a record of the documentation that is transmitted, together with instructions for disposition of the documents and other special instructions.

9. *Export declaration*   required by the United States Department of Commerce to control exports, in compliance with export licensing, and to provide export statistics.

Methods of Payment   International logistics systems must handle a wider variety of methods of payment for goods than is the case domestically. Open-account sales against established credit with customers in countries having freely convertible currencies is commonly used in international transactions, but when credit is questionable or payment in dollars is subject to government approval, letters of credit are used to guarantee payment to the seller.

A letter of credit is a document issued by a foreign bank on behalf of its client to assure the U.S. seller of payment for goods or services exported. Letters of credit can be of three types:

Irrevocable   opened by a foreign bank or by a U.S. bank at the request of a foreign correspondent, in favor of the exporter.

Confirmed irrevocable   opened by a foreign bank and confirmed (guaranteed) by a U.S. bank, in favor of the exporter.

Revocable   a pro forma document used as a guideline for the preparation of an irrevocable or confirmed irrevocable letter of credit, and therefore binding on no one.

Provided the conditions stated in an irrevocable or confirmed irrevocable letter of credit are fully observed (time limit, documents required, special conditions) a letter of credit cannot be canceled without the consent of the exporter. In order to collect the payment(s) specified in the letter of credit, the exporter is required to present the documents specified in the letter of credit to the bank to demonstrate that the goods have been delivered as promised. A bank will refuse to honor a letter of credit if there is *any* discrepancy between the conditions specified in the letter of credit and the performance of parties to the transaction. To put it another way, the bank will not turn over the funds to the payee unless it is certain all specifications have been observed. An example of a confirmed irrevocable letter of credit is shown in Figure 13–4.

Insurance

From the standpoint of carrier liability for loss and damage, international freight is totally unlike domestic freight. Ocean carriers accept no liability for loss or damage of freight, and ocean cargo insurance is therefore essential.[12] The liability of international air carriers for freight loss and damage is sharply limited by international convention and air carrier tariffs. Logistics managers must therefore arrange insurance coverage for all international air and ocean freight shipments.

Packaging and Packing

Packaging   Aside from marketing considerations concerning foreign language labeling and any labeling or carton-marking requirements of the carriers involved or the host country,

FIGURE 13–4: Confirmed irrevocable letter of credit

Hudson Trust Company
Four Wall Street
New York 15, N.Y.

Confirmed Irrevocable
Credit No. 0029/531

Dated   January 15, 1991

Universal Export Corporation
One Rockefeller Plaza, 89th Floor
NewYork, N.Y. 10020-2094

Gentlemen:

We are informed by BANCO COMMERCIAL DE LIMA, LIMA PERU, that they have issued their Irrevocable Credit No. 471 in your favor, to the extent of
—— $100,000.00 (One Hundred Thousand Dollars) ————————————————————
for account of IMPORTADORES GONZALEZ CIA., LIMA PERU
available by your drafts on us at SIGHT accompanied by the following documents (complete sets unless otherwise stated) evidencing shipment(s) of:
Complete portable aquifiers for industrial filtration, FOB Vessel New York, from New York to Callao, Peru.
Copy of invoice.
Copy of Consular Invoice including Certificate of Origin and mentioning Import Permit Number 67398.
Copy of your airmail letter to Motores Internacionales, S.A., Lima, stating the details of shipment necessary for insurance purposes.
Non-negotiable copy of onboard ocean bill of lading issued to order of Transportes Nacional, S.A., Lima, Peru.
Copy of your airmail letter to Motores Internacionales, S.A., Lima, Peru, enclosing the originals of the invoice, consular invoice, including certificate of origin, and onboard ocean bill of lading.

Drafts must clearly specify the number of this credit, and be presented at this Company not later than March 15, 1991.
Except so far as otherwise expressly stated, this credit is subject to the Uniform Customs and Practice for Commercial Documentary Credits fixed by the Thirteenth Congress of the International Chamber of Commerce. For the definitions of certain export quotations, reference is made to the general descriptions of those terms included in the "Revised American Foreign Trade Definitions, 1941." Any amendment of the terms of this credit must be in writing over an authorized signature of this Company.
The above mentioned corresondent engages with you that all drafts drawn in conformity with the conditions of this credit will be duly honored. At the request of our correspondent we confirm their credit and also engage with you that drafts drawn in conformity with the conditions of this credit will be duly honored by us.

Yours very truly,

Authorized Signature

Note
Documents must conform strictly with the terms of this Credit. If you are unable to comply with its terms, please communicate with us and/or your customer promptly with a view to having the conditions changed.

the packaging of goods for export should take into account variations in climate, uses for the empty package in poor countries (often a prime selling point), and the weight of the packaging material. Since some customs duties in some countries for some goods are based on weight rather than value, and packaging is considered part of the weight of the goods, an unnecessarily heavy package may increase customs duties substantially.

Packing for Export Goods to be shipped by ocean carrier must be packed to withstand rough handling and exposure to the elements while being loaded, unloaded, or sitting unprotected on an open dock or in a loading area. Today, of course, a very large percentage of nonbulk items shipped in international trade are packed in containers. A properly loaded container will protect goods from weather, damage, and pilferage.

Goods shipped internationally by air generally require only the same degree of packing care as domestic airfreight shipments. Goods shipped by motor carrier or rail between the United States and Mexico or Canada may be packed in the same fashion as domestic shipments.

MULTINATIONAL FINANCIAL CONSIDERATIONS FOR LOGISTICS

Currency Exchange and Fluctuation

Many corporate international financial considerations are primarily the concern of a company's financial managers. However, the logistics manager does have significant concerns with currency exchange rates and fluctuations in currency values when payment must be made for logistics services in foreign countries. A few years ago the British pound plummeted in exchange value from $1.50 to $1.09 in a few months, and then rose back up to near its former level nearly as quickly. Not all currency fluctuations are as dramatic, but when tens or possibly hundreds of thousands of dollars in transportation, warehousing and other charges will be incurred, even a modest ''wrong way'' movement in exchange rates will wreck a planned logistics budget for services that must be paid in a foreign currency.

Country Risk

The additional risks associated with international business dealings are characterized by the term ''country risk.'' This is an all-inclusive term that encompasses matters of political stability as well as economic uncertainty regarding a country's policies affecting foreign interests. As noted earlier in this chapter, a decision to engage in multinational business is a strategic decision made by top management and should take into account those factors that enter into an assessment of country risk.

Country Credit Ratings

Every six months the publishers of *Institutional Investor* magazine, a leading trade journal in the financial field, survey bankers around the world to get their opinions as to the credit worthiness of 112 countries. Shown in Table 13–11, these credit ratings reflect a judgmental combination of economic, financial, and political assessments of ''risk'' with respect to credit-based transactions with these countries. Table 13–12 shows a sample of positive and negative credit rating changes over the 10-year period from 1979 to 1989. Of course, as noted previously, a firm can protect itself financially in the case of a weak credit situation by selling only for cash in advance or on the basis of a confirmed irrevocable letter of credit.

TABLE 13–11: Country Credit Ratings

Rank	Country	Credit Rating	Rank	Country	Credit Rating	Rank	Country	Credit Rating
1	Japan	94.5	39	Greece	47.8	77	Jamaica	19.8
2	Switzerland	93.9	40	Cyprus	46.3	78	Ivory Coast	19.6
3	West Germany	92.8	41	India	46.2	79	Senegal	19.5
4	United States	88.8	42	Hungary	43.6	80	Syria	18.5
5	Netherlands	87.6	43	Turkey	41.4	81	Swaziland	18.4
6	France	87.1	44	Tunisia	38.5	82	Argentina	18.3
7	United Kingdom	86.9	45	Algeria	38.4	83	Nigeria	18.2
8	Canada	85.0	46	Barbados	38.3	84	Panama	18.0
9	Austria	84.7	47	Chile	37.8	85[a]	Iraq	17.8
10	Sweden	80.9	48	Israel	36.4	86[a]	Bangladesh	17.8
11[a]	Italy	79.8	49	South Africa	35.8	87	Ecuador	17.6
12[a]	Belgium	79.8	50	Mauritius	35.2	88	Dominican Republic	17.0
13	Finland	78.8	51	Mexico	35.0	89	Guatemala	16.9
14	Norway	78.2	52	Bulgaria	34.7	90	Seychelles	15.7
15	Singapore	77.7	53	Papau New Guinea	34.3	91	Malawi	15.6
16	Taiwan	77.6	54	Colombia	33.7	92	Congo	14.0
17	Spain	76.6	55	Venezuela	32.2	93	Honduras	13.8
18	Denmark	72.8	56	Kenya	31.6	94	Angola	13.5
19	Australia	69.8	57	Romania	31.5	95	Bolivia	13.2
20	South Korea	68.7	58	Uruguay	30.9	96	Peru	11.1
21	Ireland	67.7	59	Trinidad & Tobago	30.7	97	El Salvador	10.9
22	Hongkong	64.6	60	Pakistan	30.0	98	Tanzania	10.7
23	New Zealand	64.4	61	Zimbabwe	29.1	99	Cuba	10.5
24	Portugal	63.2	62	Morocco	28.8	100	Zaire	10.1
25	Thailand	62.3	63	Yugoslavia	28.1	101	Zambia	9.9
26	Kuwait	60.8	64	Gabon	27.7	102	Liberia	9.0
27	Malaysia	60.5	65[a]	Paraguay	27.0	103	Grenada	8.9
28	Saudi Arabia	59.8	66[a]	Cameroon	27.0	104	Haiti	8.2
29	United Arab Emirates	59.7	67	Jordan	26.6	105	Ethiopia	8.1
30	East Germany	59.6	68	Brazil	26.5	106	Lebanon	7.4
31	Qatar	55.5	69	Libya	26.3	107	Sierra Leone	7.2
32	Bahrain	55.0	70	Philippines	25.9	108	Mozambique	7.0
33	Iceland	54.8	71	Iran	24.1	109	Nicaragua	5.9
34	U.S.S.R.	52.5	72[a]	Sri Lanka	23.3	110	Uganda	5.8
35	Czechoslovakia	52.2	73[a]	Nepal	23.3	111	Sudan	5.6
36	Oman	52.1	74	Egypt	22.4	112	North Korea	4.3
37	China	51.2	75	Costa Rica	21.1			
38	Indonesia	48.0	76	Poland	20.2		Global average rating	39.0

[a]Order determined by actual results before rounding.

TABLE 13–12: 10-Year Changes in Country Credit Ratings (September 1979 to September 1989)

Who's up the most?		Who's down the most?	
Country	Change in Institutional Investor Credit Rating	Country	Change in Institutional Investor Credit Rating
Turkey	26.3	Iraq	−43.6
Taiwan	12.1	Argentina	−43.4
Portugal	9.3	Mexico	−41.5
Cyprus	6.9	Venezuela	−40.3
Spain	5.8	Brazil	−37.1
Italy	5.3	Libya	−36.6
Thailand	5.1	Nigeria	−36.3
Pakistan	4.8	Ecuador	−35.4
Finland	4.5	Yugoslavia	−31.7
Zimbabwe	4.3	Liberia	−31.6

SOURCE: *Institutional Investor*, "10th Anniversary Survey: Country Credit Ratings," (September 1989) 305. This copyrighted material is reprinted with permission from Institutional Investor, Inc.

MULTINATIONAL PHYSICAL SUPPLY

Vendor Relations

When arranging for the purchase and shipment of goods procured abroad, vendor relationships should be very carefully worked out and defined. Agreements must be clearly expressed, preferably in writing in both languages (if applicable) with both language versions being carefully checked for identical meaning by an experienced person fluent in business terminology in both languages. Even the best of intentions can founder on problems caused by miscommunication and resulting misunderstanding.

Host Country Policies

Nations strongly favor exports because exports earn foreign currency and help with the balance of trade. Generally, the only items limited or prohibited from export are such things as national art treasures, archaeologically significant items, or items deemed to affect matters of national security.

U.S. Government Policies

Import Constraints The U.S. Government limits or prohibits the importation of certain products, and as noted previously may prohibit imports entirely from certain countries. Prohibition is usually less of a problem for a logistics manager than the matter of import quotas because prohibition is absolute and requires no decisions. However, if one's firm imports goods or commodities that have import quotas, it is necessary to go through the procedures necessary for obtaining government approval (an import license) for such imports.

Tariff Considerations   Customs duties levied on most items imported into the United States are, by international standards, relatively low. However, it is critically important for logistics managers to insure that the *description* of the imported goods be accurate so as to incur no more than the proper customs duty. Lack of precision in describing goods can result in the imposition of much higher customs duties than would otherwise be the case.

When contemplating the importation of large dollar volumes of one or more items over a period of time, it is advisable either to consult a Customs Import Specialist or to obtain a binding ruling from U.S. Customs. Although the foreign consular invoice should be accurate in its description of the goods, a safer course of action is to consult a Customs Import Specialist (an employee of the U.S. Customs Service) if there is any doubt as to the classification of goods to be imported. The safest course of all is to take advantage of the Binding Ruling Program of the U.S. Customs Service. Under this Program one may request a District Director of Customs to issue in advance a binding ruling in writing that states the applicable customs duty on the goods to be imported. Such a written ruling will be issued within 30 days from the time it is requested and will be binding on all U.S. Customs officers at all U.S. ports of entry.

Import Documents

The most important import documents are:[13]

1. *Customs entries*   documents needed for goods entering the United States. There are four type of customs entries:

   Consumption entry   required for bringing goods into the United States. This document contains information about the origin of the cargo, a description of the merchandise, and the estimated duties applicable to the commodity imported; estimated duties are to be paid when the entry is filed.

   Immediate delivery entry   used to expedite the clearance of cargo. It allows 10 days for payment of estimated duty and for processing of the consumption entry. Furthermore, it allows delivery of the goods before payment of estimated duties and allows subsequent filing of the consumption entry and duty.

   Immediate transportation entry   allows cargo to be transferred from the pier to any point inland by a bonded carrier without payment of customs duties or finalization of the entry at the arrival port.

   Transportation and exportation entry   allows goods coming from or going to a third country to enter the United States for the purpose of transshipment.

2. *Carrier certificate and release order*   used to advise customs of the details of the shipment. Through this document, the carrier certifies that the company or individual named in the certificate is the owner or consignee of the cargo.

3. *Delivery order*   issued by the consignee or a customs broker to the ocean carrier, authorizing the release of the cargo to the inland carrier. It includes the necessary information for the pier delivery clerk to determine whether the cargo can be transferred to the inland carrier.

4. *Arrival notice*   sent by the carrier to inform the "notify" party of the estimated arrival date of the vessel; it identifies shipment details, and shows expiration date of free time.

5. *Freight release or freight bill receipt*   provides evidence that freight charges for the cargo have been paid. It can be used at the pier to obtain release of cargo.

6. *Special customs invoice*   required by United States Customs when the value of the cargo exceeds $500. Normally prepared by the foreign exporter, it is used by customs to determine the value of the shipment.

In the same manner that U.S. exporters may have concern for collection of monies owed for merchandise shipped abroad and use letters of credit as discussed earlier in the chapter, foreign exporters to the United States may have similar concerns. Accordingly, they, too, may arrange for a letter of credit to be established in their favor to guarantee payment to them by the U.S. importer. A sample "telex-originated" irrevocable letter of credit is shown in Figure 13–5.

Since the end of World War II there has been a substantial improvement in many countries with respect to easing the documentation and processing of shipments of imported goods. This has happened primarily as result of pressure on governments from exporters and importers to simplify, or at least make more efficient, the procedures involved. For example, through the use of electronic data interchange (EDI), shipments of many types of products being imported into the United States can be essentially "precleared" by U.S. Customs prior to their arrival from abroad by use of the Automated Manifest System (AMS) now in use by American customhouse brokers. The AMS provides for electronic transmission of customs information at the time the goods are shipped from overseas to a U.S. port of entry, and thus greatly reduces the time required for customs clearance on arrival, an advantage to all concerned. However, despite such improvements, documentation and processing of international shipments across customs borders will always involve more complex procedures than domestic shipments.

Operational Considerations

Imported Item Availability After inspecting several satisfactory samples of an item, more than one company has been unpleasantly surprised to find that its decision to purchase 10,000 "whatzits" from a foreign vendor (particularly one in an underdeveloped country) is met with a helpless response, such as, "These are handmade and the village can only turn out about two hundred a month. We never realized you would want so many." Logistics and purchasing managers should proceed with caution rather than simply assuming availability of large quantities of "unusual" items or materials.

Transportation and Delivery Times As is typical in other aspects of international activities, the management of vendor relations involving arrangements for and tracking of inbound shipments from foreign origins is often considerably more difficult and complex than is the case with typical domestic operations. Intermodal and documentary problems coupled with the irregularity of transportation schedules in many parts of the world make it difficult to predict and plan on the arrival times of inbound international shipments. In only a few cases

FIGURE 13–5: Sample telex-originated letter of credit

```
Msg : @21M / JT234     Line :   4   Hdr :   1
   153212    UNITY BANK
TRT         3911122
13478525367   03/02  GA
1122131ITWUA BR
4617812                   UNITY BANK MSG JT234
TO:         BANCO PARISO S.A., 01013 SAO PAULO, BRAZIL
FROM:       UNITY Bank of South Florida, N.A.
MIAMI, FL 33101 U.S.A.
DATE:       MARCH 2, 1988
TEST:       11 FOR USD80,202.00 DD 880302
PLEASE ADVISE:  BANCO DO BRASIL S.A.
SAO PAULO S.P. BRAZIL
WE ISSUE OUR IRREVOCABLE LETTER OF CREDIT 37001
IN THEIR FAVOR FOR ACCOUNT OF:
MOTOR SPECIALTY EQUIPMENT CO.
1234 S. FEDERAL HIGHWAY
HOMESTEAD, FL. 33030
FOR UP TO AN AGGREGATE OF USD80,202.00
AVAILABLE WITH:  UNITY BANK OF SOUTH FLORIDA, N.A.
123 N.W. 175TH STREET
MIAMI, FLORIDA 33010 UNITED STATES
BY PAYMENT AGAINST DRAFTS AT SIGHT-SEE ADDL CONDITIONS
DRAWN ON Unity Bank of South Florida, N.A.
FOR 15.0 PERCENT OF INVOICE VALUE.
PARTIAL SHIPMENT PERMITTED
TRANSSHIPMENT PERMITTED
SHIPMENT FROM SANTOS, BRAZIL
SHIPMENT TO CIF JACKSONVILLE, FLORIDA
COVERING SHIPMENT OF:
AS PER PROFORMA INVOICE NUMBER 231/88
DOCUMENTS REQUIRED:
– COMMERCIAL INVOICE ORIGINAL AND 3 COPIES
– INSURANCE POLICY OR CERTIFICATE IN DUPLICATE FOR 110 PERCENT OF INVOICE VALUE
– FULL SET CLEAN ON BOARD OCEAN BILL OF LADING ISSUED TO ORDER OF BANCO DO BRASIL S.A., BLANK ENDORSED MARKED NOTIFY MOTOR
SPECIALTY EQUIPMENT CO. 1234 S. FEDERAL HIGHWAY, HOMESTEAD, FL. 33030 AND MARKED FREIGHT PAID.
– BILL OF LADING MUST BE DATED NOT LATER THAN MARCH 31, 1988
– PACKING LIST IN DUPLICATE
– SHIPPERS SIGNED COPY OF LETTER TO APPLICANT STATING ONE SET OF NON-NEGOTIABLE SHIPPING DOCUMENTS WERE AIRMAILED TO
APPLICANT
– THIS LETTER OF CREDIT TO FACILITATE MOTOR SPECIALTY EQUIPMENT CO.'S UTILIZATION UNDER THE FINEX PROGRAM.
ADDITIONAL CONDITIONS:
– 15 PERCENT OF AMOUNT AT SIGHT AND 85 PERCENT BALANCE OF INVOICE VALUE IN SIX EQUAL DRAFTS OF $11,361.95 PRINCIPAL PLUS INTEREST
AT 6.5 PERCENT PER ANNUM ON THE DECLINING PRINCIPAL BALANCE.
– DRAFTS TO BE PRESENTED SUCCESSIVELY COMMENCING 180 DAYS AFTER BILL OF LADING DATE.
ALL BANKING CHARGES EXCEPT THOSE OF ISSUING BANK ARE FOR THE ACCOUNT OF THE BENEFICIARY
SHIPPING DOCUMENTS TO BE PRESENTED WITHIN 21 DAYS AFTER DATE OF ISSUANCE OF BILL OF LADING BUT WITHIN THE VALIDITY OF THIS
CREDIT
ALL DOCUMENTS MUST BE FORWARDED TO US IN ONE SINGLE AIR MAIL.
EXPIRATION DATE  April 15, 1991 AT THE COUNTERS OF THE ISSUING BANK.
INSTRUCTIONS TO BANK(S)
REIMBURSEMENT INSTRUCTIONS:  PAYMENT WILL BE EFFECTED UPON RECEIPT OF DOCUMENTS IN COMPLIANCE WITH THE TERMS OF THIS CREDIT
AT OUR COUNTERS IN ACCORDANCE WITH YOUR PAYMENT INSTRUCTIONS.
SUBJECT TO ICC PUBLICATION 400.
WE HEREBY AGREE WITH THE DRAWERS, ENDORSERS AND BONA FIDE HOLDERS OF DRAFTS DRAWN UNDER AND IN COMPLIANCE WITH THE
TERMS OF THIS CREDIT THAT SUCH DRAFTS WILL BE DULY HONORED ON PRESENTATION TO THE DRAWEES.  CONSIDER THIS YOUR OPERATIVE
INSTRUMENT
NNNN
   15   12     UNITY BANK
112  31PTAUA  BR . . . . .
007.9 MINS
Time: 15:40  03/01/88  EDT
Connect Time:  547 seconds
```

are services so routinely dependable that shipment arrival times may be counted upon. An example of dependable ocean transportation service is the excellent scheduled containership service between Rotterdam and New York.

SUMMARY

Multinational logistics operations are considerably more complex than domestic logistics operations, and therefore require greater knowledge and expertise in their management. The extent of U.S. import and export trade is steadily increasing, and many logistics managers are becoming increasingly involved in multinational operations.

Multinational logistics operations require dealing with different business cultures, currencies, languages, and legal systems. A logistics manager inexperienced in dealing with multinational operations is well advised to seek information and advice from knowledgeable individuals rather than making what may turn out to be very damaging and costly erroneous assumptions.

The culture of a country permeates the conduct of business with respect to business negotiations, the sense of time (urgency), and the manner in which government laws, regulations, and policies are enforced. Logistics managers should make every effort to understand the culture — particularly the business culture — of countries with whose officials or business executives they are negotiating or dealing. And, government instability in some countries may pose problems and require decisions with respect to placement of inventories, granting of credit, and so on.

Differing legal systems suggest the need for assistance of expert legal counsel when contracts are being drafted. And, although arbitration clauses in commercial contracts are generally desirable, this may not be the case if the dispute concerns a matter of law rather than, for example, the quality of the goods or whether the goods conform to samples that were agreed upon.

The logistics infrastructure in a foreign country (transportation, warehousing, communications, and such) may be *much* worse than, worse than, about the same, or even better than that of the United States, depending on the country concerned. Operational problems encountered when exporting from or importing to the United States will likely be greater in the case of underdeveloped or developing countries that have been unable to build up their logistics infrastructures.

Problems of inflation and nonconvertible foreign currencies are primarily those of a firm's financial managers; but they may affect logistics managers, particularly if inflation affects planned logistics budgets, or when nonconvertible currency results in problems of payment for goods in U.S. dollars.

Of the several types of regional economic alliances, the most important is the European Economic Community (EEC). The EEC will be a single market of 335,000,000 people when it is fully unified on December 31, 1992. For firms exporting to Europe, the greatest significance of this will be that inventories can be located anywhere in the EEC without regard to tariff barriers.

The choice of channel strategy — direct sales, distributors, or foreign direct investment — is a top management decision, but one that will affect logistics operations. The principal logistics consideration in the case of direct sales versus distributorships is that the latter will likely involve on-site inventories of finished goods and repair parts. Foreign direct investment primarily involves arrangements for shipments of materials, parts, and finished goods in one or both directions between the foreign and domestic locations of the corporation.

When responsible for exporting goods, a logistics manager must be aware of the host country's policies with respect to import constraints and customs duties. He or she must also be aware of any U.S. government limitations on exports.

Multinational physical distribution operations are far more complex than domestic operations and normally require the expertise and assistance of international freight forwarders for exports. The same is true of the need for the expertise and assistance of customhouse brokers with respect to imports.

Terms of sale for exports involve many more alternatives than is the case with domestic terms of sale. For ocean transportation they are, in sequence: (1) point of origin, (2) F.O.B. first transport vehicle, (3) F.A.S. vessel, (4) F.O.B. vessel, (5) C. & F., (6) C.I.F., and (7) at foreign destination dock. Terms of sale for airfreight movements are simpler, generally involving only considerations of local cartage to an airport followed by air movement to the foreign airport freight dock.

Customer service with respect to quick delivery, replacement of defective goods, and so on, is easier when inventory-carrying distributors are used than when direct export sales by company salespersons or sales agents who have no inventory backup are used.

The use of bonded warehouses and free trade zones enables a firm to avoid payment of customs duties on goods in transit and also on goods destined for the market in that country until those goods leave the bonded warehouse or free trade zone. Another advantage is the opportunity to inspect goods prior to having paid duty on them.

In nearly every respect, arrangements for international transportation of goods are more complex than is the case with domestic shipments. Distances are greater, transportation charges are higher, extensive documentation is required, special insurance is needed, and there are usually special requirements for labeling, marking, packaging, and packing of shipments.

Requirements for export documentation are extensive. Great care must be taken to insure that documentation is both accurate and complete, or delays will be encountered. Arrangements for payment must be set up in advance either through the granting of credit to creditworthy customers who can pay in hard currency, or by the use of letters of credit when it is believed there may be some financial risk to the transaction.

Multinational physical supply (importing goods) requires careful attention to vendor relations, host country export laws, regulations and policies, and U.S. government import constraints and tariff regulations. Import documentation requirements are just as complicated as export documentation. As mentioned above, the assistance of customhouse brokers to handle much of the administrative work in connection with processing import shipments is a virtual necessity for most firms.

Logistics managers should also be aware that supplies of foreign materials or finished goods may be limited and should not assume the availability of large quantities of such materials or finished goods. Finally, international transportation movements are subject to more delays (for example, export clearance by customs, intermodal transfers, import customs clearance) than are domestic movements, and thus delivery times will tend to vary much more than is the case with domestic shipments.

As noted at the beginning of the chapter, the globalization of business is steadily increasing. Many more firms are engaging in multinational business, and more and more logistics managers are finding themselves handling multinational transactions that require far more knowledge, skill and understanding than is the case with domestic logistics management.

DISCUSSION QUESTIONS

1. In what respects are multinational logistics operations more complex than domestic logistics operations?

2. Are U.S. imports and exports increasing or decreasing? What are the reasons for this? Table 13–5 shows the expectations for food and chemical imports to show almost no increase; why is this the case?

3. Figure 13–3 notes that Switzerland has four official languages, yet Switzerland is a very small country. Why would a very small (compared with the United States) country have four official languages?

4. What are the two principal tasks of a logistics manager if his or her firm plans to, or does, engage in multinational business?

5. What is meant by the statement, ''Culture permeates the conduct of business''? Explain.

6. Does the Foreign Corrupt Practices Act (FCPA) permit the use of bribes to officials in foreign countries? Explain.

7. What are the two basic types of legal systems found in many countries?

8. Despite the many advantages of arbitrations, are there circumstances when it might be wiser for the disputants to go to court, rather than to arbitration, to resolve a business dispute?

9. Why is a decision to export goods a top management decision?

10. What is the logistics significance of the fact that the European Common Market will have no internal trade barriers?

11. Why might a company salesperson or sales agent in a foreign country have to have more on-the-spot authority in dealing with customers than a domestic salesperson or sales agent? Explain.

12. For what reason(s) do countries have import constraints? What significance does this have for logistics managers?

13. What is a prohibitive tariff? Explain.

14. Does the United States prohibit or limit the export of any types of goods?

15. Explain the roles of foreign freight forwarders and customhouse brokers.

16. Why are the specific terms of sale so important in regard to international export shipments?

17. What roles are played by bonded warehouses and free trade zones in international trade?

18. In what respects are international transportation movements different or more complex than domestic movements?

19. From what source (document) does the United States government obtain export statistics?

20. Why do banks require absolute compliance with the provisions and conditions of a letter of credit before they will make payment?

21. Why is insurance necessary for international air and ocean shipments?

22. What is meant by the term "country risk"? Explain.

23. Why is it important to have an accurate description of goods to be imported into the United States?

24. What is the purpose of the Binding Ruling Program of the U.S. Department of Customs? When might it be advisable for a logistics manager to seek such a ruling?

25. Why might a foreign exporter require a U.S. importer to furnish a confirmed irrevocable letter of credit before shipping goods?

26. Why should a logistics manager be cautious when considering importation of large quantities of unusual items or materials? Explain.

CASE: Appointment of a Logistics Manager for a European Subsidiary

The vice president of logistics support services and the vice president of human resource services of the Mitchell Aircraft Corporation were considering two candidates for the position of logistics manager for the company's soon-to-be-established European parts distribution subsidiary.

Headquartered in Los Angeles, Mitchell Aircraft Corporation was a major producer of several widely used models of commercial jet aircraft, as well as aircraft replacement parts.* In addition to distribution of its own replacement parts in the United States and Europe, Mitchell also handled the distribution of replacement parts for several U.S. machinery manufacturers in Europe.

The reason for Mitchell's establishment of a distribution subsidiary in Europe was the unified European Economic Community (EEC) market scheduled to come into being in 1992. Mitchell's management had decided to consolidate its nine European parts inventories at a single location, probably close to a major airport on the continent. These inventories were presently managed by a designated Mitchell "tech rep"** at each location. This arrangement was not wholly satisfactory, but had been deemed necessary due to delays, difficulties, and "red tape" that would have been encountered in moving parts through customs to many countries from a single inventory location, although customer needs currently made some intercountry shipments of parts necessary. An EEC market without internal customs boundaries would eliminate customs problems within the entire EEC area.

The vice president of logistics support services and the vice president of human resource services had narrowed their search for a suitable candidate for the position of manager of the European logistics subsidiary to two persons: Patricia Robinson and Henry Warner. The vice president of human resource services had assembled a summary of the qualifications of each candidate.

---

*Replacement parts did not include engine parts. Those were the responsibility of the manufacturers of the jet engines, such as Pratt & Whitney, General Electric, and Rolls Royce.

**"Tech rep" is industry slang for the job title "technical representative." These were Mitchell employees (aeronautical engineers, or individuals with similar training and experience) stationed at airline maintenance bases to advise, consult, and assist with matters of maintenance of Mitchell aircraft.

Patricia Allen Robinson:

- Raised in Europe (father in U.S. Foreign Service).
- Languages: English, French, German (latter two rusty, but would regain fluency in a month or so).
- B.A. degree in political science (Tufts University).
- M.B.A. (Boston University).
- Tour guide for U.S. travel firm for one year in Europe between undergraduate and graduate work.
- Employment history at Mitchell: department head of inventory parts control in Mitchell Export Division in Los Angeles past three years; prior four years experience in Mitchell parts inventory warehouse in Los Angeles, rising to position of assistant warehouse manager. Excellent job performance ratings.

Henry Albert Warner:

- Four years military service in U.S. Army, including 22 months' service in Germany, following graduation from college.
- Languages: English, no fluency in German.
- B.S. degree in Business Logistics (Pennsylvania State University).
- Employment history at Mitchell: four years in Mitchell's purchased-materials warehouse in Los Angeles, rising to position of assistant warehouse manager, followed by four years as a member of Mitchell's domestic aircraft sales team. Excellent job performance ratings.

The vice president of logistics support services (VPLSS) and the vice president of human resource services (VPHRS) met to discuss which of the two candidates to choose.

VPLSS: "Well, we have to decide between Robinson and Warner. All the other candidates we considered have been eliminated, and clearly they always were the best possibilities we had for the position. What are your thoughts?"

VPHRS: "Both of them have the technical qualifications for the job. Maybe she has the edge of inventory knowledge, but he has the edge on being out in the field. Both know warehousing."

VPLSS: "I see a problem in her being a woman dealing with European managers and executives."

VPHRS: "Wish you hadn't brought that up, but I know we are going to have to consider it. Women just aren't viewed as executives in Europe. It's bias and prejudice and wrong, but it's real."

VPLSS: "Lots of people here in the States don't view women as executives either."

VPHRS: "Yes, but that's changed a lot and it's continuing to change. Appointing a woman manager or executive is getting to be pretty common in lots of firms, including ours. Two of my five department heads are women, and one of them has a real shot at my job when I retire three years from now."

VPLSS: "Let's get back to qualifications. I think Robinson's languages definitely give her an edge over Warner. With French and German, plus English, she'll be home free in dealing with most of the people she'll be in contact with in Europe. And, she knows our parts inventories."

VPHRS: "Well, Warner's also well qualified. He may not have the languages, but a lot of European managers and executives speak English; it's really becoming the international business language. Warner has warehouse supervision experience and he has been very effective in dealing with our domestic airline customers in sales. And, then there's that "woman executive in Europe" aspect of the matter. Warner wouldn't have that to worry about, and neither would we."

VPLSS: "Well, which one should it be?"

VPHRS: "I'll go with either one. Since the position will report to you, you make the decision and I'll endorse it."

ONE WEEK LATER THE TWO EXECUTIVES MET AGAIN

VPLSS: "Well, I've made up my mind."

VPHRS: "About time you did. Which one?"

VPLSS: "I've decided it will be . . . . ."

CASE QUESTION

1. Which person should be appointed to the new position? Explain and justify your answer.

SUGGESTED READINGS

LODGE, GEORGE CABOT, *Comparative Business Government Relations*, Englewood Cliffs, New Jersey: Prentice-Hall, Inc., 1990. Chapter 2, "Government Targeting and the U.S. Response," examines industrial policies in Europe, Japan and Brazil. Chapter 3, "Managing the Government Affairs Function," discusses the design, organization, and management of the government affairs function in multinational corporations, as well as the role of industry associations.

ROBESON, JAMES F., and ROBERT G. HOUSE, eds. *The Distribution Handbook*, New York: The Free Press, 1985. Section 12 by Paul S. Bender, "International Distribution," treats the international dimension of physical distribution management.

STEVENS, CHRIS, ed. *Logistics: International Issues*, Cleveland, Ohio: Leaseway Transportation, 1985. This book is the published proceedings of the 1985 Logistics Research Forum sponsored by Leaseway Transportation Corp. It contains 19 articles that focus on international logistics issues and problems.

The following texts offer a treatment of international air and ocean transportation:

BRANCH, ALAN E., *Elements of Shipping*, 5th ed., London: Chapman and Hall, 1981. This British text has been sold in over 150 countries and is regarded by many as a standard work on the subject of ocean transportation.

BUGLASS, LESLIE J., *Marine Insurance and General Average in the United States*, 2d ed., Centreville, Maryland: Cornell Maritime Press, 1981. This book offers a thorough treatment of this very complex subject.

COYLE, JOHN J., EDWARD J. BARDI, and JOSEPH L. CAVINATO, *Transportation*, 3d ed., St. Paul, Minnesota: West Publishing Company, 1990. Chapter 12 treats international air and ocean transportation.

KENDALL, LANE C., *The Business of Shipping*, 5th ed., Centreville, Maryland: Cornell Maritime Press, 1986. More oriented toward U.S. ocean shipping operations than the Branch book cited above.

MURR, ALFRED, *Export/Import Traffic Management and Forwarding*, 6th ed., Centreville, Maryland: Cornell Maritime Press, 1979. A comprehensive treatment of export/import operations with emphasis on the role of the foreign freight forwarder and customhouse broker.

STEPHENSON, FREDERICK J., JR., *Transportation USA*, Reading, Mass.: Addison-Wesley Publishing Company, 1987. Chapter 9 treats ocean transportation and Chapter 16 treats international air transportation and the U.S. air-cargo industry.

WELLS, ALEXANDER T., *Air Transportation*, 2d ed., Belmont, California: Wadsworth Publishing Company, 1989. Part Four, "The International Scene," offers a full treatment of international aviation law and international conventions.

WOOD, DONALD F., and JAMES C. JOHNSON, *Contemporary Transportation*, 3d ed., New York: Macmillan Publishing Company, 1989. Chapter 18 treats international transportation, both air and ocean.

The following general business logistics texts contain treatments of international aspects of logistics operations:

BOWERSOX, DONALD J., DAVID J. CLOSS, and OMAR K. HELFERICH, *Logistical Management*, 3d ed., New York: Macmillan Publishing Company, 1986. Chapter 15, "Dimensions of Change," contains a brief section on multinational logistics and highlights various prerequisites for global success.

COYLE, JOHN J., and EDWARD J. BARDI, *The Management of Business Logistics*, 3d ed., St. Paul, Minnesota: West Publishing Company, 1984. Chapter 11, "Traffic Management," contains a brief section on international logistics operations.

JOHNSON, JAMES C., and DONALD F. WOOD, *Contemporary Logistics*, 4th ed., New York: Macmillan Publishing Company, 1990. Chapter 11, "International Logistics," provides a comprehensive discussion of the complexities and problems inherent in international logistics management.

LAMBERT, DOUGLAS M., and JAMES R. STOCK, *Strategic Physical Distribution Management*, Homewood, Illinois: Richard D. Irwin, Inc., 1982. Chapter 13, "International Physical Distribution," discusses the key similarities and differences in the management of physical distribution in domestic and foreign environments, how to assess the physical distribution environment in international markets, and how to develop an effective international physical distribution strategy.

TYWORTH, JOHN E., JOSEPH L. CAVINATO, and C. JOHN LANGLEY, Jr., *Traffic Management*, Reading, Mass.: Addison-Wesley Publishing Company, 1987. Chapter 15, "International Traffic Management," examines export/import transportation services and facilitators, as well as treatment of pricing and cost factors, methods of payment, documentation, and marine insurance issues.

The reader interested in a broad overview treatment of international business is referred to any of the following texts:

ASHEGHIAN, PARVIZ, and BAHMAN EBRAHIMI, *International Business*, New York: Harper & Row, 1990.

CZINKOTA, MICHAEL R., PIETRA RIVOLI, and ILKKA A. RONKAINEN, *International Business*, New York: The Dryden Press, 1989.

DANIELS, JOHN D., and LEE H. RADEBAUGH, *International Business*, 5th ed., Reading, Mass.: Addison-Wesley Publishing Company, 1989.

GROSSE, ROBERT, and DUANE KUJAWA, *International Business*, Homewood, Illinois: Richard D. Irwin, 1988.

MORAN, ROBERT T., and PHILIP R. HARRIS, *Managing Cultural Differences*, 3d ed., Houston: Gulf Publishing Company, 1991. This excellent 640-page book treats cultural impacts on global management, cultural impacts on international business, cultural specifics and business service abroad, and management resources for global professionals. It is highly recommended.

ENDNOTES

1. On March 30, 1990, the U.S. government published a list of 35 countries and two blocs (the European Economic Community and the communist bloc countries) alleged to be guilty of trade discrimination against U.S. exports and announced plans to consider retaliatory actions.

2. The reader will note that, with respect to the United States, Spanish is listed as a second language. This reflects the fact that about 25,000,000 Americans are of Hispanic origin, *and* that a very large volume of business is done by sunbelt businesses with Latin American firms and much of this is conducted in Spanish.

3. The 1977 Foreign Corrupt Practices Act (FCPA) is an amendment to Section 13(b) of the 1934 Securities Exchange Act. The FCPA prohibits every domestic business concern (and foreign firms having a place of business in the United States) from making payments to a foreign official, political party, or candidate for political office for the purpose of influencing such to obtain or retain business for the company or to influence foreign government legislation or regulations. The term ''foreign official'' does not include a foreign government employee whose duties are ''essentially ministerial or clerical.'' The FCPA thus does not prohibit so-called grease payments to foreign officials if such payments are not for the purpose of influencing the actions the act prohibits. If payments are made for the purpose of speeding up paperwork administrative matters, such as customs clearance or processing of work permits, to which the business concern is legally entitled in the first place, they are not illegal. However, firms subject to Securities Exchange Commission regulation must still record such payments accurately in their books.

4. In many cultures, particularly the Middle East and Far East, it is fruitless for a woman to attempt to conduct higher-level business dealings. The culture simply will not permit it. This is less true of Europe, but even there women are still not regarded as the equal of men in the arena of business. A ''good'' example of this is Switzerland.

5. Prior to its acquisition by the United States as part of the Louisiana Purchase in 1815, Louisiana was a French colony and it has retained a legal system based on Civil Law rather than Common Law.

6. Clive Schmitthoff, *Schmitthoff's Export Trade: The Law and Practice of International Trade*, 7th ed. (London: Stevens & Sons, 1980): 411–412. Chapter 26 of this book contains an excellent treatment of commercial arbitration.

7. Some of the material in this section has been adapted from Robert Grosse and Duane Kujawa, *International Business* (Homewood, Ill.: Irwin, 1988): 255.

8. The terms defined in this section are adapted from Paul S. Bender, ''The International Distribution of Physical Distribution Management,'' *The Distribution Handbook*, James F. Robeson and Robert G. House, eds. (New York: The Free Press, 1985): 786–787.

9. Operators utilizing free trade zones are able to minimize paperwork associated with payment and subsequent ''drawback'' of customs duties paid on entry and re-export of goods.

10. Though there are over 100 free trade zones that have been authorized by the government, only about half have actually been developed and are open for business. This relatively slow but steady growth reflects the realities of economic risk associated with any development requiring substantial investment in land and buildings in the face of uncertainties of volume of business likely to be realized at any given trade zone location.

11. Bender, ''International Distribution,'' 805–806.

12. The practice of ocean carriers not being insurers of the goods they carry (contrasted with domestic common carriers, for example) derives from the fact that historically in most cases the ship carrying the goods was the only asset of any value the company possessed. If the ship went down there would be nothing left to pay the shippers the value of their cargo, hence the need for cargo insurance. This practice has carried over into modern times.

13. Bender, ''International Distribution,'' 806–807.

APPENDIX

LETTER OF CREDIT INSTRUCTIONS

Date:

TO

F R O M

NAME		
COMPANY		
ADDRESS		
CITY	STATE	ZIP CODE
TELEPHONE	TELEX	

GENTLEMEN:

Following are the particular details we wish to have included in your documentary Letter of Credit, issued in reply to our Pro Forma invoice number _____ dated _____.

Please instruct your bank to open and issue this credit, by telecommunication or by mail, in accordance with the following terms and subject to the Uniform Customs and Practices for Documentary Credits, International Chamber of Commerce Publication 400 (revision currently in force).

We have made every effort in these instructions to provide you with terms which can be easily accommodated. If you or your bank are unable to comply with these terms and conditions, please consult with our offices prior to the issuance of the credit to avoid delay or non-shipment. Thank you for your cooperation. _____

1. The Letter of Credit shall be irrevocable.

2. The credit shall be ☐ advised by _____
   ☐ confirmed by _____

3. The credit shall be payable at the counters of _____
   _____
   _____

4. The credit shall show as the beneficiary _____
   _____
   _____

5. The credit shall be payable in _____, in the amount ☐ not to exceed _____.
   (currency)   ☐ exactly _____.
   ☐ about _____.

6. The credit shall be payable ☐ at sight
   ☐ _____ days sight   upon presentation at the counters of the bank stated in item #3 above.
   ☐ _____ days from _____ Date

7. The Letter of Credit ☐ shall
   ☐ shall not   be transferrable.

8. The credit shall show that all banking charges incurred ☐ inside the beneficiary's country are for the account of the applicant.
   ☐ outside

9. The credit shall show that all charges for amendments to the credit, including related communications expenses, are for the account of ☐ applicant.
   ☐ beneficiary.

10. Partial shipments ☐ shall be allowed.
    ☐ shall not be allowed.

11. Transshipments ☐ shall be allowed.
    ☐ shall not be allowed.

12. The credit shall allow for required transport documents dated
    ☐ No later than _____.
    ☐ No later than _____ days from the advising bank's issuance of written notice to the beneficiary.

13. The credit shall allow for a minimum of _____ days after the required transport document date for presentation of documents at the counters of the bank stated in item #3.

14. The required documents should include:
    ☐ Commercial Invoice Totaled ☐ F.O.B. ☐ C. & F. _____.
    ☐ F.A.S. ☐ C.I.F.   (named point)
    ☐ Commercial invoice shall cover ☐ Pro Forma invoice # _____ or
    ☐ the following:

☐ Packing list for above
☐ Insurance certificate showing insurance/policy provided by seller in the amount of _____.
☐ Ocean Bill of Lading

☐ The credit ☐ shall / ☐ shall not allow for NVOCC bills of lading.
☐ The Bill of Lading shall be consigned ☐ to _____.
☐ to the order of _____.

☐ The Bill of Lading ☐ shall / ☐ need not be marked on board.
☐ Air Waybill consigned to _____.

_____.

☐ The credit ☐ shall / ☐ shall not allow for air consolidators Airway Bills.

☐ The transport document shall be marked freight ☐ prepaid / ☐ collect
☐ Inland straight bill of lading consigned to _____.
☐ Any shipping documents required shall show as the origin _____ and as the destination _____
☐ Other required documents: _____
_____

15. If designated, the forwarder shall be shown as _____.
16. If designated, the carrier shall be shown as _____.
17. Special instructions:

Form 18-409 Printed and Sold by *UNZCO* 190 Baldwin Ave., Jersey City, NJ 07306 • (800) 631-3098 • (201) 795-5400

UNITRAK®

LETTER OF CREDIT WORKSHEET UNITRAK™

ADVISING BANK

BENEFICIARY

FOR ACCOUNT OF NOTIFY PARTY

CONTACT NAME:

TELEPHONE NO.:

☐ CONFIRMED, IRREVOCABLE COMMERCIAL

☐ OTHER (describe) _____

AMENDMENTS ALLOWED? YES ☐ NO ☐

AMOUNT _____ CURRENCY _____

EXPIRATION DATE _____ LATEST SHIP DATE _____

PARTIAL SHIPMENTS ALLOWED? YES ☐ NO ☐

PARTIAL DRAWS ALLOWED? YES ☐ NO ☐

REQUIRED STATEMENT FROM BENEFICIARY STATING THAT A FULL SET OF ALL ORIGINAL DOCUMENTS HAS BEEN SENT DIRECTLY TO:

☐ BROKER (name) _____

(addr) _____

_____

☐ IMPORTER

☐ NOTIFY PARTY

EVIDENCING SHIPMENT OF: _____

_____

DRAFT TO BE ACCOMPANIED BY:

SIGNED COMMERCIAL INVOICE _____ COPIES _____

SPECIAL CUSTOMS INVOICE _____ COPIES _____

PACKING LIST _____ COPIES _____

INSPECTION CERTIFICATE _____ COPIES _____

OCEAN BILL OF LADING _____ COPIES _____

AIR WAY BILL OF LADING _____ COPIES ORIGINAL SENT WITH FREIGHT? YES ☐ NO ☐

_____ _____ COPIES _____

_____ _____ COPIES _____

_____ _____ COPIES _____

SPECIAL INSTRUCTIONS

SHIP DATES _____ TO _____

CARGO RECEIPT IS ACCEPTABLE IN PLACE OF OCEAN B/L? YES ☐ NO ☐

3rd PARTY SHIPPER IS ACCEPTABLE? YES ☐ NO ☐

ALL CHARGES OUTSIDE THE U.S. ARE FOR THE ACCOUNT OF:

☐ BENEFICIARY/SHIPPER

☐ IMPORTER

☐ 3rd PARTY (name) _____

(addr) _____

(addr) _____

Form 18-200 Printed and Sold by *UNACO* 190 Baldwin Ave., Jersey City, NJ 07306 • (800) 631-3098 • (201) 795-5400

DOCUMENTATION CHECKLIST
FOR LETTER OF CREDIT (L/C) SHIPMENTS

On any L/C transaction, the commercial and shipping documents must meet the conditions of the L/C exactly. In order to help you avoid costly discrepancy charges by banks, we are pleased to provide you with this checklist for use in preparing and reviewing your documents prior to shipment.

Do your documents show:

- Correct name and address of exporter?

- Correct name and address of buyer?

- Third parties or "notify" information (banks, etc.)?

- Description of goods identical to L/C?

- Unit prices and extensions identical to L/C?

- Number of packages, and consistent weight and measurements?

- Marks and numbers as stipulated in the L/C?

- Terms of Sale (FOB, C&F, etc.) as stipulated in the L/C?

- Any Import License number or other statements required by the L/C?

- Ports of loading or discharge, or ultimate destination, where required?

- "Freight Prepaid [Collect]", where required by the L/C?

- The L/C number and date of issue, or other statements as required?

- An original signature or endorsement?

Finally, have you prepared the correct number of copies, as stipulated by the L/C?

Copyright © 1988 UNZ & CO.

UNIDEK™

UNZ & CO.
U.S./GENERAL UNIFORM EXPORT DECLARATION

EXPORTER (Name and address including ZIP code)		COMMERCIAL INVOICE NO.		DATE
	ZIP CODE	DATE OF EXPORTATION	BILL OF LADING AIR WAYBILL NO.	
EXPORTER EIN (IRS) NO.	PARTIES TO TRANSACTION ☐ Related ☐ Non-related	CUSTOMER ORDER NO.		
ULTIMATE CONSIGNEE		DELIVERY TERMS, CONDITIONS OF SALE		
INTERMEDIATE CONSIGNEE				
FORWARDING AGENT		COUNTRY OF ORIGIN		
		POINT (STATE) OF ORIGIN OR FTZ NO	COUNTRY OF ULTIMATE DESTINATION	
LOADING PIER (Vessel only)	MODE OF TRANSPORT (Specify)	DOMESTIC ROUTING EXPORT INSTRUCTIONS		
EXPORTING CARRIER	PORT OF EXPORT			
PORT OF UNLOADING (Vessel and air only)	CONTAINERIZED (Vessel only) ☐ Yes ☐ No			

Record New Harmonized Schedule B Commodity Number In Gray Blocks

SCHEDULE B DESCRIPTION OF COMMODITIES MARKS, NOS., AND KIND OF PKGS.				SHIPPING WEIGHT (Kilos)		UNIT SELLING PRICE	VALUE (U.S. dollars) omit cents
D F	U.S. SCHEDULE B NUMBER 6 DIGIT H.S. NO. —4 DIGIT STAT NO	CHECK DIGIT	QUANTITY SCHEDULE B UNIT(S)	GROSS	NET		(Selling price or cost if not sold)
	—						
DESCRIPTION							
	—						
DESCRIPTION							
	—						
DESCRIPTION							
	—						
DESCRIPTION							
	—						
DESCRIPTION							

VALIDATED LICENSE NO. GENERAL LICENSE SYMBOL	ECCN (When required)	
Duly authorized officer or employee	The exporter authorizes the forwarder named above to act as forwarding agent for export control and customs purposes.	NET INVOICE VALUE

CERTIFICATIONS

Required Signatures: Be sure to sign in pen and ink the first Export Declarations and the original Commercial Invoice.

Form 10-260H Printed and Sold by *UNZCO* 190 Baldwin Ave., Jersey City, NJ 07306 • (800) 631-3098 • (201) 795-5400

EXPORT QUOTATION WORKSHEET   **UNITRAK**™

DATE _____   REF/PRO FORMA INVOICE NO. _____
COMMODITY _____   EXPECTED SHIP DATE _____
CUSTOMER _____   PACKED DIMENSIONS _____
COUNTRY _____   PACKED WEIGHT _____
PAYMENT TERMS _____   PACKED CUBE _____

PRODUCTS TO BE SHIPPED FROM _____
                                          TO _____

SELLING PRICE OF GOODS: $ _____

SPECIAL EXPORT PACKING:
    $ _____ quoted by _____
    $ _____ quoted by _____
    $ _____ quoted by _____ $ _____

INLAND FREIGHT:
    $ _____ quoted by _____
    $ _____ quoted by _____
    $ _____ quoted by _____ $ _____
Inland freight includes the following charges:
☐ unloading   ☐ pier delivery   ☐ terminal   ☐ _____

OCEAN FREIGHT			AIR FREIGHT		
quoted by	tariff item		quoted by	spec code	
$ _____	_____	# _____	$ _____	_____	# _____
$ _____	_____	# _____	$ _____	_____	# _____
$ _____	_____	# _____	$ _____	_____	# _____

Ocean freight includes the following surcharges: Air freight includes the following surcharges:
☐ Port congestion   ☐ Heavy lift   ☐ Fuel adjustment
☐ Currency adjustment ☐ Bunker   ☐ Container stuffing
☐ Container rental   ☐ Wharfage   ☐ _____
☐ _____   ☐ _____

☐ INSURANCE   ☐ includes war risk   ☐ INSURANCE   ☐ includes war risk
rate: _____ per $100 or $ _____   rate: _____ per $100 or $ _____

TOTAL OCEAN CHARGES $ _____   **TOTAL AIR CHARGES** $ _____ $ _____
notes: notes:

FORWARDING FEES: $ _____
Includes: ☐ Courier Fees ☐ Certification Fees ☐ Banking Fees ☐ _____

CONSULAR LEGALIZATION FEES: $ _____

INSPECTION FEES: $ _____

DIRECT BANK CHARGES: $ _____

OTHER CHARGES: _____ $ _____
               _____ $ _____

TOTAL: ☐ FOB _____   ☐ C&F _____
        ☐ FAS _____   ☐ CIF _____ $ _____

PACKING/TRANSPORTATION WORKSHEET
SEE REVERSE SIDE FOR INSTRUCTIONS

SPECIAL PACKING REQUIREMENTS:

HAZARDOUS MATERIAL PACKAGING REQUIRED   NO ☐   YES ☐   (SEE DANGEROUS GOODS WORKSHEET)
SPECIAL MARKINGS AND POSITION ON PACKAGE:

LOCAL TRANSPORT BY: _____

RATE QUOTED: _____ DATE: _____ BY: _____

LOCAL TRANSPORT FROM: _____

LOCAL TRANSPORT TO: _____

PICK-UP DATE: _____   PICK-UP CONFIRMED ☐

DELIVERY DATE: _____ DELIVERED TO: _____

DELIVERY CONFIRMED ☐

OCEAN/AIR TRANSPORT BY: _____

RATE QUOTED: _____ DATE: _____ BY: _____

BOOKING INFORMATION:

CARRIER: _____

VESSEL/FLIGHT: _____

CUT-OFF DATE: _____   DELIVERY CONFIRMED ☐

B/L INFORMATION SUBMITTED TO: _____ DATE: _____

B/L RECEIVED FROM FORWARDER/CARRIER: _____ DATE: _____

UNITRAK™

PACKING/TRANSPORTATION WORKSHEET

Special packing and markings often are necessary in export shipments. Pack your product to withstand possible rough handling and bad weather; also be sure to follow special customer or L/C instructions. Your freight forwarder or carrier should be able to advise you on special handling or markings for your shipment.

Depending on the terms of delivery quoted in your contract, you may be responsible for certain transportation arrangements. Make certain that you understand the terms and conditions as they apply to your responsibilities and risks. Remember that in most export contracts, responsibility for the transaction falls on the principals, that is, the buyer and seller. These two parties hold the ultimate responsibility for performance in accordance with the terms of sale and delivery, regardless of error or failure on the part of an agent or contract carrier.

Always document transportation arrangements, and confirm pickups and deliveries. It is always a good idea to note the name of the person from whom you received rate quotes or other transportation information, as well as the time and date when the information was obtained.

Form 18-400 Printed and Sold by *UNZCO* 190 Baldwin Ave., Jersey City, NJ 07306 • (800) 631-3098 • (201) 795-5400

Copyright © 1988 UNZ & CO.

COMMERCIAL INVOICE

SHIPPER/EXPORTER	COMMERCIAL INVOICE NO. / DATE
	CUSTOMER PURCHASE ORDER NO. / B/L, AWB NO.
	COUNTRY OF ORIGIN / DATE OF EXPORT
CONSIGNEE	TERMS OF PAYMENT
	EXPORT REFERENCES
NOTIFY: INTERMEDIATE CONSIGNEE	
FORWARDING AGENT	AIR/OCEAN PORT OF EMBARKATION
	EXPORTING CARRIER/ROUTE

Terms of Sale and Terms of Payment under this offer are governed by Incoterms # 322, "Uniform Rules For The Collection Of Commercial Paper" and # 400 "Uniform Customs And Practice For Documentary Credits".

PKGS.	QUANTITY	NET WT. (Kilos)	GROSS WT. (Kilos)	DESCRIPTION OF MERCHANDISE	UNIT PRICE	TOTAL VALUE

PACKAGE MARKS:

MISC. CHARGES (Packing, Insurance, etc.)

INVOICE TOTAL

CERTIFICATIONS

AUTHORIZED SIGNATURE

Form 15-320 Printed and Sold by *UNZCO* 190 Baldwin Ave., Jersey City, NJ 07306 • (800) 631-3098 • (201) 795-5400

SHIPPER *(Name and address including ZIP code)*

①

ZIP CODE

INLAND CARRIER *(See note #2 below)* **⑦** SHIP DATE   PRO NO.

EXPORTER EIN NO.

②

PARTIES TO TRANSACTION
☐ Related **③** ☐ Non-related

ULTIMATE CONSIGNEE

④

INTERMEDIATE CONSIGNEE

⑤

FORWARDING AGENT

⑥

POINT (STATE) OF ORIGIN OR FTZ NO.   **⑧**   **COUNTRY OF ULTIMATE DESTINATION**   **⑨**

SHIPPER'S LETTER OF INSTRUCTIONS

NOTE: ① IF YOU ARE UNCERTAIN OF THE SCHEDULE B COMMODITY NO.—DO NOT TYPE IT IN—WE WILL COMPLETE WHEN PROCESSING THE 7525-V.

② IF YOU HAVE SHIPPED THIS MATERIAL TO US VIA AN INLAND CARRIER—PLEASE GIVE US THE INLAND CARRIER'S NAME, SHIPPING DATE, AND RECEIPT OR PRO. NO. (IF AVAILABLE). THIS WILL HELP US EXPEDITE YOUR SHIPMENT WITH THE INLAND CARRIER.

③ BE SURE TO PICK UP TOP SHEET AND SIGN THE FIRST BUFF EXPORT DECLARATION WITH PEN AND INK.

SHIPPER'S REF. NO. **⑩**   DATE **⑪**   SHIP VIA ☐ AIR **⑫** ☐ OCEAN ☐ CONSOLIDATE **⑬** ☐ DIRECT

SCHEDULE B DESCRIPTION OF COMMODITIES

D/F	MARKS, NOS., AND KIND OF PKGS. SCHEDULE B NUMBER		QUANTITY— SCHEDULE B UNIT(S)	SHIPPING WEIGHT *(Kilos)*	SHIPPING WEIGHT *(Pounds)*	CUBIC METERS	VALUE (U.S. dollars, omit cents) *(Selling price or cost if not sold)*
⑭	**⑮**		**⑯**	**⑰**	**⑱**	**⑲**	**⑳**
	㉑						

VALIDATED LICENSE NO./GENERAL LICENSE SYMBOL **㉒**   ECCN *(When required)* **㉔**   SHIPPER MUST CHECK ► **㉕** ☐ PREPAID OR ☐ COLLECT

Duly authorized officer or employee **㉓**   The exporter authorizes the forwarder named above to act as forwarding agent for export control and customs purposes.   C.O.D. AMOUNT $

SPECIAL INSTRUCTIONS

㉖

SHIPPER'S INSTRUCTIONS IN CASE OF INABILITY TO DELIVER CONSIGNMENT AS CONSIGNED: ☐ ABANDON ☐ RETURN TO SHIPPER **㉘** ☐ DELIVER TO

BE SURE TO PICK UP TOP SHEET AND SIGN THE FIRST BUFF EXPORT DECLARATION WITH PEN & INK.

㉗

SHIPPER REQUESTS INSURANCE   ☐ NO   If Shipper has requested insurance as provided for at the left hereof. shipment is insured in the amount indicated (recovery is limited to actual loss) in accordance with the provisions as specified in the Carrier's Tariffs. Insurance is payable to Shipper unless payee is designated in writing by the shipper.
☐ YES $ **㉙**

NOTE   The Shipper or his Authorized Agent hereby authorizes the above named Company. in his name and on his behalf. to prepare any export documents. to sign and accept any documents relating to said shipment and forward this shipment in accordance with the conditions of carriage and the tariffs of the carriers employed. The shipper guarantees payment of all collect charges in the event the consignee refuses payment. Hereunder the sole responsibility of the Company is to use reasonable care in the selection of carriers. forwarders. agents and others to whom it may entrust the shipment.

Form 18-400 Printed and Sold by *UNZ&CO* 190 Baldwin Ave., Jersey City. NJ 07306 • (800) 631-3098 • (201) 795-5400

GUIDE TO PREPARING THE SHIPPER'S LETTER OF INSTRUCTION

The Shipper's Letter of Instruction is just that—a "letter" from the Shipper instructing the Freight Forwarder how and where to send the export shipment. In preparing this form, the Shipper also fills in most of the information required on the Shipper's Export Declaration, form 7525V (the Freight Forwarder will complete the rest). After the Shipper completes the form, he or she retains the blue shipper's ply and forwards the rest of the form with the shipment to the Freight Forwarder.

1. EXPORTER—the name and address of the principal party responsible for effecting export from the United States. The exporter as named on the validated export license. Report only the first five digits of the Zip Code.

2. EXPORTER EIN NO.—the exporter's Internal Revenue Service Employer Identification Number (EIN) or Social Security Number (SSN) if no EIN has been assigned.

3. PARTIES TO TRANSACTION (RELATED)—one between the U.S. exporter and the foreign consignee, when the person owns (directly or indirectly) at any time during the fiscal year, **10 percent** or more of the voting securities of the incorporated business, or an equivalent interest if an unincorporated business enterprise, including a branch.

4. ULTIMATE CONSIGNEE—the name and address of the person/company to whom the goods are shipped for the designated end use, or the party so designated on the export license.

5. INTERMEDIATE CONSIGNEE—the name and address of the party who effects delivery of the merchandise to the ultimate consignee, or the party so named on the export license.

6. FORWARDING AGENT—the name and address of the duly authorized forwarder acting as agent for the exporter.

7. INLAND CARRIER—see note 2 on form.

8. POINT (STATE) OF ORIGIN OR FTZ NO.—(a) the 2-digit U.S. Postal Service abbreviation of the state in which the merchandise actually starts its journey to the port of export, or (b) the state of the commodity of greatest value, or (c) the state of consolidation, or (d) the Foreign Trade Zone Number for exports leaving an FTZ.

9. COUNTRY OF ULTIMATE DESTINATION—the country in which the merchandise is to be consumed, further processed, or manufactured; the final country of destination as known to the exporter at the time of shipment; or the country of ultimate destination as shown on the validated export license.

10. SHIPPER'S REFERENCE NO.—Shipper's reference with freight forwarder.

11. DATE—date shipment sent to forwarder.

12. SHIP VIA—method of shipment required.

13. CONSOLIDATE/DIRECT—determines how forwarder is to instruct Carrier to ship goods. Generally, a choice between speed and economy of shipment.

14. D/F—D (domestic exports)—merchandise grown, produced or manufactured (including imported merchandise which has been enhanced in value) in the United States. F (foreign exports) merchandise that has entered the United States and is being reexported in the same condition as when it entered.

15. MARKS, NOS., & KINDS OF PACKAGES—Indicate the numbers and kinds of packages (boxes, barrels, cases) and any descriptive marks, numbers or other identification shown on the packages. Such marks and numbers are required to be placed on the outside of all packaged goods whenever feasible.

SCHEDULE B NUMBER—the commodity number as provided in Schedule B—Statistical Classification of Domestic and Foreign Commodities Exported from the United States.

16. QUANTITY—SCHEDULE B UNIT(S)—the unit(s) specified in Schedule B with the unit indicated or the unit as specified on the validated export license.

17. SHIPPING WEIGHT—(for vessel and air shipments) the gross shipping weight in pounds, including the weight of containers but excluding carrier equipment. NOTE: This requirement will change to kilograms upon passage of the Harmonized System.

18. SHIPPING WEIGHT (pounds)—the gross shipping weight in pounds of the commodities being shipped, not including weight of shipping container.

19. CUBIC METERS—length × width × height in meters, not required, but helpful.

20. VALUE (U.S. DOLLARS, OMIT CENTS)—the selling price, or cost if not sold, for the number of items recorded in the quantity field when they were sold by the vendor to the purchaser.

21. SCHEDULE B DESCRIPTION—a proper identifying description of the commodity as known in the country of production or exportation. This should be sufficient to permit verification of the Schedule B Commodity Number, or the description shown on the export license.

22. VALIDATED LICENSE NO./GENERAL LICENSE NO.—Export license number and expiration date or general license symbol.

23. DULY AUTHORIZED OFFICER—Signature of exporter authorizing the named agent to effect the export when such agent does not have formal power of attorney.

24. ECCN—(when required) Export Control Commodity Number—ECCN number of commodities listed on the Commodity Control List (commodities subject to U.S. Department of Commerce export controls) in the Export Administration Regulations.

25. SHIPPER MUST CHECK—specifies whether shipper (prepaid) or consignee (collect) will pay freight charges. If shipment is to be paid for C.O.D. by consignee, specify amount.

26. SPECIAL INSTRUCTIONS—used to inform forwarder of any special instructions, such as a specific carrier to be used, special telex notification, required certifications, etc.

27. SIGNATURES—lift up the top plies of the form and sign the first Export declaration. This certifies to the U.S. government that all information on the form is true and correct.

28. SHIPPER'S INSTRUCTIONS—instructs the forwarder in direction of the carrier's disposition of non-deliverable merchandise abroad.

29. INSURANCE—used where insurance is required, and the shipper wishes to use an insurer chosen by the Forwarder. The amount insured is usually 110% of the shipment value.

UNITRAK™

Copyright © 1988 UNZ & CO.

TO: BROKER	REFERENCE NUMBER	DATE
	FOREIGN SELLER	

FROM: IMPORTER CONSIGNEE	
	NOTIFY INTERMEDIATE CONSIGNEE

IMPORTER'S TELEPHONE	CONTACT		
IMPORTING CARRIER	FLIGHT VESSEL	ROUTE	B L AWB

IMPORTER'S LETTER OF INSTRUCTION

Enclosed you will find the documents listed below to clear referenced shipment for our account.

☐ ORIGINAL B L NO. _____

☐ NON-NEGOTIABLE B L AND _____ COPIES

☐ ORIGINAL COMMERCIAL INVOICE AND _____ COPIES

☐ PACKING LIST AND _____ COPIES

☐ GSP FORM A

☐ _____

☐ _____

☐ _____

Please prepare the necessary documents for the following entry type:

☐ CONSUMPTION ENTRY

☐ WAREHOUSE ENTRY

☐ TEMPORARY IMPORT BOND ENTRY

[ ] FREE TRADE ZONE ENTRY

☐ IMMEDIATE TRANSPORTATION ENTRY

   To: _____
   _____
   _____

☐ ARRANGE FOR INSURANCE ON CARGO

ROUTING INSTRUCTIONS

☐ STANDARD INSTRUCTIONS

☐ VIA _____
   _____

☐ TO: _____
   _____
   _____

☐ Please call prior to delivery.
   (TELEPHONE) _____
   (CONTACT) _____

☐ PREPAID   [ ] COLLECT

☐ BILL TO _____
   _____

☐ REQUEST CUSTOMS OVERTIME

☐ In the event that this merchandise is subject to examination by Customs, please deliver to CES:
   _____
   _____
   _____

SPECIAL INSTRUCTIONS

Form 16-305 Printed and Sold by *UNZCO* 190 Baldwin Ave., Jersey City, NJ 07306 • (800) 631-3098 • (201) 795-5400

IMPORTER FILE

UNZCO UNITRAK™ **EXPORT TRANSACTION SUMMARY** Copyright© 1988 Unz & Co

CUSTOMER INFORMATION

NAME
ADDR

CONTACT

TEL
FAX
TLX
ORDER #
CUST. REF. #

METHOD OF PAYMENT

TERMS OF PAYMENT
TERMS OF DELIVERY
(FOB _____ etc.)

BANK INFORMATION

ESTIMATED PAYMENT DATE

LETTER OF CREDIT #
RECEIVED ☐   REVIEWED ☐
LATEST SHIPPING DATE
PRESENT DOCUMENTS BY
EXPIRATION DATE

AMENDMENT(S) REQUESTED ☐
RECEIVED ☐
DOCUMENTS PRESENTED TO BANK

DOCUMENTS AGAINST PAYMENT ☐
DOC. AGAINST ACCEPTANCE ☐ AT _____ DAYS

DOCUMENTS PRESENTED TO BANK

OPEN ACCOUNT
TERMS
INVOICED (DATE)
PAYMENT RECEIVED

CASH IN ADVANCE   PAYMENT RCVD ☐

Form 18-400 Printed and Sold by UNZCO 190 Baldwin Ave., Jersey City, NJ 07306 · (800) 631-3098 · (201) 795-5400

PRODUCT STATUS

EST. SHPG. DATE

PRODUCT CLASSIF. #
SCHED. B/HS & DESCRIPTION
(OTHER)

EXPORT LICENSE (Individual Validated Lic.)

YES ☐   NO ☐   GENL. LIC. SYMBOL

CURRENT VALIDATED LIC. #
NEW LIC. APPLICATION FILED ☐ by
          APPLICATION REJECTED ☐ ☐ (see worksheet)
          APPLICATION APPROVED ☐
          VAL. LICENSE RECEIVED ☐ #
DEPT. OF COMMERCE (202) 377-4811

SHIPPING INFORMATION

INLAND FREIGHT

FORWARDER/
EXPORTING AGENT

CARRIER NAME
VESSEL/FLIGHT #
          ETD: ETA:

BOOKING/HOUSE AIR WAYBILL #

OCEAN BILL OF LADING/
MASTER AIR WAYBILL #
OCEAN B/L (AIR WAYBILL) RECEIVED ☐
                        REVIEWED ☐

NOTES:

IMPORTANT: ALL NECESSARY DOCUMENTS, INCLUDING INVOICE, SHIPPER'S EXPORT DECLARATION, DANGEROUS GOODS DECLARATION, BANK DRAFT, SHIPPER'S LETTER OF INSTRUCTIONS, OR ANY CERTIFICATES HAVE BEEN PROPERLY SIGNED OR ENDORSED.
          ☐ by

INSURANCE   Us   Buyer
COVERED BY   ☐   ☐
CERT. ISSUED BY
          DATED
          AMOUNT $

INSPECTION/CERTIFICATION
          (Type)   RCVD RVWD
                                      ☐   ☐
                                      ☐   ☐
                                      ☐   ☐
          WORKSHEET(S) COMPLETED ☐

INVOICE/PACKING LIST   INV   P/L
WORKSHEET(S) COMPLETED   ☐   ☐
DOCUMENT(S) REVIEWED   ☐   ☐

SHIPPER'S LETTER OF INSTRUCTIONS (SLI)
YES ☐   NO ☐
RELEASED TO FORWARDING AGENT ☐

DANGEROUS GOODS DECLARATION (HAZMAT)
YES ☐   NO ☐
RELEASED TO FORWARDER/CARRIER ☐

IMPORT TRANSACTION SUMMARY

UNZ&CO UNITRAK™

Copyright© 1988 Unz & Co

VENDOR INFORMATION

NAME

ADDR.

CONTACT

TEL

FAX

TLX

ORDER #

CUST. REF. #

TO:

ENTRY TYPE

CONSUMPTION ☐

WAREHOUSE ☐

TEMPORARY IMPORT BOND ☐

FOREIGN TRADE ZONE ☐

IMMEDIATE TRANSPORTATION ☐

ENTRY DETAILS

CUSTOMS ENTRY NO.

RECEIVED CF7501 ☐   DATE

LIQUIDATION NOTICE REC'D ☐   DATE

REFUND DUE   ☐ YES ☐ NO   DATE

ADDITIONAL DUTY DUE   ☐ YES   AMT.

NNED PROTEST   ☐ YES ☐ NO

FDA/OTHER AGENCY

RELEASE DATE

SAMPLED

EXAMINED BY CUSTOMS   ☐ YES ☐ NO

DISPOSITION

PURCHASE ORDER

NUMBER   DATE

RELEASE NO.   DATE

RELEASE NO.   DATE

RELEASE NO.   DATE

RELEASE NO.   DATE

INSURANCE

  Us ☐   Vendor ☐   Broker ☐

COVERED BY

CERT. ISSUED BY

DATED

AMOUNT $

SHIPPING DETAILS

DATE PRE-ADVICE RECEIVED FROM VENDOR

OCEAN CARRIER/AIRLINE   ETA

VESSEL/FLIGHT NO.

PORT OF DEPARTURE   ETD

PORT OF ENTRY

MASTER B/L, AWB NO.

HOUSE B/L, AWB NO.

NO. PIECES

GROSS WT.

CONTAINER NO   CY/CY   CY/CFS   CFS/CY   CFS/CFS

BREAKBULK AGENT/DEST.

DOCUMENTS

ORIGINAL INVOICE   REC'D   TO BROKER

ORIGINAL B/L   REC'D   TO BROKER

NON-NEG. B/L   REC'D   TO BROKER

PACKING LIST   REC'D   TO BROKER

GSP FORM A   REC'D   TO BROKER

INSP. CERT.   REC'D   TO BROKER

REC'D   TO BROKER

REC'D   TO BROKER

IMPORTER'S INSTRUCTIONS TO BROKER

FREIGHT

TO   ☐ OUR WAREHOUSE ☐ CONSIGNEE

RECEIPT   DATE

☐ PPD ☐ BILL TO

☐ COLLECT

☐ PROOF OF DELIVERY   DATE

☐ DATE PAID

BROKER INVOICE

NO.   PAID   AMT.

DATE

OTHER PAYMENTS

$ TO

$ TO

METHOD OF PAYMENT

TERMS OF PAYMENT

TERMS OF DELIVERY

(FOB _____, etc.)

OPEN ACCOUNT

TERMS

INVOICE NO.   DATE

AMOUNT

CASH IN ADVANCE

AMOUNT

DATE SENT   CHECK NO.

LETTER OF CREDIT

BANK

BANK CONTACT

TELEPHONE

DATE L/C APPLICATION TO BANK

L/C NO.

DATE OPENED

EXPIRATION DATE

DATE ADVICE TO VENDOR

Form 18-200 Printed and Sold by *UNZ&CO* 190 Baldwin Ave., Jersey City, NJ 07306 • (800) 631-3098 • (201) 795-5400

INTEGRATED LOGISTICS SYSTEM STRATEGY, ORGANIZATION, AND CONTROL

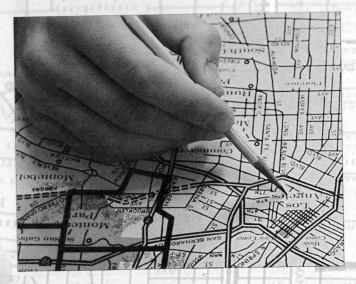

Location, whether of manufacturing or distribution facilities, is a major management decision that has great effect on logistics operations.

CHAPTER FOURTEEN

14

Location Theory and Practice

LEARNING OBJECTIVES

The objectives of this chapter are to:

➤ Review the work in the field of economic geography that led to the formulation and development of location theory.

➤ Discuss the factors that lead to the creation of market areas and market boundaries.

➤ Review and discuss the trends and changes in U.S. regional economies and the implications of these trends and chages for logistics systems and managers.

➤ Review and discuss the aspects of analysis of alternative inventory location strategies.

➤ Present and discuss the advantages and limitations of quantitative techniques for determining inventory locations.

➤ Consider the practical aspects of inventory location strategy and the limitations imposed by nonlocational factors affecting corporate decision making.

Where should a company manufacture or process products and hold inventory? The answer to this question is important because location is a major factor in determining how quickly and at what cost customer orders can be filled; location also affects the costs of processing and manufacturing. Thus, location is a basic element of competitive business strategy and, therefore, a very important aspect of logistics management.

FOUNDATIONS OF LOCATION THEORY

Location questions arise from the fact that the geography of production processes and the geography of market demands very often do not coincide. Thus, the primary determining factors in making location decisions are the cost of production and the cost and time of transportation between production and consumption points. All location theory and practice is based on these cost and time factors.

The complexity of location problems facing business firms has grown tremendously in recent decades because many firms have greatly expanded their markets geographically, expanded their product lines to include much larger numbers of SKUs (many thousands in some cases), and have responded to strong competitive pressures to locate inventory so as to provide ever higher levels of customer service. Further, the effects of the deregulation of transportation on transportation rates have changed former transportation-rate locational advantages and disadvantages for many firms, both absolutely and with respect to competition.

Von Thünen's "Isolated City-State"

The earliest recorded modern work in the field of location theory bearing directly on the influence of transportation on location was done by Johann Heinrich Von Thünen early in the 19th Century.[1] Von Thünen visualized an isolated city-state situated in a limitless plain of equal soil fertility. He then speculated on the use of the surrounding land for agricultural purposes.

Assuming a constant transportation rate for a given weight and distance, Von Thünen reasoned that those products with a low dollar-weight factor — a low value per pound — would be cultivated nearest the city because of the burdensome nature of transportation charges on low value products. He hypothesized that "the value of produce at the place of production decreases with the distance of the place of production from the market."[2] In other words, *the value of a product at the point of production is equivalent to market value less the cost of transportation from point of production to market.*

Von Thünen wrote for another time when horse-drawn wagons and ox carts brought farm products to town. But his theory offers insights into modern urban land use patterns where changes in intensity of land use are closely related to modifications of the transportation system.

Weber's Materials Orientation

Von Thünen's theory had to do with organizing production in a region surrounding a single market point. Alfred Weber's theories dealt with raw material and production points serving single or multiple markets in a region.[3] He assumed that certain materials used in manufacture would be available everywhere in his economy. These materials, of which air and water are examples, he called "ubiquities." Materials available only at certain locations, such as mineral deposits, were referred to as "localized" materials.

Weber also classified materials from the standpoint of the part they played in the manufacturing process in order to determine their importance with respect to transportation (logistics) costs. Those materials that entered into the final product without a loss in weight were called "pure" materials; others were termed "weight-losing." Weight-losing materials ranged from raw materials that entered only a portion of their weight into a finished product to fuel burned in the production process, which added nothing to the weight of the product. Equipped with these definitions, Weber attacked the problem of a firm's decision of where to locate between a source of raw materials and a market, as indicated by points A and B in Figure 14–1.

Assuming equal costs of transportation for equal weights of raw materials and finished products hauled a given distance, company V in Figure 14–1 would gain no particular advantage by locating its plant at A, or at B, or at any point in between. The cost to haul its pure raw materials would be the same as for its finished product. Oil refineries, at which crude oil is converted directly into various products during the refining process, are examples of this type of situation. In this regard, it is interesting to note the lack of noticeable concentration of refineries near either oil fields or markets. Although greater compatibility of pipeline operations with larger shipments of crude, as opposed to finished products, tends to favor market orientation of refineries, field refineries are feasible as well as refineries located neither at the oil field nor at a major market.

In Figure 14–1, Company W, utilizing ubiquities only, would have everything to gain by manufacturing only at the point of consumption, given a product made from materials available anywhere, including point B. Essentially, this is the nature of the soft-drink bottling industry where the product is about 98 percent water.

The optimum point of production for company X is at B also. Although its transportation costs would be much more important than those of company W, because of the transportation of a pure material, its problem would be much the same (avoiding the transportation of ubiquities).

Company Y's situation is similar to that of firms that make extensive use of localized fuels in the process of manufacture. In this case, localized raw materials undergo some loss of weight in process, suggesting a location for production at point A.

The last situation shown in Figure 14–1, that of company Z, is perhaps the most realistic of these five examples. Most firms utilize several types of raw material, as does company Z. Here the amount of weight-losing ubiquities in the finished product is more than balanced by the weight taken from localized weight-losing materials in the same process. The net result is a weight reduction from the total of raw material weights to the weight of the finished product. Company Z should locate its plant at point A.

To describe influences on location decisions that are exerted by the relative weights of raw materials and finished product, Weber formulated a "material index": *the proportion of the weight of localized raw materials to the weight of the finished product.* Upon this idea of a material index, Weber formulated three theorems:

1. All industries whose material index is not greater than one lie at the place of consumption.

2. Pure materials can never bind production to their deposits.

FIGURE 14–1: Examples of five firms using different types of materials in their products, showing the directional pull of plant location toward raw material sources or markets

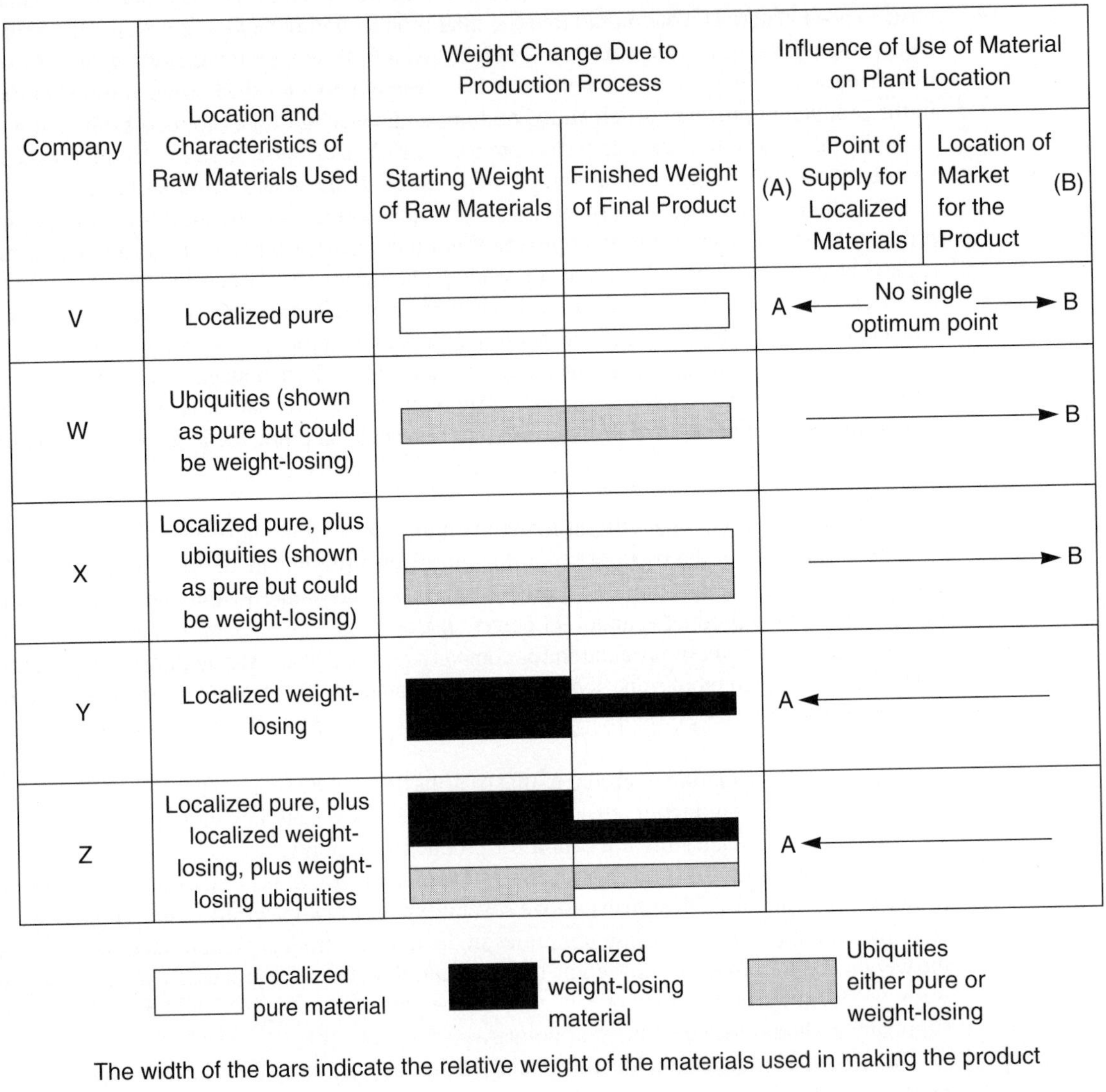

Company	Location and Characteristics of Raw Materials Used	Weight Change Due to Production Process		Influence of Use of Material on Plant Location	
		Starting Weight of Raw Materials	Finished Weight of Final Product	(A) Point of Supply for Localized Materials	Location of Market for the Product (B)
V	Localized pure			A ←—— No single ——→ B optimum point	
W	Ubiquities (shown as pure but could be weight-losing)	▆▆▆	▆▆▆	——————————→ B	
X	Localized pure, plus ubiquities (shown as pure but could be weight-losing)	☐☐☐ ▆▆▆	☐☐☐ ▆▆▆	——————————→ B	
Y	Localized weight-losing	███	██	A ←——————	
Z	Localized pure, plus localized weight-losing, plus weight-losing ubiquities	███ ▆▆▆	██ ▆▆▆	A ←——————	

☐ Localized pure material   █ Localized weight-losing material   ▆ Ubiquities either pure or weight-losing

The width of the bars indicate the relative weight of the materials used in making the product

3. Weight-losing materials, on the other hand, may pull production to their deposits. For this to happen, however, it is necessary that the material index for any one source location be greater than one, and that its portion of the material index be equal to or greater than half of the sum of the material indices for all raw material sources and the market.[4]

Hoover's Transfer Costs

As was discussed in Chapter 8, "Transportation Rates and Services," an important characteristic of transportation rates is that they are tapered. That is, a given weight is charged smaller increments per mile as the distance of a shipment increases. This tapering principle has been reinforced by one of the major effects of transportation regulation—basing rates much more on the cost of service than on the value of service. Hoover has shown that this characteristic of transportation rates tends to encourage firms using only pure materials (like company X in Figure 14–1) to locate *either* at raw material sources *or* at markets.[5]

Procurement and distribution costs (with only transfer costs graphed) for a firm locating at any point between points A and B in Figure 14–2 will taper with the transportation rate schedule. Here it is assumed that one material or combination of pure materials is available at the source. Line AC represents the cost of handling at the source. As the firm locates nearer the market, point B, its total procurement costs (in the form of handling plus transportation costs) behave in the reverse fashion, rising as the firm locates away from point B. As shown by curve EF, total transfer costs will be minimized at either the source or the market.

As Hoover noted, transit privileges may cancel out the advantages of locating at any particular point between A and B. Transit privileges tend to equalize freight charges between A and B in Figure 14–2, regardless of the particular location of plant facilities between them.

FIGURE 14–2: Costs of procurement and distribution, and total transfer cost, for locations on a direct route between A and B

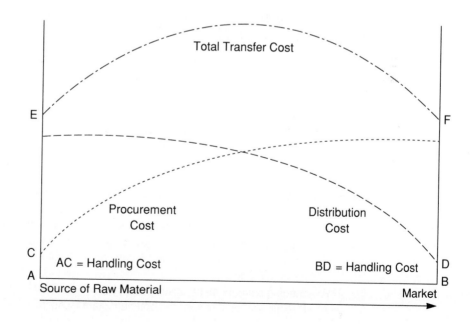

Multiple Sources and Markets

The next logical step was to develop the theory of facility location to take into account the more realistic situation of multiple sources of incoming products or multiple markets for outgoing products.

Weber approached the problem by constructing triangles encompassing two sources of raw materials and one market. The problem was to select an optimum location for a producing facility in relation to these three points.

Consider three plants producing three different products, each product using the same weights of localized raw materials, but having different finished product weights. Locational factors and statistics for each are shown in Figure 14–3. A point equidistant from each of the raw material sources and the market can be selected as a tentative location will be determined.

FIGURE 14–3: Three situations showing the influence of varying weights of raw materials and finished products on plant location decisions

---

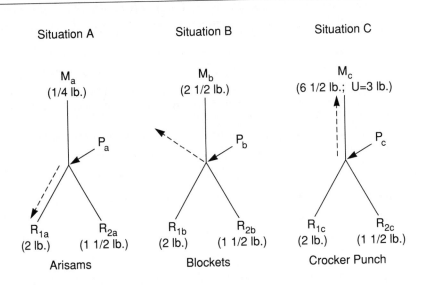

R₁ and R₂ = Locations of raw material sources. The weight of raw material to be used in each unit of finished product is indicated in parentheses.

  M = Location of the market for the finished product. The weight of raw material to be used in each unit of finished product is indicated in parentheses.

  U = Ubiquitous raw material added during the production process, per unit of finished product.

  P = Starting point for plant location analysis.

--→ Direction of "pull" toward the optimum plant location.

This is shown as P in Figure 14–3. In each case, the optimum location will be influenced by the relative weights of raw material inputs of localized raw materials from points R_1 and R_2. It will also be influenced by the resulting weight of the finished product.

Finished product weight is influenced by two factors: (1) the amount of raw material lost in the production process, and (2) the weight of ubiquitous material, if any, added during the process. The weight loss of 3.25 pounds experienced in the production of Arisams is great. The weight loss of one pound experienced in making Blockets is much less. There is actually a net weight gain in the process of making Crocker Punch, due to the addition of a great amount of ubiquitous material, perhaps water. In the following discussion, transportation costs are assumed to correspond directly to the weight of goods moving over any segment of the system under consideration.

Weber's theory can once again be applied to the situation in question. When we compute the materials index for Arisams, we find it to be 14 $[(2 + 1.5)/.25]$. Recalling Weber's theory, a result greater than 1 indicates that location at the market would not be feasible.

In order to determine whether location at any one of the raw material sources would be desirable, location weights for each source and destination can be computed. Location weights consist of the respective ratios of localized raw material to finished product weight for each source. In the case of Arisams, the location weight for source R_{1a} would be 8(2.25), and for source R_{2a}, 6(1.5/.25). In the case of the market, it would always have a location weight of 1(.25/.25). In situations where the location weight of any one source of raw materials is greater than the sum of the weights for other sources plus the market, production will gravitate to that source. This is what happens with Arisams, where the weight for R_{1a} is 8, greater than the sum of weights for the other points in the system $(6 + 1 = 7)$.

Common sense tells us that if we were to tie three strings of equal length together in the middle of a round table, run each to the edge of the table in the relationship shown in Figure 14–3, and then attach at the end of each string a lead weight proportional to the material weight of M_a, R_{1a}, and R_{2a} for Arisams, the weight for R_{1a} would pull the other two over the edge of the table at a point corresponding to R_{1a} in the figure. The same situation would prevail in the making of Crocker Punch, except that the relatively heavy weight of the finished product would suggest a plant location at the market. *The rule is that if the weight at any one nodal point exceeds the sum of the other two, the least-cost location will be at that point.*

In the case of Blockets, the materials index is 1.4 $[(2 + 1.5)/2.5]$. However, no one raw material or finished product has a location weight in excess of the sum of the others. The point of production will not be at point R_{1b}, R_{2b}, or M_b. The point will be pulled from P_b, however, in the direction that will reduce the distance that the heaviest product would have to be carried. This will be done at the expense of some increase in distance for the other two. At the point where nothing further is to be gained by "trading-off" increased transportation expense for R_{1b} and R_{2b} for decreased expense from M_b to P_b, the least-cost location for a plant will have been reached.[6]

The examples in Figure 14–3 assume an equal transportation charge for a given weight carried a given distance, regardless of the nature of the product. In reality, this is seldom the case. However, weights used in the examples could be adjusted to reflect comparative transportation charges on R_1 and R_2 and the finished product in each case. Because finished products are worth more than the sum of their component materials (and transportation charges are to some degree based on the value of the product being transported) the relative weight of the finished product in each of the cases shown in Figure 14–3 should be increased to reflect this fact. This would have the effect of drawing production sites closer to their markets, an industry-location practice that has long reflected value-of-service characteristics in the transportation rate structure.

Bulk-Gaining Commodities

Although most processing of raw materials into finished products results in either a weight loss — or at least no weight gain — there are many situations in which the conversion of raw materials to finished goods results in what is termed "bulk gaining." Examples include products as diverse as potato chips, ping pong balls, styrofoam cups, and newspapers. Further, many products not generally considered to be bulky nonetheless contain a lot of air, such as automobiles and fine furniture (bureaus and chests of drawers). Because of this gain in bulk and the fact that transportation carriers must charge for cube usage if hauling capacity is absorbed, the manufacturers of such products will tend to be market oriented. For example, potato chips can only move economically about 400 miles, while potatoes can move nearly around the world economically. On the other hand, ping pong balls can move around the world because of their high unit value and their consequent ability to absorb high transportation costs.

DETERMINATION OF MARKET BOUNDARIES

A variation of Von Thünen's transportation cost belts can be used to estimate the area that a firm might supply from a given point of storage or production. Consider the situation of the three competing firms shown in Figure 14–4. Each has a plant located equidistant from the other two.

Each firm has the same production cost per unit ($20), and transportation costs per unit are constant and equal for all firms ($.01 per mile per unit). The sum of each firm's production and transportation cost is indicated by the cost belts radiating from each production site. In this case, boundaries of the markets served by each plant (assuming completely rational economic behavior and a price policy that charges a price based on production cost plus cost of transportation to any given point) will be at the points at which the price charged by any two or more of the firms is the same. Theoretically, all of these points are situated at the intersection of comparable "cost belts" of two or three firms. By connecting these points, market boundaries are formed.

Influence on Market Boundaries

Decreased costs of transportation for one firm in comparison with another will enlarge the market territory of the first at the expense of the second. This is the relationship shown for the three firms in Figure 14–5. A combination of lower logistics costs, production costs, or both can result in a greatly increased market area for one firm at the expense of another. Thus, Firm 1 benefits in this manner at the expense of Firm 3 in Figure 14–5, enlarging its market area to encircle completely a small area surrounding Firm 3's plant.[7]

The determination of the point at which a theoretical market boundary will fall between two competing fixed facilities requires a knowledge of production costs of the two competing fixed facilities, the transportation rate per unit of distance paid by each competing firm, and the distance between competing fixed facilities.

FIGURE 14–4: Market areas for three firms with equal costs of production and transportation

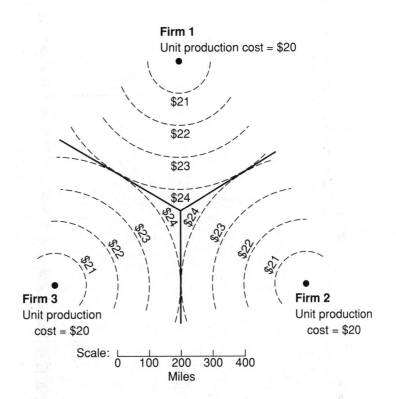

Blanket Transportation Rates and Pricing Policy

Implicit in the development of Figures 14–4 and 14–5 are two assumptions: (1) that customers will purchase from the firm offering the lowest price, and (2) that producers will price their product at an amount based directly on the cost of production and transportation. In actual practice these assumptions are commonly violated by uniform delivered pricing policies. But, even under those circumstances, Figures 14–4 and 14–5 demonstrate two things: (1) the points from which a firm with several distribution points can most economically serve a given territory, and (2) those sales that are more profitable and those that are less profitable when made from a given point on a delivered price basis.

Blanket transportation rates, discussed in Chapter 8, directly contribute to delivered uniform pricing policies. By charging a single rate beyond a "gateway" to a blanket-rate area, carriers allow uniform delivered prices to conform more directly to the shipper's actual cost.

FIGURE 14–5: Market areas for three firms having unequal costs of production and transportation

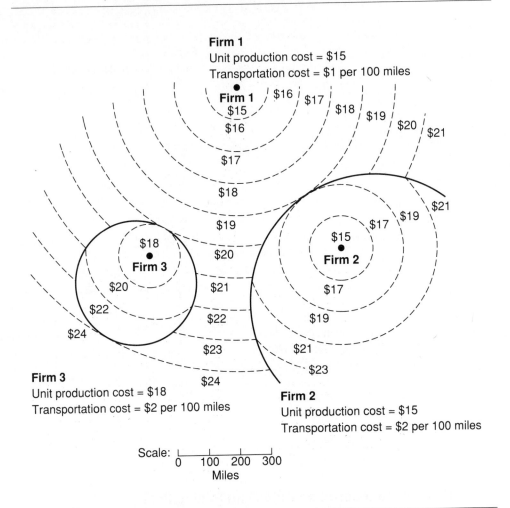

Firm 1
Unit production cost = $15
Transportation cost = $1 per 100 miles

Firm 3
Unit production cost = $18
Transportation cost = $2 per 100 miles

Firm 2
Unit production cost = $15
Transportation cost = $2 per 100 miles

Scale:
0   100   200   300
Miles

Transportation and Economies of Scale

Decreases in transportation costs in relation to competition allow a firm to expand its market territory. Increased sales allow more production at a given location. This may offer economies of scale in the production operation. These economies, in turn, may allow a company to expand further the market territory served from the plant. In cases such as this, transport cost advantages can create a self-reinforcing chain of events. Further, as sales patterns change and market areas expand or contract, some plants or distribution centers may be closed by a firm while new ones may be opened. In such cases, the resulting combination of tapering cost/distance factors and changing multiple manufacturing/inventory locations can produce extremely complex movement patterns.

Location problems can be addressed by algorithms that will yield an optimal solution, or heuristic procedures which will yield "good" solutions but not necessarily optimal ones. If a valid algorithm cannot be developed, a heuristic approach (if available) must be used.

During the past thirty years a veritable army of researchers has addressed the search for solutions to a wide range of multiple facility location problems. Many algorithms and heuristics have been developed. And, greatly expanded computer memory capabilities and high speed data manipulation have made it possible for these researchers to test a great variety of ideas. This research has produced many useful computerized analytical routines for addressing complex location problems. Some of these analytical routines are in the public domain; others are proprietary.

Trading Area Analysis

Marketing analysts have adapted location theory in developing methods of estimating the sizes of trading areas.

The decision by a potential customer to do business at one location as opposed to another is influenced only in part by the ease with which the transaction can be accomplished, a function of the distance between the customer's home, for example, and the other locations. Another important consideration is the customer's assessment of the likelihood of successfully completing the transaction at a particular location. This is true especially for goods sold at retail, so-called consumer goods. It has also given rise to a family of techniques intended to help define trading areas and the strength of "gravitational pull," which competing trading areas can exert to overcome inertial forces or "friction" created by distances between trading areas and potential customers.

William J. Reilly, in an early effort to inject scientific analysis into marketing planning, formulated a "law of retail gravitation," stated in this manner: "Two cities attract retail trade from an intermediate city or town in the vicinity of the breaking point, approximately in direct proportion to the populations of the two cities and in inverse proportion to the square of the distances from these two cities to the intermediate town."[8]

Reilly defined a breaking point as the point on a line between two competing trading centers that delineated the relative area over which each trading center would have retail trade influence. Converse and Huegy interpreted this concept in terms of the following formula:

$$\text{Breaking point between } A \text{ and } B, \text{ in miles from } B = \frac{\text{Distance between } A \text{ and } B}{1 + \sqrt{\dfrac{\text{Population of town } A}{\text{Population of town } B}}}\quad [9]$$

The law of retail gravitation resulted from the measurement of the sales of leading stores in larger cities in Texas, house-to-house interviewing to determine consumer buying habits, and retail stock checking to determine the size and breadth of assortments carried for various products.[10]

Business researchers, uncomfortable with the assumption that an invisible line separates individuals shopping at either of two competing retail outlets, have concentrated on the definition of primary, secondary, and tertiary (marginal) trading areas for competing retail operations. Estimates of the shape of such areas are based not only on the distance between the seller's location and that of the prospective buyer, but also on such factors as the type of goods being sold, the location of competing outlets, the buyer's economic capacity to buy, the buyer's life style, and any natural barriers to movement within the potential trading area.

The assumption implicit in this approach is that a store, for example, will obtain the highest proportion of the total purchases of a given type of product in its primary trading area and lesser proportions in its secondary and tertiary trading areas. Huff has formalized this into a series of models based on the probability that people will shop at one of two or more competing retail outlets, based in part on their location in relation to such outlets.[11]

LOCATION AND REGIONAL ECONOMIC DEVELOPMENT

If location theory is to be applied, it is important to have some idea of the nature of the "game board" on which actual location decisions are to be made. For the purposes of this discussion, we'll use the United States. Unlike a chess board, the map of the United States represents a changing landscape of population shifts and economic development. Among the more important trends in economic development in the United States in recent decades have been (1) shifts in population and production to regions of the country comprising the so-called Sun Belt, (2) rising regional self-sufficiency, and (3) a changing base of economic activity on a national scale.

Shifts in Population and Production

The most striking shifts in population and production in the United States in recent years have been the development of certain sections of the Sun Belt, particularly the Far West and the Southeast. Figure 14–6 shows that the population of the Pacific region (California, Oregon, and Washington) rose from 6.6 percent of the national population in 1929 to 15.1 percent in 1988. Accompanying this population growth has been a growth in the proportion of national value added by manufacturing in this region from 6.0 percent to 13.5 percent between 1929 and 1986, as shown in Figure 14–7. And, remarkable growth has occurred in those states in the West and East South Central and South Atlantic regions.

The increasing volume of demand from a growing southern and western population has led many eastern suppliers to establish distribution warehousing facilities on or closer to the West Coast. In many cases, new production facilities have been built to serve southern and western markets. It is important to put the growth of the Pacific region and Sun Belt states in some perspective. As Hoover has pointed out, the growth should not be interpreted only as a migration of industry from other states. The population of the Sun Belt has grown at a rate that has enabled that region's industry to grow at a relatively faster rate than the rest of the country.[12]

Regional Self-Sufficiency

The growth of regional populations has created local markets able to support increasing numbers of those industries in which economies of scale are important. As a consequence, regional self-sufficiency has increased in the sense that broader ranges of locally produced products are available. This trend has led to the exchange of more specialized products between regions. A striking example of the existence of the trend was the decision of several publishers of national newspapers and magazines to publish regional editions to serve not only

FIGURE 14–6: Percentage distribution of U.S. population, by regions, 1899, 1929, 1970, and 1988

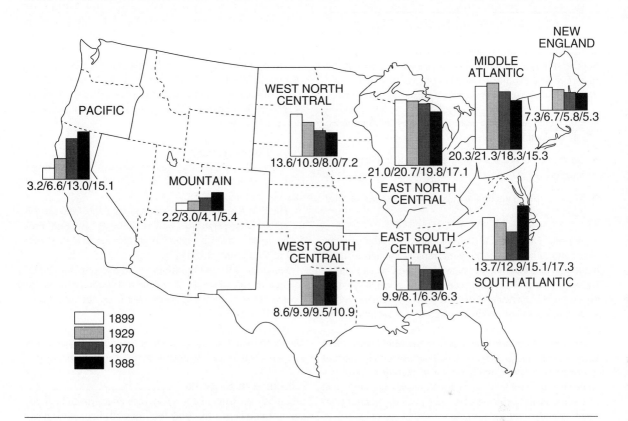

SOURCE: Department of Commerce, Bureau of the Census.

growing regional markets for readership, but also increasing numbers of firms in a region capable of supporting a substantial regional advertising program. And this is an industry where manufacturing — printing — economies of scale are tremendous.

Regional self-sufficiency is likely to continue to change the pattern of logistics in the United States. There is already some evidence of a decrease in the distances over which finished products are transported as the movement of goods *within* regions increases.[13]

This same market "magnetism" that has attracted industry to growing regions is likely to continue to pull producing facilities away from raw material sources.[14] This does not necessarily mean that the average distance any single raw material or finished goods component will have to move to reach a processing point will increase. As has been pointed out:

> The chain of processing between raw materials and final products has been growing longer and longer. The tendency of any plant in the chain to use materials which are already processed has continued to grow. As a result, in increasing degree, plants hold down their freight-in costs by locating near other plants — not near a raw material source.[15]

DISTRIBUTION FOLLOWS CONSUMER MOVEMENT

Les B. Artman and David A. Clancy

Population migration toward the coasts, especially the Southeast, has fueled growth of distribution centers (DCs) in that region according to TRANSPORTATION & DISTRIBUTION'S 1990 site selection survey. The survey also shows:

- Companies are paying more attention to distribution as a value-added function.

- Cost alone is not reason enough to select a certain DC location.

- There is still an uncertainty about the future use of third-party logistics.

Atlanta, Orlando, and Portland are the fastest growing distribution cities—each growing rapidly enough to make traditional distribution cities New York and Chicago notice. Dallas is also growing, but more slowly. Memphis, which bills itself as America's Distribution Center, remains a contender but shows some slowing in growth of facilities locating there.

Transportation hubs play a role in the selection of these sites. Atlanta and Dallas offer facilities for efficient multimodal transport. Portland has been marketing its port as a gateway to the Pacific Rim. And with Florida boasting eight of the ten fastest growing consumer markets, centrally located Orlando is a logical site to serve that region.

This growth has led to a shift in the top ten cities for DCs. The 1990 list reads (1985 rank in parenthesis):

1. Los Angeles (tied for 1)

2. Atlanta (5)

3. Chicago (tied for 1)

4. Dallas (4)

5. New York (3)

6. Philadelphia (tied for 14)

7. San Francisco (7)

8. Houston (9)

9. Denver (tied for 20)

10. Boston (8)

Falling out of the top ten for 1990 are Milwaukee (sixth in 1985), Indianapolis, Detroit, Memphis, and Minneapolis (tied for tenth in 1985).

The South Atlantic now boasts the highest percentage of DCs in the country—21.9%, up from 16.1% in 1985. The East North Central region falls from the top spot, dropping 14.3%, but still holds on to the second highest percentage of DCs with 19.1%.

Why These Areas?

Consumerwise, the South Atlantic region is growing faster than any other region. This is also reflected in the marked increase in number of DCs.

The East North Central region claims four of the top ten freight producing states, as well as 17.9% of the freight produced in the U.S. This region boasts the second highest percent of DCs in the country.

More than 13% of U.S. freight is produced in the Middle Atlantic region where 11.6% of the distribution centers are located. That region's DC percentage is up slightly, 0.8%, from five years ago.

Growth in the Pacific can be attributed to growth overseas. The Pacific Rim is quickly becoming a substantial market, and shippers want to have their distribution networks in place.

Changes in Regions

Like 1985, growth in DCs is patterned after growth in population. But other factors play roles as well. International expansion is accelerating coastal growth. Truck bans spur expansion in Los Angeles. And strict intrastate transportation regulations in Texas have fueled DC growth in areas surrounding that state.

South Atlantic. Two cities, Atlanta and Orlando, account for much of this region's growth. The area now boasts more DCs than any other region—its share of the pie is 36% higher than five years ago. Atlanta has had more DCs open in the past five years than any other city.

East North Central. Chicago slipped from a first-place tie to third in the national rankings, and the entire region's DC share was down 14.3% on number of DCs. The area still claims 19.1% of the nation's DCs, second to the South Atlantic region. Cleveland is growing significantly, as is Dayton. In the latter's case, its growth is at the expense of Cincinnati, down substantially from 1985.

Pacific. The Pacific region is seeing tremendous growth from Portland, largely from that city's efforts to attract international distribution centers. The Port of Portland is aggressively marketing itself as an international gateway, and distribution professionals are noticing. Los Angeles also continues as a focal point for international distribution, tying Dallas for second most DC openings.

Middle Atlantic. Although New York City fell from third to fifth in the city rankings, only Atlanta, Dallas, and Los Angeles had more DCs open in the past five years. This, coupled with steady growth in the Philadelphia and Pittsburgh markets, led the region to small growth of 0.8% over 1985.

West South Central. Dallas, second in DC openings, and Houston carry this region. Despite their growth, the area's percentage of DCs has dropped 17.2% from 1985 levels.

Mountain. The Mountain region, with a growth of 5.9% over five years ago, is a steady growth market. Denver, which returns to a growth pattern, and Phoenix are leading the way. Salt Lake City is also undergoing some growth.

West North Central. The West North Central region's share of the country's DCs has declined 18.2% since 1985. Only St. Louis is showing significant growth, but it slips some in the national rankings, falling to 24th overall. Minneapolis drops as well, from tenth to 12th.

East South Central. The country's biggest decliner, the East South Central region's share of the DC pie is down 27% from 1985. A shift to the South Atlantic region and Memphis' fall contribute significantly to the decline.

New England. Boston slipped slightly in the city rankings, but still held on to a strong tenth position. Hartford, CT, and Providence, RI, also benefited from the confines of New England as new facilities opened there, perhaps to ease the congestion of New York and Boston. Overall, the region grew 7.3%.

Network Size Trends

The growth many areas are seeing is occurring despite the trend toward downsizing operations. Many companies downsize the number of facilities in their distribution networks as they rationalize the trade-offs between cost and service. Often, certain locations cannot be justified because marginal service improvements cannot overcome significant fixed and inventory carrying cost penalties. Or, it may be possible to maintain, or even improve service by spending more on premium transportation and less on facilities and inventory.

Survey responses do not precisely bear out this trend. The 1990 results indicate an average of 5.9 DCs per company, versus 4.9 in 1985. This can be explained in several ways. First, respondents to both surveys were not consistently the same companies. A different mix of manufacturers, re-

tailers, and distributors impacts the precision of results in this area. Second, the tremendous number of mergers that occurred during the late 1980s was bound to increase the size of companies' distribution networks temporarily — until the rationalization process previously described has had a chance to become implemented.

There is a trend toward distribution networks of reduced size as companies react to intensifying pressure to reduce costs and improve return on asset performance while maintaining high levels of customer service.

What's Important?

Selecting a site for a new facility is a strategic decision requiring consideration of many business issues. TRANSPORTATION & DISTRIBUTION readers were asked to rate the importance of factors when making this decision — both today and five years from now.

As expected, outbound transportation issues (access and cost) consistently rank high in importance. The only major exception here is distributors — where frequent freight collect transportation terms appear to make outbound transportation economics less of a concern.

For retailers, labor availability is clearly of major importance. Retailers are quick to recognize the labor shortage problem in selected areas (like the Northeast) where their own stores are having enough difficulty attracting and retaining qualified workers at reasonable cost. A large DC, which may employ 200 or more, presents an even greater dilemma in scarce labor markets. Distributors, many of which service retail stores directly and compete for the same labor pool, also view labor as a key consideration.

For manufacturers, customer service is also a key factor when deciding on a distribution location. Service, at least from a proximity standpoint, is less important for retailers and distributors — where transit time consistency and reliability are often more important than speed.

In terms of future trends, continuing pressure on labor costs and the increasing impact of just-in-time are reflected in the ratings.

Surprises? A few:

- Lower than expected importance ranking for union environment.

- A small decrease in the significance of inbound transportation for manufacturers and retailers; a larger decrease in importance for distributors. This is somewhat at odds with the growing trend for companies to place *more* emphasis on managing the inbound side of the materials pipeline.

Continued

DISTRIBUTION FOLLOWS CONSUMER MOVEMENT CONTINUED . . .

Value-Added Services

Various forms of packaging and light assembly were the most frequently mentioned ways survey respondents described value-added functions performed in the DCs.

Companies are increasingly using DCs to add value when the economics are favorable to do so. This improves service, inventory performance, and flexibility across the materials pipeline. For suppliers, it postpones making product "customer specific" until orders are actually received. This reduced aggregate inventory levels by allowing more accurate forecasting of fewer packaging configurations at field stocking location.

For customers there is benefit as well. As the supplier's lead time becomes shorter and more predictable, customers are less compelled to carry high levels of safety stock inventory as a "hedge" against poor availability. As suppliers and customers continue to explore more creative win/win partnerships in the future, DCs will become a more important competitive weapon to help provide unique customer service programs while shrinking the total inventory investment in the pipeline.

How Far? How Fast?

Is the trend toward third-party logistics a slow migration or an immediate stampede? What are the advantages, disadvantages, and concerns? The 1990 site location survey included a series of questions that explored the third-party logistics issue, and the results are interesting, indeed. Bottom line — the jury is still out.

What is the future role of third-party logistics? Transportation and distribution managers are nearly split in their opinions regarding whether the role of third-party logistics will increase or not during the next five years. . . . These opinions hold fairly consistently across manufacturers, retailers, and distributors. Apparently the concept of third-party logistics has a way to go to convince a majority of transportation and distribution managers that benefits actually exist.

Advantages and disadvantages. . . . The most noted advantage for using third parties was reduced cost. More expertise, improved service, and enhanced flexibility were also viewed as advantages. However, 19% of respondents specifically answered "none" to this question — proving once more the lack of a true mandate. Impossible to glean from the numbers, but a possibility nonetheless, is the perceived threat that outsourcing logistics may have on today's distribution managers.

The most significant disadvantage cited relates to loss of control. Nearly half of those that had an opinion believe that relying on third parties hinders management's ability to influence day-to-day operations directly. In addition, nearly one in four believe that customer service suffers in a third-party relationship. Increased cost and reduced flexibility are viewed as other disadvantages. However, nearly one in ten saw no disadvantage at all.

Areas of importance. Transportation and warehousing are the historical areas for third-party relationships. However, . . . companies will be increasingly looking outside for help in sorting out the issue of EDI communications. EDI is a rapidly emerging reality that continues to represent a major opportunity for manufacturers, retailers, and distributors, as well as third-party providers of expertise.

How willing will companies be to share managing the business with outsiders? . . . [M]ore willing in some areas, less in others. The 100% third-party relationships will remain most common in transportation and warehousing. Fewer companies will give up total control in systems and materials management.

Note that fewer are willing to follow the "third-party management, company labor" route — although better than one in four readers see that as possible in EDI and materials management.

Based on survey results, outsourcing logistics activities will grow steadily, although not dramatically, over the next five years. Providers of third-party services have much education to complete and will need to demonstrate value and alleviate concerns about control and customer service. A major opportunity for third parties, according to respondents, is to provide help in sorting out the technological and practical issues associated with implementing EDI.

What Does This Mean?

Clearly, companies are looking at their DCs more thoroughly than ever. A DC used to be where product was stored. Today it is a flurry of activity. As space becomes more of a premium, its practical use will increase.

Companies are finding that they don't need hundreds of DCs spread across the country. A few, in strategic locations, providing necessary services, at a reasonable cost, are enough to stay competitive.

SOURCE: Reprinted with permission, *Transportation & Distribution* © June 1990, Penton Publishing Co., Cleveland, OH.

FIGURE 14–7: Percentage distribution of value added by manufacture, by regions, 1899, 1929, 1967, and 1986

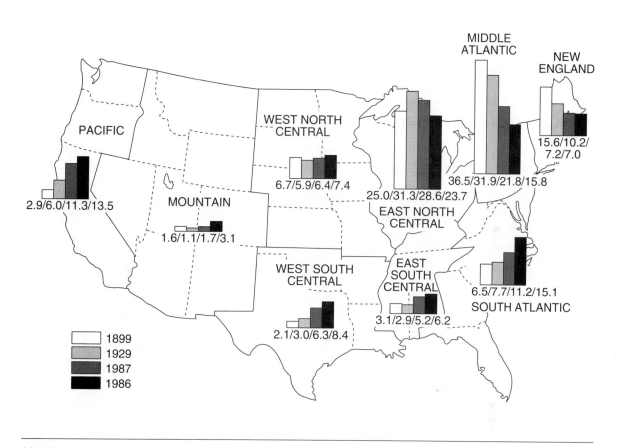

SOURCE: Department of Commerce, Bureau of the Census.

National Development

The characteristics of an economy are derived from those of its regions. Considering this, it is not surprising that the economy of the United States has undergone structural changes throughout its history. These changes, based on the general economic standard of living, can be compared directly with the developmental changes that take place in a region over a period of time.

The agricultural phase through which the United States passed is far behind us. For the past eighty years, location theorists and regional economists have concerned themselves primarily with the location and development of extractive and manufacturing industries. A more recent phase, one characteristic of a highly developed economy, is a noticeable shift in the relative importance of manufacturing, trade, and service activities in the economy. Figure 14–8 shows relative trends in employment in the major categories of activities.

Employment in agriculture and the extractive industries reached a high point as a *proportion* of total employment sometime in the nineteenth century, probably just before the Civil War. By 1870, as shown in Figure 14–8, it was already on its way downward. Manufacturing

FIGURE 14–8: Trends of U.S. employment in extractive industries, manufacturing, trade, and services, 1870–1987. Each category is stated as a percentage of total employment. Extractive occupations include agriculture, forestry, mining, and fishing. Manufacturing occupations include manufacturing and contract building construction. Trade occupations include retailing, wholesaling, finance, insurance, real estate, and transportation. Service occupations include education, other professions, domestic services, personal services, and government. Totals do not include persons in military service.

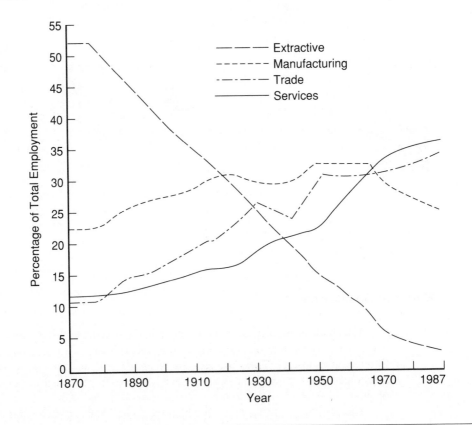

SOURCE: U.S. Department of Commerce, Office of Business Analysis, *Survey of Current Business*.

employment reached a peak in 1920 in relation to trade and service employment. Since then the latter two have been increasing in importance. The trends shown in Figure 14–8 require careful interpretation because they contain no weighting of the relative "income-generating" power per person employed in each of the categories over a period of years. For example, the growth of automation in manufacturing has increased the income-generating power per person employed, although it has led to a decline in the proportion of manufacturing employment.[16] The same is true in agriculture, mining, fishing, and forestry, where productivity increases (output per labor hour) have been continuous and dramatic over the past century.

A second major trend in the development of the U.S. economy has been the pronounced shift to a customer-oriented business philosophy. This philosophy has placed a strong emphasis on giving customers what they want, when they want it, and in the necessary quantities. It is not confined to the service of ultimate consumers, those who consume for their own benefit or pleasure. It has been extended backward slowly through the channel of logistics. Recent emphasis in retailing management has been placed on the reduction of inventories in order to increase turnover ratios. Retailers have consequently shifted many of the problems of inventory control onto the wholesalers who supply them. In many cases, wholesalers have passed some of this increased burden back to manufacturers, thus continuing the series of inventory repercussions that began at the ultimate consumer level.

A third major factor based on the level of national development can be referred to as the "technology of material." Manufacturers have attacked the "barriers" of location by utilizing lighter weight materials in a wide range of products. The greater use of aluminum, plastics, and other light materials has enabled manufacturers to increase the dollar-weight factor of goods produced.[17]

The recent emphasis on services, on customer orientation, and on improved materials technology has challenged the flexibility and adaptability of logistics systems. All three developments contribute to a trend of generally lower weights for shipments.[18] The first two developments (customer orientation and shifting of inventory position) have resulted in generally smaller shipments and "tight" inventory policies at various levels in logistics channels. The third factor (materials technology) has reduced the weight of shipments without, in many cases, influencing their cubic size. This will continue to influence the design of logistics systems in the economy to accommodate lighter shipments of the same number of product units.

INVENTORY LOCATION STRATEGY ANALYSIS

Managers entrusted with actual inventory location decisions need a set of techniques to help them make strategic decisions with long-term implications for their firms. These techniques have been supplied largely by the field of operations research.

There are a number of tools for determining favorable inventory locations from a logistical point of view. Some take into account other equally important production and marketing considerations as well. Several examples will (1) explore in a realistic manner the development of a logistics location strategy, (2) describe one or more methods for appraising each step in a system development, (3) suggest the types of information needed for proper analysis and the means of collecting it, (4) review shortcomings of the methods of analysis discussed, and (5) consider alternatives other than relocation.

The Importance of Logistics in Inventory Location Strategy

The importance of logistics considerations in inventory location strategy will vary from firm to firm. In any event, the final decision will be made on the basis of factors in addition to those of logistics. For example, a comprehensive checklist of factors to be considered in locating a manufacturing plant contains the following major categories: location; character of surrounding territory; population statistics; civic administration; climate; cost of living (per capita); labor; transportation facilities; power and fuel; water; data on present manufacturing concerns; industrial legislation; financial data; educational, recreational, and civic data; special inducements; building costs; available industrial properties and sites.[19]

In contrast, logistics factors are of great importance in warehouse location. The location of warehouse facilities will determine how fast, and at what cost, the firm's production line or its customers can be served from supply sources. Nearly all costs affected by a warehouse location decision are logistics costs. For these reasons, logistics management should play a prominent role in deciding matters of warehouse location.

The Nature of the Problem

Those writing about the location of logistics facilities are often tempted to discuss the problem in terms of a grand, sweeping redesign. Among the questions asked might be: Given the opportunity to relocate our 10 plants and 90 warehouses, where would we put them? How many would we continue to use? It would serve no purpose to devote any serious amount of time to these types of questions. Even if a firm spent the money to find the answers, it is doubtful that it would be able to carry out all resulting recommendations before they became obsolete.

The hard fact remains that the relocation or installation of fixed facilities, especially manufacturing or processing plants, is an expensive proposition. A more realistic approach to the problem might be: Given a projected demand pattern for our products 10 years from now, how should we locate new facilities as they are needed? This approach is piecemeal in character. A warehouse is opened here; two are closed there. A plant is opened at another place. These changes are more effectively made if they are part of a strategic plan. But, the plan is not realized overnight, nor is it likely that any plan will retain its validity for the full period of its projected existence; it will be modified to accommodate changing circumstances.

The optimum plant or warehouse location has never been found. Any quantitative technique developed to date that purports to identify a literally optimum location is naive. However, this assertion does not preclude the use of an organized approach to the problem of location strategy that will suggest the direction in which location planning should proceed. Such approaches have made use of optimizing and simulation techniques. The following sections describe and compare the features of each type of technique.

Optimizing Techniques

Single Inventory Problem — Center-of-Gravity Approach The center-of-gravity approach, for all its limitations, offers a straightforward, simple, and often very useful approach for estimating a good single inventory location from a logistics viewpoint.

The Method The center-of-gravity method is based on the principle that however weights may be distributed on a flat surface, a balance point between or among them can be found. This will be a point on the surface from which the sum of distances to all of the weights, multiplied by the weights themselves, is at or near a minimum. It is the point that potentially offers low transportation costs for the nodal points (weights) and the network connecting them to the center of gravity.

An Example A number of firms come into existence to serve one or several initial customers. This is the case of the Easthampton Comclean Corporation, a mythical manufacturer of an industrial cleaning compound. The product was first developed and manufactured in the garage of its founder in Easthampton, Massachusetts. The process involved two raw materials, sawdust obtained from several furniture manufacturers located in and around Pittsfield, Massachusetts, and a chemical solution, sodium trichorite supplied by an industrial jobber located in Hartford, Connecticut.* The finished product, Comclean, was supplied to a single customer on the southeast edge of Springfield, Massachusetts. The locations of suppliers, manufacturer, and customer are shown in Figure 14–9. Based on transportation costs, what is the least-cost location for the Comclean Corporation?

A determination of the least-cost location for Comclean's manufacture, from a transportation point of view, involves little more than a weighting of relative costs to move raw materials and finished product to and from sources and market, respectively. The nature of the information required to complete the weighting is shown in Table 14–1.

In this case we have assumed that the Comclean Corporation is responsible for bringing its raw materials to Easthampton from the Pittsfield and Hartford supply sources, and then delivering them to Springfield. To establish its importance from a logistics standpoint, each quantity of raw material used in a given amount of Comclean (finished product) is multiplied by its transportation cost per distance unit (5 miles) per 100 pounds (hundredweight) to determine a location cost factor that is shown in column 4 of Table 14–1.

The next weighting step is the one for distance. The map in Figure 14–9 has been divided into squares of equal size that measure vertical and horizontal distances. Although accurate diagonal distances cannot be sight-measured by this means, in all but the rarest of cases this imposes no limitation on the method. All squares on the grid have been numbered both vertically and horizontally to allow weighting of distances to find the point at which all weightings are in balance on all sides of the ultimate point selected. The process requires two steps and resembles, for each, the process by which we would move the pedestal of a seesaw to accommodate for the differences in the weight of two children seated at the ends of the board. The process by which this is accomplished consists of multiplying each location cost factor by each grid row and column number, summing the results, and dividing by the sum of the location cost factors in each case. This is done in Table 14–2.

Tracing the grid row and column coordinates, 6 and 4, respectively, to a point on Figure 14–9, we would find that they converge on some point in the square marked with an X, lying about ten miles due west of Comclean's customer rather than ten miles north as is currently the case.

---

*Chemicals, processes, proportions, and costs used in this example should not be considered accurate; they are for illustrative purposes only.

FIGURE 14–9: Plant Location Grid, Comclean Corporation

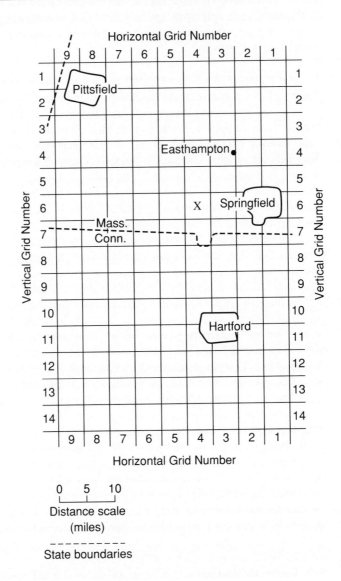

The theoretical optimum location for Comclean's plant might be in the middle of a corn field. At such location, employees might have to drive ten miles to work. The availability of land, the desire of the founder to remain in Easthampton, and many other factors would temper any recommendation to move based on transportation factors alone. Finally, the sheer cost of moving would weight against it. Nevertheless, the annual cost of remaining in Easthampton as

TABLE 14–1: Summary of Materials Used and Shipped, Transportation Costs, and Supply Source and Customer Location for Comclean Corporation

(1)	(2)	(3)	(4)	(5)	
	Material Used or Finished Product Shipped (hundredweight)	*Transportation Cost per Distance Unit (5 miles) per Hundredweight*		*Supply Source (SS) and Customer Location (C)*	
Product			*Location Cost Factor*	*Grid Row Number*	*Grid Column Number*
Sawdust	*2,000*	*$.025*	*$50.00*	*2 (SS)*	*8*
Chemicals	*500*	*.075*	*37.50*	*11 (SS)*	*3*
Comclean	*2,000[a]*	*.031*	*62.00*	*6 (C)*	*2*

[a]A weight loss occurs in the production of Comclean.

TABLE 14–2: Determination of Grid Coordinates, Comclean Location Problem

	Grid Row Determination		
	Location Cost Factor	*Grid Row Number*	*Weight*
	$ 50.00	*2*	*100.0*
	37.50	*11*	*412.5*
	62.00	*6*	*372.0*
TOTAL	*$149.50*		*884.5*
	Grid row midpoint = 884.5/149.50 = 5.9 or 6		

	Grid Column Determination		
	Location Cost Factor	*Grid Column Number*	*Weight*
	$ 50.00	*8*	*400.0*
	37.50	*3*	*112.5*
	62.00	*2*	*124.0*
TOTAL	*$149.50*		*636.5*
	Grid column midpoint = 636.5/149.50 = 4.2 or 4		

opposed to the calculated location, in terms of transportation costs, would be as shown in Table 14-3.

The possible annual saving of $78.80 in transportation costs would not appear to be great enough to outweigh other factors of location. Even though the company's plant would probably not be moved, management's attention would be brought to bear on one cost penalty incurred at its current location.

TABLE 14–3: Computation of Annual Logistics Savings from Relocation

Product	From	To	Annual Volume (hundredweight)	Distance (miles)	Transportation Cost per Distance Unit (5 miles) per Hundredweight	Transportation Cost per Hundredweight	Annual Transportation Cost
			At Present Location				
Sawdust	Pittsfield	Easthampton	2,000	27.5	$.025	$.1375	$275.00
Chemicals	Hartford	Easthampton	500	35.0	.075	.5250	262.50
Comclean	Easthampton	Springfield	2,000	11.3	.031	.0701	140.20
						TOTAL	$677.70
			At Optimum Location				
Sawdust	Pittsfield	X	2,000	28.75	.025	.1437	$287.40
Chemicals	Hartford	X	500	25.00	.075	.3075	187.50
Comclean	X	Springfield	2,000	10.00	.031	.0620	124.00
						TOTAL	$598.90

Time brought success to Comclean. Comclean's markets expanded to include many major industrial centers east of the Mississippi, with relatively little development of markets in smaller cities. Because of increased material requirements, the firm began purchasing its chemical components directly from a large manufacturer in Wilmington, Delaware. Comclean continued to purchase sawdust from Pittsfield, and to serve all customers (mill supply distributors) from its plant and warehouse at Easthampton. Ten years after its founding, the corporation's distribution pattern appears as in Figure 14–10.

FIGURE 14–10: Raw material sources, manufacturing plant, and customer locations for Comclean Corporation

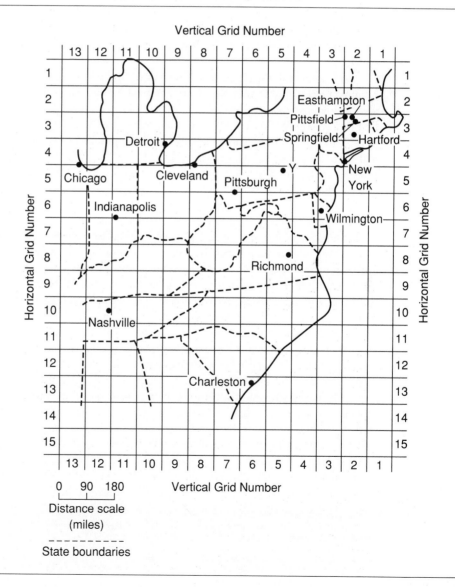

Vertical Grid Number

0   90   180
Distance scale
(miles)

– – – – – – – –
State boundaries

The problem of redetermining the effect of transportation costs on the corporation's plant location is likely to be posed in two ways. First, studies of comparative production costs and other relocation factors indicate that Pittsburgh would serve as the best location of a single plant. What effect would a move from Easthampton to Pittsburgh have on transportation costs? Or, second, what is the least-cost location under our current market situation based on transportation costs?

The first question could be answered by a series of distance measurements to which appropriate quantities and transportation costs are applied. For purposes of rough calculations, the distance scale in Figure 14–10 has been slightly reduced (map distances expanded) to compensate for the difference between airline miles and overland route distances between cities. Alternative transportation costs for Easthampton and Pittsburgh are summarized in Table 14–4. Based on results of this cost study, it appears that Pittsburgh would be a poorer location than Easthampton. If this is as far as the plant location study proceeds, Comclean will avoid incurring an extra $407,500 in annual transportation costs by remaining in Easthampton. However, the optimum plant location from the standpoint of transportation cost will go undetected.

An "optimum" location can be determined by the same method used in the less complex example preceding this one. Necessary computations are shown in Table 14–5; they indicate an optimum grid row location of 213,280/46,345 or 4.60 and an optimum grid column location of 229,400/46345 or 4.95. The location indicated by these measurements is shown as point Y in Figure 14–10, falling somewhere in central Pennsylvania.* Transportation costs to and from this point are also shown in Table 14–4. This point would appear to offer potential logistics savings of $724,200 per year when compared to Pittsburgh, and $316,700 per year when compared to the current location at Easthampton.

Limitations The center-of-gravity technique has some rather obvious limitations. First, to retain its simplicity it assumes a linear relationship between transportation cost and distance. That is, it assumes that the same transportation cost per unit is incurred with each succeeding mile of distance. We have seen that this is not the case; fixed cost elements create a tapered transportation cost and rate structure per unit over distance. Its effect will depend on the distance of input points (more than two) from each other. For example, if three input points form an equilateral triangle there will be no distortion. In other cases involving three or more input points not equally distributed on a plane, the distortion may be substantial.

Where an analysis involves large geographic areas, map distortions may result from the use of a squared as opposed to a Mercator grid conforming to the global latitudes and longitudes. However, for most problems this distortion is not significant.

Only in a very few cases does the center-of-gravity method provide a close approximation to a least-cost answer. A bias in the calculation, varying with differences in weights associated with different points, prevents this. It is most extreme when one weight exceeds the sum of all other weights. Typically, a location problem capable of analysis by the center-of-gravity method will encompass many weighted points. The greater the number and the less the dominance of any one point, the less significant is the bias of the sort we have described.[20]

---

*When map grids must be spaced a great distance apart, as in Figure 14–10, it is important that results of computations be carefully marked off. All supply and market points are given the value of the square in which they are located, thus assuming (1) they are located in the center of the square and (2) that measurement takes place from the center of the square, not its boundary lines. Thus, the center of the square in which the optimum location, Y, is found has 5 and 5 for its coordinates. A row value of 4.60 will appear near the dividing line between rows four and five. A column value of 4.95 will appear near the center of column 5.

TABLE 14–4: Computation of Annual Transportation Costs from Alternative Plant Locations for Comclean Corporation

Line	Commodity and Place	Annual Quantity (hundred-weight)	Transportation Cost per Distance Unit (5 miles) per Hundred-weight	At Easthampton Plant Site			At Pittsburgh Plant Site			At Optimum Transportation Cost Site		
				Distance from Plant Site (miles)	Transportation Cost (per hundred-weight)	Annual Transportation Cost	Distance from Plant Site (miles)	Transportation Cost (per hundred-weight)	Annual Transportation Cost	Distance from Plant Site (miles)	Transportation Cost (per hundred-weight)	Annual Transportation Cost
1	Sawdust (Pittsfield)	620,000	$.025	28	$ .14	$ 86,800	500	$2.50	$1,550,000	270	$1.35	$ 837,000
2	Chemicals (Wilmington)	155,000	.075	400	6.00	930,000	280	4.20	651,000	190	2.85	441,700
3	Comclean (Chicago)	100,000	.031	950	5.89	589,000	460	2.85	285,000	710	4.40	440,000
4	(Indianapolis)	20,000	.031	890	5.52	110,400	360	2.23	44,600	610	3.78	75,600
5	(Detroit)	80,000	.031	650	4.03	322,400	290	1.80	144,000	420	2.60	208,000
6	(Cleveland)	80,000	.031	580	3.60	288,000	120	.74	59,200	300	1.86	148,800
7	(Nashville)	10,000	.031	1,110	6.88	68,800	560	3.47	34,700	780	4.84	48,400
8	(Richmond)	40,000	.031	500	3.10	124,000	310	1.92	76,800	300	1.86	74,400
9	(Charleston)	10,000	.031	560	3.47	34,700	340	2.11	21,100	730	4.53	45,300
10	(Pittsburgh)	60,000	.031	550	3.41	204,600	—	—	—	180	1.12	67,200
11	(New York)	200,000	.031	200	1.24	248,000	390	2.42	484,000	220	1.36	272,000
12	(Hartford)	20,000	.031	35	.22	4,400	550	3.41	68,200	290	1.80	36,000
13						$3,011,100			$3,418,600			$2,694,400

TABLE 14–5: Determination of Least-Cost Location Based on Transportation Factors[a] for Comclean Corporation

(1) Product	(2) Amount Moved to or from (hundredweight)	(3) Transportation Cost per Distance Unit (5 miles) per Hundredweight	(4) Location Cost Factor	Location		Determination of Optimum Location	
				(5) Grid Row Number	(6) Grid Column Number	(7) Grid Row Weight	(8) Grid Column Weight
Sawdust (Pittsfield)	620,000	$.025	$15,500	3	3	$ 46,500	$ 46,500
Chemicals (Wilmington)	155,000	.075	11,625	6	4	69,750	46,500
Comclean							
(Chicago)	100,000	.031	3,100	5	13	15,500	40,300
(Indianapolis)	20,000	.031	620	7	11	4,340	6,820
(Detroit)	80,000	.031	2,480	4	10	9,920	24,800
(Cleveland)	80,000	.031	2,480	5	8	12,400	19,840
(Nashville)	10,000	.031	310	10	12	3,100	3,720
(Richmond)	40,000	.031	1,240	8	5	9,920	6,200
(Charleston)	10,000	.031	310	13	6	4,030	1,860
(Pittsburgh)	60,000	.031	1,860	6	7	11,160	13,020
(New York)	200,000	.031	6,200	4	3	24,800	18,600
(Hartford)	20,000	.031	620	3	2	1,860	1,240
			$46,345			$213,280	$229,400

[a]Calculations have been rounded.

The center-of-gravity method does not reflect significant differences between straight-line distances and actual practical distances, for example, around bodies of water where land transportation methods are assumed.

The cost per unit of distance to ship freight to and from a point is sometimes an elusive figure. Frequently, multiproduct and multiquantity shipments move at different transportation rates. This may require either detailed analysis of the costs of shipment components or accurate averaging of costs among segments of shipments that are "pooled" together for movement purposes.

Further, the "optimum" location may turn out to be in Central Park on Manhattan Island, smack dab in the middle of Lake Michigan, or on top of Pike's Peak. These are not very good warehouse locations. Some adjustment will have to be made.

Practical Use These limitations suggest that calculating a center-of-gravity location is only a *starting point*. Additional adjustments may be required to produce a useful final result. The following questions should be asked to evaluate the initial results obtained from the use of this technique.

1. Does the computed result place the optimum point relatively near, say within fifty miles of, a major supplier or market? A slight adjustment of location to the nearby market or source might eliminate many local transportation costs without increasing long-distance costs.

2. Can an adjustment of the outcome be made that would place the general location in one transportation rate territory as opposed to another? Such action might provide favorable rates either into or out of the location.

3. Are alternative sources of raw materials or components available that would influence logistics system adjustment?

4. Would transportation rate negotiation under the implied threat of relocation restore the attractiveness of an old location? Equalization is a term used to refer to the efforts of carriers to retain freight business even in the face of geographic handicaps by providing rates to or from a production point that would allow it to remain competitive with others in commonly served markets.

5. What is the nature of freight movement into and out of the proposed location? Is it served by several modes? Is volume sufficient to generate a balanced directional movement and favorable rates? Can the firm take advantage of an existing light backhaul situation that corresponds to the direction of heavy movement of its products or the products of suppliers?

6. What is the trend of directional growth of the company's markets? Sales trends may be used to justify a location that is less than optimum under *current* sales conditions.

Multiple Inventory Location Problem Various means of extending center-of-gravity approaches for the simultaneous location of two or more stocks of inventory, or even the location of the second inventory when one is fixed, involve a definition of the territory to be served from each inventory location. As such, they represent simple extensions of the single inventory location problem. They are of limited use in any case where the definition of the territory to be served from each location is not clear and is highly interdependent with the computed locations themselves.

The analysis of multiple inventory locations, whether to determine plants to be served from alternative raw material sources, distribution centers to be served from alternative plants, or customers to be served from alternative distribution centers, often requires more powerful optimizing techniques than the center-of-gravity approach. From those available, we have selected three greatly different ones representing the spectrum of modeling techniques available, the Bowman-Stewart model, linear programming, and dynamic programming. Although enough of each techniques is explained to allow you to evaluate their appropriate uses, please keep in mind that, unlike the center-of-gravity approach, these techniques can be solved in practical situations only by using complex computerized models. Thus, there is little value in "learning" manual solution procedures for them.

Bowman-Stewart Formulation[21] One of the most straightforward formulations of the multiple-facility location problem utilizes a mathematical model based upon the underlying concept illustrated in Figure 14–11. This model assumes that in the case of an increasing area of coverage from a given inventory location, if volume of business per unit of area (concentration of demand) is constant: (1) the warehousing cost per unit will decrease and (2) the delivery cost per unit will increase.

Factors such as the rates of warehouse labor, insurance, and other costs at different locations are assumed to be equal. However, one important influence on costs to taken into account: whether service from a given supply point involved intrafacility transportation costs, such as from a plant warehouse to a distribution warehouse. This latter feature of the overall approach forms the second of the two major components of the model because it allows a

---

FIGURE 14–11: Factors influencing the total cost to supply an area from a given location

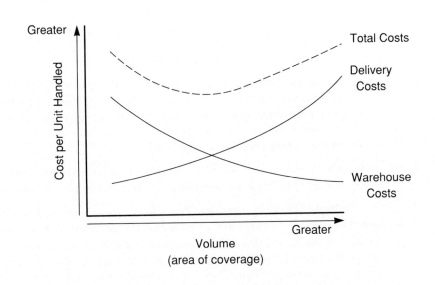

determination of areas to be served directly from plant locations as well as through distribution warehouses.

It is assumed that certain costs (associated with warehousing and material handling) vary inversely with volume, that other costs (associated with delivery) vary directly with the square root of the area served, and that other costs do not vary with changes in either volume or area. The assumption regarding delivery costs is based on the geometric principle that radius and diameter vary with the square root of the area of a circle. This allows the following mathematical expression of total costs to serve an area through a distribution warehouse:

$$C = a + \frac{b}{V} \quad c\sqrt{A},$$

where:

C = Cost (within the warehouse district) per dollar's worth of goods distributed, the measure of effectiveness

V = Volume of goods, in dollars, handled by the warehouse per unit of time

A = Area in square miles served by the warehouse

a = Cost per dollar's worth of goods distributed independent of either the warehouse's volume handled or area served

b = "Fixed" costs for the warehouse per unit of time, which, when divided by the volume, will yield the appropriate cost per dollar's worth distributed

c = The cost of the distribution that varies with the square root of the area; that is, costs associated with miles covered within the warehouse district such as gasoline, truck repairs, driver hours, and others

Next, actual data (representing C, V, and A above) for each existing warehouse in the system under analysis are determined. By the statistical method of least-squares multiple regression it is possible to use past experience to determine mathematically the values of the coefficients or parameters (a, b, and c) that make the model the closest predictor of the actual cost for all present warehouses using their individual volume and area figures.

Once determined, the coefficients a, b, and c are introduced into the formula. Actual values of V and A for each warehouse are substituted in the formula, a theoretical C is compared to the actual level of total costs at each location, and the correlation of the theoretical and actual costs is measured to determine the validity of the model thus developed.

In order to use the cost predictor, or model, as a tool of analysis to determine the most efficient location for units in a system, it is necessary to solve the model equation for A, the area to be served from any possible location. To do this, the density of sales per area (K) is expressed as $K = V/A$. It easily can be determined for each portion of the market area. Therefore, $V = KA$, and this quantity can then be substituted in the original model for V, giving:

$$C = a + \frac{b}{KA} \quad c\sqrt{A}$$

Differentiation[22] then yields a general expression that provides an optimum A for any b cost characteristic, c cost characteristic, or K density of sales:

$$A = \frac{2b}{cK}$$

Once A is determined, the distance from a branch warehouse to the boundary of its territory is computed by the formula for the radius of a circle:

$$r = \sqrt{A/\pi} \text{ (or 3.14)}$$

From time to time, many of the cost relationships and the relative densities of sales change under realistic conditions. Using existing facilities as a starting point, two or more distribution centers can be relocated simultaneously to reflect changing conditions. The degree of accuracy of the coefficients a, b, and c reflect the extent to which an optimum set of locations might be found, assuming new locations follow the same cost patterns as old.

Further, the Bowman-Stewart formulation can be expanded to reflect emphasis on customer service, measured by the distance (in miles or time) of supply points from customers. This can be accomplished by using unrealistically high values for transportation costs (coefficient c) in areas where customer service is extremely important. It would be applicable particularly where large distances or transit times characterize relationships between existing supply points in a firm's logistics system, or where a firm's marketing territory covers a wide geographic region.

Linear Programming   Linear programming is an approach to problems that assumes that the most important relationships are exactly or approximately linear in nature. For example, the most common assumption in a shipping-point allocation problem is that the transportation costs are linear in relation to volume, for example, that it costs twice as much to transport two items as to transport one. It is important to keep this assumption in mind because it imposes important limitations on the ultimate solution it provides.

Basic methods of linear programming are the distribution (transportation problem) and algebraic simplex methods. Each can be applied to problems of different structure and magnitude in logistics and other areas of management. A description of these methods can be found in any standard text in the Operations Research/Operations Management field. The distribution method is highly appropriate for use in dealing with inventory location problems.

An Appraisal of Linear Programming   Linear programming provides as many pitfalls as opportunities. Therefore, its use should be appraised in terms of the problem to be solved.

A major advantage of the technique is that it provides the framework for the systematic appraisal of many alternatives. When conditions are appropriate, linear programming methods can provide rather accurate solutions in a minimum amount of time. Because they involve repetitive calculations, computers readily can be put to the task of solving them.

On the other hand, solutions obtained by means of linear programming must be adjusted to take into account actual conditions and existing limitations. Reciprocal purchasing policies may require the allocation of purchases to vendor locations in a manner other than that indicated by formal analysis, for example.

Of course, the greatest limitation of the technique is its assumption of linearity in costs. Linear programming solutions do not take into account economies of scale. Costs are rarely linear in an exact sense of the term. Quantity discounts introduce nonlinearity into the average price per unit. Fixed costs of operating a vehicle create costs that are nonlinear with varying distances and quantities to be transported. Costs of tooling up add fixed elements to manufacturing activities that destroy their cost linearity.

Three basic approaches have been taken to cope with this limitation of linear programming. First, cost curves have been examined to determine whether they approximate linearity over certain segments. In the diagram in Figure 14–12, for example, per-unit costs of transportation approximate linearity over limited segments of the cost curve, namely AB, CD, and EF, representing ranges of volume shipped, A_1B_1, C_1D_1, and E_1F_1. Techniques discussed here would be accurate in appraising only those situations in which the range of load sizes was relatively small.

Second, nonlinear programming techniques have been developed that attempt to describe nonlinear cost functions by specially fitted equations. Because this approach requires lengthy presentation and involves advanced mathematics, it will not be discussed here.

Dynamic Programming Location decisions made today can influence the future logistics performance of the firm for years to come. Changing conditions warrant changing inventory location patterns. Less-than-optimal current locations may produce good long-term

---

FIGURE 14–12: Ranges of volume within which linearity is approximated in a typical cost curve

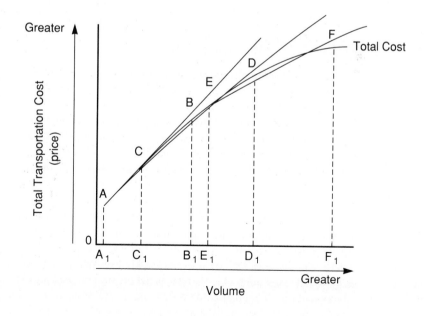

economic results. But *when* should locations be altered for optimum benefit? A technique for dealing with this problem of change over time is dynamic programming.

Dynamic programming has been implemented by only a limited number of organizations in logistics system planning. Possible reasons for this are (1) the lack of trust that managers are willing to place in long-range forecasts; (2) management perceptions of prohibitively high costs of relocation, precluding significant results from dynamic programming; and (3) an unwillingness to live with the assumptions that the proper set of alternative locations can be identified today for, say, a ten-to-fifteen-year or longer period in the future, or that one set of alternatives will remain independent of other actual or potential locations for the time frame of the projection. The concept is intriguing, but for the reasons mentioned it remains just that.[23]

SIMULATION TECHNIQUES

General Approach

Simulation can be viewed as the "counting up" of costs or profits resulting from a specified action. The comparison of results from successive trials leads to a selection of a good strategy in the simulation approach to a problem. The potential for the use of simulation in determining inventory locations has been enhanced in recent years by the development of distance estimating techniques, transport cost regressions related to distance, and other techniques for estimating costs from information about volumes of activity. Nevertheless, unless the brute force of the computer can be combined with the cunning of the human mind, simulation can be a time-consuming and expensive method of determining desirable location strategies. A further refinement of the general simulation approach, called heuristic programming, has raised the probability that the high promise of simulation for location analyses will be realized.

Heuristic Programming

Methods of simulation have been formulated to (1) allow the paper operation of a logistics system utilizing many different possible warehouse combinations or (2) duplicate the human mental process by programming an electronic computer in such a way that it uses, holds in reserve, or discards possible warehouse locations. The latter has been termed "heuristic" programming in that it (1) attempts to eliminate unnecessary or costly search and analysis, (2) reduces a problem to manageable proportions, (3) places emphasis on *working toward* optimum solution procedures rather than ever elusive optimum solutions themselves, and (4) closely parallels the thought process likely to be followed by the human mind in viewing the problem.

In their approach to the problem of warehouse location, Kuehn and Hamburger introduced three assumptions that would reduce the size of the (heuristic) problem: (1) locations with promise will be at or near concentrations of demand; (2) near-optimum warehousing systems can be developed by locating warehouses one at a time, adding at each stage of the analysis that warehouse which produces the greatest cost savings for the entire system; and (3) only a small subset of all possible warehouse locations need be evaluated in detail at each stage of the analysis to determine the next warehouse site to be added.[24] The flow diagram explaining information inputs and analytical instructions programmed into the computer is shown in Figure 14–13.

FIGURE 14–13: Flow diagram of a heuristic computer program for warehouse location

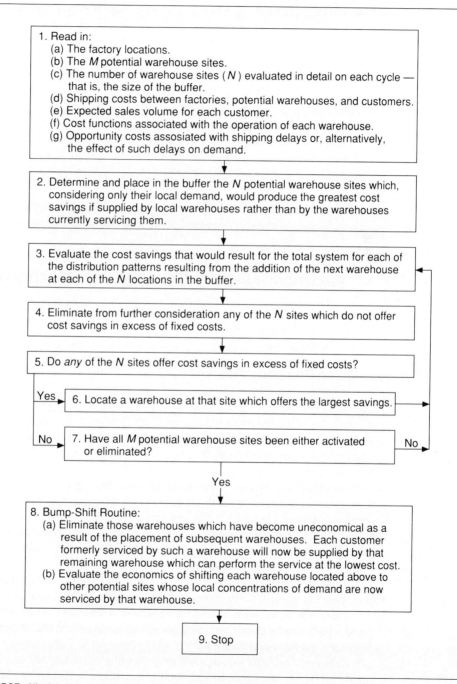

1. Read in:
   (a) The factory locations.
   (b) The *M* potential warehouse sites.
   (c) The number of warehouse sites (*N*) evaluated in detail on each cycle — that is, the size of the buffer.
   (d) Shipping costs between factories, potential warehouses, and customers.
   (e) Expected sales volume for each customer.
   (f) Cost functions associated with the operation of each warehouse.
   (g) Opportunity costs assosiated with shipping delays or, alternatively, the effect of such delays on demand.

2. Determine and place in the buffer the *N* potential warehouse sites which, considering only their local demand, would produce the greatest cost savings if supplied by local warehouses rather than by the warehouses currently servicing them.

3. Evaluate the cost savings that would result for the total system for each of the distribution patterns resulting from the addition of the next warehouse at each of the *N* locations in the buffer.

4. Eliminate from further consideration any of the *N* sites which do not offer cost savings in excess of fixed costs.

5. Do *any* of the *N* sites offer cost savings in excess of fixed costs?

Yes → 6. Locate a warehouse at that site which offers the largest savings.

No → 7. Have all *M* potential warehouse sites been either activated or eliminated? → No

Yes

8. Bump-Shift Routine:
   (a) Eliminate those warehouses which have become uneconomical as a result of the placement of subsequent warehouses. Each customer formerly serviced by such a warehouse will now be supplied by that remaining warehouse which can perform the service at the lowest cost.
   (b) Evaluate the economics of shifting each warehouse located above to other potential sites whose local concentrations of demand are now serviced by that warehouse.

9. Stop

SOURCE: Alfred A. Kuehn and Michael J. Hamburger, "A Heuristic Program for Locating Warehouses," *Management Science* (July, 1963) 647.

Microlocation and Site Selection Factors

Obviously it is not enough to conclude that a warehouse or distribution center should be located in Dallas, Detroit, or Denver. These are large metropolitan areas that will likely have been selected using market-serving criteria. Having arrived at the macrolocation decision, the task remains to select the best site possible. The process of site selection should be carried out in a careful and structured manner, taking into account all relevant factors. This is what Ackerman calls "The Final Selection Process."[25] He goes on to point out:

> Because site selection is one of the most important decisions the average distribution executive ever makes, the process of dealing with the decision cannot be discussed too often. Other distribution decisions are correctable, but a poor site for a warehouse site is a decision that, while not irreversible, is often very costly to correct. For this reason, finding the proper location for your new warehouse is one of the most challenging of decisions.[26]

The structured and systematic analysis of the relevant site selection factors is best handled using a checklist of the sort contained in the appendix to this chapter.

PRACTICAL ASPECTS OF INVENTORY LOCATION STRATEGY

Having reviewed theoretical techniques for analyzing inventory location opportunities, we turn next to several of the more practical aspects of such analyses.

Dependence on Company Policy

An inventory location decision is affected by company policy. For example, a warehouse that is owned must be sold, rented, or abandoned if a change in the logistics system eliminates the need for that facility. It is usually much easier to find a buyer or renter if a warehouse is a general-purpose facility and is located in an area of industrial and commercial concentration.

The possibility of leasing inventory facilities often presents itself to the company. The favorability of the lease from the standpoint of the lessee (such as length of lease, release penalty, and so on), however, will often vary directly with the favorability of the location, the all-purpose or specialized nature of the construction of the facility, and other factors. And, some firms may require facilities — particularly specialized facilities — that cannot be leased simply because they are not available.

Another possibility is to use public warehousing facilities. They provide space that can be rented on a short-term basis under arrangements that can be terminated on short notice.

There may be instances when, for reasons of advertising value, public relations, or service to a particular customer, it is determined by management that the company *will* stage an inventory in a particular location.

Unhappily in some cases, policies regarding customer service standards based primarily on factors other than logistics must, nevertheless, be met by a logistics system. Customer service policy serves as the greatest single determinant of the number and location of inventories.

Area of Analytic Freedom

Further constraints on solutions to inventory location problems are presented by four additional problems resulting from any proposal to relocate an inventory.

The Effect on People A move that would require the employees of the company to move their homes or find employment elsewhere will cause certain difficulties, including, but not limited to, expense. Under many circumstances there may be union-management industrial relations problems, and moves inevitably cause human relations problems. However, there are cases where a move may be precipitated by union problems. One firm consolidated two inventories at a third location in the Southwest several years ago; the decision to relocate was prompted by the desire to invalidate existing seniority ratings for union warehouse workers at the two old locations.

The Value of Being Known In addition to the public relations values of having a company operate a facility in a locality, there are important sales and promotion considerations. Customers may become familiar with an inventory location and may be satisfied and accustomed to doing business with the firm there. Further, transportation arrangements may have become stabilized, and carriers may have so adjusted their local operations as to give very good service to a particular existing location. A move to another location may well require repeating the process of getting one's operations smoothly integrated with the operations of servicing agencies (carriers) and customers, all this with an interim loss of efficiency and customer service.

Moving Costs Whenever a move is recommended and carried out, there are, in addition to the intangible costs already mentioned, certain ascertainable costs of making the move to a new location. Probably some inventory stock will have to be transferred along with office equipment, supplies, and warehouse equipment. Employees' moving expenses may also be incurred, depending on the firm's policy in this regard.

Justification of Past Decisions Costs of changes in the configuration of a logistics system must be justified to senior officers of the firm. Often some very hard questions may be asked: "Only a short while ago you decided we should relocate facilities. Now you say we should relocate them again. Why should we assume that your present decision is any better than your earlier one? Won't we just have to move again in a year or two? Aren't these moves costing us more than the operational savings you claim they will give the firm?"

A location change may be in order for one or more of the company's inventory sites, but its advocate must be prepared to defend his or her recommendation against strong counterarguments.

Centralized versus Decentralized Inventories

The long-debated question of centralized or decentralized inventory locations has not stemmed the flow of executive decisions in favor of each policy. Factors tending to favor one policy or the other change from one point in time to the next, as suggested in the enumeration of benefits of each policy presented in Table 14–6. Since World War II, the development of the Interstate Highway System and air freight services in the United States, for example, has led many firms to consolidate inventories at fewer locations without significantly reducing their customer service standards.

TABLE 14–6: Benefits of Centralized and Decentralized Inventory Location Strategies, and Determinants of Their Importance

Centralized, Consolidated Location Strategy:	Varying Directly with:
Reduction of plant-to-warehouse transport costs	*Proportion of former shipments of LTL size*
Reduction of cross-hauling of goods between warehouses	*Ineffectiveness of inventory control procedures*
Reduction of safety and dead stocks per unit of throughput	*Importance of safety and dead stocks for specific SKULs*
Creation of critical mass of business, attractive to first-class public warehouse operators	*Volume of throughput, inventory turnover*
Greater opportunity for use of private warehousing through creation of large, constant volume	*Volume, regularity of throughput*
More frequent inventory replenishment, further reducing safety stocks, and inventory program response time	*Amount of change in the volume of throughput*
Opportunity for better warehouse management, control	*Size of operation*
Improvement of in-stock position in filling customer orders	*Degree of SKUL consolidation*
Improved transportation service for beyond-warehouse distribution	*Importance of revenues to carrier*
Elimination of duplicated effort in order picking, handling	*Degree to which private warehousing is used*
Decentralized, Market-Oriented Location Strategy:	**Varying Directly with:**
Stimulation of sales	*Need of customers for proximity to stocks*
Reduction of warehouse-to-customer transport costs	*Cost of transportation variable with distance*
Greater opportunity for use of public warehousing, creating larger proportion of costs variable with volume	*Availability of, and company policies toward, public warehousing; nature of product*
Improvement in order-cycle response time for customers	*Degree to which overall transport service times are variable with distance*
Greater sales, assuming high in-stock rates	*Degree to which rapid product availability is necessary for, and substitution is practiced by, customers*

Increasing Time Pressures Affecting Location Decisions

Historically, distance and time factors involved in location decisions tended not to place excessive emphasis on speed of delivery. Dependability was enough. However, as customer demands for quick delivery of orders have increased in response to competitive market pressures, the time factor has taken on new importance as an element of the logistics location strategy.

Just-in-Time As noted in Chapter 11, "Warehousing Management," many customers are now requiring vendors to supply them on a Just-in-Time basis. This has required either the use of premium transportation, a "pipeline" of goods moving to the customer, or the warehousing of goods in close proximity to customer locations. With few exceptions, premium transportation is not a viable economic alternative for the delivery of significant quantities of goods. The "pipeline" technique — having a number of shipments in transit simultaneously — is one solution to the problem. The other solution is to locate the supplier's warehouse or storage point close to the customer's receiving point.

Premium High-Speed Delivery The development of premium high-speed delivery services such as Federal Express, DHL, UPS Air, and airline express services* has made it possible for suppliers to centralize inventories of items having one or more of the following characteristics, *provided the customer is willing to pay the cost of premium transportation*:

High value items able to bear premium transportation costs,

Items relatively low in weight,

Small items,

Slow-moving items.

The supplier can advise customers that such items are available within 24 hours for delivery anywhere in the United States. However, the use of high-speed, high-cost delivery services is not practical in the case of items such as large and heavy repair parts for heavy equipment unless the customer has a truly critical need for the item and is willing to pay a premium transportation charge to get it delivered the same or next day.

The Caterpillar Example One of the bases of success of the Caterpillar Corporation was an early strategic commitment to dispersing inventories of repair and replacement parts for its equipment at numerous locations so that the company could guarantee its customers 24-hour delivery service of such items. It was necessary for Caterpillar to adopt such a policy because of the intense pressure on its customers (mostly construction contractors) to complete projects

---

*Many airlines offer an express service whereby one goes in person to the airline counter to send the package on the airline's next flight. The recipient goes to the baggage service counter of the airline at the destination city and picks up the package about thirty minutes after the flight arrives. This is the fastest mode of freight transportation available, but it is limited to city pairs served by airlines offering such express service; interlining two or more airlines would be possible only if the matter were handled in person by the shipper's or the receiver's personal agent at the interline city.

on contractual schedules that frequently include penalty clauses for delayed completion. Caterpillar still is required to use high-speed, high-cost delivery services at times, but they have been able to avoid using them for the most part.

Dual or Multiple Distribution Systems

In firms with a wide range of products of different types, both centralization and decentralization of certain inventories may be appropriate. There is a growing trend toward this type of location strategy, which can be referred to as the use of a "dual" or "multiple" distribution system.

Fast-selling items in an inventory achieve higher turnover rates than items with slower rates of sale. One way to deal with the problem of slow sellers where it is not desirable to reduce inventory coverage for SKU groupings is to consolidate inventories for SKU groupings with lower rates of sale, expanding sales per SKU by extending the geographic territory served by a given SKU inventory, thereby increasing the inventory turn rate for these slow sellers.

A second factor supporting multiple distribution patterns is that shipper surveys have repeatedly indicated a higher shipper priority on dependability of service as opposed to speed of service. Such dependability is most feasible in a system that provides uniformly high inventory coverage for all SKUs at some geographic location known to salesmen, other employees, and perhaps customers.

Third, there is a widely held (but largely undocumented) belief that customers have lower expectations for order-cycle times for SKUs with lower rates of sale, typically "nonstandard" items, than for other SKUs. At the same time, they value dependable information about availability and shipment dates for all SKUs. Multiple distribution systems can take advantage of the former belief while meeting the latter need.

Finally, multiple distribution systems emphasize the centralization consolidation of certain SKU groupings, not the closing or opening of warehouse or plant inventories. As such, they may represent a smaller shock to the top management psyche and a smaller commitment and risk to their proponents.

SUMMARY

The theoretical foundations for the development of location strategies were provided by economic geographers, beginning with Von Thünen in the nineteenth Century. Von Thünen's work concentrated on an analysis of the types of crops produced on land located varying distances from markets and the ability of the crops to bear varying levels of transportation costs. Weber's work concentrated on the effects of production and transportation costs on the size and shape of the market in which a producing firm might price its products competitively. Hoover embellished the work of his predecessors by reflecting in his analysis the tapered nature of many transportation rate structures. One of the more practical adaptations of this theory was Reilly's effort to define the boundaries of retail trading areas by assuming that a retailing center's size determines the gravitational pull that it has on customers in relation to other retailing centers at which they might shop.

Among current trends influencing actual inventory location decisions today in the United States are significant continuing shifts of population and economic activity to the West Coast and the so-called Sun Belt regions. This has led to considerable regional self-sufficiency through the development of a market base sufficiently large to support manufacturing and distribution facility locations. The development of a postindustrial society has been accompanied by a relative decline in importance of manufacturing as opposed to service-oriented activities, influencing to a degree the nature of freight moving throughout the economy. And finally, the development of a more extensive infrastructure in the form of the Interstate Highway System and the wide availability of air freight services has allowed many firms to expand the area served from an inventory location.

Although logistics is only one of several factors taken into account in a location decision, for some products it can be most important. Logistics-oriented location techniques include optimization and simulation. Among the former is the center-of-gravity approach to the location of a single inventory, a technique that reflects directly the theoretical roots of Weber's work. Of the various approaches to the problem of locating two or more inventories simultaneously, linear programming is perhaps the most widely used. By means of a computer, it can take into account costs of production, warehousing, and transportation in determining lowest cost facility location patterns. Assumptions of linearity in costs can be modified by the careful structuring of problem analyses to reflect real world conditions as closely as possible.

While optimizing techniques search for the one best answer under somewhat restrictive assumptions, simulation produces good (but not necessarily the best) answers while often more accurately portraying the problem.

In practice, inventory location strategy may depend on matters of company policy toward the leasing or ownership of facilities, the relative emphasis placed on customer service, and the influence of inventory location on sales results. In addition, location decisions will be influenced by their effect on people, moving costs, and the context provided by past location decisions. The results produced by a logistics-oriented location model have to be evaluated and adjusted in the light of these considerations.

A number of forces in recent years have led to a trend toward the centralization of high-value and slow-selling inventory items. Chief among these forces has been the development of premium transportation, which permits 24-hour delivery provided the customer is willing to bear the cost. At the same time, stocks of more popular items have been held near concentrations of demand to meet customers' expectations for prompt service. This has led to the development of multiple inventory location strategies based on the characteristics of particular products, levels of demand for them, and expectations for customer service (such as just-in-time) associated with each.

There is no proven way of selecting the best inventory location technique for each situation. In this regard, it is important to keep in mind that *almost any systematic, organized approach to the analysis of a location problem is better than none*. In the final analysis, what counts is the degree of cost and service improvement offered by the application of a particular approach or technique.

DISCUSSION QUESTIONS

1. Why has the complexity of inventory location problems increased in recent years?

2. What are some examples of pure materials, weight-losing materials, and ubiquitous materials, other than those mentioned in the text?

3. What does the term "bulk gaining" mean? What significance does it have for location of processing plants?

4. How would you explain the location of major garment industry centers in New York and Los Angeles?

5. What is the effect of transit privileges on location?

6. How does the transportation rate tapering principle affect location?

7. How are market boundaries determined?

8. What is the relationship between blanket transportation rates and location?

9. How might a decrease in transportation costs increase a firm's market area?

10. Explain the concepts of primary, secondary, and tertiary trading areas.

11. What accounts for the relatively greater rates of population and economic growth in the Sun Belt states?

12. What are the consequences of the growing degree of economic regional self-sufficiency in the United States?

13. What has been the effect on inventory location decisions of increased levels of customer service?

14. Under what circumstances will a logistics manager in a firm have a major role in a location decision?

15. What are the limitations of the center-of-gravity technique?

16. What would a logistics manager hope to accomplish by use of the Bowman-Stewart Formulation?

17. What are the advantages and disadvantages of applying the technique of linear programming to location problems?

18. Why are managements reluctant to use dynamic programming as a technique for making location decisions?

19. What assumptions underlie the Kuehn-Hamburger heuristic approach to warehouse location? Why are they helpful?

20. What factors tend to cause a firm's management *not* to change a location?

21. What is the relationship between centralized versus decentralized inventory locations and dual distribution systems?

SUGGESTED READINGS

References for location theory and practice are a mix of classic theoretical works in the field, more recent theoretical and analytical treatments, and work that is largely applications-oriented. The references listed below are presented in the order just mentioned, but it should be noted that there is some overlap among these three groups of references.

Classic Theoretical Works

GREENHUT, MELVIN L., *Plant Location in Theory and Practice*. Chapel Hill, North Carolina: University of North Carolina Press, 1956. For a summary and integration of leading theories of plant location, see pages 3–100, for a further development of a general theory, see pages 251–291.

HOOVER, EDGAR M., *The Location of Economic Activity*. New York: McGraw-Hill Book Company, Inc., 1948. Offers one of the most sound and readable developments of modern-day work in the field of location theory, relating the theory to trends and growing problems apparent to the author at that time. See especially pages 27–115 and pages 145–212.

LÖSCH, AUGUST, *The Economics of Location*. New Haven: Yale University Press, 1954. Translated by William H. Woglom with the assistance of Wolfgang F. Stolper from the second revised edition, Jena, Germany: Gustav Fischer Verlag, 1944. A fine example of scientifically conducted research in location theory. Lösch's ingenious studies are based in large degree on information collected in the United States. That portion of his theory for which he is best noted is found on pages 103–137.

VON THÜNEN, JOHANN HEINRICH, *Der Isolierte Staat in Beziehung auf Landwirtschaft und Nationalökonomie*, 3d ed., Berlin: Schumacher-Zarchlin, 1875. This is the earliest formal work in the field of location theory bearing directly on the influence of transportation on location.

WEBER, ALFRED, *Über den Standort der Industrien*, Part I, ''Reine Theorie des Standort,'' Tübingen, Germany, 1909. Edited and translated by C. J. Friedrich as *Alfred Weber's Theory of Location of Industries*, Chicago: University of Chicago Press, 1958. Considered by many to be the most important early work in the field.

SAMPSON, ROY J., MARTIN T. FARRIS, and DAVID L. SCHROCK, *Domestic Transportation: Practice, Theory and Policy*, 6th ed., Boston: Houghton Mifflin Company, 1990. Included here because Chapter 19 of this text presents an excellent summary of the work of location theorists from Von Thünen to the present, and the bibliography at the end of the chapter is excellent.

Theoretical and Analytical Works

BECKMAN, MARTIN, *Location Theory*. New York: Random House, Inc., 1968. This lucid little book deals with most aspects of location theory covered in this chapter and offers mathematical explanations for these phenomena. Of particular interest is a final chapter reviewing the locational effects of economic growth.

BROWN, ROBERT G., *Decision Rules for Inventory Management*. New York: Holt, Rinehart and Winston, 1967. This offers one of the few descriptions of practical techniques for developing inventory location strategies.

ISARD, WALTER, *Location and Space-Economy*. New York: John Wiley & Sons, Inc., 1956. A classic work in the field, this book offers an approach to general location theory utilizing principles of econometrics that represent the greatest promise for future work in the field (and upon which subsequent methods and projects of regional analysis have been developed by Isard).

SMITH, DAVID M., *Industrial Location*, 2d ed. New York: John Wiley & Sons, Inc., 1981. A comprehensive synthesis of the contributions of economic geographers and economists to industrial location problems, this book also offers an extensive discussion of empirical applications of theory in Part Three.

Applications-Oriented Works

ACKERMAN, KENNETH B., *Practical Handbook of Warehousing*, 2d ed., Washington, D.C.: The Traffic Service Corporation, 1986. Chapter 12, ''Finding the Right Location,'' provides a concise treatment of the microlocation process.

COOPER, MARTHA C., "Freight Consolidation and Warehouse Location Strategies in Physical Distribution Systems," *Journal of Business Logistics*, 4, no. 2 (1983): 53–74.

"Distribution & Site Location Decisions," *Distribution*, 86, no. 9 (September 1987): 24–30.

MIX, HANK, "Hints on How to Move a Distribution Center," *Industrial Engineering*, 20, no. 5 (May 1988): 32–36.

PERL, JOSSEF, and MARK S. DASKIN, "A Unified Warehouse Location-Routing Methodology," *Journal of Business Logistics*, 5, no. 1 (1984): 92–111.

ROSENFIELD, DONALD B., "The Retailer Facility Site Location Problem," *Journal of Business Logistics*, 8, no. 2 (1987): 95–114.

SCHMENNER, ROGER W., *Making Business Location Decisions*. Englewood Cliffs, N.J.: Prentice-Hall, 1982. A straightforward treatment of the subject.

SODERMAN, STEN, *Industrial Location Planning*. Stockholm: Almqvist & Wiksell International, 1975. Subtitled "An empirical investigation of company approaches to the problem of locating new plants," this book offers a number of case studies drawn from European industrial experience.

ENDNOTES

1. Johann Heinrich von Thünen, *Der Isolierte Staat in Beziechung auf Landwirtschaft und Nationalökonomie*, 3d ed. (Berlin: Schumacher-Zarchlin, 1875), English edition available entitled *Von Thünen's Isolated State*, translated by C. M. Wartenburg and edited by Peter Hall (Oxford: Pergamon Press, 1966).

2. *Ibid.*, 37.

3. Alfred Weber, *Über den Standort der Industrien*, translated by C. J. Friedrich as *Alfred Weber's Theory of the Location of Industries* (Chicago: University of Chicago Press, 1958).

4. *Ibid.*, 61.

5. Edgar M. Hoover, *The Location of Economic Activity* (New York: McGraw-Hill Book Co., 1948): 26–66.

6. For a mathematical determination of the point of least transportation costs, see Friedrich, pages 227–240. Regional scientists generally regard Weber's solution as misleadingly simple and of limited value in actual problems.

7. A full description of a method for determining nonoverlapping market areas is found in C. D. Hyson and W. P. Hyson, "The Economic Law of Market Areas," *Quarterly Journal of Economics* (May 1950): 319–324.

8. William J. Reilly, *The Law of Retail Gravitation* (New York: The Knickerbocker Press, 1931): 9.

9. Paul D. Converse, Harvey W. Huegy, and Robert V. Mitchell, *Elements of Marketing*, 6th ed. (Englewood Cliffs, N.J.: Prentice-Hall, Inc., 1958): 29–30.

10. For a description of this work see William J. Reilly, *Methods for the Study of Retail Relationships* (Austin: University of Texas, 1929).

11. See David L. Huff, "A Probabilistic Analysis of Consumer Spatial Behavior," in William S. Decker, ed., *Emerging Concepts in Marketing* (Chicago: American Marketing Association, 1963): 443–461.

12. Hoover, *Economic Activity*, 148–151.

13. The clearest evidence of this is the decline (adjusted for both population increases and rate level increases) in the volume of interstate LTL freight movements since World War II.

14. The assumption that basic industry location in this country has been tied to raw material sources might well be more closely examined. There is a great deal of evidence, for example, that even an industry such as the iron and steel industry has always been "market" oriented to the extent that its production facilities have located at points strategic to markets that also offered one or more of the raw materials necessary for steel production. As more desirable raw material sites are exhausted, the locations of producing sites for basic industry are following the market, not the raw material sources.

15. Benjamin Chinitz and Raymond Vernon, "Changing Forces in Industrial Location," *Harvard Business Review* (January-February 1960): 130. Several reasons might be advanced for this trend: (1) the increasing technology, and resulting increasing number of processes requiring plant sites, needed to produce more complex products, and (2) the lessened raw material source "pull" exerted by some of the richest mineral deposits, now largely depleted.

16. Employment statistics instead of income statistics are used to show long-run trends because of the absence of detailed figures for income on a national level before 1920.

17. The dollar-weight factor is the ratio of dollar value to a given amount of weight for any product.

18. The most comprehensive information available on this question, supplied by the *Census of Transportation*, provides little indication of trend.

19. See Appendix D in *Techniques of Plant Location*, Studies in Business Policy No. 61 (New York: National Industrial Conference Board, 1953): 43–48.

20. This bias can be dealt with mathematically. For one example approach, see Robert B. Breitenbach, "A Computer Algorithm for Refining Grid Location Analysis," *Logistics and Transportation Review*, 12, no. 3 (1976): 154–169.

21. Portions of this section are reprinted from Edward H. Bowman and John B. Stewart, "A Model for Scale of Operations," *Journal of Marketing*, 20 (January 1956): 242–247.

22. The expression for differentiation is:

$$\frac{dC}{dA} = -\frac{b}{kA^2} + \frac{c}{2A} = 0$$

The technique is explained in any standard text for the calculus.

23. An exception may occur when a future event can be predicted with a high degree of certainty, for example, exhaustion of a mineral deposit at a particular location within a certain time frame.

24. Alfred A. Kuehn and Michael J. Hamburger, "A Heuristic Program for Locating Warehouses," *Management Science* (July 1963): 643–666.

25. Ackerman, Kenneth B., *Practical Handbook of Warehousing*, 2d ed. (Washington, D.C.: The Traffic Service Corporation, 1986): 130.

26. *Ibid*. 131.

APPENDIX
SITE ANALYSIS CHECKLIST

General Information

1. Site location (city, county, state):

2. Legal description of site:

3. Total Acreage: Approximate cost per acre:
   Approximate dimensions of site:

4. Owner(s) of site (give names and addresses):

Zoning

1. Current: Proposed: Master plan: Anticipated:
   Is proposed use allowed? ___ yes ___ no

2. Check which, if any, is required:
   ___ rezoning ___ variance ___ special exception
   Indicate: Approximate cost   Time required:
   Probability of success:
   ___ excellent ___ good ___ fair ___ poor

3. Applicable zoning regulations (attach copy):
   Parking/loading regulations: Open space requirements:
   Office portion: Maximum building allowed:
   Whse./DC portion: Percent of lot occupancy allowed
   Other: Setbacks, if required:
   Height restrictions: Noise limits: Odor limits:
   Are neighboring uses compatible with proposed use?
   ___ yes ___ no

4. Can a clear title be secured? ___ yes ___ no
   Describe easements, protective covenants, or mineral rights, if any:

Topography

1. Grade of slope: Lowest elevation: Highest elevation:

2. Is site: ___ level ___ mostly level ___ uneven ___ steep

3. Drainage ___ excellent ___ good ___ fair ___ poor
   Is regrading necessary? ___ yes ___ no
   Cost of regrading:

4. Are there any ___ streams ___ brooks ___ ditches ___ lakes ___ ponds
   ___ marshlands ___ on site ___ bordering site ___ adjacent to site?
   Are there seasonal variations? ___ yes ___ no

5. What is the 100-year flood plan?

6. Is any part of site subject to flooding? ____ yes ____ no

7. What is the ground water table?

8. Describe surface soil:

9. Does site have any fill? ____ yes ____ no

10. Soil percolation rate ____ excellent ____ good ____ fair ____ poor

11. Load-bearing capacity of soil: ____ PSF

12. How much of site is wooded: How much to be cleared?
    Restrictions on tree removal: Cost of clearing site:

Existing Improvements

1. Describe existing improvements.

2. Indicate whether to be ____ left as is ____ remodeled ____ renovated ____ moved
   ____ demolished
   Cost $____

Landscaping Requirements

1. Describe landscaping requirements for building parking lots, access road, loading zones, and buffer if necessary.

Access to Site

1. Describe existing highways and access roads, including distance to site. (Include height and weight limits of bridges and tunnels, if any).

2. Is site visible from highway? ____ yes ____ no

3. Describe access including distance from site to a) interstate highways b) major local roads c) central business district d) rail e) water f) airport. Describe availability of public transport.

4. Will an access road be built? ____ yes ____ no
   If yes, who will build?   Who will maintain?   Cost?
   Indicate a) curb cuts   b) median cuts   c) traffic signals
   d) turn limitations

5. Is rail extended to site? ____ yes ____ no   Name of railroad(s):
   If not, how far?   Cost of extension to site:
   Who will maintain?   Is abandonment anticipated? ____ yes ____ no

Storm Drainage

1. Location and size of existing storm sewers:

2. Is connection to them possible? ____ yes ____ no
   Tap charges:

3. Where can storm waters be discharged?

4. Where can roof drainage be discharged?

5. Describe anticipated or possible long-range plans for permanent disposal of storm waters, including projected cost to company.

Sanitary Sewage

1. Is public treatment available? ___ yes ___ no
If not, what are the alternatives?

2. Is sanitary sewage to site? ___ yes ___ no
Location of sewer mains?

3. Cost of materials (from building to main) — include surface restoration if necessary:

4. Tap charges:

5. Special requirements (describe fully):

6. Describe possible or anticipated long-range plans for permanent disposal of sewage, including projected cost to company.

Water

1. Is there a water line to site: ___ yes ___ no

2. Location of main: Size of main:

3. Water pressure: Pressure of variation:

4. Hardness of water:

5. Source of water supply: Is supply adequate? ___ yes ___ no

6. Capacity of water plant: Peak demand:

7. Who furnishes water meters?   Is master meter required?
___ yes ___ no
Preferred location of meters:
___ outside ___ inside

8. Are fire hydrants metered? ___ yes ___ no
If yes, who pays for meter installation?

9. Attach copy of water rates, including sample bill for anticipated demand if possible.

Sprinklers

1. What type of sprinkler system does code permit?

2. Is there sufficient water pressure for sprinkler system?
___ yes ___ no

3. Is water for sprinkler system metered? ___ yes ___ no

4. Is separate water supply required for sprinkler system?
____ yes ____ no

5. Where can sprinkler drainage be discharged?

Electric Power

1. Is adequate electric power available to site? ____ yes ____ no
Capacity available at site:

2. Describe high voltage lines at site:

3. Type of service available:

4. Service is ____ underground ____ overhead

5. Reliability of system ____ excellent ____ good ____ fair ____ poor

6. Metering is ____ indoor ____ outdoor

7. Is submetering permitted? ____ yes ____ no

9. Indicate if reduced rates are available for a) heat pumps ____ yes ____ no b) electric
heating ____ yes ____ no

10. Attach copy of rates, including sample bill for anticipated demand, if possible.

Fuel

Gas:

1. Type of gas available:

2. Capacity: Present: Planned:

3. Peak Demand   Present: Projected:

4. Location of existing gas lines in relation to site:

5. Pressure of gas:

6. Metering is ____ indoor ____ outdoor

7. Is submetering permitted? ____ yes ____ no

8. Is meter recess required?

9. Who furnishes gas meters?

10. Indicate limitations, if any, on new installation capacity requirements:

11. Attach copy of rates, including sample bill for anticipated demand, if possible.

Coal

1. Source of supply: Reserves:

2. Quality of coal available: Cost (per million BTU) delivered:

3. Method of delivery:

Oil

1. Source of supply: Volume available:

2. Quality of oil available: Cost (per million BTU) delivered:

3. Method of delivery:

Taxes

1. Date of most recent appraisal:

2. Real estate tax rate history, last five years:

3. History of tax assessments, last five years:

4. Proposed increases, assessments, and tax rates:

5. Are any abatement programs in effect? ___ yes ___ no   If yes, describe.

6. Is site in an Enterprise Zone? ___ yes ___ no
   Duty free zone? ___ yes ___ no

7. Have any special taxes been assessed? ___ yes ___ no
   If yes, describe:

8. Indicate anticipated or possible major public improvements:

9. Services provided for taxes paid: Local: County:
   State:

10. What is state policy on inventory tax, floor tax, etc.?
    Is it a free port state? ___ yes ___ no   If no, describe assessment dates,
    procedures and tax rates.

11. Indicate rates for: Personal income tax:
    Corporate income tax: Payroll tax:
    Unemployment compensation: Personal property tax:
    Sales and use tax: Worker's compensation:
    Franchise tax: Other taxes:

12. Indicate taxation trends:

13. Are industrial revenue bonds available? ___ yes ___ no

Reprinted by permission of Customer Service Institute, Silver Spring, MD.

CHAPTER FIFTEEN

15

Integrated Logistics System Strategy and Design

LEARNING OBJECTIVES

The objectives of this chapter are to:

➤ Explain and emphasize the relationship between logistics strategy and logistics system design.

➤ Define the requirements of a logistics system design.

➤ Discuss the concept of total cost analysis and its relationship to logistics system design.

➤ Consider the tactical alternatives of (1) cost reduction, (2) redesign, and (3) system rebalancing to improve the performance of a logistics system.

➤ Define, discuss, and analyze the nature of cost trade-offs in the design and management of a logistics system.

➤ Present and discuss alternative approaches to devising and implementing logistics system cost trade-offs.

➤ Note the variety of available approaches to the task of optimizing the process of logistics system design, including the weaknesses and limitations of these approaches and the analytical techniques associated with them.

➤ Present a systematic approach to the design and implementation of an integrated logistics system.

INTRODUCTION

Webster's Dictionary offers more than a dozen definitions of the word "system." Among them are: (1) a regularly interacting or interdependent group of items forming a unified whole, (2) an organization forming a network especially for distributing something or serving a common purpose, (3) an organized set of doctrines, ideas or principles usually intended to explain the arrangement or working of a systematic whole, (4) harmonious arrangement or pattern, and (5) bringing order out of confusion.[1] The last of these five definitions might have special appeal to a harassed logistics manager coping with the complexities of dealing with vendors, customers, transportation carriers, warehouse operators, and so on, not to mention problems of internal coordination with other functions and departments in the firm.

It is a lot easier to talk about "systems," including logistics systems, than it is to design, implement, and manage one. Imagine just trying to *describe* the total set of logistics activities of a major automobile manufacturer such as General Motors, or a retailing firm the size of Sears Roebuck. Where would one begin?

The approach we have adopted here is to follow the advice given to Alice by the Mad Hatter: "Begin at the beginning, of course." And, *the beginning of a logistics system is the logistics strategy of the firm.* That is, what is the firm attempting to accomplish by the operation of its logistics activities? What long-term logistics goal(s) does it seek? What specific logistics objectives are currently being pursued to reach the goal(s)? Questions such as these *must* be asked and answered before sensible judgments can be made concerning an appropriate design or modification of a firm's logistics system.

Examples of logistics strategy might include statements such as the following:

Because we are in an industry that is highly responsive to excellent customer service, the logistics system of this firm will be designed and operated to provide a customer service level of [definition] that matches or exceeds that offered by any competitor, our purpose being to attract and retain customers, even at the expense of lower short-term profits.

Because we are in an industry that is extremely price competitive with less customer concern with delivery times and variability, our primary strategic concern will be to minimize logistics costs so that savings resulting from our lower logistics costs can be passed on to our customers in the form of lower prices.

Because our product line is very vulnerable to product substitution of competitors' products, the primary thrust of our logistics strategy will be to focus on product availability for our customers, whether ultimate users or those buying for resale; therefore we will adopt inventory-management and transportation policies and procedures designed to all but eliminate stockouts and backorders, even at considerable cost so long as we still make a profit.

Our products are fragile and expensive. Above all, our customers want the items they have ordered to arrive unbroken; they are far less concerned with delivery times and will tolerate some amount of backordering. Therefore our primary logistics concerns will be with protective packaging and the use of transportation carriers having a superior record with respect to loss and damage.

The examples just given could be multiplied many times over. What is important is that a firm understand clearly the role its logistics activity should play. Further, the managers concerned must understand that strategy governs policies, and that policies govern procedures. Finally, they must understand that the price of inconsistency is failure: a desire to minimize transportation loss and damage cannot mix with a decision to go with the very low rates quoted by Rockem & Sockem Truckline whose dock workers treat scientific instruments as though they were anvils.

The material presented in this chapter thus assumes that:

1. The firm has consciously adopted a logistics strategy that is appropriate to its industry, its competition, and its particular circumstances.

2. This strategy is understood and accepted by all those concerned with its implementation.

3. The logistics policies adopted by the firm are consistent with its overall logistics strategy.

4. The operating procedures of the firm's logistics system are consistent with its stated logistics policies, and therefore are consistent with its logistics strategy.

First, a comprehensive logistics system design effort will involve all activities and costs of both movement and demand-supply coordination. It includes all costs of transportation, warehousing, packaging and material handling, order processing, inventory, holding and procurement. Further, it focuses on the analysis of the nature of change in these costs under varying conditions. Typically, such changes involve cost trade-offs.

Second, comprehensive logistics system design integrates the use of resources (people, machines, materials, and information) to create greater productivity in the logistics system than that suggested by the simple sum of its components. Such integration emphasizes, to the extent possible, the avoidance of suboptimization of system components (the optimization of one system component to the detriment of total system cost or performance). To do this requires a systematic approach to the analysis of a logistics system.

Third, a comprehensive design often views the movement of goods and the coordination of demand and supply not necessarily as activities carried on by or for one firm, but by and for firms at two or more levels in a channel of logistics. It recognizes that the price of a product to its ultimate user includes the total costs of a number of logistics operations repeated over and over in a channel of distribution. As such, the logistics activities of all firms in a channel are interrelated, requiring an enlightened firm in the channel to analyze channel systems in terms of logistics techniques employed by its suppliers and customers as well as itself.

Fourth, it must always be kept in mind that concurrent design of all logistics components is rarely possible because of previous commitments and perhaps mistaken emphasis on sunk costs.

The purposes of this chapter are to discuss (1) examples of environmental influences and changing managerial practices that may affect logistics strategy and system design, (2) concepts of total cost analysis, (3) the nature of system cost trade-offs, (4) methods of implementing a total cost concept, and (5) the data base on which a comprehensive logistics system planning effort relies.

ENVIRONMENTAL INFLUENCES AND CHANGING
MANAGERIAL PRACTICES

In order to formulate and pursue an effective logistics strategy, a firm must take into account forces in the environment that will affect its ongoing performance and, indeed, may determine its very survival. Further, the firm's management must constantly monitor evolving industry practices that lead to greater efficiency and effectiveness in the management of logistics systems.

Environmental Factors

A traditional approach to monitoring the environment is to focus on social, political, legal, economic, and technological developments that impact an industry in general and may have specific implications for a given firm. However, it is often difficult to fit environmental factors affecting logistics strategy neatly into just one of the above categories because many events and developments are an admixture of two or more of these categories. For example, it is impossible to separate the legal and economic consequences of transportation deregulation.

Global Competition The increase in international trade provides both a strategic opportunity and a threat. On the one hand, the logistics manager has a key role to play in efficiently handling the importation of materials and goods by the manager's firm. On the other hand, the export of goods to U.S. markets by foreign competitors results in a need for very effective management and cost control of a firm's logistics system if it is to meet the competitive challenge of such foreign firms. Likewise, as a domestic producer extends its market reach abroad, the logistics manager plays a key role in facilitating export activities or serving the sourcing requirements of direct foreign investment operations established outside the country.

Transportation Deregulation The increased complexity of the transportation marketplaces resulting from deregulation has made the task of the logistics manager even more challenging than before. Adjustments to logistics operations to reflect choices among alternative shipping arrangements in light of constantly changing industry relationships — including contracting with carriers — are major operational decisions that must mesh with the firm's logistics strategy.

Energy Impacts Since 1970, costs of petroleum-based energy have followed a roller-coaster course reflecting uncontrollable international political events. This injects a large element of uncertainty into logistics strategy and planning, particularly with respect to transportation costs.

Cost of Capital In the late 1970s and early 1980s, when the cost of capital was at very high levels, operational adjustments frequently involved cutbacks in warehouse-network investments and a concurrent shift to more direct shipments from plants to customers. Given the erratic and unpredictable shifts in capital markets, the task of the logistics manager in dealing with the financial manager of a firm to budget for logistics investments and expenses continues to be difficult. What is a wise capital investment or expense today may look like a poor decision a year or two hence.

Changing Management Practices

Although practices of competitors may rightly be regarded as uncontrollable elements in the external environment, the reality is that most firms carefully watch what others are doing and adjust their own operations as may be appropriate.

Third-Party Logistics Services Providers Use of third-party logistics services providers is increasingly a strategic option available to many firms. It requires a decision as to whether and, if so, to what extent, a firm should consider modifying its existing logistics system to make greater use of third-party logistics services. The trade-offs need to be carefully evaluated with respect to costs and benefits, particularly as they relate to customer service.

Just-in-Time Whether dealing with vendors for inbound movements, or with customers for outbound movements, the increasing adoption of JIT practices puts extensive and very detailed planning burdens on the logistics systems manager. The tight integration of delivery schedules with production schedules imposes major changes on the traditional relationships between firms in a logistics channel where JIT has been adopted by one or more members of the channel.

Materials Requirements Planning Companies that have adopted and are effectively implementing MRP pose a paradoxical problem for their logistics managers. On the one hand, the implementation of MRP will clearly show the importance of the logistics function. But, having established high expectations for inbound logistics systems performance, the burden is then on the logistics system to live up to those expectations.

Electronic Data Interchange The challenge with respect to Electronic Data Interchange (EDI) is for the logistics system to keep pace with the astonishing array of technological advances that are taking place so rapidly, and to incorporate these advances into the firm's logistics strategy. These burgeoning EDI capabilities put tremendous pressures on competing firms to respond, if not innovate faster, just to preserve their market positions.

Overseas Sourcing One aspect of the rapidly increasing globalization of business is that more and more firms are purchasing raw materials, parts, and finished goods from foreign countries. This imposes a whole new set of requirements on the logistics system of a firm with respect to expertise, global communications, dealing with new entities such as customhouse brokers, making international transportation arrangements, dealing with foreign exchange problems, and so forth.

Outsourcing Although ''make or buy'' decision alternatives have always been present in many businesses, increasingly many firms are choosing to purchase goods and services that traditionally were produced ''in house.'' This tendency reflects a growing adoption of a corporate philosophy of ''sticking to the knitting'' by concentrating on the business operations at the core of the company's mission and role. The choice of having an outside contractor such as Marriott, ARA, or Dobbs House, for examples, run the company cafeteria will relieve the logistics manager of one kind of logistics activity (ordering and storing food, tableware, and such) and allow him or her to focus on ''higher yielding'' logistics contributions. Conversely, a decision to purchase from many vendors a complex assortment of parts and components,

THE LURE OF THE EUROPEAN MARKET

J. H. van der Hoop

Every U.S. company wants a share of the fast growing European market, but wanting it isn't going to make it happen. Only a well-coordinated marketing and logistics strategy will open this burgeoning market to U.S. companies.

Logistics is eventually going to be the deciding factor that separates the winners from the losers as the emerging Single European Market becomes more competitive. However, before the right logistics strategy can be planned, the U.S. company must determine its overall market entry approach.

There are three levels of market involvement a foreign company can choose for serving Europe:

1. Export from home base — manufacturing at existing plants and selling either directly to European importer or user, or through local (national) distributors.

2. Trading from an intra-European base — manufacturing and sourcing in one or more European locations, and, if possible, exporting to other European countries.

3. Serving Europe as part of a global trading network — manufacturing and sourcing for a worldwide customer base. Any global network is driven by the principles of supply chain management, but one that serves Europe must take into account a wide range of parameters from politics to lead times.

Most larger U.S. companies are in stage two, but to become a major player in Europe, U.S. companies must quickly progress to stage three. Fortunately, the political developments pushing the Single European Market concept will make transformation from stage two to three easier. In fact, the first wave of manufacturing rationalization is already going on in Europe.

Regardless of which level of involvement a U.S. company expects to have in Europe, the marketing and logistics plan must take into account key customer service requirements. Here are the four:

■ There will continue to be greater product variety than in the U.S.

■ Customer service will have to be at a high level, but diversified since national or regional sensitivity to its components varies considerably

■ Total order lead time reliability will be crucial

■ Orders will be minimal and small but frequent.

With these requirements in mind, what are the chances of success for the U.S. competitor? Generally, the likelihood of success increases as the company works its way up from a simple stage one export operation to a complex, stage three supply chain. At the higher stages of involvement, logistics strategies not only can support customer service requirements, but can better control costs to improve overall profitability.

Here are the logistics issues to consider for each stage of involvement in the European market:

1. Export from U.S. home base. A potential problem in Europe is the continuous availability of specific items for each market within Europe. Stock-outs will be hard to avoid if your U.S.-made products have to be adapted and specially packaged for these submarkets. Filling back orders can also be a problem because production planning favors long runs. U.S. companies must choose between several expensive solutions to keep customer service levels high. It can use expedited transportation to fill back orders. It can shorten production runs and incur the cost of machine adaptation. Or it can produce large quantities of the export products and warehouse them until the goods are ordered.

Complying with the need for reliable and consistent lead times is harder to achieve from a U.S. stocking point. The customers most easily served with an export strategy are the one-time orders (except when urgency is involved) and the customers with regular orders on fixed frequency. Door-to-door transit times for full containers are almost always within an acceptable time frame.

For LCL shipments, the service levels from Non-Vessel Operating Common Carriers (NVOCCs) have improved in recent years, but the actual transit times are not as predictable for full container operators.

To serve a wide customer base with variable demand, however, it eventually becomes necessary to have stock support from within the market area, under your control or through stock-holding distributors.

In other words, the further market penetration is aimed, the sooner the next stage will be reached.

The export alternative will always be a viable option with less risk and also less stake in the European marketplace. It can only be done effectively if it is done for the longer term. It is not a market to be entered when the domestic market weakens and then abandoned when the home market strengthens.

2. Trading from intra-European bases. Europe has developed many single markets, each protected by border obstacles and bureaucracy. Most European companies traditionally have manufactured in each country to minimize border problems and to cope with product differentiation. With 1992 fast approaching, the general strategy is now to have only one or two manufacturing locations. While this makes economic and marketing sense, it presents several logistics challenges. Having only one or two locations serving all of Europe can lead to the same problems discussed above for the export strategy.

Being closer to submarkets, of course, makes these problems easier to solve. Accommodating special requirements and dealing with shortened lead times becomes easier because all production is directed at the European market. Transit times are shorter so customer service problems are fewer and less severe. Production planning is simplified because components are generally sourced locally.

Marketing can be handled through national stock-holding distributors, but by using an in-house sales force the company gains a better understanding of the national marketplace. Transportation can usually be restricted to one or two modes (truck, and to a smaller extent, rail). Increasingly, transportation is handled through long-term contract arrangements.

Private carriage is not a very attractive proposition in view of national regulations and the difficulty in organizing backhauls.

3. Serving Europe as part of a "global" network. Logistically, this is probably the most challenging, but also the most rewarding alternative. However, it pre-supposes a large-scale company that has the information, resources and expertise to operate a global supply chain.

The key requirement for a network to successfully serve Europe is a rationalized manufacturing base. Plants with a narrow product range must serve all of Europe and perhaps the Middle East, Asia and even the U.S. Strategic decisions will have to be made in the areas of location, the extent of plant networking, sourcing, product/market combinations and above all, coordinated planning.

Sourcing very likely will be worldwide, but can be restricted to only a few contractors. Inventory levels for the entire network should be substantially reduced by limiting stock locations to only a few points. This requires a strategic decision about splitting off the physical product flow from the national sales channels. Interestingly, this also requires a fresh look at the performance criteria applicable to these national profit centers.

Also, an important location decision will have to be made regarding the stock points. The most likely place is not necessarily the plant location—as it often was before—since

different plants will have to supply the same customers with different parts of the product range. In view of the cost of money and a desire to concentrate on the core business, there is a tendency to contract out the operation of a central warehouse to a third party. Efforts to share warehouse operations with other non-competitive manufacturers have hardly met with success.

Another point is that in Europe, even in the '90s, the distribution location is subject to more factors than the center of gravity in the market or transport weight and distance vectors.

The location of the central distribution location should be based on the ability to meet customer requirements. Broad areas must be able to be served with regularly scheduled deliveries. Larger customers should be served with direct delivery.

A centralized distribution location, however, must have the capability to make minor modifications to products and packaging to customize them as orders come in. Attempting to produce exact quantities of specialized items for each market ultimately pushes a company back to the stage one level of sophistication.

In stage three, inventory is traded off with transport and information. Both will need central management attention.

In the transport arena, the question arises as to what the optimal balance is between partnerships with one or two vast distribution service companies covering a large part of Europe, and using regional specialists or networks of independents. One-stop shopping may not always be the optimal solution in an area where transportation and increasingly distribution service supply has always been abundant and highly competitive. Systematic service management, on the basis of longer-term agreements spelling out each party's obligations well beyond the more usual rate agreements, are an essential part of European logistics strategy.

Under the above scenario, transport flows will increase, both in the supply lines and in the final distribution to the customers. Consolidation will be a key part of cost-effective distribution. The strategic aspect is how far consolidation, with its implicit extra handling and transit time, can penetrate the distribution network without impairing the required customer service levels. However, there is another important reason for elevating consolidation (and deconsolidation) to an art. European transport volumes have been rising spectacularly in recent years and are forecasted to continue increasing. This is leading to saturation of the available infrastructure in densely populated and industrialized areas.

While creating a new source of delays (when Europe is just trying to solve its border problems), it also is creating a

Continued

nearly unbearable environmental burden. Strong political and regulatory pressure (now from governments, but soon from under the EC aegis as well) is brought to bear to better utilize intermodal means and increase trucking productivity. Road transport is still the major mode for finished goods, components and parts in Europe. So the choice of a European logistics strategy will have to include environmental considerations. Imaginative solutions will have to include optimal use of consolidations.

One aspect of strategic concern will have to be considered: training and education. Players in the European logistics management field will have to be aware that considerable differences in European cultures and business environments exist. In order to effectively manage, a solid base of know-how and experience will have to be built. Professor James Foggin of the University of Tennessee concludes that international effectiveness depends on a combination of primary (''in the field'') and secondary (education-related) information. Gathering local experience, he adds, will be most effective when preceded by training. This aspect is often overlooked as an essential component of sophisticated international management.

Going for the European market means the logistics operations must be made an integral part of the corporate European strategy.

SOURCE: *Distribution* (October 1990): 48–52. Reprinted by permission of Chilton Company.

rather than purchasing raw materials from a few vendors and making the parts and components, will make the logistics task more complex.

Postponement   Deferring various assembly and packaging operations until the last feasible point in the channel of distribution, referred to as postponement, generally will ease the task of a logistics manager by reducing the number of SKUs at earlier points in the channel of distribution. This form of logistics strategy is being increasingly adopted where it is practicable to do so.

Continuous Monitoring versus Triggering Events

All too often, a firm becomes complacent with an existing logistics system that has been operating successfully. Such complacency can be very costly. Without a commitment to continuous monitoring of its environment and the actions of competitors, a firm can be caught by surprise by some innovative thrust by a competitor or significant development in the environment, so-called ''trigger events.'' And, if caught unprepared, the firm winds up responding to such a trigger event without the benefit of time to organize resources in a manner that will ward off the threat or allow taking advantage of an opportunity. Clearly, it is desirable for a logistics manager to take a proactive rather than reactive posture with respect to designing or modifying a firm's logistics strategy.

TOTAL COST ANALYSIS

Total cost analysis is, as its name implies, the analysis of a logistics system taking into consideration all costs of the system. It was first described in detail by Lewis, Culliton, and Steele,[2] although imaginative managers had certainly used such an approach at many times and in many firms prior to its formal presentation in print.

Total cost analysis can take a variety of forms, ranging from a listing of cost estimates valid for any point in time to the construction of elaborate models based on observed input-output relationships. Basically, whether dealing with a simple tabulation of costs or a more complex model, we can identify cost elements as fixed or variable with changes in volume of sales, distance of movement, size of order, or some other dimension. So-called $y = a + bx$ relationships, where y represents a total cost, a the fixed portion of the cost regardless of changes in the variable x, and b the cost per unit of x or the variable portion of the cost structure, are convenient to construct for logistics system analysis, regardless of the complexity of the approach used. They make it possible to employ powerful analytical techniques, such as linear programming, in the analysis by using only the variable portion of the cost estimate in the model itself and manually factoring into the calculation the fixed changes, particularly where such changes are relatively small. Such simple models often describe quite accurately a variety of logistics cost relationships.

An Example

A classic example of early thinking regarding total cost analysis can be provided by Brunswick Floors, Inc., a company distributing finished decorative wood products from its plant at Brunswick, New Jersey, to, among other places, the distribution center which it leases and operates in San Francisco, California.

Executives of the company had gathered cost data and prepared estimates that indicated that a change from the use of rail transportation to either truck or air transportation, coupled with a considerable reduction of the inventory in both Brunswick and San Francisco, could provide total cost savings. Questions were raised regarding the amount of such savings at the current volume of business of 280,000 pounds per year and the stages in the development of the company's San Francisco regional market, at which each combination of transportation and warehousing alternatives would be most economical.

Cost information for the company's current volume of business is shown in Table 15–1. Once costs are stated in terms of fixed and variable components in the form of $y = a + bx$, they can be estimated for any future volume of business by graphing them, as shown in Figure 15–1, for systems utilizing air and truck transportation.

Comparing alternative methods graphed in Figure 15–1 or described in Table 15–1, we can set the total costs of any two (y_1 and y_2) equal to each other to find the point of volume (x), if any, at which the total cost lines described by the functions intersect. This produces the following result:

$$a_1 + b_1x = a_2 + b_2x,$$

thus,

$$x = \frac{a_1 - a_2}{b_2 - b_1}.$$

Further, we can be sure of computing least-cost line intersections if we rank the alternatives in terms of the amounts of fixed costs incurred under each, from smallest to largest. In the example, annual fixed costs for air = \$34,680, truck = \$69,380, and rail = \$84,280. In

TABLE 15–1: Annual Total Logistics Costs, Current and Proposed Systems, San Francisco Region, Brunswick Floors, Inc.[a]

Cost Item	Method of Transportation, Warehousing		
	Air	Highway	Railroad
Fixed costs:			
Fixed cost element, freight bill	$ 5,000	$15,000	$15,000
Warehousing, Brunswick	14,680	14,680	14,680
Warehousing, San Francisco	–	14,700	29,600
Total fixed	$ 34,680	$69,380	$84,280
Costs variable with volume:			
Freight cost element, variable	$ 70,000	$18,000	$ 7,000
Local delivery, San Francisco	10,000	10,000	10,000
Brunswick warehousing	4,100	4,100	4,100
San Francisco warehousing	–	8,200	12,300
Order preparation and placement	9,250	2,250	2,250
Capital investment in inventory	3,300	6,000	7,800
Product obsolescence and damage	2,480	5,200	2,480
Insurance	620	1,010	1,300
Taxes	420	560	650
Total variable	$100,000	$55,320	$47,880
Annual volume (pounds)	400,000	400,000	400,000
Variable cost per pound	$.250	$.138	$.119
Total cost per pound	$.337	$.312	$.330

[a]Each of the three systems under comparison provides the same level of service to customers: 30 percent of all orders delivered within 72 hours of order receipt, 80 percent within 96 hours; and 90 percent within 120 hours.

order to find the first pertinent least-cost line intersection, we would compare air with truck. In this case, our computations would be based on the following information from Table 15–1:

$$a_1 = \$34,680$$

$$b_1 = \$.250$$

$$a_2 = \$69,380$$

$$b_2 = \$.138$$

For example in the question:

$$x = \frac{34,680 - 69,380}{.138 - .250}$$

$$= \frac{-34,700}{-.112}$$

$$= 309,821 \text{ pounds.}$$

FIGURE 15–1: Graphic method of total cost logistics system analysis, San Francisco region, Brunswick Floors, Inc.

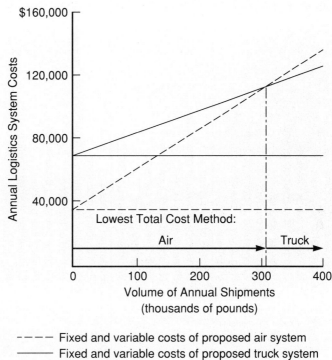

In other words, at an annual volume of 309,821 pounds, it would be economical to switch from air to truck. This is the same result shown in Figure 15–1, although the latter is less accurate, even if graphed with extreme precision.

Other Cost and Activity Relationships

What was just considered is an abstraction of a complex total cost analysis useful for illustrating the concept. In an actual situation, many logistics cost and activity relationships must be identified and measured in a comprehensive system analysis. These relationships are shown in Figure 15–2, together with the major determinants of each.

For example, transportation costs per unit decrease with larger shipment sizes, increase with shipment distance, and do so in relation to the costs of the various methods of transportation utilized. Shipment size, in turn, largely varies directly with the total volume of business, other things being constant. It varies inversely with the number of stock locations, the level of customer service desired, and the frequency of shipment, again assuming volume and other characteristics constant.

FIGURE 15–2: Some of the interrelationships in a comprehensive logistics system analysis

Cost Categories	Vary With:	Which Vary With:	Which Vary With:
Transportation costs per unit	Shipment size	Number of stock locations Frequency of shipment Total volume	
	Shipment distance	Number of stock locations Geographic market coverage	
	Cost of various modes of transportation	Value of product Density of product Geographic shipping patterns Regularity in availability of freight Shipment size	
Warehousing costs per unit	Method of warehousing	Volume of throughput Constancy of volume of activity Physical size of inventory	
	Volume of throughput	Number of stock locations Size of territory served	
	Inventory turnover rate	Inventory policy Volume of sales per SKUL	
Inventory carring costs	Inventory control, forecasting method	Pattern of demand Predictability of demand Desirability or routinizing replenishment procedures	
	Order-cycle length	Method of transport Order-processing procedures	
	Volume of sales per SKUL	Product line policies Engineering standardization Sales volume	
	Replenishment shipment size per SKUL	Frequency of replenishment	
Order processing costs per unit	Number of line items per order	Size of product line Nature of market	
	Average order size	Quantity discount incentives Nature of use	
	Method of order processing	Volume of orders Accuracy of inventory data file	
	Rate of initial order fill	Inventory coverage policy	
Lost sale costs	Willingness of customers to substitute	Nature of competition Type of customer need	
	Rate of contribution on sales	Ability to differentiate product, service from competition	

If we were to fill in the far right column of Figure 15–2, we might conclude that the total volume of business, among other things, is influenced by the level of logistics service mentioned elsewhere in the figure. Likewise, the number of stock locations will vary with the desired customer service level, which depends on other factors. As the tabulation is developed out to the right, the interrelationships in a logistics system become more and more apparent.

Clearly, even a comprehensive system analysis must limit itself to an accounting of only the major influences on cost and service. And the task of data collection and revision to fit an analytic format, even with these types of simplifications, can be tough and expensive. If the analysis is carried out properly, however, it can yield relatively accurate estimates of the cost trade-offs under various alternative system designs. Before turning to methods for achieving this type of result, it is important to consider some recurring patterns of cost trade-offs.

AN INTEGRATED VIEW

An integrated view of logistics costs separates them into discernible and roughly equal areas:

1. Transportation costs are those costs that are most visible and most easily controlled. Most companies have a good idea what these are.

2. Costs associated with inventory are often underestimated. The annual cost of holding stock in inventory can run as high as one-third or more of its value.

3. Overhead costs of running a logistics system are the least obvious and often are ignored. These include the cost of capital, allocations of general and administrative expenses, training and development expenses, and even allocable legal costs.

These costs, sensitive to such factors as increased fuel costs (transportation) and interest rates (inventory carrying costs), may run anywhere from 10 percent to 20 percent of sales, frequently almost double management's estimate.

Other sensitive costs that lie beyond management's control, or have proven difficult to control, are those costs occurring as a result of functional managers striving to improve their own performance. They have a tendency to increase lead times and to build up buffer stocks, a process that feeds on itself, and these protective measures are costly. This self-generating cycle in a "make-to-order" business can result in engineering and production increasing lead times and stretching delivery periods beyond those offered by competitors.

Marketing and production in a "make-to-order" business is often a dynamic relationship requiring very disciplined short-term planning and control systems designed to prevent crash changes in production schedules and to avoid costly expediting as a way of life. Accurate sales forecasting for individual product models is difficult for marketers. This leads to errors that inevitably lead to stockouts of some models and stock surpluses of others, resulting in costly changes in production and volume and mix.

Stockouts and stock surpluses will grow worse as the factory turns out the model mix for which it has parts and materials, but this is not likely to meet the sales requests from the field. Marketing reacts by expanding buffer inventories as a shield against the risk of stockouts while the factory piles up semifinished parts so that the next flurry of change requests will not set off another factory floor crisis.

This kind of escalation can be brought under effective control only by implementing an integrated approach to logistics. Implicit in such an approach are important choices between continuous and batch production, between manual and automated warehousing, and between centralized and decentralized stocking. Taken together, these choices constitute a given level of customer service for a given level of cost.

Three main routes are available for improving an existing logistics system: straightforward reduction of costs, system redesign, and system rebalancing.

Cost Reduction

Traditional cost reduction is an obvious route to improved logistics performance. It involves such actions as disposal of dead stocks, monitoring minimum order size rules, cutting warehouse costs, consolidating shipments, and so on. These measures can enhance a system's efficiency without altering a company's logistics system.

Redesign

Redesign, a more radical route for achieving a superior performance, can be developed and implemented, thereby enabling a company to meet the competitive challenges of market, industry, and regulatory changes. However, by itself, redesigning a logistics system will seldom prevent the inflation of buffer stocks at the various points of linkage between functions in a company's business.

Rebalancing

This involves rebalancing the system, identifying possible trade-offs, adjusting the priorities of the functions involved, and changing the planning and control systems as necessary to lock the new trade-offs into place. The order penetration (OP) point has been identified by Sharman as the one key variable in every logistics configuration.[3] Downstream of the OP point, customer orders drive the system that controls orders and materials flow; upstream, forecasts and plans do the driving; and in most cases, the OP is where product specifications get frozen. It is also the last point at which inventory is held.

Figure 15–3 outlines how the OP varies from industry to industry as does the location of intermediate stocks. We see that for every product design, the optimum logistics configuration including the OP point depends on a balance between competitive pressures and product cost and complexity; a company's optimal OP will change as market and industry conditions change. Emphasis should be placed on the importance of managers first calculating the optimum cost-service trade-off and, prior to rebalancing the level of stocks, to arrive at the best trade-off between marketing's objectives of maximizing inventories to avoid lost sales and finance's objective of minimizing inventories to reduce capital and related costs. Managers must know which value/cost trade-offs are critical and how to bring the array of plans for product development, material procurement, master production schedules, movement of goods and sales plans into harmony for a logistics system to function effectively.[4]

FIGURE 15–3: Order penetration points

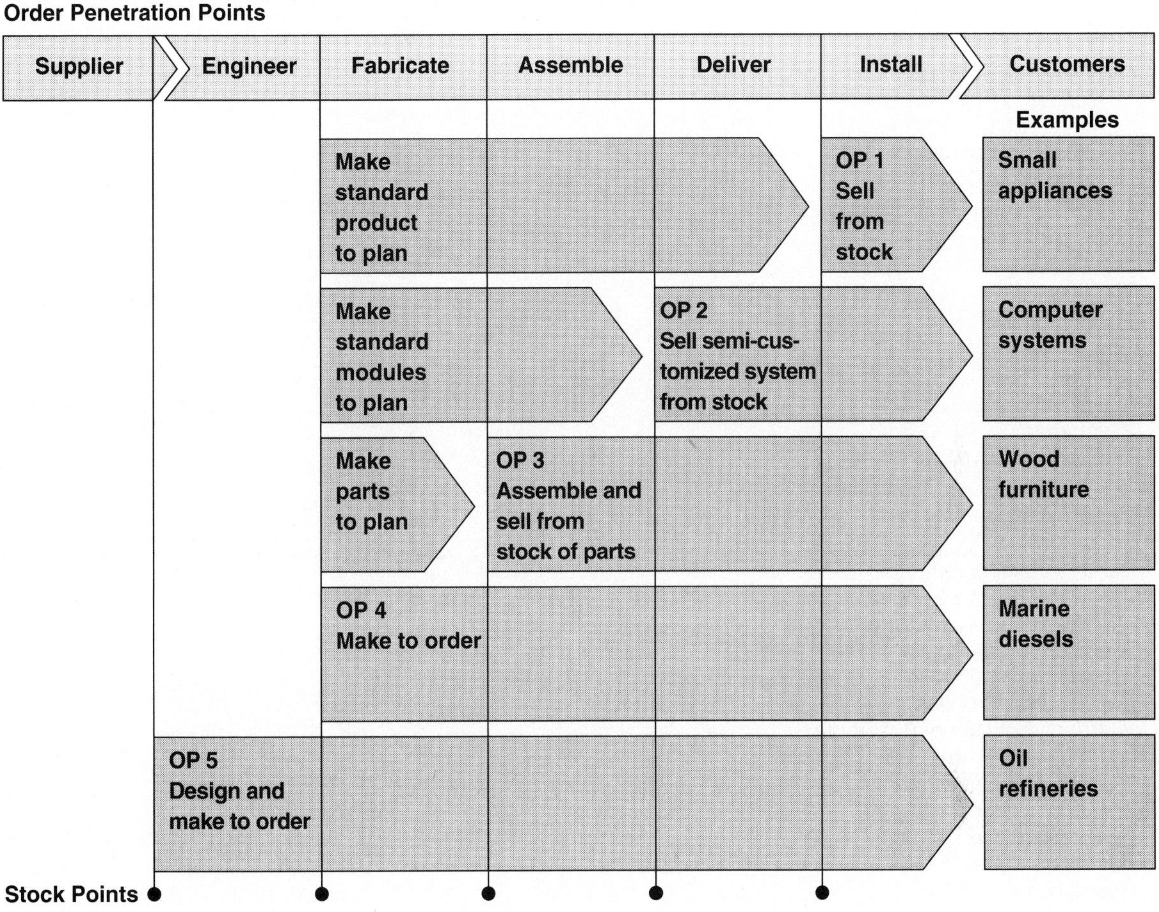

Order Penetration Points

Supplier	Engineer	Fabricate	Assemble	Deliver	Install	Customers

Examples

		Make standard product to plan			OP 1 Sell from stock	Small appliances
		Make standard modules to plan		OP 2 Sell semi-customized system from stock		Computer systems
		Make parts to plan	OP 3 Assemble and sell from stock of parts			Wood furniture
		OP 4 Make to order				Marine diesels
	OP 5 Design and make to order					Oil refineries

Stock Points

LOGISTICS COST TRADE-OFFS

Many examples of logistics system changes can be cited. A number of these are listed in Figure 15–4. They have been placed opposite the various kinds of costs with which they are associated in vendor, company, and customer organizations. Each example of change, based on actual industry experience, has resulted in the reduction of certain costs of logistics and an increase in others. In a sense, cost increases are traded for cost decreases presumably when a

FIGURE 15–4: Examples of logistics cost trade-offs reported in actual situations

These costs often change	As this action is taken											
	1	2	3	4	5	6	7	8	9	10	11	12
Long-Distance Transportation From:												
Vendor to Facility[a]		-[c]		+[d]	+							-
Intra-Facility	-	+					-	-	-			
Facility to Customer	+			-		+	-	-				+
(Nature of Cost):												
For-Hire Carrier Charges	+											
Private Carriage Costs												
Local Delivery At:												
Origin(s)												
Destination(s)										-		
Material Handling:												
Vendor		-										
Company[b]	-	-				-				-		+
Customer						-						
(Nature of Cost):												
Equipment	-					+						
Labor	-					-						
Supplies	-					+						
Inventory Holding In:												
Vendors' Facilities		+	-		-							
Company Assembly Warehouses		+	-		-							-
Company Factories			-				-	-				+
Company Distribution Warehouses	-			+				+	+		-	+
Customers' Facilities	-			-				-		-		
Carriers' Equipment (En Route)	-						-					
(Nature of Cost):												
Interest on Investment												
Obsolescence										-		
Pilferage and Damage							-					
Inventory Taxes										-		
Insurance												
Rehandling										-		
All of the Above	-[c]	+[d]	-		-						-	
Warehousing:												
Vendor		+										
Company Assembly[b]		+	+		-							-
Company Distribution	-			+	-			+				+
Customer	-			-	-		-					
All of the Above												
(Nature of Cost):												
Fixed-Private Facilities[a]										-		
Variable-Public Facilities										+		
Packing:												
Vendor Packing		-	+				+					
Company Unpacking-Packing						-	+					
Customer Unpacking	-					-	+					

Continued

FIGURE 15–4 (continued): Examples of logistics cost trade-offs reported in actual situations

	As this action is taken											
These costs often change	1	2	3	4	5	6	7	8	9	10	11	12
Order Processing:												
Vendor		-	+		+							
Company	+	-	+		+						+	
Customer	+											
Manufacturing (If Applicable):												
Fixed					-							-
Labor Variable			+									
Equipment Variable												-
Sales Losses Due to Logistics:												
Customer Service Deficiencies				-	-		-	-	-		-	
Market Territory Restrictions	-				-			-	-		-	

1. Use of premium methods of transporataion for outgoing finished products (accompanied by a reduction in warehouses, overhaul of communications).
2. Purchasing and shipping supplies and components by means of fewer orders of greater quantity.
3. Consolidation of shipments from supply points (allowing smaller, but requiring better timing of, purchases).
4. Increase in the number of distribution warehouses (reducing service times to customers).
5. Increase in the use of "split" shipments on supplies to meet manufacturing requirements.

6. Change from hand methods to palletization in handling of finished product (requiring customer compatibility for optimum savings).
7. Increase in the protective characteristics of packing containers (allowing shipment under different freight classification).
8. Establishment of distribution warehouses as mixing points for shipments between plants and customers (allowing volume shipments to customers).
9. Shifting packing and/or packaging operations from plant to distribution warehouse (allowing shipment in bulk).
10. Use of public vs. private warehousing facilities.
11. Use of faster communications and mechanized procedures in handling orders from customers.
12. Stabilization of labor requirements for manufacturing by establishing constant production schedule (creating inventory level fluctuations).

[a]Facility (plant or warehouse) of the company whose procedures are under study.
[b]Company taking action.
[c]Costs which are reduced by the action.
[d]Costs which are increased by the action.

net gain results to the company instituting the change. This exchange has become more popularly known as the "trade-off" of one cost for another.

Consider action 5 in Figure 15–4, where change is represented by an increase in the use of "split shipments" to provide better supply service to the manufacturing line. It is typical of the policy pursued by several automobile manufacturers. That is, in circumstances where planned transportation services do not appear likely to meet the time requirements for the provision of supplies or components to the manufacturing line, a part of the shipment is split off and shipped by faster or more dependable methods. This is likely to result in increases in (1) transportation costs from the vendor to the company's manufacturing facility and (2) order-processing costs of both the vendor and the company under consideration. At the same time, however, inventory holding costs of both the vendor and the company are likely to be reduced.

More important, an interruption of manufacturing processes, with the attendant possibility of a customer back-order situation, will be avoided. Its identification requires knowledge of system objectives and existing costs.

System Objectives and Costs

Identification of the nature of logistics cost trade-offs is a function of the objectives of the system in which change is proposed. In action 4 of Figure 15–4, for instance, any decision to change the number of distribution warehouses would be based on the number and location of those already in operation in relation to company markets and manufacturing facilities. If a high degree of customer service were already being rendered by the system, the cost trade-off would involve an increase in warehousing and inventory holding costs for a reduction in transportation cost from warehouse facilities to customers. If customer service levels were relatively low, trade-off calculation would include gains from an improvement in customer service.

The objectives of a given system further determine the nature of cost trade-offs in a logistics problem. For example, two basic objectives might have prompted the action in action 5 of Figure 15–4: (1) improvement of service to the production line and hence to customers, or (2) maintenance of the current level of service to the production line and to customers with some reduction in total logistics costs. Given the first objective, the cost trade-offs are essentially those pointed out above. The presence of the second objective, however, would simplify the nature of the trade-offs to an increase in inbound transportation costs for a reduction in inventory holding and warehousing costs.

METHODS OF IMPLEMENTING A TOTAL COST ANALYSIS

Total cost analysis of logistics systems may be accomplished by a series of intuitive probes or by more formal operations research techniques. The most successful efforts often result from a combination of the two approaches.

Intuitive Probes

Questions can be raised that help bring order out of the jumble of information collected concerning a logistics system. Further, the answers provide direction for the selective and economical application of more formal, often more expensive operations research techniques. Intuitive probes implicitly honor such rules of thumb as (1) reduce the element of greatest cost, (2) minimize handling, or (3) maximize freight consolidation. In practice, however, it is often found that the most cost-, service-, or profit-effective systems do not minimize or maximize any single characteristic, but strike a balance between sometimes conflicting rules of thumb.

Priority Attention to the Largest or Fastest Growing Cost Items One way of developing an analytic strategy is to identify the largest or fastest growing item of cost in the logistics system and attempt to reduce it.

Measurement against Standards   System performance can be measured against standards reflecting both system inputs (such as cost budgets) and system outputs (including customer service and other performance standards, competitors's performance, or industry averages).

Cost budgets, to the extent they are based on past performance, whether good or bad, may make poor standards against which to measure system performance because they may not reflect actual current or projected future costs. However, to the extent that they do truly reflect the costs of a company's logistics system, cost budgets may have validity as standards.

Customer service or other performance standards, perhaps derived from observations of competitors' accomplishments, may well be useful measures. This is particularly true where little competition exists in regard to other important dimensions, such as price. If service can differentiate one company's product from another's, the meeting of competitive standards can have an important influence on sales and profits.

Industry averages for logistics costs in relation to sales (to the extent they can be found) are often misleading when applied to a specific company in an industry. A company with a regional sales territory may have relatively low logistics costs in comparison with one serving a national sales territory. Companies at different stages in their growth cycles may have significantly different relative costs, even in the same industry.

Review of the Transport-Inventory Cost Mix   In industries where the value of inventory is high and costs of transportation low in relation to sales, it may pay (in terms of improved customer service) to spend more for transportation in order to reduce inventory costs to the point where inventory cost savings just equal added transportation expenditures. In industries where the reverse is true, it may pay to stock larger amounts of inventory in many market-oriented locations to provide acceptable levels of customer service while using less expensive and slower means of transportation. The point is that adjustments are made in the design of well managed logistics systems to bring transportation and inventory costs into a lowest total cost equilibrium.

Opportunities for Economies of Scale through Consolidation   Consolidation of shipments, inventories, or orders can result in significant economies of scale in a logistics system. Deregulation of rates, particularly in the trucking industry, has resulted in significant and continuing rate increases for "minimum shipments" (commonly those under 100 pounds). This has resulted in ever closer attention being paid by shippers to freight consolidation.

In this regard, for example, customer service policies, excessive numbers of distribution center stock points, or inventory management practices that preclude shipment from the plant of vehicle-load shipments (which usually carry dramatically lower rates per unit than smaller shipments) should be questioned.

By making use of economies that arise from big production volumes, volume discounts in purchasing, and shipping full truck loads or rail carloads of goods, a company can design its logistics system and associated operating policies to minimize cost while keeping customer service at an acceptable level. From the mid-1970s on, rising costs of energy, raw materials, transportation, and capital have made an overall strategy of logistics cost leadership increasingly attractive. As a result, managers have turned to logistics in the fight against eroding margins, and rightly so. On average, logistics costs consume more than 21 cents of every U.S.

sales dollar.[5] More than 20 percent of the gross national product was spent by industry on the physical distribution of goods in 1982, representing a total cost of $650 billion that year, including transportation ($300 billion), storage and warehousing ($180 billion), inventory carrying costs ($130 billion), and administration ($40 billion).[6]

Economies in material handling might be achieved through the consolidation of warehouse stocks at fewer points. A decision to attempt to gain such economies would be based on the analysis of a number of related costs. Just as in our previous example, economies of scale from the standpoint of the user are somewhat greater when private as opposed to public warehousing is employed. This increases the risk of owning and operating a private warehouse where volumes of freight are sufficient to allow the realization of scale economies.

The variable costs of processing an order may be reduced significantly by centralizing such activities in one or two points in a logistics system. However, an attendant increase in fixed costs associated with communications, as well as information sending and receiving equipment, usually accompanies such a move. As Sharman notes:

> Companies can centralize inventories as much as possible, especially for low-volume items, in a manner that is consistent with required levels of service. For example, Montgomery Ward recognized that nationwide inventory reductions could be achieved by consolidating all slower moving items into one central warehouse seven miles from Chicago's O'Hare Airport. Lower inventory costs far outweigh higher transportation charges from airfreighting items when rapid delivery is essential.[7]

Review of System Effectiveness in Assorting and Sorting Closely allied to questions of consolidation are those concerning product handling; most typical are the questions about meeting the needs of related organizational entities for different assortments of components, raw materials, and finished product. It is unrealistic to set an objective of minimizing product handling. If we were to do that, we would attempt to ship each part or machine directly and separately to customers, producing only to customer order regardless of competitive practice.

Mixing points intermediate to plants and distribution centers or customers essentially add another set of handling activities to the logistical sequence. And yet, companies where each of several multiple plants specializes in the production of certain items in a related line of products sold to customers in common, mixing points may facilitate consolidated shipping, as shown in Figures 15–5 and 15–6.

Another relevant tactic is to strive for the lowest cost routing of products from plants to warehouses to customers. This tactic is often of great importance to large companies late in their life-cycles, when service has grown spotty and geographic expansion and multiple levels of warehouses have created a logistics nightmare.

In recent years, International Paper had twenty million acres of woodlands and operated 124 manufacturing facilities and some 100 storage and transfer facilities in North America, France, Italy, and Brazil. Its network of raw materials suppliers and customers was worldwide in scope. An optimizing-based system allowed them to rationalize this multifacility operational structure to ensure a cost effective attack that would have been impossible without such a logistics-based decision aid.[8]

Handling that does not produce a significant change in product assortment can be questioned. Much of this takes place within the walls of a warehouse or manufacturing facility. It often occurs as a result of a lack of space or of poorly planned facilities.

FIGURE 15–5: Product flows in a logistics system employing direct plant-to-customer transportation, where company plants do not produce a full line of company products

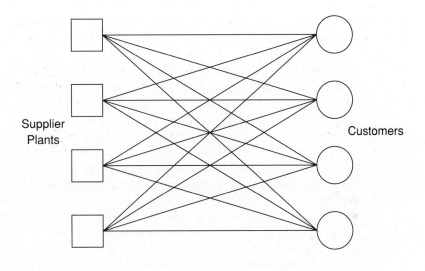

FIGURE 15–6: Product flows in a logistics system employing a shipment mixing point between plants and customers

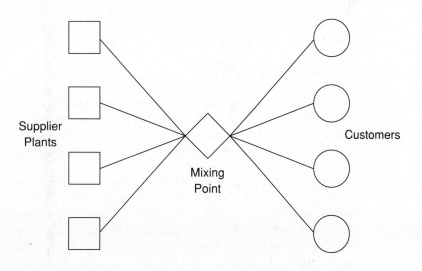

Package design and item assortments that are convenient for a plant shipping department anxious to get the product "off the dock," but that do not conform to customer desires, inevitably produce excessive handling costs for assorting and sorting. To counter this, some companies have attempted to sell standard item assortments based on an identification of repeated customer demand patterns. For example, sized merchandise, such as wearing apparel, is purchased in various sizes with predictable frequency; this allows manufacturers to pack standard sized assortments requiring no further handling of individual units until a carton is unpacked at the retail store.

Evaluation of Commitment Delay To what extent does the system use an inventory of semiassembled components, each for use in multiple finished items, instead of a stock of finished items? To what extent does allowing for assembly delay shipment in relation to the time of receipt of an order? Provision for commitment delay anywhere in a logistics system will reduce costs associated with the carrying of inventory, particularly dead stocks.

However, commitment delay must take into account the costs of delay as well as customer buying behavior and needs. It is much more feasible in a firm that has adopted a policy of using, when possible, standardized parts or subassemblies in the company's product line. Two examples of commitment delay are the restaurant business and automobile assembly plants. In both industries, standard components are combined "at the last minute" to produce a large variety of finished products, whether meals or automobiles.

Provision for Product and Market Differentiation Cost reductions may be achieved by differentiating logistics practices for various products, portions of a product line, or markets. Not every product or market requires the same logistics treatment.

Provision for System Balance To what extent are system elements, indicated by their performance, compatible with one another? To illustrate this concept, consider the use of customer-requested air freight for shipments whose billing terms to customers were not changed, thereby increasing transportation costs while not collecting for them. Symptoms of system imbalance include accumulations of inventory, unnecessary information, unsent customer invoices, idle equipment or personnel, services not billed, and so on.

Analytic Techniques

The wide variety of analytic techniques appropriate for logistics system design can be categorized rather simply. First, all techniques serve either to *optimize or simulate* a given situation. Second, all of them can be categorized basically as falling into one of two families, according to the nature of the problem they address: location or inventory control.

Optimizing Techniques Typical of optimizing techniques are linear programming and economic order quantity (EOQ) inventory models. These techniques provide "the one best" answer, an optimum solution of a problem for which a specific objective function has been stated, most often in terms of minimization of transportation, production, or total costs, or maximization of profit. Further, the economy of problem statement and the power of the mathematical approaches possible for optimizing techniques usually allow their use at a much lower cost for computing time than for simulation models, at least at the current state of the computing art. Problems involving up to several hundred origins and destinations can be solved, for example, by linear programming techniques in just several minutes of computer time.

However, optimizing approaches such as linear programming tend to oversimplify the problem statement. The range of costs and activities that can be included in such analysis is limited. Further, they require the use of restrictive assumptions. An illustration of this is the assumption of cost linearity regardless of volume in linear programming. Although there are ways of dealing with some of these restrictions, overall they constitute significant compromises for many applications.

Simulation Techniques In contrast to optimization, simulation provides relative freedom of problem expression. Whether dealing with location or inventory problems, simulation techniques emphasize a more detailed, accurate description of the way in which problem elements interact. For example, rather than emphasizing the calculation of optimum inventory management rules, simulation techniques would attempt to describe the receipt and shipment of orders and related activities in such a way that various inventory management rules could be tried (for example, *what if . . . ?*) and the resulting costs and service measures could be compared.

Simulation techniques allow for the inclusion of more types of costs or physical activities than do analytic models. For this reason, they may have broad application to a wide range of problems. Inherently, they may have a particular appeal to managers who like to know more about the nature of the analytic technique with which they are working. An inquisitive manager can learn a great deal about the assumptions inherent in a simulation model by trying out different sets of policies and comparing results produced by the simulation.

To the extent that the practical application of simulation prevents the explicit description of all elements of a system, certain simplifying assumptions or calculations are included even in large-scale simulations. To the extent they are necessary, they reflect the views of the model builder, views that may or may not reflect reality. Perhaps the biggest drawback of simulation approaches is that they do not provide any guarantee that the best answer will be found, much less that the best answer has been found. In a sense, they leave a lot to the imagination and creativity of the user, a feature that managers may find either attractive or unattractive. And, any manager who places blind faith in the results produced by either an optimizing or simulation model is a fool.

A third major problem formerly associated with many large-scale simulations was the large amount of computing time and expense they required. Fortunately, due to the extraordinary increase in computing power and speed that has taken place recently and the drastically lower costs (prices) of computers, simulation is no longer significantly "cost limited" for most business logistics applications.

Characteristics in Common Formalized analytical techniques for logistics system design have certain characteristics in common. Their "results" or "answers" tend to be over-rated by some managers. In fact, they often raise more questions than they answer. For this reason, they both require and contribute to a higher level of problem understanding on the part of management. Further, in many cases, they may suggest a complete restatement of the original problem. The most significant inputs to most problem analyses are the managerial response to questions posed by results produced by the model.

A good illustration is provided by the situation confronted by the Bay Area Bakery Company.[9] In that case the question, ''Should we build a new bakery at San Jose?'' suggested the use of linear programming for the analysis of delivery costs from seven bakeries to eleven major markets in the San Francisco Bay area. After the analysis, the original question was put aside and replaced by questions such as, ''Should we reallocate our current production in a more effective pattern?'' and ''Should we close one or two of our less efficient or less well located existing bakeries, regardless of whether we elect to build a new one at San Jose?''

A Common Pitfall A basic, sometimes critical, mistake made by managements in the application of analytic techniques to logistics problems is the tendency to compare model output, particularly from optimizing models, with the results produced by the company's current methods of doing things, without regard to whether the results are the best that could be obtained under the current method. All too often, poor current results are not the fault of the system, but rather are due to poor management of a (good) system. An old cliche illustrates the point: if all else fails, read the instructions.

We have discussed the capabilities of optimizing and simulation approaches. What, in fact, has been accomplished in the use of these techniques for logistics system design? This brings us to the two basic types of problems that various analytic techniques have addressed, those associated with location and inventory.

Location Models In addition to the location of facilities, location models are used to allocate activities, equipment, or product to various locations, all with the intent of fulfilling some stated objectives, such as cost minimization or profit maximization. Whether optimizing or simulating in character, location models require certain information inputs for their execution. Included among them are all or most of the following:

1. Market demands, by location, stated in terms of units per period of time.

2. Warehouse capacities and costs, by location, stated in terms of units of capacity per period of time and cost per unit, respectively.

3. Plant capacities and costs, by location, stated in terms of units of capacity per period of time and cost per unit, respectively.

4. Transport capacities and costs, by origin-destination pair, stated in terms of units per period of time and cost per unit, respectively.

5. Sources of supply, capacities, and costs, by location, stated in terms of units per period of time and cost per unit, respectively.

6. A statement of the objective that the model is to fulfill (explicitly stated in the case of optimizing models and implicitly stated for simulations).

Inventory Models Inventory models are used to deal with the questions of how much, where, and when individual stock-keeping units (SKUs) should be stocked, typically on an SKUL-by-SKUL basis. In cases where demand exceeds supply, such models incorporate rationing or allocation rules not unlike those used in location models. Inventory models use as inputs all or most of the following types of information:

1. Demand levels, stated in terms of units per period of time.

2. Order or setup costs, stated in terms of dollars per order or machine setup.

3. Value per unit of the item for which inventory is controlled.

4. Inventory carrying costs, expressed as a percentage of the value of the average inventory on hand over a given period of time.

5. The cost of a stockout, in dollars per unit out of stock.

6. The length of the order cycle, stated in terms of a range of days and the probability of an order cycle of given length.

7. The probability of demand of varying levels over short periods of time, often expressed in units per day.

This brief exercise points up the basic problems of logistics system design efforts employing operations research techniques to date, particularly optimizing techniques for which inputs must be structured and restricted to those we have listed. It is with such techniques that location theorists and inventory theorists have concerned themselves. Their mutual failure to take a broader view in their work, and in fact to communicate across theoretical boundaries of regional science on the one hand and inventory theory and operations research on the other, has led us to the current dilemma: there is no optimizing technique capable of dealing with comprehensive logistics system design problems. If you doubt this statement, and in any case as a useful review exercise, position the various analytical approaches discussed here with the matrix in Figure 15–7.

STATE OF THE ART IN SYSTEM DESIGN TECHNIQUES

No one has yet reached the elusive goal of developing an optimizing model that encompasses both inventory (temporal) and location (spatial) solutions. Instead, procedures have been developed that deal with problems of similar scope in alternative ways.

Significant progress has been made in the development of optimizing techniques for managing the location of multi-item inventories and for managing location problems over time (with dynamic programming). And the creation of large-scale simulation models has somewhat muted interest in the quest for a comprehensive logistics system optimizer.

Perhaps the greatest promise lies in combining optimizing and simulation approaches in a creative interactive mode.

Multi-Item Location Optimization Techniques

Optimum location models often are constrained to use with one or a small number of products. However, through the creative use of mixed integer linear programming, several models have begun to appear that do allow for a more realistic treatment of multi-item product lines.[10] For the most part, they are somewhat cumbersome from a computing standpoint. But they offer opportunity for further achievement along this useful dimension.

FIGURE 15–7: Basic categories of analytic techniques for logistics system design

	Types of Techniques	
Types of Models Relevant for Logistics	**Optimizing**	**Simulation**
	Features: 1. Yield "optimum" results 2. Require many restrictive assumptions 3. Conserve computer time 4. Raise many additional questions	Features: 1. Do not yield recognizable optimum results 2. Require few restrictive assumptions 3. Require extensive computer time 4. Raise many additional questions

Location Models, typical inputs:
   Market demands, by location
   Warehouse capacities and costs, by location
   Plant capacities and costs, by location
   Transport capacities and costs, by origin-destination pair
   Sources of supply, capacities, and costs, by location
   Statement of objective toward which solution is directed		

Inventory Models, typical inputs:
   Demand levels
   Order or set-up costs
   Value per unit of controlled SKUL
   Inventory carrying costs
   Stock-out costs
   Cost of lost sales
   Order-cycle length and variability
   Demand level and variability		

Dynamic Analysis

In recent years, perhaps greater emphasis has been placed on the development of dynamic as opposed to static analytic techniques. Dynamic techniques measure the impact of current decisions on future results and future decisions by using outputs from one period of time as inputs for the next in an interactive computational procedure.

Dynamic Optimizing Techniques   Dynamic programming[11] was developed as an extension of linear programming not only to optimize location and other types of decisions for various points in time, but also to revise what might appear to be optimal near-term decisions to provide more optimal long-term results. For example, a linear programming analysis might indicate the desirability of closing a plant or warehouse at the present time. Dynamic programming would assess the future need for the facility, perhaps because of increasing demand levels for periods of time in the future, and take into account the costs of closing and subsequently opening the facility, before presenting the cost implications of a current decision. Thus, dynamic programming is particularly useful in considering the timing of decisions, invariably involving location in a logistical context.[12]

Dynamic Simulation Techniques   Dynamic simulation techniques describe rather than optimize system performance over time, incorporating decision rules determined by the user. They may range from models constructed for a special purpose to general-purpose problem-describing devices. Ballou's simulation of the interrelationships between inventory management programs at two or more levels in a channel of distribution is typical of the first of these.[13] Forrester's development of "industrial dynamics," including modeling rules, special-purpose language, and even a specially developed computer, is an example of the broader application of dynamic simulation.[14]

Perhaps the most comprehensive example of a dynamic simulation model is one designed by Bowersox and others, called LREPS (Long-Range Environmental Planning Simulator).[15] Among other features, this model allows a decision maker either to describe the system in the following terms or to assume changes resulting from managerial decisions along the following dimensions, among others: order characteristics, product mix, new product introduction policies, the mix of customers served by the system, the location of facilities, varying the number of echelons in a distribution channel through which various shipments may pass, inventory management policies, transportation methods, communication methods, and material-handling methods. The model measures the effectiveness of any combination of descriptors or decisions in terms of overall cost and customer service levels. LREPS provides the richest output detail of any logistics simulation analytic device developed to date. Perhaps unavoidably, however, it currently shares the shortcomings outlined earlier for all simulation techniques, including being cumbersome, having large data input requirements, and involving relatively high user expense.

Combined Approaches

Thus far we have concentrated on comprehensive approaches to logistics system design, incorporating both location and inventory models by means of either optimizing or simulation approaches. Perhaps the greatest promise lies in combining optimizing and simulation models in a creative interactive mode that can capitalize on the strengths and minimize the weaknesses of each. Mentzer and Schuster have termed these hybrid models.[16]

COMPREHENSIVE LOGISTICS SYSTEM DESIGN PROCESS

System design modeling efforts do not take place in a vacuum. They have to be authorized and endorsed by a senior management that often does not understand them fully. This requires an approach that engages management, defines the problem, and meets its objectives most effectively. Whether the effort involves an outside consultant or not, the following steps in a comprehensive system design process have proven useful to many managers. Basic questions associated with each step are included as an example of issues to be addressed.

Engaging Management and Defining the Effort

The single most important element of a successful effort to analyze and design a logistics system is top management interest and support. An early indicator of this is the willingness of senior management to meet to discuss objectives, scope, and constraints associated with the study. Useful questions to be posed at this point include the following:

Why is this question being addressed now?

What led to a decision to support a study effort?

What should its objectives be?

> Improved customer service?
>
> Reduced costs of transportation or inventory holding?
>
> Which takes highest priority if conflicting objectives can't be achieved?

What form should study outputs take?

> A one-time analysis and set of recommendations?
>
> A package of software and procedures for the continued management of the system?

What scope should the study take?

What questions should it answer? Some or all of the following?:

> What form of order-processing system and information-processing procedures, in terms of general characteristics described by time lags of various types, should be utilized by the company?
>
> What type of inventory control policy should be used?
>
> Which products should be stocked at various locations in the system?

What form of transportation, in terms of its general characteristics, should be used?

How many warehouses should be operated?

Where should they be located?

To what extent should each plant and warehouse be utilized, in terms of throughput?

What warehouses should be supplied from each plant?

What customers should be supplied from each warehouse?

How should customer service be defined?

What levels of customer service should be sought and achieved?

What constraints may be placed on the study? For example, would the following types of possible recommendations be acceptable?

Closing a manufacturing facility?

Altering customer service standards?

Altering basic modes of transportation employed in the system?

Completely altering the inventory control and forecasting procedures?

Changing the organization for the management of logistics activities?

Based on this early effort to define the study and at the same time gauge and engage the support of senior management, it is useful to turn to the question of organization for the study.

Organization for the Study

A comprehensive logistics system design effort requires continuing involvement and commitment of an organization's top management because it deals with matters of strategic long-run importance. Further, because logistics touches such a wide range of activities, a company will benefit from adopting an integrative, cost trade-off approach to logistics decision making.

Top management must understand and accept the need for day-to-day decisions to be the responsibility of functional managers. Yet, at the same time, the authority of functional managers may have to be constrained if corporate objectives are to be achieved. It is precisely because logistics touches on so wide a range of activities that it is essential for top-level management to acknowledge the ''subtle but powerful effects on logistics of the decisions made within and between the regular functional areas. Manufacturing and marketing people have to accept constraints on some day-to-day decisions. This may require senior management intervention in the beginning.''[17]

For logistics managers to support a strategy of overall cost leadership,

> . . . the key management tasks are to get the elements of the system right, and to locate logistics planning in the appropriate organizational context. A low-cost strategy, for example, requires that such planning be designed, controlled, and administered as a centralized

staff function. By contrast, innovation and differentiation based strategies, for which cost minimization is not a primary goal, require that line management be involved in the design and administration of the logistics system.[18]

Membership on a study steering committee may provide the right level of opportunity for top management to learn what is going on and to provide occasional inputs to the process.

In addition, a study task force comprising those managers expected to provide the sources of data important to the study can be useful. Although a minority of the membership of the task force may be responsible for actually carrying out the study, everyone on the group might be expected to contribute significantly at one point or another.

It is the responsibility of the managers directing the study to ensure that each participant understands precisely what the company is trying to do and to bring logistical capabilities in line with corporate purposes. For example, for the company that has adopted a strategy of leverage from logistics, an awareness of how the company might gain leverage in the market through a good fit between its logistics system and its competitive strategy[19] can help provide an effective framework for the study. Figure 15–8 summarizes the operational details of that fit.

Planning for the Study

Basic planning for a comprehensive study may include the identification of the steps to be followed and the types of effort to be put forth, a timetable, and a budget.

The timetable is dependent on the efforts determined necessary for the study. Important questions sometimes left unanswered at this point (to the later regret of the study team) include:

Does data necessary to the study exist in a form that is readily available and usable with a minimum of additional processing?

What skills does the organization have in house for the study?

What outside skills may have to be engaged?

Is there sufficient in-house computing capacity to handle the necessary processing of data?

By what date must the study be completed?

Is there a definite budgetary constraint on the study or is this dependent on the amount to be proposed for it?

An example of a timetable showing the relative timing of various steps in one comprehensive system design effort is shown in Figure 15–9.

Selection of Analytical Devices

The selection of analytical techniques to be used in a study may depend on answers to the following questions:

FIGURE 15–8: Leverage through logistics

CHOSEN MODES OF COMPETITION:	PRODUCT INNOVATION	CUSTOMER SERVICE	COST LEADERSHIP
GOALS OF LOGISTICS SYSTEM	Availability Flexibility to volume shifts Flexibility to product changes Ability to handle small orders Ability to handle erratic order frequencies	Rapid delivery Consistent delivery Availability Flexibility to customer changes	Minimum cost with an acceptable service level
LOCUS OF PLANNING	Line management	Line management	Staff
PROCUREMENT	Seek vendors who can ensure: Supply continuity Quality Flexibility to changes in specifications	Seek vendors who can ensure: Consistent delivery Full-line availability Responsiveness	Make maximum use of volume purchase economies Centralized purchasing organization Seek vendors offering low prices
INVENTORY POLICY	Tensions between the need for high safety stocks kept locally to ensure availability and the need to keep inventories low to retain flexibility and guard against obsolescence: a compromise between these two extremes is required; the form of that compromise will depend on a variety of technological, physical, economic, and competitive factors; most important are pace of product change and competitive intensity	For the company that produces to inventory, local inventories will be required for "market presence" and rapid, consistent delivery	Investment in inventory at minimal levels that ensure "acceptable" service
TRANSPORT POLICY	Premium, rapid transport (air freight if sensible) Use of common carrier rather than investment in private fleet LTL shipments common	For normal supply, a mix of short-haul LTL (for customer delivery) and long-haul TL or CL (for warehouse restocking)	Low-cost transport (rail or piggyback) High utilization (TL or CL shipments) Volume discounts to encourage direct from-the-plant carload shipments Private fleet may be desirable for better control, lower transport costs
FACILITIES NETWORK	Almost non-existent in most cases - - delivery from plant to customer When warehouses required, public or leased warehouses used	For the company that produces to inventory, a multiechelon system (plant or national warehouses, regional warehouses, local warehouses) will be likely	Centralized and consolidated (minimize number of local facilities) Rationalized (number, size, scale) and sourcing decisions made to minimize cost Automated as much as is sensible

FIGURE 15–9: Suggested tasks and their time sequence for completion of a proposed logistics system study

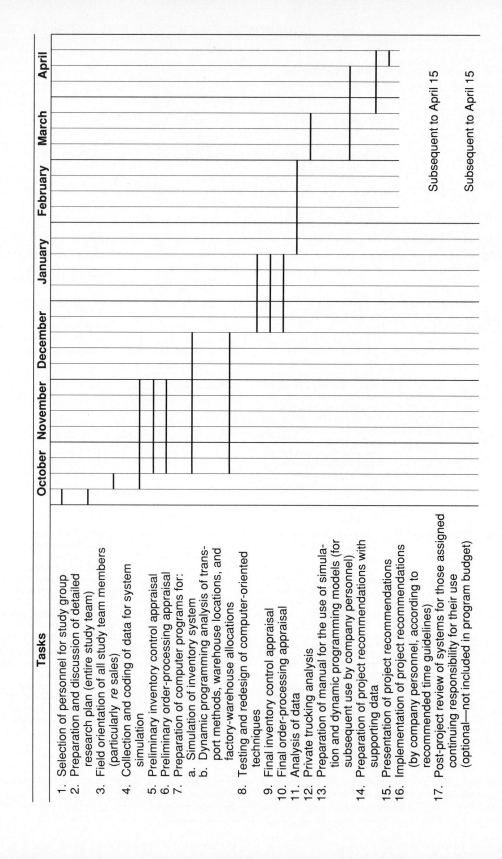

What are the questions to be addressed by the study?

With what frequency will the technique be employed during the study? After the study?

What data can be found or developed for use with a particular model?

Are off-the-shelf models or methods sufficient, or will customized approaches have to be developed?

Who will update and maintain the analytic technique at the conclusion of the study, if it is important?

Analysis and Reporting

The data base established for a comprehensive logistics system design effort can serve several functions. It can afford a baseline measurement of the status quo, the basis for analysis, a capability for performance tracking, and a tool for subsequent management control. Some or all of these might be important in a particular study.

Information important to a broad-based study can be organized in terms of management inputs and outputs or results shown in Figure 15–10. As you can see, this is not confined to numbers, but encompasses a number of elements of what has come to be referred to by some as a logistics management audit. Important types of information to be collected at this stage include statements of procedure and organization charts as well as numerical measures of results.

For the effective measurement of progress resulting from the system redesign effort, it may be useful to establish and implement several indicators of progress even before the presentation of findings and recommendations from the study.

Given the organization suggested earlier for the study, the reporting of findings and recommendations may become something of a formality. But it can afford an opportunity for an additional exchange of views among senior management as well as an interaction between the study steering committee and task force.

Implementation

Just as it is impossible to put the affairs of a business organization ''on hold'' while it is being studied, there may be no need to delay the implementation of the more obvious study recommendations before the study is completed. Implementation begins at the first meeting with senior management to set the objectives for the effort. It takes a big step forward with the organization of the steering committee and the task force.

Among the most important recommendations are those that concern (1) the individual(s) who are to be given major responsibility for implementing study recommendations, (2) the methods to be used for measuring progress, and (3) the way in which models and methods resulting from the study are to be maintained and updated periodically.

This general approach often is time-consuming and expensive. But if the desired result is a comprehensive logistics system design, unless management is willing to make the type of commitment implied in the process outlined here, experience suggests that the results of the effort might well fall short of management expectations.

FIGURE 15–10: Important elements of a logistics system audit

Review of System Inputs	Review of System Outputs

	Physical Configuration of the System
	  Locations, Capacities of Facilities
	  Volumes of Product Shipped
	  Methods of Transportation Used

Company Organization
  General
  Logistics
	Product Line Characteristics
	  Sales Volume
	  Physical Characteristics

Marketing Policies
  Product Line
  Channels of Distribution
  Sales Compensation
  Pricing
	Raw Materials and Components
	  Usage Rates
	  Physical Characteristics

Order Processing System	Markets
	  Nature of Customer Orders
	  Customers' Logistics Needs
	  Service Levels
	  Seasonal or Other Sales Patterns
	  Competition

Inventory Control Program
  Control Model
  Forecasting Procedures	

Transportation Methods	Service Standards
	  Methods of Measurement
	  Levels Achieved

Warehousing Methods	

Material Handling and
  Packaging Methods
	Time Lags
	  Order Cycle
	  Replenishment Cycle
	  Procurement Cycle
	  Inventory Update Cycle
	  Billing Cycle
	  Payment Cycle

Production Planning Methods	

Purchasing
  Policies
  Methods
	Costs

	Executive Concerns

SUMMARY

A comprehensive logistics system design effort is distinguished by its attention to costs of both movement and demand-supply coordination. It seeks an integration of interrelated parts that results in greater productivity for the resulting system than could be achieved by the sum of its parts. And it views problems in terms of logistics activities carried on by firms at two or more levels in a channel of distribution often with a need to coordinate their efforts.

One of the earliest steps toward a comprehensive system design was the total cost approach stimulated by advances in air freight, an approach that suggested that the way to achieve lowest total costs of distribution might be to spend greater amounts for premium transportation methods in order to achieve savings in the holding of inventory. This gave rise to more detailed explorations of many types of logistics cost trade-offs that have become a common characteristic of system design efforts.

System design and redesign efforts may be prompted by the type of intuitive probe that may suggest the need for a study. Such intuitive probes include questions concerning the largest or fastest growing logistics cost items incurred by a firm, some type of measurement against industry or company standards, a review of the transportation-inventory cost mix in an industry or in the firm, an appraisal of opportunities for achieving economies of scale through a consolidation of shipments or inventory locations, a review of the effectiveness with which the system performs assorting and sorting activities, an evaluation of the extent to which the system allows for the delay of commitment of raw material to particular product or a product to a particular location, the extent to which the system provides for special logistics treatment of products or markets, and the degree to which system balance is being achieved.

Models employed for the analysis of logistics systems can be categorized as dealing with inventories or locations by means of optimizing techniques or simulation. Optimizing models provide the best answers to problems of limited definition within many constraints and assumptions. Simulation allows for a more complete problem description, but cannot guarantee that the best solution to the problem will be found. Approaches combining the use of optimizing and simulation models in the same package in an interactive mode offer the best promise for the effective analysis of comprehensive logistics systems in the foreseeable future.

A process for managing a comprehensive system design effort may include a number of steps, including (1) engaging senior management and defining the effort; (2) organizing for the study itself, including the establishment of a study steering committee (sounding board of senior managers) and a task force (comprising managers with responsibility for important sources of information and various aspects of design and implementation); (3) the assessment of available resources and the development of a timetable and budget for the study; (4) the selection of appropriate devices for system analysis; (5) analysis and reporting efforts; and (6) implementation of the study recommendations, including the designation of managers responsible for maintaining machinery for analysis and control created by the study. The first of these steps may well be the most important. Without top management cooperation and support, the best efforts of a logistics system design study team may be wasted.

DISCUSSION QUESTIONS

1. Explain the relationship between logistics strategy and logistics system design.

2. What are four characteristics of a comprehensive logistics system design effort?

3. Why is total cost analysis necessary? Why is it often difficult?

4. What types of logistics costs are usually more easily ascertained? What types are more difficult to pin down, and why?

5. As among "cost reduction," "redesign," and "rebalancing," can it be said that one of these approaches is best or better than the others? Why or why not?

6. What is the significance of the "Order Penetration Point" as shown in Figure 15–3 in relation to logistics system design?

7. Why must one approach an analysis of cost trade-offs with care and caution?

8. Explain the difference between "optimizing" and "simulating" analytic techniques. Is one superior to the other? Explain. What are the weaknesses of these techniques?

9. What is the underlying purpose of "dynamic" logistics system design approaches?

10. What are the basic steps in a comprehensive logistics system design process?

CASE: WHAT LOGISTICS STRATEGY TO ADOPT?

As the chapter points out, companies vary greatly in their logistics strategies. Primarily, these strategies are customer oriented. Strategies must be adapted to competition, the size of markets served, the places of firms in industry channels of distribution, and so forth.

What logistics strategy for physical distribution would be appropriate for each of the following types of companies? In formulating your answers make whatever reasonable assumptions you consider necessary or helpful, and state them.

A MANUFACTURER OF FINE CHINA TABLEWARE

This firm manufactures and distributes place setting pieces and serving pieces of fine china tableware in 14 different patterns. In addition it produces, on a semiannual basis, replacement pieces for 37 obsolete patterns that have been special ordered during the preceding six months by customers through retail stores that carry the firm's line of china. Its plant is located in upper New York State. The firm's products are distributed directly to large retail chain warehouses and to many independent retailers throughout the United States and Canada.

A MAJOR MANUFACTURER OF CHILDREN'S TOYS

This firm produces a very broad line of toys and distributes them directly to large toy merchandising chains such as Toys Я Us™, to other retail chains of department stores and "drugstores," and to several small corporate groups of "upscale" toy stores. The firm's plant is in St. Louis, Missouri. Toy sales are very seasonal. Manufacturers take orders from major retail chain buyers at national toy merchandising exhibitions in February and March of each year, and on the basis of these orders, they plan production quantities of each toy. Heavy shipments of toys for the Christmas season begin in October and continue until early December. Certain "hot numbers" result in rush reorders that are shipped during November and up to as little as ten days before Christmas.

A LOCAL WHOLESALE DISTRIBUTOR OF FROZEN AND CHILLED FOODS

This firm carries a broad line of branded food items, including packaged frozen vegetables, fruits (strawberries, raspberries, and so forth), and prepared items such as frozen dinners, frozen pies, and other frozen desserts. Chilled products included a variety of juices, fruit salad, cottage cheese, other cheeses, butter, margarine, prepared uncooked meats, such as bacon and sausage, and prepared cooked meats, such as bologna, ham slices, and so forth. The firm distributes its products to independent grocery stores, free-standing restaurants, hotel restaurants and college dining halls in a metropolitan area of approximately 600 square miles.

A REGIONAL MANUFACTURER OF ALUMINUM LAWN FURNITURE, SCREEN DOORS, SCREEN WINDOWS, AND PATIO SCREENING (INCLUDING BOTH SCREENING AND THE CHANNEL BARS TO WHICH SCREENING IS ATTACHED)

The firm's plant is located in Los Angeles, and it markets its products in the western states, primarily California, Arizona, New Mexico, Utah, and Nevada, with some sales in western Texas, Oregon, Idaho, and Washington. It sells its products to hardware chains, "do-it-yourself" chains, major building contractors, and "home and garden" chains. It does not sell to individual retail stores. It has one warehouse for finished goods, located next door to its plant.

SUGGESTED READINGS

In a practical sense, almost any well written book or article dealing with any meaningful aspect of logistics operations management would be a relevant reference for logistics systems strategy and design. Clearly, therefore, the various readings suggested at the end of all other chapters may be considered as specific additional references to those that follow.

The Annual Conference Proceedings of the Council of Logistics Management (CLM) typically contain articles and current comment on the topic of this chapter. Examples from the 1989 CLM annual conference include the following:

DAVID B. LIVINGSTON, "Logistics as a Competitive Weapon, Part II: Total Logistics Cost and Corporate Strategy," vol. I, 375–398.

FREDERICK J. BEIER, "The ABC's of Integrated Logistics," vol. II, 81–91.

C. JOHN LANGLEY, Jr., et al., "Logistics and the Concept of Value Added," vol. II, 157–166.

BOWERSOX, DONALD J., DAVID J. KLOSS, and OMAR KEITH HELFERICH, *Logistical Management*, 3d ed. New York: Macmillan Publishing Co., Inc., 1986. This book presents especially relevant discussions of logistical strategy and decision processes in Chapter 2, planning and design methodology in Chapter 12 and design and analysis techniques in Chapter 13.

COYLE, JOHN J., and EDWARD J. BARDI, *The Management of Business Logistics*, 3d ed. St. Paul: West Publishing Company, 1984. Chapter 14 (Logistics Strategy) is a particularly useful treatment of the macroeconomic environment within which logistics strategy is formulated.

JOHNSON, JAMES C., and DONALD F. WOOD, *Contemporary Physical Distribution and Logistics*, 3d ed. New York: Macmillan Publishing Company, 1986. Chapter 12 deals with logistics system analysis and design.

LAMBERT, DOUGLAS M., and JAMES R. STOCK, *Strategic Physical Distribution Management*, Homewood, Illinois, Richard D. Irwin, Inc., 1982. Chapters 2 ("The Integrated Physical Distribution Management Concept") and 3 ("The Strategic Physical Distribution Plan") together constitute a useful treatment of logistics system design.

LEWIS, HOWARD T., JAMES W. CULLITON, and JACK D. STEELE, *The Role of Air Freight in Physical Distribution*, Boston: Division of Research, Graduate School of Business Administration,

Harvard University, 1956. After more than thirty-five years, this book remains a classic pioneering study in total cost analysis applied to physical distribution.

MENTZER, JOHN T., and ALLAN D. SCHUSTER, "Computer Modelling in Logistics," vol. 3, no. 1 (1982): 1–55. Published as a special supplement to an issue of the *Journal of Business Logistics*, this monograph-length piece offers one of the most comprehensive reviews of logistics system design techniques prepared thus far. In addition to an extensive bibliography, it contains an interesting projection of future trends in design efforts.

ROBESON, JAMES F., and ROBERT G. HOUSE, eds., *The Distribution Handbook*, New York: The Free Press, 1985. A comprehensive volume that treats a wide variety of topics related to logistics system design and strategy.

SHAPIRO, ROY D., and JAMES L. HESKETT, *Logistics Strategy: Concepts and Cases*, St. Paul, Minnesota: West Publishing Company, 1985. Part II ("Designing an Integrated Logistics System") focuses on the managerial decisions relevant to logistics systems design.

ENDNOTES

1. *Webster's Seventh New Collegiate Dictionary*, G. & C. Merriam Company. Springfield, Massachusetts, 1971.

2. Howard T. Lewis, James W. Culliton, and Jack D. Steele, *The Role of Air Freight in Physical Distribution* (Boston: Division of Research, Graduate School of Business Administration, Harvard University, 1956).

3. Graham Sharman, "The Rediscovery of Logistics," *Harvard Business Review* (September-October 1984): 75.

4. *Ibid.*

5. Roy D. Shapiro, "Getting Leverage from Logistics," *Harvard Business Review* (May-June 1984): 124.

6. National Council of Physical Distribution Management, *Measuring and Improving Productivity in Physical Distribution*, an A. T. Kearney study undertaken for NCPDM (Chicago: NCPDM, 1984).

7. Shapiro, "Getting Leverage."

8. *Ibid.*

9. See James L. Heskett, Lewis M. Schneider, Nicholas A. Glaskowsky, Jr., and Robert M. Ivie, *Case Problems in Business Logistics* (New York: The Ronald Press Co., 1973).

10. For a description of one of the more widely used of these, see A. M. Geoffrion and G. W. Graves, "Multicommodity Distribution System Design by Bender's Composition," *Management Science* (January 1974): 822–44.

11. For a detailed general exploration of dynamic programming, see R. E. Bellman and S. E. Dreyfus, *Applied Dynamic Programming* (Princeton, N.J.: Princeton University Press, 1962), and Ronald A. Howard, "Dynamic Programming," *Management Science* (January 1966): 317–18.

12. For a more detailed discussion of dynamic programming, see Ronald H. Ballou, *Business Logistics Management* (Englewood Cliffs, N.J.: Prentice-Hall, Inc., 1973): 259–266.

13. Ronald H. Ballou, *Multi-Echelon Inventory Control for Interrelated and Vertically Integrated Firms* (Columbus: The Ohio State University, unpublished dissertation, 1965).

14. Jay W. Forrester, *Industrial Dynamics* (Cambridge and New York: The M.I.T. Press and John Wiley & Sons, Inc., 1961).

15. See Donald J. Bowersox, "Planning Physical Distribution Operations With Dynamic Simulation," *Journal of Marketing* (January 1972): 17–25.

16. John T. Mentzer and Allan D. Schuster, "Computing Modeling in Logistics: Existing Models and Future Outlook," *Journal of Business Logistics* 3, no. 1 (1982): 1–55.

17. Sharman, "Rediscover."

18. Shapiro, "Getting Leverage."

19. *Ibid.*, 126.

Increasingly, top management is recognizing the importance of logistics in formulating corporate strategy.

CHAPTER SIXTEEN

16

Organization for Logistics Management

LEARNING OBJECTIVES

The objectives of this chapter are to:

- ➤ Present, discuss, and explain various reasons for the difficulties encountered in organizing for effective logistics management.

- ➤ Discuss general principles of management organization and their application to the management of logistics functions.

- ➤ Consider the factors that influence and determine the significance of logistics functions in an organization.

- ➤ Determine the resulting amount of management concern and attention that should be devoted to the place of logistics functions in the structure of the organization.

- ➤ Present and discuss alternatives for organizing logistics functions in the organization.

- ➤ Note the special circumstances that apply to the organization of logistics functions in the multinational firm.

- ➤ Discuss the staffing needs for logistics management.

- ➤ Consider the role of the logistics manager as an integrator in the organization.

Organizing for effective logistics management is often a frustrating task and seldom an easy one.* The pioneers in the logistics field had to define, build, and defend new organization arrangements against difficult odds because effective management of logistics functions tends to collide head on with traditional business organization structures found in many firms.

We could, in this chapter, limit our discussion to the principles of organization of basic importance to any business function. However, that would overlook major questions of implementation that should accompany any discussion of principles, concepts, and questions of implementation that are of paramount importance to the manager in a developing and evolving field such as logistics.

One student of organization recognized this when he wrote:

> It must be remembered that there is nothing more difficult to plan, more doubtful of success, nor more dangerous to manage, than the creation of a new system. For the initiator has the enmity of all who would profit by the preservation of the old institutions and merely lukewarm defenders in those who would gain by the new ones.

The author was Niccolo Machiavelli. He wrote it in 1513. His words are as valid today as when they were written.

With this in mind, we can benefit from a review of responsibilities for logistics activities to be organized, some basic organizational principles applicable to any function of a business, factors influencing the structure of organization for logistics, organizational alternatives in use in large companies today, and the types of skills important for logistics management. Questions unique to the organization of firms with substantial multinational logistics activities will be noted as well.

There are only a few useful generalizations that can be made about organization for logistics. Among those you might keep in mind as you read the material in this chapter are the following: (1) however they are assigned, logistics functions and responsibilities are present in any organization, whether recognized or not, (2) there is no one right answer to the so-called "organization problem," (3) however, it is likely that some organizational arrangements are better than others, (4) there are as many organizational schemes for logistics as there are organizations, and (5) what works today might not work as well tomorrow.

THE BASIC ORGANIZATIONAL PROBLEM

Whenever two or more people combine efforts to achieve one or more goals, organization (division of effort) is required. This then requires careful identification and assignment of responsibilities and reporting relationships in order to make the total effort of the group more effective and efficient.

Logistics functions must be managed in any organization, regardless of how or where in the organization this is done. Some are recognized formally, appearing on the ever-present but often misleading organization charts that at least provide a *crude* map of an organization. Some never appear on an organization chart and must be recognized and managed by less formal means.

---

*Portions of this chapter are based on James L. Heskett, "Organization," in James Robeson, ed., *Distribution Handbook* (New York: The Free Press, 1985).

Formal responsibilities encompassed by the term logistics are shown on the vertical bars in Figure 16–1. They often are found on organization charts and may be assigned to one or more managers in an organization. This may lead to managerial conflict as discussed below.

Less formal, but nonetheless important, logistics-related responsibilities often never appear on organization charts. Several are shown circled in Figure 16–2. They are of interest and concern to several major functional groups within an organization, as suggested by the maze of lines connecting functions with the responsibilities circled in Figure 16–2.

In a broad sense, logistics involves the physical flow of material that takes place in response to signals in the form of flows of information. The process is diagrammed in simplified form in Figure 16–1.

Information that flows from the market, in the form of orders or other indicators, provides the basis for forecasts of future demand. The forecasts, in turn, trigger replenishment orders that produce inventories at factories or distribution centers. These orders influence production schedules that in turn help determine the timing and quantities with which raw materials are procured. At each stage in the process, this information provides the basis for purchasing transportation from carriers or arranging in-company transportation service, calculating storage requirements, and so on.

Information flows trigger material flows — beginning with the shipment of raw materials, parts, and such to company facilities and continuing with the transfer of these materials to the production plant — the handling of materials through the production process, and their transportation to distribution centers for holding and subsequent shipment to markets or direct shipment from finished goods inventories held at the factory.

Figuratively speaking, we can view these as "horizontal" flows of information in one direction and of material in the other. Organizational problems and conflicts begin when we attempt to impose on this scheme the traditional "vertical" organization oriented around business functions. This type of organization, typified by the traditional functions shown at the top of Figure 16–1, is based on the concept of specialization as the key to the effective management of diverse functions, especially in a large enterprise.

The specialization of management tasks leads to many perplexing questions for effective logistics management. Whose province is the management of finished-product distribution centers? Who should manage finished-product inventories? Is transportation of inbound materials properly the responsibility of purchasing, traffic, or production? Who should take the lead in establishing customer service standards? In short, specialization can lead not only to jurisdictional questions, but also to the duplication *or* neglect of an area of responsibility.

So much for our introduction to some of the general questions of logistics management organization. Before turning to factors influencing the importance and nature of logistics in the organization, we'll review briefly several basic organization principles and terms.

BASIC ORGANIZATION PRINCIPLES AND TERMS

Over the years, practice has suggested the value of a relatively small number of principles in the development of any organization. While it rarely is possible or desirable to adhere strictly to all of them in any given situation, it is useful to keep them in mind. A relatively few such principles and terms provide us with all the shorthand notation we will need for this discussion.

FIGURE 16–1: Basic conflicts created by the imposition of a traditionally "vertical" organization structure on the logistics function involving "horizontal" flows

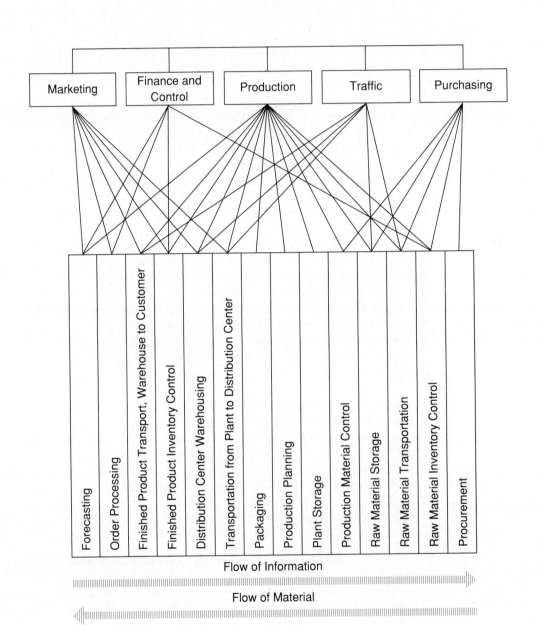

FIGURE 16–2: Logistics related responsibilities seldom found on organization charts and the functional areas often taking a strong interest in them

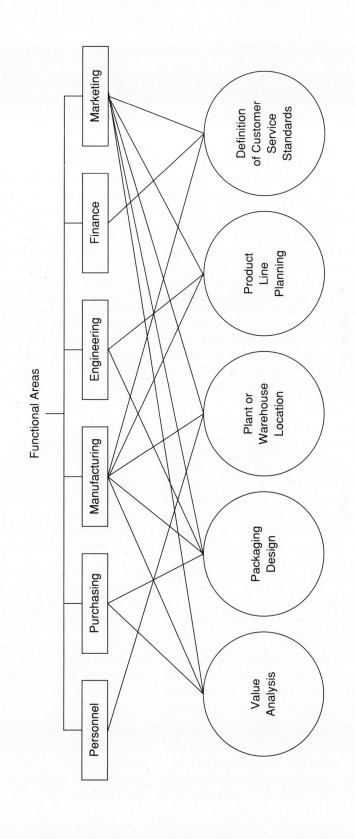

HOW TOP MANAGEMENT REALLY VIEWS LOGISTICS: PART I

E. J. Muller

Back when American manufacturing ruled the domestic roost, the traffic and distribution function was typically the hind end of companies obsessed with production.

Usually, a middle management beancounter was assigned to monitor physical distribution costs to ensure that expenses weren't eroding profit margins. The only time traffic functionaries made it to the corporate boardroom was when they were called on the carpet. And when it came to interacting with executives in finance, operations or marketing, the traffic department couldn't share the washroom key, let alone strategic concepts. Those dark days appear to be over.

Consulting firm Temple Barker & Sloane (TBS) has conducted a pair of major studies aimed at determining what top management expects from the transportation and distribution functions. TBS Vice President David Anderson sums up the results: "Senior management is worrying about logistics. They don't always understand how it works, but practically all of them are asking, 'What is it doing for me?' They are expecting radical change, but they aren't sure their distribution department can provide it. To top executives, the people in logistics still have an overwhelming cost mentality. Not enough, they believe, are looking at the service side."

In the past two months Anderson has met with four company chairmen. Each one was troubled by the time involved in taking a product from concept to market. In the past the process might have spanned five years, but company chiefs now believe it must be compressed to a year or less to gain a decent market footing.

The Roots of Awakening

The genesis of logistics' increased significance was the energy crisis of the early 1970s. That was the end of predictable freight rates. A bright new spotlight on transportation costs began to evaporate the business-as-usual attitude in corporate traffic departments. By the end of the '70s, two other factors impacted the profession: advanced information systems and deregulation. Suddenly, transportation and distribution, separate functions in many companies, were being consolidated and managed with greater efficiency. Today, the globalization of business has reinforced the service value of logistics in many companies. These companies realize that the product often is not enough. The ability to penetrate new markets and service all international customers equally is an essential competitive advantage.

Robert Wayman, chief financial officer of Hewlett-Packard Corporation, offers an even more vital explanation of top management's new interest in logistics. "The main thing that's changed is our sensitivity to the customer," he says. "In the past few years we've been actively seeking customer satisfaction information, and we've learned that they really care about the whole transaction process, not only the product.

"We are not a company classically dependent on physical distribution in a major way. That's not usually a big concern in companies with high value goods," Wayman says. "But by viewing logistics as a vital aspect of customer satisfaction we're getting a better appreciation of it. When somebody pays $500,000 for equipment, they're not tolerant of poor delivery. They want it in a timely, complete fashion." As Hewlett-Packard's market grows, the closeness of longstanding customer relationships diminishes. Service must speak for the company.

Prominent companies adopting a higher level approach to logistics include Colgate-Palmolive USA and Quaker Oats. In 1987, Colgate realigned its domestic business along product channel lines. The result was vertically integrated functions based on each product line, rather than the traditional horizontal staff structure.

At Colgate USA, logistics includes purchasing, operations planning, distribution operations (including field DCs), transportation, logistics planning and technical services. According to VP of Logistics Nicholas LaHowchic, Colgate's logistics mission is to plan, implement and control the purchasing and flow of all material, product and information from origin to consumption.

LaHowchic told an audience at this year's Council of Logistics Management conference that "Colgate understood the need to change. It understood that Purchasing *is* Transportation, and vice versa." He also stressed that where top management is concerned, "logistics is many things, and one of those things is a sell job. It is always a sell job."

Quaker Oats has shown its commitment by creating a National Customer Service Center to link sales and logistics more closely. This includes making logistics personnel available to sales representatives when addressing a customer's supply and delivery concerns.

Not all companies are progressive. In most, logistics continues to be viewed as a cost center. When he was vice president of distribution and logistics at Nabisco Corp., Richard Price had people in the corporate traffic department telling him every month how much they saved in negotiations. "You must be able to relate costs as a percentage of sales if it's to have any significance," he says. "And to impress upper management you must show that through improved service you are gaining additional sales opportunities."

Price, now president of Itel Distribution Systems, is a 25-year veteran in the distribution industry. He's witnessed first-hand the transformation in management's view of the profession. "Distribution was never of paramount importance in any corporation I was in," he says. "When I was at Nabisco, it rose to prominence when Standard Brands and Nabisco merged. When the decision was made to separate the units, however, management ignored the savings available on the distribution side." He says there were valid management reasons for Nabisco chiefs making that decision, but that the experience is a strong indicator of logistics' stature in the corporate hierarchy. He believes that logistics is understood in theory, but in application, "companies find it very hard to accomplish." What's critical is that senior management spread the concept across the company. "It's not always to the corporation's advantage to put someone in charge of the function at a high corporate level," he adds. "That often leads to turf battles."

He doesn't think it is necessary for large corporations to create a logistics operation encompassing purchasing, operations, marketing, and so forth. "What's essential is a common thread. I like to think of it as a railroad track running through the corporation," he says.

The importance of that railroad track has increased at Hewlett-Packard, although management doesn't feel compelled to hammer the ties in place. "There are few formal vehicles for interaction between functions," relates CFO Wayman. "Our Delivery Performance Task Force would be the most obvious example, where an operations committee comprised of marketing, manufacturing, transportation, distribution and information systems people works on improving our service 'from quote to customer.' Most of the time, however, we don't even think much about it. This is a fairly fluid company. We don't depend on a formal overlay. Interaction is bred into the corporate culture."

Unity of Command

The principle of unity of command is used to emphasize the need for no more than one superior with direct authority over a subordinate. This "one boss of a subordinate" rule allows for so-called *functional* supervision, generally intended to provide expert support without injecting a second boss into the relationship.

Span of Control

Span of control refers to the number of subordinates a manager can supervise. Naturally, limits have to be placed on span of control in an effectively managed organization. While such limits sometimes are stated in terms like "no more than five to seven subordinates per manager," in fact they are determined by the type of people and tasks being supervised and the manner in which supervision is carried out. If there were no limits on span of control, all subordinates would report to the chief executive officer, a situation tolerable only in the smallest organizations.

Responsibility and Authority

The terms responsibility and authority are two that are used and often misused in discussions of organization. We'll use responsibility to mean the results for which a manager is held accountable, whether measured in quantitative or nonquantitative ways. Authority is the right to direct the actions of subordinates and hold them accountable for results.

Theorists have long debated whether a manager's authority should be commensurate with his or her responsibility. As a matter of fact, authority without commensurate responsibility or accountability can lead to arbitrary, uncontrollable actions. But the reverse, responsibility without commensurate authority, is a *fact of life* for many corporate logistics managers today. It means they must often seek alternatives to direct authority as a means of discharging their responsibilities and reaching their goals.

Line and Staff Relationships and Functional Authority

Two other terms, line and staff, referring to types of responsibility and authority, will crop up repeatedly in our discussion. We use the term "line" to refer to those relationships in which the superior has direct authority over a subordinate and is responsible for using that action-oriented authority to get things done. Staff relationships, by contrast, are advisory or coordinative in nature and should not be confused with functional authority. A suggestion from the public relations department on when and how to conduct distribution center visitor tours would be "staff advice." However, a directive from the finance vice president specifying how distribution center cost records are to be kept would be an exercise of functional authority.

Little direct authority can be applied in a staff relationship, although a person in a staff relationship *may well be held responsible for achieving results* by means of the advice or coordinative support provided to managers with line authority and responsibility. Responsibility without authority may seem "unfair," but, as previously noted, this is a fact of life in many firms and managers must cope with it.

Centralization and Functional Organization

These terms refer to the relative levels in an organization to which responsibility, particularly for profits, is assigned. Top management in a centralized organization typically reserves that responsibility for itself. In order to carry out profit responsibility, often it is necessary in a centralized organization for all important decisions to be made or coordinated at the top, requiring that information flows be directed to and from the highest levels.

A centralized organization often is structured along functional lines, with senior executives in charge of finance, marketing, manufacturing, and other major functions reporting directly to a chief executive officer responsible for coordinating major functional decisions.

Decentralization and Business-Oriented Organization

Responsibilities, particularly for profit, are delegated to lower ranks of management in a decentralized organization. Profit responsibility often is centered around so-called strategic business units, each with control over its own operating functions, such as marketing, manufacturing, and logistics. Such organizations often include in their top management senior executives who are responsible for major staff or advisory functions, as well as the activities involved in allocating corporate assets (particularly money in the form of approved budgets) to the strategic business units.

FACTORS INFLUENCING THE IMPORTANCE AND NATURE OF LOGISTICS IN THE ORGANIZATION

Among factors influencing the importance and nature of logistics in an organization are the type of business transacted; the importance of logistics in relation to total costs of doing business; the need to manage trade-offs between important logistics cost categories of transportation, inventory holding, and lost sales (customer service); the complexity of the logistics network; the need for flexibility in management; the nature of the overall corporate strategy; and the capacities of people available to manage.

Type of Business Transacted

In organizations that do not manufacture the products in which they deal, logistics assumes a greater *relative* importance in the firm's operations. Thus, in a wholesaling or retailing organization, it may be called operations and be found alongside accounting and sales (or merchandising and store management), as shown in the organization for a wholesaling firm in Figure 16–3.

Importance of Logistics Costs

Logistics costs of transportation, inventory holding, and lost sales may range from 2 percent of total costs in a firm manufacturing high technology equipment and components to 40 percent in a firm producing basic raw materials or agricultural products. Studies have shown some correlation between the level of the most senior logistics executive in an organization and the importance of logistics in a firm's total cost structure. However, the number of deviations from this relationship suggest that other factors may be even more important determinants of the importance of the function. And, it is quite certain that they are more important than cost levels in determining the nature of responsibilities assigned to the most senior logistics manager. Foremost among these is the need to manage trade-offs among important logistics cost categories.

The Need to Manage Trade-Offs among Important Logistics Cost Categories

Logistics cost trade-offs influence greatly the complexity and nature of the manager's task. Consider these case examples.

A producer of high technology components used in the manufacture of computers sells to a limited number of OEMs (original equipment manufacturers). Because of their high value, such products incur high inventory holding costs. However, failure to meet delivery schedules results in severe strains on customer relations and potentially high costs of lost sales. Thus, there is a potential conflict between inventory holding costs and prompt customer order filling. Transportation costs in relation to total costs are, however, so low that even if airfreight service is used consistently the cost is relatively insignificant. In this business, logistics costs not only are relatively low, but the nature of cost trade-offs suggests that high-cost transportation is preferable to build-ups in inventory or lost sales. While the scheduling of production may be

FIGURE 16–3: An example organization for the management of a large wholesaling firm

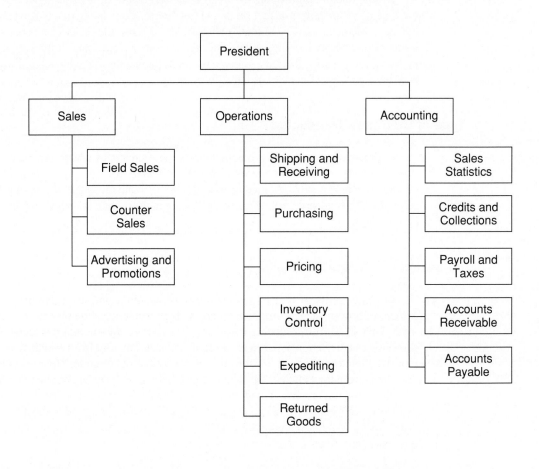

important, the outbound logistics tasks are carried out by a shipping manager with relatively little authority, little need to exercise judgment, and having low standing in the organization.

In a firm mining and shipping coal, logistics costs may reach 40 percent of the total cost of doing business. Here, however, the cost of transportation outweighs by a large margin inventory holding or customer service costs. The cost of carrying inventory is so low in relation to transportation costs that large stockpiles of coal are established at both the shipping point and at customer locations. The objective is to do whatever is necessary to ship the lowest-cost quantity by the lowest-cost method of transportation. In this firm, a vice president of transportation reporting to the president manages the important transportation function. The title "vice president" is often conferred to lend stature to this officer with respect to carrier relationships, including rate negotiation. However, the nature of the task involves so few trade-offs between transportation and other costs that this high-ranking manager oversees a department immersed

How Top Management Really Views Logistics: Part II

A Sweet Approach to Logistics

In the 1970s Hershey Chocolate Company had its functions scattered throughout the business structure. It was almost haphazard; warehousing reported directly to the chairman, traffic reported to the secretary of the corporation, and "production scheduling was done on the back of an envelope," says Michael Wells, Hershey USA's VP of Logistics.

Management consultants helped Hershey restructure. In the process, Earl Spangler, whose background was manufacturing, became director of distribution. He applied many of the integrated planning concepts common in manufacturing to distribution. Wells, who would be Spangler's successor, was hired in 1976. Spangler went on to become president of Hershey USA and has since retired. Wells moved up to VP of Distribution, then VP of Purchasing. Was his being named VP of Logistics indicative of Hershey's management enlightenment? "Hell no," says Wells, "I gave myself the title."

Wells relates that upper management "hears the buzzwords—channel integration, JIT, all that—and wonders if there's something we should be doing. But the only time they really take a close look at the operation is when a major capital project is proposed." But Wells likes it this way. "At Hershey, there's no need for a logistics person at the corporate level," he says. "Top management as well as the divisional levels realize that customer service is a serious element of our business. We have many selling advantages because of our logistics. Corporate understands the trade-off between cost and service."

Departmental interaction is both formal and informal at Hershey. Weekly "changing ideas" meetings are held between sales, marketing, operations and logistics. These are essential because as much as 20 percent of Hershey's product line is in transition at any given time due to seasonality, packaging changes and phase-outs.

Among Hershey USA's logistics successes are corporate decisions to give Wells's department order processing control and to create an inbound transportation group to ease the purchasing burden on his division's buyers. "The only purchasing done at the corporate level is of cocoa and sugar," Wells explains. "We buy everything else. We work so closely with corporate that logistics is like an arm of commodities purchasing."

Two years ago Hershey bought Luden's, the famed cough drop maker, and absorbed its $100 million purchasing and logistics unit into the Hershey USA fold. "We added only two staff people," Wells says, "and reduced the percentage of distribution cost against sales by about two percent." Wells is now planning to work the same magic with the even larger Cadbury Chocolate Co., a recent Hershey acquisition.

Logistical Chemistry

Mobay Corp., one of the nation's largest chemical companies, created the Information Logistics Marketing Group (ILM) three years ago to bring logistics greater prominence within the company. There is now an understanding that from procurement to end user, logistics is involved at every stage. "The corporate emphasis for this restructuring," says VP of Purchasing Robert Christman, "was to make Mobay an easier company to do business with."

Mobay's concept of logistics includes purchasing product and delivering it to nine different plants, channeling orders to those plants, and final distribution to customers. Materials handling and inventory is each plant's responsibility. Data processing ties it all together.

Christman believes that the increased emphasis on integrated logistics is a direct result of Mobay's commitment to a formal Quality process. Walt Becker, VP of Mobay's ILM Group, sees the company's commitments to Quality and logistics as "two parallel streets that have come together." Both are based on optimal communication, internally and externally, and customer service. "Quality circles aren't enough," Christman says. "A Quality culture is what is needed."

---

in coal tariffs and is seldom considered a serious candidate for general management because of his or her specialization.

In contrast to these two examples, a manufacturer of grocery products distributes a line of processed and packaged foods. In total, logistics costs may represent 15 percent of the cost of doing business for this firm. Costs of transportation are substantial, costs of holding inventory on a per-pound basis are high, and failure to meet customer orders may result in substantial sales lost through the substitution of other manufacturers' brands. The necessity of coordinating transportation and inventory decisions with those involving customer service requires that all three of these responsibilities be vested in one position, a manager of physical distribution responsible for managing trade-offs among three important cost areas. While this position may not report to the chief executive officer, it involves complexities sufficient to qualify it as a good training ground for general management.

Complexity of the Logistics Network

The logistics management task requires the servicing of a network of suppliers and customers, few of whom may be selected by the logistics manager. Service may be provided through varying number of collection points, plants, mixing points, and distribution warehouses. The addition of each "node" increases the network's complexity as well as the opportunity for error in analysis or management of the network and loss of control over logistics costs. Sooner or later, such loss of control may lead to focusing attention on the situation, thus encouraging management to pay more attention to the logistics function in the organization.

Nature of the Corporate Strategy

Goals for the logistics function in a firm may shift from time to time, for example, from cost minimization to a maximization of customer service. Such shifts reflect management's desires to achieve the highest profits in the long run and the perceptions of various senior managers as to the most effective ways of achieving profits under varying conditions. In industries typified by wide cyclical swings in the relation of supply and demand, such as paper manufacturing, the emphasis may change relatively rapidly from that of providing a high level of customer service during periods of excess supply to that of minimizing costs during periods of high customer demand. When such a change occurs, it is important to maintain a direct line of communication between those managers setting corporate strategy and those managing logistics operations. This suggests the desirability of a direct reporting relationship to top management by the senior logistics manager.

Factors such as the number of businesses or divisions represented in a company's operating portfolio, the extent to which each is run as a profit center, and the degree to which logistics is regarded as a profit center influence the location and nature of the logistics function. All are elements reflecting corporate strategy. They determine whether a corporate staff advising divisions on logistics matters is necessary. They determine the extent to which logistics management is carried out in the divisions or business units. And they influence the extent to which common logistics facilities, such as private transportation fleets and warehouses, are used jointly by two or more businesses divisions and how the logistics services are paid for or the costs divided.

Where logistics is treated as a profit center, business units or divisions typically are charged a prorated portion of the costs, or better yet, a market rate less a discount for the transportation, warehousing, or other service that is provided. The performance of the logistics function is judged on the extent to which its costs are kept in line with its charges for services provided. The use of "market prices" introduces a desirable discipline into the management picture. The "using division" cannot complain that "we could get it cheaper outside." However, the logistics services group also must perform as efficiently and effectively as potential outside vendors of logistics services or risk losing internal corporate business to such vendors if this is permitted by company policy.

Capacities of People Available to Manage

The textbook approach to organization suggests that the structure (or organization) should reflect a company's strategy and should follow from it. As a practical matter, management capability is often a major constraint on a business. A lack of capacity or talent in the logistics management of a company may require that it adopt a strategy that minimizes the complexity of the management task, delegate responsibility for logistics activities to managers primarily responsible for other functions, or otherwise reduce the impact that any one logistics manager or department may have on the performance of the company. Conversely, the presence of a strong logistics capability may induce general management to develop a strategy based in (large) part on its logistics capability.

ALTERNATIVES FOR ORGANIZING LOGISTICS MANAGEMENT

In sorting through many available alternatives, management must decide whether to adopt a decentralized or centralized organization, place logistics in a line or staff capacity, assign various functions to logistics for management, or employ matrix organization concepts. In addition, in the multinational firm, basic decisions have to be made about whether to organize around geographic areas or products. All of these have a profound impact on the way logistics activities are managed, and by whom.

Centralization versus Decentralization

Logistics activities can be managed from corporate headquarters in the centralized firm or from the plant, sales office, or business units in a decentralized firm.

Basic advantages of centralized management, often organized around functions, tend to result in a more effective use of warehouse and private transport facilities, coordination of the purchase of transportation and other services, and central control over inventories supporting two or more business units. An example of functionally oriented, centralized organization is shown in Figure 16–4.

In a decentralized approach to logistics management, two or more divisions or business units might house such groups, as shown in Figure 16–5. Here, responsibilities for profits are delegated to the divisional or business unit level, with corporate officers responsible for advice on such matters as personnel, labor relations, and legal matters, and having line responsibility for the acquisition and allocation of funds to divisions.

FIGURE 16–4: An organization chart for a manufacturing firm with a centralized organization

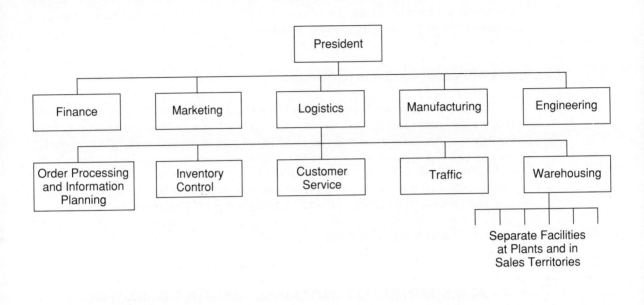

Benefits of this type of organization are that it may complement a corporate strategy encompassing distinctly different types of business units with little need for coordination or had a divisionalized organization with a corporate staff logistics function advisory to line common facilities. It delegates profit responsibility to lower levels of the organization, facilitating the development of talent capable of assuming senior general management responsibilities. And, it makes available to all divisions or business units a common pool of experts housed in various corporate staff departments.

According to a survey of 379 members of the Council of Logistics Management conducted in 1989, 108 (28.5 percent) had a functional organization with logistics responsibilities being dispersed to several functional areas, 93 (24.5 percent) had a functional organization with consolidated logistics responsibilities, 59 (15.6 percent) had a divisional organization with logistics responsibilities consolidated with business units, 41 (10.8 percent) had a divisionalized organization with centrally consolidated logistic responsibilities, 59 (15.8 percent) logistics functions in the business units, and 19 firms (5.0 percent) had some other type of organization for logistics management.[1] One would presume, or at least hope, that each of these groupings of firms have sound reasons, such as those discussed in this chapter, for the particular organization structure each has adopted.

As in most aspects of business, it is hard to find the pure examples of logistics organizational alternatives that exist so often in theory and management texts. Given the complexity of logistics functions, this should be no surprise.

FIGURE 16–5: The organization for logistics (physical distribution) management in a decentralized firm

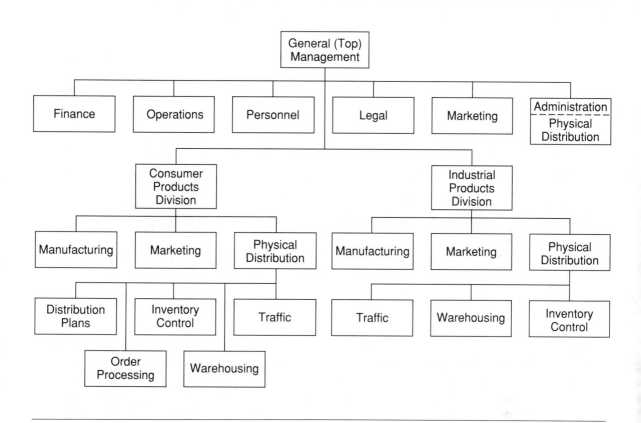

Line versus Staff

Line, operating, or action responsibilities within the logistics function typically are concerned with the management of transportation, warehousing, order processing, or procurement activities. Depending on the degree of decentralization, they may be managed either at the divisional or corporate level.

Staff advisory responsibilities most commonly are concerned with traffic management (particularly the negotiation and administration of rate matters and mode and carrier selection) and system design, including inventory control and materials management or physical distribution on a shorter-term basis. Whether such staff activities are positioned at the corporate or divisional level in an organization tends to vary with the size of the organization and the extent to which two or more divisions can utilize the same staff support.

The organization of a large manufacturing firm showing the presence of line and staff logistics groups at both the corporate and divisional levels is shown in Figure 16–6.

FIGURE 16–6: The organization of a large firm manufacturing packaged grocery products with Line and Staff Logistics responsibilities assigned at both Corporate and Division levels
Note: Line management responsibilities for logistics in italics.

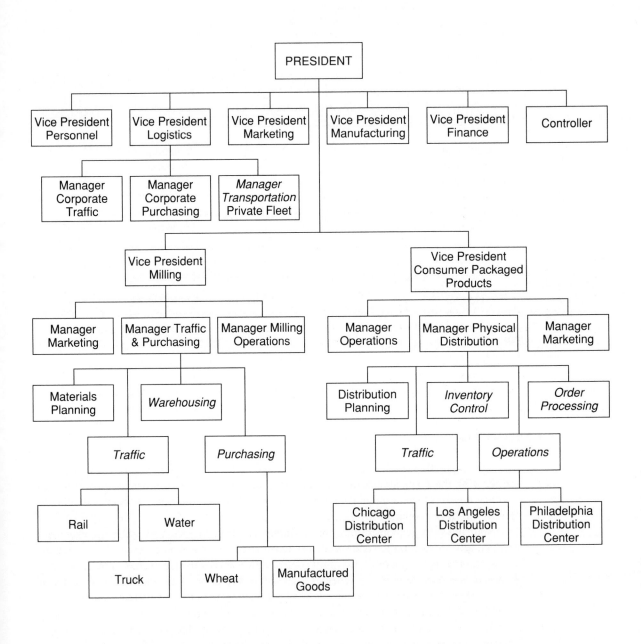

Scope and Positioning of Responsibility

Table 16–1 presents the results of a major recent survey of the logistics functions most and least commonly found under the line authority of logistics managers in manufacturing, wholesaling, retailing, and hybrid organizations.

Reporting relationships for those holding primary responsibility for logistics activities vary greatly as well. For example, where physical distribution is viewed as a supporting activity in a marketing-oriented firm, its management often is responsible to senior marketing management. Similarly, materials management may be established in support of, and be responsible to, manufacturing management. Organizations in which logistics is viewed primarily as the arbitrator between conflicting needs of marketing, manufacturing, and finance often assign logistics activity coordination to general management. This is reflected in the results of the recent organization survey shown in Table 16–2.

Matrix Organization

In recent years matrix organizations have been formed to foster coordination among managers organized on some combination of functional, geographic, product, or customer bases. For example, product managers with responsibility for the profitability of designated product groupings might have to marshal resources for the proper distribution of their products from physical distribution, advertising, and sales departments with either profit or cost responsibility. The abilities to coordinate and manage conflict are prized highly in a matrix organization.

One such matrix organization proposed solely for logistics activities in an aluminum manufacturing firm is shown in Figure 16–7. In this firm, the flows of raw materials such as coal and bauxite were thought to be so important that product managers with responsibility for the procurement and associated logistical activities for each raw material were appointed to bring together the resources of the traffic, transportation, and functionally oriented departments on behalf of their particular commodity.

Matrix organization concepts have achieved some popularity as a means of fostering coordination and management dialogue in complex organizations. However, they tend to violate the ''one boss to a subordinate'' rule and often prove very difficult to implement effectively, as in the old saying ''too many cooks spoil the broth.''

The Multinational Firm—A Special Case

Contrasting organizational alternatives have arisen among the growing number of firms engaged in multinational or global business activities. Some firms with important costs associated with product flows, such as the aluminum producer shown in Figure 16–7, have organized on a product basis with strong emphasis on the central planning and management of such flows across national boundaries. In such firms, a central logistics function with high visibility and broad responsibility is quite common.

Other firms facing highly differentiated marketing and manufacturing tasks among nations or regions have tended to organize accordingly by having separate, self-contained organizations for the ''French'' or ''German'' subsidiary. Area organizations predominate, for

TABLE 16-1: Common Logistics Line Functions Ranked by Business Type by Firms Reporting Direct Logistics Line Authority for Each of the Listed Functions[a]

Line Function	Manufacturer	Wholesaler	Retailer	Hybrid
Outbound transportation	1	2	2	1.5
Intracompany transportation	2	3.5	5	4
Warehousing	3	1	1	1.5
Inbound transportation	4	—	3	5
Logistics administration	5	—	—	—
Materials handling	—	3.5	4	3
Inventory management	—	5	—	—
Logistics systems planning	—	—	—	13.5
Customer service	—	—	14	—
Purchasing	—	—	15.5	13.5
Facilities design	—	14	15.5	15
Capital equipment procurement	—	15	—	—
Data processing/Distribution applications	—	17	—	10
Production planning	14	—[b]	—[b]	—
International logistics	15	18	17	17
Raw materials WIP inventory	16	—[b]	—[b]	—
Logistics engineering	17	—[b]	—[b]	—
Sales forecasting	18	16	18	16

[a]Ranked from five most common (1–5) and five least common (14–18). Blanks indicate a ranking somewhere between 5 and 14.

[b]These functions would not likely exist in these types of firms.

SOURCE: Adapted from Table 3-3 and Table 3-4 of *Leading Edge Logistics Competitive Positioning for the 1990's*, (Oak Brook, Illinois: Council of Logistics Management, 1989) 74 and 76.

TABLE 16-2: Level of the Executive to Whom Senior Logistics Executive Reports by Business Type and CAI Group[a]

Reports to	Manufacturer L.E./Norm	Wholesaler L.E./Norm	Retailer L.E./Norm	Hybrid L.E./Norm
Chairman	0.0/ 0.0%	4.8/13.5%	0.0/ 7.1%	20.0/12.2%
President	39.7/24.5	61.9/51.0	50.0/51.8	60.0/40.8
Executive vice president	27.0/24.5	23.8/12.5	43.8/25.0	13.3/ 8.2
Senior vice president	0.0/ 0.0	0.0/ 3.1	0.0/14.3	6.7/10.2
Vice president	31.8/41.9	9.5/10.4	0.0/ 1.8	0.0/12.2
Director	1.6/ 4.7	0.0/ 2.1	0.0/ 0.0	0.0/ 4.1
Manager	0.0/ 3.2	0.0/ 1.0	0.0/ 0.0	0.0/ 2.0
Supervisor	0.0/ 0.0	0.0/ 0.0	0.0/ 0.0	0.0/ 2.0
Other	0.0/ 1.2	0.0/ 6.3	6.3/ 0.0	0.0/ 8.2

[a]The Common Attributes Index (CAI) was developed by the research staff that conducted the study from which this table was taken. The CAI differentiates between "Leading Edge" and "Normal" business firms with respect to their management of logistics activities.

SOURCE: *Leading Edge Logistics Competitive Positioning for the 1990's* (Oak Brook, Illinois: Council of Logistics Management, 1989) 185.

FIGURE 16–7: Proposed matrix organization for logistics management in a large, integrated, multinational aluminum manufacturing firm

Functional Group (Managers)

	Raw Materials	Capital Goods	Consulting	Quality Control	Market Survey	Expediting		Planning/Research	Inventory Control	Rail	Truck	Ship	Port	Navigation Charts	Chartering Bulk Space	Claims/Marine Insurance	Leasing/Purch. of Ships	Monitoring Performance	Scheduling	Freight Forwarding	Terminal Management	Marine Management	Rail/Truck Management	Accounting	Insurance/Treasury	Office Management	Systems	RIMS
Bauxite & Alumina																												
Special Aluminas																												
Carbon Materials																												
Alloys																												
Smelter Materials																												
Ingot																												
Electrolite Mat'ls & Chemicals																												
Other Raw Materials																												
Fabricated Products																												

Product Line (Managers)

SOURCE: Adapted from the case study, ALCAN ALUMINUM LIMITED (B), (Boston: Intercollegiate Case Clearing House, Harvard University Graduate School of Business Administration, 1980).

HOW TOP MANAGEMENT REALLY VIEWS LOGISTICS: PART III

A Chance for Champions

Is it possible for a logistics crusader in the divisional ranks to garner top brass commitment for these concepts? Hewlett-Packard's Wayman certainly believes so. "It must come from the divisional level up," he says. "There are just too many ideas coming too fast in logistics. Top management is not always aware of the changes. Of course, if top management is always beating on them, they'll never get that type of input.

"Maybe you go out and get a consultant to plant just the right idea in a VP's mind," Wayman adds, "but I just don't think it works that way." He credits Hewlett-Packard's corporate distribution manager, Dennis Colard, with communicating a broader view of how logistics can tie together various department goals. "What also helped," he asserts, "was that he was able to make the costs of the whole process visible to us. Before that we did not have a cost figure. It's important to wave a number. In our case, that number was bigger than we ever imagined."

Prior to taking the distribution reins at H-P, Colard spent almost 20 years on the manufacturing side, most recently as manager of H-P's Puerto Rico plant operations. "We had made real progress improving our manufacturing process, and the company felt that the same principles could be applied to distribution," he says. He explains his pitch to his bosses: "I talked about dollars and cents, about productivity as a process, and about the need to eliminate unnecessary transactions." He presented his ultimate boss, CFO Wayman, with what he calls the department's "stretch goal": improving the efficiency and effectiveness of delivery performance, while limiting growth of distribution costs to less than one-fourth of revenue growth.

"That is a *powerful* statement," says Wayman. As a measure of Colard's success in bringing logistics a higher level of recognition, management is on the verge of transforming many traffic and distribution titles to logistics, according to Wayman.

What do executives lacking logistics knowledge look for when determining whether or not that function is performing up to par? Wayman says: "We have performance measurements. We push our people to get a better sense of their competitive performance. We need that because I'll never be able to have a gut feel for that part of the business."

On the financial side Wayman looks at inventory levels, expense levels and regulatory compliance. Manufacturing judges the logistics operation on cost and timing measures. The company keeps charts on projected delivery times. Because of the growing global nature of the business, it also looks at import/export issues. "The sales and marketing area is where we are most sensitive to logistics' impact, making sure our customers get what they want, when they want it," says Wayman. "I recently met our director of distribution management for Europe. He had charts on all his goals for supplies sourced globally. He tracked the time between receipt and delivery of orders and was getting good regular measurements that way. This kind of thing is much more prevalent now."

Maybe it's more prevalent within Hewlett-Packard, but it still hasn't been absorbed by the majority of America's chief executives. Mobay's Robert Christman says, "A lot of the judgmental stuff is hip shooting. Sometimes a singular point of achievement will be noticed. But in truth, it's the failures that management remembers."

The Grass Isn't Always Greener

Itel's Richard Price has an interesting view of these logistics trends. When top management grasps the value of logistics, he believes it will then be free "to concentrate on what it really enjoys — manufacturing and marketing."

As president of a contract logistics supplier, Price has a vested interest in that visionary scenario. But he has also seen things from the other side of the fence, and as a logistics professional, the grass wasn't always greener over there. "When a company comes up with a hot item," he maintains, "it is concerned with the item, not with the distribution of the item."

He recalls meeting with a corporate chairman, who claimed that the quality of his company's distribution "was a given" when discussing a product rollout. Having worked in the trenches, Price was hurt by the comment. He didn't believe this chief knew whether his distribution was good or not; it was merely taken for granted.

That's one of the main reasons Price decided to leave corporate logistics and move into contract logistics. "Now, my business *is* distribution," he says. The challenge, for Itel and the many other logistics suppliers, is to convince corporations that logistics is so important it shouldn't be handled in-house.

Ironically, outside firms persuade the chiefs the same way Hewlett-Packard's Dennis Colard convinced his bosses. Says Price: "It's nothing new. You have to show them where they can save the money, and where they can improve the service."

Will corporate bosses continue to trust the "good old company traffic staff" in the face of increased high-level marketing by contract suppliers? "It's not really a question of trusting employees," Price says, "it's a question of where management wants to spend its time." He firmly believes that when it comes to logistics, the chiefs want to spend their time enjoying results, not running an extensive distribution operation.

Contract logistics suppliers aren't ready to launch the major campaign on top management just yet, Price notes. These suppliers are fragmented at present. "The industry is gearing up," he says, "by improving information systems, hiring a higher caliber of personnel, and expanding its geographic capabilities to address the U.S. as a whole, not on a regional basis."

Says Hewlett-Packard's Wayman: "I can't imagine third parties handling the type of integrated logistics we're talking about, particularly on a global basis. Conceptually, I'm open to it. Practically, I have my doubts."

---

example, in companies facing strongly national consumer markets and restricted opportunities for importing that require local manufacture as well. Thus, the aluminum manufacturer utilizing a product-oriented organization with a strong central logistics function for the management of its raw material production was found to have an "area organization" for the fabrication and sale of consumer products manufactured from the basic aluminum. Each area supported its own logistics function in the manner that a firm confining its activities to any one country might have done.

STAFFING THE LOGISTICS FUNCTION

Successful staffing of the logistics function requires job definition, an inventory of available people and skills, and matching of people with jobs. Given the nature of the logistics management task, it may be important that those selected for senior responsibilities possess strong integrative abilities.

Job Definition and Description

Perhaps the most important, yet most detested, task in organizing any function is that of writing job descriptions. That may account for the fact that few job descriptions prove helpful or are ever referred to after they are prepared. However, there are ways of simplifying the task of writing a job description and making its product more useful.

Basic elements of a job description include the title, reporting relationship, scope of responsibility, and measure(s) of performance associated with the job. Titles and reporting relationships depend on factors cited earlier.

The scope of responsibility will reflect the size and complexity of various tasks to be performed. It can be described very simply, eliminating flowery, useless language. Each task can be designated by an action verb and an object noun. For example, a transportation manager may be responsible for hiring and firing owner-operators, scheduling loads, allocating equipment, or establishing internal private transport transfer prices.

Measures of performance are an integral part of the job description. Bases on which performance is to be measured as well as specific goals to be achieved on each may be agreed on by supervisor and subordinate, thus obtaining the approval of the former and the commitment of the latter.

Inventorying People and Skills

In assessing available skills for logistics management within an organization, it is important to look beyond current managers of logistics activities. In fact, the desirability of a broad educational and experience in several functional areas of the firm is implied by information shown in Table 16–3. This suggests that an important qualification for senior logistics management is the sort of multifunctional experience that is so important to the successful coordination of material and information flows across functions. Other skills thought to be useful for logistics management, based on responses of managers themselves, are shown in Table 16–3.

TABLE 16–3: Educational Background and Areas Identified for Further Study by Logistics Executives

Credentials			
High school diploma			12%
Baccalaureate			46%
Graduate degree			42%
Special certification			17%

Major Field of Study	Logistics	Other Business	Non Business
Baccalaureate	16%	55%	29%
Graduate degree	9%	81%	10%

Areas Identified for Further Study	
Finance	20%
Computers	19%
Logistics	11%
Leadership	9%
Quantitative methods	8%
Marketing	7%
Management	6%
International distribution	4%
Strategic planning	3%
Accounting	3%
Quality control	2%
Miscellaneous	8%

SOURCE: James Masters and Bernard J. LaLonde, "The 1988 Ohio State University Survey of Career Patterns in Logistics," *Annual Conference Proceedings*, Boston, Massachusetts, October 9-12, 1988, Vol. 1, (Oak Brook, Illinois: Council of Logistics Management) 38–40.

HOW TOP MANAGEMENT REALLY VIEWS LOGISTICS: PART IV

Plotting the Future

A potentially negative factor in logistics' bid for more corporate level recognition is the precariousness of long-range planning brought on by American business's takeover mania. An alarming number of well-known companies, many of which have touted a progressive commitment to logistics during the past few years, declined to participate in this story. Privately, all the ranking logistics executives in these companies expressed concern about boardroom shakeups possibly upsetting their company's long-term logistics plans.

So perhaps it's best for the logistics profession to maintain a presence just outside the boardroom, a safer distance from the merciless blade of modern commerce. In this environment, a structure such as Hershey's where the logistics control of each division is fairly immune from corporate turnover, seems all the more logical.

In 10 years time, it's a safe bet that logistics will have filtered into almost every executive suite. "In the food business," Hershey's Mike Wells asserts, "logistics will become more important. That's because there'll be fewer and fewer food manufacturers, and they'll all be struggling to improve customer service. They must improve, or have their brains kicked out."

Mobay's Walt Becker doesn't believe that the true value of logistics has yet been experienced. "When energy costs rise again, and they will, companies with quality logistics won't be hurt as much," he says. "And although American business has done a good job cutting its inventories, the benefits aren't as noticeable when interest rates are down, like they are now. When those rates go back up, it will be the companies with the best logistics that will succeed."

SOURCE: *Distribution* (December 1988): 23–30. Reprinted with permission of Chilton Company.

Matching People and Jobs

Organizational life often dictates an interactive process of job definition, inventorying of skills, and some adjustment of jobs and titles to fit the realities of available personnel. Only where major gaps or duplication in abilities exist should people have to be hired from outside or relocated within the firm to meet position needs.

The Logistics Manager as Integrator

In many organizations, logistics is a coordinative function. Its successful performance requires the cooperation of marketing, manufacturing, and finance. Its stock-in-trade is the trade-off of one type of cost for another. The logistics manager often must serve as referee and adjudicator among other functional managers, providing objectivity to the decision-making process. And, at times, this role must be performed without direct authority over those whose efforts are to be coordinated. This has come to be known as the role of an integrator, and it pervades much of logistics management today.

Research suggests the qualities that integrators possess, qualities that might well describe many successful logistics managers today. One study concludes that:

1. Integrators need to be seen as contributing to important decisions on the basis of their competence and knowledge, rather than on their positional authority.

2. Integrators must have balanced orientations (as, for example, between production and sales, short-range and long-range thinking, etc.) and behavior patterns (as, for example, between people-oriented and task-oriented jobs).
3. Integrators need to feel that they are being rewarded for their total product responsibility, not solely on the basis of their performance as individuals.
4. Integrators must have a capacity for resolving inter-departmental conflicts and disputes.[2]

TRENDS IN ORGANIZATION FOR LOGISTICS

Logistics management in the future will reflect trends in management in general. At least in American firms, it will become more multinational in its orientation. It will concentrate less on the development of new techniques of analysis and more on the utilization of available technology for computing and communicating information. It will place more emphasis on the ability to interpret and act on data rather than generating it.

As a growing number of senior managers count logistics responsibilities among those from which they graduated to their current jobs, the logistics function should be integrated more effectively into the strategic planning of the business. It will, to an increasing extent, become a training ground for general managers.

SUMMARY

Organization is essential to the performance of work and the accomplishment of goals. It is important that logistics tasks inherent to any business organization reflect the complexity and importance of the logistics function in that firm as well as the need to integrate logistics into business strategy.

Whether oriented around inbound materials or physical distribution activities, or both, logistics involves the management of flows of material and information across several more traditional functions. Thus, coordination is a by-word for logistics management, whether it is achieved by the assignment of line responsibility for some or all logistics activities to one manager, or by the assignment of an integrator with many responsibilities but limited authority to accomplish the tasks.

The most important factors influencing the importance and nature of the logistics function in an organization are the type of business being managed; the importance of logistics in relation to total costs of doing business; the need to manage trade-offs between important logistics cost categories of transportation, inventory holding, and lost sales (customer service); the complexity of the logistics network; the nature of the overall corporate strategy, and the capacities of people available to manage.

These factors account for the wide array of organizational alternatives found for the management of logistics in American industry today. Few organizations have comprehensive line authority for both materials and physical distribution management. The most commonly-found arrangement combines centralized responsibility for the line management, for example, of private transportation and staff support for traffic, inventory, and facility planning with decentralized or divisionalized line responsibility for warehousing, inventory management, order processing, and traffic. The growth of matrix organizational arrangements has enhanced opportunities for coordination so important to effective logistics management, although it is no panacea.

As organizations grow more complex and the forces leading to the differentiation of tasks increase, the tasks of integrators capable of coordinating actions of managers with potentially conflicting interests will become more important. Logistics management, because of its many intra- and interfirm relationship, is becoming an important source of such integrative capabilities, capabilities that, to an increasing extent, may be required for the more effective general management of the firm. Those sought out for logistics management will be evaluated to an increasing degree on their integrative skills.

The difference between simply having an organization structure that is assigned responsibility for carrying out certain activities, and actually carrying out activities in an organized manner, is the difference between form and substance. The editors of a business magazine devoted at the time to the coverage of logistics topics put it bluntly:

> . . . we would venture to say that many companies which are not "organized" for physical distribution management — either by chart or by use of the term — are in fact doing a first-rate physical distribution job because they understand the function, while other companies with beautifully drawn charts encompassing a physical distribution hierarchy are falling down on the job because they still haven't learned what physical distribution is all about.[3]

As this quotation suggests, to have an organization structure without actually carrying out the functions of the organization is to achieve a triumph of technique over purpose.

The important thing is to insure that appropriate levels of attention and coordination for all logistics activities are encouraged by the form of organization adopted, not necessarily that they all be grouped under one manager in the organization.

DISCUSSION QUESTIONS

1. Why does the management of logistics functions tend to conflict with traditional organization structures?

2. Why are the "circled" activities shown in Figure 16–2 seldom found on organization charts?

3. What problems are created by the fact that information flows and physical flows go in opposite directions?

4. Distinguish between staff advice and the exercise of functional authority? When is the use of functional authority appropriate?

5. What factors influence (or determine) the importance of logistics in an organization? Explain.

6. Should a company attempt to "fit a person to a job" or "fit the job to the person"? Explain your answer.

7. What arguments can be made in favor of centralized management? Decentralized management? Is one better than the other? Explain.

8. What accounts for the wide variety of differing placements of logistics functions in organization structures?

9. Reference Figure 16–6, explain what you would believe to be the relationships between the managers of corporate traffic and corporate purchasing with the managers of traffic and purchasing in the milling and consumer products divisions.

10. What are the advantages and disadvantages of the matrix organization approach to logistics management? How might some of the disadvantages be overcome?

11. What effect does strong "nationalism" tend to have on the organization of the logistics function in multinational firms?

12. What is meant by the term *integrator*? Why is this concept often of particular importance to logistics management?

CASE: ESTABLISHMENT OF A LOGISTICS DEPARTMENT

At what size or stage of development should a firm establish a logistics department, assuming that the firm is a manufacturer that uses purchased inbound materials to manufacture its goods and that also manages the distribution of its outbound finished goods?

With the above question in mind, review the material in Chapter 14 concerning the Easthampton Comclean Corporation. At what point — if any, so far — in the company's growth and development would the creation of a logistics department have been justified?

In assessing this situation you should:

1. Make whatever assumptions about the company and its operations that seem reasonable to you and state them.

2. Make whatever assumptions about competing firms that seem reasonable to you and state them.

3. Make whatever other reasonable assumptions you believe necessary or useful to assessing this situation and state them.

Given your assumptions and the information presented and discussed in this chapter and elsewhere in this book, present and justify your case for or against the establishment of a logistics department at the Easthampton Comclean Corporation at some time in the past, the present, or at some time in the future (assuming further growth of the company).

CASE QUESTIONS

1. If you recommend against establishment of a logistics department at Comclean now or in the past, state how the firm's logistics activities would be assigned within the management structure of the corporation and justify your answer.

2. If you recommend establishment of a logistics department at Comclean at its present state of development, state what activities you would place under the direction and control of a logistics department and justify your answer.

3. If you recommend establishment of a logistics department at Comclean only at some time in the future, what developments would have to occur to lead you to make such a recommendation?

SUGGESTED READINGS

Leading Edge Logistics Competitive Positioning for the 1990's, Oakbrook, Illinois: Council of Logistics Management, 1989. This landmark study shows clearly the directions in which firms that are leaders in logistics management are going. It is highly recommended to any person having an interest in present and future trends in the field of logistics.

AMMER, DEAN S., *Materials Management and Purchasing*, Homewood, Illinois: Richard D. Irwin, Inc., 1980. This text emphasizes both the current principles of organization for materials management (in Chapter 4) and future organizational developments, such as the impact of automation on the supply process, changes created by automation in the office, and the creation of the materials management profit center (in Chapter 20).

BALLOU, RONALD H., *Basic Business Logistics*, Englewood Cliffs: Prentice-Hall, Inc., 1978. The material on organization in this basic text contains an interesting discussion of the organization and management of two or more independently-owned companies dealing with one another in a channel of distribution.

BOWERSOX, DONALD J., DAVID J. CLOSS, and OMAR K. HELFERICH, *Logistical Management*, 3d. ed. New York: Macmillan Publishing Co., Ltd., 1986. Included in the discussion of organization (Chapter 10) is a description of the several stages through which logistics organizations typically evolve.

COLEMAN, EUNICE C., "Is International Distribution Management Any Different from Domestic Distribution Management?", *Logistics: International Issues*, Cleveland, Ohio: Leaseway Transportation Corp., 1985, pages 81–94. This article is primarily devoted to the challenges facing managers in the organizational context of multinational logistics operations.

COYLE, JOHN J., and EDWARD J. BARDI, *The Management of Business Logistics*, 3d. ed. St. Paul: West Publishing Company, 1986. This book includes a description of a systems approach to logistics organization (in Chapter 13).

FIRTH, DON, F. R. DENHAM, KENNETH R. GRIFFIN, JOE HEFFERNAN, STUART H. PRESS, NEIL CORMACK ROBSON, and ALAN I. SAIPE, *Distribution Management Handbook*, Toronto: McGraw-Hill Ryerson Limited, 1980. Chapter 2, "Organizing for Effective P.D. Management," contains several interesting examples drawn from Canadian firms showing differences in organization influenced by the type of business engaged in and changes in organization for logistics over time.

JOHNSON, JAMES C., and DONALD F. WOOD, *Contemporary Logistics*, 4th ed. New York: Macmillan Publishing Company, 1990. Chapter 14 includes a series of organization charts depicting the organizational evolution of the logistics function in a paint company as the firm grows.

LAMBERT, DOUGLAS M., and JAMES R. STOCK, *Strategic Physical Distribution Management*, Homewood, Illinois: Richard D. Irwin, Inc., 1982. Chapter 12 includes a good treatment of strategies for improving communication effectiveness in managing logistics activities.

SHAPIRO, ROY D., and JAMES L. HESKETT, *Logistics Strategy: Cases and Concepts*, St. Paul: West Publishing Company, 1985. Chapter 8 contains an excellent summary of the nature of the challenges involved in organizing for effective logistics management.

ENDNOTES

1. *Leading Edge Logistics Competitive Positioning for the 1990s* (Oak Brook, Illinois: Council of Logistics Management, 1989): 87.

2. Lawrence, Paul R., and Jay W. Lorsch, "New Management Job: The Integrator," *Harvard Business Review* (November-December 1967): 142–51.

3. "Organization vs. Function in Physical Distribution Management," *Transportation and Physical Distribution Management* (February 1962): 3.

Constant monitoring and effective feedback of information is essential to maintain the desired performance level of a logistics system.

CHAPTER SEVENTEEN

17

System Performance Measurement and Control

LEARNING OBJECTIVES

The objectives of this chapter are to:

➤ Explain the relationship of performance measurement and control to planning.

➤ Present and discuss the features of an effective logistics performance measurement and control system.

➤ Identify and explain the significance of several important productivity measures in a logistics system.

➤ Identify the essential features of program management of a logistics performance measurement and control system.

➤ Present the steps necessary for the establishment of a practical logistics control program.

➤ Discuss and explain the nature of logistics project planning and control.

➤ Treat profitability control with respect to logistics costs incurred by products, territories, and customers.

Are we meeting our customer service standards? What are our costs? Are we moving in the right direction? Are we where we should be at this point? How well are we doing? How well should we be doing? Can we do better? Should we be doing better? How could we do better? Such questions are constantly asked by boards of directors of presidents, by presidents of vice presidents, by vice presidents of managers, and by managers of supervisors.

Logistics activities, like those of any other management function, should make a cost-effective, value-added contribution to the attainment of a company's goals. Effective measurement and control of the ongoing performance of logistics managers is essential to insure that this happens.

The basic task of logistics management is to meet a predetermined customer service standard, or set of standards, at the lowest practicable cost. In a manufacturing firm there are two types of customers: those to whom the firm sells its products, and the firm's production department, which is supplied with purchased raw materials, parts, components, and such.

In Chapter 4 we discussed customer service standards and emphasized the care with which they must be defined. From outside customers of the firm, the two key customer service standard questions are: (1) How soon do I receive orders after I've placed them? and (2) Are my orders filled completely? From the production manager (the "internal customer"), the question is: Do I always have the raw materials, parts, and components needed to keep my production lines going? These questions, as might be expected, all relate to place and time utility.

It is against a background of clearly stated and well understood customer service standards that measures of logistics performance and techniques of control are properly developed and applied. Logistics performance measurement in practice is thus concerned with the simultaneous measurement of the logistics costs being incurred and the degree to which customer service standards are being met. Achievement of "low" logistics costs is at best a Pyrrhic victory if customer service standards are sacrificed in the process.

Regardless of the difficulty of devising and implementing a performance measurement and control program, it is essential for a function such as logistics. In our discussion of organization in the preceding chapter, we concluded that it may be unrealistic to think that problems of coordination necessary for the achievement of a least total cost (or maximum profit) result can be achieved in very many cases by centralizing full responsibility for all logistics activities under one manager. However, if this is in fact the case, such an organization will still have to resort to coordinated control and performance measurement to achieve its logistics objectives. Further, as we will see, efforts to implement an effective performance measurement and control program provide perhaps the best avenue of approach to improved logistics planning.

RELATIONSHIP OF PERFORMANCE MEASUREMENT AND CONTROL TO PLANNING

The relationship between planning and performance measurement and control is one of a closed loop, the nature of which is shown by the diagram in Figure 17–1.

A logistics system plan should include both a set of goals and limits around those goals that represent the bounds of acceptable performance. Periodic performance measures will determine the relationship between goals and actual performance. Where the differences be-

FIGURE 17–1: Relationship between planning and performance measurement and control in the management process

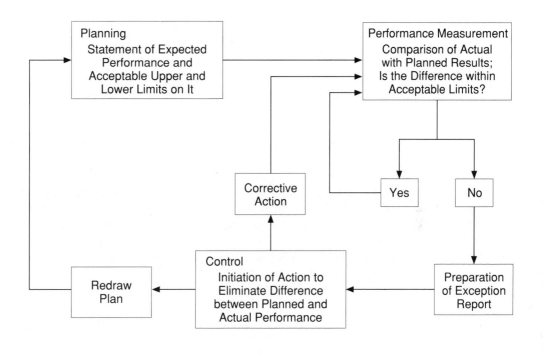

tween planned and actual performance levels are unacceptably large, an exception report or review audit will call that fact to the attention of management for appropriate action. The cumulative effect of such exception reports will influence future planning effort to the extent that it points out flaws in past efforts that need to be avoided, or provided for, in future plans.

This is the basic relationship between these important management functions. We will see next how this general statement can be applied to day-to-day management of logistics activities as well as to the planning and control of major projects.

FEATURES OF AN EFFECTIVE PERFORMANCE MEASUREMENT AND CONTROL PROGRAM

During the 1980s, seven studies concerned with various aspects of logistics accounting, control, and productivity were carried out under the auspices of the Council of Logistics Management. Published as hardbound books, these studies present an exhaustive collection of industry practices and data on the subjects of their concern. Collectively, they are the best available source of comprehensive industry information with respect to a wide range of factors relevant to logistics system performance measurement and control.*

Use the following subheadings in this section as a checklist to spot-check the usefulness of logistics performance measurement and control programs. It will assist you in pinpointing certain shortcomings in existing programs without losing sight of the benefits.

Emphasis on Productivity and Quality Rather than Production

The number of ton-miles of freight moved by a private trucking fleet during May is a measure of production. The cost per ton-mile or ratio of ton-miles to driver labor hours are measures of productivity.

But, the bottom line would be the *quality* of the service delivered by the firm's private fleet. Volume of freight carried and the ton-mile operating costs of the fleet will mean little — however "productive" the operation may be — unless the *correct quantities* of inbound materials or outbound finished goods are delivered *on time and undamaged*. Increasingly, customers are demanding high quality in goods and services. To put it another way, they want what they are paying for. In the discussion that follows, we include *quality of service* as being inherent in any meaningful definition of "logistics productivity."

Production measures, signifying amounts of output, are of value for control purposes if the sole objective of such production is output. But, they provide a very limited frame of reference for evaluating output figures, even when there are successive output measurements over time with which to establish trends. In contrast, *productivity* measures relate outputs to inputs. The resulting ratios provide indicators of what must be paid for outputs in terms of time, costs, or other inputs. As a result, productivity measures often are more useful than production measures. In the reports shown in Tables 17–1 and 17–2, you may wish to identify production as opposed to productivity measures and evaluate the relative frequency of the latter.

Proper Identification of Cost Inputs

The second feature of an effective performance measurement and control system is the proper identification of cost inputs. Functional cost accounting, which identifies costs in such a way that they can be attributed to logistics, production, and marketing activities, is an art that is yet to be developed in many organizations. Instead, costs are collected in so-called "natural" accounts, such as labor or materials, without regard to whether labor costs incurred, for example at a manufacturing complex, were incurred for activities of actual manufacture, plant material handling, or movement of product into or out of the warehouse located near the plant.

---

*For students interested in investigating further, these studies are: *Leading Edge Logistics: Competitive Positioning for the 1990's* (1989). *Partnerships in Providing Customer Service: A Third Party Perspective* (1989). *Customer Service: A Management Perspective* (1988). *Corporate Profitability and Logistics* (1987). *Warehouse Accounting and Control: Guidelines for Distribution and Financial Managers* (1985). *Measuring and Improving Productivity in Physical Distribution* (1984). *Transportation Accounting and Control: Guidelines for Distribution and Financial Management* (1983).

Comment on the content of each of these works is included in their complete citations under "Suggested Readings" at the end of this chapter. Their value is that they offer very detailed guidelines for the gathering and presentation of information required for comprehensive logistics system performance measurement and control. All belong in the personal library of any aspiring logistics manager.

TABLE 17–1: Proposed Format for a Physical Distribution Reporting and Control Problem

System-Wide Report

Company: *National Radiator Corp.*
Period: *March*

	This Month	Last Month	This Month Last Year	Goal
Transportation				
Plant to warehouses, cost per hundredweight	$ 1.58	$ 1.62	$ 1.56	$ 1.56
Plant to customers, cost per hundredweight	$ 3.34	$ 3.26	$ 3.20	$ 3.24
Field warehouse to customers, cost per hundredweight	$ 2.86	$ 2.98	$ 2.94	$ 2.94
Between warehouses, cost per hundredweight, shipped from plant	$ .16	$ .08	$ .06	$ .06
Warehousing				
Plant warehouse, cost per case handled out	$ .28	$ .28	$ .26	$ .28
Field warehouses, cost per case handled in and out	$ 1.06	$ 1.10	$ 1.10	$ 1.10
Plant, storage cost per case in average (annualized) inventory	$ .50	$ .44	$ .42	$ .42
Field warehouses, storage cost per case in average inventory	$ .60	$ .52	$ .54	$ .52
Inventory Control				
Inventory turn, plant and field warehouses, on annualized basis	7.3	6.6	6.6	6.6
Values of total average inventory at cost (in millions)	$17.84	$20.04	$18.84	$19.00
Order Entry/Processing				
Cost per order processed at plant	$19.80	$19.20	$19.00	$19.00
Cost per order processed at field warehouse	$24.60	$22.50	$22.90	$22.80
Customer Service				
Percentage of line-item fill, field warehouse	86%	92%	89%	90%
Percentage of order fill, field warehouse	63%	75%	74%	75%
Air freight transport cost as percentage of warehouse-to-customer transport cost	3.2%	1.6%	1.5%	1.5%
Total Distribution Cost				
Per case shipped to customer	$ 2.16	$ 2.04	$ 2.02	$ 2.00
As a percentage of sales	13.5%	12.7%	12.6%	12.5%

Once lost, functional costs have to be reconstructed by allocating categories of costs in natural accounts on the basis of activity measurements, use of space, or some other *assumed* relationship between levels of activities and costs.

Some logistics costs are buried in other accounts. Freight on raw materials inbound to a plant or on finished products inbound to a wholesaling or retailing operation most often is charged off as part of "raw materials" or "cost of goods sold," respectively. The cost-identification problem is compounded when companies that purchase such items on a delivered basis receive no record of freight as a part of the total landed cost. Warehousing costs may be

TABLE 17–2: Proposed Format for a Physical Distribution Reporting and Control Problem

Warehouse Report

Company: *National Radiator Corp.*
Location: *Newark, New Jersey*
Period: *March*

	This Month	Last Month	This Month Last Year	Goal
Transportation				
Plant to warehouses, cost per hundredweight	$ 1.16	$ 1.12	$ 1.18	$ 1.20
Warehouse to customers, cost per hundredweight	$ 2.72	$ 2.80	$ 2.98	$ 2.90
Warehousing				
Cost per case handled in and out	$ 1.24	$ 1.26	$ 1.26	$ 1.26
Storage cost per case in average inventory	$ .48	$ .50	$ .62	$ .56
Inventory Control				
Inventory turn, on annualized basis	5.7	5.9	6.1	6.0
Values of total average inventory at cost (in millions)	$ 1.35	$ 1.29	$ 1.23	$ 1.25
Cost per order processed at warehouse (include all extra charges here)	$21.90	$21.90	$23.10	$22.50
Customer Service				
Percentage of line-item fill	92%	90%	87%	90%
Percentage of order fill	77%	75%	70%	75%
Percentage of on-time shipment (within 48 hours of receipt of order)	98%	96%	97%	96%
Plant direct transportation costs to territory as percentage of warehouse-to-customer transport cost	8.3%	10.2%	16.1%	12.0%

charged either to production (for plant-oriented facilities) or to marketing (for distribution centers). The "loss" of inventory costs represents such a glaring example that we will consider it separately.

A typical breakdown of functional costs from a set of natural accounts is shown in Figures 17–2, 17–3, and 17–4.

During the last ten years there has been a steady increase in the use of computers to record elements of cost at their most fundamental level and to then aggregate these costs in a variety of output formats and reports. To accomplish this, a computer program is written that will, for example, take a labor hour in the shipping room of a manufacturing plant and classify that labor hour in a variety of ways. Out of this process can come a number of different types of computer-generated information, each including that labor hour. This information might then be incorporated:

1. As part of the firm's payroll records, including issuance of payroll checks, accounting for tax withholding, other payroll deductions, and such;

2. As part of a total labor hours report for that plant location;

3. As part of a departmental report on total costs of the shipping department;

FIGURE 17–2: Translation of natural cost accounts into a financial statement for external reporting

Natural Accounts (Accounting)			For External Reporting: Profit and Loss Statement		
Account	Amount ($000)		Account	Amount ($000)	
Sales	$121,500	(A)[a]	Net Sales (Y)	$120,000	(A-B)
Returns and Allowances	1,500	(B)	Less: Cost of Goods Sold (Z)	80,000	(C+D+E+F+H)
Manufacturing:			Gross Profit	$ 40,000	(Y-Z)
Supervision	2,500	(C)			
Labor	30,000	(D)	Operating Expenses:		
Materials	33,000	(E)			
Supplies	5,700	(F)	General and Administrative	$ 7,500	(P+Q+R+S)
Research and Development	2,500	(G)	Selling	12,500	(J+K+L+M)
Overhead Other Than R&D	6,300	(H)	Advertising and Sales	3,500	(N)
Selling:			Promotion		
Supervision	1,000	(J)	Research and Development	2,500	(G)
Salaries	2,800	(K)			
Transportation	5,000	(L)			
Overhead	3,700	(M)			
Advertising and Sales Promotion	3,500	(N)	Other Expense:		
Insurance	800	(P)	Interest	3,500	(T)
General and Administrative:			Depreciation	4,000	(X)
Salaries	1,000	(Q)	Property Taxes	1,200	(U)
Office	2,700	(R)	Employment Taxes	1,300	(V)
Overhead	3,000	(S)			
Interest	3,500	(T)			
Taxes:			Net Profit Before Tax	$ 4,000	
Property	1,200	(U)	Income Taxes	2,000	(W)
Employment	1,300	(V)			
Income	2,000	(W)			
Depreciation	4,000	(X)	Net Profit After Tax	$ 2,000	

[a]Capital letters identify natural accounts which are rearranged, and sometimes aggregated, in the Profit and Loss Statement as shown above.

4. As a labor hour specifically associated with the shipment of goods sent to individual customers rather than on to the company's distribution warehouses;

5. As part of a report summarizing logistics costs at that plant location;

6. As part of a productivity report relating labor hours to various volume measures of order processing.

The above list could be extended and multiplied many times over. The point is that with modern computer systems, if one captures and identifies each piece of information at its "lowest" level, those pieces of information can be arranged, rearranged, aggregated, and summarized in a wide variety of ways in order to meet management's information needs for the purposes of logistics system performance measurement and control.

FIGURE 17–3: Descriptors of functional logistics costs as portions of natural cost accounts

Natural Accounts (Accounting)			Basis for Allocation to Functional Accounts[a]
Account	Amount	($000)	Manufacturing payroll records for supervision of handling, packaging, and packing
Sales	$121,500		
Returns and Allowances	1,500		Plant warehouse payroll records for raw material handling, finished product handling, packaging, and packing
Manufacturing:			
Supervision	2,500	(C)	Freight bills for incoming raw materials (explicit) and estimated freight on goods bought delivered (implicit)
Labor	30,000	(D)	Bills for packing, packaging supplies, pallets, fuel for material-handling equipment, other warehouse supplies
Materials	33,000	(E)	Labor fringe benefits according to proportion of total manufacturing payroll; supervisory fringe benefits according to total supervision bill; heat on basis of square footage of warehouse to total; light and water estimated at 30% of the rate per sq. ft. for average of all manufacturing operations
Supplies	5,700	(F)	
Research and Development	2,500	(G)	
Overhead Other Than R&D	6,300	(H)	
Selling:			
Supervision	1,000	(J)	Freight bills and vouchers for private fleet services
Salaries	2,800	(K)	Payroll records for distribution center supervision, order processing, material handling, inventory control, communications on basis of supervisory estimate, other utilities, rent on basis of square footage in office vs. warehouse and proportion of official payroll for sales vs. distribution labor, public warehouse bills
Transportation	5,000	(L)	
Overhead	3,700	(M)	
Advertising and Sales Promotion	3,500	(N)	
			Insurance payments for owned warehouse facilities, transportation and material-handling equipment, and raw materials and finished product in stock
Insurance	800	(P)	Payroll records for logistics management
General and Administrative:			Payroll records for headquarters personnel engaged in order processing, inventory control, forecasting, and production planning activities
Salaries	1,000	(Q)	
Office	2,700	(R)	
			Communications and computer facility expenses on basis of executive estimate of percentage of facility use for order processing, inventory update and control, forecasting and production planning
Overhead	3,000	(S)	
			Estimated on basis of proportion of total investment (at book value) devoted to warehouses, transportation, and handling equipment, and inventory (for explicit costs), imputed cost of capital applied to above investment (for explicit and implicit costs)
Interest	3,500	(T)	
			Estimated as proportion of book value on real property plus inventory taxes
Taxes:			
Property	1,200	(U)	Estimated as proportion of labor bill, executive salaries attributed to logistics
Employment	1,300	(V)	
Income	2,000	(W)	Book value depreciation on warehouse facilities, transportation, and material-handling equipment and inventories
Depreciation	4,000	(X)	

[a]The Basis for Allocation to Functional Accounts describes for each natural account the reason for allocating a portion of that natural account to a functional account (in this case, logistics).

FIGURE 17–4: Translation of natural cost accounts into a functional account (logistics) for internal management use

Natural Accounts (Accounting)			For Internal Company Use: Functional Accounts (Logistics in Detail)	
Account	Amount ($000)		Account	Amount ($000)
Sales	$121,500	(A)	Manufacturing	
Returns and Allowances	1,500	(B)	Accounting	
Manufacturing:			Marketing	
Supervision	2,500	(C)	Finance	
Labor	30,000	(D)	Research and Development	
Materials	33,000	(E)	Labor Relations and Personnel Administration	
Supplies	5,700	(F)	Other	
Research and Development	2,500	(G)	Logistics:	
Overhead Other Than R&D	6,300	(H)	Headquarters Management (q, r)[a]	$ 437
			Headquarters Other (s, v):	
Selling:			Computer	420
Supervision	1,000	(J)	Communications	260
Salaries	2,800	(K)	Procurement (q)	72
Transportation	5,000	(L)	Raw Material:	
Overhead	3,700	(M)	Transport—Explicit and (Implicit) (e, t, v)	350
Advertising and Sales Promotion	3,500	(N)	Handling (c, d, h)	622
Insurance	800	(P)	Inventory:	
			Interest—Explicit and (Implicit) (t)	270
General and Administrative:			Warehousing (h, x, v)	217
Salaries	1,000	(Q)	Tax (u)	14
Office	2,700	(R)	Insurance (p)	17
Overhead	3,000	(S)	Obsolescence	7
Interest	3,500	(T)	Production Planning	32
			Packaging (f)	2,421
Taxes:			Finished Product Transport (t):	
Property	1,200	(U)	Plants to Customers (l)	840
Employment	1,300	(V)	Plants to Dist. Centers (DCs) (l, x)	1,420
Income	2,000	(W)	Plants to Plants (l)	170
Depreciation	4,000	(X)	DCs to DCs (l)	160
			DCs to Customers (l)	2,410
			Finished Product Inventory:	
			Interest—Explicit and (Implicit) (t)	1,400
			Warehousing (m, x, v)	1,107
			Tax (u)	79
			Insurance (p)	102
			Obsolescence (x)	832
			Order Processing (m, r, s)	237
			Forecasting (r, s)	73
			Total	$13,969

[a]Lower-case letters used to indicate that only an allocated portion of the corresponding capital letter natural account is assigned to one or more logistics functional accounts.

HOW TO CALCULATE THE TOTAL COST OF QUALITY

Robert A. Novack

Transportation costs, warehousing costs and inventory costs are just a few ways that managers measure logistics performance. However, today many managers are adding a new yardstick: the costs of quality. These aren't as easy to identify or manage, because accounting systems are not really set up to capture quality costs. So what are the costs of quality and how are they managed? Let's take a look.

Quality in the Abstract

Quality? Here's a word that has probably been used more in the past 10 years than it has since the development of the English language. But do we really know what it means? Its meaning will be determined by who is defining it. To some individuals a 1973 Volkswagen Beetle in good working condition represents quality, while to others, a 1990 Rolls Royce is the only way to travel. Both vehicles provide transportation and both are perceived by their owners as being of a high quality.

So what's the meaning of all of this? In a nutshell, quality is achieved when a customer's expectations are met, regardless of what those expectations might be. In other words, quality is achieved when the customer is satisfied.

Quality is also an abstract concept. That is, for it to exist someone has to perceive it. "If a tree falls in the woods and there is nobody around to hear it, does it make a sound?" can be turned around to read, "If a firm provides what it thinks to be a quality product but there are no customers around to recognize it, has quality really been achieved?"

Although quality is an abstract concept and is a goal to be achieved, it is also something that can be added to the firm's product. Adding quality means that every activity or process that a firm undertakes to get a product to the customer, from selecting raw material suppliers to stocking retail shelves, must be performed in the manner that it was intended. This attention to detail so that customer expectations can be met is not difficult to do nor is it something that is new to logistics managers. Making things work as they were intended is the goal and purpose of control.

If quality, or meeting customer expectations, is a goal of the firm and control helps ensure that things work the way they're supposed to, it is safe to say that a requirement for achieving quality is the existence of control systems. The total costs of quality, then, are really the costs associated with trying to make things work as they were intended, plus the costs incurred when they don't.

Total Cost of Quality

If you buy into this last statement, then your costs of quality are somewhat dependent on the success of your controls. Control systems within a firm are not necessarily cheap, and the cost of these systems will increase as the amount of control needed increases.

Think for a moment about the collection of freight bill data. A manual collection and storage system will probably be cheaper than a computerized one. However, if freight costs begin to get out of hand, which system would give the traffic manager more flexibility to analyze the cause of the rising costs and initiate management action to prevent them from getting worse? The more expensive computerized system. So control does cost money and management time. These costs can be generalized as prevention costs, appraisal costs, internal failure costs and external failure costs. Each of these will be discussed in the context of a supplier evaluation example.

Prevention costs are those incurred to prevent a failure in quality from occurring. These costs happen because you try to set up a process so that it works as it should.

Let's assume that you have identified a new need within your company (this could mean a new product, a new market, or both; for this example, we'll use a new market). Meeting this new need will require using a new and untried carrier.

You have now entered the selection portion of the supplier evaluation process. Before you try to find this new carrier, you must identify exactly the needs of this new market: speed in transit time, claim-free delivery, etc. Then you must quantify these so you can give prospective carriers detailed requirements: 48-hour transit time, 98 percent claim-free delivery, etc. Be sure to give yourself and your carrier a little room to breathe by adding tolerances to these requirements.

Now the requirements might look like this: 48-hour transit time $+/- 4$ hours, and 98 percent claim-free delivery, $+/- .5$ percent. With these requirements in hand, you can select your carrier.

For the purposes of this discussion, we'll make some assumptions; some far-fetched, some not. First, the carrier you selected just happened to make a cold call on you that morning and was waiting in your office when you found out about a new market opening up. Because you want to make sure that your firm's entry into the new market is successful, you decide to enter into a "partnership" with this carrier and decide that the carrier should be "certified" and develop Statistical Process Control (SPC) capabilities.

Every action you have taken so far — defining requirements, choosing a carrier, setting up a partnership, certifying the carrier — has used management time and required information systems to be developed or strengthened. The costs incurred to do these things are prevention costs. Money and time spent here will reduce the money and time spent for the other costs of quality.

Appraisal or **evaluation costs** are those costs incurred while monitoring how well things are working. If the costs you incurred for prevention gave you perfect service from the carrier, you wouldn't have any appraisal costs or failure costs. Since this won't happen, get ready to spend some time and money here.

By the way, you have now entered the performance evaluation phase of the supplier evaluation process. Once the carrier starts to deliver product in the new market, you can start to collect data on transit times and claims. This data base will enable you to compare the carrier's actual performance with the requirements you set back at the beginning. If the carrier is operating as it promised, then everyone is happy and you can get on with other things.

However, if the actual performance is different from what was expected, you, as the manager, must find out why. If the variance was caused by something out of the carrier's control — bad weather, for example — relax, because there is nothing you or the carrier can do about it; it was an unpreventable occurrence. If the variance was caused by something within the carrier's control — poor routing, for example — then you must take some type of action, along with the carrier, to prevent it from happening again.

By now you have noticed that the word "prevent" has been used in this section. That's because the prevention of variances should also happen in the appraisal stage. If you are using control charts to monitor the carrier's performance and notice an upward trend in transit time, you and the carrier can take some type of action to prevent transit time from exceeding the 52-hour maximum. So in this situation, prevention costs and appraisal costs are incurred at the same time. All the activities you have undertaken in the appraisal stage — data collection, comparison of actual versus standards, variance analysis and corrective action — have used both management time and information resources.

The Cost of Failure

Both prevention costs and appraisal costs are the costs of control. Money and time spent on these control costs could be spent somewhere else if the alternative investment would yield a higher return than that of satisfying the customer's expectations. The more investment made in these two areas, the less likely failure costs will occur. However, even the best laid plans sometimes fail. When this happens, you will experience failure costs.

There are two types of failure costs. **Internal failure costs** are incurred when a failure occurs within the firm; that is, before a product gets delivered to the customer. **External failure costs** are incurred when a failure occurs after the product is delivered to the consumer. Internal failure costs are incurred within or between the firm's plants or warehouses, and within or between any other channel members the firm might use to deliver its product to the customer. Examples of internal failures that would incur costs are claims and inaccurate order picking. External failure costs are incurred when the failure occurs in the customer's hands. Claims or inaccurate order picking for an industrial customer might cause that customer to stop production. Costs then would be incurred to make the situation whole again (resupplying the product). Costs might also be incurred from the loss of future sales to that customer.

The biggest difference between these two types of costs is that external failure costs include the cost of lost sales. The farther down the delivery channel the failure travels toward the customer, the higher the costs associated with that failure.

If the money and time you spent on the prevention and appraisal portions of your evaluation process resulted in your ability to detect service failures before they occurred, and enabled you to take preventive action, there would be no failure costs. You must be ready to address failures.

Failures, whether internal or external, have one of two causes. First, your prevention and appraisal systems tell you that the carrier is not performing as expected when, in fact, the carrier is performing as it should, causing you to take corrective action when none is needed. This is also known as a Type I error.

Second, the prevention and appraisal systems you have are not sensitive enough to detect the carrier's unacceptable performance, causing you to conclude that everything is functioning properly. This is known as a Type II error. Regardless of the cause, failures and the associated costs of

Continued

rectifying them will happen. So don't panic when failures occur.

If the carrier fails to meet the transit time and/or claims requirements for the new market, you should first try to rectify the damage this failure has produced. This might mean another shipment using a higher priced alternate mode. Second, you will need to find out why this failure occurred and take action to prevent it.

Notice that here you will be incurring appraisal costs along with failure costs. The difference between these costs and those discussed in the appraisal section is that these costs are incurred to prevent a failure from happening *again*, while the appraisal costs discussed previously are incurred to prevent a failure from occurring the first time. Believe it or not, addressing failures also becomes part of your supplier evaluation process, because you are still trying to make the carrier perform as it was intended.

In this whole concept of the total cost of quality, the bottom line is that if you are managing transportation, warehousing and inventory costs with the intention of satisfying your customers, then you are also managing the costs of quality.

SOURCE: *Distribution* (August 1989): 108–110. Reprinted with permission of Chilton Company.

Some firms have achieved this degree of data processing sophistication. Other firms are still struggling with the process of translating traditional natural accounts into functional accounts, as previously discussed. The trend, however, is clear. Within the next several years, any firm in a highly competitive industry that is not applying the full power of electronic data processing to this problem will find itself at a significant disadvantage with respect to analyzing and controlling the cost performance of its logistics system.

Balance in Cost Inputs Reported

There is a further dichotomy in the identification of costs between explicit logistics costs, such as purchased transportation and public warehousing costs, for which documentation is readily available, and implicit logistics costs, such as inventory carrying and internal handling costs, for which documentation is not naturally accumulated.

Several years ago, a professor of logistics addressed a national meeting of the Grocery Manufacturers of America, attended by approximately 100 senior executives of companies in an industry noted for its progressive approach to logistics, especially physical distribution. During the course of the presentation, the audience was asked to respond to four questions.

1. How many of you (senior executives) know whom to hold responsible in your organization if transportation costs are too high? [In response to this question, approximately 80 chief and senior executives raised their hands.]

2. How many of you receive a periodic, monthly, quarterly, or even annual report of transportation costs? [Again, about 80 hands went up.]

3. How many of you know whom to hold responsible for inventory levels in your organization? [This time, only about 25 hands were raised.]

4. How many of you receive a periodic report of some or all costs of holding inventory, identified as such on the report? [A number of the members of the audience glanced over their shoulders to check the responses of their colleagues. Slowly, 7 hands came up.]

Effective Cost Allocation

Costs must be allocated in those cases in which they are not, or cannot be, accumulated in a manner that identifies costs by causes, profit centers, or functions. Typically, they are known as indirect costs. The less definitive a cost collection and accounting system, the greater the proportion of costs that requires allocation.

There are two basic stages in the logistics cost allocation effort.

1. Allocating costs in natural accounts to functional accounts.

2. Assigning logistics costs, once identified, to cost responsibility centers.

The saying, "You can't satisfy all of the people all of the time," can be applied to cost allocation, and the problems associated with cost allocation probably predate written human history. Anthony put it this way: "Whenever allocated costs are involved, the resulting . . . cost cannot be said to be accurate.[1]

The perfect procedure for allocating costs has never been found. Realization of this at the outset of the logistics cost allocation effort will encourage "satisficing" behavior and save a lot of hopeless searching for the perfect cost allocation system.

Allocating Natural Costs to Functional Accounts

Problems at this first stage typically include the following:

1. Determining plant warehousing costs (as opposed to production facility costs) for:

   a. Heat, light, and other power;

   b. Interest on investment in facilities;

   c. Depreciation on facilities and equipment;

   d. Labor fringe benefits.

2. Determining distribution center (as opposed to field sales office) costs for:

   a. Heat, light, and other power;

   b. Interest on investment in shared facilities;

   c. Depreciation on shared facilities;

   d. Communication costs in order processing and inventory control activities;

   e. Labor costs for order processing.

3. Determining central computer and communication (as opposed to uses of shared facilities for other administrative activities) costs for:

   a. Inventory control;

   b. Order processing;

   c. Forecasting;

   d. Production planning.

4. Determining interest expense for:

    a. Investment in facilities;

    b. Investment in inventories (as opposed to accounts receivable and other uses of working capital).

The allocation procedure, particularly for indirect costs, requires the following:

1. Collection of the cost in a separate account;

2. Identification of the functional activity to which it is to be allocated;

3. Establishment of a logical basis (such as square feet of space used, in the case of functional activities carried out in shared facilities) on which to allocate costs;

4. Calculation of cost per unit used for the allocation basis (in the case above, cost per square foot for a natural cost category like property tax);

5. Assignment of costs on the basis of the number of units (in this case, square feet) used by an activity center.

Authorities on distribution cost accounting have suggested guidelines for simplifying the allocation job while retaining the usefulness of results.[2] Among these are:

1. The creation of functional cost centers designed to provide management with facts required for the resolution of known policy issues or recurring system design needs;

2. Grouping of activity centers, products, or customers to which costs are to be allocated in such a manner that expenses fluctuate similarly and in a significantly different manner than for other such groupings;

3. Grouping of bases for allocation when they closely resemble one another;

4. Elimination of the separate allocation of expenses too minor to influence results;

5. Selection of bases of allocation on the criterion of the extent to which the basis is measurable without undue expense.

Logistics costs lose their meaning if they are averaged over territories, origin-destination pairs, or distribution centers. For this reason, distribution center costing is gaining in popularity. Through the coding of expenses as they are incurred, facility-oriented costs as well as transportation to and from each distribution center can be accumulated. Transportation costs on shipments directly from plants to customers may even be coded by the distribution center territory in which such customers are located, particularly if these shipments often are occasioned by customer service deficiencies at the distribution center.

Specific bases for determining logistics cost allocations are suggested in Figure 17–1. The identification of other costs can be accomplished by analyzing information often collected but otherwise unidentified in the accounting process, as suggested in Figures 17–2, 17–3, and 17–4.

Both explicit costs (those appearing in identifiable dollar expense accounts for financial reporting purposes), and implicit costs (such as inventory carrying costs assessed on the basis of a minimum acceptable rate of return to the company), are estimated in Figures 17–2, 17–3, and 17–4. For system analysis and design purposes, both are important. For management performance measurement purposes, implicit costs are so subjective and difficult to justify to those whose performance is being measured that they are best put aside, or at least treated separately. The same is true for the allocation of overhead costs over which a logistics manager has no control, such as the company president's salary or real estate taxes on a warehouse facility, as discussed below.

Assigning Functional Costs to Responsibility Centers

Problems at this stage may be less severe than those encountered at the previous one. Typically, the responsibility centers for entire categories of costs reside in functional groups at headquarters under centralized administration, or under a group of facility traffic and warehouse managers at plants and field warehouse locations under decentralized management.

Transportation and order communication costs between company facilities may have to be allocated to managers at both the destination and origin. At a more detailed level of allocation, reasons for holding inventory may be identified so that the relative amounts of inventory accumulated to accommodate logistics (transit, safety, and some speculative stock) can be related to individuals responsible for inventory control at each control point.

Separation of Controllable and Noncontrollable Measures of Inputs and Outputs

George C. Smith has pointed out that "all costs are controllable by someone. This concept refers to the level of management that is responsible for the approval of the expenditures. . . . But all costs are not controllable to the same degree."[3]

In the relative short run, over which managerial performances most often are measured and compared, many measures of logistics system output cannot be influenced by managers responsible for them. The basic nature of the problem is illustrated in Figure 17–5. Here we see that those decisions that have the greatest impact on logistics performance often are made with the least participation by logistics management.

Because managers are most effectively judged primarily by the way in which they manage controllable elements of their business, it is important to identify the controllable elements and report them separately, or at least to establish performance measures on elements that largely are controllable. Controllable and noncontrollable cost elements for one logistics organization are shown in Table 17–3.

Unless there is wide latitude in the time during which logistics activities can be scheduled and accomplished in an organization, work outputs, such as cases handled in and out of a warehouse, ton-miles of private transportation activity accomplished, or orders processed, are largely the result of demands created by marketing and production effort. Thus, output levels rarely will be controllable over all but the shortest period of time. For this reason, the comparison of outputs to controllable inputs often will yield a measure of the manager's ability to anticipate and adjust to various demands for output activity, or putting it another way, managerial as well as labor and material inputs.

FIGURE 17–5: Decisions with varying impact on logistics performance and the
degree to which logistics management typically participates in them

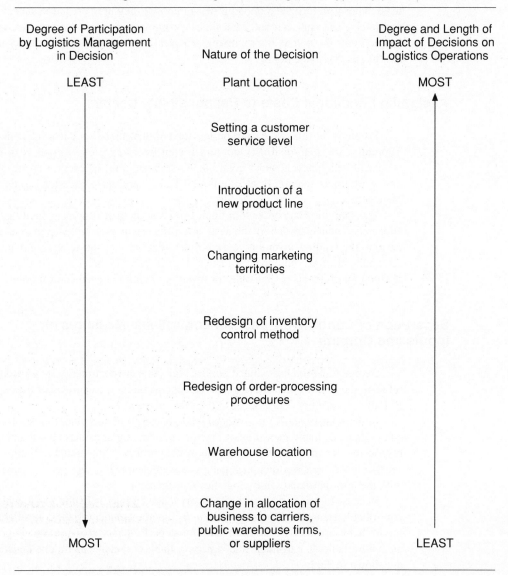

Degree of Participation by Logistics Management in Decision	Nature of the Decision	Degree and Length of Impact of Decisions on Logistics Operations
LEAST	Plant Location	MOST
	Setting a customer service level	
	Introduction of a new product line	
	Changing marketing territories	
	Redesign of inventory control method	
	Redesign of order-processing procedures	
	Warehouse location	
MOST	Change in allocation of business to carriers, public warehouse firms, or suppliers	LEAST

Once identified, controllable costs or other inputs can be compared with units of output on some logical basis. Naturally, every attempt should be made to relate outputs to those inputs from which they result. The relationship never will be perfect, but the goal is to achieve as much logical explanation as possible.

For measures of the effectiveness of all inputs, including those of capital, it can be useful occasionally to compare gross overall outputs with both controllable and noncontrollable inputs.

TABLE 17–3: Controllable and Noncontrollable Nature of Logistics Costs (Over Period of Performance Measurement)

Logistics Cost Account	Basic Action Responsibility (if decentralized)[a]	Amount Controllable	Amount Noncontrollable
Headquarters management	Headquarters Logistics Management	$ 50,000	$ 387,000
Headquarters, other:			
Computer	Manager, Computer Center	140,000	280,000
Communications	Manager, Computer Center	60,000	200,000
Procurement	Plant Procurement Manager	7,000	65,000
Raw material:			
Transport (explicit only)	Plant Traffic Manager	350,000	—
Handling	Plant Manager	522,000	100,000
Inventory:			
Interest (explicit only)	Headquarters Administration	270,000	—
Warehousing	Plant Manager	30,000	187,000
Tax	Headquarters Administration	14,000	—
Insurance	Headquarters Administration	17,000	—
Obsolescence	Plant Manager	7,000	—
Production planning	Plant Manager or Headquarters Administration	—	32,000
Packaging	Plant Manager	770,000	1,651,000
Finished product transport:			
Plants to customers	Plant or Field Sales Manager	840,000	—
Plants to distribution centers (DCs)	DC Manager	1,420,000	—
Plants to plants	Plant Manager	170,000	—
DCs to DCs	DC Manager (at destination)	160,000	—
DCs to customers	DC Manager	2,410,000	—
Finished product inventory:			
Interest (explicit only)	Headquarters Administration	1,400,000	—
Warehousing	DC or Field Sales Manager	836,000	281,000
Tax	Headquarters Administration	79,000	—
Insurance	Headquarters Administration	102,000	—
Obsolescence	DC Manager or Headquarters Administration	416,000	416,000
Order processing	Field Sales or DC Manager	50,000	187,000
Forecasting	Field Sales or Headquarters Marketing Management	—	73,000
		$10,120,000	$3,849,000

[a]If centralized, action responsibilities may be divided among logistics (more traditionally traffic and procurement), production, marketing and control groups. Centralized advisory responsibility may be shared by logistics, inventory control, production planning, and forecasting groups.

Transfer Pricing

The existence of more than one functional activity within an organization gives rise to the question of absorption of costs associated with operations. Whenever a performance measurement system attempts to capture information about expenses incurred by one department in support of the operations of another functional unit, the question of how the expenses are accounted for must be addressed. The interdepartmental transactions are accounted for on the basis of "transfer pricing." As pointed out in a CLM study:

> Although its importance depends on the volume of internal transactions, pricing a substantial number of transactions can affect performance significantly because of the financial impact on responsibility centers.[4]

> Transfer pricing supports the management control of a number of diverse activities and elements within the company through two primary purposes: (1) it ensures management is working towards the objectives of the organization, and (2) it evaluates the progress of managers in meeting the objectives.[5]

Figure 17–6 shows four criteria that should be considered in deciding upon a transfer pricing strategy. There are basically three methods for setting transfer prices. As shown in Figure 17–7, transfer prices may be set on the basis of the cost of the service, the market price of the service, or a combination of the two. Although simple in concept, the actual development of the transfer prices to be used becomes quite complex and difficult to administer

---

FIGURE 17–6: Criteria to Consider in Deciding Upon a Transfer Pricing Strategy

---

- *Fairness and Equity.* The transfer pricing strategy should be perceived by managers as being fair and equitable. It should provide confidence that the pricing of transportation services is consistent for all users, and represents the correct allocation of costs.

- *Contribution to Decisionmaking.* The pricing strategy should provide effective information for evaluating transportation service trade offs; i.e., using the private fleet or purchased transportation.

- *Goal Congruence.* The pricing stategy should assist in meeting the goals of the organization. The impacts on the firm of internal pricing should be consistent and predictable.

- *Accuracy for Performance Measurement.* The pricing strategy should allocate costs and profits correctly. This allows the division, department, or subsidiary to be evaluated as a profit, cost, or investment center without its performance distorted by invalid charges.

SOURCE: *Transportation Accounting & Control: Guidelines for Distribution and Financial Management* (Oak Brook, Illinois: NCPDM, 1983) 96.

FIGURE 17–7: Approaches to Setting Transfer Pricing Strategies

- *Transfer Pricing Techniques Based on Cost*
    - Actual Full Cost
    - Standard Full Cost
    - Variable Cost

- *Transfer Pricing Techniques Based on Market Price*
    - Market Price
    - Adjusted Market Price

- *Transfer Pricing Techniques Based on a Combination of Cost and Market Price*
    - Negotiated Price
    - Target Profit

SOURCE: *Transportation Accounting & Control: Guidelines for Distribution and Financial Management* (Oak Brook, Illinois: NCPDM, 1983) 97.

because of the inherent problems associated with accurate cost determination and acceptance of allocations between departments. As to market prices, there may be no single market price or no closely equivalent product or service available in the marketplace.

IDENTIFICATION OF PRODUCTIVITY RELATIONSHIPS

Experience gained in the collection of cost and other information will provide the basis on which to estimate the way productivity measures should vary, for example, in relation to changes in the volume of an organization's activity or in relation to one another.

Performance-Volume Relationships

Output, input, and productivity measures (relating outputs to inputs) vary with the volume of activity taking place in an organization. For example, an increasing volume of sales from a distribution center should, other things equal, produce a lower handling cost per unit of product handled for a company operating its own distribution center. This is because certain fixed work elements and a fixed labor requirement, unvarying regardless of volume, can be spread over a greater amount of volume with increased material-handling activity, at least up to a point near the theoretical capacity of a given work force.

In many situations, fixed elements of input as well as the level of output are predetermined and outside the control of an individual manager responsible for an activity. For example, the volume of shipments from a distribution center is determined by the level of sales generated in the territory served by the center as well as by the percentage of the demand the distribution center is designed to supply. Further, certain fixed elements of cost or other work inputs for material-handling activity are based on decisions outside the control of the distribution center manager responsible for the activity. In fact, only variable inputs (perhaps measured in terms of cost or man-hours) can be controlled to any degree by the manager. This requires that inputs that are fixed or variable with regard to output be identified separately for purposes of budgeting and other goal setting.

A simple approach to the identification of relationships between productivity and output involves the actual measurement of productivity at different levels of activity. In the case of material-handling activity at a distribution center, readings of tons handled in and out per hour of material-handling labor can be taken at different rates of throughput. A line or curve fitted to the resulting measurements, plotted in the form shown in Figure 17–8, can provide estimates of the fixed and variable elements of the measure necessary for estimating the expected productivity results at various levels of throughput.

FIGURE 17–8: Estimating fixed and variable elements of a productivity measure in relation to volume of activity (tons per man-hour of materials handled into and out of a distribution center, in relation to the volume of tonnage handled in and out)

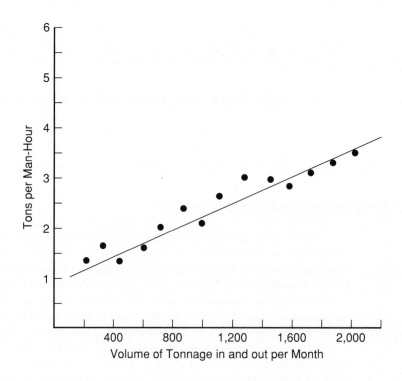

Fixing Productivity Measures in Time

Many performance measures for logistics activities relate logistics costs to sales levels for a given period. This type of measure can produce puzzling results because it relates current logistics costs to products sold during the current sales period, for which logistics costs may have been incurred largely in some preceding period. Thus, during a period of heavy sales and inventory reductions, a company might experience a ratio of transportation costs for shipments from plants to warehouses that is very low when compared with sales, especially in contrast to the high ratio incurred during a preceding period when warehouse stocks were being built in anticipation of seasonal demand.

This problem can be avoided either by eliminating performance measures relating sales outputs to logistics cost inputs or by adopting the accountant's matching concept in the collection and reporting of cost information. Under the latter alternative, attempts can be made to charge logistics costs against goods as they are sold, accruing such costs until the time of sale. Because of the complexities of assigning logistics costs under the matching concept, it is perhaps more practical to restrict the use of sales/logistics cost ratios to longer periods of time (three to twelve months) over which sales and logistics activity peaks and valleys can be averaged. Such periods may be based on the length of time required for a product to pass through the entire pipeline from procurement to production line or from production line to actual sale, or the inventory cycle that a company might experience, particularly in a seasonal business.

One final note: to the extent that costs are allocated on the basis of output measures, productivity measures relating such outputs and costs will be rendered meaningless. It is hard to avoid "productivity averaging" completely, but the design of subsequent performance measures should avoid heavily averaged relationships.

RECOGNITION OF THE IMPACT OF A CONTROL PROGRAM ON MANAGERIAL BEHAVIOR

A control program influences managerial behavior. When performance measures, goals, and review and reward procedures are established in such a way that different functions of an organization work at cross purposes, they may be less desirable than none at all.

The identification of cost relationships, either within or between separate managerial groups in an organization, should lead eventually to coordinated planning and performance measurement. Coordinated planning of interfunctional strategies can in turn encourage the establishment of goals that create a minimum of conflict among production, marketing, finance, and logistics management. This is a characteristic of a well-conceived, well-implemented program of planning and control.

Although many organizations are working toward such coordinated planning, all but a handful are still establishing performance goals and measuring performance without regard for underlying implications of interfunctional strategies determined at the top management level. Consider the following situation, which developed several years ago in the European subsidiary of a large multinational company.

This company, manufacturing a wide range of ceramic bathroom fixtures, among other items, found that its inventories of fixtures were badly out of balance. Stocks of colored fixtures were far too large, while white fixtures were back-ordered constantly. Although the logistics group within the organization had responsibility for establishing inventory control methods, plant managers were responsible for the quantities of items produced in their respective plants. Upon investigating for possible causes of the situation, the corporate logistics staff found that plant managers were being evaluated in relation to a goal based on the dollar value of goods produced at each facility. Because colored units of a given fixture invariably carried a higher value, even though their manufacture required approximately the same labor and material input as white units, plant managers were giving priority to the manufacture of colored units in order to meet their manufacturing value-added goals.

Production, marketing, and finance functions, in the absence of a coordinating group such as logistics, all have a deep and somewhat conflicting interest in inventory policy. Increased inventories of SKUs result in longer, less frequent, and less expensive (per unit) production costs. For seasonal items, increased speculative stocks will allow production an opportunity to maintain a constant output in spite of seasonality in sales, thus maintaining a level, less expensive work force per unit of output.

At the same time, an increase in safety stocks can produce a larger buffer against out-of-stock situations, particularly if such safety stocks are held close to markets. For this reason, a policy leading to increased safety stocks would be highly favored by marketing management.

The third party to this interrelationship, finance, often is concerned with maintaining as little inventory as possible in relation to sales, in order to conserve the working capital of the organization.

Unless the result of an inventory policy decision can be determined, or at least reasonably estimated, in terms of its impact on production set-up costs, per-unit production costs, inventory carrying costs, and sales, it will be impossible to select a policy that will produce the best total result for the company as a whole.

In the past, this has not been a relevant argument in many organizations. The inventory policy was set to accommodate production management in production- and engineering-oriented organizations, marketing management in marketing-oriented organizations, and the finance department in financially oriented organizations.

The emergence of the logistics function, systems thinking, and company-wide planning are forcing companies to face the problem. Increasingly, business firms are introducing policies and practices that charge ''abnormal'' logistics costs to the department that causes them to be incurred. For example, if a salesperson wants an order shipped ''rush'' (air freight instead of motor carrier) the extra cost of shipping by air will be charged directly to the sales department just as the cost of entertaining a customer would be charged.

The authors of this book have witnessed a variety of examples of the dramatic effect that the institution of such policies has on salespersons' requests for rush orders, stockpiling of inventory by production managers to accommodate badly planned machine maintenance schedules, and so on. *The moral is that when the beneficiary must pay the cost, the value of the benefit is scrutinized much more closely.*

PROGRAM MANAGEMENT

The management of a performance measurement and control program for logistics requires that jobs be defined, performance measures established, budgets and goals set, and performance review implemented.

Job Definition

Many organizations have established position descriptions for all executive and clerical personnel. In many, perhaps most, of these same organizations, few individuals ever refer to descriptions of jobs that they, their superiors, or their subordinates are to perform. Too often, the writing of job descriptions is a time-consuming, expensive, and useless task. Perhaps the greatest factor in the nonuse of position descriptions, once they are formulated within an organization, is that they are written in such broad terms that they are impossible to interpret and administer on a day-to-day or even periodic basis.

A job definition should be short, somewhat general with respect to duties and responsibilities (as opposed to a statement of specific procedures to be followed on a job), and quite detailed in its specification of performance measures and review procedures. The most successful ones we have encountered contain the following elements: job title, the individual to whom the person holding the job is to report, responsibilities attendant to the job, measures by which performance in the job will be evaluated, the individual responsible for reviewing performance in the job, and the frequency and manner in which such review will be conducted.

Establishment of Performance Measures

Measures to be used in evaluating performance on a job should reflect the responsibilities of the position. Beyond this, however, there are additional guidelines that successful organizations have applied in establishing performance measures:

1. Be very selective in the development of quantitative measures. It is difficult for a manager to concentrate on more than a few such measures in addition to nonquantitative measures, such as employee morale and the development of talent for job succession.

2. Select quantitative measures on the basis of those that reflect:

    a. important costs or other inputs;

    b. scarce resources, such as facilities with limited capacities; and

    c. measures involving inputs and outputs over which the manager being measured has the greatest control.

In establishing performance measures, it is important to obtain recommendations from the person for whom the measures are being established. This question, ''How would you like to be measured on your job?'' can elicit valuable information from individuals about the way they see their jobs and their sense of perspective. It may also enlist cooperation in and support of the measurement and evaluation process.

Measures that have been established successfully, with adaptations, in several logistics organizations were shown in Tables 17–1 and 17–2. The set of measures in Table 17–1 can be applied to a company's overall logistics activity. At a lower level of management, the measures shown in Table 17–2 can be applied to a company manager's distribution center. In each case, they reflect the scope and nature of logistics operations for a specific company.

Budgeting and Goal Setting

Budgets not only inject discipline into the managerial process, but they provide the basis for intermediate-term financial planning, particularly the planning of cash flow. Typically budgets are confined to the items over which a particular manager has immediate control. In a staff-oriented logistics organization with advisory responsibility, for example, such items usually include only the salaries and related administrative items for a central office staff. Clearly in this situation, the budget has limited meaning (as opposed to broader measures of performance) for the logistics manager who can meet a budgetary goal by hiring or firing a secretary or a rate clerk.

The budgeting of logistics costs for an entire organization may be the responsibility of the corporate staff, even though this group may not be responsible for managing all logistics activities directly. Regardless of responsibility, the budgetary measures used for such activities should be flexible. That is, they should take into account the portions of a given cost that are fixed and variable in regard to the volume of logistics activity the organization is required to carry out. If the operation of a warehouse requires a fixed charge of $100,000 per year in addition to roughly 20 cents for every case handled into and out of the facility, the budget goal should reflect the fact that on-target performance will be represented by an expenditure of $300,000 if 1,000,000 cases are handled into and out of the facility and $400,000 if the volume of such activity is 1,500,000 cases.

Budgets and performance goals should include not only a target figure for each item, but also upper and lower limits that, if violated during the course of the period for which they are established, will lead to the creation of an exception, or red-flag, report of the fact. Performance may go "out of control," or violate limits, for a variety of reasons, all of which warrant immediate review. Causes may range from poor management to a basic change in the economics of an operation that may require an adjustment in the budget or the performance goal.

Goals for performance have broader-reaching implications than budgetary estimates. A logistics organization directly responsible for only a small administrative budget may nevertheless be measured on the basis of its ability to plan and implement a system design through others that will produce a certain result. In this case, the characteristic evaluated on the basis of such indirect measures may well be the ability of the staff advisory organization to communicate or, in the terms of Lawrence and Lorsch, to integrate.[6]

Performance Review

The failure to follow up performance measurement with a periodic review and evaluation can negate an otherwise well-devised program. The frequency of the review may depend on the importance of good performance in the job, the length of time during which the person being reviewed has held the job, or other factors. Typically, such reviews are held more often than salary and promotion reviews, perhaps every six months. In addition, impromptu reviews may take place when budgetary or performance measures go "out of control."

There are many possible approaches to performance review. All should involve advance knowledge on the part of the person being reviewed of the bases on which his or her performance is being evaluated. One effective approach to the actual review is to have *both* the subordinate and superior each prepare an evaluation, based on performance figures and other information, of both qualitative and quantitative criteria. The evaluations can then be compared and discussed. Participation in the process on the part of the person being reviewed leads to greater acceptance of the actual evaluation.

Third-Party Performance Measurement and Control

The emergence of third-party logistics service providers has been discussed in previous chapters. The fundamental reality that such services represent a growing trend across a wide spectrum of logistics management practice brings into focus the need for measuring and controlling the performance and costs of third-party providers in much the same way as internally managed logistics services are held accountable for efficiency and ultimate impacts on customer satisfaction.

The scope and nature of services contracted to be provided must be clearly set forth in the service contracts. Assuming that the contract is sufficiently clear on all relevant matters, the task becomes one of monitoring the third party's performance against the standards agreed upon in the contract. Monitoring third party performance is likely to be more difficult to accomplish than monitoring a firm's own internal performance since the third party is not under the active control of the contractor.[7] For this reason, the contract itself should provide for the means of determining compliance with the customer service standards that have been set for the third party's performance of its contracted services.

PRACTICAL STEPS IN ESTABLISHING A LOGISTICS CONTROL PROGRAM

It has always seemed to us that the higher executives rise in an organization, the more uneasy they become about the adequacy of measures and controls at their disposal for guiding those responsible to them. To a degree, top management is an easy mark for those in middle management concerned about establishing visibility for themselves and their management areas. They only need address themselves to the creation of a productivity control program. Even though some members of top management may not know what logistics is, at least they'll agree that it ought to be controlled.

The possible steps in the establishment of a logistics control program sound formidable when arrayed in the manner we have discussed them above. Sometimes the gap between ideal and actual is so great that we are discouraged from taking the first steps to bridge it. And yet the pay-off, in terms of increased recognition for the importance of logistics activities within an organization and the individuals responsible for them, is so great that it is important to take the first steps toward the creation of such a program.

First, with a pencil and paper and the help of our preceding discussion, identify all important logistics cost categories along with other inputs of effort that the organization incurs. At this stage, the objective is to be complete. The only investment is a little of your time. There is no risk.

Second, begin collecting the cost and input data. At first, this might be done on a one-shot basis, for example, for the preceding year. Later, of course, the objective is to have such reporting carried out on a periodic, routine basis. This task may test an executive's skill in obtaining assistance from colleagues in an organization. If top management's support must be enlisted to accomplish one of these early steps in the process, it may be necessary to proceed directly to step four, below.

It is important that the cost input collection process begin as soon as possible. Most executives we have observed have learned a great deal about the lack or adequacy of cost information and the magnitude of the task of proper identification and collection of such information within their organizations merely by attempting to collect it. A degree of control may result just from the identification and collection process.

Third, identify and begin collecting important output measures. Production measures may be more easily obtained than those of inputs. For example, cases shipped in palletized form from a warehouse may be recorded on a shipping document. If they are not, they can be estimated from the weight shipped by a mode of transportation in which pallets are employed.

The collection of both input and output data may require a long lead time. That is why it is important to start early in the entire process. It is essential to the fourth step.

Fourth, prepare a set of desired measures by which the logistics activities within the organization might be evaluated. Such measures, rather than reflecting the nature of an individual's job, should encompass all logistics activities, regardless of the assignment of responsibility for them. They might reflect the scope of those in Table 17–1, including various measures for transportation, warehousing, inventory control, order entry and processing, customer service, and total logistics cost performance.

Fifth, these measures can then be presented to top management, along with an estimate of the importance of the logistics costs which have been collected in step two. With such justification, it would take a closed top-management mind to veto the recommended control. In one presentation, which might take place months after the collection of the first information, a concerned logistics manager can:

1. Highlight the importance of logistics to top management;

2. Provide, in a practical context, an explanation of the scope of the logistics function;

3. Stress the importance of measuring logistics management performance, regardless of responsibility;

4. Propose a step-by-step program for such measurement and control;

5. Enlist top management support in the implementation of the program; and

6. Project herself or himself as the most likely candidate for the position of manager in charge of some or all logistics activities.

Sixth, assuming top management's support, a program regularly reporting productivity measures, such as those presented in Table 17–1, can be instituted. In all likelihood, even at this stage, sufficient information required for all of these measures will not be available on a regular basis.

Seventh, assuming support for the program is continued, organizations will develop a need for someone in the accounting or controller's function to serve as liaison between those departments and individuals responsible for logistics activities.[8] This will facilitate the regular collection and reporting of necessary information. In most cases, this effort will require that monetary and physical measures of activity be recorded and coded to the point where they are captured for entry into the company's management information system, a basic escalation in effort requiring a policy commitment as well as the investment of funds sufficient to support the activity.

Eighth, organizations in an industry with similar interests in the measurement and control of productivity may establish cooperative efforts to exchange information, probably through a third party able to maintain confidentiality of the data.

Ninth, as productivity measures for budgeting and performance measurement and review purposes are collected, involved executives will begin to develop a "feel" for interrelationships among various types of outputs, inputs, and measures and goals developed for sister departments within the organization. Not until this stage of development is reached can an organization develop the type of coordinated planning that will consistently utilize cross-departmental cost-benefit analyses. The stage will be set for the development of interfunctional planning teams to help in the preparation of budgets and performance goals that take into account and attempt to reduce the magnitude of goal conflicts so common to production, marketing, finance, and logistics management.

Tenth, the development of a coordinated program for performance and control also will facilitate more sophisticated efforts, such as those to plan and control particular logistics projects and to measure the relative profitability of various types of business activity.

PROJECT PLANNING AND CONTROL

The requirements for control of ongoing logistics activities are quite different from those for the selection and periodic review of efforts to implement major projects or programs that typically involve the basic redesign of all or some aspects of a logistics system. Many of the problems of project control begin in the planning process; for this reason, it is useful to consider features of an effective project control process in conjunction with planning efforts that precede it.

Standard Format for Planning and Audit Purposes

A standard format for estimating the impact of a proposed change in logistics system design can provide a checklist against which planners may compare the scope and coverage of their efforts as well as a vehicle for the systematic audit of planning and implementation efforts at a later date. One such format, which can be adjusted to meet the needs of a specific project effort, is shown in Table 17–4.

Effective Capital Budgeting Procedures

Most organizations establish cut-off points, typically expressed in terms of minimum returns on investments, below which capital investments for proposed projects will not be approved. It is useful for a project planner to have these cut-off points in mind when evaluating the usefulness of a proposed project before it is submitted to an organization's top management for consideration. It provides the basis for structuring the actual planning effort, regardless of whether there are substantial investments required for a particular project.

Capital budgeting needs require that a total cost analysis of a proposed logistics system change be accompanied by an estimate of the required capital investment, the net impact on related major costs, and an estimate of the effect on sales.[9]

TABLE 17–4: Format for Requesting Logistics Projects Authorization

	Timing of Cash Inflows or Outflows			
Items to Be Described	*Year 1*	*Year 2*	*Year 3*	*Year 4*
Summary statement of proposed project:				
Creation of an additional product distribution point by using public warehousing space at Denver, Colorado				
Required capital expenditures for:				
New facilities				
Inventory	$ 50,000	$ 10,000[a]	$ 10,000[a]	$ 10,000[a]
Working capital				
Cost of implementing project	8,000			
Other				
Less capital receipts from:				
Sales of equipment				
Sales of facilities				
Other				
New capital investment required	$ 58,000	$ 10,000	$ 10,000	$ 10,000
Additional costs for, and amount:				
Order processing	$ 7,000	$ 7,000	$ 8,000	$ 9,000
Warehousing charges (in addition to current charges)	$ 5,000	$ 6,000	$ 7,000	$ 8,000
Less cost savings from, and amount:				
Warehouse-to-customer transportation	$ 26,000	$ 28,000	$ 30,000	$ 32,000
Net effect on logistics costs	− $ 14,000	− $ 15,000	− $ 15,000	− $ 15,500
Net effect on sales levels	+ $200,000	+ $250,000	+ $250,000	+ $300,000
Net effect on production costs	None			
Percentage of order fill				
Estimated before-tax return on investment, calculated on a discounted cash-flow basis, assuming a ten-year project life	11% (payback period is slightly less than 6 years)			

[a]Additional after the first year.

Projects involving the expenditure of money for physical facilities typically fall within the capital budgeting requirements for organized analysis and presentation set up within many organizations. However, a revision of an inventory control policy or procedure may require no new physical facilities but may have a great effect on inventories and working capital. In addition, most projects of any magnitude require capital investments, whether in the form of computer programming effort or the relocation of personnel, for their implementation. All of these considerations should be taken into account in establishing the investment required for a specific project.

While it may be impossible to provide a realistic estimate of the impact of a system change on profits, it is useful to identify effects that the change may have on major related production costs and sales levels. This will require top management personnel responsible for those activities to commit themselves to projections that can be reviewed at a later date.

Finally, all cash inflows and outflows must be positioned in time so that the estimated return on investment from the project can be calculated on a discounted cash-flow basis, taking into account the value of money today as opposed to some time in the future. The format in Table 17–4 has been designed to provide the basic inputs for the calculation of rate of return on investment on a discounted cash-flow basis.

Linkage between Project Planning and Implementation

In most cases, the responsibilities for planning and implementing a project are divided. Central staff personnel with advisory capacity typically do the planning, handing it over to line managers having action responsibility for implementation. This, coupled with the fact that planning and implementation, especially for major projects, can be disconnected in time as well, often leads to an interruption in the vital feedback loop between control and planning shown in Figure 17–1. When this occurs, and it occurs often, (1) planning and control of a given effort may be carried out under totally different assumptions, (2) those responsible for planning on the one hand and control on the other are given a wonderful opportunity to point their fingers at each other for subpar performance, and (3) many opportunities to improve subsequent planning efforts in the light of past successes or failures are lost.

There are several ways of creating the necessary linkage. Planning personnel may be involved in the implementation process. Those responsible for implementation and control may be engaged to help plan a project. Planning and control may be linked organizationally under one manager. Or, a project audit routine may be established for the assessment and communication of planning and control efforts associated with a given project.

Regardless of the method or combination of methods used to establish a linkage between project planning and control, a systematic project audit routine can serve a useful purpose.

Project Audit Routine

Projects of minimum size, involving a minimum capital investment or minimum potential savings to warrant the cost of an audit should be formally reviewed to determine the quality of planning and control and ways in which each could have been improved. Although such an audit should be conducted by an objective group within the organization (perhaps the finance, control, or engineering group), it should involve representatives from groups responsible for logistical planning and control.

The audit routine should be designed to determine:

1. How well the plan has been fulfilled.

2. Reasons for the relative success or failure of the project.

3. Whether the project should be continued in the light of the findings.

4. Ways in which future planning and control efforts can be improved.

An effective audit requires that planners be able to formulate the project plan in such a way that underlying assumptions on which the plan was based can be identified, even several years after the implementation phase was initiated. It requires also that those responsible for implementation be able to verbalize the assumptions, procedures, and policies with which the plan was implemented and the operating environment in which it was done.

The timing of the audit will depend on the period of time required for the plan to register its full impact. In the case of a new warehouse facility, it might require a year's time to assess its impact on sales in the territory it serves. A change to private from common carrier operation and its resulting impact on customer service might warrant a review after no more than six months.

Postproject Feedback and Review

Reports tend to get filed and not read. As a part of the audit procedure, it is useful to include a postaudit debriefing for selected members of the organization responsible for logistical planning and control activities. Audit reports, along with other project documents and the minutes of the debriefing meeting, might then be placed in a reference file to be used by those involved in future projects.

PROFITABILITY CONTROL

Logistics, to a greater extent than other basic business functions, is spatially oriented. From the standpoint of profitability, it makes a lot of difference where products are sold, stored, and shipped. Lewis' summary of the view held by one of his colleagues makes the point well:

> . . . by allocating total costs among the various activities of marketing [including logistics] on the basis of standards or standard costs, rather than building up the individual charges at the source of their occurrence, the accountant fails to allow for the variability of . . . costs that result from locational differences.[10]

Logistics costs, to a greater extent than costs incurred in production, marketing, and financing activities, can be associated with specific sales. This provides an opportunity to relate costs to individual customers, types or groups of customers, sales territories, warehouse territories, plant territories, or specific products or product lines.

Product Profitability

The profitability of a product or product line often is influenced primarily by the margin between the allocated cost of the product sold and the sale price a company is able to command for it in the market. Typically, the importance of logistics costs as determinants of product profitability varies inversely with the value of the product per unit of weight, notwithstanding the fact that inventory costs are related directly to product value.

One of our friends once encountered a shipping clerk for a computer manufacturer who shipped everything air express, in part because the clerk didn't realize that air express cost approximately twice what air freight did on a comparable shipment. However inadvertently the clerk may have arrived at this policy, it was probably right: a modest additional cost was incurred that likely resulted in a very high level of customer service and satisfaction. In contrast, a similar investigation of the distribution of ceramic building tile disclosed that logistics costs were not only a major factor in product profitability, but also were the most important determinants of marketing territories.

Transportation and public warehouse rates are quoted on the basis of the physical characteristics of a product, among other things. On a company-wide basis, inventory turnover rates can be developed for each product. For these reasons, it is not difficult to associate a large portion of total logistics costs with a product, at least on an estimated basis. Those that remain, typically order entry and processing costs, can be assigned with the use of a surrogate, such as a heavier cost per unit for items found, by sample, to be out-of-stock more often than others in relation to the number of units sold.

What to do with the knowledge that certain product-line items are unprofitable, perhaps even without taking marketing costs into account, is something else. There may be many reasons for retaining an unprofitable item, among them the need to spread overhead costs over an extensive line and fulfill customers' expectations of product coverage. Nevertheless, it is useful to be able to make such decisions with the full knowledge that an item might be unprofitable.

Territory Profitability

The overall logistical profitability of a plant, warehouse, or sales territory will be influenced largely by the geographic relationship among plants, warehouse, and sales territories in question; the operational effectiveness at each facility location; and differences in customer behavior.

Costs against which to assess the relative profitability of territories can be built up starting at their origin. Beginning with a plant, warehousing and inventory costs can be determined and allocated to various categories of product. The process of cost building can then continue through the subsequent phases of the distribution process, including transportation between facilities and markets, and the storage, material-handling, inventory-carrying, and order-processing activities that take place at each facility.

In a company with excess production and marketing capacity, any operational territory that produces revenues in excess of the variable costs attributed to the revenue (termed "contribution to overhead and profit" by accountants) can be justified. However, in situations where production and marketing resources are scarce, a company may want to have knowledge of the actual and potential profitability of all feasible operational territories in order to be able to structure its effort to obtain the maximum profit from a limited production or sales volume.

Customer Profitability

Customers served through identical channels of physical product flow may have significantly different profitability for a supplier. Customer profitability varies with the size and complexity of orders placed for a given destination, the nature of the product-line items ordered, and customer demands for special logistical services.

In some cases, customer behavior may be a major determinant of the relative profitability of a sales or warehouse territory. For example, regional sales managers who do or do not encourage their salesmen to emphasize standard, high-sales-volume items as opposed to special items for which they might be substituted can have a major impact on logistics costs on a territory-wide basis. In this case, the resulting remedy may have more to do with changing sales policies than logistics procedures.

SUMMARY

We have traced the subject of profit measurement and control from the features of an effective program to the more detailed application of such a program in the identification of profitability for products, operating territories, and customers. At its most sophisticated level of use, such a system can provide the means to identify cost relationships, not only over varying levels of activity, but also between functions of the organization. In this way, it can provide the eventual means to assess the implications of a given policy for various functional areas, thus providing for the establishment of realistic expectations for performance in situations where compromises in performance levels between functions are necessary if the organization is to operate in the most effective manner.

Meal has summed it up nicely:

> One of the most important responsibilities of distribution management is to show the general management of any firm the implications of the alternative choices available to it in resolving the conflicts of interests between the various parts of an organization. It is the set of policy statements which control the routine or day-to-day decisions which will most importantly influence the face which a company presents to the outside world and which, in turn, will determine the operating results which are recorded at the end of the year. Distribution management has the responsibility for showing how the operating statement results can be influenced and will be influenced by the choice of policy statement.[11]

In the process of accomplishing this objective, a manager can achieve important byproduct results of informing top management in a practical sense of the scope and importance of logistics activities in general and, in particular, the logistics manager's value to the organization.

DISCUSSION QUESTIONS

1. Why should the production line be viewed as a customer of the firm's logistics system?

2. Explain the relationships among production, productivity, and quality with respect to logistics system performance.

3. Explain the process of "translation" of traditional cost accounts into functional logistics cost accounts.

4. Professor Anthony is quoted as saying, "Whenever allocated costs are involved, the . . . resulting cost cannot be said to be accurate." Why is this so? Explain.

5. Why is it important to separate controllable and noncontrollable costs? Explain.

6. Why is it likely to be undesirable to relate logistics costs to sales over comparatively short periods of time?

7. With respect to the length and type of production runs and levels of finished goods inventories, there are "natural conflicts" among production, marketing, and finance executives. What accounts for this? Can such conflicts be resolved? If so, how? If not, why not?

8. What factors should govern the selection of quantitative measures of logistics system performance? Explain.

9. How often should logistics system performance be reviewed and evaluated? Explain, and justify your answer.

10. The text presents a ten-step process for establishing a logistics control program. Which of these would you consider to be easier to accomplish than others? Which more difficult? Explain your reasons for your answers.

11. Reference the preceding question, would your answers depend on the type of firm or industry being considered? Why or why not? Explain.

12. How does logistics project planning and control differ from logistics operational system planning and control?

13. What is (are) the purpose(s) of a logistics project audit?

14. In what ways are logistics costs related to product profitability, territory profitability, and customer profitability?

CASE: ASSESSING MANAGERIAL PERFORMANCE

Elizabeth Pope was disappointed and angry at the size of her annual bonus check. She'd been expecting something in a nice four-figure number but had received ''a lousy three hundred bucks!''

She knew she was doing a good job as the company's physical distribution manager. She had negotiated good rates with each of the carriers the company used and had steadily improved the productivity of her warehouse and office staff. She had installed and was using modern technology, including extensive use of bar coding and electronic data interchange with customers and carriers. Her inventory management program was well designed and fully computerized. What bothered her so much was her belief that the company's performance measurement system was loaded against her despite her good management of the company's physical distribution department.

Determined to do something about the situation, she sat down and wrote out a list of examples of expenses charged to her department during the past year that seemed to her to be either unfair or at least unreasonable.

1. Costs of overtime for warehouse personnel during ''rush season'' just prior to holiday periods when company sales were higher than at other times.

2. Costs of premium transportation for ''rush orders'' that the sales department said had to be sent by one of the express companies or by air freight, instead of by regular surface transportation.

3. Costs of temporary employees who were brought in when, for example, several of her people were out with the flu or were on vacation.

4. Freight damage claims (not many, but some) that were not paid by the carriers and eventually had to be made good to the customer who had received the shipment from the company.

5. The cost of property and liability insurance carried on the distribution warehouse and the portion of the company's other property and liability insurance costs allocated to her department on the basis of nonwarehouse office space occupied by her department.

6. The cost of converting the warehouse overhead lighting fixtures from incandescent to fluorescent.

7. The cost of merchandise that had been stolen in a break-in by thieves when the warehouse alarm system was not "armed" due to an oversight by the shift foreman.

8. The costs incurred in rehandling several truckloads of returned goods that had been recalled by the company because of a product defect. The defective parts had been replaced by the manufacturing department and the goods placed back in inventory.

"This ought to stir up the finance and personnel people," she thought. "If they take away these unjustified charges I'll be evaluated the way I *should* be evaluated."

CASE QUESTIONS

1. Should some, all, or none of these costs be considered when assessing the managerial performance of Ms. Pope as the company's distribution manager? Why or why not? Explain.

SUGGESTED READINGS

The Council of Logistics Management, headquartered in Oak Brook, Illinois, was formerly known as the National Council of Physical Distribution Management (see Chapter 1). This organization of approximately 6,000 members has taken the lead in the area of research into logistics management practices in American industry. As noted early in this chapter, CLM sponsored seven major research studies that were published during the 1980s. These studies, listed in order of publication dates, represent a comprehensive treatment of every major aspect of logistics system performance, measurement, and control.

Transportation Accounting and Control: Guidelines for Distribution and Financial Management (prepared by Ernst & Whinney in collaboration with Cleveland Consulting Associates), 1983. As noted in the Executive Summary, this report:

Describes the evolving needs of financial and distribution managers for improved timeliness and accuracy of transportation cost information.

Assesses the state of the art of current practices of the industry in applying methods and techniques for transportation accounting, cost control, and information management.

Describes guidelines for the important issues related to transportation costing, planning, and budgeting; responsibility accounting and performance reporting; and special concerns such as standards, cost allocation, transfer pricing, and internal controls.

Suggests guidelines for companies to design or improve transportation information systems to support transportation and distribution decision making in the 1980s.

The report also provides guidelines for transportation charts of accounts; includes a glossary of commonly used management accounting and transportation terms; and summarizes the results of an in-depth industry survey that has contributed to the research underlying this report.

Measuring and Improving Productivity in Physical Distribution (prepared by A. T. Kearney, Inc.), 1984. An introductory summary of the study results highlights findings in the following areas:

The productivity crisis [of the 1980s].

The continuing opportunity for improvements in logistics productivity.

The positive climate for change in logistics productivity, particularly with respect to changes in logistics organization and responsibilities, transportation deregulation, and exploding computer capabilities.

Progress made since a similar study of logistics productivity was made in 1978.

Identification and analysis of companies that have been particularly successful in improving logistics productivity.

The processes used to achieve logistics productivity improvements.

The benefits derived from improved logistics productivity.

Warehouse Accounting and Control: Guidelines for Distribution and Financial Managers (prepared by Ernst & Whinney in collaboration with Cleveland Consulting Associates), 1985. The results of this study are highlighted in an Executive Overview, which points out seven "critical success factors."

The proper role of warehousing in the company is recognized in strategic planning.

Warehousing operations are integrated with the other functions of distribution, and with marketing and production.

The costs of warehousing — the total costs associated with the storage and handling of materials, goods, and products — are planned, measured, allocated, and reported properly.

The information provided to warehousing managers is timely, reliable, and comprehensive, and it is supportive of warehousing decisions.

The applications of management accounting and financial techniques (for example, net present value investment analysis) are commonplace and contribute to sound warehousing business decisions.

Efficiency in warehousing operations is maintained through productivity and effective human resource practices.

Warehousing performance is monitored regularly and corrective actions are taken as a result.

Corporate Profitability & Logistics (prepared by Ernst & Whinney), 1987. This study focuses on the bottom line impact on corporate profitability of successful logistics system management. It provides an analysis of basic principles of logistics excellence, which are practiced by preeminently successful firms whose logistics management practices contribute significantly to their high levels of profitability. Specifically, Chapter 12 ("Measuring and Reacting to Performance") treats logistics system performance measurement and control.

Customer Service: A Management Perspective (prepared by Bernard J. LaLonde, Martha C. Cooper, and Thomas G. Noordewier of the College of Business, The Ohio State University), 1988. In conjunction with the next cited work, this study reveals the significant relationship between well performing logistics systems and high levels of customer service and satisfaction.

Partnerships in Providing Customer Service: A Third Party Perspective (prepared by Bernard J. LaLonde and Martha C. Cooper of the College of Business, The Ohio State University), 1989. Closely related to the previously cited study, the work provides further insight into the character of the relationship between logistics system performance and customer service when third party services (transportation carriers, public/contract warehouses, electronic data interchange, and other third party services) are involved in a firm's logistics system.

Leading Edge Logistics Competitive Positioning for the 1990's (prepared by Donald J. Bowersox, Patricia J. Daugherty, Cornelia L. Droge, Dale S. Rogers, and Daniel L. Wardlow of Michigan State University), 1989. This landmark study shows clearly the directions in which firms that are leaders in logistics management are going. Chapter 5 ("Management Behavior") emphasizes the relationships between logistics strategy, planning, and performance measurement with respect to assets, costs, customer service, productivity, and quality.

ENDNOTES

1. Robert N. Anthony, *Management Accounting, Text and Cases*, 4th ed. (Homewood, Illinois: Richard D. Irwin, Inc., 1970): 381.

2. See J. Brooks Heckert and Robert B. Miner, *Distribution Costs* (New York: The Ronald Press Co., 1953), especially at page 26; and Donald R. Longman and Michael Schiff, *Practical Distribution Cost Analysis* (Homewood, Illinois: Richard D. Irwin, Inc., 1955), especially at pages 193–199 and 227.

3. George C. Smith, "Knowing Your P.D. Costs." *Distribution Age* (January 1966): 21–27.

4. *Transportation Accounting & Control: Guidelines for Distribution and Financial Management* (Oak Brook, Illinois: NCPDM, 1983): 95.

5. *Ibid.* 96.

6. Paul R. Lawrence and Jay W. Lorsch, "New Management Job: The Integrator." *Harvard Business Review* (November-December 1967): 142–151.

7. The risks involved in a third party relationship, including loss of control, are discussed in *Partnerships in Providing Customer Service: A Third Party Perspective*, Bernard J. LaLonde, and Martha C. Cooper (Oak Brook, Illinois: Council of Logistics Management, 1989): 116–118.

8. It is perhaps significant that one of the major recommendations of the Schiff report, cited earlier in this chapter, was for the designation of a person with responsibilities for maintaining just such liaison.

9. For an interesting discussion of this subject, see John R. Grabner, Jr., and James F. Robeson, "Distribution System Analysis: A Problem in Capital Budgeting," in David McConaughy and C. Joseph Clawson (eds.), *Business Logistics-Politics and*

Decisions (Los Angeles: University of Southern California Research Institute for Business and Economics, 1968): 143–156.

10. Ronald J. Lewis, "Strengthening Control of Physical Distribution Costs," *Management Services* (January-February 1968): 39. In this article Lewis summarizes a point of view expressed in what is perhaps the most intensive investigation of the subject: Richard Lewis, *A Logistical Information System for Marketing Analysis* (Cincinnati: South-Western Publishing Co., 1970).

11. Harlan C. Meal, "The Formulation of Distribution Policy," *Transportation & Distribution Management* (January 1965): 21–27.

CHAPTER EIGHTEEN

A Look to the Future

LEARNING OBJECTIVES

The objectives of this chapter are to:

➤ Point out and evaluate the factors leading to the shift in logistics management emphasis that are causing institutional change.

➤ Present, discuss, and evaluate the several types of institutional and organizational change that allow greater cooperation between and among member firms in channels of distribution.

➤ Assess the impact and significance of computers and data communication on logistics management.

➤ Assess the impact and consequences of the deregulation of transportation on logistics management.

➤ Discuss and evaluate carrier responses to the challenges posed by deregulation and increased shipper expectations

➤ Highlight the need for creative problem solving that will result in mutual benefits accruing to both shippers and carriers.

INTRODUCTION

So far as the future of logistics management is concerned, there is good news and bad news. Some of the present trends and possible future developments in the field of logistics will bring smiles to the faces of logistics managers; others will cause severe headaches, or at least significant operational concerns.

Attempts to predict future developments in almost any area of endeavor frequently founder from one of several causes. Either the problems that will be encountered are not accurately forecasted or, if the problems are accurately forecasted, the means that will become available for dealing with them are not accurately forecasted. For example, one of the greatest concerns of the city of New York at the turn of this century was the very large and rapidly increasing amount of horse manure accumulating on city streets — so much that its removal posed a mighty and steadily worsening logistics problem for which there appeared to be no feasible solution. The problem was solved by the arrival of the automobile. Of course, the automobile eventually became the major source of air pollution in the city, thereby creating a new problem that has yet to be solved.

Opportunities, on the other hand, pose a different type of forecasting problem because the sources of opportunities are so varied. For examples, an opportunity may arise in terms of a new technology that would lower logistics costs or from a change in economic regulation that would allow greater flexibility in logistics system operations.

The ancient Greeks had their oracles and today's fortune tellers have crystal balls, ouija boards, tarot cards, and palms to read. However, our attempts to assess the future as it is likely to affect logistics management must be based on a reasonable extrapolation of present trends and developments rather than prophecy.

Changes in logistics management practice are brought about in two basic ways. One is the adoption of improved business practices that occurs due to pressures for lowering costs, improving service, improving profits, and so on. This includes the application of new technology. A second source of change is the translation of social and political forces into actions that result in legislation or other national and international events that change the rules of the game.

So far as the application of existing technology and improved management methods in the area of logistics are concerned, some firms are clearly ''ahead of the pack'' and can correctly be regarded as pacesetters for the future. Out of a total of 695 manufacturers, wholesalers, and retailers whose logistics practices were surveyed in detail, researchers of the Council of Logistics Management identified 117 who were exploiting their logistics competency to the ''leading edge firms.'' The results of this 1989, 517-page, CLM study show that:

> These [leading edge] companies use logistics as a competitive weapon to secure and maintain customer loyalty. They are more responsive and flexible, are more committed to their customers, are more aware of their results, work more closely with their suppliers, are more likely to embrace technology and are more involved with their firms' strategic direction, . . . Analysis of these organizations revealed significant differences between the leading edge firms' approach to logistics organization structure, strategy and behavior than that of more typical firms.[1]

An understanding of the forces at work in our global society provides something of a reasonable guide to understanding what is likely to occur, and thereby affect, the field of logistics during the last decade of this century and on into the beginning of the twenty-first century.

We have grouped the topics to be considered into two classifications: (1) environmental factors and developments, including technology, that are impacting or will likely impact logistics management either favorably or unfavorably, and (2) management practices that will improve logistics system efficiency and effectiveness.

It is not always possible to separate cause and effect when dealing with relationships among changes in the law, advances in technology, effects of social and political forces, and managerial innovations with respect to the organization and operation of logistics functions. Clearly, there are overlaps among these topics as well as a number of cross-relationships.

Managements must adapt to environmental factors and developments over which they have no control, and we will treat these first before dealing with issues of organizational change.

ENVIRONMENTAL FACTORS AND DEVELOPMENTS HAVING IMPLICATIONS FOR LOGISTICS MANAGEMENT

Computers

The room is not brightly lit because too much light would make it a bit hard to view the CRTs (computer TV screens). In one part of the room, traffic specialists are monitoring their industrial firm's inbound and outbound shipments with information electronically furnished by the carriers. In another part of the room, inventory control specialists are monitoring the firm's inventories of finished goods and raw materials. They are updating the inventory numbers based on up-to-the-minute (or hour) sales and production figures, inbound arrivals, outbound shipments to customers and distribution centers, and so on.

This is not Buck Rogers stuff. It is happening or starting to happen in hundreds of firms and will, within a few years, be commonplace. What has happened is a fortuitous marriage of humans and machines (computers and electronic communications). Despite an occasional claim to the contrary, it is not yet possible, and it is truly not foreseeable, that a computer program can be as efficient and effective as a trained and experienced human mind with respect to monitoring and acting on logistics information.

The important emergent figures in logistics practice during the next decade will include a new type of (senior) specialist: the ''logistics controller.'' Using a CRT, and being responsible for some sectors of inventory, a logistics controller will continually integrate all of the information bearing on that inventory and will order feasible adjustments made to keep it balanced against known needs and probable or possible contingencies. Computers simply can't be programmed to handle unforeseen changes or contingencies, and the human brain can't even begin to handle data in computer-like fashion. But, when one works with the other, the results are as described above. By the mid-1990s, logistics controllers will be the backbone of the logistics system in many firms.

Electronic Data Interchange

It is hard to overestimate the impact of this technology on logistics operations. By the end of this decade, electronic data interchange will be the dominant means of transmitting logistics information, both intercompany and intracompany. When and where ''hard copy'' is required, it will be produced by computer printout. Firms will continue to be able to choose between operating their own systems or using the services of third-party providers, with use of the translation capabilities of the latter being mandatory when the primary parties use different codes in their systems.

Barcoding

Barcoding is the third part of the computer-EDI-barcoding triumvirate. Those innocuous little symbols on products, packages, and cartons are the key to faster and more efficient material handling and order picking, shipment tracing, and more accurate and timely recording of inventory record changes. We will see almost universal use of barcoding before this decade is out.

Expert Systems and Artificial Intelligence

Thus far, the primary application of expert systems to logistics has been in the area of inventory management and control. Computer models have been developed that take into account variations in demand and increase or decrease order sizes and inventory levels. Other models are used to consolidate inbound and outbound shipments. Still others have application with respect to loading of ships, taking into account weight and balance as well as cargo destinations.[2] Much work continues to be done on the development of expert systems in the field of logistics, although much has been accomplished.[3] However, true artificial intelligence applied to business is still over the horizon; its achievement awaits theory not yet conceived and formulated, much less developed.[4]

Transportation

As of 10 years ago, current developments with respect to transport vehicle technology appeared to have topped out. Now, a decade later, that observation has proved largely correct. Current developments in transport vehicle technology consist primarily of minor refinements and fine tuning. Examples include such things as satellite tracking of vehicles; on-board computers with peripheral equipment, such as bar code readers; aerodynamic shapes, such as curved windscreens on top of truck tractors; and more widespread use of double and triple bottoms (twin or triple trailers). However, there is no technology on the horizon that is likely to see application in this century with respect to new methods of propulsion or any significant change in the design or operation of transport vehicles.

Certain transportation modes, such as rail and highway, have constraints imposed by existing physical facilities. The height of a rail car can be increased only to a point. Any further increase, except on a few specific routes where the volume of double-stacking COFC (container on flatcar) traffic might justify large-scale alterations, would require massive expenditures for greater clearances at bridges, tunnels, and underpass or overpass intersections that have replaced grade-level railroad crossings. Truckers now speak only of very small increments of increased length or gross weight.

Public attitude comprises a growing constraint on the further development of other transportation technologies. The refusal to support the development of the supersonic transport, was an important indicator. It may be significantly more difficult in the foreseeable future to obtain funds for the development of an ecologically and economically uncertain device, such as the supersonic transport, than for, say, an expanded system of bicycle paths for urban commuters.

A decade ago it was popular to look ahead to the "era of the 747 freighter," a great hope of air freight advocates. These "boxcars of the sky" were to eliminate the economic barriers to the use of air freight. However, few anticipated the problems of assembling a sufficient volume of freight in one place at one time to meet the vastly greater requirements of the 747 for efficient operation. And, with their attention diverted to developments in the sky, most air freight advocates paid too little attention to the significant improvements that would be needed in problem areas of far greater magnitude, such as customs clearance and the handling of air freight on the ground.

What has made international airfreight increasingly useful to and used by logistics managers is the careful *integration* of domestic and international airfreight movement capability into the *logistics systems* of their firms. The air/ground interface has been vastly improved, mainly through preloading of airfreight containers at the shippers' facilities. Shipping schedules have been tailored to maximize utilization of aircraft that today cost more than $125 million each (the 747–400). Efforts of the International Civil Aviation Organization (IACAO) and the International Air Transport Association (IATA) to achieve rapid customs clearance of international airfreight have been very well rewarded. Without such integration, 747s could have become white elephants so far as airfreight is concerned.

The same marine architects who have produced 500,000-ton ULCCs (ultra large crude carriers) now tell us that, although designs of one million tons are possible, the safety factors and economics of building and operating such ships quite likely preclude any possibility of their construction. Even if construction were feasible, the public attitude toward environmental concerns such as oil spills would discourage interest.

With respect to deregulation, the picture is unclear. Deregulation of the motor carrier industry has produced chaotic competition in the truckload sector and is tending to result in oligopoly in the less-than-truckload sector. The airline industry also shows a strong trend toward oligopoly. Major railroad mergers continue to take place. Whether these trends will lead to any degree of reregulation is a possibility that will continue to be debated in Congress and elsewhere, but the outcome of the debate is impossible to predict. The effects of transportation deregulation will be treated at greater length later in this chapter.

Energy

There is a very important question that hovers over the entire logistics scene: the cost of energy in general, and particularly the cost of oil fuels, which are the lifeblood of transportation. In this area we will attempt no predictions or forecasts, other than to note that if the cost of transportation increases disproportionately to other logistics costs, then it is almost certain that the cost trade-offs affected will result in increased economic order quantities, and there will be much greater consolidation of shipments into full vehicle loads.

Should international developments *severely* curtail world oil supplies, the resultant economic dislocations would be so great that an analysis of the consequences is beyond the scope of this book. For example, coal-burning steamships and coal-fired steam locomotives would return as major forms of transport propulsion technology and be part of a changed logistics scene that can be imagined, but will not be dealt with here.

ARE YOU READY FOR THE NEXT BREAKTHROUGH?

Walter E. Goddard and Oliver Wight

Breakthroughs, by definition, create a tremendous impact. Unique solutions which produce outstanding results instantaneously change the standard of performance. In sports, the highjump is a classic example. For years, the Scissor Kick was the best way over the bar. The Western Roll made it obsolete. The Fosbury Flop was the next breakthrough.

Becoming the best scissor kicker in the world will no longer earn a gold medal. To reach maximum heights today, you must either perfect the Flop or figure out a better approach.

The same is true in business. Breakthroughs become such an advantage that all competitors are forced to follow the leader. Within the past 25 years there have been a number of significant breakthroughs in how we manage the logistics pipeline, controlling the flow of raw materials through the manufacturing and the distribution activities to the final consumer.

In the 1960s, the reorder point approach was the Scissor Kick of its day. For every item in the pipeline, it determined when to reorder. The formula has three ingredients: an estimate of the replenishment lead time, a forecast of anticipated usage over this period of time, and some extra inventory called "safety stock" to protect against fluctuations in both time and demand.

Back then, I was inventory manager for a manufacturing company that had 14 warehouses, resupplied from multiple manufacturing locations. In turn, our warehouses supplied wholesalers that supplied distributors that sold to the ultimate customer. Each layer in this pipeline was managed independently. Consequently, each was forecasting the next higher level, striving to have enough of the right items for good customer service, while minimizing money tied up in inventory.

The same was true within our manufacturing operation. Each level in the bill of material became a separate layer and was controlled by the reorder point approach. Our suppliers did the same.

To visualize how it worked, picture a pipeline with many valves, each representing reorder points for every layer. Next, imagine managers opening and closing them independently. It's not hard to see how these stops and starts would frequently and randomly interrupt the flow.

MRP II Improves Service

Manufacturing Resource Planning (MRP II) was the breakthrough in the 1970s. By tying together the products and their components, this approach eliminated the vast bulk of their components, and this approach eliminated the vast bulk of forecasting. Demand for lower level components could be calculated by analyzing the needs for the parents. Less inventory and better customer service were the results.

By the late 1970s the logical extension of this approach, both above and below the manufacturing facilities, occurred. Distribution Resource Planning (DRP) became the new means for integrating the resources required at distribution centers. By reducing the uncertainty between these two layers in the pipeline, costs dropped further and customer service rose higher. To help suppliers in a similar manner, vendor scheduling was initiated. Instead of the suppliers having to forecast material and capacity, companies using MRP II could provide their long-term, time-phased requirements as far beyond lead times as needed.

Immediate benefits occur as you link layers, customer to supplier. Providing reliable information from the customer to the supplier enables the supplier to manage his business in a better manner, resulting in better service and lower prices to the customer.

Going beyond DRP

Just-in-time/total quality control (JIT/TQC) has been the breakthrough of the 1980s. It's a process for achieving continuous improvements. It does so by attacking wasteful activities, those which add no value to the product. By simplifying and eliminating wasteful activities and improving those that are necessary, quality improves, lead times shrink, customer service increases, and costs decrease. When JIT/TQC is coupled to the planning capabilities of DRP and MRP II, dramatic improvements not thought possible a few years ago are produced. Today, this combination is similar to the Fosbury Flop in the highjump — it's the best way to clear the highbar.

Are you ready for the next breakthrough?

A number of leading-edge companies are putting together a shorter, faster pipeline. They have established a strategic plan which embraces three elements:

■ *CONNECTING ALL LAYERS IN THE PIPELINE*. This chain of information enables the requirements for each to be in lockstep, synchronized so that deliveries can be done quickly, economically, and when needed.

■ *LEARNING HOW TO MANAGE WITH THE FORMAL SYSTEM*. Valid plans must be maintained and executed in order to replace order launching and expediting.

■ *WORKING AS PARTNERS*. Customers and suppliers must join together to eliminate wasteful activities, such as eliminating layers and reducing lead times between the remaining ones.

Putting It All Together

Connecting all layers is the easiest element to put in place. Electronic Data Interchange (EDI) and MRP II/DRP software are widely available. Although important, this is equivalent to giving an athlete the equipment that he or she needs. Using it properly is more difficult.

The next element, utilizing a formal system to manage, is not easy to implement. Many managers have not made the transition from being good firefighters to being good fire preventers. Maintaining valid schedules — ones that correctly reflect the needs of the company and are possible to carry out — is the alternative to the enormous waste of time and energy plus the extra costs caused by hot lists.

Having everyone within your company aware of what they must do to carry out the company's game plan and working hard to accomplish it are both highly productive and personally satisfying.

Working as partners to help the other guy is also tough to do. Too often, marketing tends to be distrustful of manufacturing; manufacturing is uncertain about engineering; engineering is suspicious of purchasing, all of which generates a bad case of fingerpointing. It's tougher still to develop an open and honest relationship between customers and suppliers. Each party is typically worried about the other's intentions. To make progress, the most important issue to be addressed is "What's in it for me?" When the answer is seen as a competitive advantage, attitudes will change and good headway can be made.

Welding these elements together raises the highbar of performance. A handful of companies are now successfully operating in this manner. Just envision the benefits gained by:

■ eliminating the need for forecasting

■ knowing continuously the demands of your customers

■ having suppliers deliver reliably

■ working as a team to reduce lead times

■ working together to reduce costs and improve quality for both information and products.

Or, just imagine if your best competitor has just done it. Motivation comes from such visions.

Breakthroughs do not occur overnight. Rather, they come from managers dissatisfied with the status quo and a conviction that there must be a much better way. A great deal of work, often trial and error, follows.

An observant manager often finds inspiration from innovation in another industry. Being able to see how innovations may apply to your company, having the ability to assess the potential consequences, and then fostering a climate that's receptive to change are characteristics of effective managers. The competitive race is not necessarily won by the inventor of the breakthrough. Rather, the winners are those who swiftly convert it to its full potential.

There's no doubt in my mind that within a few years we'll look back upon the 80s and wonder why it took us so long to implement the better approach — just as we do today for the decades preceding us. The only question is, will you be looking back as a strong leader or as a struggling follower?

Automation

The hoped for promise of fully automated warehousing is yet to be realized. In fact, the requirements it imposes on the need for regularity and volume of product flow for effective utilization of highly automated facilities in many cases may be achieved only through major advances in the type of institutional cooperation discussed later in this chapter. However, partial automation has been achieved in many modern warehousing operations by the use of "driverless forklifts" that are controlled by computers and retrieve and stow away in high racks without human supervision. We also have "Automated Guided Vehicles" (AGVs) that can even board a truck at a loading dock and load or unload cargo.

Recycling

Legal requirements for recycling of packages and containers will continue to increase and will place ever more pressure on firms to insure that these legal requirements are met. This is both an opportunity and a threat. The opportunity is for innovation; the threat is that recyclability requirements may increase the costs of packaging and material handling. The need will be for innovation in packaging that will at least not increase costs, while meeting stringent recycling requirements.

Metric Conversion

Already well underway, the process of converting to metric weights and measures will continue. Metrification will become mandatory for American firms doing business internationally. Domestically, the changeover will proceed at a slower pace.

Education and Training

The day of the green-eyeshade traffic manager is long since past. Increasingly, the field of logistics requires that its managers be well educated and that they be highly trained in inventory management, data processing, carrier negotiations, electronic communication, international logistics operations, and JIT practices and, above all, have a clear understanding of the meaning and importance of customer service.

Productivity

There is a clear shift from a production orientation to a *productivity* orientation in logistics operations. This shift in emphasis is cost-driven and will gain even more momentum as pressures to reduce logistics costs and improve efficiency continue to increase.

Quality and Customer Service

Increasingly, customers are demanding high quality in the services and products that they purchase. With respect to logistics, customers are becoming increasingly intolerant of order-filling errors, backorders, goods damaged in transit, delays in delivery, failure to respond promptly to order-tracing inquiries, and so on. They want quality logistics service and, given a choice, they will do business only with firms that offer it and produce it.

Just-in-Time

Whether dealing with what are truly just-in-time inbound movement systems, or simply firms tightening up their inventory control systems, suppliers and carriers will have to provide increasingly dependable service to their customers. Further, and the point is often overlooked, just-in-time systems also put considerable pressure on logistics management in the receiving firm. The practitioner of JIT must coordinate very closely with vendors and carriers to insure that the instructions given to them are carried out and produce the desired JIT results.

Globalization of Business

Logistics managers may expect a continuing increase in the number and types of international transactions for which they must provide logistics services. This imposes a whole new set of requirements for skills and knowledge and, in many firms, will give a substantial career advantage to those logistics managers who acquire such skills and knowledge.

THE SHIFT OF EMPHASIS TO INSTITUTIONAL CHANGE[5]

The primary focus of logistics management during the 1990s will be a continuation of institutional change for a variety of reasons. Included among these are (1) existing technologies, to a growing extent, require for their success a rationalization of logistics activity that can be brought about through institutional cooperation and new types of institutions, (2) there are changing attitudes toward interorganizational coordination among individuals in business as well as government, (3) continued organizational development of logistics management will yield information necessary to justify institutional change, and (4) perhaps most important, the economic benefits from institutional coordination and change far exceed the benefits that foreseeable technological developments will offer.

This represents a logical progression in logistics thinking and management from emphasis on decision making based on internal total cost analyses to emphasis on internal total profit analyses and interorganizational total cost and profit analyses of the sort suggested in Figure 18–1.

Rationalization Required by Existing Technologies

Rationalization, typified by improved division of effort and responsibility among cooperating and even competing institutions, is required by the introduction of new technologies. However, technological advances have outstripped institutional changes to such a degree that the absence of the latter now often imposes significant constraints on the former.

The capabilities of current computers and information-processing technology are nowhere near fully utilized in most firms. Those firms whose managers most clearly understand and are able to apply such technology will gain a competitive advantage in their industry.

Innovation coupled with improved production technologies and new materials has made possible smaller, lighter products that perform jobs better than their larger, heavier predecessors. Examples include products as diverse as vacuum cleaners and computers. At the same time, improvements to our intercity transportation systems have made it easier and less expensive to transport larger quantities of smaller shipments, at least to the outskirts of large metropolitan areas. What happens then? In a growing number of cities we have congestion and chaos. This is clearly a case in which technology has contributed to a problem that will be solved either by more technological development, perhaps in the form of subterranean freight access routes, or by institutional cooperation to create more efficient freight flows, perhaps by consolidating multiple-retail store shipments inbound to a central business district.

FIGURE 18–1: Stages in the scope of analyses for logistics decision making

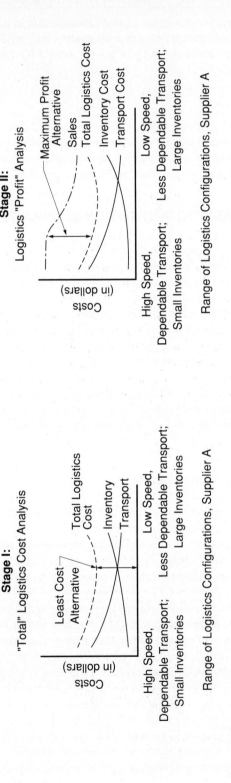

Stage I:
"Total" Logistics Cost Analysis

Costs (in dollars)

Least Cost Alternative

Total Logistics Cost

Inventory
Transport

High Speed, Dependable Transport; Small Inventories

Low Speed, Less Dependable Transport; Large Inventories

Range of Logistics Configurations, Supplier A

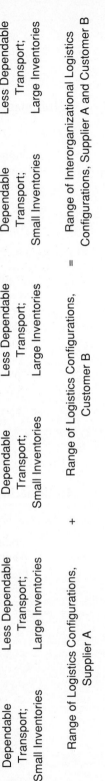

Stage II:
Logistics "Profit" Analysis

Costs (in dollars)

Maximum Profit Alternative
Sales
Total Logistics Cost
Inventory Cost
Transport Cost

High Speed, Dependable Transport; Small Inventories

Low Speed, Less Dependable Transport; Large Inventories

Range of Logistics Configurations, Supplier A

Maximum Profit Alternative, Supplier A + Customer B
Sales
Logistics Costs

Costs (in dollars)

High Speed, Dependable Transport; Small Inventories

Low Speed, Less Dependable Transport; Large Inventories

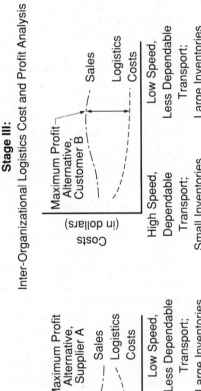

Stage III:
Inter-Organizational Logistics Cost and Profit Analysis

Maximum Profit Alternative, Customer B
Sales
Logistics Costs

Costs (in dollars)

High Speed, Dependable Transport; Small Inventories

Low Speed, Less Dependable Transport; Large Inventories

Maximum Profit Alternative, Supplier A
Sales
Logistics Costs

Costs (in dollars)

High Speed, Dependable Transport; Small Inventories

Low Speed, Less Dependable Transport; Large Inventories

Range of Logistics Configurations, Supplier A
+
Range of Logistics Configurations, Customer B
=
Range of Interorganizational Logistics Configurations, Supplier A and Customer B

Changing Attitudes toward Interorganizational Cooperation

Many forms of interorganizational coordination not only are legal, but are becoming more and more attractive as problem-solving means to businessmen and government officials alike. The growing interest in encouraging the coordination of inbound freight movements to congested city centers mentioned above is just one example of a response by government and industry leaders to a difficult problem.

Continued Organizational Development for Logistics

A number of studies have documented the organizational evolution and growth of logistics management. Clearly, the field has expanded from primary concern for fragmented activities, such as transportation or inventory control, to include warehousing, material handling, inventory control, order processing, and procurement activities. While organizational growth has not fulfilled the expectations of all projections made for it, certain identifiable patterns of past growth, which we cited earlier, should continue. Organizational change, at first apparent in some larger corporations, now appears to be spreading to other companies in certain industries.

What types of industries? Several characteristics can be identified. Industries where substantial costs of logistics, compared to sales, must be balanced against rigorous demands for customer service have provided a spawning ground for logistics management. Included among these are grocery and chemical product manufacturing. Other industries facing severe pressures of expanded product lines have supported organizational development. These include manufacturers and distributors of products requiring extensive distribution activities for replacement/repair parts.

Responsibility for Coordinated Product Flow

Concepts of postponement and speculation provide a means to assess future changes resulting from the analysis of overall product flows in a firm or a channel of distribution. Postponement is the practice of waiting until the last practicable moment to put a product into its final form, while speculation entails holding inventory in anticipation of sales. These practices are responses to various physical flow problems experienced by companies, and as such are useful for the logistics manager to keep in mind. A ready example of one such problem is that of expanded product lines.

Expanded product lines increase the cost of speculation for whoever is holding inventories. As a result, retailers and wholesalers have limited their speculative risk by reducing stocks of any one item (or investing the same amount of money in inventory for a broader product line) while at the same time expecting, and in fact depending upon, excellent response time to orders from manufacturers in order to maintain a given level of customer service. This customer expectation, stated in the form of a willingness to substitute one manufacturer's product for another's in the event of the latter's inability to meet the customer's expectations, in effect raises the incentive for speculation by raising the penalties for postponement on the part of the manufacturer.

Thus caught in a squeeze between increasingly large product lines and increasing demands for service from channel institutions, a number of manufacturers have responded by holding larger quantities of stock in *semifinished form* closer to market, typically in distribution centers. Here, such stock can be cut, assembled, packaged to order, and so on, thus postponing commitment to final form until the last possible moment. At the same time speculation (measured in terms of the elapsed time between customer order and delivery) is reduced for the customer.

To a growing degree, logistics management will involve the operation of light manufacturing as well as distribution facilities. Perhaps the automobile assembly plant offers the most extreme example of this phenomenon. It is the closest thing to a distribution center in the channel of distribution for automobiles produced in the United States; it also houses light manufacturing activities. Because of the complexity of the latter, however, these plants typically fall under the responsibility of production management. However, in other industries with less complex field manufacturing requirements, such as the cutting to order of plate glass, paper products, lumber, and steel, and the packaging to order of common commodities using different materials, light manufacturing in the field may become a functional responsibility of logistics management.

Principles of postponement and speculation, like total cost analysis, suggest reasons for shifting functions between facilities (in a sense, intraorganizational institutions) within the firm. They also suggest reasons for shifting such functions between the firms and for creating new and eliminating old firms in a channel of distribution. Clearly, this family of concepts will have a significant impact on the future organizational growth of logistics.

Conversely, continued organizational development for logistics management will provide further support for institutional change to the extent that it will foster (1) continued emphasis on the system (including related services provided by other companies) as the appropriate unit for analysis, redesign, and control, (2) the development of information necessary for the appraisal of new institutional arrangements, and (3) the development of a cadre of managers capable of analyzing and dealing with interorganizational problems.

Relatively Great Economic Benefits

Technological change can make more efficient the performance of a function by a company in a channel of distribution. Institutional change typically can eliminate entirely the cost of performing a function by shifting it from a company to another point in the channel, where it can be absorbed by integrating it with other activities. Only occasionally, as with momentous developments such as containerization, can technology accomplish as much. And even then, it can do this only when accompanied by the institutional change necessary to implement its introduction and growth.

INSTITUTIONAL CHANGE AND INTERORGANIZATIONAL MANAGEMENT

Early in our discussion (Chapter 1) we suggested that the basic functions performed in a channel of distribution, such as selling, buying, storing, transporting, financing, providing information, and others, can be shifted, but not eliminated. They must be performed by some institutions at some points in a channel. Improved distribution opportunities can be pinpointed by identifying which of the basic functions can be performed most effectively by each institution in the channel and the types of institutional change needed to accommodate efficient product flow. This matter is of growing concern to companies with great dependence on, and the opportunity to assume leadership of, channels of distribution. Their concern will trigger the implementation of pricing mechanisms, implied threats, or other means to produce a coordinated channel effort that leads to the ultimate sale of more goods at a lower price and a higher per-unit profit margin for the sum of the firms cooperating in the channel.

What types of institutional change will interorganizational management call for? Indications suggest that changes may encompass several types, arrayed in terms of their organizational impact on firms in a channel: (1) the coordination of policies and practices to facilitate the more effective performance of existing functions by cooperating channel members, (2) the shifting of functions from one institution to another in a channel of distribution, (3) the creation of joint venture or "third-party" institutions to eliminate duplicated performance of functions in such channels, and (4) the vertical integration of channel functions performed by existing organizations. Improved economics of operation will be the incentive, and anything from incentive pricing mechanisms to acquisition will be the vehicle for such change.

Coordination of Policies and Practices

It has been shown that, at a given level of demand for a product in a channel of distribution, there is a quantity of goods a customer should order, a transportation firm should carry, and a supplier should ship, to produce the lowest total cost to the sum of the channel members.[6] However, this is different from the quantity each party to the transaction would calculate if each were to analyze the problem shown in Figure 18–2.

In fact, only by the greatest coincidence would all firms arrive at a decision to deal in quantities optimum to the channel without direction from two or more cooperating companies.

Further, pricing mechanisms necessary to achieve the desired interorganizational result can be calculated by those organizations supplying product or services to the channel. Because these mechanisms may have the effect of redistributing profits among members of the channel, supplementary actions such as rebates may be necessary to distribute the benefits of interorganizational action to all parties to such a transaction.

Where the buyer-seller relationship is a continuing one, and the volume of product moving between them is sufficiently large, an interorganizational approach to the problem of product flow is clearly warranted. In some cases, the introduction of technology providing distinct and strong incentives to carry out the interorganizational transaction in a given fashion has produced the desired coordination of policies and practices.

Consider, for example, the impact of palletization on interorganizational coordination. In order to reap the maximum benefits of palletization, buyers and sellers have to coordinate their material-handling systems to make use of the same size pallet, or at least pallet sizes with modular compatibility. Thus, industry standards for pallet sizes have been established for the shipment of such things as tin cans and paper products. Where standards have not been established, wholesalers, for example, have adapted their material-handling systems to conform with those of a dominant supplier. Companies electing not to abide by such standards do so at a price, reflected in increased costs for handling goods.

What is the potential payoff from such coordination? One retailing organization selling about $200 million in goods per year estimated that its total logistics bill came to about $6.3 million, not including the cost of inbound transportation. However, on goods purchased it was estimated that suppliers were incurring logistics costs (buried in the retailer's cost of goods

FIGURE 18–2: Graph of profit curves for seller, carrier, buyer, and channel of distribution as a whole (the sum of the seller, carrier, and buyer) dealing in various order quantities, based on assumed data

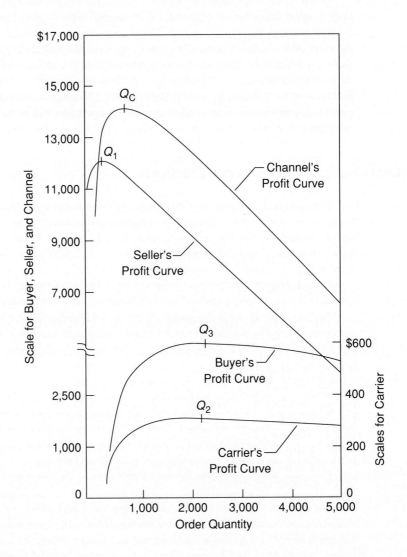

Source: James L. Heskett and Ronald H. Ballou, "Logistical Planning in Inter-Organization Systems," in Michael P. Hottenstein and R. William Millman, *Papers and Proceedings of the 26th Annual Meeting of the Academy of Management* (Academy of Management, 1966) 131.

sold) of nearly $15 million. This prompted a shift in emphasis from a search for opportunities largely for internal cost savings to a more balanced emphasis to include possibilities for achieving much larger savings through improved supplier-retailer coordination.

Shifting of Functions between Organizations

A large distributor of personal care and houseware products through a network of direct sales personnel desired to gain greater control over the delivery of product to its distributors without actually going into the trucking business. It offered truckers an interesting proposition: a guaranteed high return on their investment in return for the full authority to schedule and control their trucks, a 40 percent reduction in existing charges, and access to the truckers' books to verify profit levels. The 40 percent reduction in charges combined with the guaranteed high profit suggest the tremendous potential benefits made possible by a shift of functions and responsibilities in this case.

We have already mentioned the general shift of stock-keeping responsibility from inventory-turnover-conscious retailers to wholesalers and manufacturers. This has resulted in part from the desire of retailers to reduce speculation and dead or unsalable stocks in an age of expanding product lines, as well as a realization that warehousing and material-handling costs may be significantly lower per unit for manufacturers and wholesalers than for their retailer customers. If this is the case, the shift of responsibility for the performance of these functions in the channel of distribution is a logical result of formal or informal interorganizational analysis and management.

Third-Party Distribution

Third-party distribution is supplanting the private warehousing and shipping process for many U.S. manufacturing companies. This allows the manufacturer's marketing organization to concentrate on selling. Due to the extensive economic deregulation of trucking, these firms are increasingly directly engaged in the transportation function for their customers.

There is also a steady trend toward the formation of third-party "chains" having widespread geographic coverage under a common, coordinated corporate umbrella. The many rapid and continuing developments in computer and communications technology are providing the necessary operational controls to enable managers of these firms to coordinate widespread multiwarehouse networks.

However, some firms are rethinking the use, or possible use, of third-party providers. Their concern is loss of direct control over distribution operations and some loss of direct customer contact.

Consolidated Distribution

Consolidated distribution, involving the movement of carload quantities of stocks directly from the production lines of competing manufacturers into common regional distribution centers for consolidated delivery direct to retail stores, has been discussed for some time, particularly in the grocery products industry. Until now, objections regarding loss of control over the product, possible disclosure of competitive information, and the elimination of an area of potential competitive advantage have overruled the economic advantages of averting both the manufacturer-operated and the retailer-operated distribution center, as shown in Figure 18–3.

But, consolidated distribution of this type is now a reality. The concept has been implemented in Canada with the creation of a distribution center in Vancouver shared jointly by leading manufacturers and their chain-store customers. The success of this experiment by a

FIGURE 18–3: The impact of consolidated distribution on the product flow of three competing manufacturers supplying three competing retail chain store organizations

Product Flow Without Consolidated Distribution to a Regional Market Area

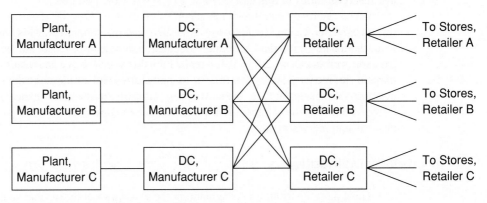

Product Flow With Consolidated Distribution to a Regional Market Area

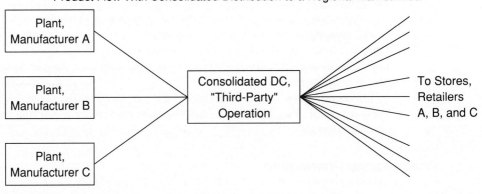

DC = distribution centers

task force of the Canadian Grocery Manufacturers Association, which reported that it reduced the cost of dry grocery distribution by at least 10 percent led to its expansion of the practice to other Canadian provinces.

Central Distribution Facilities

The benefits of consolidating outbound freight can usually be achieved by a well-managed medium-sized or large manufacturer. However, companies receiving small shipments from many sources have found that they must establish cooperative arrangements to enjoy similar benefits.

Thus far, such arrangements have been confined to the formation of shippers' cooperatives for the consolidation at origin of merchandise purchased by several companies for delivery to the same destination (a metropolitan area). Transportation cost savings, in the form of pro rata rebates, from the replacement of small-package shipments by carload and truckload shipments, have been remarkable.

These same companies continue to explore, with the urging of city officials, the creation of consolidated storage and merchandise processing facilities, located in low-cost suburban areas, as well as coordinated delivery to store sites. A private study in which one of us participated several years ago indicated that central distribution facilities could be operated at a satisfactory profit by a third party charging retailer customers only 80 percent of their current costs of receiving, processing, and delivering such goods themselves, typically in crowded, expensive space and traffic-clogged shipping facilities.

THE IMPACT OF TRANSPORTATION DEREGULATION

The wholesale economic deregulation of transportation is having significant effects on carriers and shippers alike, and these effects will continue to multiply in the next few years. The primary intent of Congress (and several state legislatures) was to foster price competition in the case of motor and air freight, and to enable carriers to make a profit in the case of the railroads. However, one of the by-products of deregulation likely to have a more profound long-range effect than ''mere'' price competition is competitive flexibility on the part of the carriers.

A whole host of carrier actions and carrier-shipper relationships formerly forbidden are now condoned or even encouraged. Railroads may make long-term *secret* contracts with individual shippers. Intracorporate truck hauling is now permitted. In the case of motor carriers, the previous sharp distinctions between private, contract, and common carriage are now so blurred as to be nonconstraining. Air freight is all but wide open as to points served and rates charged.

Thus, most of the barriers to interorganizational cooperation between carriers and shippers have been removed. Mutually advantageous cost trade-offs, which were formerly legally unattainable, can now be negotiated.

All this calls for increased sophistication on the part of carriers and shippers alike when negotiating rates and services. As might be expected, there is considerable variance among shippers and carriers in their ability to cope with this dramatic change in the transportation marketplace. The next ten years will witness the evolution of a new pattern of carrier-shipper relationships. Inevitably there will be some discrimination among shippers by carriers, and public opinion is sharply divided over whether or not such effects of deregulation are worth the hoped for benefits. Only time will tell whether the pendulum of deregulation has swung too far.

IMPLICATIONS FOR CARRIER MANAGEMENT

In the first part of this chapter, we considered a wide variety of environmental factors and developments that will impact logistics management in this decade and on into the twenty-first century. Similarly, those developments have specific implications for carriers as well. We recommend a test for a carrier manager to determine how aware he or she is. Ask the manager to answer the following five questions.

Ten years from now:

1. Do you expect your company to be offering the same services as it does now?

2. Do you expect your company's customers to be roughly the same?

3. Do you expect their approaches to the purchase of transportation and other logistics services to be the same?

4. Do you expect your company's organization to be the same?

5. Do you expect your company's ownership to be the same?

If the reply is "yes" to as many as three of these questions, ask a sixth question:

6. Are you really equipped to serve your organization well during an era of institutional change?

Clearly, there is no place for "status quo" thinking within carrier managements at the present time.

The impact of conscious or unconscious adherence to the logistics system concept on the part of those responsible for the management of logistics activities in industrial and commercial enterprises has been felt during the last decade by those firms providing services to such systems. Principal among these service groups is the freight carrier. Problems and opportunities created for carriers extend also to suppliers of material-handling equipment and to those dealing in packaging and packing services, equipment and supplies. We will confine our discussion to implications for carrier management; it is easily translated and transferred to other service and supply firms.

Change in Response to Demand

In the past, industrial and commercial management has placed great emphasis on the reduction of explicit costs of transportation. Since deregulation, carriers have responded with intense price competition in seeking the favor of existing and potential customers. Yet, the demand for transportation services among organizations that emphasize and coordinate the management of logistics activities is typified by emphasis on dependability of service and other cost-oriented logistics considerations rather than on lower carrier rates *per se*.

New shipper policies have given rise to a shift of emphasis among carrier organizations from price competition alone to the design of new services that reduce the costs of logistics for customers without seriously affecting the return per unit of service to the carrier. Intense price competition among carriers probably will continue, but it will be confined more strictly to those industries that continue to emphasize transportation cost reduction to the exclusion of service improvement.

Selling Transportation as a System Component

Most recent attempts by carriers to establish marketing techniques in tune with increasing emphasis on the logistics system concept have included the following steps: (1) reorganization and reallocation of sales effort, (2) the development of customized consulting programs utilizing the total cost approach to physical supply and distribution systems analysis, and (3) the establishment of groups consisting of consulting analysts commissioned to work alongside regular sales representatives to compare customer needs with carrier capability for meeting them.

Reorganization of Sales Effort The expense involved in conducting total cost appraisals of customer logistics systems requires that carriers first reorganize their sales efforts to allow less attention to some customers and more to others. This is accomplished in four steps.

1. An analysis and understanding of the capabilities of a given carrier and the types of shippers most logically attracted to its services.

2. A survey of all potential shippers that might be expected reasonably to utilize services of the carrier.

3. Specific identification of customers by the following types:

   a. Customers firmly committed to the use of other methods of transportation;

   b. "Captive" or "automatic" customers of the carrier in question;

   c. Current and potential customers with little knowledge of their total costs of logistics;

   d. Current and potential customers with an interest in and a knowledge of various costs of logistics activities.

4. The assignment of additional selling effort, particularly in the form of system analysis, to existing and prospective customers.

Usually, it is the cost-conscious customer who is most receptive to a consulting sales approach. It is precisely this type of customer who, in the process of appraising current movement systems, is most likely to alter a firm's utilization of different transportation services. It is this firm that should be the target of the greatest amount of creative sales effort on the part of carriers.

The shipper who is interested in the results of a carrier consulting sales study, but who cannot provide information for such a study or permission for carrier analysts to procure it, has posed many problems for advanced carrier sales effort. This has proven particularly troublesome for air freight sales effort, as indicated by Lewis, Culliton, and Steele in their pioneering study.[7] Where there is shipper interest, there is a prospect for carrier consulting sales efforts utilizing total cost analysis. Only limited use has been made of the total cost system analysis effort directed toward receptive clients.

Automatic customers are those bound to ship by certain methods because of location, product characteristics, or other. Because of the nature of automatic customers, carrier sales effort could be limited to a periodic review of their current and potential needs. Even less attention can be afforded those customers automatic to other carriers. However, experience indicates that considerable time is devoted to automatic or captive customers simply because they don't present any problems for the freight sales representative. This is human nature; it is also wasted effort.

Of those carriers currently attempting to analyze customers' logistics systems as part of their sales effort, no two have taken the same approach. For example, one railroad, recognizing that fewer than a dozen basic industries provide it with over three-quarters of its potential traffic revenue, has organized its market development group to pay special attention to these basic industries and then largely to key customers within these industries. Another railroad has analyzed the needs only of those shippers initiating a request for such analysis.

An air carrier that pioneered in the total cost analysis of shippers' logistics problems still makes some attempt to encourage its sales representatives to sell the idea of the analysis, as well as the company's service itself, to likely candidates for the use of air freight service.

Establishment of Policies   Carrier consulting sales programs, to be successful in their use of total cost analysis techniques, should be operated under the following guidelines:

1. Selective sales effort, as outlined above;

2. Emphasis on the necessity for sales representatives to take action that will enhance, rather than damage, the standing of individuals representing prospective customer organizations in the eyes of their colleagues;

3. Stress on the need to give the shipper-client an opportunity to voice his needs in regard to carrier equipment, freight handling, schedules, rates, and auxiliary services;

4. Inclusion of transportation, storage, material handling, packing and packaging, order processing, and inventory carrying costs in an appraisal of shipper needs;

5. Objective analysis of shippers' needs in regard to the transportation and material-handling components of their logistics systems, including recommendation of the use of competing services and equipment, where necessary;

6. Emphasis on the importance of studying the needs of both shippers and receivers in a logistics system;

7. Realization of the need to bring to bear on shippers' problems as wide a range of knowledge as a carrier marketing organization can provide;

8. Continued reliance on the traditional carrier sales representatives to:

   a. Locate likely candidates for total cost analyses;

   b. Provide the main contact between consulting sales talent and the shipper-customer.

Organization of Effort   To date, those carriers emphasizing consulting sales techniques have tried different organizational approaches. Most work through their regular sales representatives, to whom client accounts are assigned, supplementing their effort with that of more highly trained sales analysts or consultants. Some carrier sales consulting groups, however, have the power to initiate studies and carry out all necessary contact work.

The type of back-up support made available to regular carrier sales representatives and their accounts varies widely. One airline emphasizing its air freight service reduced the size of its consulting sales staff to two in anticipation of training all sales representatives to carry out total cost analyses.

Another airline has developed a ''dual'' sales organization with one group of sales representatives concentrating on the development of new business through the application of total cost and other more complex sales techniques, and one group concentrating on providing closer attention to the needs of existing air freight users. The theory behind this approach is that the two tasks require essentially different levels of analytical ability and different sales personalities.

Several railroads have provided their sales representatives with engineering support to cope with problems of the design of shippers' material-handling systems and carriers' equipment. Others have organized their analytic efforts on an industry-by-industry basis to devise new equipment, service schedules, and rates to meet the needs of specific industries.

Actual and Potential Results   The development of total cost approaches to the analysis of shipper problems by both shippers and carriers has opened up interesting opportunities for the latter. For example, sophisticated shippers are using piggyback service, largely because it bypasses traditional railroad classification (sorting) yards. Many shippers will continue to use it regardless of its speed of service, because they have developed the analytic and organizational mechanisms to appraise the value of *dependable* transit-time service.

Adapting Prices and Services to Interorganizational Needs

Pricing   Selective rate adjustments based on the combined costs of services to shippers, carriers, and receivers have led to greater emphasis on types of rates designed to: (1) offer shippers lower cost transportation service, (2) better utilize existing carrier equipment and service schedules, and (3) produce greater overall profit for all parties to the transaction.

For example, a railroad whose customers took full advantage of a five-day free-time provision in its demurrage rules for the unloading of 50-ton carloads of coal estimated that each day of delay cost the railroad about $8 per car. Further, it concluded that its customers, through improved scheduling, could accomplish faster unloading with an increase in storage and handling cost of perhaps no more than 5 cents per ton for each day by which car turnaround time was reduced. This would cost the customer 15 cents a ton (5 cents × 3 days).

Based on a load of about 50 tons per car, the railroad estimated its value of a reduction in free time from five days to two to be 48 cents per ton ($8 $\times$ 3 days/50 tons). It changed its tariff to reduce free time to two days in exchange for a 30 cents-per-ton reduction in rate. The customer thus received a 30 cent rate reduction in return for increasing its costs by only 15 cents, while the railroad gave a 30 cent rate reduction in return for a saving of 48 cents.

Design of Service "Packages" Several years ago, based on a comprehensive analysis of the economics of moving grain from producing areas in the Midwest to customers in the Southeast, a railroad proposed to reduce its rates by 60 percent for grain consigned in quantities of no less than 450 tons (five-car quantities) for transportation in newly designed Big John hopper cars. Because of the relatively low rate for moving grain as opposed to milled products such as flour or feed, the equipment and associated rates offered the potential of restructuring the milling industry by: (1) encouraging the relocation of milling facilities from production- oriented to market-oriented sites, and (2) providing a stimulus to animal-feeding industries in the Southeast.

The study of appliance movements and shipment dimensions by another railroad resulted in the introduction of high-cube rail boxcars capable of carrying twice as many units as their predecessors. This, combined with a rate offering significant cost savings to manufacturers willing and able to load the cars to capacity, allowed manufacturers to lower their costs of appliance distribution.

Consulting Sales Approaches in Perspective

Analysis of shipper-customer movements systems has been performed by relatively few carriers. What are the reasons for this? First, as with many kinds of research, the benefits from a consulting sales program employing total cost analysis may not be immediately apparent. Second, the requirement of a certain amount of objectivity in analysis has made the technique vulnerable to criticism if it does not tie a customer to the carrier spending time and money doing the analysis. Once the overall benefits of using a certain mode and carrier are understood by a customer, there is no guarantee the shipper will utilize the service of the carrier sponsoring the analysis. This has been a particularly acute problem in air freight services where serious sales efforts have been made by only a few airlines, but the advantages of their efforts have accrued to the entire industry. Further, carrier personnel sometimes carry biases into consulting sales studies, and this affects their objectivity.

The availability of, or the necessity to train, people qualified for the demanding job of consulting sales analysis has proven a barrier to the development of more than a handful of such groups. The policies of some firms prevent the hiring of sufficient talent from outside the carrier organization to staff a new department. Organizational conflict has developed in several instances within more traditional carrier sales organizations. This conflict has revolved around the consultant-analyst's function, and the scope of his or her authority in customer contact. Problems have grown out of insufficient communication of ideas and coordination of effort among the carrier personnel involved.

To its credit, the consulting sales approach has helped individuals in shipper-customer firms build their own prestige to the point where more information for total cost system analysis has become available.

To accomplish significant results, it is essential that a carrier consulting sales program have the continuity of effort that stems from long-run organizational support. In return, there is evidence that a logistics system, once designed, is likely to tie a customer to one mode or supplier of transportation services longer than routine sales effort placing almost exclusive emphasis on rates. This is particularly true where the system is centered around specialized equipment or methods developed solely for the system. Once performed, a system analysis can be updated with a relatively small increment of effort.

CREATIVE INTERORGANIZATIONAL PROBLEM SOLVING IN LOGISTICS

Despite the constraints sometimes imposed by managerial inertia or biases, creative interorganization logistics problem-solving efforts can prevail. Individuals and companies that adopt the attitudes necessary to foster creative approaches to interorganizational problems will have an edge on their competitors. What are these attitudes and approaches? Research in the field of interorganization management has yielded some suggestions.[8]

Companies likely to be recognized as leaders during an era of institutional change and interorganizational problem solving will have the following characteristics.

First, they will employ ''win-win'' approaches in their dealings. They will tend to seek what bargaining theorists have termed ''non-zero sum results from negotiations.'' Essentially, a non-zero sum result is one that reduces the total costs of the negotiating organizations, regardless of how they divide the resulting benefits. As we have seen from preceding examples, non-zero sum results can be achieved only through a basic change in procedure. Examples of this are the design of quantity price discounts to reflect efficient handling and shipping quantities, or the implementation of incentives to encourage the faster unloading and turnaround of cars in our previous example. In contrast, zero sum results produce no such net benefits. Changes in prices with no accompanying changes in procedure only transfer costs and profits from one company's profit and loss statement to another's with no net economic benefit to the channel system.

Second, leading firms will be willing to absorb risk for the mutual benefit of participants in a channel system. Consider the common problem of congestion at shippers' truck docks. The addition of extra truck bays might reduce truck waiting time significantly, thereby producing a high return on investment. To add more truck bays the shipping or receiving firms would have to make the investment to alter their facilities, the benefits of which would accrue to truckers supplying pickup and delivery services. Fortunately, the regulatory barriers that would have prevented such a mutually advantageous cost trade-off have now been broken. Transportation deregulation at the Federal level and the complete elimination of all economic regulation of trucking in some states, for example, Arizona and Florida, has now made it possible to implement cost trade-off agreements between shippers and carriers that formerly would have been unlawful. We will see much more of this in the next few years.

Third, these companies are willing to innovate on behalf of the channel. Some companies are known as innovators in their respective business spheres, either in the testing of new technologies, organization relationships, or contractual relationships. For example, a company first to establish a pool of pallets for the economic handling of goods in a channel of distribution is likely to be regarded as such an innovator, with resulting long-term rewards for successful experiments (and perhaps losses for unsuccessful ones).

Fourth, they may establish mechanisms for collecting and transmitting information and skills throughout a channel. Information that provides an early warning of inventory buildups at the retail level can be of use to all participants in a channel system. Manufacturers of products as diverse as drugs and fertilizers have provided their distributors with inventory control systems and educated them in the use of these systems. Expectations of long-term improvements in distributor profitability and loyalty motivate such manufacturers with enlightened interorganizational practices.

Fifth, there is an exchange of personnel among parallel industries. For example, railroads hire experienced industrial traffic managers from shipper companies, and vice versa; private truck fleets hire operations managers from motor carriers; and so forth. A factor that distinguishes management in the United States from that in most other parts of the world is executive mobility. American executives not only expect relatively frequent moves, they rarely plan to spend a lifetime working for a single firm. For example, the migration of railroad traffic personnel into the traffic departments of major industrial firms in recent years has set the stage for important interorganizational achievements by executives in cooperating organizations who understand each others' problems and economic constraints.

SUMMARY AND CONCLUSION

Many technological advances that were merely speculation as recently as a decade ago are now practically taken for granted. In fact, the rate of technological change in transportation, material handling, and data handling and analysis has been so great that a period of even more rapid institutional change will be required just to realize the benefits of recent technological advances. What we could do has currently far outstripped what we are doing.

Organizational and attitudinal changes are fostering the creation of institutional arrangements designed to capitalize on technology and the opportunities afforded by transportation deregulation. Now we see growing constraints on the types of technological change which may be possible in the intermediate future. These factors suggest that we may be entering a period in which institutional change will occupy a more important place alongside technological advances in the field of logistics.

Improved organization for and costing of logistics activities and their management will require appropriate responses from carriers in the development of equipment, services and rates to meet the needs of increasingly sophisticated logistics managers in industry. It will require selective carrier marketing effort designed to allow greater attention to the needs of the "nonautomatic" customer capable of taking advantage of several competing logistics system service packages.

As is so often the case in many fields of endeavor, there are firms at the "leading edge" of logistics practice. It is these firms that will lead in realizing the benefits of new technology and economic deregulation.

Shippers and carriers alike, who understand the total cost and service implications of alternative logistics systems and who are prepared to negotiate rates, services, equipment designs, and facility locations that require significant economies or service improvements will not only survive but prosper. In the process, new jobs, new types of businesses, and new institutional arrangements will be created, promising continued excitement and opportunity in the truly dynamic field we have come to call business logistics.

DISCUSSION QUESTIONS

1. What is meant by "topping out" of technologies? What are the consequences of this?

2. Why and how are attitudes toward interorganizational cooperation changing?

3. What is meant by a "win-win" philosophy of negotiation?

4. What can be gained by shifting functions between organizations in a channel of distribution?

5. Explain the rationale for and role played by third-party distribution companies. Will they grow in popularity? Why or why not?

6. What factors might inhibit the implementation of central distribution facilities designed to reduce congestion problems in central business districts?

7. Why is the combination of the computer and the human mind such a powerful tool in the management of logistics systems?

8. What has been the effect of transportation deregulation on interorganizational cooperation? What implications does this have for carrier management?

9. Why do the sales consulting activities of carriers frequently "go to waste"?

10. Should a carrier completely ignore its captive customers? Why or why not? Explain.

11. Should a carrier completely ignore the captive customers of other carriers or modes of transportation? Why or why not?

SUGGESTED READINGS

Leading Edge Logistics Competitive Positioning for the 1990s, Oak Brook, Illinois: Council of Logistics Management, 1989. This landmark study shows clearly the directions in which firms that are leaders in logistics management are going. It is highly recommended to any person having an interest in present and future trends in the field of logistics.

Putting Expert Systems to Work in Logistics, Oak Brook, Illinois: Council of Logistics Management, 1990. A state of the art summary of the applications of expert systems in the field of logistics.

ALLEN, MARY KAY, *The Development of an Artificial Intelligence System for Inventory Management*, Oak Brook, Illinois: Council of Logistics Management, 1986. An extensively researched state of the art study of the applications of expert systems in the area of inventory control.

BLANDING, WARREN, *Practical Handbook of Distribution/Customer Service*, Washington, D.C.: Traffic Service Corporation, 1985. Although earlier included as a suggested reading for Chapter 4, "Customer Logistics Service," Blanding's book stresses the importance of customer service, which has become a hallmark of firms using logistics service as a strategic competitive weapon.

HERTZ, DAVID B., *The Expert Executive: Using AI and Expert Systems for Financial Management, Marketing, Production, and Strategy*, New York: John Wiley & Sons, 1988. A highly readable text aimed at the practicing business executive.

LALONDE, BERNARD J., MARTHA C. COOPER, and THOMAS G. NOORDEWIER, *Customer Service: A Management Perspective*, Oak Brook, Illinois: Council of Logistics Management, 1988. This work focuses on the managerial concerns with the implementation, maintenance, and monitoring of customer service strategies. It represents the most comprehensive treatment of customer service from a logistics management point of view.

LALONDE, BERNARD J., and MARTHA C. COOPER, *Partnerships in Providing Customer Service: A Third-Party Perspective*, Oak Brook, Illinois, Council of Logistics Management, 1989. This up-to-date study considers transportation carriers, public/contract warehouses and electronic data interchange as the principal partners in newly emerging logistics system modification and development.

The articles cited below from the noted proceedings treat various aspects of future directions in logistics management.

Proceedings of the Annual Meeting, Council of Logistics Management, St. Louis, Missouri, October 22–25, 1989, Volumes I and II:

BOWERSOX, DONALD J., and PATRICIA J. DAUGHERTY, ''Achieving and Maintaining Logistics Leadership: Logistics Organizations of the Future,'' vol. I, 59–72.

GREGORY, WILLIAM D., ''Planning the Distribution Center for the Nineties,'' vol. I, 177–214.

VAN DER HOOP, J. H., ''The Single European Market: Optimizing Logistics Operations in Post 1992 Europe,'' vol. I, 271–282.

BISHOP, DARYL, ''Outsourcing Transportation and Traffic Management Services,'' vol. II, 207–212.

GODDERIE, CYRIEL L., ''European Distribution Management: Practical Advice for the 90's,'' vol. II, 289–300.

Proceedings of the Annual Meeting, Council of Logistics Management, Boston, Mass., October 9–12, 1988, Volumes I and II:

BISHOP, THOMAS, and STEVEN H. WUNNING, ''Third Party Logistics: A Competitive Advantage,'' 1–14.

HESKETT, JAMES L., ''Leadership through Integration: The Special Challenge of Logistics Management,'' 15–22.

BOULAIS, PETER D., ''Consolidated Freightways, Inc. Strategic Development in the 1980's and 1990's to Meet Customer Needs,'' 55–66.

WARK, JOE E., ''Logistics Issues in the 1990's,'' 225–230.

Proceedings of the Annual Meeting, Council of Logistics Management, Atlanta, Georgia, September 27–30, 1987, Volumes I and II:

LIVINGSTON, DAVID B., and GREGORY LANE, ''Integrating Customer Service into the Firm's Strategy: The Times They Are a Changing,'' 16–31.

ANDERSON, DAVID L., and ROBERT CALABRO, ''Logistics Productivity through Strategic Alliances,'' 61–74.

BOWERSOX, DONALD J., and ROBERT E. MURRAY, ''Logistics Strategic Planning for the 1990's,'' 231–244.

ROBERTS, MICHAEL A., ''Selling Airfreight in the Deregulated Domestic Environment,'' 371–378.

ENDNOTES

1. *Leading Edge Logistics Positioning for the 1990's*, Donald J. Bowersox, Principal Researcher (Oak Brook, Illinois: Council of Logistics Management, 1989) i.

2. See *Putting Expert Systems to Work in Logistics* (Oak Brook, Illinois: Council of Logistics Management, 1990). This report, prepared by Intellogistics, Inc. and

Dialog Systems Division of A. T. Kearney, Inc. includes a summary listing of one 105 logistics expert systems in one of its six appendixes.

3. See Mary Kay Allen, *The Development of an Artificial Intelligence System for Inventory Management* (Oak Brook, Illinois: Council of Logistics Management, 1986). Dr. Allen (Major, U.S. Air Force, Ret.) extensively researched the state of the art in the development of expert systems in the area of inventory control.

4. See David B. Hertz, *The Expert Executive: Using AI and Expert Systems for Financial Management, Marketing, Production, and Strategy* (New York: John Wiley & Sons, 1988). Dr. Hertz's book is addressed to business executives and is very readable.

5. Some of the material in this section is based on earlier work by Professor James L. Heskett, whose article ''Sweeping Changes in Distribution,'' *Harvard Business Review* (March-April, 1973): 123–132, has proven to be remarkably prophetic.

6. See James L. Heskett and Ronald H. Ballou, ''Logistical Planning in Inter-Organization Systems,'' in Michael P. Hottenstein and R. William Millman, *Papers and Proceedings of the 26th Annual Meeting of the Academy of Management* (Academy of Management: 1966) 124–136. This represents some of the earliest work done in this area and remains as relevant today as when this landmark paper was first presented.

7. Howard T. Lewis, James W. Culliton, and Jack D. Steele, *The Role of Air Freight in Physical Distribution* (Boston: Division of Research, Graduate School of Business Administration, Harvard University, 1956).

8. Much of what follows in this section is based on J. L. Heskett, Louis W. Stern, and Frederick J. Beier, ''Bases and Uses of Power in Interorganization Relations,'' in Louis P. Bucklin, ed., *Vertical Marketing Systems* (Glenville, Illinois: Scott, Foresman and Co., 1970): 75–93. For an interesting collection of papers on the subject, see Matthew Tuite, Roger Chisholm, and Michael Radnor, *Interorganizational Decision Making* (Chicago: Adline Publishing Co., 1972). These classic early works continue to provide valuable insights for today's logistics practitioner.

INDEX